Rethinking the Western Tradition

*The volumes in this series
seek to address the present debate
over the Western tradition
by reprinting key works of
that tradition along with essays
that evaluate each text from
different perspectives.*

An Essay on the Principle of Population

Population

The 1803 Edition

THOMAS ROBERT MALTHUS

Edited and with an
Introduction by
Shannon C. Stimson
with essays by
Niall O'Flaherty
Deborah Valenze
E. A. Wrigley
Kenneth Binmore
Karen O'Brien

Yale

UNIVERSITY PRESS

New Haven & London

Yale University Press books may be purchased in quantity for educational,
business, or promotional use. For information, please e-mail
sales.press@yale.edu (U.S. office) or
sales@yaleup.co.uk (U.K. office).

Set in Times Roman type by Newgen North America.
Printed in the United States of America.

Library of Congress Control Number: 2017935592

ISBN 978-0-300-17741-1 (paperback : alk. paper)

A catalogue record for this book is available from the
British Library.

This paper meets the requirements of
ANSI/NISO Z39.48–1992 (Permanence of Paper).

10 9 8 7 6 5 4 3 2 1

Contributors

Kenneth Binmore, CBE, FES, FBA, is Research Fellow in Economics, Finance and Management, Bristol University.

Karen O'Brien is Head of Humanities and Professor of English Literature, University of Oxford.

Dr. Niall O'Flaherty is Lecturer in the History of European Political Thought, King's College London.

Shannon C. Stimson is Thomas and Dorothy Leavey Professor, Georgetown University, and Professor Emerita, University of California Berkeley.

Deborah Valenze is Ann Whitney Olin Professor of History, Barnard College, Columbia University.

E. A. Wrigley is former Professor of Population Studies, London School of Economics; Professor of Economic History, University of Cambridge; and cofounder of the Cambridge Group for the History of Population and Social Structure.

Contents

Acknowledgments

This volume has had a lengthy gestation, and the editor wishes to acknowledge the intellectual and critical assistance of several individuals of special importance to its completion. The project has received both critical advice and continued encouragement from four valued friends and colleagues: Ruth Collier, Murray Milgate, James Moore, and Ian Shapiro. The manuscript received careful and immensely helpful readings from two anonymous press reviewers. It was brought to completion with the excellent and timely assistance of Samuel Garrett Zeitlin and Joanna Williamson. Finally, I wish to express my gratitude for the exceptional patience and unfailing cooperation of the five scholars whose essays accompany and inform this complete edition of Malthus's 1803 *Essay*.

Introduction

SHANNON C. STIMSON

Thomas Robert Malthus, called Bob or Robert within his family, was born in 1766 at The Rookery, a country house in Wescott, near Dorking in Surrey, the sixth child of Daniel and Henrietta Malthus. Daniel Malthus was a country gentlemen of independent means and moderately radical opinions, an acquaintance of both David Hume and Jean-Jacques Rousseau, and an inspired devotee of the latter. The details of the young Malthus's life in the bosom of his large and closely intermarried family circle are reminiscent of a Jane Austen novel: the "affectionate and indulgent" mother of well-established societal standing; the mercurial, imperative, and peripatetic father.[1] Add to this inner circle the sensitive but dissolute older brother living abroad and who, dying prematurely, left six stepchildren, four legitimate heirs, and one "natural child";[2] the four sisters and seemingly endless numbers of intermarried, maiden, and widowed aunts, together with many cousins with their numerous offspring, several of whom did not survive infancy.[3] Malthus's parents were second cousins and were themselves the product of more than a century of intermarriage among four families: the Daltons, Eckersalls, Malthuses, and Grahams. Malthus's mother was a Graham; his eventual wife and cousin, Harriet, an Eckersall. Many of these marriages arose from the proximity of professional association, as the Daltons, Eckersalls, and Malthuses were historically in some form of royal service, some from the time of Charles II. Daniel Graham (1695–1778) was Apothecary to George II and George III, and Malthus's grandfather on his mother's side, while Thomas Graham, Apothecary to George I and George II, was a direct lineal forebear of both of Malthus's parents.

Daniel Malthus kept his family in a state of almost perpetual movement from one country house to another from 1768 until 1787. In the midst of his family's continual dislocations, young Robert's education was largely entrusted to others and mostly away from home. His early education fell under the guidance of Rev. Richard Graves at the Claverton Rectory near Bath, and from 1782 under the personal direction of Gilbert Wakefield at the Warrington Dissenting Academy and in Wakefield's own home in

Lancashire. From 1784, Malthus studied – as Wakefield had done – at Jesus College, Cambridge, until graduating as Ninth Wrangler in mathematics, attaining the ninth highest First Class degree in that subject, in 1788. Malthus would later be elected a Fellow of the college in 1793.

Shortly after leaving Cambridge, in 1789, Malthus became a country curate in the Church of England, licensed by the Bishop of Winchester to serve the remote curacy of Okewood in the parish of Wotton, Surrey. Such an unlikely choice of career by such an obviously talented young intellect met with Malthus's own expressed desire for "a retired living in the country," and has been partially explained by the fact that Malthus suffered from birth from a devastating physical handicap due to a harelip and cleft palate.[4] While his personal appearance was very little affected, and his deformity almost never discussed in public or private communications, the physical challenge of speaking must have been great, and his speech in the few rare instances it has been noted in print by his contemporaries was described as "stammering" and "horrid," or more generously as "the vowels sonorous, whatever might become of the consonants."[5]

As his biographer the late Patricia James has noted, it was "impossible to tell from the records how long young Robert actively served this curacy."[6] However, the parish records of Okewood contain other pieces of information of relevance concerning Malthus's time there. The curate at Okewood, with its remote but beautiful thirteenth-century chapel, was so poor it lacked even a heating stove for the chapel until the mid-nineteenth century.[7] Until 1829, there was no residence for the curate, and Malthus would have had to ride horseback nine miles to serve his parishioners. Too isolated to be licensed to perform marriages, Okewood Chapel's eighteenth-century register chronicled relatively few burials but a "prodigious number of baptisms, all children of the poor."[8] As the entire Register of Okewood is reported to have contained not one individual described as "Esquire," the country folk who labored through Malthus's sermons and who brought their infants for baptism from a pewter bowl would have been basically those common laborers at the very bottom of a subsistence economy, and whose children survived on a basic diet of bread. Malthus would thus powerfully describe them in 1798:

> The sons and daughters of peasants will not be found such rosy cherubs in real life, as they are described in romances. It cannot fail to be remarked by those who live much in the country, that the sons of labourers are very apt to be stunted in their growth, and are a long while arriving at maturity. Boys that you would guess to be fourteen or fifteen, are, upon enquiry, frequently found to be eighteen or nineteen.[9]

Despite the obvious personal challenges of public speaking, Malthus was also made Rector of Walesby in Lincolnshire in 1803, with its living of just over three hundred pounds per annum, which when combined with other sources of income enabled him in 1804 to marry his second cousin Harriet Eckersall, and provided him with a permanent income for the remainder of his life.[10] A year later, Malthus additionally took up a position as Professor of Political Economy at the newly founded East-India College of Haileybury in Hertfordshire, a position which he also held until his death. Malthus's post at the East-India College was the first of its kind in England, and his movement from curate to professor of political economy reflected little alteration in the importance or content of his theological commitments. Historian Boyd Hilton has described the outset of the nineteenth century as one of an "age of atonement" positioned between Britain's two great ages of empire.[11] Malthus's more than two decades of training the young (between the ages of fifteen and eighteen), soon-to-be civil servants of the East India Company have been argued to be largely synchronous with his ever-closer alignment to the theological-utilitarian beliefs of the noted clergyman, natural theologian, and moral and political philosopher William Paley.

Paley's theology has been characterized by some historians of the period as essentially a mainstream Church of England position which saw the world as a state of trial and one that gave believers a chance to change their ways and modify their behavior.[12] The Paleyite position, suggesting a belief in the need for measuring man's commitment to moral principle by his strict attention to the consequences of his actions, would seem heuristically well-matched to the mission of imbuing newly minted administrators for the Indian service with the values of a practical theology of discipline and moral restraint. In drawing on a kind of Paleyite utilitarianism, Malthus adopted an understanding of Christian moral life that was indeed utilitarian in character, yet could never be epitomized by the terms of "implicit secular utilitarianism" that would render him "indistinguishable from those Benthamites who were to provide the early mainstay of neo-Malthusianism."[13] Nevertheless, the Christian values or theodicy which Malthus espoused might be as easily discovered through attention to the first (1798) and second editions (1803) of his *Essay on the Principle of Population,* and his classes on political economy, as through his observance of any strictly formal religious theology. Indeed, much contemporary scholarship on Malthus has persuasively argued that considerations of Malthus's writings on population and political economy should not be sharply disengaged from his theological commitments.[14] While questions of religion and theodicy remained important in the development of Malthus's principle of population, certainly of great if not equal importance in shaping Malthus's demographic, moral, and political economic thinking in the period between 1798 and 1803 were writings of the political economist Adam Smith and the utopian writer William Godwin. Malthus's engagement with the work of both Smith and Godwin serve to place the 1803 edition of the *Essay* within the context of social, political, and economic reform in the early decades of the nineteenth century.

Malthus assigned the work of Adam Smith a most important place in his thought and writing, and for many years harbored the idea of bringing out his own edition of the *Wealth of Nations*.[15] Whether serving as the anvil in forging Malthus's attack in the first edition of the *Essay on Population* on the speculative visions ("phantom of the imagination") of William Godwin and Condorcet, or as his later point of departure in writing the *Principles of Political Economy* (1820) in offering critical commentary on David Ricardo's new political economy, Smith's orienting influence is there.[16] This is not surprising, as Malthus was consistently a reactive and critical thinker, rather than a consummate theorist. His very first and unpublished work, "The Crisis," as well as the unsigned first *Essay,* were reactive precisely in this sense. However, despite what might be described as Smith's formative influence in Malthus's work, this is not, of course, how many of his critics and commentators from his own time to the present have tended to see their relationship.[17] For example, when Malthus chose in the pages of the 1824 *Quarterly Review* to openly claim Smith as his ally in an emerging disciplinary divide between old and "new" schools of political economy,[18] John Stuart Mill returned fire in the pages of the *Westminster Review* arguing that the difficulty of reconciling Malthus and Smith was insuperable.[19]

The debate was joined, and then as now Malthus has been required to carry a twin burden. On the one hand, the *Essay* in his own time was seen as opposing Smith's systematic thought with a loosely and erroneously labeled "dismal science," and of functioning as a demoralizer of an existing moral economy.[20] Beginning with Karl Polanyi in the twentieth century, commentators on the Smith-Malthus debate have persistently maintained this focus on the *Essay* in order to highlight Malthus's moral impoverishment of Smith's political economy through the introduction of a form of naturalism understood as biological reductionism. On the other hand, it has been suggested that Malthus's political economy presented a more extreme version of Smithian concepts such as the invisible hand, unintended consequences, or even, in his opposition to the Poor Law, laissez-faire. Although scholars recognize that this was not perhaps Malthus's own perception of his enterprise, they have argued that in his hands, "more harshly than Smith, more practically than Mandeville," private virtue had become "apparently pernicious" and "vice a source of benefit."[21] Certainly, Malthus's theory of population is read fairly by some scholars to have exceeded Smith's own reliance on unintended consequences, perhaps even to serve as a veritable test case for that "doctrine."[22] Thus, opinion remains sharply divided over whether Malthus's effort in the first edition of the *Essay* should be understood as a direct challenge and subversion of Smith's theory of progress,[23] or as at least originally, an actual defense of Smith's moral and political economy from the critique leveled by another leading thinker of the eighteenth century, William Godwin.

Malthus's initial, unpublished consideration of this question was inspired by social and political upheaval, as its title – "The Crisis" – readily confirms.[24] The crisis confronting Malthus appeared to take two forms: the continued political threat to Britain of the effects of an imploding French Revolution and war with France, and the visible "distresses and dissatisfactions" of a growing and increasingly immiserated rural laboring class at home.[25] The two were being dramatically brought together in his mind by a series of events involving the splits and defections occurring in the William Pitt administration in opposition to the war, public repression of protest, and high taxation consequent to it, and the simultaneous political debate engendered by "Mr. Pitt's Poor Law Bill." Malthus had yet to arrive at or at least record any systematic understanding of a population principle that might inform these debates.

At the time, Malthus had no theoretical or even systematic answer to this question. To address the immediate political crisis which French politics and the war were engendering in Britain under Pitt's administration, he proposed a purely practical solution – "the revival of the true Whig principles in a body of the community sufficiently numerous and powerful to snatch the object of contention from the opposing factions," which was to be found, he believed, in the "sense and reason of the country gentleman, and the middle classes of society."[26] On the question of the means by which the crisis of the rural poor was to be alleviated, Malthus was more circumspect, supporting the Pitt proposal for continued parish relief but registering uncertainty about the principles that supported it. Acknowledging England's growing number of indigent laboring poor, Malthus had at this point nothing systematic to say and could only comment in passing: "On the subject of population, I cannot agree with Archdeacon Paley, who says, that the quantity of happiness in any country is best measured by the

number of people. Increasing population is the most certain possible sign
of the happiness and prosperity of a state; but the actual population may
only be a sign of the happiness that is past."[27]

However, when Malthus turned to Godwin's essay on "Avarice and Profusion," in *The Enquirer* (1797), together with Godwin's *An Enquiry into
Political Justice and Its Influence on General Virtue and Happiness* (1793),
he found just such an effort to offer a principled analysis of the very political and economic crises he was observing. It was in his opinion, however,
a deeply flawed and – in the context of the times – unsettling proposal to
connect a theory of man's perfectible nature to a principle of diminishing
population, and to enunciate a root-and-branch reform of both the constitution and the advancing commercial society over which it governed. In
what might be described as Godwin's futuristic utopia of Enlightenment
rationalism, reason would so triumph over selfish interest that

> The men therefore who exist when the earth shall refuse itself to a more
> extended population, will cease to propagate, for they will no longer
> have any motive, either of error or duty, to induce them. In addition to
> this they will perhaps be immortal. The whole will be a people of men,
> and not of children. Generation will not succeed generation, nor truth
> have in a certain degree to recommence her career at the end of every
> thirty years. There will be no war, no crimes, no administration of jus-
> tice as it is called, and no government.[28]

Malthus published a response. He found Godwin's claims wholly lacking in
either empirical or genuine logical thought, and felt Godwin's "beautiful"
system was "little better than a dream, a beautiful phantom of the imagination."[29] Malthus chose to counter Godwin in a small, polemical, and unsigned piece, *An Essay on the Principle of Population*, which Malthus chose
to publicly acknowledge five years after its original publication in 1798.
The reaction to the *Essay* was immediate and in most instances vitriolic.[30]

While Malthus published but one edition of his *Principles of Political
Economy* (1820) during his lifetime,[31] he produced no fewer than six editions of the *Essay,* and in 1803 offered that "collection of a greater number
of facts in elucidation of the general argument," which he acknowledged
in his original preface remained to be supplied.[32] Indeed, while Malthus
continued to make changes and adjustments through all the editions, it
was clearly the second, 1803 edition that massively revised and reordered
the original *Essay* to nearly four times its original length and has since
been characterized as effectively a "separate work."[33] It is this edition that
remains the most fundamental statement of his work on population – the

Great Quarto – and it is upon this edition that all later corrections and revisions of the four following editions on which he spent the remainder of his life (1806, 1807, 1817, 1826) would be based. Thus, it must be considered the definitive text upon which Malthus placed his imprimatur and to which his innumerable critics responded. Importantly, it is the 1803 edition that confirmed Malthus's reputation as the leading political economist of the day until Ricardo's remarkable *Principles of Political Economy and Taxation* appeared in 1817. Malthus's population principle was to remain a basic assumption of the writings of all the classical political economists up to and including John Stuart Mill.

The Great Quarto reflected a significant period of travel, as well as an extensive body of historical research and empirical observation of the demographics, climatic conditions, commodity prices, laws, and public services undertaken by Malthus in Scandinavia and continental Europe between 1799 and 1803. This material would become the basis of the two entirely new books 1 and 2 of the 1803 edition, and drew extensively upon his journals made during a six-month tour of Hamburg, the Duchies of Schleswig-Holstein, Denmark, Norway, Sweden, and Russia in 1799. He then traveled to France and Switzerland with his family and Harriet Eckersall between May and October 1802. Reaching beyond the material of his own observations and travel journals of the period, Malthus filled the twenty-six chapters of these two new books 1 and 2 with material prodigiously mined from the empirical, statistical, and historical research of others, including François Le Vaillant's personal 1790 account, *Voyage dans l'intérieur de l'Afrique;* Peter Simon Pallas's volumes of the 1780s on discoveries and voyages in different parts of the Russian Empire; Sir George Staunton's *Embassy to China* of 1797; and Jean Baptiste Duhalde's massive eighteenth-century account of China, *The General History of China Containing Geographical, Historical, Chronological, Political and Physical Description of the Empire of China. Chinese-Tartary, Corea and Tibet, Including an Exact and Particular Account of Their Customs, Manners, Ceremonies, Religion, Arts and Sciences.*[34] As his footnotes to the 1803 *Essay* document, Malthus drew also from the historical research of others on Ancient Greece and Rome, as well as from his exploration of the writings of Plato, Aristotle, Dionysius of Halicarnassus, Julius Caesar, Plutarch, Tacitus, and Livy, and on comments upon climate in China by Montesquieu, and upon Roman and Greek cultural and political practices by David Hume and Edward Gibbon.

Stung by the charges of unoriginality and intellectual borrowing made about the 1798 *Essay,* or perhaps simply inspired to massively enlarge the

support for its fundamental argument, Malthus not only extended his project but undertook significant alterations in argument and inductive method,
rewrote as well as added entirely new sections to the work, and widely
acknowledged the work of others both in the preface and in copious notes
to the work. The preface of the 1803 edition went to some length to re-
iterate for readers that in writing the original edition of the *Essay* while
tucked away in the country, Malthus had had only available to him the likes
of David Hume, Adam Smith, and the Revs. Robert Wallace and Richard
Price. However, Malthus acknowledged that in the revisions undertaken
for the 1803 edition, he had consulted as well the writings of Benjamin
Franklin, the French économistes, Montesquieu, Sir James Steuart, Arthur
Young, and Rev. Joseph Townsend. Indeed, Benjamin Franklin might le-
gitimately be claimed to have anticipated several of Malthus's early ideas
on population. However, with the publication of the second, 1803 edition,
which Malthus produced – as Patricia James informs us – in an unknown
"series of garrets" rented in London, Malthus moved far beyond these earlier thinkers in his own ability to collect and process an unparalleled research trove of demographic and economic data, and to connect population
theory to poverty, wealth, and the growth of capital.[35]

Malthus signaled the important advancement of his aims and contribution in the Great Quarto with the significant alteration of its title from that
of a consideration of the principle of population "as it effects the future
improvement of society, with remarks on the speculations of Mr Godwin,
M. Condorcet, and other writers," to its ambitious restatement of 1803: *An
Essay on the Principle of Population; or, A View of Its Past and Present Effects on Human Happiness; with an Inquiry into Our Prospects Respecting
the Future Removal or Mitigation of the Evils Which It Occasions.* Commentators reflecting on the alteration and expansion of the 1803 edition,
such as E. A. Wrigley, have noted that it consolidated Malthus's mature
position, and that despite new material added to the later editions and the
significant later alteration of the order of chapters, the work as a whole
after the 1803 edition remained "recognizably the same"[36] The caesura created between his original polemic and the nearly quadrupled enlargement
and alterations made in 1803 is definitive.[37] Malthus himself acknowledged
the newness of the work at the conclusion of its preface, suggesting that
"[t]hroughout the whole of the present work, I have so far differed in principle from the former, as to suppose another check to population possible,
which does not strictly come under the head either of vice or misery."[38]
Malthus continued to maintain, throughout all the editions, his principle
that population, if unchecked, had the tendency to outstrip the means of

subsistence. Yet, importantly, Malthus proceeded in the first chapter of the 1803 to formally label this new preventive check as "moral restraint," arguing that "of the preventive checks, that which is not followed by irregular gratifications, may properly be termed moral restraint."[39]

The locus of this more complex preventive check was to be found in the regulating powers of a restraint from marriage, and Malthus clearly intended that the imputation of such a forward-thinking capacity in the laboring poor would not only "soften some of the harshest conclusions of the first essay" but also elevate the perception of his judgment of their capacity to address what were not unforeseen consequences of very early marriage.[40] The intended conclusion was that "the poverty and misery which prevail among the lower classes of society" was *not* "absolutely irremediable."[41] Certainly other scholars have noted that Malthus followed in these aims a kind of "theological utilitarian" belief in the need for measuring man's commitment to moral principle by his "strict attention" to the consequences of his actions.[42]

The impact of the Great Quarto of 1803 was immediately registered with positive, if not uncritical, reviews in the *Monthly Review,* the *Imperial Review,* and the Anglican periodical *British Critic.* And while Malthus's harshest critics persisted among poets and literary essayists such as Robert Southey and William Hazlitt, among moralists such as William Cobbett, and economic reformers such as Robert Owen, and, later, by Nassau William Senior, the 1803 edition was now recognized as having moved beyond "a brilliant a priori polemic" to "a weighty empirical treatise and a third and fourth edition followed in 1806 and 1807."[43] In Europe, the Quarto found readers through its German (1807) and French (1809) translations. In America, Thomas Jefferson wrote to Joseph Priestley in January 1804 offering the following assessment of Malthus's Quarto: "Have you seen the new work of Malthus on population? It is one of the ablest I have ever seen. Although his main object is to delineate the effects of redundancy of population, and to test the poor laws of England, and other palliations for that evil, several important questions in political economy, allied to his subject incidentally, are treated with a masterly hand."[44] Jefferson wrote in a similarly laudatory vein only a few days later to the French political economist Jean Baptiste Say, suggesting that he found it a work of "sound logic, in which some of the opinions of Adam Smith as well as of the economists, are examined."[45]

The influence and importance of Malthus's work on population as definitively developed in the 1803 Quarto has been historically recognized to reach well into the middle and later decades of the nineteenth century in the writings of Charles Darwin and Herbert Spencer, and well beyond them to the debates over the "population bomb" of the mid-late twentieth century. Malthus's twentieth-century biographer Patricia James alluded to his immediate influence in the first three decades of the nineteenth century when she wrote that the "currency" of the word "Malthusian" in the first three decades of that century could perhaps "be compared with the 'Freudian' about a century later, which was used by people who had little idea who Freud was, when or where he worked, or even what tenets he held."[46] Malthus's thought, and most importantly his "principle," seemed to be assumed ever after, by writers of literature and of political and social thought, to be commonly understood.

Yet, more systematic studies of the tremendous resonance and impact of Malthus's *Essay* are even now appearing, as with the five original, critical, and interpretive essays which accompany this complete edition of Malthus's Great Quarto of 1803, *An Essay on the Principle of Population,* by scholars in the fields of economic, political, and social history; demography; economics; and English literature.[47] The contributors to this volume were each tasked with addressing, in a set of new essays for readers and students of Malthus, what might be taken to be a signal or important contribution with regard to their own fields. What emerges in the essays that follow is a wide-ranging consideration of Malthus's legacy which makes no pretense to be synoptic, but rather to suggest the remarkably creative and interdisciplinary significance of Malthus's impact both in its scope and character. In the view of many at work in these and other scholarly disciplines, the 250th anniversary of Malthus's birth has reinforced the need for a relaunch of his most famous work in its entirety, reissuing a complete version of his benchmark text that restores parts of the original now of current and particular interest both to historians and interdisciplinary scholars of the academic world concerned with what can be described as "global" issues.

In this volume, the importance of the 1803 *Essay* is the subject of renewed historical interest taken up in the essays by Niall O'Flaherty and Deborah Valenze. O'Flaherty's essay, "Malthus and the History of Population," successfully reorients contemporary scholarly understanding of just what Malthus might be understood to have been doing in terms of both his method and his political thought in the 1803 revision, by giving greater weight to the historical context of his theory, particularly as the principle of population purports to be an argument based on historical observation. It is this record of human experience, O'Flaherty suggests, "that comprises the 'scientific' underpinning" of all Malthus's practical and policy recommendations. The essay by Deborah Valenze, "The Tortoise and the Hare:

Thomas Robert Malthus as Natural Philosopher," enlarges upon the theme of Malthus's focus on methodology in "natural philosophy" by placing his revisions of the first *Essay* within the framework of his need to "reinforce" history with hard data, and thus to follow "two paths" of research into the natural world. Malthus's tours of Scandinavia, first through Germany and Denmark, then northward into Sweden and Norway, offered Malthus an opportunity "of gleaning information on reproduction and survival shaped by minimal interference of modernizing forces." Valenze offers a fascinating look at Malthus's methods of correlating vast amounts of meteorological data on European weather patterns and temperature fluctuations to buttress his more general theories on the power of nature and the balance of "prudential restraint" necessary to sustainable population growth. As Valenze notes, "Malthus's understanding of rural life, supported by his empirical natural philosophy, belonged to a universe in which nature held the trump card capable of negating all efforts to match agricultural output with the level of population." This view of nature was the basis of Malthus's comparison of the relative speed of productive growth to that of population as a race between a tortoise and a hare. However, Valenze demonstrates that over time and in his more focused political economic writing, "the fury of Malthus's concept of nature diminished, as it hovered over a carefully planned notion of economic life only distantly related to the communal table in Norway."

E. A. Wrigley picks up the population principle as an element of emerging classical political economy in his essay "The Preventive Check and the Poor Law: The Malthusian Model and Its Implications." Wrigley notes that Malthus "shared with the other classical economists the same concern about the implications of the impossibility of overcoming the ceiling set to material production by the limited amount of cultivatable land, but he added a further consideration that reinforced and extended his concern." This consideration was his belief in the nature of two progressions – population growth and diminishing agricultural output – which would produce an ineliminable tension between population and production without the operation of either preventive checks or moral restraint. However, as Wrigley notes, the nature of the relationship between productive capacity and population was changing during Malthus's lifetime "in ways that made his model of their linkages increasingly inapplicable." Yet Wrigley also notes that one of Malthus's most admired characteristics by later economists such as John Maynard Keynes was his willingness to modify his views based on empirical evidence. And evidence for this can be found in the 1803 edition, which Wrigley touches upon in his essay.

The contemporary economist and game theorist Kenneth Binmore reconsiders the question "Malthusian Economics: Right or Wrong?" in a quintessentially modern economic theorist's consideration for the volume. Binmore suggests that no equations or other technicalities are needed to confirm that a properly stated version of this Malthusian doctrine is necessarily correct. Binmore rehearses some of the strongest contemporary claims resisting what he interprets as the most general Malthusian principle – that something cannot grow without bound if there is a bound which it cannot exceed. He suggests that contemporary resistance to this principle has rested on technological growth and advances in scientific food production rather than a continued focus on population control. In a fascinating yet contrarian argument, Binmore suggests that the wager on technology growth rather than population restraint is a very uncertain one. In an important sense, Binmore's reflections on the continuing contemporary policy relevance of Malthus's perspective revive something of the spirit of those who remarked that Malthus and his concerns with scarcity had been buried many times, but that "anyone who has been buried so often cannot be entirely dead."[48]

The final essay for the volume reaches beyond Malthus's influence in either natural science or economics and takes up his afterlife in literature. In "The Cultural and Literary Significance of the 1803 *Essay,*" Karen O'Brien explores the considerable cultural and literary influence of Malthus's work when set in the political, social, and cultural contexts of the first few decades after its publication: "The Napoleonic wars, political controversy about poverty and food scarcity, cultural debate about the rate and age of marriage, and, more specifically, the significance of the findings of the first British censuses of 1801, 1811, and 1821." O'Brien notes that the "disconnected subhistory of the poorer part of mankind," together with the significance of the "cognitive deficit" which Malthus ascribed to those members of society most likely to be affected by the "positive check," was not lost on the Romantic anti-Malthusians and other early critics of the *Essay* such as William Wordsworth in the *Lyrical Ballads* of 1798. However, Wordsworth's perspective altered by 1814 to offer more a plea for moral and religious education, which Malthus shared in *The Excursion.* Juxtaposed to a Romantic conservatism that found its origins "in the powerful negative inspiration of Malthus's ideas," O'Brien chronicles other kinds of literary and didactic writings of the period that drew upon Malthus for a new type of literary realism and advocated for individual moral responsibility in the face of hostile economic and social conditions. Beyond the more frequently referenced Evangelical economists thought to take up the

Malthusian problem, O'Brien focuses on the work of literary figures, such as the poet George Crabbe, a great favorite with Jane Austen, and Austen herself, as well as other women writers of importance – Maria Edgeworth (*Castle Rackrent,* 1800), Elizabeth Hamilton, George Eliot (*Adam Bede,* 1859), Elizabeth Gaskell (*Mary Barton,* 1848), and Harriet Martineau (*Illustrations of Political Economy,* 1832–1834) – to suggest the depth and range of the *Essay*'s literary and cultural reach.

The volume's editor has taken the position that the contributors' essays are intended to introduce educated readers and scholars to a diverse set of contemporary interdisciplinary understandings and approaches to the wide-reaching impact of Malthus's work, rather than to attempt to settle in a single place a myriad of interpretive debates. The very breadth of impact of the 1803 edition of the *Essay* on so many fields of the humanities and social sciences has stimulated multiple approaches to thinking about this pivotal work and has mitigated against the effort either to impose a single interpretive framework or to attempt to weave one connective tissue through the interpretive essays. As such, this volume captures the renewed intervention into the political and cultural impact of a profoundly influential work of political economic thinking in the early and mid-decades of the nineteenth century. It is our hope that this volume will be of great use to both students and scholars of Malthus, of the history of political and economic thought, and of the intellectual and social history of the period. It conveys as well our confidence in the continued resonance and significance of T. R. Malthus's thought to scholarly and contemporary debate even in the twenty-first century.

NOTES

1. Patricia James, *Population Malthus: His Life and Time* (London: Routledge and Kegan Paul, 1979), 13. Malthus died after a brief illness on 29 December 1834 from what is generally believed to have been heart disease or some disorder of the heart. He is buried in Bath Abbey. Many of the most important details of Malthus's life and family, and much of what we know of the personal context of his work, we know thanks to this monumental biography by James, based on nearly twenty years of biographical research into his personal and family papers, and in the public records. James has given us not only Malthus's definitive biography but also a definitive, two-volume variorum edition of his masterwork, *An Essay on the Principle of Population,* based on the 1803 edition with the variora of 1806, 1807, 1816, and 1826 (Cambridge: Cambridge University Press, 1989). James has given us

as well an immensely valuable edition of *The Travel Diaries of T. R. Malthus* (Cambridge: Cambridge University Press, 1966), including the Scandinavian journal from 1799, when the second edition of the *Essay* was already in the planning, and from his Continental travels in 1810, 1825, and 1826. James's unrivalled research as presented in these three scholarly resource works has been drawn upon for a number of details concerning Malthus's life and travels discussed below. In addition, important contemporary reflections on Malthus's life and his historical significance have been recently brought to light by Robert Mayhew's biography, *Malthus: The Life and Legacies of an Untimely Prophet* (Cambridge, Mass.: Harvard University Press, 2014). Any errors of fact or interpretation that remain are the responsibility of this author alone.

2. James, *Population Malthus*, 39.

3. Ibid., 6–9.

4. James Bonar, *Malthus and His Work*, 2nd ed. (London: Allen and Unwin, 1924), 9, cited in James, *Population Malthus*, 3.

5. Henry Holland, *Recollections of Past Life* (London: Longmans, 1872), 4; Maria Edgeworth quoted in *Maria Edgeworth: Letters from England, 1813–1844*, ed. Christina Colvin (Oxford: Oxford University Press, 1971), 331; Harriet Martineau, *Harriet Martineau's Autobiography*, 2nd ed. (London: Smith, Elder, 1877), 1:327–328, cited in James, *Population Malthus*, 3.

6. Malthus, *An Essay on the Principle of Population*, ed. James, 1:ix. As James notes there, Malthus obtained the title to the curacy in 1824 and held it until his death.

7. James, *Population Malthus*, 45.

8. Malthus, *An Essay on the Principle of Population*, ed. James, 1:ix.

9. T. R. Malthus, *An Essay on the Principle of Population as It Affects the Future Improvement of Society with Remarks on the Speculations of Mr. Godwin, M. Condorcet, and Other Writers* (1798), in *The Works of Thomas Robert Malthus*, ed. E. A. Wrigley and David Souden (London: W. Pickering, 1986), 1:29–30 (original pagination, 71–76; hereafter First *Essay*). One topic of contemporary as well as historical concern, that of Malthus's objections to birth control in the form of artificial methods of contraception, are briefly addressed by two of the contributors to this volume (Binmore and O'Brien). Both consider aspects of an answer offered most frequently by historians, which is to recur to Malthus's status as an Anglican priest. It would seem important to add as well that Malthus's objections to effective birth control were consonant with his theological opinions about the providential purposes served by population pressures, and would not be fairly dismissed as the emanations of any personal shyness or prudery. Indeed, I am reminded that

Malthus was certainly aware that his proposals for the delay of marriage could not entirely alleviate the pressures of population growth as he understood them, and that the vices of prostitution and abortion were the likely byproducts of this dilemma. The editor wishes to thank an anonymous press reader for emphasizing the importance of this aspect of Malthus's theological perspective.

10. A. M. C. Waterman, *Revolution, Economics, and Religion: Christian Political Economy, 1798–1833* (Cambridge: Cambridge University Press, 1991), 83–85. As Waterman notes, there was no record either of Malthus giving up the stipendiary curacy of Okewood nor of a new curate's appointment being made there. See also Donald Winch, *Malthus: A Very Short Introduction* (Oxford: Oxford University Press, 2013), 14. Winch is the editor of the abridged, one-volume version of the 1803 *Essay* based on Patricia James's variorum edition together with a separate editor's introduction. See T. R. Malthus, *An Essay on the Principle of Population; or, A View of Its Past and Present Effects on Human Happiness,* ed. Donald Winch (Cambridge: Cambridge University Press, 1992). This edition did not print large sections of books 1 and 2, which this present complete edition has now restored.

11. Boyd Hilton, *The Age of Atonement: The Influence of Evangelicalism on Social and Economic Thought, 1795–1865* (Oxford: Oxford University Press, 1988).

12. For a classic statement of this position, see Waterman, *Revolution, Economics, and Religion,* 146–147, 172. But see also the important work on this subject by Donald Winch in "Robert Malthus: Christian Moral Scientist, Arch-Demoralizer, or Implicit Secular Utilitarian?" *Utilitas* 5, no. 2 (November 1993): 239–253, and *Riches and Poverty: An Intellectual History of Political Economy in Britain, 1750–1834* (Cambridge: Cambridge University Press, 1996).

13. For a discussion of Malthus in the context of his secular opponents and followers, as well as his contemporary interpretation by economic historians, see Winch, *Riches and Poverty,* 243.

14. The relationship of Malthus's developing ideas on population to religious orthodoxy and theodicy, from their first expression in 1798 to their suggested reformulation by 1803 as well as later, has been one of considerable debate in the literature on all the editions of the *Essay.* This debate reflects importantly on an understanding of the critical reactions to Malthus's *Essay* within both the Church of England and by Christian political economists and reformers, which has been productively discussed by these authors, as well as others, and is not developed further here. However, for two important examples of this debate, see J. M. Pullen, "Malthus' Theological Ideas and Their

Influence on His Principle of Population," *History of Political Economy*, 13, no. 1 (1981): 39–54, and Boyd Hilton, "Malthus and the Dismal Science," *Times Literary Supplement*, 16 August 1996, 9.

15. Donald Winch, *Malthus: A Very Short Introduction*, 15

16. First *Essay*, 65 (original pagination, 175). Malthus's considerations of the work of Robert Owen would usurp Malthus's earlier focus on Godwin by the 1817 edition. See also Malthus, *An Essay on the Principle of Population*, ed. James, 1:xii.

17. E. A. Wrigley has written an important essay on the pitfalls of drawing an extreme distinction between the interests of Smith and Malthus in the limits to growth and the implications of "population, resources and environment, a viewpoint they shared with David Ricardo." See Wrigley, "The Limits to Growth: Malthus and the Classical Economists," in *Population and Resources in Western Intellectual Traditions*, ed. M. S. Teitelbaum and J. M. Winter (Cambridge: Cambridge University Press, 1989), 30–48, 30–31.

18. See Malthus's critical review of J. R. McCulloch's "Essay on 'Political Economy,' *Supplement to the Encyclopaedia Britannica*, vol. VI, part I (Edinburgh, 1823)," *Quarterly Review* 30, no. 6 (1828): 297–334.

19. Mill's exact words are, "The difficulty of serving God and Mammon is proverbial, but it is a mere trifle in comparison with that of reconciling Mr. Malthus and Adam Smith." See John Stuart Mill, "The Quarterly Review, no. LX, Art. 1 'On the Essay on Political Economy, in the Supplement to the Encyclopaedia Britannica,'" *Westminster Review* 3, no. 5 (January 1825): 213–232, reprinted in Bernard Semmel, ed., *Occasional Papers of T. R. Malthus on Ireland, Population, and Political Economy from Contemporary Journals Written Anonymously and Hitherto Uncollected* (New York: Burt Franklin, 1963), 211–230.

20. For a valuable discussion of the contemporary literature on Malthus as "arch demoralizer," see Winch, "Robert Malthus."

21. John Burrow, *Whigs and Liberals* (Oxford: Clarendon, 1988), 59

22. Ibid., 59. Burrow adds, "In embracing Political Economy and defending Malthus, the Philosophic Radicals accepted the doctrine of unintended consequences in economic life as one of their chief defining characteristics, and so won a large part of their reputation for being harsh, unfeeling, and coldly mechanical" (59).

23. Gertrude Himmelfarb, *The Idea of Poverty* (New York: Knopf, 1984), 107–122.

24. "The Crisis, a View of the Present State of Britain, by a Friend to the Constitution." Surviving paragraphs of his unpublished pamphlet of 1796 may be seen in Bernard Semmel's reprint of William Empson's memoir, "Life,

Writings, and Character of Mr. Malthus," as originally published in the *Edinburgh Review,* January 1837, 469–506. See Semmel, ed., *Occasional Papers of T. R. Malthus,* 231–268.

25. Patricia James notes that at the close of the eighteenth century, the poor of England were "near starvation," and their condition in 1800 was to be exacerbated by another late harvest. In Yorkshire, robberies of storehouses and inns were increasing as one local observer noted: "That want must surely be dreadful, which would brave the gallows to obtain a single meal." James, *Population Malthus,* 86. Indeed, William Empson noted in his 1837 *Edinburgh Review* memoir that as of 1796, Malthus's position on population was at best at its "threshold," and that "he had seen so little of his way" that Malthus was at that point a "warm advocate of Mr. Pitt's Poor Law bill and of the *jus trium liberorum,*" which in the tradition of the Roman Empire rewarded families producing three or more children with state supplements. See Semmel, ed., *Occasional Papers of T. R. Malthus,* 244, 246. James Bonar quoted William Pitt's 1796 speech in Parliament reprising the principle: "Let us make relief a matter of right and honor. This will make a large family a blessing and not a curse; this will draw a proper line of distinction between those who are to provide for themselves by their labour and those who after enriching their country with a number of children, have claim upon its assistance for their support." Bonar, *Malthus and His Work* (London: Macmillan, 1885), 127.

26. "The Crisis," quoted in Semmel, ed., *Occasional Papers of T. R. Malthus,* 241.

27. Ibid., 244.

28. William Godwin, *An Enquiry Concerning Political Justice and Its Influence on General Virtue and Happiness* (London: G. G. Robinson, 1793), vol. 2, book 8, chap. 7, p. 871. William Godwin, *The Enquirer. Reflections on Education, Manners, and Literature. In A Series of Essays* (London: G. G. and J. Robinson, 1797).

29. First *Essay,* 1:64–65 (original pagination, 173–178).

30. Notable among his many savage critics, which famously included the poets Samuel Coleridge, William Wordsworth, and Robert Southey, were also Karl Marx and Friedrich Engels, who characterized the principle of population as "this vile, infamous theory, this hideous blasphemy against nature and mankind." See Karl Marx, *Capital,* ed. Ernest Mandel (New York: Vintage, 1977), 1:472–473n27. See also Friedrich Engels, "Outlines of a Critique of Political Economy," in *Collected Works of Karl Mark and Frederick Engels* (New York: International Publishers, 1975), 3:437. Of course, Malthus's supporters have characterized the work otherwise, though hardly less extremely, as when John Maynard Keynes praised the *Essay* as a landmark in

economic thought and one "profoundly in the English tradition of human science . . . a tradition marked by the love of truth and most noble lucidity, by a prosaic sanity free from sentiment and metaphysic, and by an immense disinterestedness and public spirit." See Keynes, *Essays in Biography,* in *The Collected Writings of John Maynard Keynes,* ed. Elizabeth Johnson and Donald Moggridge (London: Macmillan, 1972), 10:86.

31. The second, 1836 edition, with his substantial changes all but complete, appeared shortly after his death.

32. First *Essay,* 1:i (original pagination, i–iii).

33. T. R. Malthus, *An Essay on the Principle of Population; or, A View of Its Past and Present Effects on Human Happiness; with an Inquiry into Our Prospects Respecting the Future Removal or Mitigation of the Evils Which It Occasions. A New Edition, Very Much Enlarged* (London: J. Johnson, 1803; reprint New Haven, Conn.: Yale University Press, 2017) (hereafter *Essay of 1803*); James, *Population Malthus,* 81.

34. James, *Population Malthus,* 94 nn. 34–35.

35. Ibid., 79, 81.

36. First *Essay,* 1:8.

37. James, *Population Malthus,* 81.

38. *Essay of 1803,* 5. Throughout, the page numbers cited for this work are to the present edition.

39. Ibid., 19.

40. Ibid., 5. Debate exists over whether moral restraint is perhaps implied in the first *Essay.* However, the specific terminology and the direct clarification of this preventative appears first in the much more mature and comprehensive work of the Great Quarto. William Empson, in particular, emphasized the importance to Malthus of the introduction of moral restraint in the 1803 edition, in that "he hoped that he had 'not violated the principles of just reasoning, nor expressed any opinion respecting the probable improvement of society, in which he was not borne out by the experience of the past.'" (Ibid.) For Empson, its introduction in the second edition was a recognition that "as civilization practically descended into the mass of the people, the influence of moral restraint upon the course of the population might become more and more perceptible." Semmel, ed., *Occasional Papers of T. R. Malthus,* 250.

41. *Essay of 1803,* 5. Malthus's belief in the potential of moral restraint persisted within his theory and perhaps sought to reach beyond his own experience as a rural rector. Church records document that Malthus presided over two marriages of poor and illiterate couples at his parish in May 1804. The same records also indicate that he christened the first child of one of the couples on

2 September. The Walesby register records that this same mother gave birth to thirteen children over the course of her lifetime, losing four to infant death before the age of six months. James, *Population Malthus,* 164.

42. See Hilton, *The Age of Atonement;* Winch, *Riches and Poverty,* 243; and Timothy L. Alborn, "Boys to Men: Moral Restraint at Haileybury College," in *Malthus, Medicine, and Morality: "Malthusianism" after 1798,* ed. Brian Dolan (Amsterdam: Rodopi, 2000), 33–55.

43. Lord Robbins, foreword, in James, ed., *Travel Diaries of T. R. Malthus,* viii. Robert Southey published a withering review of the work in the *Annual Review* for 1803 (London: T. N. Longman and O. Rees, 1804), 292–300.

44. Thomas Jefferson to Joseph Priestly, 29 January 1804, in *Writings of Jefferson,* ed. A. E. Bergh (Washington, D.C.: Jefferson Memorial Association, 1903), 10:447–448.

45. Thomas Jefferson to Jean Baptiste Say, 1 February 1804, in ibid., 11:1–3. Say would hold fundamental disagreements with Malthus on the political economic question of effectual demand and the possibility of systemic gluts, on which themes, later economists such as John Maynard Keynes, writing in the aftermath of the Great Depression, held Malthus to have had the better of the argument. For discussions of American antebellum attitudes supporting or opposing Malthus's population principle, see C. Vann Woodward, *American Counter-Point: Slavery and Racism in the North-South Dialogue* (Boston: Little, Brown, 1971), chap. 3; Robert Fogel, *Without Consent or Contract: The Rise and Fall of American Slavery* (New York: Norton, 1989), chap. 5; and Eugene Genovese and Elizabeth Genovese, "Slavery, Economic Development, and the Law: The Dilemma of Southern Political Economists, 1800–1860," *Washington and Lee Law Review* 41, no. 1 (Winter 1984): 1–29.

46. James, *Population Malthus,* 346.

47. See Robert Mayhew, *Malthus: The Life and Legacies of an Untimely Prophet* (Cambridge, Mass.: Harvard University Press, 2014). The remarkable new contribution to Malthus scholarship by Alison Bashford and Joyce E. Chaplin, *The New Worlds of Thomas Robert Malthus: Rereading the Principle of Population,* appeared too late to be incorporated in the considerations of the volume. It is clear, however, that Bashford and Chaplin have focused important and new attention on Malthus's fundamental reworking of the first *Essay* in the Great Quarto of 1803 as "altogether different in both scale and content," and on the need for a new edition and reprinting of the 1803 *Essay,* which it is hoped this new edition goes some way to provide. Bashford and Chaplin, *The New Worlds of Thomas Robert Malthus: Rereading the Principle of Population* (Princeton, N.J.: Princeton University Press, 2016), 10.

48. Remarks to this effect have been attributed both to the late ecologist Garrett Hardin, perhaps best known as author of "The Tragedy of the Commons," *Science,* 13 December 1968, 1243–1248, and quoted again by the late Herman E. Daly, *Steady-State Economics: The Economics of Biophysical Equilibrium and Moral Growth,* 2nd ed. (Washington, D.C.: Island Press, 1991), 42–43.

Note on the Text

This volume reproduces Malthus's original 1803 text with very few changes. The nineteenth-century practice of enlarged letters to begin paragraphs or sections is eliminated; the list of errata to the 1803 edition is incorporated; the use of stacked quotation marks in the left column (e.g., p. 25) to indicate a block of quoted material is retained. The long "s" has been modernized. Obvious printers' errors have been silently corrected when the correction did not interfere with the meaning of the text.

AN ESSAY

ON THE

PRINCIPLE OF POPULATION;

OR,

A VIEW OF ITS PAST AND PRESENT EFFECTS

ON

HUMAN HAPPINESS;

WITH AN INQUIRY INTO OUR PROSPECTS RESPECTING THE FUTURE REMOVAL
OR MITIGATION OF THE EVILS WHICH IT OCCASIONS.

A NEW EDITION, VERY MUCH ENLARGED.

By T. R. MALTHUS, A.M.

FELLOW OF JESUS COLLEGE, CAMBRIDGE.

LONDON:

PRINTED FOR J. JOHNSON, IN ST. PAUL'S CHURCH-YARD,

BY T. BENSLEY, BOLT COURT, FLEET STREET.

1803.

PREFACE.

THE Essay on the Principle of Population, which I published in 1798, was suggested, as is expressed in the preface, by a paper in Mr. Godwin's Inquirer. It was written on the spur of the occasion, and from the few materials which were within my reach in a country situation. The only authors from whose writings I had deduced the principle, which formed the main argument of the essay, were Hume, Wallace, Dr. Adam Smith, and Dr. Price; and my object was to apply it to try the truth of those speculations on the perfectibility of man and society, which at that time excited a considerable portion of the publick attention.

In the course of the discussion, I was naturally led into some examination of the effects of this principle on the existing state of society. It appeared to account for much of that poverty and misery observable among the lower classes of people in every nation, and for those reiterated failures in the efforts of the higher classes to relieve them. The more I considered the subject in this point of view, the more importance it seemed to acquire; and this consideration, joined to the degree of publick attention which the essay excited, determined me to turn my leisure reading towards an historical examination of the effects of the principle of population on the past and present state of society; that, by illustrating the subject more generally, and drawing those inferences from it, in application to the actual state of things which experience seemed to warrant, I might give it a more practical and permanent interest.

In the course of this inquiry, I found that much more had been done, than I had been aware of, when I first published the essay. The poverty and misery arising from a too rapid increase of population, had been distinctly seen, and the most violent remedies proposed, so long ago as the times of Plato and Aristotle. And of late years, the subject had been treated in such a manner, by some of the French Economists, occasionally by Montesquieu, and, among our own writers, by Dr. Franklin, Sir James Steuart, Mr. Arthur Young, and Mr. Townsend, as to create a natural surprise, that it had not excited more of the publick attention.

Much, however, remained yet to be done. Independently of the comparison between the increase of population and food, which had not perhaps been stated with sufficient force and precision; some of the most curious and interesting parts of the subject had been either wholly omitted or treated very slightly. Though it had been stated distinctly, that population must always be kept down to the level of the means of subsistence; yet few inquiries had been made into the various modes by which this level is effected; and the principle had never been sufficiently pursued to its consequences, and those practical, inferences drawn from it, which a strict examination of its effects on society appears to suggest.

These are therefore the points which I have treated most in detail in the following essay. In its present shape, it may be considered as a new work, and I should probably have published it as such, omitting the few parts of the former which I have retained, but that I wished it to form a whole of itself, and not to need a continual reference to the other. On this account, I trust that no apology is necessary to the purchasers of the first edition. I should hope that there are some parts of it, not reprinted in this, which may still have their use; as they were rejected, not because I thought them all of less value than what has been inserted, but because they did not suit the different plan of treating the subject which I had adopted.

To those who either understood the subject before, or saw it distinctly on the perusal of the first edition, I am fearful that I shall appear to have treated some parts of it too much in detail, and to have been guilty of unnecessary repetitions. These faults have arisen partly from want of skill, and partly from intention. In drawing similar inferences from the state of society in a number of different countries, I found it very difficult to avoid some repetitions; and in those parts of the inquiry which led to conclusions different from our usual habits of thinking, it appeared to me, that, with the slightest hope of producing conviction, it was necessary to present them to the reader's mind at different times, and on different occasions. I was willing to sacrifice all pretensions to merit of composition, to the chance of making an impression on a larger class of readers.

The main principle advanced is so incontrovertible, that, if I had confined myself merely to general views, I could have entrenched myself in an impregnable fortress; and the work, in this form, would probably have had a much more masterly air. But such general views, though they may advance the cause of abstract truth, rarely tend to promote any practical good; and I thought that I should not do justice to the subject, and bring it fairly under discussion, if I refused to consider any of the consequences which appeared necessarily to flow from it, whatever these consequences might be. By pursuing this plan, however, I am aware that I have opened a door to many objections; and, probably, to much severity of criticism: but I console myself with the reflection, that even the errors into which I may have fallen, by affording a handle to argument, and an additional excitement to examination, may be subservient to the important end, of bringing a subject so nearly connected with the happiness of society into more general notice.

Throughout the whole of the present work, I have so far differed in principle from the former, as to suppose another check to population possible, which does not strictly come under the head either of vice or misery; and, in the latter part, I have endeavoured to soften some of the harshest conclusions of the first essay. In doing this, I hope that I have not violated the principles of just reasoning; nor expressed any opinion respecting the probable improvement of society, in which I am not borne out by the experience of the past. To those who shall still think that any check to population whatever, would be worse than the evils which it would relieve, the conclusions of the former essay will remain in full force; and if we adopt this opinion, we shall be compelled to acknowledge that the poverty and misery which prevail among the lower classes of society are absolutely irremediable.

I have taken as much pains as I could to avoid any errors in the facts and calculations which have been produced in the course of the work. Should any of them nevertheless turn out to be false, the reader will see, that they will not materially affect the general tenour of the reasoning.

From the crowd of materials which presented themselves in illustration of the first branch of the subject, I dare not flatter myself that I have selected the best, or arranged them in the most perspicuous method. To those who take an interest in moral and political questions, I hope that the novelty and importance of the subject will compensate the imperfections of its execution.

LONDON, June 8, 1803.

CONTENTS.

BOOK I.

Of the Checks to Population in the less civilized parts of the world, and in past times.

BOOK II.

Of the Checks to Population in the different States of Modern Europe.

BOOK III.

Of the different Systems or Expedients which have been proposed or have prevailed in Society, as they affect the Evils arising from the Principle of Population.

BOOK IV.

Of our future Prospects respecting the removal or mitigation of the Evils arising from the Principle of Population.

ESSAY, &c.

BOOK I.

OF THE CHECKS TO POPULATION IN THE LESS CIVILIZED PARTS OF THE WORLD, AND IN PAST TIMES.

CHAP. I.

Statement of the Subject. Ratios of the Increase of Population and Food.

In an inquiry concerning the future improvement of society, the mode of conducting the subject which naturally presents itself, is

1. An investigation of the causes that have hitherto impeded the progress of mankind towards happiness; and

2. An examination into the probability of the total or partial removal of these causes in future.

To enter fully into this question, and to enumerate all the causes that have hitherto influenced human improvement, would be much beyond the power of an individual. The principal object of the present essay is to examine the effects of one great cause intimately united with the very nature of man, which, though it has been constantly and powerfully operating since the commencement of society, has been little noticed by the writers who have treated this subject. The facts which establish the existence of this cause have, indeed, been repeatedly stated and acknowledged; but its natural and necessary effects have been almost totally overlooked; though probably among these effects may be reckoned a very considerable portion of that vice and misery, and of that unequal distribution of the bounties of nature, which it has been the unceasing object of the enlightened philanthropist in all ages to correct.

The cause to which I allude, is the constant tendency in all animated life to increase beyond the nourishment prepared for it.

It is observed by Dr. Franklin, that there is no bound to the prolific nature of plants or animals, but what is made by their crowding and interfering with each others means of subsistence. Were the face of the earth, he says, vacant of other plants, it might be gradually sowed and overspread with one kind only; as, for instance, with fennel: and were it empty of other inhabitants, it might in a few ages be replenished from one nation only; as, for instance, with Englishmen.[1]

This is incontrovertibly true. Through the animal and vegetable kingdoms Nature has scattered the seeds of life abroad with the most profuse and liberal hand; but has been comparatively sparing in the room and the nourishment necessary to rear them. The germs of existence contained in this spot of earth, with ample food, and ample room to expand in, would fill millions of worlds in the course of a few thousand years. Necessity, that imperious all-pervading law of nature, restrains them within the prescribed bounds. The race of plants and the race of animals shrink under this great restrictive law; and the race of man cannot by any efforts of reason escape from it.

In plants and animals the view of the subject is simple. They are all impelled by a powerful instinct to the increase of their species; and this instinct is interrupted by no reasoning or doubts about providing for their offspring. Wherever, therefore, there is liberty, the power of increase is exerted; and the superabundant effects are repressed afterwards by want of room and nourishment, which is common to plants and animals; and among animals, by their becoming the prey of each other.

The effects of this check on man are more complicated. Impelled to the increase of his species by an equally powerful instinct, reason interrupts his career, and asks him whether he may not bring beings into the world, for whom he cannot provide the means of support. If he attend to this natural suggestion, the restriction too frequently produces vice. If he hear it not, the human race will be constantly endeavouring to increase beyond the means of subsistence. But as by that law of our nature which makes food necessary to the life of man, population can never actually increase beyond

1. Franklin's Miscell. p. 9.

the lowest nourishment capable of supporting it; a strong check on population, from the difficulty of acquiring food, must be constantly in operation.
This difficulty must fall somewhere; and must necessarily be severely felt
in some or other of the various forms of misery, or the fear of misery, by a
large portion of mankind.

That population has this constant tendency to increase beyond the means
of subsistence, and that it is kept to its necessary level by these causes, will
sufficiently appear from a review of the different states of society in which
man has existed. But before we proceed to this review, the subject will perhaps be seen in a clearer light, if we endeavour to ascertain, what would be
the natural increase of population if left to exert itself with perfect freedom;
and what might be expected to be the rate of increase in the productions
of the earth, under the most favourable circumstances of human industry.
A comparison of these two rates of increase will enable us to judge of the
force of that tendency in population to increase beyond the means of subsistence, which has been stated to exist.

It will be allowed, that no country has hitherto been known, where the
manners were so pure and simple, and the means of subsistence so abundant, that no check whatever has existed to early marriages from the difficulty of providing for a family; and no waste of the human species has
been occasioned afterwards by vicious customs, by towns, by unhealthy
occupations, or too severe labour. Consequently in no state that we have
yet known, has the power of population been left to exert itself with perfect
freedom.

Whether the law of marriage be instituted, or not, the dictate of nature
and virtue seems to be an early attachment to one woman; and where there
were no impediments of any kind in the way of an union to which such
an attachment would lead, and no causes of depopulation afterwards, the
increase of the human species would be evidently much greater than any
increase which has been hitherto known.

In the northern states of America, where the means of subsistence have
been more ample, the manners of the people more pure, and the checks
to early marriages fewer, than in any of the modern states of Europe, the
population was found to double itself for some successive periods every
twenty-five years. Yet even during these periods, in some of the towns, the
deaths exceeded the births;[2] and they consequently required a continued
supply from the country to support their population.

2. Price's Observ. on Revers. Pay. vol. i. p. 274.

In the back settlements, where the sole employment was agriculture, and vicious customs and unwholesome occupations were unknown, the population was found to double itself in fifteen years.[3] Even this extraordinary rate of increase is probably short of the utmost power of population. Very severe labour is requisite to clear a fresh country; such situations are not in general considered as particularly healthy; and the inhabitants were probably occasionally subject to the incursions of the Indians, which might destroy some lives, or at any rate diminish the fruits of their industry.

According to a table of Euler, calculated on a mortality of 1 in 36, if the births be to the deaths in the proportion of 3 to 1, the period of doubling will be only 12 $\frac{4}{5}$ years.[4] And these proportions are not only possible suppositions, but have actually occurred for short periods in more countries than one.

Sir William Petty supposes a doubling possible in so short a time as ten years.[5]

But to be perfectly sure that we are far within the truth, we will take the slowest of these rates of increase; a rate, in which all concurring testimonies agree, and which has been repeatedly ascertained to be from procreation only.

It may safely be pronounced therefore, that population when unchecked goes on doubling itself every twenty-five years, or increases in a geometrical ratio.

The rate according to which the productions of the earth may be supposed to increase, it will not be so easy to determine. Of this, however, we may be perfectly certain, that the ratio of their increase must be totally of a different nature from the ratio of the increase of population. A thousand millions are just as easily doubled every twenty-five years by the power of population as a thousand. But the food to support the increase from the greater number will by no means be obtained with the same facility. Man is necessarily confined in room. When acre has been added to acre till all the fertile land is occupied, the yearly increase of food must depend upon the amelioration of the land already in possession. This is a stream, which, from the nature of all soils, instead of increasing, must be gradually diminishing. But population, could it be supplied with food, would go on with unexhausted vigour; and the increase of one period would furnish the power of a greater increase the next, and this, without any limit.

3. Id. p. 282.   4. See this table at the end of chap. iv. book ii.
5. Polit. Arith. p. 14.

From the accounts we have of China and Japan, it may be fairly doubted, whether the best directed efforts of human industry could double the produce of these countries even once in any number of years. There are many parts of the globe, indeed, hitherto uncultivated, and almost unoccupied; but the right of exterminating, or driving into a corner where they must starve, even the inhabitants of these thinly peopled regions, will be questioned in a moral view. The process of improving their minds and directing their industry, would necessarily be slow; and during this time, as population would regularly keep pace with the increasing produce, it would rarely happen that a great degree of knowledge and industry would have to operate at once upon rich unappropriated soil. Even where this might take place, as it does sometimes in new colonies, a geometrical ratio increases with such extraordinary rapidity, that the advantage could not last long. If America continue increasing, which she certainly will do, though not with the same rapidity as formerly, the Indians will be driven further and further back into the country, till the whole race is ultimately exterminated.

These observations are, in a degree, applicable to all the parts of the earth, where the soil is imperfectly cultivated. To exterminate the inhabitants of the greatest part of Asia and Africa, is a thought that could not be admitted for a moment. To civilize and direct the industry of the various tribes of Tartars, and Negroes, would certainly be a work of considerable time, and of variable and uncertain success.

Europe is by no means so fully peopled as it might be. In Europe, there is the fairest chance that human industry may receive its best direction. The science of agriculture has been much studied in England and Scotland; and there is still a great portion of uncultivated land in these countries. Let us consider, at what rate the produce of this island might be supposed to increase under circumstances the most favourable to improvement.

If it be allowed, that by the best possible policy, and great encouragements to agriculture, the average produce of the island could be doubled in the first twenty-five years, it will be allowing probably a greater increase than could with reason be expected.

In the next twenty-five years, it is impossible to suppose that the produce could be quadrupled. It would be contrary to all our knowledge of the properties of land. The improvement of the barren parts would be a work of time and labour; and it must be evident to those who have the slightest acquaintance with agricultural subjects, that in proportion as cultivation extended, the additions that could yearly be made to the former average produce, must be gradually and regularly diminishing. That we may be the better able to compare the increase of population and food, let us make a supposition, which, without pretending to accuracy, is clearly more favourable to the power of production in the earth, than any experience that we have had of its qualities will warrant.

Let us suppose that the yearly additions which might be made to the former average produce, instead of decreasing, which they certainly would do, were to remain the same; and that the produce of this island might be increased every twenty-five years, by a quantity equal to what it at present produces: the most enthusiastic speculator cannot suppose a greater increase than this. In a few centuries it would make every acre of land in the island like a garden.

If this supposition be applied to the whole earth, and if it be allowed that the subsistence for man which the earth affords, might be increased every twenty-five years by a quantity equal to what it at present produces, this will be supposing a rate of increase much greater than we can imagine that any possible exertions of mankind could make it.

It may be fairly pronounced therefore, that, considering the present average state of the earth, the means of subsistence, under circumstances the most favourable to human industry, could not possibly be made to increase faster than in an arithmetical ratio.

The necessary effects of these two different rates of increase, when brought together, will be very striking. Let us call the population of this island eleven millions; and suppose the present produce equal to the easy support of such a number. In the first twenty-five years the population would be twenty-two millions, and the food being also doubled, the means of subsistence would be equal to this increase. In the next twenty-five years, the population would be forty-four millions, and the means of subsistence only equal to the support of thirty-three millions. In the next period the population would be eighty-eight millions, and the means of subsistence just equal to the support of half of that number. And at the conclusion of the first century, the population would be a hundred and seventy-six millions, and the means of subsistence only equal to the support of fifty-five millions; leaving a population of a hundred and twenty-one millions totally unprovided for.

Taking the whole earth instead of this island, emigration would of course be excluded; and supposing the present population equal to a thousand millions, the human species would increase as the numbers 1, 2, 4, 8, 16, 32, 64, 128, 256, and subsistence as 1, 2, 3, 4, 5, 6, 7, 8, 9. In two centuries the population would be to the means of subsistence as 256 to 9; in three centuries as 4096 to 13, and in two thousand years the difference would be almost incalculable.

In this supposition no limits whatever are placed to the produce of the earth. It may increase for ever, and be greater than any assignable quantity; yet still the power of population being in every period so much superior, the increase of the human species can only be kept down to the level of the means of subsistence by the constant operation of the strong law of necessity acting as a check upon the greater power.

CHAP. II.

Of the general Checks to Population, and the Mode of their Operation.

THE checks to population, which are constantly operating with more or less force in every society, and keep down the number to the level of the means of subsistence, may be classed under two general heads; the preventive and the positive checks.

The preventive check, is peculiar to man, and arises from that distinctive superiority in his reasoning faculties, which enables him to calculate distant consequences. Plants and animals have apparently no doubts about the future support of their offspring. The checks to their indefinite increase, therefore, are all positive. But man cannot look around him, and see the distress which frequently presses upon those who have large families; he cannot contemplate his present possessions or earnings, which he now nearly consumes himself, and calculate the amount of each share, when with very little addition they must be divided, perhaps, among seven or eight, without feeling a doubt, whether if he follow the bent of his inclinations, he may be able to support the offspring which he will probably bring into the world. In a state of equality, if such can exist, this would be the simple question. In the present state of society other considerations occur. Will he not lower his rank in life, and be obliged to give up in great measure his former society? Does any mode of employment present itself by which he may reasonably hope to maintain a family? Will he not at any rate subject himself to greater difficulties, and more severe labour than in his single state? Will he not be unable to transmit to his children the same advantages of education and improvement that he had himself possessed? Does he even feel secure that, should he have a large family, his utmost exertions can save them from rags, and squalid poverty, and their consequent degradation in the community? And may he not be reduced to the grating necessity of forfeiting his independence, and of being obliged to the sparing hand of charity for support?

These considerations are calculated to prevent, and certainly do prevent, a great number of persons in all civilized nations from pursuing the dictate of nature in an early attachment to one woman.

If this restraint do not produce vice, as in many instances is the case, and very generally so among the middle and higher classes of women, it is undoubtedly the least evil that can arise from the principle of population.

Considered as a restraint on an inclination, otherwise innocent, and always natural, it must be allowed to produce a certain degree of temporary unhappiness; but evidently slight, compared with the evils which result from any of the other checks to population.

When this restraint produces vice, as it does most frequently among men, and among a numerous class of females, the evils which follow are but too conspicuous. A promiscuous intercourse to such a degree as to prevent the birth of children, seems to lower in the most marked manner the dignity of human nature. It cannot be without its effect on men, and nothing can be more obvious than its tendency to degrade the female character, and to destroy all its most amiable and distinguishing characteristics. Add to which, that among those unfortunate females with which all great towns abound, more real distress and aggravated misery are perhaps to be found, than in any other department of human life.

When a general corruption of morals, with regard to the sex, pervades all the classes of society, its effects must necessarily be, to poison the springs of domestic happiness, to weaken conjugal and parental affection, and to lessen the united exertions and ardour of parents in the care and education of their children; effects, which cannot take place without a decided diminution of the general happiness and virtue of the society; particularly, as the necessity of art in the accomplishment and conduct of intrigues, and in the concealment of their consequences, necessarily leads to many other vices.

The positive checks to population are extremely various, and include every cause, whether arising from vice or misery, which in any degree contributes to shorten the natural duration of human life. Under this head therefore may be enumerated, all unwholesome occupations, severe labour and exposure to the seasons, extreme poverty, bad nursing of children, great towns, excesses of all kinds, the whole train of common diseases and epidemics, wars, pestilence, plague, and famine.

On examining these obstacles to the increase of population which I have classed under the heads of preventive, and positive checks, it will appear that they are all resolvable into moral restraint, vice, and misery.

Of the preventive checks, that which is not followed by irregular gratifications, may properly be termed moral restraint.

Promiscuous intercourse, unnatural passions, violations of the marriage bed, and improper arts to conceal the consequences of irregular connexions, clearly come under the head of vice.

Of the positive checks, those which appear to arise unavoidably from the laws of nature may be called exclusively misery; and those which we obviously bring upon ourselves, such as wars, excesses, and many others which it would be in our power to avoid, are of a mixed nature. They are brought upon us by vice, and their consequences are misery.[1]

In every country, some of these checks are, with more or less force, in constant operation; yet notwithstanding their general prevalence, there are few states in which there is not a constant effort in the population to increase beyond the means of subsistence. This constant effort as constantly tends to subject the lower classes of society to distress, and to prevent any great permanent amelioration of their condition.

These effects, in the present state of society, seem to be produced in the following manner. We will suppose the means of subsistence in any country just equal to the easy support of its inhabitants. The constant effort towards population, which is found to act even in the most vicious societies, increases the number of people before the means of subsistence are increased. The food therefore which before supported eleven millions, must now be divided among eleven millions and a half. The poor consequently must live much worse, and many of them be reduced to severe distress. The number of labourers also being above the proportion of work in the market, the price of labour must tend to fall; while the price of provisions would at the same time tend to rise. The labourer therefore must do more work, to earn the same as he did before. During this season of distress, the discouragements to marriage, and the difficulty of rearing a family are so great, that population is nearly at a stand. In the mean time, the cheapness of labour, the plenty of labourers, and the necessity of an increased industry among them, encourage cultivators to employ more labour upon their land;

1. As the general consequence of vice is misery, and as this consequence is the precise reason why an action is termed vicious, it may appear that the term misery alone would be here sufficient, and that it is superfluous to use both. But the rejection of the term vice would introduce a considerable confusion into our language and ideas. We want it particularly to distinguish that class of actions, the general tendency of which is to produce misery, but which, in their immediate or individual effects, may produce perhaps exactly the contrary. The gratification of all our passions in its immediate effect is happiness, not misery; and in individual instances even the remote consequences (at least in this life) come under the same denomination. I have little doubt that there have been some irregular connexions with women, which have added to the happiness of both parties, and have injured no one. These individual actions therefore cannot come under the head of misery. But they are still evidently vicious, because an action is so denominated, the general tendency of which is to produce misery, whatever may be its individual effect; and no person can doubt the general tendency of an illicit intercourse between the sexes, to injure the happiness of society.

to turn up fresh soil, and to manure and improve more completely what is already in tillage; till ultimately the means of subsistence may become in the same proportion to the population, as at the period from which we set out. The situation of the labourer being then again tolerably comfortable, the restraints to population are in some degree loosened; and, after a short period, the same retrograde and progressive movements, with respect to happiness, are repeated.

This sort of oscillation will not probably be obvious to common view; and it may be difficult even for the most attentive observer to calculate its periods. Yet that, in the generality of old states, some such vibration does exist, though in a much less marked, and in a much more irregular manner, than I have described it, no reflecting man who considers the subject deeply can well doubt.

One principal reason why this oscillation has been less remarked, and less decidedly confirmed by experience than might naturally be expected, is, that the histories of mankind which we possess, are, in general, histories only of the higher classes. We have not many accounts, that can be depended upon, of the manners and customs of that part of mankind where these retrograde and progressive movements chiefly take place. A satisfactory history of this kind, of one people and of one period, would require the constant and minute attention of many observing minds in local and general remarks on the state of the lower classes of society, and the causes that influenced it; and to draw accurate inferences upon this subject, a succession of such historians for some centuries would be necessary. This branch of statistical knowledge has of late years been attended to in some countries,[2] and we may promise ourselves a clearer insight into the internal

2. The judicious questions which Sir John Sinclair circulated in Scotland, and the very valuable accounts which he has collected in that part of the island, do him the highest honour; and these accounts will ever remain an extraordinary monument of the learning, good sense, and general information of the clergy of Scotland. It is to be regretted that the adjoining parishes are not put together in the work, which would have assisted the memory both in attaining and recollecting the state of particular districts. The repetitions and contradictory opinions which occur are not in my opinion so objectionable, as, to the result of such testimony, more faith may be given than we could possibly give to the testimony of any individual. Even were this result drawn for us by some master hand, though much valuable time would undoubtedly be saved, the information would not be so satisfactory. If, with a few subordinate improvements, this work had contained accurate and complete registers for the last 150 years, it would have been inestimable, and would have exhibited a better picture of the internal state of a country, than has yet been presented to the world. But this last most essential improvement no diligence could have effected.

structure of human society from the progress of these inquiries. But the science may be said yet to be in its infancy, and many of the objects, on which it would be desirable to have information, have been either omitted or not stated with sufficient accuracy. Among these perhaps may be reckoned, the proportion of the number of adults to the number of marriages; the extent to which vicious customs have prevailed in consequence of the restraints upon matrimony; the comparative mortality among the children of the most distressed part of the community, and of those who live rather more at their ease; the variations in the real price of labour; the observable differences in the state of the lower classes of society with respect to ease and happiness, at different times during a certain period; and very accurate registers of births, deaths, and marriages, which are of the utmost importance in this subject.

A faithful history, including such particulars, would tend greatly to elucidate the manner in which the constant check upon population acts; and would probably prove the existence of the retrograde and progressive movements that have been mentioned; though the times of their vibration must necessarily be rendered irregular from the operation of many interrupting causes; such as, the introduction of or failure of certain manufactures, a greater or less prevalent spirit of agricultural enterprize; years of plenty, or years of scarcity; wars, sickly seasons, poor laws, emigration, and other causes of a similar nature.

A circumstance which has perhaps more than any other contributed to conceal this oscillation from common view, is, the difference between the nominal and real price of labour. It very rarely happens that the nominal price of labour universally falls; but we well know that it frequently remains the same, while the nominal price of provisions has been gradually rising. This is, in effect, a real fall in the price of labour; and, during this period, the condition of the lower classes of the community must be gradually growing worse. But the farmers and capitalists are growing rich from the real cheapness of labour. Their increasing capitals enable them to employ a greater number of men; and, as the population had probably suffered some check from the greater difficulty of supporting a family, the demand for labour, after a certain period, would be great in proportion to the supply, and its price would of course rise, if left to find its natural level; and thus the wages of labour, and consequently the condition of the lower classes of society, might have progressive and retrograde movements, though the price of labour might never nominally fall.

In savage life, where there is no regular price of labour, it is little to be doubted that similar oscillations take place. When population has increased nearly to the utmost limits of the food, all the preventive and the positive checks will naturally operate with increased force. Vicious habits with respect to the sex will be more general, the exposing of children more frequent, and both the probability, and fatality, of wars and epidemicks, will be considerably greater; and these causes will probably continue their operation till the population is sunk below the level of the food; and then the return to comparative plenty will again produce an increase, and, after a certain period, its further progress will again be checked by the same causes.[3]

But without attempting to establish in all cases these progressive and retrograde movements in different countries, which would evidently require more minute histories than we possess, the following propositions are proposed to be proved:

1. Population is necessarily limited by the means of subsistence.

2. Population invaribly increases, where the means of subsistence increase, unless prevented by some very powerful and obvious checks.

3. These checks, and the checks which repress the superior power of population, and keep its effects on a level with the means of subsistence, are all resolvable into moral restraint, vice, and misery.

The first of these propositions scarcely needs illustration. The second and third will be sufficiently established by a review of the past and present state of society.

This review will be the subject of the following chapters.

---

3. Sir James Steuart very justly compares the generative faculty to a spring loaded with a variable weight, (Polit. Econ. vol. i. b. i. c. 4. p. 20.) which would of course produce exactly that kind of oscillation which has been mentioned. In the first book of his Political Economy, he has explained many parts of the subject of population very ably.

C H A P . III.

Of the Checks to Population in the lowest Stage of Human Society.

THE wretched inhabitants of Terra del Fuego have been placed by the general consent of voyagers at the bottom of the scale of human beings.[1] Of their domestic habits and manners, however, we have few accounts. Their barren country, and the miserable state in which they live, have prevented any intercourse with them that might give such information; but we cannot be at a loss to conceive the checks to population among a race of savages, whose very appearance indicates them to be half starved, and who, shivering with cold, and covered with filth and vermin, live in one of the most inhospitable climates in the world, without having sagacity enough to provide themselves with such conveniences as might mitigate its severities, and render life in some measure more comfortable.[2]

Next to these, and almost as low in genius and resources, have been placed, the natives of Van Diemen's land;[3] but some late accounts have represented the islands of Andaman in the east, as inhabited by a race of savages still lower in wretchedness even than these. Every thing that voyagers have related of savage life, is said to fall short of the barbarism of this people. Their whole time is spent in search of food; and as their woods yield them few or no supplies of animals, and but little vegetable diet, their principal occupation is that of climbing the rocks, or roving along the margin of the sea, in search of a precarious meal of fish, which, during the tempestuous season, they often seek for in vain. Their stature seldom exceeds five feet; their bellies are protuberant, with high shoulders, large heads, and limbs disproportionably slender. Their countenances exhibit the extreme of wretchedness, a horrid mixture of famine and ferocity; and their extenuated and diseased figures plainly indicate the want of wholesome nourishment. Some of these unhappy beings have been found on the shores in the last stage of famine.[4]

In the next scale of human beings perhaps we may place the inhabitants of New Holland, of a part of whom we have some accounts that may be depended upon, from a person who resided a considerable time at Port Jackson, and had frequent opportunities of being a witness to their habits

1. Cook's First Voy. vol. ii. p. 59.   2. Second Voy. vol. ii. p. 187.
3. Vancouver's Voy. vol. ii. b. iii. c. i. p. 13.
4. Syme's Embassy to Ava, ch. i. p. 129. and Asiatic Researches, vol. iv. p. 401.

and manners. The narrator of Captain Cook's first voyage having mentioned the very small number of inhabitants that was seen on the eastern coast of New Holland, and the apparent inability of the country, from its desolate state, to support many more, observes, "By what means the inhab-
"   itants of this country are reduced to such a number as it can subsist, is
"   not perhaps very easy to guess; whether, like the inhabitants of New
"   Zealand, they are destroyed by the hands of each other in contests for
"   food, whether they are swept off by accidental famine, or whether there
"   is any cause that prevents the increase of the species, must be left for
"   future adventurers to determine."[5]

The account which Mr. Collins has given of these savages will, I hope, afford in some degree a satisfactory answer. They are described as, in general, neither tall nor well made. Their arms, legs, and thighs, are thin, which is ascribed to the poorness of their mode of living. Those who inhabit the sea-coast depend almost entirely on fish for their sustenance, relieved occasionally by a repast on some large grubs which are found in the body of the dwarf gum tree. The very scanty stock of animals in the woods, and the very great labour necessary to take them, keep the inland natives in as poor a condition as their brethren on the coast. They are compelled to climb the tallest trees after honey, and the smaller animals, such as the flying squirrel and the opossum. When the stems are of great height, and without branches, which is generally the case, in thick forests, this is a process of great labour, and is effected by cutting a notch with their stone hatchets for each foot successively, while their left arm embraces the tree. Trees were observed notched in this manner to the height of eighty feet before the first branch, where the hungry savage could hope to meet with any reward for so much toil.[6]

The woods, exclusive of the animals occasionally found in them, afford but little sustenance. A few berries, the yam, the fern root, and the flowers of the different banksia, make up the whole of the vegetable catalogue.[7]

A native with his child, surprised on the banks of the Hawksbury river by some of our colonists, launched his canoe in a hurry, and left behind him a specimen of his food, and of the delicacy of his stomach. From a piece of water-soken wood, full of holes, he had been extracting and eating a large worm. The smell both of the worm and its habitation was in the highest degree offensive. These worms, in the language of the country, are called cah-bro; and a tribe of natives dwelling inland, from the circumstance of

5. Cook's First Voy. vol. iii. p. 240.
6. Collins's Account of New South Wales, Appendix, p. 549. 4to.
7. Id. Appen. p. 557.

eating these loathsome worms, is named Cah-brogal. The wood natives also make a paste formed of the fern root, and the large and small ants bruised together, and, in the season, add the eggs of this insect.[8]

In a country, the inhabitants of which are driven to such resources for subsistence, where the supply of animal and vegetable food is so extremely scanty, and the labour necessary to procure it is so severe, it is evident, that the population must be very thinly scattered in proportion to the territory. Its utmost bounds must be very narrow. But when we advert to the strange and barbarous customs of these people, the cruel treatment of their women, and the difficulty of rearing children; instead of being surprised that it does not more frequently press to pass these bounds, we shall be rather inclined to consider even these scanty resources as more than sufficient to support all the population that could grow up under such circumstances.

The prelude to love in this country is violence, and of the most brutal nature. The savage selects his intended wife from the women of a different tribe, generally one at enmity with his own. He steals upon her in the absence of her protectors, and having first stupified her with blows of a club, or wooden sword, on the head, back, and shoulders, every one of which is followed by a stream of blood, he drags her through the woods by one arm, regardless of the stones and broken pieces of trees that may lie in his route, and anxious only to convey his prize in safety to his own party, where a most brutal scene ensues. The woman thus ravished becomes his wife, and is incorporated into the tribe to which he belongs, and but seldom quits him for another. The outrage is not resented by the relations of the female, who only retaliate by a similar outrage when it is in their power.[9]

The union of the sexes takes place at an early age, and instances were known to our colonists of very young girls having been much and shamefully abused by the males.[10]

The conduct of the husband to his wife, or wives, seems to be nearly in character with this strange and barbarous mode of courtship. The females bear on their heads the traces of the superiority of the males, which is exercised almost as soon as they find strength in their arms to inflict a blow. Some of these unfortunate beings have been observed with more scars on their shorn heads cut in every direction, than could well be counted. Mr. Collins feelingly says, "The condition of these women is so wretched, " that I have often, on seeing a female child borne on its mothers shoul-

8. Id. Appen. p. 558.   9. Collins's N. S. Wales, Appen. p. 559.
10. Appen p. 563.

" ders, anticipated the miseries to which it was born, and thought it would
" be a mercy to destroy it."[11] In another place, speaking of Bennilong's
wife being delivered of a child, he says, "I here find in my papers a note
" that for some offence Bennilong had severely beaten this woman in the
" morning, a short time before she was delivered."[12]

Women treated in this brutal manner must necessarily be subject to frequent miscarriages, and it is probable that the abuse of very young girls,
mentioned above as common, and the too early union of the sexes in general, would tend to prevent the females from being prolifick. Instances of a
plurality of wives were found more frequent than of a single wife; but what
is extraordinary, Mr. Collins did not recollect ever to have noticed children
by more than one. He had heard from some of the natives, that the first wife
claimed an exclusive right to the conjugal embrace, while the second was
merely the slave and drudge of both.[13]

An absolutely exclusive right in the first wife to the conjugal embrace
seems to be hardly probable; but it is possible that the second wife might
not be allowed to rear her offspring. At any rate, if the observation be generally true, it proves that a great part of the women are without children,
which can only be accounted for from the very severe hardships which they
undergo, or from some particular customs which may not have come to the
knowledge of Mr. Collins.

If the mother of a sucking child die, the helpless infant is buried alive in
the same grave with its mother. The father himself places his living child
on the body of his dead wife, and having thrown a large stone upon it, the
grave is instantly filled by the other natives. This dreadful act was performed by Co-le-be, a native well known to our colonists, and who, on
being talked to on the subject, justified the proceeding by declaring that
no woman could be found who would undertake to nurse the child, and
that therefore it must have died a much worse death than that which he had
given it. Mr. Collins had reason to believe that this custom was generally
prevalent, and observes, that it may in some measure account for the thin-
ness of the population.[14]

Such a custom, though in itself perhaps it might not much affect the
population of a country, places in a strong point of view the difficulty of
rearing children in savage life. Women, obliged by their habits of living to
a constant change of place, and compelled to an unremitting drudgery for
their husbands, appear to be absolutely incapable of bringing up two or

---

11. Collins's N. S. Wales, Appen. p. 583.   12. Appen. note p. 562.
13. Appen. p. 560.   14. Collins's N.S. Wales, Appendix, p. 607.

three children nearly of the same age. If another child be born before the one above it can shift for itself, and follow its mother on foot, one of the two must almost necessarily perish for want of care. The task of rearing even one infant, in such a wandering and laborious life, must be so troublesome and painful, that we are not to be surprised that no woman can be found to undertake it, who is not prompted by the powerful feelings of a mother.

To these causes, which forcibly repress the rising generation, must be added those which contribute subsequently to destroy it; such as the frequent wars of these savages with different tribes, and their perpetual contests with each other; their strange spirit of retaliation and revenge which prompts the midnight murder, and the frequent shedding of innocent blood; the smoke and filth of their miserable habitations, and their poor mode of living, productive of loathsome cutaneous disorders, and above all, a dreadful epidemic like the small-pox, which sweeps off great numbers.[15]

In the year 1789 they were visited by this epidemic which raged among them with all the appearance and virulence of the small-pox. The desolation that it occasioned was almost incredible. Not a living person was to be found in the bays and harbours that were before the most frequented. Not a vestige of a human foot was to be traced on the sands. They had left the dead to bury the dead. The excavations in the rocks were filled with putrid bodies, and in many places the paths were covered with skeletons.[16]

Mr. Collins was informed, that the tribe of Co-le-be, the native mentioned before, had been reduced by the effects of this dreadful disorder to three persons; who found themselves obliged to unite with some other tribe to prevent their utter extinction.[17]

Under such powerful causes of depopulation, we should naturally be inclined to suppose that the animal and vegetable produce of the country would be increasing upon the thinly scattered inhabitants, and, added to the supply of fish from their shores, would be more than sufficient for their consumption; yet, it appears upon the whole, that the population is in general so nearly on a level with the average supply of food, that every little deficiency from unfavourable weather, or other causes, occasions distress. Particular times, when the inhabitants seemed to be in great want, are mentioned as not uncommon, and at these periods, some of the natives were found reduced to skeletons, and almost starved to death.[18]

---

15. See generally, the Appendix to Collins's Account of the English Colony in New South Wales.

16. Collins's N. S. Wales, Appendix, p. 597.   17. Id. Appendix, p. 598.

18. Id. c. iii. p. 34. and Appendix, p. 551

C H A P .   IV.

Of the Checks to Population among the American Indians.

WE may next turn our view to the vast continent of America, the greatest part of which was found to be inhabited by small independent tribes
of savages, subsisting nearly in a similar manner to the natives of New
Holland on the productions of unassisted nature. The soil was covered by
an almost universal forest, and presented few of those fruits and esculent
vegetables which grow in such profusion in the islands of the South Sea.
The produce of a most rude and imperfect agriculture, known to some of
the tribes of hunters, was so trifling as to be considered only as a feeble
aid to the subsistence acquired by the chace. The inhabitants of this new
world, therefore, might be considered as living principally by hunting and
fishing;[1] and the narrow limits to this mode of subsistence are obvious. The
supplies derived from fishing could extend only to those who were within
a certain distance of the lakes, the rivers, or the sea-shore; and the ignorance and indolence of the improvident savage would frequently prevent
him from extending the benefits of these supplies much beyond the time
when they were actually obtained. The great extent of territory required for
the support of the hunter has been repeatedly stated and acknowledged.[2]
The number of wild animals within his reach, combined with the facility
with which they might be either killed or ensnared, must necessarily limit
the number of his society. Tribes of hunters, like beasts of prey, whom they
resemble in their mode of subsistence, will consequently be thinly scattered over the surface of the earth. Like beasts of prey, they must either
drive away, or fly from, every rival, and be engaged in perpetual contests
with each other.[3]

Under such circumstances, that America should be very thinly peopled
in proportion to its extent of territory, is merely an exemplification of the
obvious truth, that population cannot increase without the food to support
it. But the interesting part of the inquiry, that part, to which I would wish
particularly to draw the attention of the reader, is, the mode by which the
population is kept down to the level of this scanty supply. It cannot escape
observation, that an insufficient supply of food to any people, does not

1. Robertson's History of America, vol. ii. b. iv. p. 127. et seq. octavo edit.
1780.   2. Franklin's Miscell. p. 2.   3. Robertson, b. iv. p. 129.

shew itself merely in the shape of famine, but in other more permanent forms of distress, and in generating certain customs, which operate sometimes with greater force in the suppression of a rising population, than in its subsequent destruction.

It was generally remarked, that the American women were far from being prolific, their marriages seldom producing above two or three children.[4] This unfruitfulness has been attributed by some to a want of ardour in the men towards their women; a feature of character, which has been considered as peculiar to the American savage. It is not however peculiar to this race; but probably exists in a great degree among all barbarous nations, whose food is poor and insufficient, and who live in a constant apprehension of being pressed by famine, or by an enemy. Bruce frequently takes notice of it, particularly, in reference to the Galla and Shangalla, savage nations on the borders of Abyssinia;[5] and Le Vaillant mentions the phlegmatic temperament of the Hottentots as the chief reason of their thin population.[6] It seems to be generated by the hardships and dangers of savage life, which take off the attention from the sexual passion. And that these are the principal causes of it among the Americans, rather than any absolute constitutional defect, appears probable, from its diminishing, nearly in proportion to the degree in which these causes are mitigated, or removed. In those countries of America, where, from peculiar situation or further advantages in improvement, the hardships of savage life are less severely felt, the passion between the sexes becomes more ardent. Among some of the tribes seated on the banks of rivers well stored with fish, or others that inhabit a territory greatly abounding in game or much improved in agriculture, the women are more valued and admired; and as hardly any restraint is imposed on the gratification of desire, the dissolution of their manners is sometimes excessive.[7]

If we do not then consider this apathy of the Americans as a natural defect in the bodily frame, but merely as a general coldness, and an infrequency of the calls of the sexual appetite, we shall not be inclined to give

4. Robertson, b. iv. p. 106. Burke's America, vol. i. p. 187. Charlevoix, Hist. de la Nouvelle France, tom. iii. p. 304. Lafitau, Mœurs des Sauvages, tom. i. p. 590. In the course of this chapter I often give the same references as Robertson; but never, without having examined and verified them myself. Where I have not had an opportunity of doing this, I refer to Robertson alone.

5. Travels to discover the Source of the Nile, vol. ii. p. 223. 559.

6. Voyage dans l'Interieur de l'Afrique, tom. i. p. 12, 13.

7. Robertson, b. iv. p. 71. Lettres Edif. & Curieuses, tom vi. p. 48. 322, 330, tom. vii. p. 20. 12mo. edit. 1780. Charlevoix, tom. iii. p. 303, 423. Hennepin, Mœurs des Sauvages, p. 37.

much weight to it as affecting the number of children to a marriage; but shall be disposed to look for the cause of this unfruitfulness in the condition and customs of the women in a savage state. And here we shall find reasons amply sufficient to account for the fact in question.

It is finely observed by Dr. Robertson, that "Whether man has been
" improved by the progress of arts and civilization, is a question, which in
" the wantonness of disputation has been agitated among philosophers.
" That women are indebted to the refinement of polished manners for a
" happy change in their state, is a point, which can admit of no doubt."[8] In every part of the world, one of the most general characteristics of the savage is to despise and degrade the female sex.[9] Among most of the tribes in America their condition is so peculiarly grievous, that servitude is a name too mild to describe their wretched state. A wife is no better than a beast of burthen. While the man passes his days in idleness or amusement, the woman is condemned to incessant toil. Tasks are imposed upon her without mercy, and services are received without complacence or gratitude.[10] There are some districts in America where this state of degradation has been so severely felt, that mothers have destroyed their female infants, to deliver them at once from a life in which they were doomed to such a miserable slavery.[11]

This state of depression and constant labour added to the unavoidable hardships of savage life must be very unfavourable to the office of child-bearing;[12] and the libertinage which generally prevails among the women before marriage, with the habit of procuring abortions, in which they rarely fail, must necessarily render them more unfit for bearing children afterwards.[13] One of the missionaries speaking of the common practice among the Natchez of changing their wives, adds, unless they have children by them, a proof, that these marriages were in general unfruitful, which may be accounted for from the libertine lives of the women before wedlock, which he had previously noticed.[14]

8. Robertson, b. iv. p. 103.

9. Robertson, b. iv. p. 103. Lettres Edif. passim. Charlevoix Hist. Nouv. Fr. tom. iii. p. 287. Voy. de Perouse, c. ix. p. 402. 4to. London.

10. Robertson, b. iv. p. 105. Lettres Edif, tom. vi, p. 329. Major Roger's North America, p. 211. Creuxii Hist. Canad. p. 57.

11. Robertson, b. iv. p. 106. Raynal, Hist. des Indes, tom. iv. c. vii. p. 110. 8vo. 10 vol. 1795.

12. Robertson, b. iv. p. 106. Creuxii Hist. Canad. p. 57. Lafitau, tom. i. p. 590.

13. Robertson, b. iv. p. 72. Ellis's Voyage, p. 198. Burke's America, vol. i. p. 187.

14. Lettres Edif. tom. vii. p. 20. 22.

The causes, that Charlevoix assigns, of the sterility of the American women, are, the suckling their children for several years, during which time they do not cohabit with their husbands; the excessive labour to which they are always condemned in whatever situation they may be; and the custom established in many places of permitting the young women to prostitute themselves before marriage. Added to this, he says, the extreme misery to which these people are sometimes reduced, takes from them all desire of having children.[15] Among some of the ruder tribes it is a maxim not to burden themselves with rearing more than two of their offspring.[16] When twins are born, one of them is commonly abandoned, as the mother cannot rear them both; and when a mother dies during the period of suckling her child, no chance of preserving its life remains, and, as in New Holland, it is buried in the same grave with the breast that nourished it.[17]

As the parents are frequently exposed to want themselves, the difficulty of supporting their children becomes at times so great, that they are reduced to the necessity of abandoning or destroying them.[18] Deformed children are very generally exposed; and among some of the tribes in South America, the children of mothers who do not bear their labours well, experience a similar fate, from a fear that the offspring may inherit the weakness of its parent.[19]

To causes of this nature we must ascribe the remarkable exemption of the Americans from deformities of make. Even when a mother endeavours to rear all her children without distinction, so great a proportion of the whole number perishes under the rigorous treatment that must be their lot in the savage state, that probably none of those who labour under any original weakness or infirmity can attain the age of manhood. If they be not cut off as soon as they are born, they cannot long protract their lives under the severe discipline that awaits them.[20] In the Spanish provinces, where the Indians do not live so laborious a life, and are prevented from destroying their children, great numbers of them are deformed, dwarfish, mutilated, blind, and deaf.[21]

Polygamy seems to have been generally allowed among the Americans, but the privilege was seldom used, except by the Caciques and chiefs, and now and then by others in some of the fertile provinces of the South, where

15. Charlevoix, N. Fr. tom. iii. p. 304.
16. Robertson, b. iv. p. 107. Lettres Edif. tom. ix. p. 140.
17. Robertson, b. iv. p. 107. Lettres Edif. tom. viii. p. 86.
18. Robertson, b. iv. p. 108.   19. Lafitau, Mœurs des Sauv. tom, i. p. 592.
20. Charlevoix, tom. iii. p. 303. Raynal, Hist. des Indes, tom. viii. l.xv. p. 22.
21. Robertson, b. iv. p. 73. Voyage d'Ulloa, tom. i. p. 232.

subsistence was more easily procured. The difficulty of supporting a family confined the mass of the people to one wife;[22] and this difficulty was so generally known and acknowledged, that fathers, before they consented to give their daughters in marriage, required unequivocal proofs in the suitor of his skill in hunting, and his consequent ability to support a wife and children.[23] The women, it is said, do not marry early;[24] and this seems to be confirmed by the libertinage among them before marriage, so frequently taken notice of by the missionaries and other writers.[25]

The customs above enumerated, which appear to have been generated principally by the experience of the difficulties attending the rearing of a family, combined with the great proportion of children that must necessarily perish under the hardships of savage life, in spite of the best efforts of their parents to save them,[26] must, without doubt, most powerfully repress the rising generation.

When the young savage, by a fortunate train of circumstances, has passed safely through the perils of his childhood, other dangers scarcely less formidable await him on his approach to manhood. The diseases to which man is subject in the savage state, though fewer in number, are more violent and fatal than those which prevail in civilized society. As savages are wonderfully improvident, and their means of subsistence always precarious, they often pass from the extreme of want to exuberant plenty, according to the vicissitudes of fortune in the chace, or to the variety in the productions of the seasons.[27] Their inconsiderate gluttony in the one case, and their severe abstinence in the other, are equally prejudicial to the human constitution; and their vigour is accordingly at some seasons impaired by want, and at others by a superfluity of gross aliment, and the disorders arising from indigestions.[28] These, which may be considered as the unavoidable consequence of their mode of living, cut off considerable numbers in the prime of life. They are likewise extremely subject to consumptions, to pleuretic, asthmatic, and paralytic disorders, brought on by the immoderate hardships and fatigues which they endure in hunting and war, and by the inclemency of the seasons to which they are continually exposed.[29]

22. Robertson, b. iv. p. 102. Lettres Edif. tom. viii. p. 87.

23. Lettres Edif. tom. ix. p. 364. Robertson, b. iv. p. 115.

24. Robertson, b. iv. p. 107.   25. Lettres Edif. passim. Voyage d'Ulloa, tom. i. p. 343. Burke's America, vol. i. p. 187. Charlevoix, tom. iii. p. 303, 304.

26. Creuxius says, that scarcely one in thirty reach manhood. (Hist. Canad. p. 57); but this must be a great exaggeration.   27. Robertson, b. iv. p. 85.

28. Charlevoix, tom. iii. p. 302, 303.   29. Robertson, b. iv. p. 86. Charlevoix, tom. iii. p. 364. Lafitau, tom. ii. p. 360, 361.

The missionaries speak of the Indians in South America as subject to perpetual diseases for which they know no remedy.[30] Ignorant of the use of the most simple herbs, or of any change in their gross diet, they die of these diseases in great numbers. The jesuit Fauque says, that, in all the different excursions which he had made, he scarcely found a single individual of an advanced age.[31] Robertson determines the period of human life to be shorter among savages than in well-regulated and industrious communities.[32] Raynal, notwithstanding his frequent declarations in favour of savage life, says of the Indians of Canada, that few are so long lived as our people, whose manner of living is more uniform and tranquil.[33] And Cook and Perouse confirm these opinions in the remarks which they make on some of the inhabitants of the northwest coast of America.[34]

In the vast plains of South America, a burning sun operating on the extensive swamps and the inundations that succeed the rainy season, sometimes generates dreadful epidemics. The missionaries speak of contagious distempers as frequent among the Indians, and occasioning at times a great mortality in their villages.[35] The small-pox every where makes great ravages, as, from want of care, and from confined habitations, very few that are attacked recover from it.[36] The Indians of Paraguay are said to be extremely subject to contagious distempers, notwithstanding the care and attentions of the Jesuits. The small-pox and malignant fevers, which, from the ravages they make, are called plagues, frequently desolate these flourishing missions, and, according to Ulloa, are the cause that they had not increased in proportion to the time of their establishment, and the profound peace which they had enjoyed.[37]

These epidemics are not confined to the south. They are mentioned as if they were not uncommon among the more northern nations;[38] and, in a late voyage to the northwest coast of America, captain Vancouver gives an account of a most extraordinary desolation apparently produced by some distemper of this kind. From New Dungeness he traversed a hundred and fifty miles of the coast without seeing the same number of inhabitants. Deserted villages were frequent, each of which was large enough to contain all the scattered savages that had been observed in that extent of country. In the different excursions which he made, particularly about Port Discovery,

30. Lettres Edif, tom. viii. p. 83.   31. Lettres Edif, tom. vii. p. 317. et seq.
32. b. iv. p. 86.   33. Raynal, b. xv. p. 23.
34. Cook, third Voy. vol. iii. ch. ii. p. 520. Voy. de Perouse, ch. ix.
35. Lettres Edif. tom. viii. p. 79. 339. tom. ix. p. 125.
36. Voyage d'Ulloa, tom. i. p. 349.   37. Id. tom. i. p. 549.
38. Lettres Edif. tom. vi. p. 335.

the skulls, limbs, ribs, and backbones, or some other vestiges of the human body, were scattered promiscuously in great numbers; and, as no warlike scars were observed on the bodies of the remaining Indians, and no particular signs of fear and suspicion, the most probable conjecture seems to be, that this depopulation must have been occasioned by pestilential disease.[39] The small-pox appears to be common and fatal among the Indians on this coast. Its indelible marks were observed on many, and several had lost the sight of one eye from it.[40]

In general, it may be remarked of savages, that, from their extreme ignorance, the dirt of their persons, and the closeness and filth of their cabins,[41] they lose the advantage which usually attends a thinly peopled country, that, of being more exempt from pestilential diseases, than those which are fully inhabited. In some parts of America the houses are built for the reception of many different families, and fourscore or a hundred people are crowded together under the same roof. When the families live separately, the huts are extremely small, close, and wretched, without windows, and with the doors so low, that it is necessary to creep on the hands and knees to enter them.[42] On the northwest coast of America, the houses are in general of the large kind; and Meares describes one of most extraordinary dimensions belonging to a chief near Nootka Sound, in which eight hundred persons ate, sat, and slept.[43] All voyagers agree with respect to the filth of the habitations, and the personal nastiness of the people on this coast.[44] Captain Cook describes them as swarming with vermin, which they pick off and eat;[45] and the nastiness and stench of their houses, he says, is equal to their confusion.[46] Perouse declares that their cabins have a nastiness and stench, to which the den of no known animal in the world can be compared.[47]

Under such circumstances, it may be easily imagined what a dreadful havoc an epidemic must make, when once it appears among them; and it does not seem improbable, that the degree of filth described should generate distempers of this nature, as the air of their houses cannot be much purer than the atmosphere of the most crowded cities.

39. Vancouver's Voy. vol. i. b. ii. c. v. p. 256.   40. Id. c.iv. p. 242.

41. Charlevoix speaks in the strongest terms of the extreme filth and stench of the American cabins, "On ne peut entrer dans leur cabanes qu'on ne soit impesté"; and the dirt of their meals, he says, "vous feroit horreur." Vol. iii. p. 338.

42. Robertson, b. iv. p. 182. Voyage d' Ulloa, tom. i. p. 340.

43. Meares's Voyage, ch. xii. p. 138.   44. Id. ch. xxiii. p. 252. Vancouver's Voy. vol. iii. b.vi. c. i. p. 313.   45. Cook's 3d Voyage, vol. ii. p. 305.

46. c. iii. p. 316.   47. Voy. de Perouse, ch. ix. p. 403.

Those who escape the dangers of infancy and of disease are constantly exposed to the chances of war; and notwithstanding the extreme caution of the Americans in conducting their military operations, yet as they seldom enjoy any interval of peace, the waste of their numbers in war is considerable.[48] The rudest of the American nations are well acquainted with the rights of each community to its own domains.[49] And as it is of the utmost consequence to prevent others from destroying the game in their hunting grounds, they guard this national property with a jealous attention. Innumerable subjects of dispute necessarily arise. The neighbouring nations live in a perpetual state of hostility with each other.[50] The very act of increasing in one tribe, must be an act of aggression on its neighbours, as a larger range of territory will be necessary to support its increased numbers. The contest will in this case naturally continue, either till the equilibrium is restored by mutual losses, or till the weaker party is exterminated, or driven from its country. When the irruption of an enemy desolates their cultivated lands, or drives them from their hunting grounds, as they have seldom any portable stores, they are generally reduced to extreme want. All the people of the district invaded are frequently forced to take refuge in woods or mountains which can afford them no subsistence, and where many of them perish.[51] In such a flight each consults alone his individual safety. Children desert their parents, and parents consider their children as strangers. The ties of nature are no longer binding. A father will sell his son for a knife or a hatchet.[52] Famine, and distresses of every kind, complete the destruction of those whom the sword had spared; and in this manner whole tribes are frequently extinguished.[53]

Such a state of things has powerfully contributed to generate that ferocious spirit of warfare observable among savages in general, and most particularly among the Americans. Their object in battle is not conquest, but destruction.[54] The life of the victor depends on the death of his enemy; and, in the rancour and fell spirit of revenge with which he pursues him, he seems constantly to bear in mind the distresses that would be consequent on defeat. Among the Iroquois, the phrase by which they express their resolution of making war against an enemy, is, "Let us go and eat that nation." If they solicit the aid of a neighbouring tribe, they invite it to eat broth made

---

48. Charlevoix, Hist. N. Fr. tom. iii. 202, 203, 429.
49. Robertson, b. iv. p. 147.   50. Ibid. Lettres Edif. tom. viii. p. 40, 86, & passim. Cook's 3d Voy. vol. ii. p. 324. Meares's Voy. ch. xxiv. p. 267.
51. Robertson, b. iv. p. 172. Charlevoix, N. Fr. tom. iii. p. 203.
52. Lettres Edif. tom. viii. p. 346.   53. Robertson, b. iv. p. 172. Account of N. America, by Major Rogers, p. 250.   54. Robertson, b. iv. p. 150.

of the flesh of their enemies.[55] Among the Abnakis, when a body of their warriors enters an enemy's territory, it is generally divided into different parties of thirty or forty; and the chief says to each, to you is given such a hamlet to eat, to you such a village,[56] &c. These expressions remain in the language of some of the tribes, in which the custom of eating their prisoners taken in war no longer exists. Cannibalism, however, undoubtedly prevailed in many parts of the new world;[57] and, contrary to the opinion of Dr. Robertson, I cannot but think that it must have had its origin in extreme want, though the custom might afterwards be continued from other motives. It seems to be a worse compliment to human nature, and to the savage state, to attribute this horrid repast to malignant passions, without the goad of necessity, rather than to the great law of self-preservation, which has, at times, overcome every other feeling even among the most humane and civilized people. When once it had prevailed, though only occasionally, from this cause, the fear that a savage might feel of becoming a repast to his enemies, might easily raise the passion of rancour and revenge to so high a pitch, as to urge him to treat his prisoners in this way, though not prompted at the time by hunger.

The missionaries speak of several nations, which appeared to use human flesh whenever they could obtain it, as they would the flesh of any of the rarer animals.[58] These accounts may perhaps be exaggerated, though they seem to be confirmed, in a great degree, by the late voyages to the northwest coast of America, and by Captain Cook's description of the state of society in the southern island of New Zealand.[59] The people of Nootka Sound appear to be cannibals,[60] and the chief of the district Maquinna is said to be so addicted to this horrid banquet, that, in cold blood, he kills a slave every moon to gratify his unnatural appetite.[61]

The predominant principle of self-preservation, connected in the breast of the savage, most intimately, with the safety and power of the community to which he belongs, prevents the admission of any of those ideas of honour and gallantry in war, which prevail among more civilized nations. To fly from an adversary that is on his guard, and to avoid a contest where he cannot contend without risk to his own person, and consequently to his

---

55. Id. p. 164.   56. Lettres Edif. tom. vi. p. 205.

57. Robertson, b. iv. p. 164.   58. Lettres Edif. tom. viii. p. 105, 271. tom. vi. p. 266.

59. Cautious as Captain Cook always is, he says of the New Zealanders, "it was but too evident that they have a great liking for this kind of food." Second Voy. vol. i. p. 246. And in the last voyage, speaking of their perpetual hostilities, he says, "and perhaps the desire of a good meal may be no small incitement." Vol. i. p. 137.

60. Cook's Third Voy. vol. ii. p. 271.   61. Meares's Voy. ch. xxiii. p. 255.

community, is the point of honour with the American. The odds of ten to one are necessary to warrant an attack on a person who is armed and prepared to resist, and even then, each is afraid of being the first to advance.[62] The great object of the most renowned warrior, is, by every art of cunning and deceit, by every mode of stratagem and surprize, that his invention can suggest, to weaken and destroy the tribes of his enemies with the least possible loss to his own. To meet an enemy on equal terms is regarded as extreme folly. To fall in battle, instead of being reckoned an honourable death,[63] is a misfortune, which subjects the memory of a warrior to the imputation of rashness and imprudence. But to lie in wait day after day, till he can rush upon his prey, when most secure, and least able to resist him; to steal in the dead of night upon his enemies, set fire to their huts, and massacre the inhabitants, as they fly naked and defenceless from the flames,[64] are deeds of glory, which will be of deathless memory in the breasts of his grateful countrymen.

This mode of warfare is evidently generated by a consciousness of the difficulties attending the rearing of new citizens under the hardships and dangers of savage life. And these powerful causes of destruction may, in some instances, be so great, as to keep down the population even considerably below the means of subsistence; but the fear that the Americans betray of any diminution of their society, and their apparent wish to increase it, are no proofs that this is generally the case. The country could not probably support the addition that is coveted in each society; but an accession of strength to one tribe, opens to it new sources of subsistence in the comparative weakness of its adversaries; and, on the contrary, a diminution of its numbers, so far from giving greater plenty to the remaining members, subjects them to extirpation or famine from the irruptions of their stronger neighbours.

The Chiriguanes, originally only a small part of the tribe of Guaranis, left their native country in Paraguay, and settled in the mountains towards Peru. They found sufficient subsistence in their new country, increased rapidly, attacked their neighbours, and, by superior valour, or superior fortune, gradually exterminated them, and took possession of their lands, occupying a great extent of country; and having increased, in the course of some years, from three or four thousand, to thirty thousand,[65] while the tribes of their weaker neighbours were daily thinned by famine and the sword.

62. Lettres Edif. tom. vi. p. 360.   63. Charlevoix, N. Fr. tom. iii. p. 376.
64. Robertson, b. iv. p. 155. Lettres Edif. tom. vi. p. 182, 360.
65. Lettres Edif. tom. viii. p. 243. Les Chiriguanes multiplierent prodigieusement, et en assez peu d'années leur nombre monta a trente mille ames.

Such instances prove the rapid increase, even of the Americans, under favourable circumstances, and sufficiently account for the fear in every tribe of diminishing its numbers, and the frequent wish to increase them,[66] without supposing a superabundance of food in the territory actually possessed.

That the increase of the Americans is regulated more by the means of subsistence, than by any of the other causes that have been mentioned as affecting their population; or rather, perhaps, I should say, that these causes themselves are principally regulated by the plenty or scarcity of subsistence, is sufficiently evinced, from the greater frequency of the tribes, and the greater numbers in each, throughout all those parts of the country, where, from the vicinity of lakes or rivers, the superior fertility of the soil, or further advances in improvement, food becomes more abundant. In the interior of the provinces bordering on the Oronoco, several hundred miles may be traversed in different directions, without finding a single hut, or observing the footsteps of a single creature. In some parts of North America, where the climate is more rigorous, and the soil less fertile, the desolation is still greater. Vast tracts of some hundred leagues have been crossed through uninhabited plains and forests.[67] The missionaries speak of journies of twelve days without meeting with a single soul,[68] and of immense tracts of country, in which scarcely three or four scattered villages were to be found.[69] Some of these deserts did not furnish game,[70] and were therefore entirely desolate; others, which were to a certain degree stocked with it, were traversed in the hunting seasons, by parties, who encamped, and remained in different spots, according to the success they met with, and were therefore really inhabited in proportion to the quantity of subsistence which they yielded.[71]

Other districts of America are described as comparatively fully peopled; such as the borders of the great northern lakes, the shores of the Missisippi, Louisiana, and many provinces in South America. The villages here were large, and near each other, in proportion to the superior fruitfulness of the territory in game and fish, and the advances made by the inhabitants in agriculture.[72] The Indians of the great and populous empires of Mexico and Peru, sprung undoubtedly from the same stock, and originally

66. Lafitau, tom. ii. p. 163.   67. Robertson, b. iv. p. 129, 130.

68. Lettres Edif. tom. vi. p. 357.   69. Lettres Edif. tom. vi. p. 321.

70. Lettres Edif. tom. ix. p. 145.   71. Lettres Edif. tom. vi. p. 66, 81, 345. tom. ix. p. 145.   72. Lettres Edif. tom. ix. p. 90, 142. Robertson, b. iv. p. 141.

possessed the same customs, as their ruder brethren; but the moment that, by a fortunate train of circumstances, they were led to improve and extend their agriculture, a considerable population rapidly followed, in spite of the apathy of the men, or the destructive habits of the women. These habits would, indeed, in a great measure yield to the change of circumstances; and the substitution of a more quiet and sedentary life, for a life of perpetual wandering and hardship, would immediately render the women more fruitful, and enable them at the same time to attend to the wants of a larger family.

In a general view of the American continent, as described by historians, the population seems to have been spread over the surface very nearly in proportion to the quantity of food, which the inhabitants of the different parts, in the actual state of their industry and improvement, could obtain; and that, with few exceptions, it pressed hard against this limit, rather than fell short of it, appears, from the frequent recurrence of distress for want of food in all parts of America.

Remarkable instances occur, according to Dr. Robertson, of the calamities which rude nations suffer by famine. As one of them, he mentions an account given by Alvar Nugnez Cabeca de Vaca, one of the Spanish adventurers, who resided almost nine years among the savages of Florida. He describes them as unacquainted with every species of agriculture, and living chiefly upon the roots of different plants, which they procure with great difficulty, wandering from place to place in search of them. Sometimes they kill game, sometimes they catch fish, but in such small quantities, that their hunger is so extreme, as to compel them to eat spiders, the eggs of ants, worms, lizards, serpents, a kind of unctuous earth, and, I am persuaded, he says, that, if in this country there were any stones, they would swallow them. They preserve the bones of fishes and serpents, which they grind into powder and eat. The only season when they do not suffer much from famine, is when a certain fruit like the opuntia, or prickly-pear, is ripe; but they are sometimes obliged to travel far from their usual place of residence in order to find it. In another place, he observes, that they are frequently reduced to pass two or three days without food.[73]

Ellis, in his voyage to Hudson's Bay, feelingly describes the sufferings of the Indians in that neighbourhood from extreme want. Having mentioned the severity of the climate, he says, "Great as these hardships are " which result from the rigour of the cold, yet it may justly be affirmed, " that they are much inferior to those which they feel from the scarcity of

73. Robertson, note 28. to p. 117. b. iv.

" provisions, and the difficulty they are under of procuring them. A story
" which is related at the factories, and known to be true, will sufficiently
" prove this, and give the compassionate reader a just idea of the miseries
" to which these unhappy people are exposed." He then gives an account
of a poor Indian and his wife, who, on the failure of game, having eaten up
all the skins which they wore as clothing, were reduced to the dreadful
extremity of supporting themselves on the flesh of two of their children.[74]
In another place he says, "It has sometimes happened, that the Indians who
" come in summer to trade at the factories, missing the succours they ex-
" pected, have been obliged to singe off the hair from thousands of beaver
" skins in order to feed upon the leather."[75]

The Abbé Raynal, who is continually reasoning most inconsistently in
his comparisons of savage and civilized life, though in one place he speaks
of the savage as morally sure of a competent subsistence, yet in his account of the nations of Canada, he says, that though they lived in a country
abounding in game and fish, yet in some seasons, and sometimes for whole
years, this resource failed them; and famine then occasioned a great destruction among a people who were at too great a distance to assist each other.[76]

Charlevoix, speaking of the inconveniences and distresses to which the
missionaries were subject, observes, that not unfrequently the evils which
he had been describing are effaced by a greater, in comparison of which
all the others are nothing. This is famine. It is true, says he, that the savages can bear hunger with as much patience, as they shew carelessness in
providing against it; but they are sometimes reduced to extremities beyond
their power to support.[77]

It is the general custom among most of the American nations, even those
which have made some progress in agriculture, to disperse themselves in
the woods at certain seasons of the year, and to subsist for some months
on the produce of the chace, as a principal part of their annual supplies.[78]
To remain in their villages, exposes them to certain famine;[79] and in the
woods they are not always sure to escape it. The most able hunters sometimes fail of success, even where there is no deficiency of game;[80] and in
their forests, on the failure of this resource, the hunter or the traveller is
exposed to the most cruel want.[81] The Indians, in their hunting excursions,
are sometimes reduced to pass three or four days without food;[82] and a

74. p. 196.   75. p. 194.   76. Raynal, Hist. des Indes, tom. viii. 1. xv. p. 22.
77. Hist. N. Fr. tom. iii. p. 338.   78. Lettres Edif. tom. vi. p. 66, 81, 345. ix. 145.
79. Lettres Edif. tom. vi. 82, 196, 197, 215. ix. 151.
80. Charlevoix, N. Fr. tom. iii. p. 201. Hennessin, Mœurs des Sauv. p. 78.
81. Lettres Edif. tom. vi. p. 167, 220.   82. Id. tom. vi. p. 33.

missionary relates an account of some Iroquois who, on one of these occasions, having supported themselves as long as they could, by eating the
skins which they had with them, their shoes, and the bark of trees, at length,
in despair, sacrificed some of the party to support the rest. Out of eleven,
five only returned alive.[83]

The Indians, in many parts of South America, live in extreme want,[84]
and are sometimes destroyed by absolute famines.[85] The islands, rich as
they appeared to be, were peopled fully up to the level of their produce. If a
few Spaniards settled in any district, such a small addition of supernumerary mouths soon occasioned a severe dearth of provisions.[86] The flourishing Mexican empire was in the same state in this respect; and Cortez often
found the greatest difficulty in procuring subsistence for his small body of
soldiers.[87] Even the Missions of Paraguay, with all the care and foresight
of the Jesuits, and notwithstanding that their population was kept down by
frequent epidemicks, were by no means totally exempt from the pressure
of want. The Indians of the Mission of St. Michael are mentioned as having at one time increased so much, that the lands, capable of cultivation in
their neighbourhood, produced only half of the grain necessary for their
support.[88] Long droughts often destroyed their cattle,[89] and occasioned a
failure of their crops; and on these occasions some of the Missions were
reduced to the most extreme indigence, and would have perished from famine, but for the assistance of their neighbours.[90]

The late voyages to the northwest coast of America, confirm these accounts of the frequent pressure of want in savage life, and shew the uncertainty of the resource of fishing, which seems to afford, in general, the
most plentiful harvest of food that is furnished by unassisted nature. The
sea on the coast near Nootka Sound is seldom or never so much frozen as
to prevent the inhabitants from having access to it. Yet from the very great
precautions they use in laying up stores for the winter, and their attention
to prepare and preserve whatever food is capable of it, for the colder seasons, it is evident that the sea at these times yields no fish; and it appears,
that they often undergo very great hardships from want of provisions in the
cold months.[91] During a Mr. Maccay's stay at Nootka Sound, from 1786 to
1787, the length and severity of the winter occasioned a famine. The stock
of dried fish was expended, and no fresh supplies of any kind were to be

83. Id. tom. vi. p. 71.   84. Id. tom. vii. p. 383. ix. 140.   85. Id. tom. viii. p. 79.
86. Robertson, b. iv. p. 121. Burke's America, vol. i. p. 30.
87. Robertson, b. viii. p. 212.   88. Lettres Edif. tom. ix. p. 381.
89. Id. tom. ix. p. 191.   90. Id. tom. ix. p. 206, 380.
91. Meares's Voy. ch. xxiv. p. 266.

caught, so that the natives were obliged to submit to a fixed allowance, and the chiefs brought every day to our countrymen the stated meal of seven dried herrings' heads. Mr. Meares says, that the perusal of this gentleman's journal would shock any mind tinctured with humanity.[92]

Captain Vancouver mentions some of the people to the north of Nootka Sound, as living very miserably on a paste made of the inner bark of the pine tree, and cockles.[93] In one of the boat excursions, a party of Indians was met with who had some halibut, but, though very high prices were offered, they could not be induced to part with any. This, as Captain Vancouver observes, was singular, and indicated a very scanty supply.[94] At Nootka Sound in the year 1794, fish had become very scarce, and bore an exorbitant price; as, either from the badness of the season, or from neglect, the inhabitants had experienced the greatest distress for want of provisions during the winter.[95]

Perouse describes the Indians in the neighbourhood of Port Francois, as living during the summer in the greatest abundance by fishing, but exposed in the winter to perish from want.[96]

It is not, therefore, as Lord Kaimes imagines, that the American tribes have never increased sufficiently to render the pastoral or agricultural state necessary to them;[97] but, from some cause or other, they have not adopted in any great degree these more plentiful modes of procuring subsistence, and therefore, cannot have increased so as to become populous. If hunger alone could have prompted the savage tribes of America to such a change in their habits, I do not conceive that there would have been a single nation of hunters and fishers remaining; but it is evident, that some fortunate train of circumstances, in addition to this stimulus, is necessary for this purpose; and it is undoubtedly probable, that these arts of obtaining food, will be first invented and improved in those spots that are best suited to them, and where the natural fertility of the situation, by allowing a greater number of people to subsist together, would give the fairest chance to the inventive powers of the human mind.

Among most of the American tribes that we have been considering, so great a degree of equality prevailed, that all the members of each community would be nearly equal sharers in the general hardships of savage life, and in the pressure of occasional famines. But in many of the more southern nations, as in Bagota,[98] and among the Natchez,[99] and particularly

92. Id. ch. xi. p. 132.   93. Vancouver's Voy. vol. ii. b. ii. c. ii. p. 273.

94. Id. p. 282.   95. Id. vol. iii. b. vi. c. i. p. 304.

96. Voy. de Perouse, ch. ix. p. 400.   97. Sketches of the Hist. of Man. vol. i. p. 99, 105. 8vo. 2d edit.   98. Robertson, b. iv. p. 141.

99. Lettres Edif. tom. vii. p. 21. Robertson, b. iv. p. 139.

in Mexico and Peru, where a great distinction of ranks prevailed, and the lower classes were in a state of absolute servitude,[100] it is evident that, on occasion of any failure of subsistence, these would be the principal sufferers, and the positive checks to population would act almost exclusively on this part of the community.

The very extraordinary depopulation that has taken place among the American Indians, may appear to some to contradict the theory which is intended to be established; but it will be found that the causes of this rapid diminution may all be resolved into the three great checks to population that have been stated; and it is not asserted, that these checks, operating from particular circumstances with unusual force, may not in some instances be more powerful even than the principle of increase.

The insatiable fondness of the Indians for spirituous liquors,[101] which, according to Charlevoix, is a rage that passes all expression,[102] by producing among them perpetual quarrels and contests, which often terminate fatally, by exposing them to a new train of disorders which their mode of life, unfits them to contend with, and, by deadening and destroying the generative faculty in its very source, may alone be considered as a vice adequate to produce the present depopulation. In addition to this, it should be observed, that almost every where the connexion of the Indians with Europeans, has tended to break their spirit, to weaken or to give a wrong direction to their industry, and in consequence to diminish the sources of subsistence. In St. Domingo, the Indians neglected purposely to cultivate their lands in order to starve out their cruel oppressors.[103] In Peru and Chili, the forced industry of the natives was fatally directed to the digging into the bowels of the earth, instead of cultivating its surface; and among the northern nations, the extreme desire to purchase European spirits, directed the industry of the greatest part of them, almost exclusively, to the procuring of peltry for the purpose of this exchange,[104] which would prevent their attention to the more fruitful sources of subsistence, and at the same time tend rapidly to destroy the produce of the chace. The number of wild animals, in all the known parts of America, is probably even more diminished than the number of people.[105] The attention to agriculture has every where slackened, rather than increased, as might at first have been expected, from

---

100. Robertson, b. vii. p. 190, 242.   101. Major Rogers's Account of North America, p. 210.   102. Charlevoix, tom. iii. p. 302.   103. Robertson, b. ii. p. 185. Burke's America, vol. i. p. 300.   104. Charlevoix, N. Fr. tom. iii. p. 260.

105. The general introduction of fire-arms among the Indians, has probably greatly contributed to the diminution of the wild animals.

European connexion. In no part of America, either North or South, do we hear of any of the Indian nations living in great plenty, in consequence of their diminished numbers. It may not, therefore, be very far from the truth, to say, that even now, in spite of all the powerful causes of destruction that have been mentioned, the average population of the American nations is, with few exceptions, on a level with the average quantity of food, which in the present state of their industry they can obtain.

C H A P . V.

Of the Checks to Population in the Islands of the South Sea.

THE Abbé Raynal speaking of the ancient state of the British isles, and of islanders in general, says of them: "It is among these people that we " trace the origin of that multitude of singular institutions that retard the " progress of population. Anthropophagy, the castration of males, the in- " fibulation of females, late marriages, the consecration of virginity, the " approbation of celibacy, the punishments exercised against girls who " become mothers at too early an age,"[1] &c. These customs, caused by a superabundance of population in islands, have been carried, he says, to the continents, where philosophers of our days are still employed to investigate the reason of them. The Abbé does not seem to be aware, that a savage tribe in America, surrounded by enemies, or a civilized and populous nation, hemmed in by others in the same state, is in many respects in a similar situation. Though the barriers to a further increase of population be not so well defined, and so open to common observation, on continents, as on islands, yet they still present obstacles that are nearly as insurmountable: and the emigrant, impatient of the distresses which he felt in his own country, is by no means secure of finding relief in another. There is probably no island yet known, the produce of which could not be further increased. This is all that can be said of the whole earth. Both are peopled up to their actual produce. And the whole earth is in this respect like an island. But as the bounds to the number of people on islands, particularly when they are of small extent, are so narrow, and so distinctly marked, that every person must see and acknowlege them, an inquiry into the checks to population on those of which we have the most authentic accounts may perhaps tend considerably to illustrate the present subject. The question that is asked in captain Cook's first voyage, with respect to the thinly scattered savages of New Holland, "By what means the inhabitants of this country are reduced to such a num- " ber as it can subsist?"[2] may be asked with equal propriety of the most populous islands in the South Sea, or of the best peopled countries in Europe and Asia. The question, applied generally, appears to me to be highly curious, and to lead to the elucidation of some of the most obscure,

1. Raynal, Hist. des Indes, vol. ii, liv. iii. p. 3. 10 vols. 8vo. 1795.
2. Cook's First Voyage, vol. iii. p. 240. 4to.

yet important points, in the history of human society. I cannot so clearly and concisely describe the precise aim of the first part of the present work, as by saying, that it is an endeavour to answer this question so applied.

Of the large islands of New Guinea, New Britain, New Caledonia, and the New Hebrides, little is known with certainty. The state of society in them is probably very similar to that which prevails among many of the savage nations of America. They appear to be inhabited by a number of different tribes who are engaged in frequent hostilities with each other. The chiefs have little authority; and private property being in consequence insecure, provisions have been rarely found on them in abundance.[3] With the large island of New Zealand we are better acquainted; but not in a manner to give us a favourable impression of the state of society among its inhabitants. The picture of it drawn by captain Cook in his three different voyages, contains some of the darkest shades that are any where to be met with in the history of human nature. The state of perpetual hostility in which the different tribes of these people live with each other, seems to be even more striking than among the savages of any part of America;[4] and their custom of eating human flesh, and even their relish for that kind of food, are established beyond a possibility of doubt.[5] Captain Cook, who is by no means inclined to exaggerate the vices of savage life, says of the natives in the neighbourhood of Queen Charlotte's Sound, "If I had followed
" the advice of all our pretended friends, I might have extirpated the whole
" race; for the people of each hamlet or village, by turns, applied to me to
" destroy the other. One would have thought it almost impossible that so
" striking a proof of the divided state in which these miserable people
" live, could have been assigned."[6] And in the same chapter further on, he
" says, "From my own observations, and the information of Taweiharooa,
" it appears to me, that the New Zealanders must live under perpetual ap-
" prehensions of being destroyed by each other; there being few of their
" tribes that have not, as they think, sustained wrongs from some other
" tribes, which they are continually upon the watch to revenge. And
" perhaps the desire of a good meal may be no small incitement.****Their
" method of executing their horrible designs, is by stealing upon the

---

3. See the different accounts of New Guinea and New Britain, in the *Histoire des Navigations aux terres Australes*; and of New Caledonia and the New Hebrides in Cook's Second Voyage, vol. ii. b. iii.

4. Cook's First Voyage, vol. ii. p. 345. Second Voyage, vol i. p 101. Third Voyage, vol. i. p. 161, &c.   5. Second Voyage, vol. i. p. 246.   6. Third Voyage, vol. i p. 124.

"   adverse party in the night; and if they find them unguarded (which,
"   however, I believe is very seldom the case) they kill every one indis-
"   criminately, not even sparing the women and children. When the mas-
"   sacre is completed, they either feast and gorge themselves on the spot,
"   or carry off as many of the dead bodies as they can, and devour them at
"   home with acts of brutality too shocking to be described.****To give
"   quarter, or to take prisoners, makes no part of the military law, so that
"   the vanquished can only save their lives by flight. This perpetual state of
"   war, and destructive method of conducting it, operates so strongly in
"   producing habitual circumspection, that one hardly ever finds a New
"   Zealander off his guard, either by night or by day."[7]

As these observations occur in the last voyage, in which, the errors
of former accounts would have been corrected, and as a constant state of
warfare is here represented as prevailing to such a degree, that it may be
considered as the principal check to the population of New Zealand, little
need be added on this subject. We are not informed whether any customs
are practised by the women unfavourable to population. If such be known,
they are probably never resorted to, except in times of great distress; as
each tribe will naturally wish to increase the number of its members, in
order to give itself greater power of attack and defence. But the vagabond
life which the women of the southern island lead, and the constant state
of alarm in which they live, being obliged to travel and work with arms in
their hands,[8] must undoubtedly be very unfavourable to gestation, and tend
greatly to prevent large families.

Yet, powerful as these checks to population are, it appears, from the
recurrence of seasons of scarcity, that they seldom repress the number of
people below the average means of subsistence. "That such seasons there
"   are (Captain Cook says) our observations leave us no room to
"   doubt."[9] Fish is a principal part of their food, which, being only to be
procured on the sea coast, and at certain times,[10] must always be considered
as a precarious resource. It must be extremely difficult to dry and preserve
any considerable stores in a state of society subject to such constant alarms;
particularly, as we may suppose, that the bays and creeks most abounding
in fish would most frequently be the subject of obstinate contest, to people
who were wandering in search of food.[11] The vegetable productions are, the
fern root, yams, clams, and potatoes.[12] The three last are raised by cultiva-

7. Cook's Third Voy. vol. i. p. 137.   8. Id. Second Voy. vol. i. p. 127.
9. Id. First Voy. vol. iii. p. 66.   10. Id. p. 43.
11. Cook's Third Voy. vol. i. p. 157.   12. Id. First Voy. vol. iii. p. 43.

tion, and are seldom found on the southern island, where agriculture is but little known.[13] On the occasional failure of these scanty resources from unfavourable seasons, it may be imagined that the distress must be dreadful. At such periods it does not seem improbable, that the desire of a good meal should give additional force to the desire of revenge, and that they should be "perpetually destroying each other by violence, as the only alter-" native of perishing by hunger."[14]

If we turn our eyes from the thinly scattered inhabitants of New Zealand, to the crowded shores of Otaheite and the Society Islands, a different scene opens to our view. All apprehension of dearth seems at first sight to be banished from a country that is described to be fruitful as the garden of the Hesperides.[15] But this first impression would be immediately corrected by a moment's reflection. Happiness and plenty have always been considered as the most powerful causes of increase. In a delightful climate, where few diseases are known, and the women are condemned to no severe fatigues, why should not these causes operate with a force unparalleled in less favourable regions? Yet, if they did, where could the population find room and food in such circumscribed limits? If the numbers in Otaheite, not 40 leagues in circuit, surprised Captain Cook, when he calculated them at two hundred and four thousand,[16] where could they be disposed of in a single century, when they would amount to above three millions, supposing them to double their numbers every twenty-five years.[17] Each island of the group would be in a similar situation. The removal from one to another, would be a change of place, but not a change of the species of distress. Effectual emigration, or effectual importation, would be utterly excluded, from the situation of the islands, and the state of navigation among their inhabitants.

The difficulty, here, is reduced to so narrow a compass, is so clear, precise, and forcible, that we cannot escape from it. It cannot be answered in the usual vague and inconsiderate manner, by talking of emigration, and further cultivation. In the present instance we cannot but acknowledge, that

13. Id. First Voy. vol. ii. p. 405.   14. Id. First Voy. vol. iii. p. 45.

15. Missionary Voy. Appendix, p. 347.

16. Cook's Second Voy. vol. i. p. 349.

17. I feel very little doubt that this rate of increase is much slower than would really take place, supposing every check to be removed. If Otaheite, with its present produce, were peopled only with an hundred persons, the two sexes in equal numbers, and each man constant to one woman, I cannot but think, that for five or six successive periods, the increase would be more rapid than in any instance hitherto known, and that they would probably double their numbers in less than fifteen years.

the one is impossible, and the other glaringly inadequate. The fullest conviction must stare us in the face, that the people on this group of islands could not continue to double their numbers every twenty-five years; and before we proceed to inquire into the state of society on them, we must be perfectly certain, that, unless a perpetual miracle render the women barren, we shall be able to trace some very powerful checks to population in the habits of the people.

The successive accounts that we have received of Otaheite and the neighbouring islands, leave us no room to doubt the existence of the Eareeoie societies[18] which have justly occasioned so much surprise among civilized nations. They have been so often described, that little more need be said of them here, than that promiscuous intercourse and infanticide appear to be their fundamental laws. They consist exclusively of the higher classes; "and (according to Mr. Anderson[19]) so agreeable is this licentious
" plan of life to their disposition, that the most beautiful of both sexes thus
" commonly spend their youthful days, habituated to the practice of enor-
" mities that would disgrace the most savage tribes.****When an Eareeoie
" woman is delivered of a child, a piece of cloth dipped in water is applied
" to the mouth and nose which suffocates it."[20] Captain Cook observes, "It is certain, that these societies greatly prevent the increase of the superior
" classes of people of which they are composed."[21] Of the truth of this observation there can be no doubt.

Though no particular institutions of the same nature have been found among the lower classes; yet the vices which form their most prominent features are but too generally spread. Infanticide is not confined to the Eareeoies. It is permitted to all; and as its prevalence, among the higher classes of the people, has removed from it all odium, or imputation of poverty, it is probably often adopted, rather as a fashion, than a resort of necessity, and appears to be practised familiarly and without reserve.

It is a very just observation of Hume, that the permission of infanticide generally contributes to increase the population of a country.[22] By removing the fears of too numerous a family, it encourages marriage, and the

---

18. Cook's First Voy. vol. ii. p. 207. & seq. Second Voy. vol. i. p. 352. Third Voy. vol. ii. p. 157. & seq. Missionary Voy. Appendix, p. 346. 4to.

19. Mr. Anderson acted in the capacity of naturalist and surgeon in Cook's last voyage. Captain Cook and all the officers of the expedition seem to have had a very high opinion of his talents and accuracy of observation. His accounts therefore may be looked upon as of the first authority.

20. Cook's Third Voy. vol. ii. p. 158, 159.　　21. Id. Second Voy. vol. i. p. 352.

22. Hume's Essays, vol. i. essay xi. p. 431. 8vo. 1764.

powerful yearnings of nature prevent parents from resorting to so cruel an expedient, except in extreme cases. The fashion of the Eareeoie societies in Otaheite and its neighbouring islands, may have made them an exception to this observation, and the custom has probably here a contrary tendency.

The debauchery and promiscuous intercourse which prevail among the lower classes of people, though in some instances they may have been exaggerated, are established to a great extent, on unquestionable authority. Captain Cook, in a professed endeavour to rescue the women of Otaheite from a too general imputation of licentiousness, acknowledges that there are more of this character here, than in other countries, making at the same time a remark of a most decisive nature, by observing, that the women who thus conduct themselves, do not in any respect lower their rank in society, but mix indiscriminately with those of the most virtuous character.[23]

The common marriages in Otaheite are without any other ceremony than a present, from the man to the parents of the girl. And this seems to be rather a bargain with them for permission to try their daughter, than an absolute contract for a wife. If the father should think that he has not been sufficiently paid for his daughter, he makes no scruple of forcing her to leave her friend, and to cohabit with another person who may be more liberal. The man is always at liberty to make a new choice. Should his consort become pregnant, he may kill the child, and after that continue his connexion with the mother or leave her, according to his pleasure. It is only when he has adopted a child, and suffered it to live, that the parties are considered as in the marriage state. A younger wife, however, may afterwards be joined to the first; but the changing of connexions is much more general than this plan, and is a thing so common, that they speak of it with great indifference.[24] Libertinage before marriage, seems to be no objection to a union of this kind ultimately.

The checks to population from such a state of society would alone appear sufficient to counteract the effects of the most delightful climate and the most exuberant plenty. Yet these are not all. The wars between the inhabitants of the different islands, and their civil contentions among themselves, are frequent, and sometimes carried on in a very destructive manner.[25] Besides the waste of human life in the field of battle, the conquerors generally ravage the enemy's territory, kill or carry off the hogs and poultry, and reduce as much as possible the means of future subsistence. The island of Otaheite which, in the years 1767 and 1768, swarmed with

---

23. Cook's Second Voy. vol. i. p. 187.   24. Id. Third Voy. vol. ii. p. 157.
25. Bouganville, Voy. autour du Monde, ch. iii. p. 217. Cook's First Voy. vol. ii. p. 244. Missionary Voy. p. 224.

hogs and fowls, was, in 1773, so ill supplied with these animals, that hardly any thing could induce the owners to part with them. This was attributed by Captain Cook principally to the wars which had taken place during that interval.[26] On Captain Vancouver's visit to Otaheite in 1791, he found that most of his friends that he had left in 1777, were dead; that there had been many wars since that time, in some of which, the chiefs of the western districts of Otaheite had joined the enemy; and that the king had been for a considerable time completely worsted, and his own districts entirely laid waste. Most of the animals, plants, and herbs, which Captain Cook had left, had been destroyed by the ravages of war.[27]

The human sacrifices which are frequent in Otaheite, though alone sufficient strongly to fix the stain of barbarism on the character of the natives, do not probably occur in such considerable numbers as materially to affect the population of the country; and the diseases, though they have been dreadfully increased by European contact, were before peculiarly lenient; and even for some time afterwards, were not marked by any extraordinary fatality.[28]

The great checks to increase, appear to be the vices of promiscuous intercourse, infanticide, and war, each of these operating with very considerable force. Yet powerful in the prevention and destruction of life as these causes must be, they have not always kept down the population to the level of the means of subsistence. According to Mr. Anderson, "Notwithstanding
" the extreme fertility of the island, a famine frequently happens in which
" it is said many perish. Whether this be owing to the failure of some
" seasons, to over-population, which must sometimes almost necessarily
" happen; or wars, I have not been able to determine; though the truth of
" the fact may fairly be inferred from the great economy that they observe
" with respect to their food, even when there is plenty."[29] After a dinner with a chief at Ulietea, Captain Cook observed, that, when the company rose, many of the common people rushed in, to pick up the crumbs which had fallen, and for which they searched the leaves very narrowly. Several people daily attended the ships, and assisted the butchers for the sake of the entrails of the hogs which were killed. In general, little seemed to fall to their share except offals. "It must, however, be owned," Captain Cook says,
" that they are exceedingly careful of every kind of provision, and waste
" nothing that can be eaten by man, flesh and fish especially."[30]

26. Cook's Second Voy. vol. i. p. 182, 183.   27. Vancouver's Voy. vol. i. b.i. c. 6. p. 98. 4to.   28. Cook's Third Voy. vol.ii. p. 148.   29. Cook's Third Voy. vol. ii. p. 153, 154.   30. Id. Second Voy. vol. i. p. 176.

From Mr. Anderson's account, it appears, that a very small portion of animal food falls to the lot of the lower class of people, and then, it is either fish, sea-eggs, or other marine productions; for they seldom or never eat pork. The king or principal chief, is alone able to furnish this luxury every day; and the inferior chiefs, according to their riches, once a week, fortnight, or month.[31] When the hogs and fowls have been diminished by wars, or too great consumption, a prohibition is laid upon these articles of food, which continues in force sometimes for several months, or even for a year or two, during which time, of course, they multiply very fast, and become again plentiful.[32] The common diet even of the Earecoies, who are among the principal people of the islands, is, according to Mr. Anderson, made up of at least nine tenths of vegetable food.[33] And, as a distinction of ranks is so strongly marked, and the lives and property of the lower classes of people appear to depend absolutely on the will of their chiefs, we may well imagine that these chiefs will often live in plenty while their vassals and servants are pinched with want.

From the late accounts of Otaheite, in the Missionary Voyage, it would appear, that the depopulating causes above enumerated, have operated with most extraordinary force since Captain Cook's last visit. A rapid succession of destructive wars, during a part of that interval, is taken notice of in the intermediate visit of Captain Vancouver;[34] and, from the small proportion of women remarked by the Missionaries,[35] we may infer that a greater number of female infants had been destroyed than formerly. This scarcity of women would naturally increase the vice of promiscuous intercourse, and, aided by the ravages of European diseases, strike most effectually at the root of population.[36]

It is probable that Captain Cook, from the data on which he founded his calculation, may have overrated the population of Otaheite, and perhaps the Missionaries have rated it too low;[37] but I have no doubt that the population has very considerably decreased since Captain Cook's visit, from the different accounts that are given of the habits of the people, with regard to economy, at the different periods. Captain Cook and Mr. Anderson agree in describing their extreme carefulness of every kind of food; and Mr. Anderson, apparently after a very attentive investigation of the subject, mentions the frequent recurrence of famines. The Missionaries, on the contrary, though they strongly notice the distress from this cause in the Friendly Islands and

---

31. Id. Third Voy. vol. ii. p. 154.   32. Id. p. 155.   33. Id. p. 148.
34. Vancouver's Voy. vol. i. b. i. c. 7. p. 137.   35. Missionary Voyage, p. 192, & 385.   36. Id. Appen. p. 347.   37. Id. ch. xiii. p. 212.

the Marquesas, speak of the productions of Otaheite as being in the greatest profusion; and observe, that, notwithstanding the horrible waste committed at feastings, and by the Eareeoie society, want is seldom known.[38]

It would appear from these accounts, that the population of Otaheite is at present repressed considerably below the average means of subsistence, but it would be premature to conclude that it will continue long so. The variations in the state of the island which were observed by Captain Cook, in his different visits, appear to prove that there are marked oscillations in its prosperity and population.[39] And this is exactly what we should suppose from theory. We cannot imagine that the population of any of these islands has, for ages past, remained stationary at a fixed number, or that it can have been regularly increasing, according to any rate, however flow. Great fluctuations must necessarily have taken place. Overpopulousness would at all times increase the natural propensity of savages to war; and the enmities occasioned by aggressions of this kind, would continue to spread devastation, long after the original inconvenience, which might have prompted them, had ceased to be felt.[40] The distresses experienced from one or two unfavourable seasons, operating on a crowded population, which was before living with the greatest economy, and pressing hard against the limits of its food, would, in such a state of society, occasion the more general prevalence of infanticide and promiscuous intercourse;[41] and these depopulating causes would, in the same manner, continue to act with increased force, for some time after the occasion which had aggravated them was at an end. A change of habits to a certain degree, gradually produced by a change of circumstarices, would soon restore the population, which could not long be kept below its natural level, without the most extreme violence. How far European contact may operate in Otaheite with this extreme violence, and prevent it from recovering its former population, is a point which experience only can determine. But should this be the case, I have no doubt that on tracing the causes of it, we should find them to be aggravated vice and misery.

Of the other islands in the Pacific Ocean we have a less intimate knowledge than of Otaheite; but our information is sufficient to assure us, that the state of society in all the principal groups of these islands is, in most respects, extremely similar. Among the Friendly and Sandwich islanders, the

---

38. Missionary Voy. p. 195. Appen. p. 385.   39. Cook's Second Voy. vol. i. p. 182, & seq. & 346.   40. Missionary Voy. p. 225.

41. I hope I may never be misunderstood with regard to some of these preventive causes of overpopulation, and be supposed to imply the slightest approbation of them, merely because I relate their effects. A cause which may prevent any particular evil may be beyond all comparison worse than the evil itself.

same feudal system, and feudal turbulence, the same extraordinary power of the chiefs, and degraded state of the lower orders of society, and nearly the same promiscuous intercourse among a great part of the people, have been found to prevail, as at Otaheite.

In the Friendly Islands, though the power of the king was said to be unlimited, and the life and property of the subject at his disposal; yet it appeared, that some of the other chiefs acted like petty sovereigns, and frequently thwarted his measures, of which he often complained. "But how-
" ever independent (Captain Cook says) on the despotic power of the king
" the great men may be, we saw instances enough to prove, that the lower
" orders of people have no property nor safety for their persons, but at the
" will of the chiefs, to whom they respectively belong."[42] The chiefs often beat the inferior people most unmercifully,[43] and when any of them were caught in a theft on board the ships, their masters, far from interceding for them, would often advise the killing of them,[44] which, as the chiefs themselves appeared to have no great horror of the crime of theft, could only arise from their considering the lives of these poor people as absolutely of no value.

Captain Cook, in his first visit to the Sandwich Islands, had reason to think that external wars, and internal commotions, were extremely frequent among the natives.[45] And Captain Vancouver, in his later account, strongly notices the dreadful devastations in many of the islands from these causes. Incessant contentions had occasioned alterations in the different governments since Captain Cook's visit. Only one chief of all that were known at that time was living; and, on inquiry, it appeared that few had died a natural death, most of them having been killed in these unhappy contests.[46] The power of the chiefs over the inferior classes of the people in the Sandwich Islands appears to be absolute. The people, on the other hand, pay them the most implicit obedience; and this state of servility has manifestly a great effect in debasing both their minds and bodies.[47] The gradations of rank seem to be even more strongly marked here, than in the other islands, as the chiefs of higher rank behave to those who are lower in this scale in the most haughty and oppressive manner.[48]

It is not known that, either in the Friendly, or Sandwich Islands, infanticide is practised, or that any institutions are established similar to the Eareeoie societies in Otaheite; but it seems to be stated on unquestionable

42. Cook's Third Voy. vol. i. p. 406.   43. p. 232.   44. p. 233.
45. Id. vol. ii. p. 247.   46. Vancouver, vol. i. b. ii. c. ii. p. 187, 188.
47. Cook's Third Voyage, vol. iii. p. 157.   48. Ibid.

authority, that prostitution is extensively diffused, and prevails to a great degree among the lower classes of women,[49] which must always operate as a most powerful check to population. It seems highly probable, that the toutous, or servants, who spend the greatest part of their time in attendance upon the chiefs,[50] do not often marry; and it is evident that the polygamy allowed to the superior people, must tend greatly to encourage and aggravate the vice of promiscuous intercourse among the inferior classes.

Were it an established fact, that in the more fertile islands of the Pacific Ocean, very little, or nothing, was suffered from poverty and want of food; as we could not expect to find among savages in such climates any great degree of virtuous restraint, the theory on the subject would naturally lead us to conclude, that vice, including war, was the principal check to their population. The accounts which we have of these islands strongly confirm this conclusion. In the three great groups of islands which have been noticed, vice appears to be a most prominent feature. In Easter Island, from the great disproportion of the males to the females,[51] it can scarcely be doubted that infanticide prevails, though the fact may not have come to the knowledge of any of our navigators. Perouse seemed to think that the women in each district were common property to the men of that district,[52] though the numbers of children which he saw,[53] would rather tend to contradict this opinion. The fluctuations in the population of Easter Island appear to have been very considerable, since its first discovery by Roggewein in 1722, though it cannot have been much affected by European intercourse. From the description of Perouse, it appeared, at the time of his visit, to be recovering its population, which had been in a very low state, probably either from drought, civil dissensions, or the prevalence in an extreme degree of infanticide, and promiscuous intercourse. When Captain Cook visited it in his second voyage, he calculated the population at six or seven hundred,[54] Perouse at two thousand;[55] and, from the number of children which he observed, and the number of new houses that were building, he conceived that the population was on the increase.[56]

In the Marianne Islands, according to Pere Gobien, a very great number[57] of the young men remained unmarried, lived like the members of the

---

49. Cook's Third Voy. vol. i. p. 401. Vol. ii. p. 543. Vol. iii. p. 130. Missionary Voy. p. 270.   50. Cook's Third Voy. vol. i. p. 394.   51. Cook's Second Voy. vol. i. p. 289. Voyage de Perouse, c. iv. p. 323. c. v. p. 336. 4to. 1794.

52. Perouse, c. iv. p. 326. c. v. p. 336.   53. Perouse, c. v. p. 336.

54. Cook's Second Voy. vol. i. p. 289.   55. Perouse, c. v. p. 336.

56. Ibid.   57. Une infinité de jeunes gens. Hist. des Navigations aux terres Australes, vol. ii. p. 507.

Eareeoie society in Otaheite, and were distinguished by a similar name.[58] In the island of Formosa, it is said, that the women were not allowed to bring children into the world before the age of thirty-five. If they were with child prior to that period, an abortion was effected by the priestess, and till the husband was forty years of age, the wife continued to live in her father's house, and was only seen by stealth.[59]

The transient visits that have been made to some other islands, and the imperfect accounts that we have of them, do not enable us to enter into any particular detail of their customs; but, from the general similarity of these customs, as far as has been observed, we have reason to think, that, though they may not be marked by some of the more atrocious peculiarities which have been mentioned, vicious habits with respect to women, and wars, are the principal checks to their population.

These, however, are not all. On the subject of the happy state of plenty in which the natives of the South Sea islands have been said to live, I am inclined to think, that our imaginations have been carried beyond the truth, by the exuberant descriptions which have sometimes been given of these delightful spots. The not unfrequent pressure of want, even in Otaheite, mentioned in Captain Cook's last voyage, has undeceived us with regard to the most fertile of all these islands; and from the Missionary Voyage it appears, that at certain times of the year, when the bread fruit is out of season, all suffer a temporary scarcity. At Oheitahoo, one of the Marquesas, it amounted to hunger, and the very animals were pinched for want of food. At Tongataboo, the principal of the Friendly Islands, the chiefs, to secure plenty, changed their abodes to other islands,[60] and at times many

---

58. Cook's Third Voyage, vol. ii. p. 158. note of the Editor.

59. Harris's Collection of Voyages, 2 vols. folio. edit. 1744. vol. i. p. 794. This relation is given by John Albert de Mandesloe, a German traveller of some reputation for fidelity, though I believe, in this instance, he takes his account from the Dutch writers quoted by Montesquieu, (Esprit des Loix, liv. 23. ch. 17.) The authority is not perhaps sufficient to establish the existence of so strange a custom, though I confess that it does not appear to me wholly improbable. In the same account, it is mentioned, that there is no difference of condition among these people, and that their wars are so bloodless, that the death of a single person generally decides them. In a very healthy climate, where the habits of the people were favourable to population, and a community of goods was established, as no individual would have reason to fear *particular poverty* from a large family, the government would be in a manner compelled to take upon itself the suppression of the population by law; and as this would be the greatest violation of every natural feeling, there cannot be a more forcible argument against a community of goods.

60. Missionary Voy. Appen. p. 385.

of the natives suffered much from want.[61] In the Sandwich Islands, long droughts sometimes occur;[62] hogs and yams are often very scarce,[63] and visitors are received with an unwelcome austerity very different from the profuse benevolence of Otaheite. In New Caledonia, the inhabitants feed upon spiders,[64] and are sometimes reduced to eat great pieces of steatite to appease the cravings of their hunger.[65]

These facts strongly prove, that in whatever abundance the productions of these islands may be found at certain periods, or however they may be checked by ignorance, wars, and other causes, the average population, generally speaking, presses hard against the limits of the average food. In a state of society, where the lives of the inferior orders of the people seem to be considered by their superiors as absolutely of no value, it is evident that we are very liable to be deceived with regard to the appearances of abundance; and we may easily conceive, that hogs and vegetables might be exchanged in great profusion for European commodities by the principal proprietors, while their vassals and slaves were suffering severely from want.

I cannot conclude this general review of that department of human society, which has been classed under the name of savage life, without observing, that the only advantage in it above civilized life that I can discover, is the possession of a greater degree of leisure by the mass of the people. There is less work to be done, and consequently there is less labour. When we consider the incessant toil to which the lower classes of society in civilized life are condemned, this cannot but appear to us a striking advantage; but it is probably overbalanced by greater disadvantages. In all those countries where provisions are procured with facility, a most tyrannical distinction of rank prevails. Blows, and violations of property, seem to be matters of course; and the lower classes of the people are in a state of comparative degradation much below what is known in civilized nations.

In that part of savage life where a great degree of equality obtains, the difficulty of procuring food, and the hardships of incessant war, create a degree of labour not inferior to that which is exerted by the lower classes of the people in civilized society, though much more unequally divided. But though we may compare the labour of these two classes of human society, their privations and sufferings will admit of no comparison. Nothing appears to me to place this in so striking a point of view, as the whole tenor

---

61. Id. p. 270.   62. Vancouver's Voy. vol. ii. b. iii. c. viii. p. 230.
63. Id. c. vii. and viii.   64. Voyage in search of Perouse, ch. xiii. p. 420. Eng. transl. 4to.   65. Id. ch. xiii, p. 400.

of education among the ruder tribes of savages in America. Every thing that can contribute to teach the most unmoved patience under the severest pains and misfortunes, every thing that tends to harden the heart, and narrow all the sources of sympathy, is most sedulously inculcated in the savage. The civilized man, on the contrary, though he may be advised to bear evil with patience when it comes, is not instructed to be always expecting it. Other virtues are to be called into action besides fortitude. He is taught to feel for his neighbour, or even his enemy in distress; to encourage, and expand his social affections; and in general, to enlarge the sphere of pleasurable emotions. The obvious inference from these two different modes of education is, that the civilized man hopes to enjoy, the savage expects only to suffer.

The preposterous system of Spartan discipline, and that unnatural absorption of every private feeling in concern for the public, which has sometimes been so absurdly admired, could never have existed but among a people, exposed to perpetual hardships and privations from incessant war, and in a state, under the constant fear of dreadful reverses of fortune. Instead of considering these phenomena as indicating any peculiar tendency to fortitude and patriotism in the disposition of the Spartans, I should merely consider them as a strong indication of the miserable and almost savage state of Sparta, and of Greece in general at that time. Like the commodities in a market, those virtues will be produced in the greatest quantity for which there is the greatest demand; and where patience, under pain and privations, and extravagant patriotic sacrifices, are the most called for, it is a melancholy indication of the misery of the people, and the insecurity of the state.

CHAP. VI.

Of the Checks to Population among the ancient Inhabitants of the North of Europe.

A HISTORY of the early migrations and settlements of mankind, with the motives which prompted them, would illustrate in a striking manner the constant tendency in the human race to increase beyond the means of subsistence. Without some general law of this nature, it would seem as if the world could never have been peopled. A state of sloth, and not of restlessness and activity, seems evidently to be the natural state of man; and this latter disposition could not have been generated but by the strong goad of necessity, though it might afterwards be continued by habit, and the new associations that were formed from it, the spirit of enterprize, and the thirst of martial glory.

We are told, that Abram and Lot had so great substance in cattle, that the land would not bear them both, that they might dwell together. There was strife between their herdsmen. And Abram proposed to Lot to separate, and said, "Is not the whole land before thee? If thou wilt take the left hand, then " I will go to the right; if thou depart to the right hand, then I will go to the " left."[1]

This simple observation and proposal is a striking illustration of that great spring of action which overspread the whole earth with people, and in the progress of time, drove some of the less fortunate inhabitants of the globe, yielding to irresistible pressure, to seek a scanty subsistence in the burning deserts of Asia and Africa, and the frozen regions of Siberia and North America. The first migrations would naturally find no other obstacles than the nature of the country; but when a considerable part of the earth had been peopled, though but thinly, the possessors of these districts would not yield them to others without a struggle; and the redundant inhabitants of any of the more central spots, could not find room for themselves without expelling their nearest neighbours, or at least passing through their territories, which would necessarily give occasion to frequent contests.

The middle latitudes of Europe and Asia, seem to have been occupied at an early period of history, by nations of shepherds. Thucydides gave it as his opinion, that the civilized states of Europe and Asia, in his time, could

---

1. Genesis, ch. xiii.

not resist the Scythians united. Yet a country in pasture cannot possibly support so many inhabitants as a country in tillage; but what renders nations of shepherds so formidable, is the power which they possess of moving altogether, and the necessity they frequently feel of exerting this power in search of fresh pasture for their herds. A tribe that is rich in cattle has an immediate plenty of food. Even the parent stock may be devoured in case of absolute necessity. The women live in greater ease than among nations of hunters, and are consequently more prolific. The men, bold in their united strength, and confiding in their power of procuring pasture for their cattle by change of place, feel probably but few fears about providing for a family. These combined causes soon produce their natural and invariable effect, an extended population. A more frequent and rapid change of place then becomes necessary. A wider and more extensive territory is successively occupied. A broader desolation extends all around them. Want pinches the less fortunate members of the society; and at length the impossibility of supporting such a number together, becomes too evident to be resisted. Young scions are then pushed out from the parent stock, and instructed to explore fresh regions, and to gain happier seats for themseves by their swords.

"The world is all before them where to chuse."

Restless from present distress, flushed with the hope of fairer prospects, and animated with the spirit of hardy enterprize, these daring adventurers are likely to become formidable adversaries to all who oppose them. The inhabitants of countries long settled, engaged in the peaceful occupations of trade and agriculture, would not often be able to resist the energy of men acting under such powerful motives of exertion. And the frequent contests with tribes in the same circumstances with themselves, would be so many struggles for existence, and would be fought with a desperate courage, inspired by the reflection, that death would be the punishment of defeat, and life the prize of victory.

In these savage contests, many tribes must have been utterly exterminated. Many probably perished by hardships and famine. Others, whose leading star had given them a happier direction, became great and powerful tribes, and in their turn sent off fresh adventurers in search of other feats. These would at first owe allegiance to their parent tribe; but in a short time the ties that bound them would be little felt, and they would remain friends, or become enemies, according as their power, their ambition, or their convenience, might dictate.

The prodigious waste of human life occasioned by this perpetual struggle for room and food, would be more than supplied by the mighty power of population, acting in some degree unshackled from the constant habit of migration. A prevailing hope of bettering their condition by change of place, a constant expectation of plunder, a power, even, if distressed, of selling their children as slaves, added to the natural carelesness of the Barbaric character, would all conspire to raise a population which would remain to be repressed afterwards by famine, or war.

The tribes that possessed themselves of the more fruitful regions, though they might win them and maintain them by continual battles, rapidly increased in number and power, from the increased means of subsistence; till at length the whole territory, from the confines of China to the shores of the Baltic, was peopled by a various race of barbarians, brave, robust, and enterprising, enured to hardships, and delighting in war.[2] While the different fixed governments of Europe and Asia, by superior population and superior skill, were able to oppose an impenetrable barrier to their destroying hordes, they wasted their superfluous numbers in contests with each other; but the moment that the weakness of the settled governments, or the casual union of many of these wandering tribes, gave them the ascendant in power, the storm discharged itself on the fairest provinces of the earth; and China, Persia, Egypt, and Italy, were overwhelmed at different periods in this flood of barbarism. These remarks are strongly exemplified in the fall of the Roman empire. The shepherds of the north of Europe were long held in check by the vigour of the Roman arms, and the terror of the Roman name. The formidable irruption of the Cimbri in search of new settlements, though signalized by the destruction of five consular armies, was at length arrested in its victorious career by Marius; and the barbarians were taught to repent their rashness by the almost complete extermination of this powerful colony.[3] The names of Julius Cæsar, of Drusus, Tiberius, and Germanicus, impressed on their minds by the slaughter of their countrymen, continued to inspire them with a fear of encroaching on the Roman territory. But they were rather triumphed over, than vanquished;[4] and though the armies, or colonies, which they sent forth, were either cut off, or forced back into their original seats, the vigour of the great German nation remained un-

---

2. The various branchings, divisions, and contests, of the great Tartar nation are curiously described in the genealogical history of the Tartars by the Khan Abul Ghazi; (translated into English from the French, with additions, in 2 vols. 8vo.) but the misfortune of all history is, that while the motives of a few princes and leaders, in their various projects of ambition, are sometimes detailed with accuracy, the motives which often crowd their standards with willing followers, are totally overlooked.   3. Tacitus de Moribus Germanorum, s. 37.
    4. Tacitus de Moribus Germanorum, s. 37.

impaired, and ready to pour forth her hardy sons in constant succession, wherever they could force an opening for themselves by their swords. The feeble reigns of Decius, Gallus, Æmilianus, Valerian, and Gallienus, afforded such an opening, and were in consequence marked by a general irruption of barbarians. The Goths, who were supposed to have migrated in the course of some years from Scandinavia to the Euxine, were bribed to withdraw their victorious troops, by an annual tribute. But no sooner was the dangerous secret of the wealth and weakness of the Roman empire thus revealed to the world, than new swarms of barbarians spread devastation through the frontier provinces, and terror as far as the gates of Rome.[5] The Franks, the Allemanni, the Goths, and adventurers of less considerable tribes, comprehended under these general appellations, poured like a torrent on different parts of the empire. Rapine and oppression destroyed the produce of the present, and the hope of future harvests. A long and general famine was followed by a wasting plague, which for fifteen years ravaged every city and province of the Roman empire; and, judging from the mortality in some spots, it was conjectured, that in a few years, war, pestilence, and famine, had consumed the moiety of the human species.[6] Yet the tide of emigration still continued at intervals to roll impetuously from the north, and the succession of martial princes, who repaired the misfortunes of their predecessors, and propt the falling fate of the empire, had to accomplish the labours of Hercules in freeing the Roman territory from these barbarous invaders. The Goths, who, in the year 250, and the following years, ravaged the empire both by sea and land, with various success, but in the end, with the almost total loss of their adventurous bands,[7] in the year 269, sent out an emigration of immense numbers with their wives and families for the purposes of settlement.[8] This formidable body, which was said to consist at first of 320,000 barbarians,[9] was ultimately destroyed and dispersed by the vigour and wisdom of the emperor Claudius. His successor, Aurelian, encountered and vanquished new hosts of the same name that had quitted their settlements in the Ukraine; but one of the implied conditions of the peace, was, that he should withdraw the Roman forces from Dacia, and relinquish this great province to the Goths and Vandals.[10] A new and most formidable invasion of the Allemanni threatened soon after to sack the mistress of the world, and three great and bloody battles

---

5. Gibbon's Decline and Fall of the Roman Empire, vol. i. c. x. p. 407. et seq. 8vo. edit, 1783.   6. Id. vol. i. c. x. p. 455, 456.

7. Gibbon, vol. i. c. x. p. 431.   8. Id. vol. ii. c. xi. p. 13.   9. Id. p. 11.

10. Id. p. 19. A. D. 270.

were fought by Aurelian before this destroying host could be exterminated, and Italy be delivered from its ravages.[11]

The strength of Aurelian had crushed on every side the enemies of Rome. After his death, they seemed to revive with an increase of fury and numbers. They were again vanquished on all sides by the active vigour of Probus. The deliverance of Gaul alone from German invaders is reported to have cost the lives of four hundred thousand barbarians.[12] The victorious emperor pursued his successes into Germany itself, and the princes of the country, astonished at his presence, and dismayed and exhausted by the ill success of their last emigration, submitted to any terms that the conquerors might impose.[13] Probus, and afterwards Diocletian,[14] adopted the plan of recruiting the exhausted provinces of the empire, by granting lands to the fugitive or captive barbarians, and disposing of their superfluous numbers where they might be the least likely to be dangerous to the state; but such colonizations were an insufficient vent for the population of the north, and the ardent temper of the barbarians would not always bend to the slow labours of agriculture.[15] During the vigorous reign of Diocletian, unable to make an effectual impression on the Roman frontiers, the Goths, the Vandals, the Gepidæ, the Burgundians, and the Allemanni, wasted each other's strength by mutual hostilities, while the subjects of the empire enjoyed the bloody spectacle, conscious, that whoever vanquished, they vanquished the enemies of Rome.[16]

Under the reign of Constantine the Goths were again formidable. Their strength had been restored by a long peace, and a new generation had arisen, who no longer remembered the misfortunes of ancient days.[17] In two successive wars great numbers of them were slain. Vanquished on every side, they were driven into the mountains; and, in the course of a severe campaign, above a hundred thousand were computed to have perished by cold and hunger.[18] Constantine adopted the plan of Probus and his successors, in granting lands to those suppliant barbarians who were expelled from their own country. Towards the end of his reign, a competent portion in the provinces of Pannonia, Thrace, Macedonia, and Italy, was assigned for the habitation and subsistence of three hundred thousand Sarmatians.[19]

The warlike Julian had to encounter and vanquish new swarms of Franks and Allemanni, that, emigrating from their German forests during the civil wars of Constantine, settled in different parts of Gaul, and made the scene of their devastations three times more extensive than that of their

11. Id. p. 26.   12. Id. vol. ii. c. xii. p. 75.   13. Id. p. 79. A. D. 277.
14. Id. c. xiii. p. 132. A. D. 296.   15. Gibbon, vol. ii. c. xii. p. 84.
16. Id. c. xiii. p. 130.   17. Id. c. xiv. p. 254. A. D. 322.
18. Id. vol. iii. c. xviii. p. 125. A. D. 332.   19. Id. p. 127.

conquests.[20] Destroyed and repulsed on every side, they were pursued, in five expeditions, into their own country;[21] but Julian had conquered, as soon as he had penetrated into Germany; and in the midst of that mighty hive which had sent out such swarms of people, as to keep the Roman world in perpetual dread, the principal obstacles to his progress were, almost impassable roads, and vast unpeopled forests.[22]

Though thus subdued and prostrated by the victorious arms of Julian, this hydra-headed monster rose again after a few years; and the firmness, vigilance, and powerful genius of Valentinian were fully called into action, in protecting his dominions from the different irruptions of the Allemanni, the Burgundians, the Saxons, the Goths, the Quadi, and Sarmatians.[23]

The fate of Rome was at length determined by an irresistible emigration of the Huns from the east and north, which precipitated on the empire the whole body of the Goths;[24] and the continuance of this powerful pressure on the nations of Germany, seemed to prompt them to the resolution, of abandoning to the fugitives of Sarmatia their woods and morasses, or at least, of discharging their superfluous numbers on the provinces of the Roman empire.[25] An emigration of four hundred thousand persons issued from the same coast of the Baltic, which had poured forth the myriads of Cimbri and Teutones during the vigour of the Republic.[26] When this host was destroyed by war and famine, other adventurers succeeded. The Suevi, the Vandals, the Alani, the Burgundians, passed the Rhine never more to retreat.[27] The conquerors who first settled, were expelled or exterminated by new invaders. Clouds of barbarians seemed to collect from all parts of the northern hemisphere. Gathering fresh darkness and terror as they rolled on, the congregated bodies at length obscured the sun of Italy, and sunk the western world in night.

In two centuries from the flight of the Goths across the Danube, barbarians of various names and lineage had plundered and taken possession of Thrace, Pannonia, Gaul, Britain, Spain, Africa, and Italy.[28] The most horrible devastations, and an incredible destruction of the human species, accompanied these rapid conquests; and famine and pestilence, which always march in the train of war, when it ravages with such inconsiderate cruelty, raged in every part of Europe. The historians of the times, who beheld these

20. Id. vol. iii. c. xix. p. 215. A. D. 356.

21. Id. p. 228. and vol. iv. c. xxii. p. 17. from A. D. 357 to 359.

22. Gibbon, vol. iv. c. xxii. p. 17. and vol. iii. c. xix. p. 229.

23. Id. vol. iv. c. xxv. from A. D. 364 to 375.   24. Id. vol iv. c. xxvi. p. 382. et seq. A. D. 376.   25. Id. vol. v. c. xxx. p. 213.   26. Id. p. 214. A. D. 406.

27. Id. p. 224.   28. Robertson's Charles V. vol. i. sect. i. p. 7. 8vo. 1782.

scenes of desolation, labour, and are at a loss for expressions, to describe them; but beyond the power of language, the numbers and the destructive violence of these barbarous invaders were evinced by the total change which took place in the state of Europe.[29] These tremendous effects, so long, and so deeply felt, throughout the fairest portions of the earth, may be traced to the simple cause of the superiority of the power of population to the means of subsistence.

Machiavel, in the beginning of his history of Florence, says, "The people who inhabit the northern parts that lie between the Rhine and the
" Danube, living in a healthful and prolific climate, often increase to such
" a degree, that vast numbers of them are forced to leave their native
" country, and go in search of new habitations. When any one of those
" provinces begins to grow too populous, and wants to disburthen itself,
" the following method is observed. In the first place, it is divided into
" three parts, in each of which, there is an equal portion of the nobility and
" commonalty, the rich and the poor. After this they cast lots, and that di-
" vision on which the lot falls, quits the country and goes to seek its for-
" tune, leaving the other two more room and liberty to enjoy their posses-
" sions at home. These emigrations proved the destruction of the Roman
" empire."[30] Gibbon is of opinion that Machiavel has represented these emigrations too much as regular and concerted measures;[31] but I think it highly probable that he has not erred much in this respect, and that it was a foresight of the frequent necessity of thus discharging their redundant population, which gave occasion to that law among the Germans, taken notice of by Cæsar and Tacitus, of not permitting their cultivated lands to remain

29. Id. p. 10, 11, 12.   30. Istorie Fiorentine Machiavelli, l. i. p. 1, 2.

31. Gibbon, vol. i. c. ix. p. 360. note. Paul Diaconus, from whom it is supposed that Machiavel has taken this description, writes thus: Septentrionalis plaga quantò magis ab æstu solis remota est, et nivali frigore gelida, tantò salubrior corporibus hominum et propagandis gentibus magis coaptata. Sicut e contrario, omnis meridiana regio, quò solis est fervori vicinior eo morbis est abundantior, et educandis minus apta mortalibus*****. Multæque quoque ex eâ, eo quod tantas mortalium turmas germinat, quantas alere vix sufficit, sæpe gentes egressæ sunt, quæ non solum partes Asiæ, sed etiam maxime sibi contiguam Europam afflixere. (De gestis Longobardorum, l. i. c. i.)

Intra hanc ergo constituti populi, dum in tantam multitudinem pullulassent, ut jam simul habitare non valerent, in tres (ut fertur) partes omnem catervam dividentes, quænam ex illis patriam esset relictura, ut novas sedes exquirerent, forte disquirunt. Igitur ea pars, cui sors dederit genitale solum excedere, exteraque arva sectari, constitutis supra se duobus ducibus, lbore scilicet, et Agione, qui et Germani erant, et juvenili. ætate floridi, ceterisque prestantiores, ad exquirandas quas possint incolere terras, sedesque statuere, valedicentes suis simul et patriæ iter arripiunt. (c. ii.)

longer than a year under the same possessors.[32] The reasons which Cæsar mentions as being assigned for this custom, seem to be hardly adequate; but if we add to them, the prospect of emigration, in the manner described by Machiavel, the custom will appear to be highly useful, and a double weight will be given to one of the reasons that Cæsar mentions, namely, lest they should be led, by being accustomed to one spot, to exchange the toils of war for the business of agriculture.[33]

Gibbon very justly rejects, with Hume and Robertson, the improbable supposition, that the inhabitants of the north were far more numerous formerly, than at present;[34] but he thinks himself obliged at the same time to deny the strong tendency to increase in the northern nations,[35] as if the two facts were necessarily connected. But a careful distinction should always be made, between a redundant population, and a population actually great. The Highlands of Scotland are probably more redundant in population than any other part of Great Britain; and though it would be admitting a palpable absurdity, to allow that the north of Europe, covered in early ages with immense forests, and inhabited by a race of people who supported themselves principally by their herds and flocks,[36] was more populous in those times than in its present state; yet the facts detailed in the Decline and Fall of the Roman empire, or even the very slight sketch of them that I have given, cannot rationally be accounted for, without the supposition of a most powerful tendency in these people to increase, and to repair their repeated losses by the prolific power of nature.

From the first irruption of the Cimbri, to the final extinction of the western empire, the efforts of the German nations to colonize or plunder were unceasing.[37] The numbers that were cut off during this period by war and famine were almost incalculable, and such as could not possibly have been supported with undiminished vigour by a country thinly peopled, unless the stream had been supplied by a spring of very extraordinary power.

Gibbon describes the labours of Valentinian in securing the Gallic frontier against the Germans, an enemy, he says, whose strength was renewed by a stream of daring volunteers which incessantly flowed from the most distant tribes of the north.[38] An easy adoption of strangers was probably a mode by which some of the German nations renewed their strength so

---

32. De bello Gallico, vi. 22. De moribus German, s. xxvi.
33. De bello Gallico vi. 22.   34. Gibbon, vol. i. c. ix. p. 361.   35. Id. p. 348.
36. Tacitus de moribus German. s. v. Cæsar de bell. Gall. vi. 22.
37. Cæsar found in Gaul a most formidable colony under Ariovistus, and a general dread prevailing that in a few years all the Germans would pass the Rhine. De bell. Gall. i. 31.   38. Gibbon, vol. iv. c. xxv. p. 283.

suddenly,[39] after the most destructive defeats; but this explanation only re-moves the difficulty a little further off. It makes the earth rest upon the tor-toise; but does not tell us, on what the tortoise rests. We may still ask, what northern reservoir supplied this incessant stream of daring adventurers ? Montesquieu's solution of the problem, will, I think, hardly be admitted. The swarms of barbarians which issued formerly from the north, appear no more, he says, at present; and the reason which he gives is, that the violences of the Romans had driven the people of the south into the north. As long as this force continued, they remained there; but as soon as it was weakened, they spread themselves again over every country.

The same phenomenon appeared after the conquests and tyrannies of Charlemagne, and the subsequent dissolution of his empire; and if a prince, he says, in the present days were to make similar ravages in Europe, the nations driven into the north, and resting on the limits of the universe,[40] would there make a stand, till the moment when they would inundate, or conquer, Europe a third time. In a note he observes, we see to what the famous question is reduced – why the north is no longer so fully peopled as in former times?

If the famous question, or rather the answer to it, be reduced to this, it is reduced to a miracle; for without some supernatural mode of obtaining food, how these collected nations could support themselves in such barren regions, for so long a period, as during the vigour of the Roman empire, it is a little difficult to conceive; and one can hardly help smiling at the bold figure of these prodigious crowds making their last determined stand on the limits of the universe, and living, as we must suppose, with the most patient fortitude on air and ice for some hundreds of years, till they could return to their own homes, and resume their usual more substantial mode of subsistence.

The whole difficulty, however, is at once removed, if we apply to the German nations at that time, a fact, which is so generally known to have occurred in America, and suppose, that, when not checked by wars and famine, they increased at a rate that would double their numbers in twenty-five or thirty years. The propriety, and even the necessity, of applying this rate of increase to the inhabitants of ancient Germany, will strikingly ap-pear from that most valuable picture of their manners which has been left us by Tacitus. He describes them as not inhabiting cities, or even admitting

39. Ibid. note.
40. Les nations adossées au limites de l'univers y tiendroient ferme. Grandeur et Decad. des Rom. c. xvi. p. 187.

of contiguous settlements. Every person surrounds his house with a vacant space,[41] a circumstance, which besides its beneficial effect as a security from fire, is strongly calculated to prevent the generation, and check the ravages, of epidemics. They content themselves almost universally with one wife. Their matrimonial bond is strict and severe, and their manners in this respect deserving of the highest praise.[42] They live in a state of well-guarded chastity, corrupted by no seducing spectacles, or convivial incitements. Adultery is extremely rare, and no indulgence is shewn to a prostitute. Neither beauty, youth, nor riches can procure her a husband; for none there looks on vice with a smile, nor calls mutual seduction the way of the world. To limit the increase of children, or put to death any of the husband's blood, is accounted infamous; and virtuous manners have there more efficacy than good laws elsewhere.[43] Every mother suckles her own children, and does not deliver them into the hands of servants and nurses. The youths partake late of the sexual intercourse, and hence pass the age of puberty unexhausted. Nor are the virgins brought forward. The same maturity, the same full growth is required: the sexes unite equally matched and robust, and the children inherit the vigour of their parents. The more numerous are a man's kinsmen and relations, the more comfortable is his old age; nor is it any advantage to be childless.[44]

With these manners, and a habit of enterprise and emigration, which would naturally remove all fears about providing for a family, it is difficult to conceive a society with a stronger principle of increase in it; and we see at once that prolific source of successive armies and colonies, against which, the force of the Roman empire so long struggled with difficulty, and under which, it ultimately sunk. It is not probable that for two periods together, or even for one, the population within the confines of Germany ever doubled itself in twenty-five years. Their perpetual wars, the rude state of agriculture, and particularly the very strange custom adopted by most of the tribes, of marking their barriers by extensive desarts,[45] would absolutely prevent any very great actual increase of numbers. At no one period could the country be called well-peopled, though it was often redundant in population. They abandoned their immense forests to the exercise of hunting, employed in pasturage the most considerable part of their lands, bestowed on the small remainder a rude and careless cultivation, and when the return of famine severely admonished them of the insufficiency of their scanty resources, they accused the sterility of a country which refused to

41. Tacitus de moribus Germ. s. xvi.   42. Id. s. xviii.   43. Id. s. xix.
44. Id. s. xx.   45. Cæsar de bell. Gall. vi. 23.

supply the multitude of its inhabitants;[46] but instead of clearing their forests, draining their swamps, and rendering their soil fit to support an extended population, they found it more congenial to their martial habits and impatient dispositions, to go "in quest of food, of plunder, or of " glory,"[47] into other countries. These adventurers either gained lands for themselves by their swords, or were cut off by the various accidents of war; were received into the Roman armies, or dispersed over the Roman territory; or perhaps, having relieved their country by their absence, returned home laden with spoils, and ready, after having recruited their diminished numbers, for fresh expeditions. The succession of human beings appears to have been most rapid, and as fast as some were disposed of in colonies, or mowed down by the scythe of war and famine, others rose in increased numbers to supply their place.

According to this view of the subject, the North could never have been exhausted; and when Dr. Robertson, describing the calamities of these invasions, says, that they did not cease, till the North, by pouring forth successive swarms, was drained of people, and could no longer furnish instruments of destruction,[48] he will appear to have fallen into the very error which he had before laboured to refute, and to speak as if the northern nations were actually very populous. For they must have been so, if the number of their inhabitants at any one period, had been sufficient, besides the slaughter of war, to people in such a manner Thrace, Pannonia, Gaul, Spain, Africa, Italy, and England, as in some parts not to leave many traces of their former inhabitants. The period of the peopling of these countries, however, he himself mentions as two hundred years,[49] and in such a time new generations would arise that would more than supply every vacancy.

The true cause which put a stop to the continuance of northern emigration was the impossibility any longer of making an impression on the most desirable countries of Europe. They were then inhabited by the descendants of the bravest and most enterprising of the German tribes; and it was not probable, that they should so soon degenerate from the valour of their ancestors, as to suffer their lands to be wrested from them by inferior numbers and inferior skill, though perhaps superior hardihood.

Checked for a time by the bravery and poverty of their neighbours by land, the enterprising spirit and overflowing numbers of the Scandinavian nations soon found vent by sea. Feared before the reign of Charlemagne,

46. Gibbon, vol. i. c. ix. p. 360.   47. Id. c. x. p. 417.
48. Robertson's Charles V. vol. i. s. i. p. 11.   49. Id. vol. i. s. i. p. 7.

they were repelled with difficulty by the care and vigour of that great prince, but during the distractions of the empire under his feeble successors, they spread like a devouring flame over Lower Saxony, Friezeland, Holland, Flanders, and the banks of the Rhine as far as Mentz.

After having long ravaged the coasts, they penetrated into the heart of France, pillaged and burnt her fairest towns, levied immense tributes on her monarchs, and at length obtained, by grant, one of the finest provinces of the kingdom. They made themselves even dreaded in Spain, Italy, and Greece, spreading every where desolation and terror. Sometimes they turned their arms against each other, as if bent on their own mutual destruction; at other times transported colonies to unknown or uninhabited countries, as if they were willing to repair, in one place, the horrid destruction of the human race occasioned by their furious ravages, in others.[50]

The mal-administration and civil wars of the Saxon kings of England produced the same effect as the weakness which followed the reign of Charlemagne in France,[51] and for two hundred years the British isles were incessantly ravaged, and often in part subdued, by these northern invaders. During the eighth, ninth, and tenth centuries, the sea was covered with their vessels from one end of Europe to the other,[52] and the countries, now the most powerful in arts and arms, were the prey of their constant depredations. The growing and consolidating strength of these countries, at length, removed all further prospect of success from such invasions.[53] The nations of the north were slowly and reluctantly compelled to confine themselves within their natural limits, and to exchange their pastoral manners, and with them the peculiar facilities of plunder and emigration which they afforded, for the patient labours, and slow returns of trade and agriculture. But the slowness of these returns necessarily effected an important change in the manners of the people.

In ancient Scandinavia, during the time of its constant wars and emigrations, few or none, probably, were ever deterred from marrying by the fear of not being able to provide for a family. In modern Scandinavia, on the contrary, the frequency of the marriage union is continually checked by

---

50. Mallet, Introd. a l'Histoire de Dannemarc, tom. i. c. x. p. 221, 223, 224. 12mo. 1766.   51. Id. p. 226.   52. Id. p. 221.

53. Perhaps the civilized world could not be considered as perfectly secure from another northern or eastern inundation, till the total change in the art of war, by the introduction of gunpowder, gave to improved skill and knowledge the decided advantage over physical force.

the most imperious and justly founded apprehensions of this kind. This is most particularly the case in Norway, as I shall have occasion to remark in another place; but the same fears operate in a greater or less degree, though every where with considerable force, in all parts of Europe. Happily, the more tranquil state of the modern world does not demand such rapid supplies of human beings, and the prolific powers of nature cannot therefore be so generally called into action.

Mallet, in the excellent account of the northern nations which he has prefixed to his history of Denmark, observes, that he had not been able to discover any proofs that their emigrations proceeded from want of room at home;[54] and one of the reasons which he gives, is, that, after a great emigration, the countries often remained quite deserted and unoccupied for a long time.[55] But instances of this kind I am inclined to think were rare, though they might occasionally happen. With the habits of enterprize and emigration which prevailed in those days, a whole people would sometimes move in search of a more fertile territory. The lands, which they before occupied, must of necessity be desart for a time; and if there were any thing particularly inelegible in the soil or situation, which the total emigration of the people would seem to imply, it might be more congenial to the temper of the surrounding barbarians, to provide for themselves better by their swords, than to occupy immediately these rejected lands. Such total emigrations proved the unwillingness of the society to divide, but by no means that they were not straitened for room and food at home.

The other reason which Mallet gives is, that, in Saxony, as well as Scandinavia, vast tracts of land lay in their original uncultivated state, having never been grubbed up or cleared ; and that, from the descriptions of Denmark in those times, it appeared, that the coasts alone were peopled, but the interior parts formed one vast forest.[56] It is evident, that he here falls into the common error of confounding a superfluity of inhabitants with great actual population. The pastoral manners of the people, and their habits of war and enterprize, prevented them from clearing and cultivating their lands;[57] and then these very forests, by restraining the sources of subsis-

---

54. Hist. Dan. tom. i. c. ix. p. 206.   55. Id. p. 205, 206.
56. Hist. Dan. tom. i. c. ix. p. 207.   57. Nec arare terram aut expectare annum tam facile persuaseris, quam vocare hostes et vulnera mereri; pigrum quinimò et iners videtur sudore acquirere-quod possis sanguine parare. Tacitus de mor. Germ. Nothing, indeed, in the study of human nature, is more evident than the extreme difficulty with which habits are changed; and no argument therefore can be more fallacious than to infer, that those people are not pinched with want, who do not make a proper use of their lands.

tence within very narrow bounds, contributed to a superfluity of numbers, that is, to a population beyond what the scanty supplies of the country could support.

There is another cause, not often attended to, why poor, cold, and thinly-peopled countries tend generally to a superfluity of inhabitants, and are strongly prompted to emigration. In warmer and more populous countries, particularly those abounding in great towns and manufactures, an insufficient supply of food can seldom continue long without producing epidemics, either in the shape of great and ravaging plagues, or of less violent, though more constant, sicknesses. In poor, cold, and thinly-peopled countries, on the contrary, from the antiseptic quality of the air, the misery arising from insufficient or bad food, may continue a considerable time without producing these effects, and, consequently, this powerful stimulus to emigration continues to operate for a much longer period.[58]

I would by no means, however, be understood to say, that the northern nations never undertook any expeditions unless prompted by straitened food or circumstances at home. Mallet relates, what was probably true, that it was their common custom to hold an assembly every spring, for the purpose of considering in what quarter they should make war;[59] and among a people who nourished so strong a passion for war, and who considered the right of the strongest as a right divine, occasions for it would never be wanting. Besides this pure and disinterested love of war and enterprize, civil dissensions, the pressure of a victorious enemy, a wish for a milder climate, or other causes, might sometimes prompt to emigration; but, in a general view of the subject, I cannot help considering this period of history as affording a very striking illustration of the principle of population; a principle, which appears to me, to have given the original impulse and spring of action, to have furnished the inexhaustible resources, and often prepared the immediate causes, of that rapid succession of adventurous irruptions and emigrations, which occasioned the fall of the Roman empire; and afterwards pouring from the thinly-peopled countries of Denmark and Norway, for above two hundred years ravaged and over-ran a great part of Europe. Without the supposition of a tendency to increase almost as great

---

58. Epidemics have their seldomer or frequenter returns according to their sundry soils, situations, air, &c. Hence, some have them yearly, as Egypt and Constantinople; others, once in four or five years, as about Tripoli and Aleppo; others, scarce once in ten, twelve, or thirteen years, as England; others, not in less than twenty years, as *Norway and the Northern islands*. Short, History of Air, Seasons, &c. vol. ii. p. 344.   59. Hist. Dan. c. ix. p. 209.

as among the Americans, the facts appear to me not to be accounted for;[60] and with such a supposition, we cannot be at a loss to name the checks to the actual population, when we read the disgusting details of those unceasing wars, and of that prodigal waste of human life, which marked these barbarous periods.

Inferior checks would undoubtedly concur; but we may safely pronounce, that among the shepherds of the north of Europe, war and famine, were the principal checks that kept the population down to the level of their scanty means of subsistence.

60. Gibbon, Robertson, and Mallet, seem all rather to speak of Jornandes's expression *vagina nationum* as incorrect and exaggerated; but to me it appears exactly applicable, though the other expression, officina gentium, at least their translation of it, *storehouse of nations*, may not be quite accurate.

Ex hac igitur Scanziâ insulâ, quasi officina gentium, aut certè velut vagina nationum egressi, &c. Jornandes de rebus Geticis, p. 83.

CHAP. VII.

Of the Checks to Population among modern Pastoral Nations.

THE pastoral tribes of Asia, by living in tents and moveable huts, instead of fixed habitations, are still less connected with their territory than the shepherds of the north of Europe. The camp, and not the soil, is the native country of the genuine Tartar. When the forage of a certain district is consumed, the tribe makes a regular march to fresh pastures. In the summer, it advances towards the north, in the winter returns again to the south; and thus, in a time of most profound peace, acquires the practical and familiar knowledge of one of the most difficult operations of war. Such habits would strongly tend to diffuse among these wandering tribes the spirit of emigration and conquest. The thirst of rapine, the fear of a too powerful neighbour, or the inconvenience of scanty pastures, have in all ages been sufficient causes to urge the hordes of Scythia boldly to advance into unknown countries, where they might hope to find a more plentiful subsistence, or a less formidable enemy.[1]

In all their invasions, but more particularly when directed against the civilized empires of the south, the Scythian shepherds have been uniformly actuated by a most savage and destructive spirit. When the Moguls had subdued the northern provinces of China, it was proposed, in calm and deliberate council, to exterminate all the inhabitants of that populous country, that the vacant land might be converted to the pasture of cattle. The execution of this horrid design was prevented by the wisdom and firmness of a Chinese mandarin;[2] but the bare proposal of it exhibits a striking picture, not only of the inhuman manner, in which the rights of conquest were abused, but of the powerful force of habit among nations of shepherds, and the consequent difficulty of the transition from the pastoral to the agricultural state.

To pursue, even in the most cursory manner, the tide of emigration and conquest in Asia, the rapid increase of some tribes, and the total extinction of others, would lead much too far. During the periods of the formidable irruptions of the Huns, the wide-extended invasions of the Moguls, the sanguinary conquests of Tamerlane and Aurengzebe, and the dreadful convulsions which attended the dissolution, as well as the formation, of their empires, the checks to population are but too obvious. In reading of the

1. Gibbon, vol. iv. c. xxvi. p. 348.   2. Gibbon, vol. vi. ch. xxxiv. p. 54.

devastations of the human race in those times, when the slightest motive of caprice or convenience, often involved a whole people in indiscriminate massacre,[3] instead of looking for the causes which prevented a further progress in population, we can only be astonished at the force of that principle of increase, which could furnish fresh harvests of human beings for the scythe of each successive conqueror. Our inquiries will be more usefully directed to the present state of the Tartar nations, and the ordinary checks to their increase, when not under the influence of these violent convulsions.

The immense country inhabited at present by those descendants of the Moguls and Tartars, who retain nearly the same manners as their ancestors, comprises in it almost all the middle regions of Asia, and possesses the advantage of a very fine and temperate climate. The soil is in general of great natural fertility. There are comparatively but few genuine deserts. The wide-extended plains without a shrub, which have sometimes received that appellation, and which the Russians call steppes, are covered with a luxuriant grass, admirably fitted for the pasture of numerous herds and flocks. The principal defect of this extensive country is a want of water; but it is said that the parts which are supplied with this necessary article, would be sufficient for the support of four times the number of its present inhabitants, if it were properly cultivated.[4] Every Orda, or tribe, has a particular canton belonging to it, containing both its summer and winter pastures; and the population of this vast territory, whatever it may be, is probably distributed over its surface nearly in proportion to the degree of actual fertility in the different districts.

Volney justly describes this necessary distribution in speaking of the Bedoweens of Syria: – "In the barren cantons, that is, those which are ill
"   furnished with plants, the tribes are feeble, and very distant from each
"   other; as in the desert of Suez, that of the Red Sea, and the interior part
"   of the Great Desert. When the soil is better covered, as between Damas-
"   cus and the Euphrates, the tribes are stronger and less distant. And in the
"   cultivable cantons, as the Pachalic of Aleppo, the Hauran, and the coun-
"   try of Gaza, the incampments are numerous and near each other."[5] Such
a distribution of inhabitants, according to the quantity of food which they can obtain in the actual state of their industry and habits, may be applied to Grand Tartary, as well as to Syria and Arabia, and is, in fact, equally applicable to the whole earth, though the commerce of civilized nations prevents it from being so obvious, as in the more simple stages of society.

3. Id. p. 55.   4. Geneal. Hist. of Tartars, vol. ii. sec. i. 8vo. 1730.
5. Voy. de Volney, tom. i. ch. xxiii. p. 351. 8vo. 1787.

The Mahometan Tartars, who inhabit the western parts of Grand Tartary, cultivate some of their lands; but this, in so slovenly and insufficient a manner, as not to afford a principal source of subsistence.[6] The slothful and warlike genius of the Barbarian every where prevails, and he does not easily reconcile himself to the acquiring by labour what he can hope to acquire by rapine. When the annals of Tartary are not marked by any signal wars and revolutions, its domestic peace and industry are constantly interrupted by petty contests, and mutual invasions for the sake of plunder. The Mahometan Tartars are said to live almost entirely by robbing and preying upon their neighbours, as well in peace as in war.[7]

The Usbecks, who possess as masters the kingdom of Chowarasm, leave to their tributary subjects, the Sarts and Turkmans, the finest pastures of their country, merely, because their neighbours on that side are too poor, or too vigilant, to give them hopes of successful plunder. Rapine is their principal resource. They are perpetually making incursions into the territories of the Persians, and of the Usbecks of Great Bucharia; and neither peace nor truce can restrain them; as the slaves, and other valuable effects, which they carry off, form the whole of their riches. The Usbecks, and their subjects the Turkmans, are perpetually at variance; and their jealousies, fomented often by the princes of the reigning house, keep the country in a constant state of intestine commotion.[8] The Turkmans are always at war with the Curds and the Arabs, who often come and break the horns of their herds, and carry away their wives and daughters.[9]

The Usbecks of Great Bucharia are reckoned the most civilized of all the Mahometan Tartars, yet are not much inferior to the rest in their spirit of rapine.[10] They are always at war with the Persians, and laying waste the fine plains of the province of Chorasan. Though the country which they possess is of the greatest natural fertility, and some of the remains of the ancient inhabitants practise the peaceful arts of trade and agriculture; yet neither the aptitude of the soil, nor the example which they have before them, can induce them to change their antient habits; and they would rather pillage, rob, and kill, their neighbours, than apply themselves to improve the benefits which nature so liberally offers them.[11]

The Tartars of the Casatshia Orda in Turkestan, live in a state of continual warfare with their neighbours to the north and east. In the winter

6. Geneal. Hist. Tar. vol. ii. p. 382.   7. Geneal. Hist. Tart. vol. ii. p. 390.
8. Id. p. 430, 431.   9. Id. p. 426.   10. Id. p. 459.
11. Geneal. Hist. Tart. vol. ii. p. 455.

they make their incursions towards the Kalmucks, who, about that time, go to scour the frontiers of Great Bucharia, and the parts to the south of their country. On the other side, they perpetually incommode the Cosacks of the Yaik, the Nogai Tartars, and the Kalmuck tribes which obey Ajuka Chan. In the summer they cross the mountains of Eagles, and make inroads into Siberia. And though they are often very ill treated in these incursions, and the whole of their plunder is not equivalent to what they might obtain with very little labour from their lands, yet they chuse rather to expose themselves to the thousand fatigues and dangers necessarily attendant on such a life, than apply themselves seriously to agriculture.[12]

The mode of life among the other tribes of Mahometan Tartars, presents the same uniform picture, which it would be tiresome to repeat, and for which, therefore, I refer the reader to the Genealogical History of the Tartars, and its valuable notes. The conduct of the author of this history himself, a Chan of Chowarasm, affords a curious example of the savage manner in which the wars, of policy, of revenge, or plunder, are carried on in these countries. His invasions of Great Bucharia were frequent, and each expedition was signalized by the ravage of provinces, and the utter ruin and destruction of towns and villages. When, at any time, the number of his prisoners impeded his motions, he made no scruple to kill them on the spot. Wishing to reduce the power of the Turkmans who were tributary to him, he invited all the principal people to a solemn feast, and had them massacred to the number of two thousand. He burnt and destroyed their villages with the most unsparing cruelty, and committed such devastations, that the effect of them returned on their authors, and the army of the victors suffered severely from dearth.[13]

The Mahometan Tartars in general hate trade, and make it their business to spoil all the merchants who fall into their hands.[14] The only commerce that is countenanced is the commerce in slaves. These form a principal part of the booty which they carry off in their predatory incursions, and are considered as a chief source of their riches. Those which they have occasion for themselves, either for the attendance on their herds, or as wives and concubines, they keep, and the rest they sell.[15] The Circassian and Daghestan Tartars, and the other tribes in the neighbourhood of Caucasus, living in a poor and mountainous country, and, on that account, less subject to invasion, generally overflow with inhabitants; and when they cannot obtain slaves in the common way, steal from one another, and even sell their own

12. Id. p. 573, et seq.   13. Geneal. Hist. Tart. vol. i. c. xii.
14. Id. vol. ii. p. 412.   15. Id. p. 413.

wives and children.[16] This trade in slaves, so general among the Mahometan Tartars, may be one of the causes of their constant wars; as, when a prospect of a plentiful supply for this kind of traffick offers itself, neither peace nor alliance can restrain them.[17]

The heathen Tartars, the Kalmucks, and Moguls, do not make much use of slaves, and are said, in general, to lead a much more peaceable and harmless life, contenting themselves with the produce of their herds and flocks, which form their sole riches. They rarely make war for the sake of plunder; and seldom invade the territory of their neighbours, unless to revenge a prior attack. They are not, however, without destructive wars. The inroads of the Mahometan Tartars oblige them to constant defence and retaliation; and feuds subsist between the kindred tribes of the Kalmucks and Moguls, which, fomented by the artful policy of the emperor of China, are carried on with such animosity, as to threaten the entire destruction of one or other of these nations.[18]

The Bedoweens of Arabia and Syria do not live in greater tranquillity than the inhabitants of Grand Tartary. The very nature of the pastoral state, seems to furnish perpetual occasions for war. The pastures which a tribe uses at one period, form but a small part of its possessions. A large range of territory is successively occupied in the course of the year; and as the whole of this is absolutely necessary for the annual subsistence of the tribe, and is considered as appropriated, every violation of it, though the tribe may be at a great distance, is held to be a just cause of war.[19] Alliances and kindred make these wars more general. When blood is shed, more must expiate it; and as such accidents have multiplied in the lapse of years, the greatest part of the tribes have quarrels between them, and live in a state of perpetual hostility.[20] In the times which preceded Mahomet, seventeen

16. Id. vol. ii. p. 413, 414, and ch. xii.

17. "They justify it as lawful to have many wives, because they say they bring us
" many children, which we can sell for ready money, or exchange for necessary
" conveniences; yet when they have not wherewithal to maintain them, they hold it
" a piece of charity to murder infants new born, as also they do such as are sick,
" and past recovery, because they say they free them from a great deal of misery."
Sir John Chardin's Travels. Harris's Col. b. iii. c. ii, p. 865.

18. Geneal. Hist. Tart. vol. ii. p. 545.

19. Ils se disputeront la terre inculte comme parmi nous les citoyens se disputent les heritages. Ainsi ils trouveront de frequentes occasions de guerre pour la nourriture de leur bestiaux, &c. **** ils auront autant de choses a regler par le droit des gens qu'ils en auront peu a decider par le droit civil. Montes. Esprit des Loix, l. xviii. c. xii.

20. Voy. de Volney, tom. i. c. xxii. p. 361, 362, 363.

hundred battles are recorded by tradition; and a partial truce of two months, which was religiously kept, might be considered, according to a just re-mark of Gibbon, as still more strongly expressive of their general habits of anarchy and warfare.[21]

The waste of life, from such habits, might alone appear sufficient to repress their population; but probably their effect is still greater in the fatal check which they give to every species of industry, and particularly to that, the object of which is to enlarge the means of subsistence. Even the con-struction of a well, or a reservoir of water, requires some funds and labour in advance; and war may destroy in one day, the work of many months, and the resources of a whole year.[22] The evils seem mutually to produce each other. A scarcity of subsistence might at first perhaps give occasion to the habits of war, and the habits of war in return powerfully contribute to nar-row the means of subsistence.

Some tribes, from the nature of the deserts in which they live, seem to be necessarily condemned to a pastoral life;[23] but even those which inhabit soils proper for agriculture, have but little temptation to practise this art, while surrounded by marauding neighbours. The peasants of the frontier provinces of Syria, Persia, and Siberia, exposed as they are to the constant incursions of a devastating enemy, do not lead a life that is to be envied by the wandering Tartar or Arab. A certain degree of security, is perhaps still more necessary, than richness of soil, to encourage the change from the pastoral to the agricultural state; and where this cannot be attained, the sedentary labourer is more exposed to the vicissitudes of fortune, than he who leads a wandering life, and carries all his property with him.[24] Under the feeble, yet oppressive government of the Turks, it is not uncommon for peasants to desert their villages and betake themselves to a pastoral state, in which they expect to be better able to escape from the plunder of their Turkish masters and Arab neighbours.[25]

It may be said, however, of the shepherd, as of the hunter, that if want alone could effect a change of habits, there would be few pastoral tribes remaining. Notwithstanding the constant wars of the Bedoween Arabs, and the other checks to their increase, from the hardships of their mode of life, their population presses so hard against the limits of their food, that they are compelled from necessity to a degree of abstinence, which nothing but early and constant habit could enable the human constitution to support.

---

21. Gibbon, vol. ix. c. l. p. 238, 239.   22. Voy. de Volney, tom. i. c. xxiii. p. 353.
23. Id. p. 350.   24. Id. p. 354.   25. Id. p. 350.

According to Volney, the lower classes of the Arabs live in a state of habitual misery and famine.[26] The tribes of the desert deny that the religion of Mahomet was made for them. For how, they say, can we perform ablutions, when we have no water; how can we give alms, when we have no riches; or what occasion can there be to fast during the month of Ramadan, when we fast all the year?[27]

The power and riches of a Chaik consist in the number of his tribe. He considers it therefore as his interest to encourage population, without reflecting how it maybe supported. His own consequence much depends on a numerous progeny, and kindred;[28] and in a state of society where power generally procures subsistence, each individual family derives strength and importance from its numbers. These ideas act strongly as a bounty upon population, and co-operating with a spirit of generosity which almost produces a community of goods,[29] contribute to push it to its utmost verge, and to depress the body of the people in the most rigid poverty.

The habits of polygamy, where there have been losses of men in war, tend perhaps also to produce the same effect. Niehbuhr observes that polygamy multiplies families till many of their branches sink into the most wretched misery.[30] The descendants of Mahomet are found in great numbers all over the east, and many of them in extreme poverty. A Mahometan is in some degree obliged to polygamy from a principle of obedience to his prophet, who makes one of the great duties of man to consist in procreating children to glorify the Creator. Fortunately, individual interest, corrects in some degree, as in many other instances, the absurdity of the legislator, and the poor Arab is obliged to proportion his religious obedience to the scantiness of his resources. Yet still the direct encouragements to population are extraordinarily great; and nothing can place, in a more striking point of view, the futility and absurdity of such encouragements, than the present state of these countries. It is universally agreed, that if their population be not less than formerly, it is indubitably not greater; and it follows as a direct consequence, that the great increase of some families has absolutely pushed the others out of existence. Gibbon, speaking of Arabia, observes, that "The measure of population is regulated by " the means of subsistence, and the inhabitants of this vast peninsula, " might be out-numbered by the subjects of a fertile and industrious

26. Voy. de Volney, tom. i. c. xxiii. p. 359.
27. Id. p. 380.   28. Id. p. 366.   29. Id. p. 378.
30. Niehbuhr's Travels, vol. ii. c. v. p. 207.

" province."[31] Whatever may be the encouragements to marriage, this measure cannot be passed. While the Arabs retain their present manners, and the country remains in its present state of cultivation, the promise of Paradise to every man who had ten children, would but little increase their numbers, though it might greatly increase their misery. Direct encouragements to population have no tendency whatever to change these manners, and promote cultivation. Perhaps, indeed, they have a contrary tendency, as the constant uneasiness from poverty and want which they occasion, would encourage the marauding spirit[32] and multiply the occasions of war.

Among the Tartars, who, from living in a more fertile soil, are comparatively richer in cattle, the plunder to be obtained in predatory incursions, is greater than among the Arabs. And as the contests are more bloody, from the superior strength of the tribes, and the custom of making slaves is general, the loss of numbers in war will be more considerable. These two circumstances united, enable some hordes of fortunate robbers to live in a state of plenty, in comparison of their less enterprising neighbours. Professor Pallas gives a particular account of two wandering tribes subject to Russia, one of which supports itself almost entirely by plunder, and the other lives as peacefully as the restlessness of its neighbours will admit. It may be curious to trace the different checks to population that result from these different habits.

The Kirgisiens, according to Pallas,[33] live at their ease in comparison of the other wandering tribes that are subject to Russia. The spirit of liberty and independence which reigns amongst them, joined to the facility with which they can procure a flock sufficient for their maintenance, prevents any of them from entering into the service of others. They all expect to be treated as brothers, and the rich, therefore, are obliged to use slaves. It may be asked what are the causes which prevent the lower classes of people from increasing till they become poor?

31. It is rather a curious circumstance, that a truth so important which has been stated, and acknowledged, by so many authors, should so rarely have been pursued to its consequences. People are not every day dying of famine. How then is the population regulated to the measure of the means of subsistence?

32. Aussi arrive-t'il chaque jour des accidens, des enlèvements de bestiaux; et cette guerre de maraude est une de celles qui occupent d'avantage les Arabes. Voy. de Volney, tom. i. c. xxiii. p. 364.

33. Not having been able to procure the work of Pallas on the history of the Mongol nations, I have here made use of a general abridgement of the works of the Russian travellers, in 4 vols. oct. published at Berne and Lausanne in 1781 and 1784, entitled, Decouvertes Russes, tom. iii. p. 399.

Pallas has not informed us how far vicious customs with respect to women, or the restraints on marriage from the fear of a family, may have contributed to this effect; but, perhaps, the description which he gives of their civil constitution, and licentious spirit of rapine, may be alone almost sufficient to account for it. The Chan cannot exercise his authority but through the medium of a council of principal persons, chosen by the people; and even the decrees thus confirmed are continually violated with impunity.[34] Though the plunder and capture of persons, of cattle, and of merchandize, which the Kirgisiens exercise on their neighbours the Kazalpacs, the Bucharians, the Persians, the Truchemenes, the Kalmucks, and the Russians, are prohibited by their laws, yet no person is afraid to avow them. On the contrary, they boast of their successes in this way, as of the most honourable enterprizes. Sometimes they pass their frontiers alone, to seek their fortune, sometimes collect in troops under the command of an able chief, and pillage entire caravans. A great number of Kirgisiens, in exercising this rapine, are either killed, or taken into slavery; but about this the nation troubles itself very little. When these ravages are committed by private adventurers, each retains what he has taken, whether cattle or women. The male slaves and the merchandize are sold to the rich, or to foreign traders.[35]

With these habits, in addition to their national wars, which, from the fickle and turbulent disposition of the tribe, are extremely frequent,[36] we may easily conceive that the checks to population from violent causes may be so powerful as nearly to preclude all others. Occasional famines may sometimes attack them in their wars of devastation,[37] their fatiguing predatory incursions, or from long droughts, and mortality of cattle; but, in the common course of things, the approach of poverty would be the signal for a new marauding expedition; and the poor Kirgisien would either return with sufficient to support him, or lose his life or liberty in the attempt. He who determines to be rich, or die, and does not scruple the means, cannot long remain poor.

The Kalmucks, who, before their migration in 1771, inhabited the fertile steppes of the Wolga, under the protection of Russia, lived, in general, in a different manner. They were not often engaged in any very bloody wars;[38]

34. Decouv. Russ. tom. iii. p. 389.   35. Decouv. Russ. tom. iii. p. 396, 397, 398.
36. Id. p. 378.
37. Cette multitude devaste tout se qui se trouve sur son passage, ils emmenent avec eux tout le betail qu'ils ne consomment pas, et reduisent a l'esclavage les femmes, les enfans, et les hommes, qu'ils n'ont par massacrés. Id. p. 390.
38. Decouv. Russ. tom. iii. p. 221. The tribe is described here under the name of the Torgots, which was their appropriate appellation. The Russians called them by the more general name of Kalmucks.

and the power of the Chan being absolute;[39] and the civil administration better regulated than among the Kirgisiens, the marauding expeditions of private adventurers were checked. The Kalmuck women are extremely prolific. Barren marriages are rare, and three or four children are generally seen playing round every hut. From which it may naturally be concluded, Pallas observes, that they ought to have multiplied greatly during the hundred and fifty years that they inhabited tranquilly the steppe of the Wolga. The reasons which he gives for their not having increased so much as might be expected, are, the many accidents occasioned by falls from horses, the frequent petty wars between their different princes, and with their different neighbours; and, particularly, the numbers among the poorer classes who die of hunger, of misery, and every species of calamity, of which the children are most frequently the victims.[40]

It appears that when this tribe first put itself under the protection of Russia, it had separated from the Soongares, and was by no means numerous. The possession of the fertile steppe of the Wolga, and a more tranquil life, soon increased it, and in 1662 it amounted to fifty thousand families.[41] From this period to 1771, the time of its migration, it seems to have increased very slowly. The extent of pastures possessed, would not probably admit of a much greater population, as at the time of its flight from these quarters, the irritation of the Chan at the conduct of Russia, was seconded by the complaints of the people, of the want of pasture for their numerous herds. At this time the tribe amounted to between 55 and 60,000 families. Its fate in this curious migration, was what has probably been the fate of many other wandering hordes, who, from scanty pastures, or other causes of discontent, have attempted to seek for fresh seats. The march took place in the winter, and numbers perished on this painful journey from cold, famine, and misery. A great part was either killed or taken by the Kirghises; and those who reached their place of destination, though received at first kindly by the Chinese, were afterwards treated with extreme severity.[42]

Before this migration, the lower classes of the Kalmucks had lived in great poverty and wretchedness, and had been reduced habitually to make use of every animal, plant, or root, from which it was possible to extract

39. Id. p. 327.   40. Decouv. Russ. tom. iii. p. 319, 320, 321.

41. Id. p. 221. Tooke's View of Russian Empire, vol. ii. b. ii. p. 30. Another instance of rapid increase presents itself in a colony of baptized Kalmucks, who received from Russia a fertile district to settle in. From 8695, which was its number in 1754, it had increased in 1771 to 14,000. Tooke's View of Rus. Em. vol. ii. b. ii. p. 32, 33.

42. Tooke's View of Rus. Emp. vol. ii. b. ii. p. 29, 30, 31. Decouv. Rus. tom. iii. p. 221.

nourishment.[43] They very seldom killed any of their cattle that were in health, except indeed they were stolen, and then they were devoured immediately for fear of a discovery. Wounded, or worn out horses, and beasts that had died of any disease, except a contagious epidemic, were considered as most desireable food. Some of the poorest Kalmucks would eat the most putrid carrion, and even the dung of their cattle.[44] A great number of children perished of course from bad nourishment.[45] In the winter all the lower classes suffered severely from cold and hunger.[46] In general, one third of their sheep, and often much more, died in the winter, in spite of all their care; and if a frost came late in the season after rain and show, so that the cattle could not get at the grass, the mortality among their herds became general, and the poorer classes of the Kalmucks were exposed to inevitable famine.[47]

Malignant fevers, generated principally by their putrid food and the putrid exhalations with which they were surrounded, and the small-pox, which is dreaded like the plague, sometimes thinned their numbers;[48] but in general, it appears, that their population pressed so hard against the limits of their means of subsistence, that want, with the diseases arising from it, might be considered as the principal check to their increase.

A person travelling in Tartary during the summer months, would probably see extensive steppes unoccupied, and grass in profusion, spoiling for want of cattle to consume it. He would infer, perhaps, that the country could support a much greater number of inhabitants, even supposing them to remain in their shepherd state. But this might be a hasty and unwarranted conclusion. A horse, or any other working animal, is said to be strong only in proportion to the strength of his weakest part. If his legs be slender and feeble, the strength of his body will be but of little consequence; or if he wants power in his back and haunches, the strength which he may possess in his limbs can never be called fully into action. The same reasoning must be applied to the power of the earth to support living creatures. The profusion of nourishment which is poured forth in the seasons of plenty, cannot all be consumed by the scanty numbers that were able to subsist through the season of scarcity. When human industry and foresight are directed in the best manner, the population that the soil can support is regulated by the average produce throughout the year; but among animals, and in the uncivilized states of man, it will be much below this average. The Tartar would find it extremely difficult to collect and carry with him such a quantity of

43. Id. p. 275, 276.   44. Id. p. 272, 273, 274.   45. Id. p. 324.
46. Id. p. 310.   47. Ibid. and p. 270.   48. Id. p. 311, 312, 313.

hay, as would feed all his cattle well during the winter. It would impede his motions, expose him to the attacks of his enemies, and an unfortunate day might deprive him of the labours of a whole summer, as in the mutual invasions which occur, it seems to be the universal practice to burn and destroy all the forage and provisions which cannot be carried away.[49] The Tartar, therefore, provides only for the most valuable of his cattle during the winter, and leaves the rest to support themselves by the scanty herbage which they can pick up. This poor living, combined with the severe cold, naturally destroys a considerable part of them.[50] The population of the tribe is measured by the population of its herds; and the average numbers of the Tartars, as of the horses that run wild in the desart, are repressed so low by the annual returns of the cold and scarcity of winter, that they cannot consume all the plentiful offerings of summer.

Droughts and unfavourable seasons have, in proportion to their frequency, the same effect as the winter. In Arabia,[51] and a great part of Tartary,[52] droughts are not uncommon; and if the periods of their return be not above six or eight years, the average population can never much exceed what the soil can support during these unfavourable times. This is true in every situation; but perhaps in the shepherd state, man is peculiarly exposed to be affected by the seasons; and a great mortality of parent stock is an evil more fatal and longer felt, than the failure of a crop of grain. Pallas and the other Russian travellers speak of epizooties, as very common in these parts of the world.[53]

As among the Tartars, a family is always honourable, and women are reckoned very serviceable in the management of the cattle and the household concerns, it is not probable that many are deterred from marriage, from the fear of not being able to support a family.[54] At the same time, as all wives are bought of their parents, it must sometimes be out of the power of the poorer classes to make the purchase. The monk Rubruquis, speaking of this custom, says, that as parents keep all their daughters till they can

---

49. On mit le feu a toutes les meules de bled et de fourrage.**** Cent cinquante villages egalement encendies. Memoires du Baron de Tott, tom. i. p. 272. He gives a curious description of the devastations of a Tartar army, and of its sufferings in a winter campaign. Cette journée couta a l'armée plus de 3,000 hommes, et 30,000 chevaux, qui perirent de froid, p. 267.

50. Decouvertes Russes, vol. iii. p. 261.   51. Voy. de Volney, vol. i. c. 23. p. 353.

52. Decouv. Russ. tom. i. p. 467. ii. p. 10, 11, 12, &c. &c.

53. Id. tom. i. p. 290, &c. ii. p. 11. iv. p. 304.

54. Geneal. Hist. Tartars, vol. ii. p. 407.

sell them, their maids are sometimes very stale before they are married.[55] Among the Mahometan Tartars female captives would supply the place of wives;[56] but among the pagan Tartars, who make but little use of slaves, the inability of buying a wife, must frequently operate on the poorer classes as a check to marriage, particularly as their price would be kept up by the practice of polygamy among the rich.[57]

The Kalmucks are said not to be jealous,[58] and, from the general prevalence of the venereal disease among them,[59] we may infer that a certain degree of promiscuous intercourse prevails.

On the whole, therefore, it would appear, that in that department of the shepherd life which has been considered in this chapter, the principal checks which keep the population down to the level of the means of subsistence, are, restraint, from inability to obtain a wife, vicious customs with respect to women, epidemics, wars, famine, and the diseases arising from extreme poverty. The three first checks and the last appear to have operated with much less force among the shepherds of the north of Europe.

---

55. Travels of Wm. Rubruquis in 1253. Harris's Collection of Voy. b. i. c. ii. p. 561.   56. Decouv. Russ. tom. iii. p. 413.

57. Pallas takes notice of the scarcity of women, or the superabundance of males among the Kalmucks, notwithstanding the more constant exposure of the male sex to every kind of accident. Decouv. Russ. tom. iii. p. 320.

58. Decouv. Russ. tom. iii. p. 239.   59. Id. p. 324.

CHAP. VIII.

Of the Checks to Population in different Parts of Africa.

THE parts of Africa visited by Park, are described by him as neither well cultivated, nor well peopled. He found many extensive and beautiful districts entirely destitute of inhabitants; and in general, the borders of the different kingdoms were either very thinly peopled, or perfectly deserted. The swampy banks of the Gambia, the Senegal, and other rivers towards the coast, appeared to be unfavourable to population, from being unhealthy;[1] but other parts were not of this description; and it was not possible, he says, to behold the wonderful fertility of the soil, the vast herds of cattle proper both for labour and food, and reflect on the means which presented themselves of vast inland navigation, without lamenting that a country so abundantly gifted by nature, should remain in its present savage and neglected state.[2]

The causes of this neglected state clearly appear, however, in the description which Park gives of the general habits of the negroe nations. In a country divided into a thousand petty states, mostly independent and jealous of each other, it is natural to imagine, he says, that wars frequently originate from very frivolous provocations. The wars of Africa are of two kinds, one called killi, that which is openly avowed; and the other, tegria, plundering or stealing. These latter are very common, particularly about the beginning of the dry season, when the labours of harvest are over, and provisions are plentiful. These plundering excursions always produce speedy retaliation.[3]

The insecurity of property arising from this constant exposure to plunder, must necessarily have a most baneful effect on industry. The deserted state of all the frontier provinces, sufficiently proves to what a degree it operates. The nature of the climate is unfavourable to the exertion of the negroe nations; and, as there are not many opportunities of turning to advantage the surplus produce of their labour, we cannot be surprised that they should in general content themselves with cultivating only as much ground as is necessary for their own support.[4] These causes appear adequately to account for the uncultivated state of the country.

1. Park's Interior of Africa, c. xx. p. 261. 4to.   2. Id. c. xxiii. p. 312.
3. Park's Africa, c. xxii. p. 291. & seq.   4. Id. c. xxi. p. 280.

The waste of life in these constant wars and predatory incursions must be considerable; and Park agrees with Buffon in stating, that, independent of violent causes, longevity is rare among the negroes. At forty, he says, most of them became greyhaired and covered with wrinkles, and but few of them survive the age of fifty-five, or sixty.[5] Buffon attributes this shortness of life to the premature intercourse of the sexes, and the very early and excessive debauchery.[6] On this subject perhaps he has been led into exaggerations; but, without attributing too much to this cause, it seems agreeable to the analogy of nature to suppose, that, as the natives of hot climates arrive much earlier at maturity than the inhabitants of colder countries, they should also perish earlier.

According to Buffon, the negroe women are extremely prolific; but, it appears from Park, that they are in the habit of suckling their children two or three years, and as the husband, during this time, devotes the whole of his attention to his other wives, the family of each wife is seldom numerous.[7] Polygamy is universally allowed among the negro nations,[8] and consequently without a greater superabundance of women than we have reason to suppose, many will be obliged to live unmarried. This hardship will probably fall principally on the slaves, who, according to Park, are in the proportion of three to one to the free men.[9] A master is not permitted to sell his domestic slaves, nor those born in his own house, except in case of famine, to support himself and family. We may imagine, therefore, that he will not suffer them to increase beyond the employment which he has for them. The slaves which are purchased, or the prisoners taken in war, are entirely at the disposal of their masters.[10] They are often treated with extreme severity, and in any scarcity of women arising from the polygamy of the free men, would of course be deprived of them without scruple. Few or no women, probably, remain in a state of strict celibacy; but, in proportion

5. Id. p. 274.

6. L'usage prematuré des femmes est peut-être la cause de la brieveté de leur vie; les enfans sont si debauches, et si peu contraints par les peres et meres, que des leur plus tendre jeunesse ils se livrent à tout ce que la nature leur suggère, rien n'est si rare que de trouver dans ce peuple quelque fille qui puise se souvenir du tems auquel elle a cessé d'etre vierge. Histoire Naturelle de l'Homme, vol. vi. p. 235. 5th edit. 12mo. 31 vols.

7. Park's Africa, c. xx. p. 265. As the accounts of Park, and those on which Buffon has founded his observations, are probably accounts of different nations, and certainly at different periods, we cannot infer that either is incorrect because they differ from each other: but as far as Park's observations extend, they are certainly entitled to more credit than any of the travellers which preceded him.

8. Id. c. xx. p. 267.   9. Id. c. xxii. p. 287.   10. Id 288.

to the number married, the state of society does not seem to be favourable to increase.

Africa has been at all times the principal mart of slaves. The drains of its population in this way have been great and constant, particularly since their introduction into the European colonies; but perhaps, as Dr. Franklin observes, it would be difficult to find the gap that has been made by a hundred years exportation of negroes which has blackened half America.[11] For, notwithstanding this constant emigration, the loss of numbers from incessant war, and the checks to increase from vice and other causes, it appears, that the population is continually passing beyond the means of subsistence. According to Park, scarce years and famines are frequent. Among the four principal causes of slavery in Africa, he mentions famine next to war;[12] and the express permission given to masters to sell their domestic slaves for the support of their family, which they are not allowed to do on any less urgent occasion,[13] seems to imply the not infrequent recurrence of severe want. During a great scarcity, which lasted for three years in the countries of the Gambia, great numbers of people became slaves. Park was assured by Dr. Laidley, that at that time many free-men came, and begged with great earnestness, to be put upon his slave chain to save them from perishing with hunger.[14] While Park was in Manding, a scarcity of provisions was severely felt by the poor, as the following circumstance painfully convinced him. Every evening during his stay, he observed five or six women come to the Mansa's house, and receive each of them a certain quantity of corn. "Observe that boy," said the Mansa to him, pointing to a fine child about five years of age – "his mother has sold him to me for forty days provision " for herself and the rest of her family. I have bought another boy in the " same manner."[15] In Sooseeta, a small Jallonka village, Mr. Park was informed by the master, that he could furnish no provisions, as there had lately been a great scarcity in that part of the country. He assured him, that before they had gathered in their present crops, all the inhabitants of Kullo had been for twenty-nine days without tasting corn; during which time they had supported themselves entirely on the yellow powder which is found in the pods of the nitta, so called by the natives, a species of mimosa, and upon the seeds of the bamboo cane, which, when properly pounded and dressed, taste very much like rice.[16]

11. Franklin's Miscell. p. 9.   12. Park's Africa, c. xxii. p. 295.
13. Id. p. 288. note.   14. Id. p. 295.   15. Id. c. xix. p. 248.
16. Park's Africa, c. xxv. p. 336.

It may be said, perhaps, that as, according to Park's account, much good land remains uncultivated in Africa, the dearths may be attributed to a want of people; but if this were the case, we can hardly suppose that such numbers would yearly be sent out of the country. What the negroe nations really want, is, security of property, and its general concomitant, industry; and without these, an increase of people would only greatly aggravate their distresses. If, in order to fill up those parts that appeared to be deficient in inhabitants, we were to suppose a high bounty given on children, the effects would probably be, the increase of wars, the increase of the exportation of slaves, and a great increase of misery, but little or no real increase of population.

The customs of some nations, and the prejudices of all, operate in some degree like a bounty of this kind. The Shangalla negroes, according to Bruce, hemmed in on every side by active and powerful enemies, and leading a life of severe labour, and of constant apprehension, feel but little desire for women. It is the wife and not the man, that is the cause of their polygamy. Though they live in separate tribes or nations, yet these nations are again subdivided into families. In fighting, each family attacks and defends by itself, and their's is the spoil and plunder who take it. The mothers, therefore, sensible of the disadvantages of a small family, seek to multiply it by all the means in their power; and it is by their importunity, that the husband suffers himself to be overcome.[17] The motives to polygamy among the Galla, are described to be the same, and in both nations, the first wife courts the alliance of a second, for her husband; and the principal argument that she makes use of, is, that their families may be joined together and be strong, and that her children, by being few in number, may not fall a prey to their enemies in the day of battle.[18] It is highly probable that this extreme desire of having large families, defeats its own purpose; and that the poverty and misery which it occasions, cause fewer children to grow up to maturity than if the parents had confined their attention to the rearing of a smaller number.

Bruce is a great friend to polygamy, and defends it in the only way in which it is capable of being defended, by asserting, that, in the countries in which it principally prevails, the proportion of girls to boys born, is two or three to one. A fact so extraordinary, however, cannot be admitted upon the authority of those vague inquiries on which he founds his opinion. That there are considerably more women living, than men, in these climates,

17. Bruce's Travels to discover the Source of the Nile, vol. ii. p. 556. 4to.
18. Bruce's Travels to discover the Source of the Nile, vol. ii. p. 223.

is in the highest degree probable. Even in Europe, where it is known with certainty that more boys are born than girls, the women in general exceed the men in number; and we may imagine, that, in hot and unhealthy climates, and in a barbarous state of society, the accidents to which the men are exposed must be very greatly increased. The women by leading a more sedentary life, would suffer less from the effects of a scorching sun and swampy exhalations. They would in general be more exempt from the disorders arising from debauchery; but above all, they would escape in great measure the ravages of war. In a state of society in which hostilities never cease, the drains of men, from this cause alone, must occasion a great disproportion of the sexes, particularly where it is the custom, as related of the Galla in Abyssinia,[19] to massacre indiscriminately all the males, and save only the marriageable women from the general destruction. The actual disproportion of the sexes arising from these causes, probably, first gave rise to the permission of polygamy, and has, perhaps, contributed to make us more easily believe, that the proportion of male and female children, in hot climates, is very different from what we have experienced it to be, in the temperate zone.

Bruce, with the usual prejudices on this subject, seems to think that the celibacy of a part of the women is fatal to the population of a country. He observes of Jidda, that, on account of the great scarcity of provisions which is the result of an extraordinary concourse of people to a place almost destitute of the necessaries of life, few of the inhabitants can avail themselves of the privilege granted by Mahomet. They cannot, therefore, marry more than one wife; and from this cause arises, he says, the want of people and the large number of unmarried women.[20] But it is evident, that the want of people in this barren spot arises solely from the want of provisions, and that if each man had half a dozen wives, the number of people could not be much increased by it.

In Arabia Felix, according to Bruce, where every sort of provision is exceedingly cheap, where the fruits of the ground, the general food of man, are produced spontaneously, the support of a number of wives costs no more than that of so many slaves or servants; their food is the same, and a blue cotton shirt, a habit common to them all, is not more chargeable for the one than for the other. The consequence is, he says, that celibacy in women is prevented, and the number of people increased in a fourfold ratio by polygamy, to what it is in those countries that are monogamous.[21] And

19. Id. vol. iv. p. 411.   20. Bruce, vol. i. c.xi. p. 280.
21. Id. vol. i. c. xi. p. 281.

yet, notwithstanding this fourfold increase, it does not appear that any part of Arabia is really very populous.

The effect of polygamy in increasing the number of married women and preventing celibacy, is beyond dispute; but how far this may tend to increase the actual population, is a very different consideration. It may perhaps contribute to press the population harder against the limits of the food; but the squalid and hopeless poverty which this occasions, is by no means favourable to industry; and in a climate in which there appears to be many predisposing causes of sickness, it is difficult to conceive that this state of wretchedness does not powerfully contribute to the extraordinary mortality which has been observed in some of these countries.

According to Bruce, the whole coast of the Red Sea, from Suez to Babelmandel, is extremely unwholesome, but more especially between the tropics. Violent fevers, called there nedad, make the principal figure in this fatal list, and generally terminate the third day in death.[22] Fear frequently seizes strangers upon the first sight of the great mortality which they observe on their first arrival.

Jidda and all the parts of Arabia adjacent to the eastern coast of the Red Sea, are in the same manner very unwholesome.[23]

In Gondar, fevers perpetually reign, and the inhabitants are all the colour of a corpse.[24]

In Sirè, one of the finest countries in the world, putrid fevers of the very worst kind are almost constant.[25] In the low grounds of Abyssinia, in general, malignant tertians occasion a great mortality.[26] And every where, the small-pox makes great ravages, particularly among the nations bordering on Abyssinia, where it sometimes extinguishes whole tribes.[27]

The effect of poverty, bad diet, and its almost constant concomitant want of cleanliness, in aggravating malignant distempers, is well known; and this kind of wretchedness seems generally to prevail. Of Tchagassa, near Gondar, Bruce observes, that the inhabitants, notwithstanding their threefold harvests, are miserably poor.[28] At Adowa, the capital of Tigré, he makes the same remark, and applies it to all the Abyssinian farmers. The land is let yearly to the highest bidder, and, in general, the landlord furnishes the seed on condition to receive half of the produce; but, it is said, that he is a very indulgent master who does not take another quarter

22. Bruce, vol. iii. p. 33.   23. Id. vol. i. 279.   24. Id. vol. iii. p. 178.
25. Id. p. 153.   26. Id. vol. iv. p. 22.
27. Id. vol. iii. c. iii. p. 68. c. vii. p. 178. vol. i. c. xiii. p. 353.
28. Id. vol. iii. c. vii. p. 195.

for the risk he has run; so that the quantity which comes to the share of the husbandman is not more than sufficient to afford a bare sustenance to his wretched family.[29] The Agows, one of the most considerable nations of Abyssinia in point of number, are described by Bruce as living in a state of misery and penury scarcely to be conceived. We saw a number of women, he says, wrinkled and sunburnt, so as scarcely to appear human, wandering about under a burning sun, with one and sometimes two children upon their backs, gathering the seeds of bent grass to make a kind of bread.[30] The Agow women begin to bear children at eleven years old. They marry generally about that age, and there is no such thing as barrenness known among them.[31] In Dixan, one of the frontier towns of Abyssinia, the only trade is that of selling children. Five hundred are exported annually to Arabia; and in times of scarcity, Bruce observes, four times that number.[32]

In Abyssinia, polygamy does not regularly prevail. Bruce, indeed, makes rather a strange assertion on this subject, and says, that though we read from the Jesuits a great deal about marriage and polygamy, yet that there is nothing which may be averred more truly, than that there is no such thing as marriage in Abyssinia.[33] But, however this may be, it appears clear, that few or no women live a life of celibacy in Abyssinia, and that the prolific powers of nature are nearly all called into action, except as far as they are checked by promiscuous intercourse. This, however, from the state of manners described by Bruce, must operate very powerfully.[34]

The check to population from war, appears to be excessive. For the last four hundred years, according to Bruce, it has never ceased to lay desolate this unhappy country;[35] and the savage manner in which it is carried on, surrounds it with tenfold destruction. When Bruce first entered Abyssinia, he saw on every side ruined villages destroyed to the lowest foundation, by Rass Michael in his march to Gondar.[36] In the course of the civil wars, while Bruce was in the country, he says, "The rebels had begun to lay waste
"   Dembea, and burnt all the villages in the plain, from south to west; mak-
"   ing it like a desert between Michael and Fasil.**** The king often as-
"   cended to the top of the tower of his palace, and contemplated, with the
"   greatest displeasure, the burning of his rich villages in Dembea."[37] In another place, he says, "the whole country of Degwessa was totally de-
"   stroyed; men, women, and children, were entirely extirpated, without
"   distinction of age or sex; the houses rased to the ground, and the country

29. Bruce, vol. iii. c. v. p. 124.   30. Id. c. xix. p. 738.   31. Id. p. 739.
32. Id. vol. iii. c. iii. p. 88.   33. Id. c. xi. p. 306.   34. Id. p. 292.
35. Id. vol. iv. p. 119.   36. Bruce, vol. iii. c. vii. p. 192.
37. Id. vol. iv. c. v. p. 112.

" about it left as desolate as after the deluge. The villages belonging to the
" king were as severely treated; a universal cry was heard from all parts,
" but no one dared to suggest any means of help."[38] In Maitsha, one of the
provinces of Abyssinia,, he was told, that if ever he met an old man, he
might be sure that he was a stranger, as all that were natives died by the
lance young.[39]

If the picture of the state of Abyssinia, drawn by Bruce, be in any degree
near the truth, it places, in a strong point of view, the force of that principle
of increase which preserves a population fully up to the level of the means
of subsistence, under the checks of war, pestilential diseases, and promiscuous intercourse, all operating in an excessive degree.

The nations which border on Abyssinia are universally short-lived. A
Shangalla woman at twenty-two, is, according to Bruce, more wrinkled
and deformed by age than is an European woman at sixty.[40] It would appear
therefore, that, in all these countries, as among the northern shepherds, in
the times of their constant emigrations, there is a very rapid succession of
human beings, and the difference in the two instances is, that our northern
ancestors died out of their own country, whereas these die at home. If accurate registers of mortality were kept among these nations, I have little
doubt that it would appear, that, including the mortality from wars, 1 in 17
or 18 at the least, die annually, instead of 1 in 34 or 36, as in the generality
of European states.

The description which Bruce gives of some parts of the country which
he passed through on his return home, presents a picture more dreadful
even than the state of Abyssinia, and shews how little population depends
on the birth of children, in comparison of the production of food, and of
those circumstances of natural and political situation which influence this
produce.

"At half past six," Bruce says, "we arrived at Garigana, a village whose
" inhabitants had all perished with hunger the year before; their wretched
" bones being all unburied, and scattered upon the surface of the ground
" where the village formerly stood. We encamped among the bones of the
" dead, no space could be found free from them."[41]

Of another town or village in his route, he observes, "The strength of
" Teawa was 25 horse. The rest of the inhabitants might be 1200, naked,
" miserable, and despicable Arabs, like the rest of those which live in
" villages.****Such was the state of Teawa. Its consequence was only to

---

38. Id.vol. iv. p. 258.   39. Id. c. i. p. 14.   40. Id. vol. ii. p. 559.
41. Bruce, vol. iv. p. 349.

" remain till the Daveina Arabs should resolve to attack it, when its corn-
" fields being burnt and destroyed in a night, by a multitude of horsemen,
" the bones of its inhabitants scattered upon the earth, would be all its
" remains like those of the miserable village of Garigana."[42]

"There is no water between Teawa and Beyla. Once Ingedidema and
" a number of villages were supplied with water from wells, and had large
" crops of Indian corn sown about their possessions. The curse of that
" country the Arabs Daveina have destroyed Ingedidema, and all the vil-
" lages about it; filled up their wells, burnt their crops, and exposed all the
" inhabitants to die by famine."[43]

Soon after leaving Sennaar, he says, "We began now to see the effects
" of the quantity of rain having failed. There was little corn sown, and that
" so late, as to be scarcely above ground. It seems the rains begin later as
" they pass northward. Many people were here employed in gathering
" grass-seeds to make a very bad kind of bread. These people appear per-
" fect skeletons, and no wonder, as they live upon such fare. Nothing in-
" creases the danger of travelling and prejudice against strangers, more
" than the scarcity of provisions in the country through which you are
" to pass.[44]

"Came to Eltic, a straggling village about half a mile from the Nile, in
" the north of a large bare plain; all pasture, except the banks of the river
" which are covered with wood. We now no longer saw any corn sown.
" The people here were at the same miserable employment as those we
" had seen before, that of gathering grass-seeds."[45]

Under such circumstances of climate and political situation, though
a greater degree of foresight, industry, and security, might considerably
better their condition, and increase their population, the birth of a greater
number of children without these concomitants, would only aggravate their
misery, and leave their population where it was.

The same may be said of the once flourishing and populous country of
Egypt. Its present depressed state has not been caused by the weakening of
the principle of increase, but by the weakening of the principle of industry
and foresight, from the insecurity of property consequent on a most tyrannical and oppressive government. The principle of increase in Egypt, at
present, does all that is possible for it to do. It keeps the population fully
up to the level of the means of subsistence; and, were its power ten times
greater than it really is, it could do no more.

42. Id. p. 353.   43. Bruce, vol. iv. p. 411.   44. Id. p. 511.   45. Ibid.

The remains of ancient works, the vast lakes, canals, and large conduits for water destined to keep the Nile under controul, serving as reservoirs to supply a scanty year, and as drains and outlets to prevent the superabundance of water in wet years, sufficiently indicate to us, that the ancients by art and industry contrived to fertilize a much greater quantity of land from the overflowings of their river, than is done at present; and to prevent, in some measure, the distresses which are now so frequently experienced from a redundant or insufficient inundation.[46] It is said of the governor Petronius, that, effecting by art what was denied by nature, he caused abundance to prevail in Egypt under the disadvantage of such a deficient inundation, as had always before been accompanied by dearth.[47] A flood too great is as fatal to the husbandman, as one that is deficient; and the ancients had, in consequence, drains and outlets to spread the superfluous waters over the thirsty sands of Lybia, and render even the desert habitable. These works are now all out of repair, and by ill management often produce mischief instead of good. The causes of this neglect, and consequently of the diminished means of subsistence, are obviously to be traced to the extreme ignorance and brutality of the government, and the wretched state of the people. The Mamelukes, in whom the principal power resides, think only of enriching themselves, and employ for this purpose what appears to them to be the simplest method, that of seizing wealth wherever it may be found, of wresting it by violence from the possessor, and of imposing continually new and arbitrary contributions.[48] Their ignorance and brutality, and the constant state of alarm in which they live, prevent them from having any views of enriching the country; the better to prepare it for their plunder. No public works therefore are to be expected from the government, and no individual proprietor dares to undertake any improvement which might imply the possession of capital, as it would probably be the immediate signal of his destruction. Under such circumstances, we cannot be surprised, that the ancient works are neglected, that the soil is ill cultivated, and that the means of subsistence, and consequently the population, are greatly reduced. But such is the natural fertility of the Delta from the inundations of the Nile, that even without any capital employed upon the land, without a right of succession, and consequently almost without a right of property, it still maintains a considerable population in proportion to its extent; sufficient, if property were secure, and industry well directed,

46. Bruce, vol. iii. c. xvii. p. 710.   47. Voyage de Volney, tom. i. c. iii.
p. 33. 8vo.   48. Id. c. xii. p. 170.

gradually to improve and extend the cultivation of the country, and restore it to its former state of prosperity. It may be safely pronounced of Egypt, that it is not the want of population that has checked its industry, but the want of industry that has checked its population.

The causes which keep down the population to the level of the present contracted means of subsistence are but too obvious. The peasants are allowed for their maintenance only sufficient to keep them alive.[49] A miserable sort of bread made of doura without leaven or flavour, cold water, and raw onions, make up the whole of their diet. Meat and fat, of which they are passionately fond, never appear but on great occasions, and among those who are more at their ease. Their habitations are huts made of earth, where a stranger would be suffocated with the heat and smoke; and where the diseases that are generated by want of cleanliness, by moisture, and by bad nourishment, often visit them and commit great ravages. To these physical evils are added, a constant state of alarm, the fear of the plunder of the Arabs, and the visits of the Mamelukes, the spirit of revenge that is transmitted in families, and all the evils of a continued civil war.[50]

In the year 1783 the plague was very fatal; and in 1784 and 1785, a dreadful famine reigned in Egypt, from a deficiency in the inundations of the Nile. Volney draws a frightful picture of the misery that was suffered on this occasion. The streets of Cairo, which at first were full of beggars, were soon cleared of all these objects, who either perished or fled. A vast number of unfortunate wretches, in order to escape death, spread themselves over all the neighbouring countries, and the towns of Syria were inundated with Egyptians. The streets, and public places were crowded with extenuated and dying skeletons. All the most revolting modes of satisfying the cravings of hunger were resorted to; the most disgusting food was devoured with eagerness; and Volney mentions the having seen, under the walls of ancient Alexandria, two miserable wretches seated on the carcase of a camel, and disputing with the dogs its putrid flesh. The depopulation of the two years was estimated at one sixth of all the inhabitants.[51]

---

49. Voyage de Volney, tom. i. c. xii. p. 172.
50. Volney, tom. i. c. xii. p. 173. This sketch of the state of the peasantry in Egypt, given by Volney, seems to be nearly confirmed by all the other writers on the subject; and particularly in a valuable paper intitled, *Considerations generales sur l'Agriculture de l'Egypte, par L. Reynier.* (Memoirs sur L'Egypte, tom. iv. p. 1.)
51. Voy. de Volney, tom. i. c. xii. s. ii.

Of the Checks to Population in Siberia, Northern and Southern.

THE inhabitants of the most northern parts of Asia subsist chiefly by hunting and fishing; and we may suppose, therefore, that the checks to their increase are of the same nature as those which prevail among the American Indians; except that the check from war is considerably less, and the check from famine, perhaps, greater than in the temperate regions of America. M. de Lesseps, who travelled from Kamtschatka to Petersburgh with the papers of the unfortunate Perouse, draws a melancholy picture of the misery that is sometimes suffered in this part of the world from a scarcity of food. He observes, while at Bolcheretsk, a village of Kamtschatka, "very
" heavy rains are injurious in this country, because they occasion floods,
" which drive the fish from the rivers. A famine, the most distressing to
" the poor Kampschadales, is the result, as it happened last year in all the
" villages along the western coast of the peninsula. This dreadful calamity
" occurs so frequently in this quarter, that the inhabitants are obliged to
" abandon their dwellings, and repair with their families to the borders of
" the Kamtschatka river, where they hope to find better resources, fish
" being more plentiful in this river. M. Kasloff (the Russian officer who
" conducted M. de Lesseps) had intended to proceed along the western
" coast; but the news of this famine determined him, contrary to his
" wishes, to return, rather than be driven to the necessity of stopping half
" way, or perishing with hunger."[1] Though a different route was pursued, yet in the course of the journey almost all the dogs which drew the sledges died for want of food; and every dog, as soon as he failed, was immediately devoured by the others.[2]

Even at Okotsk, a town of considerable trade, the inhabitants wait with hungry impatience for the breaking up of the river Okhota in the spring. When M. de Lesseps was there, the stock of dried fish was nearly exhausted. Meal was so dear, that the common people were unable to purchase it. On drawing the seine prodigious numbers of small fish were caught, and the joy and clamour redoubled at the sight. The most famished were first served. M. de Lesseps feelingly says, "I could not refrain from tears on

---

1. Travels in Kamtschatka, vol. i. p. 147. 8vo. Eng. trans. 1790.
2. Id. p. 264.

"   perceiving the ravenousness of these poor creatures;**** whole fami-
"   lies contended for the fish, which were devoured raw before my eyes."[3]

Throughout all the northern parts of Siberia, the small-pox is very fatal. In Kampschatka, according to M. de Lesseps, it has carried off three
fourths[4] of the native inhabitants.

Pallas confirms this account; and, in describing the Ostiacks on the Obi
who live nearly in the same manner, observes, that this disorder makes
dreadful ravages among them, and may be considered as the principal
check to their increase.[5] The extraordinary mortality of the small-pox
among these people, is very naturally accounted for, from the extreme heat,
filth, and putrid air, of their underground habitations. Three or four Ostiack
families are crowded together in one yourt, and nothing can be so disgusting as their mode of living. They never wash their hands, and the putrid
remains of the fish, and the excrements of the children, are never cleared
away. From this description, says Pallas, one may easily form an idea of the
stench, the fœtid vapours, and humidity of their yourts.[6] They have seldom
many children. It is a rare thing to see three or four in one family. The reason which Pallas gives, is, that so many die young on account of their bad
nourishment.[7] To this, perhaps, should be added the state of miserable and
laborious servitude to which the women are condemned,[8] which certainly
prevents them from being prolific.

The Samoyedes, Pallas thinks, are not quite so dirty as the Ostiacks,
because they are more in motion during the winter in hunting; but he describes the state of the women amongst them as a still more wretched and
laborious servitude;[9] and consequently the check to population from this
cause would be greater.

Most of the natives of these inhospitable regions live nearly in the same
miserable manner, which it would be, therefore, mere repetition to describe.
From what has been said, we may form an idea of the principal checks that
keep the actual population down to the level of the scanty means of subsistence which these dreary countries afford.

In some of the southern parts of Siberia, and in the districts adjoining
the Wolga, the Russian travellers describe the soil to be of extraordinary
fertility. It consists in general of a fine black mould of so rich a nature as
not to require, or even to bear, dressing. Manure only makes the corn grow
too luxuriantly, and subjects it to fall to the ground and be spoiled. The

---

3. Id. vol. ii. p. 252, 253.   4. Id. vol. i. p. 128.
5. Voy. de Pallas, tom. iv. p. 68. 4to. 5 vols. 1788. Paris.   6. Id. p. 60.
7. Voy. de Pallas, tom. iv. p. 72.   8. Id. p. 60.   9. Id. p. 92.

only mode of recruiting this kind of land which is practised, is, by leaving it one year out of three in fallow, and proceeding in this way, there are some grounds, the vigour of which is said to be inexhaustible.[10] Yet notwithstanding the facility with which, as it would appear, the most plentiful subsistence might be procured, many of these districts are thinly peopled, and in none of them, perhaps, does population increase in the proportion that might be expected from the nature of the soil.

Such countries seem to be under that moral impossibility of increasing, which is well described by Sir James Steuart.[11] Man, though he may often be produced without a sufficient demand for him, cannot really multiply and prosper unless his labour be wanted; and the reason that the population goes on so slowly in these countries, is, that there is very little demand for men. The mode of agriculture is described to be extremely simple, and to require very few labourers. In some places the seed is merely thrown on the fallow.[12] The buck-wheat is a common culture; and though it is sown very thin, yet one sowing will last five or six years, and produce every year twelve or fifteen times the original quantity. The seed which falls during the time of the harvest is sufficient for the next year, and it is only necessary to pass a harrow once over it in the spring. And this is continued, till the fertility of the soil begins to diminish. It is observed, very justly, that the cultivation of no kind of grain can so exactly suit the indolent inhabitants of the plains of Siberia.[13]

With such a system of agriculture, and with few or no manufactures, the demand for men must be very easily satisfied. Corn will undoubtedly be very cheap; but labour will be in proportion still cheaper. Though the farmer may be able to provide an ample quantity of food for his own children, yet the wages of his labourer will not be sufficient to enable him to rear up a family with ease.

If, from observing the deficiency of population, compared with the fertility of the soil, we were to endeavour to remedy it by giving a bounty upon children, and thus enabling the labourer to rear up a greater number; what would be the consequence? Nobody would want the work of these supernumerary labourers that were thus brought into the market. Though the ample subsistence of a man for a day might be purchased for a penny, yet nobody will give these people a farthing for their labour. The farmer is able to do all that he wishes, all that he thinks necessary in the cultivation

10. Id. p. 5. 11. Polit. Econ. b. i. c. v. p. 30. 4to.
12. Voy. de Pallas, tom. i. p. 250.
13. Decouv. Russ. vol. iv. p. 329. 8vo. 4 vols. Berne.

of the soil, by means of his own family, and the one or two labourers which he might have before. As these people, therefore, can give him nothing that he wants, it is not to be expected that he should overcome his natural indolence, and undertake a larger and more troublesome concern, merely to provide them gratuitously with food. In such a state of things, when the very small demand for manufacturing labour is satisfied, what are the rest do? They are, in fact, as completely without the means of subsistence, as if they were living upon a barren sand. They must either emigrate to some place where their work is wanted, or perish miserably of poverty. Should they be prevented from suffering this last extremity by a scanty subsistence given to them, in consequence of a scanty and only occasional use of their labour, it is evident, that though they might exist themselves, they would not be in a capacity to marry, and continue to increase the population.

It might be supposed, perhaps, that if there were much good land un-used, the redundant population would naturally betake itself to the culti-vation of it, and raise its own food. But though there are many countries where good land remains uncultivated, there are very few where it may be obtained by the first person who chuses to occupy it. Even were this the case, there would be still some obstacles remaining. The supernumerary labourer whom I have described, has no funds whatever, that can enable him to build a house, to purchase stock and utensils, and to subsist till he has brought his new land into proper order, and obtained an adequate return. Even the children of the farmer, when they grow up, would find it very difficult to obtain these necessary funds. In a state of society where the market for corn is extremely narrow, and the price very low, the culti-vators are always poor; and though they may be able amply to provide for their family, in the simple article of food; yet they cannot realise a capital to divide among their children, and enable them to undertake the culti-vation of fresh land. Though this necessary capital might be very small, yet even this small sum, the farmer perhaps cannot acquire; for when he grows a greater quantity of corn than usual, he finds no purchaser for it,[14] and cannot convert it into any permanent article, which will enable any of his children to command an equivalent portion of subsistence or labour in future. In general, therefore, he contents himself with growing only what is sufficient for the immediate demands of his family, and the narrow market to which he is accustomed. And if he has a large family, many of his chil-dren probably fall into the rank of labourers, and their further increase is

14. Il y a fort peu de debit dans le pays, parce que le plupart des habitans son cultivateurs et elevent eux memes des bestiaux. Voy. de Pallas, tom. iv. p. 4.

checked, as in the case of the labourer before described, by a want of the means of subsistence.

It is not therefore a direct encouragement to the procreation and rearing of children that is wanted in these countries, in order to increase their population; but the creation of an effectual demand for the produce of the soil, by promoting the means of its distribution. This can only be effected, either by the introduction of manufactures, and by inspiring the cultivator with a taste for them, which must necessarily be a work of time; or by assisting new colonists and the children of the old cultivators with capital to enable them to occupy successively, and bring into cultivation, all the land that is fit for it.

The late Empress of Russia adopted both these means of increasing the population in her dominions. She encouraged both manufacturers and cultivators; and furnished to foreigners of either description, capital, and funds for subsistence, free of all interest for a certain term of years.[15] These well-directed efforts, added to what had been done by Peter I. had, as might be expected, a considerable effect; and the Russian territories, particularly the Asiatic part of them, which had slumbered for centuries, with a population nearly stationary, or at most increasing very languidly, seem to have made a sudden start of late years. Though the population of the more fertile provinces of Siberia be still very inadequate to the richness of the soil; yet in some of them, agriculture flourishes in no inconsiderable degree, and great quantities of corn are grown. In a general dearth which happened in 1769, the province of Isetsk was able, notwithstanding a scanty harvest, to supply, in the usual manner, the founderies and forges of Ural, besides preserving from the horrors of famine all the neighbouring provinces.[16] And in the territory of Krasnoyarsk, on the shores of the Yenissey, in spite of the indolence and drunkenness of the inhabitants, the abundance of corn is so great, that no instance has ever been known of a general failure.[17] Pallas justly observes, if we consider that Siberia, not two hundred years ago, was a wilderness utterly unknown, and, in point of population, was even far behind the almost desert tracts of North America, we may justly be astonished at the present state of this part of the world, and at the multitude of its Russian inhabitants, who in numbers greatly exceed the natives.[18]

When Pallas was in Siberia, provisions in these fertile districts, particularly in the environs of Krasnoyarsk, were most extraordinarily cheap. A pood, or forty pounds, of wheaten flour, was sold for about twopence

15. Tooke's View of Russian Empire, vol. ii. p. 242.
16. Voy. de Pallas, tom. iii. p. 10.   17. Id. tom. iv. p. 3.   18. Id. p. 6.

halfpenny, an ox for five or six shillings, and a cow for three or four.[19] This unnatural cheapness, owing to a want of vent for the products of the soil, was perhaps the principal check to the population. In the period which has since elapsed, the prices have risen considerably;[20] and we may conclude, therefore, that the object principally wanted has been attained, and that the population proceeds with rapid strides.

Pallas, however, complains, that the intentions of the Empress respecting the peopling of Siberia, were not always well fulfilled by her subordinate agents, and that the proprietors, to whose care this was left, often sent off colonists, in every respect unfit for the purpose, in regard to age, diseases, and want of industrious habits.[21] Even the German settlers in the districts near the Wolga, are, according to Pallas, deficient in this last point,[22] and this is certainly a most essential one. It may, indeed, be safely asserted, that the importation of industry is of infinitely more consequence to the population of a country, than the importation of men and women considered only with regard to numbers. Were it possible at once to change the habits of a whole people, and to direct its industry at pleasure, no government would ever be reduced to the necessity of encouraging foreign settlers. But to change long-existing habits is of all enterprizes the most difficult. Many years must elapse under the most favourable circumstances, before the Siberian boor will possess the industry and activity of an English labourer. And though the Russian government has been incessant in its endeavours, to convert the pastoral tribes of Siberia to agriculture; yet many obstinately persist in bidding defiance to any attempts that can be made to wean them from their injurious sloth.[23]

Many obstacles concur to prevent that rapid growth of the Russian colonies which the procreative power would permit. Some of the low countries of Siberia are unhealthy, from the number of marshes which they contain,[24] and great and wasting epizooties are frequent among the cattle.[25] In the districts near the Wolga, though the soil is naturally rich, yet droughts are so frequent, that there is seldom more than one good harvest out of three.[26] The colonists of Saratof, after they had been settled for some years, were obliged to remove on this account to other districts, and the whole expence of building their houses, amounting to above a million of rubles, was remitted to them by the Empress.[27] For purposes either of safety or

---

19. Id. p. 3.   20. Tooke's View of Russian Empire, vol. iii. p. 239.
21. Voy. de Pallas, tom. v. p. 5.   22. Voy. de Pallas, tom. v. p. 253.
23. Tooke's Russian Empire, vol. iii. p 313.
24. Voy. de Pallas, tom. iii. p. 16.   25. Id. p. 17. tom. v. p. 411.
26. Id. p. 252, et seq.   27. Tooke's Russian Empire, vol. ii. p. 245.

convenience, the houses of each colony are all built contiguous, or nearly so, and not scattered about upon the different farms. A want of room is, in consequence, soon felt in the immediate neighbourhood of the village, while the distant grounds remain in a state of very imperfect cultivation. On observing this in the colony of Kotschesnaia, Pallas proposed that a certain part should be removed by the Empress to other districts, that the remainder might be left more at their ease.[28] This proposal seems to prove that spontaneous divisions of this kind did not often take place, and that the children of the colonists might not always find an easy mode of settling themselves, and rearing up fresh families. In the flourishing colony of the Moravian brethren at Sarepta, it is said, that the young people cannot marry without the consent of their priests; and that their consent is not in general granted till late.[29] It would appear, therefore, that among the obstacles to the increase of population, even in these new colonies, the preventive check has its share. Population can never increase with great rapidity but when the price of common labour is very high, as in America; and from the state of society in this part of the Russian territories, and the consequent want of a proper vent for the produce of industry, this effect, which usually accompanies new colonies, and is essential to their rapid growth, does not take place in any considerable degree.

28. Voy. de Pallas, tom. v. p. 253.   29. Id. p. 175.

CHAP. X.

Of the Checks to Population in the Turkish Dominions, and Persia.

IN the Asiatic parts of the Turkish dominions, it will not be difficult, from the accounts of travellers, to trace the checks to population, and the causes of its present decay; and as there is little difference in the manners of the Turks, whether they inhabit Europe or Asia, it will not be worth while to make them the subject of distinct consideration.

The fundamental cause of the low state of population in Turkey, compared with its extent of territory, is undoubtedly the nature of the government. Its tyranny, its feebleness, its bad laws, and worse administration of them, with the consequent insecurity of property, throw such obstacles in the way of agriculture, that the means of subsistence are necessarily decreasing yearly, and with them, of course, the number of people. The miri, or general land tax, paid to the sultan, is in itself moderate;[1] but by abuses inherent in the Turkish government, the pachas, and their agents, have found out the means of rendering it ruinous. Though they cannot absolutely alter the impost which has been established by the sultan, they have introduced a multitude of changes, which, without the name, produce all the effects of an augmentation.[2] In Syria, according to Volney, having the greatest part of the land at their disposal, they clog their concessions with burdensome conditions, and exact the half, and sometimes even two thirds, of the crop. When the harvest is over, they cavil about losses, and, as they have the power in their hands, they carry off what they think proper. If the season fail, they still exact the same sum, and expose every thing that the poor peasant possesses to sale. To these constant oppressions, are added a thousand accidental extortions. Sometimes a whole village is laid under contribution for some real or imaginary offence. Arbitrary presents are exacted on the accession of each governor; grass, barley, and straw, are demanded for his horses; and commissions are multiplied, that the soldiers who carry the orders may live upon the starving peasants, whom they treat with the most brutal insolence and injustice.[3]

The consequence of these depredations is, that the poorer class of inhabitants, ruined, and unable any longer to pay the miri, become a burden

---

1. Voy. de Volney, tom. ii. c. xxxvii. p. 373. (8vo. 1787.)   2. Ibid.
3. Voy. de Volney, tom. ii. c. xxxvii.

to the village, or fly into the cities; but the miri is unalterable, and the sum to be levied must be found somewhere. The portion of those who are thus driven from their homes falls on the remaining inhabitants, whose burden, though at first light, now becomes insupportable. If they should be visited by two years of drought and famine, the whole village is ruined and abandoned; and the tax, which it should have paid, is levied on the neighbouring lands.[4]

The same mode of proceeding takes place, with regard to the tax on the Christians, which has been raised by these means from three, five, and eleven piastres, at which it was first fixed, to thirty-five and forty, which absolutely impoverishes those on whom it is levied, and obliges them to leave the country. It has been remarked, that these exactions have made a rapid progress during the last forty years, from which time are dated the decline of agriculture, the depopulation of the country, and the diminution in the quantity of specie carried to Constantinople.[5]

The peasants are every where reduced to a little flat cake of barley, or doura, onions, lentils, and water. Not to lose any part of their corn, they leave in it all sorts of wild grain, which often produces bad consequences. In the mountains of Lebanon and Nablous, in time of dearth, they gather the acorns from the oaks, which they eat after boiling, or roasting them on the ashes.[6]

By a natural consequence of this misery, the art of cultivation is in the most deplorable state. The husbandman is almost without instruments, and those he has, are very bad. His plough is frequently no more than the branch of a tree cut below a fork, and used without wheels. The ground is tilled by asses and cows; rarely by oxen, which would bespeak too much riches. In the districts exposed to the Arabs, as in Palestine, the countryman must sow with his musket in his hand; and scarcely does the corn turn yellow, before it is reaped and concealed in subterraneous caverns. As little as possible is employed for seed corn, because the peasants sow no more than is barely necessary for their subsistence. Their whole industry is limited to a supply of their immediate wants; and to procure a little bread, a few onions, a blue shirt, and a bit of woollen, much labour is not necessary. "The peasant lives therefore in distress; but at least he does not enrich his " tyrants, and the avarice of despotism is its own punishment."[7]

This picture, which is drawn by Volney, in describing the state of the peasants in Syria, seems to be confirmed by all the other travellers in these

4. Id. c. xxxvii. p. 375.   5. Id. p. 376.
6. Voy. de Volney, tom. ii. c. xxxvii. p. 377.   7. Id. p. 379.

countries; and, according to Eton, it represents very nearly the condition of the peasants in the greatest part of the Turkish dominions.[8] Universally, the offices of every denomination are set up to public sale, and in the intrigues of the seraglio, by which the disposal of all places is regulated, every thing is done by means of bribes. The pachas, in consequence, who are sent into the provinces, exert to the utmost their power of extortion; but are always outdone by the officers immediately below them, who, in their turn, leave room for their subordinate agents.[9]

The pacha must raise money to pay the tribute, and also to indemnify himself for the purchase of his office; support his dignity, and make a provision in case of accidents; and, as all power, both military and civil, centers in his person, from his representing the sultan, the means are at his discretion, and the quickest are invariably considered as the best.[10] Uncertain of to-morrow, he treats his province as a mere transient possession, and endeavours to reap, if possible, in one day, the fruit of many years, without the smallest regard to his successor, or the injury that he may do to the permanent revenue.[11]

The cultivator is necessarily more exposed to these extortions than the inhabitants of the towns. From the nature of his employment, he is fixed to one spot, and the productions of agriculture do not admit of being easily concealed. The tenure of the land and the right of succession are besides uncertain. When a father dies, the inheritance reverts to the sultan, and the children can only redeem the succession by a considerable sum of money. These considerations naturally occasion an indifference to landed estates. The country is deserted, and each person is desirous of flying to the towns, where he will not only in general meet with better treatment, but may hope to acquire a species of wealth, which he can more easily conceal from the eyes of his rapacious masters.[12]

To complete the ruin of agriculture, a maximum is in many cases established, and the peasants are obliged to furnish the towns with corn at a fixed price. It is a maxim of Turkish policy, originating in the feebleness of the government, and the fear of popular tumults, to keep the price of corn low in all the considerable towns. In the case of a failure in the harvest, every person who possesses any corn is obliged to sell it at the price fixed, under pain of death; and if there be none in the neighbourhood, other districts are

8. Eton's Turkish Emp. c. viii. 2d edit. 1799.
9. Eton's Turkish Emp. c. ii. p. 55.   10. Voy. de Volney, tom. ii. c. xxxiii. p. 347.   11. Id. p. 350.   12. Id. c. xxxvi. p. 369.

ransacked for it.[13] When Constantinople is in want of provisions, ten provinces are perhaps famished for a supply.[14] At Damascus, during a scarcity in 1784, the people paid only one penny farthing a pound for their bread, while the peasants in the villages were absolutely dying with hunger.[15]

The effect of such a system of government on agriculture, need not be insisted upon. The causes of the decreasing means of subsistence are but too obvious; and the checks which keep the population down to the level of these decreasing resources, may be traced with nearly equal certainty; and will appear to include almost every species of vice and misery that is known.

It is observed, in general, that the Christian families consist of a greater number of children, than the Mahometan families where polygamy prevails.[16] This is an extraordinary fact; because, though polygamy, from the unequal distribution of women which it occasions, be naturally unfavourable to the population of a whole country; yet the individuals who are able to support a plurality of wives, ought certainly, in the natural course of things, to have a greater number of children, than those who are confined to one. The way in which Volney principally accounts for this fact is, that, from the practice of polygamy, and very early marriages, the Turks are enervated while young, and impotence at thirty is very common.[17] Eton notices an unnatural vice, as prevailing in no inconsiderable degree among the common people, and considers it as one of the checks to the population;[18] but the five principal causes of depopulation which he enumerates, are,

1. The plague, from which the empire is never entirely free.
2. Those terrible disorders which almost always follow it, at least in Asia.
3. Epidemic and endemic maladies in Asia, which make as dreadful ravages as the plague itself, and which frequently visit that part of the empire.
4. Famine.
5. And lastly, the sicknesses which always follow a famine, and which occasion a much greater mortality.[19]

He afterwards gives a more particular account of the devastations of the plague in different parts of the empire, and concludes by observing,

13. Voy. de Volney, tom. ii. c. xxxviii. p. 38.   14. Id. c. xxxiii. p. 345.
15. Id. c. xxxviii. p. 381.   16. Eton's Turkish Emp. c. vii. p. 275.
17. Voy. de Volney, tom. ii, c. xl. p. 445.   18. Eton's Turkish Emp. c. vii.
p. 275.   19. Eton's Turkish Emp. c. vii. p. 264.

that if the numbers of the Mahometans have decreased, this cause alone is adequate to the effect;[20] and that, things going on in their present train, the Turkish population will be extinct in another century.[21] But this inference, and the calculations which relate to it, are without doubt erroneous. The increase of population in the intervals of these periods of mortality, is probably greater than he is aware of. At the same time, it must be remarked, that in a country where the industry of the husbandman is confined to the supply of his necessary wants, where he sows only to prevent himself from starving, and is unable to accumulate any surplus produce, a great loss of people is not easily recovered, as the natural effects from the diminished numbers cannot be felt in the same degree, as in countries where industry prevails, and property is secure.

According to the Persian legislator, Zoroaster, to plant a tree, to cultivate a field, to beget children, are meritorious acts; but it appears, from the account of travellers, that many among the lower classes of people cannot easily attain the latter species of merit; and in this instance, as in numberless others, the private interest of the individual corrects the errors of the legislator. Sir John Chardin says, that matrimony in Persia is very expensive, and that only men of estates will venture upon it, lest it prove their ruin.[22] The Russian travellers seem to confirm this account, and observe, that the lower classes of people are obliged to defer marriage till late; and that it is only among the rich that this union takes place early.[23]

The dreadful convulsions to which Persia has been continually subject for many hundred years, must have been fatal to her agriculture. The periods of repose from external wars, and internal commotions, have been short and few, and even during the times of profound peace, the frontier provinces have been constantly subject to the ravages of the Tartars.

The effect of this state of things is such as might be expected. The proportion of uncultivated, to cultivated land, in Persia, Sir John Chardin states to be, ten to one;[24] and the mode in which the officers of the Shah and private owners let out their lands to husbandmen, is not that which is best calculated to reanimate industry. The grain in Persia is, besides, much subject to be destroyed by hail, drought, locusts, and other insects,[25] which probably tends rather to discourage the employment of capital in the cultivation of the soil.

20. Id. p. 291.   21. Id. p. 280.
22. Sir John Chardin's Travels. Harris's Collect, b. iii. c. ii. p. 870.
23. Decouv. Russ. tom. ii, p. 293.
24. Chardin's Travels. Harris's Collect. b. iii. c. ii. p. 902.   25. Ibid.

The plague does not extend to Persia; but the small-pox is mentioned by the Russian travellers, as making very fatal ravages.[26]

It will not be worth while to enter more minutely on the checks to population in Persia, as they seem to be nearly similar to those which have been just described in the Turkish dominions. The superior destruction of the plague in Turkey, is, perhaps, nearly balanced by the greater frequency of internal commotions in Persia.

26. Decouv. Russ. tom. ii. p. 377.

CHAP. XI.

Of the Checks to Population in Indostan and Tibet.

In the ordinances of Menu, the Indian legislator, which Sir Wm. Jones has translated and called the *Institutes of Hindu Law,* marriage is very greatly encouraged, and a male heir is considered as an object of the first importance.

"By a son, a man obtains victory over all people; by a son's son, he en-
" joys immortality; and afterwards, by the son of that grandson, he reaches
" the solar abode."

"Since the son delivers his father from the hell, named put, he was
" therefore called puttra, by Brahma himself."[1]

Among the different nuptial rites, Menu has ascribed particular qualities to each.

"A son of a *Bráhmì,* or wife, by the first ceremony, redeems from sin, if
" he perform virtuous acts, ten ancestors, ten descendants, and himself,
" the twenty-first person."

"A son born of a wife by the *Daiva* nuptials, redeems seven and seven,
" in higher and lower degrees; of a wife by the *Arsha,* three and three; of
" a wife by the *Prájápatya,* six and six."[2]

A housekeeper is considered as of the most eminent order. "The divine
" sages, the manes, the gods, the spirits, and guests, pray for benefits to
" masters of families."[3] An elder brother not married before the younger is mentioned among the persons who are particularly to be shunned.[4]

Such ordinances would naturally cause marriage to be considered as a religious duty; yet it seems to be rather a succession of male heirs, than a very numerous progeny, that is the object so much desired.

"The father having begotten a son, discharges his debt to his own
" progenitors."

---

1. Sir Wm. Jones's Works, vol. iii. c. ix. p. 354. Speaking of the Indian laws, the Abbé Raynal says, "La population est un devoir primitif, un ordre de la nature si
" sacré, que la loi permet de tromper, de mentir, de se parjurer pour favoriser un
" marriage." Hist. des Indes, tom. i. l. i. p. 81. 8vo. 10 vols. Paris 1795.
2. Sir Wm. Jones's Works, vol.iii. c. iii. p. 124.
3. Sir Wm. Jones's Works, vol. iii. c. iii. p. 130.   4. Id. p. 141.

"That son alone, by whose birth he discharges the debt, and through
" whom he attains immortality, was begotten from a sense of duty; all the
" rest are considered by the wife as begotten from love of pleasure."[5]

A widow is, on some occasions, allowed to have one son by the brother,
or some appointed kinsman of the deceased husband, but on no account a
second. "The first object of the appointment being obtained, according to
" law, both the brother and the sister must live together like a father and
" daughter by affinity."[6]

In almost every part of the ordinances of Menu, sensuality of all kinds is
strongly reprobated, and chastity inculcated as a religious duty.

"A man by the attachment of his organs to sensual pleasure incurs cer-
" tain guilt; but having wholly subdued them, he thence attains heavenly
" bliss."

"Whatever man may obtain all those gratifications, or whatever man
may resign them completely, the resignation of all pleasures is far better
than the attainment of them."[7]

It is reasonable to suppose, that such passages might, in some degree,
tend to counteract those encouragements to increase, which, have been before mentioned, and might prompt some religious persons to desist from
further indulgencies when they had obtained one son, or to remain more
contented than they otherwise would have been, in an unmarried state.
Strict and absolute chastity, seems, indeed, to supersede the obligation of
having descendants.

"Many thousands of Brahmens having avoided sensuality from their
" early youth, and having left no issue in their families, have ascended
" nevertheless to heaven."

"And, like those abstemious men, a virtuous wife ascends to heaven,
" though she have no child, if, after the decease of her lord, she devote
" herself to pious austerity."[8]

The permission to a brother, or other kinsman, to raise up an heir for
the deceased husband, which has been noticed, extends only to women of
the servile class.[9] Those of the higher classes are not even to pronounce the
name of another man, but to

"Continue till death forgiving all injuries, performing harsh duties,
" avoiding every sensual pleasure, and cheerfully practising the incompa-
" rable rules of virtue."[10]

5. Id. c. ix. p. 349.   6. Id. p. 343.   7. Id. c. ii. p. 96.   8. Sir Wm. Jones's
Works, vol. iii. c. v. p. 221.   9. Id. c. ix. p. 343.   10. Id. c. v. p. 221.

Besides these strict precepts relating to the government of the passions, other circumstances would perhaps concur to prevent the full effect of the ordinances which encourage marriage.

The division of the people into classes, and the continuance of the same profession in the same family, would be the means of pointing out to each individual, in a clear and distinct manner, his future prospects respecting a livelihood; and from the gains of his father, he would be easily enabled to judge whether he could support a family by the same employment. And though, when a man cannot gain a subsistence in the employments appropriate to his class, it is allowable for him, under certain restrictions, to seek it in another; yet some kind of disgrace seems to attach to this expedient, and it is not probable that many persons would marry with the certain prospect of being obliged thus to fall from their class, and to lower in so marked a manner their condition in life.

In addition to this, the choice of a wife seems to be a point of considerable difficulty. A man might remain unmarried for some time, before he could find exactly such a companion as the legislator prescribes. Ten families of a certain description, be they ever so great, or ever so rich in kine, goats, sheep, gold, and grain, are studiously to be avoided. Girls with too little or too much hair, who are too talkative, who have bad eyes, a disagreeable name, or any kind of sickness, who have no brother, or whose father is not well known, are all, with many others, excluded; and the choice will appear to be in some degree confined, when it must necessarily rest upon

"A girl, whose form has no defect; who has an agreeable name; who
" walks gracefully, like a phenicopteros, or a young elephant; whose hair
" and teeth are moderate respectively in quantity and size; whose body
" has exquisite softness."[11]

It is observed, that a woman of the servile class is not mentioned, even in the recital of any ancient story, as the wife of a Brahmen or of a Cshatriya, though in the greatest difficulty to find a suitable match; which seems to imply that such a difficulty might sometimes occur.[12]

Another obstacle to marriage arising from the Hindoo customs, is, that an elder brother who does not marry, seems in a manner to confine all his other brothers to the same state; for a younger brother who marries before the elder incurs disgrace, and is mentioned among the persons who ought to be shunned.[13]

---

11. Sir William Jones's Works, vol. iii. c. iii. p. 120.   12. Id. p. 121.
13. Id. p. 141.

The character which the legislator draws of the manners and disposition of the women in India is most extremely unfavourable. Among many other passages expressed with equal severity, he observes, that,

"Through their passion for men, their mutable temper, their want of
" settled affection, and their perverse nature, (let them be guarded in
" this world ever so well), they soon become alienated from their
" husbands."[14]

This character, if true, probably proceeded from their never being allowed the smallest degree of liberty,[15] and from the state of degradation to which they were reduced by the practice of polygamy; but however this may be, such passages tend strongly to shew, that illicit intercourse between the sexes was frequent notwithstanding the laws against adultery. These laws are noticed as not relating to the wives of public dancers or singers, or of such base men as lived by the intrigues of their wives;[16] a proof that these characters were not uncommon, and were to a certain degree permitted. Add to this, that the practice of polygamy[17] among the rich, would sometimes render it difficult for the lower classes of people to obtain wives; and this difficulty would probably fall particularly hard on those who were reduced to the condition of slaves.

From all these circumstances combined, it seems probable, that among the checks to population in India, the preventive check would have its share; but from the prevailing habits and opinions of the people, there is reason to believe, that the tendency to early marriages was still always predominant, and in general prompted every person to enter into this state, who could look forward to the slightest chance of being able to maintain a family. The natural consequence of this was, that the lower classes of people were reduced to extreme poverty, and were compelled to adopt the most frugal and scanty mode of subsistence. This frugality was still further increased, and extended in some degree to the higher classes of society, by its being considered as an eminent virtue.[18] The population would thus be pressed hard against the limits of the means of subsistence, and the food of the country would be meted out to the major part of the people in the smallest shares that could support life. In such a state of things, every failure in the crops from unfavourable seasons would be felt most severely; and India, as might be expected, has in all ages been subject to the most dreadful famines.

14. Sir William Jones's Works, vol. iii. c. ix. p. 337.   15. Id. c. v. p. 219.
16. Id. c. viii. p. 325.   17. Id. c. ix. p. 346, 347.
18. Sir William Jones's Works, vol. iii. c. iii. p. 133.

A part of the ordinances of Menu is expressly dedicated to the consideration of times of distress, and instructions are given to the different classes respecting their conduct during these periods. Brahmens pining with hunger and want are frequently mentioned;[19] and certain ancient and virtuous characters are described, who had done impure and unlawful acts, but who were considered by the legislator as justified, on account of the extremities to which they were reduced.

"Ajígarta, dying with hunger, was going to destroy his own son by sell-
" ing him for some cattle; yet he was guilty of no crime, for he only
" sought a remedy against famishing."

"Vámadéva, who well knew right and wrong, was by no means rendered
" impure, though desirous, when oppressed by hunger, of eating the flesh
" of dogs."

"Viswámitra too, than whom none knew better the distinctions between
" virtue and vice, resolved, when he was perishing with hunger, to eat the
" haunch of a dog, which he had received from a *Chandála.*"[20]

If these great and virtuous men of the highest class, whom all persons were under the obligation of assisting, could be reduced to such extremities, we may easily conjecture what must have been the sufferings of the lowest class.

Such passages clearly prove the existence of seasons of the most severe distress, at the early period when these ordinances were composed; and we have reason to think that they have occurred at irregular intervals ever since. One of the Jesuits says, that it is impossible for him to describe the misery to which he was witness, during the two years famine in 1737 and 1738;[21] but the description which he gives of it, and of the mortality which it occasioned, is sufficiently dreadful without further detail. Another Jesuit, speaking more generally, says, "Every year we baptize a thousand children,
" whom their parents can no longer feed, or who, being likely to die, are
" sold to us by their mothers in order to get rid of them."[22]

The positive checks to population would of course fall principally upon the Sudrá class, and those still more miserable beings, who are the outcasts of all the classes, and are not even suffered to live within the towns.[23]

On this part of the population the epidemics which are the consequences of indigence and bad nourishment, and the mortality among young children, would necessarily make great ravages; and thousands of these un-

19. Id. c. iv. p. 165. c. x. p. 397.   20. Id. c. x. p. 397, 398.
21. Lettres Edif. tom. xiv. p. 178.   22. Id. p. 284.
23. Sir William Jones's Works, vol. iii. c. x. p. 390.

happy wretches would probably be swept off in a period of scarcity, before any considerable degree of want had reached the middle classes of the society. The Abbé Raynal says, on what authority I know not, that when the crops of rice fail, the huts of these poor outcasts are set on fire, and the flying inhabitants shot by the proprietors of the grounds, that they may not consume any part of the produce.[24]

The difficulty of rearing a family, even among the middle and higher classes of society, or the fear of sinking from their cast, has driven the people in some parts of India to adopt the most cruel expedients to prevent a numerous offspring. In a tribe on the frontiers of Junapore, a district of the province of Benares, the practice of destroying female infants has been fully substantiated. The mothers were compelled to starve them. The reason that the people gave for this cruel practice, was, the great expence of procuring suitable matches for their daughters. One village only furnished an exception to this rule, and in this village several old maids were living. It would naturally occur, that the race could not be continued upon this principle; but it appeared, that the particular exceptions to the general rule, and the intermarriages with other tribes, were sufficient for this purpose. Our East India Company obliged these people to enter into an engagement not to continue this inhuman practice.[25]

On the coast of Malabar the Nayrs do not enter into regular marriages, and the right of inheritance and succession rests in the mother of the brother, or otherwise goes to the sister's son, the father of the child being always considered as uncertain.

Among the Brahmens, when there are more brothers than one, only the elder, or eldest of them, marries. The brothers who thus maintain celibacy cohabit with Nayr women without marriage in the way of the Nayrs. If the eldest brother has not a son, then the next brother marries.

Among the Nayrs, it is the custom for one Nayr woman to have attached to her two males, or four, or perhaps more.

The lower casts, such as carpenters, ironsmiths, and others, have fallen into the imitation of their superiors, with this difference, that the joint concern in one woman is confined to brothers and male relations by blood, to the end that no alienation may take place in the course of the succession.[26]

Montesquieu takes notice of this custom of the Nayrs on the coast of Malabar, and accounts for it on the supposition that it was adopted in order to weaken the family ties of this cast, that, as soldiers, they might be more

24. Hist. des Indes, tom. i. liv. i. p. 97. 8vo. 10 vols. Paris, 1795.
25. Asiatic Researches, vol. iv. p. 354.   26. Id. vol. v. p. 14.

at liberty to follow the calls of their profession; but I should think that it originated, more probably, in a fear of the poverty arising from a large family, particularly, as the custom seems to have been adopted by the other classes.[27]

In Tibet, according to Turner's late account of it, a custom of this kind prevails generally. Without pretending absolutely to determine the question of its origin, Mr. Turner leans to the supposition that it arose from the fear of a population too great for an unfertile country. From travelling much in the east, he had probably been led to observe the effects necessarily resulting from an overflowing population, and is in consequence one among the very few writers who see these effects in their true light. He expresses himself very strongly on this subject, and, in reference to the custom above mentioned, says, "It certainly appears, that a superabundant population in
"   an unfertile country must be the greatest of all calamities, and produce
"   eternal warfare or eternal want. Either the most active and the most able
"   part of the community must be compelled to emigrate, and to become
"   soldiers of fortune, or merchants of chance; or else, if they remain at
"   home, be liable to fall a prey to famine, in consequence of some acci-
"   dental failure in their scanty crops. By thus linking whole families to-
"   gether in the matrimonial yoke, the too rapid increase of population was
"   perhaps checked, and an alarm prevented, capable of pervading the
"   most fertile region upon the earth, and of giving birth to the most inhu-
"   man and unnatural practice, in the richest, the most productive, and the
"   most populous country in the world. I allude to the empire of China,
"   where a mother, not foreseeing the means of raising or providing for a
"   numerous family, exposes her newborn infant to perish in the fields; a
"   crime, however odious, by no means, I am assured, unfrequent."[28]

In almost every country of the globe individuals are impelled, by considerations of private interest, to habits which tend to repress the natural increase of population; but Tibet is perhaps the only country where these habits are universally encouraged by the government, and where to repress, rather than to encourage population, seems to be a public object.

In the first career of life the Bootea is recommended to distinction by a continuance in a state of celibacy, as, on the contrary, any matrimonial contract proves almost a certain hindrance to his rise in rank, or his advancement to offices of political importance. Population is thus opposed by the two powerful bars of ambition and religion; and the higher orders

27. Esprit des Loix, liv. xvi. c. 5.
28. Turner's Embassy to Tibet, part ii. c. x. p. 351.

of men, entirely engrossed by political or ecclesiastical duties, leave to the husbandman and labourer, to those who till the fields and live by their industry, the exclusive charge of propagating the species.[29]

Hence religious retirement is frequent,[30] and the number of monasteries and nunneries is considerable. The strictest laws exist to prevent a woman from accidently passing a night within the limits of the one, or a man within those of the other; and a regulation is framed, completely to obviate abuse, and establish respect towards the sacred orders of both sexes.

The nation is divided into two distinct and separate classes, those who carry on the business of the world, and those who hold intercourse with heaven. No interference of the laity ever interrupts the regulated duties of the clergy. The latter, by mutual compact, take charge of all spiritual concerns; and the former, by their labours, enrich and populate the state.[31]

But, even among the laity, the business of population goes on very coldly. All the brothers of a family, without any restriction of age or of numbers, associate their fortunes with one female, who is chosen by the eldest, and considered as the mistress of the house; and whatever may be the profits of their several pursuits, the result flows into the common store.[32]

The number of husbands is not, apparently, defined or restricted within any limits. It sometimes happens that in a small family there is but one male; and the number, Mr. Turner says, may seldom exceed that which a native of rank at Teshoo Loomboo pointed out to him in a family resident in the neighbourhood, in which five brothers were then living together very happily with one female under the same connubial compact. Nor is this sort of league confined to the lower ranks of people alone, it is found also frequently in the most opulent families.[33]

It is evident that this custom, combined with the celibacy of such a numerous body of ecclesiastics, must operate in the most powerful manner as a preventive check to population. Yet notwithstanding this excessive check, it would appear, from Mr. Turner's account of the natural sterility of the soil, that the population is kept up to the level of the means of subsistence, and this seems to be confirmed by the number of beggars in Teshoo Loomboo. On these beggars, and the charity which feeds them, Mr. Turner's remark, though common, is yet so just and important, that it cannot be too often repeated.

29. Turner's Embassy, part ii. c. i. p. 172.   30. Ibld.
31. Id. c. viii. p. 312.   32. Turner's Embassy, part ii. c. x. p. 348. 350.
33. Id. p. 349.

"Thus I unexpectedly discovered," he says, "where I had constantly
" seen the round of life moving in a tranquil regular routine, a mass of
" indigence and idleness of which I had no idea. But yet it by no means
" surprised me, when I considered that wherever indiscriminate charity
" exists, it will never want objects on which to exercise its bounty, but will
" always attract expectants more numerous than it has the means to grat-
" ify. No human being can suffer want at Teshoo Loomboo. It is on this
" humane disposition that a multitude even of Musselmen, of a frame
" probably the largest and most robust in the world, place their reliance
" for the mere maintenance of a feeble life; and besides these, I am in-
" formed, that no less than three hundred Hindoos, Goseins, and Sun-
" niasses, are daily fed at this place by the Lama's bounty."[34]

34. Turner's Embassy, part ii. c. ix. p. 330.

CHAP. XII.

Of the Checks to Population in China and Japan.

THE account which has lately been given of the population of China is so extraordinary, as to startle the faith of many readers, and tempt them to suppose, either that some accidental error must have crept into the calculations from an ignorance of the language, or that the mandarin who gave Sir George Staunton the information, must have been prompted by a national pride, which is common every where, but is particularly remarkable in China, to exaggerate the power and resources of his country. It must be allowed, that neither of these circumstances is very improbable; at the same time it will be found, that the statement of Sir George Staunton, does not very essentially differ from other accounts of good authority; and so far from involving any contradiction, is rendered probable, by a reference to those descriptions of the fertility of China in which all the writers who have visited the country agree.

According to Duhalde, in the poll made at the beginning of the reign of Kang-hi, there were found 11,052,872 families, and 59,788,364 men able to bear arms; and yet, neither the princes, nor the officers of the court, nor the mandarins, nor the soldiers who had served and been discharged; nor the literati, the licentiates, the doctors, the bonzas, nor young persons under twenty years of age; nor the great multitudes living either on the sea, or on rivers in barks, are comprehended in this number.[1]

The proportion which the number of men of a military age, bears to the whole population of any country, is generally estimated as 1 to 4. If we multiply 59,788,364 by 4, the result will be 239,153,456; but in the general calculations on this subject, a youth is considered as capable of bearing arms before he is twenty. We ought therefore to have multiplied by a higher number. The exceptions to the poll seem to include almost all the superior classes of society, and a very great number among the lower. When all these circumstances are taken into consideration, the whole population, according to Duhalde, will not appear to fall very short of the 333,000,000 mentioned by Sir George Staunton.[2]

---

1. Duhalde's Hist. of China, 2 vols. folio, 1738. vol. i. p. 244.
2. Embassy to China, vol. ii. Appen. p. 615. 4to.

The small number of families, in proportion to the number of persons able to bear arms, which is a striking part of this statement of Duhalde, is accounted for by a custom noticed by Sir George Stauntton as general in China. In the inclosure belonging to one dwelling, he observes, that a whole family of three generations, with all their respective wives and children, will frequently be found. One small room is made to serve for the individuals of each family, sleeping in different beds, divided only by mats hanging from the ceiling. One common room is used for eating.[3] In China there is, besides, a prodigious number of slaves,[4] who will, of course, be reckoned as part of the families to which they belong. These two circumstances may perhaps be sufficient to account for what at first appears to be a contradiction in the statement.

To account for this population, it will not be necessary to recur to the supposition of Montesquieu, that the climate of China is in any peculiar manner favourable to the production of children, and that the women are more prolific than in any other part of the world.[5] The causes which have principally contributed to produce this effect, appear to be the following:

First, the excellence of the natural soil, and its advantageous position in the warmest parts of the temperate zone; a situation the most favourable to the productions of the earth. Duhalde has a long chapter on the plenty which reigns in China, in which he observes, that almost all that other kingdoms afford, may be found in China; but that China produces an infinite number of things which are to be found no where else. This plenty, he says, may be attributed as well to the depth of the soil, as to the painful industry of its inhabitants, and the great number of lakes, rivers, brooks, and canals, wherewith the country is watered.[6]

Secondly, The very great encouragement that from the beginning of the monarchy has been given to agriculture, which has directed the labours of the people to the production of the greatest possible quantity of human subsistence. Duhalde says, that what makes these people undergo such incredible fatigues in cultivating the earth, is not barely their private interest, but rather the veneration paid to agriculture, and the esteem which the emperors themselves have always had for it, from the commencement of the monarchy. One emperor of the highest reputation was taken from the plough to sit on the throne. Another found out the art of draining water from several low countries, which were, till then, covered with it, of conveying it in canals to the sea, and of using these canals to render the soil

3. Id. p. 155.   4. Duhalde's China, vol. i. p. 278.
5. Esprit des Loix, liv. viii. c. xxi.   6. Duhalde's China, vol. i. p. 314.

fruitful.[7] He besides wrote several books on the manner of cultivating land, by dunging, tilling, and watering it. Many other emperors expressed their zeal for this art, and made laws to promote it; but none raised its esteem to a higher pitch than Ven-ti, who reigned 179 years before Christ. This prince, perceiving that his country was ruined by wars, resolved to engage his subjects to cultivate their lands, by the example of ploughing with his own hands the land belonging to his palace, which obliged all the ministers and great men of his court to do the same.[8]

A great festival, of which this is thought to be the origin, is solemnized every year in all the cities of China on the day that the sun enters the fifteenth degree of Aquarius, which the Chinese consider as the beginning of their spring. The emperor goes himself in a solemn manner to plough a few ridges of land, in order to animate the husbandman by his own example; and the mandarins of every city perform the same ceremony.[9] Princes of the blood, and other illustrious persons, hold the plough after the emperor, and the ceremony is preceded by the spring sacrifice which the emperor, as chief pontiff, offers to Shang-ti to procure plenty in favour of his people.

The reigning emperor, in the time of Duhalde, celebrated this festival with extraordinary solemnity, and in other respects shewed an uncommon regard for husbandmen. To encourage them in their labours, he ordered the governors of all the cities to send him notice every year of the person in this profession, in their respective districts, who was most remarkable for his application to agriculture, for unblemished reputation, for preserving union in his own family, and peace with his neighbours, and for his frugality and aversion to all extravagance.[10] The mandarins in their different provinces encourage with honours the vigilant cultivator, and stigmatize with disgrace the man whose lands are neglected.[11]

In a country, in which the whole of the government is of the patriarchal kind, and the emperor is venerated as the father of his people, and the fountain of instruction, it is natural to suppose, that these high honours paid to agriculture should have a powerful effect. In the gradations of rank, they have raised the husbandman above the merchant or mechanic,[12] and the great object of ambition among the lower classes, is, in consequence, to become possessed of a small portion of land. The number of manufacturers bears but a very inconsiderable proportion to that of husbandmen in China;[13] and the whole surface of the empire is, with trifling exceptions,

---

7. Id. p. 274.   8. Id. p. 275.   9. Duhalde's China, vol. i. p. 275.

10. Id. p 276.   11. Lettres Edif. tom. xix. p. 132.   12. Duhalde's China, vol. i. p. 272.   13. Embassy to China, Staunton, vol, ii. p. 544.

dedicated to the production of food for man alone. There is no meadow, and very little pasture; neither are the fields cultivated in oats, beans, or turnips, for the support of cattle of any kind. Little land is taken up for roads, which are few and narrow, the chief communication being by water. There are no commons, or lands suffered to lie waste by the neglect, or the caprice, or for the sport, of great proprietors. No arable land lies fallow. The soil, under a hot and fertilizing sun, yields annually, in most instances, double crops, in consequence of adapting the culture to the soil, and of supplying its defects by mixture with other earths, by manure, by irrigation, and by careful and judicious industry of every kind. The labour of man is little diverted from that industry, to minister to the luxuries of the opulent and powerful, or in employments of no real use. Even the soldiers of the Chinese army, except during the short intervals of the guards which they are called upon to mount, or the exercises, or other other occasional services, which they perform, are mostly employed in agriculture. The quantity of subsistence is increased also by converting more species of animals and vegetables to that purpose, than is usual in other countries.[14]

This account, which is given by Sir George Staunton, is confirmed by Duhalde, and the other Jesuits, who agree in describing the persevering industry of the Chinese, in manuring, cultivating, and watering their lands, and their success in producing a prodigious quantity of human subsistence.[15] The effect of such a system of agriculture on population must be obvious.

Lastly, The extraordinary encouragements that have been given to marriage, which have caused the immense produce of the country to be divided into very small shares, and have consequently rendered China more populous in proportion to its means of subsistence, than perhaps any other country in the world.

The Chinese acknowledge two ends in marriage;[16] the first is, that of perpetuating the sacrifices in the temple of their fathers; and the second, the multiplication of the species. Duhalde says, that the veneration and submission of children to parents, which is the grand principle of their political government, continues even after death, and that the same duties are paid to them as if they were living. In consequence of these maxims, a father feels some sort of dishonour, and is not easy in his mind, if he do not marry off all his children; and an elder brother, though he inherit nothing from his

14. Embassy to China, Staunton, vol. ii. p. 545.
15. Duhalde, chapter on agriculture, vol. i. p. 272. chapter on plenty, p. 314.
16. Lettres Edif. et Curieuses, tom. xxiii. p. 448.

father, must bring up the younger children, and marry them, lest the family should become extinct, and the ancestors be deprived of the honours and duties they are entitled to from their descendants.[17]

Sir George Staunton observes, that whatever is strongly recommended, and generally practised, is at length considered as a kind of religious duty, and that the marriage union, as such, takes place in China, wherever there is the least prospect of subsistence for a future family. This prospect, however, is not always realized, and the children are then abandoned by the wretched authors of their being;[18] but even this permission given to parents thus to expose their offspring, tends undoubtedly to facilitate marriage, and encourage population. Contemplating this extreme resource beforehand, less fears are entertained of entering into the married state, and the parental feelings will always step forwards to prevent a recurrence to it, except under the most dire necessity. Marriage with the poor is, besides, a measure of prudence, because the children, particularly the sons, are bound to maintain their parents.[19]

The effect of these encouragements to marriage among the rich, is to subdivide property, which has in itself a strong tendency to promote population. In China, there is less inequality in the fortunes than in the conditions of men. Property in land has been divided into very moderate parcels, by the successive distribution of the possessions of every father equally among his sons. It would rarely happen that there was but one son to enjoy the whole property of his deceased parents; and, from the general prevalence of early marriages, this property would not often be increased by collateral succession.[20] These causes constantly tend to level wealth, and few succeed to such an accumulation of it, as to render them independent of any efforts of their own for its increase. It is a common remark among the Chinese, that fortunes seldom continue considerable in the same family beyond the third generation.[21]

The effect of the encouragements to marriage on the poor, is to keep the reward of labour as low as possible, and consequently to press them down to the most abject state of poverty. Sir George Staunton observes, that the price of labour is generally found to bear as small a proportion every where to the rate demanded for provisions as the common people can suffer; and that notwithstanding the advantage of living together in large families, like soldiers in a mess, and the exercise of the greatest economy in

---

17. Duhalde's China, vol. i. p. 303.   18. Embassy to China, vol. ii. p. 157.
19. Ibid.   20. Embassy to China, Staunton, vol. ii. p. 151.
21. Id. p. 152.

the management of these messes, they are reduced to the use of vegetable food, with a very rare and scanty relish of any animal substance.[22]

Duhalde, after describing the painful industry of the Chinese, and the shifts and contrivances, unknown in other countries, to which they have recourse in order to gain a subsistence, says, "yet it must be owned, that
" notwithstanding the great sobriety and industry of the inhabitants of
" China, the prodigious number of them occasions a great deal of misery.
" There are some so poor, that being unable to supply their children with
" common necessaries, they expose them in the streets."****"In the
" great cities, such as Pekin and Canton, this shocking sight is very
" common."[23]

The Jesuit Premare, writing to a friend of the same society, says, "I will
" tell you a fact, which may appear to be a paradox,[24] but is nevertheless
" strictly true. It is, that the richest and most flourishing empire of the
" world, is, notwithstanding, in one sense, the poorest and the most miser-
" able of all. The country, however extensive and fertile it may be, is not
" sufficient to support its inhabitants. Four times as much territory would
" be necessary to place them at their ease. In Canton alone, there is, with-
" out exaggeration, more than a million of souls, and in a town three or
" four leagues distant, a still greater number. Who then can count the in-
" habitants of this province? But what is this to the whole empire, which
" contains fifteen great provinces all equally peopled. To how many mil-
" lions would such a calculation amount. A third part of this infinite popu-
" lation would hardly find sufficient rice to support itself properly."

"It is well known that extreme misery impels people to the most dread-
" ful excesses. A spectator in China, who examines things closely, will
" not be surprised that mothers destroy, or expose, many of their children;
" that parents sell their daughters for a trifle; that the people should be
" interested; and that there should be such a number of robbers. The sur-
" prise is, that nothing still more dreadful should happen, and that, in the
" times of famines, which are here but too frequent, millions of people
" should perish with hunger, without having recourse to those dreadful
" extremities, of which we read examples in the histories of Europe."

"It cannot be said in China, as in Europe, that the poor are idle, and
" might gain a subsistence if they would work. The labours and efforts of
" these poor people are beyond conception. A Chinese will pass whole
" days in digging the earth, sometimes up to his knees in water, and in the

22. Id. p. 156.　　23. Duhalde's China, vol. i. p. 277.
24. Lettres Edif. et Curieuses, tom. xvi. p. 394.

" evening is happy to eat a little spoonful of rice, and to drink the insipid
" water in which it was boiled. This is all that they have in general."[25]

A great part of this account is repeated in Duhalde, and, even allowing for some exaggeration, it shews, in a strong point of view, to what
degree population has been forced in China, and the wretchedness which
has been the consequence of it. The population which has arisen naturally
from the fertility of the soil, and the encouragements to agriculture, may
be considered as genuine and desireable; but all that has been added by
the encouragements to marriage, has not only been an addition of so much
pure misery in itself, but has completely interrupted the happiness which
the rest might have enjoyed.

The territory of China is estimated at about eight times the territory of
France.[26] Taking the population of France only at 26 millions, eight times
that number will give 208,000,000; and when the three powerful causes
of population, which have been stated, are considered, it will not appear
incredible, that the population of China should be to the population of
France, according to their respective superficies, as 333 to 208, or a little
more than 3 to 2.

The natural tendency to increase is every where so great, that it will
generally be easy to account for the height at which the population is found
in any country. The more difficult, as well as the more interesting part of
the inquiry, is to trace the immediate causes which stop its further progress.
The procreative power would, with as much facility, double, in twenty-five
years, the population of China, as that of any of the states of America;
but we know that it cannot do this, from the palpable inability of the soil
to support such an additional number. What then becomes of this mighty
power in China? and what are the kinds of restraint, and the forms of premature death, which keep the population down to the level of the means of
subsistence?

Notwithstanding the extraordinary encouragements to marriage in
China, we should perhaps be led into an error, if we were to suppose that
the preventive check to population does not operate. Duhalde says, that the
number of bonzas is considerably above a million, of which there are two
thousand unmarried, at Pekin, besides three hundred and fifty thousand
more in their temples established in different places by the emperor's patents, and that the literary bachelors alone are about ninety thousand.[27]

25. Lettres Edif. et Curieuses, tom. xvi. p. 394. et seq.
26. Embassy to China, Staunton, vol. ii, p. 546.
27. Duhalde's China, vol. i. p. 244.

The poor, though they would probably always marry when the slightest prospect opened to them of being able to support a family, and, from the permission of infanticide, would run great risks in this respect; yet they would undoubtedly be deterred from entering into this state under the certainty of being obliged to expose all their children, or to sell themselves and families as slaves; and from the extreme poverty of the lower classes of people, such a certainty would often present itself. But it is among the slaves themselves, of which, according to Duhalde, the misery in China produces a prodigious multitude, that the preventive check to population principally operates. A man sometimes sells his son, and even himself and wife, at a very moderate price. The common mode is, to mortgage themselves with a condition of redemption, and a great number of men and maid servants are thus bound in a family.[28] Hume, in speaking of the practice of slavery among the ancients, remarks very justly, that it will generally be cheaper to buy a full grown slave, than to rear up one from a child. This observation appears to be particularly applicable to the Chinese. All writers agree in mentioning the frequency of the dearths in China, and, during these periods, it is probable that slaves would be sold in great numbers for little more than a bare maintenance. It could very rarely therefore answer to the master of a family to encourage his slaves to breed; and we may suppose, in consequence, that a great part of the servants in China, as in Europe, remain unmarried.

The check to population arising from a vicious intercourse with the sex, does not appear to be very considerable in China. The women are said to be modest and reserved, and adultery is rare. Concubinage is however generally practised, and, in the large towns, publick women are registered; but their number is not great, being proportioned, according to Sir George Staunton, to the small number of unmarried persons, and of husbands absent from their families.[29]

The positive checks to population from disease, though considerable, do not appear to be so great as might be expected. The climate is in general extremely healthy. One of the missionaries goes so far as to say, that plagues, or epidemic disorders, are not seen once in a century;[30] but this is undoubtedly an error, as they are mentioned by others, as if they were by no means so infrequent. In some instructions to mandarins relating to the

---

28. Id. p. 278. La misere et le grand nombre d'habitans de l'empire y causent cette multitude prodigieuse d'esclaves: presque tous les valets, et generalement toutes les filles de service d'une maison sont esclaves. Lettres Edif. tom. xix. p. 145.

29. Embassy to China, vol. ii. p. 157.   30. Lettres Edif. tom. xxii. p. 187.

burying of the poor, who have in general no regular places of sepulture, it is observed, that, when epidemic diseases prevail, the roads are found covered with bodies sufficient to infect the air to a great distance;[31] and the expression of years of contagion,[32] occurs soon after, in a manner which seems to imply that they are not uncommon. On the first and fifteenth day of every month, the mandarins assemble, and give their people a long discourse, wherein every governor acts the part of a father who instructs his family.[33] In one of these discourses which Duhalde produces, the following passage occurs: "Beware of those years which happen from time to time,
"   when epidemic distempers, joined to a scarcity of corn, make all places
"   desolate. Your duty is then to have compassion on your fellow citizens,
"   and assist them with whatever you can spare."[34]

It is probable that the epidemics, as is usually the case, fall severely on the children. One of the Jesuits, speaking of the number of infants whom the poverty of their parents condemns to death the moment that they are born, writes thus: "There is seldom a year in which the churches at Pekin
"   do not reckon five or six thousand of these children purified by the wa-
"   ters of baptism. This harvest is more or less abundant according to the
"   number of catechists which we can maintain. If we had a sufficient
"   number, their cares need not be confined alone to the dying infants that
"   are exposed. There would be other occasions for them to exercise their
"   zeal, particularly at certain times of the year, when the small-pox, or
"   epidemic disorders, carry off an incredible number of children."[35] It is indeed almost impossible to suppose, that the extreme indigence of the lower classes of people, should not produce diseases, that would be fatal to a considerable part of those children, whom their parents might attempt to rear in spite of every difficulty.

Respecting the number of infants which are actually exposed, it would be difficult to form the slightest guess; but, if we believe the Chinese writers themselves, the practice must be very common. Attempts have been made at different times by the government to put a stop to it, but always without success. In a book of instructions before alluded to, written by a mandarin celebrated for his humanity and wisdom, a proposal is made for the establishment of a foundling hospital in his district, and an account is given of some antient establishments of the same kind,[36] which appear to have fallen into disuse. In this book, the frequency of the exposure of children, and the

---

31. Id. tom. xix. p. 126.   32. Id. p. 127.   33. Duhalde's China, vol. i. p. 254.   34. Duhalde's China, vol. i. p. 256.   35. Lettres Edif. tom. xix. p. 100.   36. Id. p. 110.

dreadful poverty which prompts it, are particularly described. We see, he says, people so poor, that they cannot furnish the nourishment necessary for their own children. It is on this account that they expose so great a number. In the metropolis, in the capitals of the provinces, and in the places of the greatest commerce, their number is the most considerable; but many are found in parts that are less frequented, and even in the country. As the houses in towns are more crowded together, the practice is more obvious; but every where these poor unfortunate infants have need of assistance.[37]

In the same work, part of an edict to prevent the drowning of children, runs thus: "When the tender offspring just produced, is thrown without pity
" into the waves, can it be said, that the mother has given, or that the child
" has received life, when it is lost as soon as it is begun to be enjoyed? The
" poverty of the parents is the cause of this crime. They have hardly
" enough to support themselves, much less are they able to pay a nurse,
" and provide for the expences necessary for the support of their children.
" This drives them to despair, and not being able to bring themselves to
" suffer two people to die that one may live, the mother, to preserve the
" life of her husband, consents to sacrifice her child. It costs much, how-
" ever, to the parental feelings; but the resolution is ultimately taken, and
" they think that they are justified in disposing of the life of their child to
" prolong their own. If they exposed their children in a secret place, the
" babe might work upon their compassion with its cries. What do they do
" then? They throw it into the current of the river, that they may lose sight
" of it immediately, and take from it at once all chance of life."[38]

Such writings appear to be most authentick documents respecting the general prevalence of infanticide.

Sir George Staunton has stated, from the best information which he could collect, that the number of children exposed annually at Pekin is about two thousand;[39] but it is highly probable, that the number varies extremely from year to year, and depends very much upon seasons of plenty or seasons of scarcity. After any great epidemic or destructive famine, the number is probably very small; it is natural that it should increase gradually on the return to a crowded population, and is, without doubt, the greatest, when an unfavourable season takes place, at a period in which the average produce is already insufficient to support the overflowing multitude.

These unfavourable seasons do not appear to be infrequent, and the famines which follow them, are perhaps the most powerful of all the posi-

---

37. Lettres Edif. tom. xix. p. 111.   38. Id. p. 124.
39. Embassy to China, vol. ii. p. 159.

tive checks to the Chinese population; though at some periods, the checks from wars and internal commotions have not been inconsiderable.[40] In the annals of the Chinese monarchs, famines are often mentioned;[41] and it is not probable that they would find a place among the most important events and revolutions of the empire, if they were not desolating and destructive to a great degree.

One of the Jesuits remarks, that the occasions when the mandarins pretend to shew the greatest compassion for the people are, when they are apprehensive of a failure in the crops, either from drought, from excessive rains, or from some other accident, such as a multitude of locusts, which sometimes overwhelms certain provinces.[42] The causes here enumerated, are probably those which principally contribute to the failure of the harvests in China; and the manner in which they are mentioned, seems to shew that they are not uncommon.

Meares speaks of violent hurricanes, by which whole harvests are dissipated, and a famine follows. From a similar cause, he says, accompanied by excessive drought, a most dreadful dearth prevailed in 1787, throughout all the southern provinces of China, by which an incredible number of people perished. It was no uncommon thing at Canton, to see the famished wretch breathing his last, while mothers thought it a duty to destroy their infant children, and the young to give the stroke of fate to the aged, to save them from the agonies of such a dilatory death.[43]

The Jesuit Parennin, writing to a member of the Royal Academy of Sciences, says, "another thing that you can scarcely believe, is, that dearths " should be so frequent in China;"[44] and in the conclusion of his letter he remarks, that if famine did not, from time to time, thin the immense number of inhabitants which China contains, it would be impossible for her to live in peace.[45] The causes of these frequent famines, he endeavours to investigate, and begins by observing, very justly, that, in a time of dearth, China can obtain no assistance from her neighbours, and must necessarily draw the whole of her resources from her own provinces.[46] He then describes the delays and artifices which often defeat the emperor's intentions to assist from the public granaries those parts of the country which are the most distressed. When a harvest fails in any province, either from excessive drought, or a sudden inundation, the great mandarins have recourse to the

40. Annals of the Chinese Monarchs. Duhalde's China, vol. i. p. 136.

41. Ibid.   42. Lettres Edif. tom. xix. p. 154.   43. Meares's Voyage, ch. vii. p. 92.   44. Lettres Edif. et Curieuses, tom. xxii. p. 174.   45. Id. p. 186.

46. Id. p. 175.

public granaries; but often find them empty, owing to the dishonesty of the inferior mandarins, who have the charge of them. Examinations and researches are then made, and an unwillingness prevails to inform the court of such disagreeable intelligence. Memorials are however at length presented. These memorials pass through many hands, and do not reach the emperor till after many days. The great officers of state are then ordered to assemble, and to deliberate on the means of relieving the misery of the people. Declarations, full of expressions of compassion for the people, are in the mean time published throughout the empire. The resolution of the tribunal is at length made known; but numberless other ceremonies delay its execution; while those who are suffering, have the time to die with hunger before the remedy arrives. Those who do not wait for this last extremity, crawl as well as they can into other districts, where they hope to get support, but leave the greatest part of their number dead on the road.[47]

If, when a dearth occurs, the court do not make some attempt to relieve the people, small parties of plunderers soon collect, and their numbers increase by degrees, so as to interrupt the tranquillity of the province. On this account, numerous orders are always given, and movements are continually taking place, to amuse the people, till the famine is over; and as the motives to relieve the people are generally rather reasons of state, than genuine compassion, it is not probable that they should be relieved at the time, and in the manner, that their wants require.[48]

The last cause of famine, which is mentioned in this investigation, and on which the writer lays considerable stress, is the very great consumption of grain in making spirits;[49] but in stating this as a cause of famine, he has evidently fallen into a very gross error; yet, in the Abbé Grosier's general description of China, this error has been copied, and the cause above mentioned has been considered as one of the grand sources of the evil.[50] But, in reality, the whole tendency of this cause is in a contrary direction. The consumption of corn in any other way but that of necessary food, checks the population before it arrives at the utmost limits of subsistence; and as the grain may be withdrawn from this particular use in the time of a scarcity, a public granary is thus opened, richer, probably, than could have been formed by any other means. When such a consumption has been once established, and has become permanent, its effect is exactly as if a piece of land with all the people upon it were removed from the country. The rest of the people would certainly be precisely in the same state as they were

---

47. Lettres Edif. tom. xxii. p. 180.   48. Id. p. 187.   49. Id. p. 184.
50. Vol. i. b. iv. c. iii. p. 396. 8vo. Eng tran.

before, neither better nor worse in years of average plenty; but in a time of dearth the produce of this land would be returned to them, without the mouths to help them to eat it. China, without her distilleries, would certainly be more populous, but on a failure of the seasons, would have still less resource than she has at present, and as far as the magnitude of the cause would operate, would in consequence be more subject to famines, and those famines would be more severe.

The state of Japan resembles in so many respects that of China, that a particular consideration of it would lead into too many repetitions. Montesquieu attributes its populousness to the birth of a greater number of females;[51] but the principal cause of this populousness is, without doubt, as in China, the persevering industry of the natives, directed, as it has always been, principally to agriculture.

In reading the preface to Thunberg's account of Japan, it would seem extremely difficult to trace the checks to the population of a country, the inhabitants of which are said to live in such happiness and plenty; but the continuation of his own work contradicts the impression of his preface; and, in the valuable history of Japan by Kæmpfer, these checks are sufficiently obvious. In the extracts from two historical chronicles published in Japan, which he produces,[52] a very curious account is given of the different mortalities, plagues, famines, bloody wars, and other causes of destruction which have occurred since the commencement of these records. The Japanese are distinguished from the Chinese, in being much more warlike, seditious, dissolute, and ambitious; and it would appear, from Kæmpfer's account, that the check to population from infanticide, in China, is balanced by the greater dissoluteness of manners with regard to the sex, and the greater frequency of wars and intestine commotions, which prevail in Japan. With regard to the positive checks to population from disease and famine, the two countries seem to be nearly on a level.

---

51. Liv. xxiii. c. xii. It is surprising that Montesquieu, who appears sometimes to understand the subject of population, should at other times make such observations as this.

52. Book ii.

CHAP. XIII.

Of the Checks to Population among the Greeks.

IT has been generally allowed, and will not indeed admit of a doubt, that the more equal division of property among the Greeks and Romans, in the early period of their history, and the direction of their industry principally to agriculture, must have tended greatly to encourage population. Agriculture is not only, as Hume states,[1] that species of industry, which is chiefly requisite to the subsistence of multitudes, but it is in fact the *sole* species by which multitudes can exist; and all the numerous arts and manufactures of the modern world, by which such numbers appear to be supported, have no tendency whatever to increase population, except as far as they tend to increase the quantity, and to facilitate the distribution, of the products of agriculture.

In countries where, from the operation of particular causes, property in land is divided into very large shares, these arts and manufactures are absolutely necessary to the existence of any considerable population. Without them, modern Europe would be unpeopled. But where property is divided into small shares, the same necessity for them does not appear. The division itself attains immediately one great object, that of distribution; and if the demand for men be constant, to fight the battles, and support the power and dignity of the state, we may easily conceive that this motive, joined to the natural love of a family, might be sufficient to induce each proprietor to cultivate his land to the utmost, in order that it might support the greatest number descendants.

The division of people into small states, during the early periods of Greek and Roman history, gave additional force to this motive. Where the number of free citizens did not perhaps exceed ten or twenty thousand, each individual would naturally feel the value of his own exertions, and knowing that the state to which he belonged, situated in the midst of envious and watchful rivals, must depend chiefly on its population for its means of defence and safety, would be sensible, that in suffering the lands which were allotted to him to lie idle, he would be deficient in his duty as a citizen. These causes appear to have produced a considerable attention

---

1. Essay xi. p. 467. 4to. edit.

to agriculture without the intervention of the artificial wants of mankind to encourage it. Population followed the products of the earth with more than equal pace; and when the overflowing numbers were not taken off by the drains of war or disease, they found vent in frequent and repeated colonization. The necessity of these frequent colonizations, joined to the smallness of the states, which brought the subject immediately home to every thinking person, could not fail to point out to the legislators and philosophers of these times, the strong tendency of population to increase beyond the means of subsistence; and they did not, like the statesmen and projectors of modern days, overlook the consideration of a question which so deeply affects the happiness and tranquillity of society. However we may justly execrate the barbarous expedients which they adopted to remove the difficulty, we cannot but give them some credit for their penetration in seeing it; and in being fully aware, that, if not considered and obviated, it would be sufficient of itself to destroy their best planned schemes of republican equality and happiness.

The power of colonization is necessarily limited, and after the lapse of some time, it might be extremely difficult, if not impossible, for a country, not particularly well situated for this purpose, to find a vacant spot proper for the settlement of its expatriated citizens. It was necessary, therefore, to consider of other resources besides colonization.

It is probable that the practice of infanticide had prevailed from the earliest ages in Greece. In the parts of America where it was found to exist, it appears to have originated from the extreme difficulty of rearing many children in a savage and wandering life, exposed to frequent famines and perpetual wars. We may easily conceive that it had a similar origin among the ancestors of the Greeks, or the native inhabitants of the country. And when Solon permitted the exposing of children, it is probable that he only gave the sanction of law to a custom already prevalent.

In this permission he had, without doubt, two ends in view. First, that which is most obvious, the prevention of such an excessive population as would cause universal poverty and discontent; and, secondly, that of keeping the population up to the level of what the territory could support, by removing the terrors of too numerous a family and, consequently, the principal obstacle to marriage. From the effect of this practice in China, we have reason to think that it is better calculated to attain the latter, than the former purpose. But if the legislator, either did not see this, or if the barbarous habits of the times prompted parents invariably to prefer the murder of their children to poverty, the practice would appear to be very particularly calculated to answer both the ends in view, and to preserve, as completely and as constantly as the nature of the thing would permit, the requisite proportion between the food and the numbers which were to consume it.

On the very great importance of attending to this proportion, and the evils that must neccssarily result, of weakness on the one hand, or of poverty on the other, from the deficiency or the excess of population, the Greek political writers strongly insist; and propose in consequence various modes of maintaining the relative proportion desired.

Plato, in the republick which he considers in his books of laws, limits the number of free citizens, and of habitations, to five thousand and forty; and this number he thinks may be preserved, if the father of every family chuse one out of his sons for his successor to the lot of land which he has possessed, and disposing of his daughters in marriage according to law, distribute his other sons, if he have any, to be adopted by those citizens who are without children. But if the number of children, upon the whole, be either too great or too few, the magistrate is to take the subject particularly into his consideration, and to contrive so, that the same number of five thousand and forty families should still be maintained. There are many modes, he thinks, of effecting this object. Procreation, when it goes on too fast, may be checked, or when it goes on too slow, may be encouraged, by the proper distribution of honours and marks of ignominy, and by the admonitions of the elders to prevent or promote it according to circumstances.[2]

In his philosophical republick[3] he enters more particularly into this subject, and proposes that the most excellent among the men should be joined in marriage to the most excellent among the women, and the inferior citizens matched with the inferior females; and that the offspring of the first should be brought up; of the others, not. On certain festivals appointed by the laws, the young men and women who are betrothed, are to be assembled, and joined together with solemn ceremonies. But the number of marriages is to be determined by the magistrates, that, taking into consideration the drains from wars, diseases, and other causes, they may preserve, as nearly as possible, such a proportion of citizens as will be neither too numerous nor too few, according to the resources and demands of the state. The children who are thus born from the most excellent of the citizens are to be carried to certain nurses destined to this office, inhabiting a separate part of the city; but those which are born from the inferior citizens, and any

2. Plato de Legibus, lib. v.   3. Plato de Republicâ, lib. v.

from the others which are imperfect in their limbs, are to be buried in some obscure and unknown place.

He next proceeds to consider the proper age for marriage, and determines it to be twenty for the woman, and thirty for the man. Beginning at twenty, the woman is to bear children for the state till she is forty, and the man is to fulfil his duty in this respect, from thirty to fifty-five. If a man produce a child into publick either before or after this period, the action is to be considered in the same criminal and profane light as if he had produced one without the nuptial ceremonies, and instigated solely by incontinence. The same rule should hold, if a man, who is of the proper age for procreation, be connected with a woman who is also of the proper age, but without the ceremony of marriage by the magistrate; he is to be considered as having given to the state a spurious, profane, and incestuous offspring. When both sexes have passed the age assigned for presenting children to the state, Plato allows a great latitude of intercourse, but no child is to be brought to light. Should any infant by accident be born alive, it is to be exposed in the same manner as if the parents could not support it.[4]

From these passages it is evident, that Plato fully saw the tendency of population to increase beyond the means of subsistence. His expedients for checking it are indeed execrable; but the expedients themselves, and the extent to which they were to be used, shew his conceptions of the magnitude of the difficulty. Contemplating, as he certainly must do in a small republick, a great proportional drain of people by wars; if he could still propose to destroy the children of all the inferior and less perfect citizens; to destroy also all that were born not within the prescibed ages, and with the prescribed forms; to fix the age of marriage late, and after all to regulate the number of these marriages; his experience and his reasonings must have strongly pointed out to him the great power of the principle of increase, and the necessity of checking it.

Aristotle appears to have seen this necessity still more clearly. He fixes the proper age of marriage at thirty-seven for the men, and eighteen for the women; which must of course condemn a great number of women to celibacy, as there never can be so many men of thirty-seven as there are women of eighteen. Yet though he has fixed the age of marriage for the men at so late a period, he still thinks that there may be too many children, and proposes that the number allowed to each marriage should be regulated; and if

4. Plato de Repub. lib. v.

any woman be pregnant after she has produced the prescribed number, that an abortion should be procured before the fœtus has life.

The period of procreating children for the state, is to cease with the men at fifty-four or fifty-five, because the offspring of old men, as well as of men too young, is imperfect both in body and mind. When both sexes have passed the prescribed age, they are allowed to continue a connexion; but, as in Plato's republick, no child which may be the result, is to be brought to light.[5]

In discussing the merits of the republick proposed by Plato in his books of laws, Aristotle is of opinion, that he has by no means been sufficiently attentive to the subject of population; and accuses him of inconsistency, in equalizing property without limiting the number of children. The laws on this subject, Aristotle very justly observes, require to be much more definite and precise in a state where property is equalized than in others. Under ordinary governments an increase of population would only occasion a greater subdivision of landed property; whereas in such a republick the supernumeraries would be altogether destitute, because the lands, being reduced to equal, and as it were elementary, parts, would be incapable of further partition.[6]

He then remarks, that it is necessary, in all cases, to regulate the proportion of children that they may not exceed the proper number. In doing this, deaths and barrenness are of course to be taken into consideration. But, if, as in the generality of states, every person be left free to have as many children as he pleases, the necessary consequence must be poverty; and poverty is the mother of villany and sedition. On this account Pheidon of Corinth, one of the most ancient writers on the subject of politicks, introduced a regulation directly the reverse of Plato's, and limited population without equalizing possessions.[7]

Speaking afterwards of Phaleas of Chalcedon, who proposed as a most salutary institution, to equalize wealth among the citizens, he adverts again to Plato's regulations respecting property, and observes, that those who would thus regulate the extent of fortunes, ought not to be ignorant that it is absolutely necessary at the same time to regulate the number of children. For, if children multiply beyond the means of supporting them, the law will

5. Aristotelis Opera. De Repub. lib. vii. c. xvi.
6. De Repub. lib. ii. c. vi. Gillies's Aristotle, vol. ii. b. ii. p. 87. For the convenience of those who may not chuse the trouble of consulting the original, I refer at the same time to Gillies's translation; but some passages he has wholly omitted, and of others he has not given the literal sense, his object being a free version.
7. De Repub. lib. ii. c. vii. Gillies's Aristot. vol. ii. b. ii. p. 87.

necessarily be broken, and families will be suddenly reduced from opulence to beggary; a revolution always dangerous to publick tranquillity.[8]

It appears from these passages, that Aristotle clearly saw, that the strong tendency of the human race to increase, unless checked by strict and positive laws, was absolutely fatal to every system founded on equality of property; and there cannot surely be a stronger argument against any system of this kind, than the necessity of such laws as Aristotle himself proposes.

From a remark which he afterwards makes respecting Sparta, it appears still more clearly that he fully understood the principle of population. From the improvidence of the laws relating to succession, the landed property in Sparta had been engrossed by a few, and the effect was greatly to diminish the populousness of the country. To remedy this evil, and to supply men for continual wars, the kings preceding Lycurgus had been in the habit of naturalizing strangers. It would have been much better, however, according to Aristotle, to have increased the number of citizens by a nearer equalization of property. But the law relating to children was directly adverse to this improvement. The legislator wishing to have many citizens, had encouraged as much as possible the procreation of children. A man who had three sons was exempted from the night-watch; and he who had four, enjoyed a complete immunity from all publick burdens. But it is evident, Aristotle most justly observes, that the birth of a great number of children, the division of the lands remaining the same, would necessarily cause only an accumulation of poverty.[9]

He here seems to see exactly the error, into which many other legislators besides Lycurgus have fallen, and to be fully aware, that, to encourage the birth of children, without providing properly for their support, is to obtain a very small accession to the population of a country at the expence of a very great accession of misery.

The legislator of Crete[10] as well as Solon, Pheidon, Plato, and Aristotle, saw the necessity of checking population in order to prevent general poverty; and, as we must suppose that the opinions of such men, and the laws founded upon them, would have considerable influence, it is probable, that the preventive check to increase from late marriages and other causes, operated to a considerable degree among the free citizens of Greece.

For the positive checks to population, we need not look beyond the wars in which these small states were almost continually engaged, though we

8. De Repub. lib. ii. c. vii. Gillies's Aristot. vol. ii. b. ii. p. 91.
9. De Repub. lib. ii. c. ix. Gillies's Aristot. vol. ii. b. ii. p. 107.
10. Aristot, de Repub. lib. ii, c. x. Gillies's Aristot. vol. ii. b. ii. p. 113.

have an account of one wasting plague at least, in Athens; and Plato supposes the case of his republick being greatly reduced by disease.[11] Their wars were not only almost constant, but extremely bloody. In a small army, the whole of which would probably be engaged in close fight, a much greater number in proportion would be slain, than in the large modern armies, a considerable part of which often remains untouched;[12] and as all the free citizens of these republicks were generally employed as soldiers in every war, losses would be felt very severely, and would not appear to be very easily repaired.

11. De legibus, lib. v.   12. Hume, Essay xi. p. 451.

C H A P . XIV.

Of the Checks to Population among the Romans.

THE havock made by war in the smaller states of Italy, particularly during the first struggles of the Romans for power, seems to have been still
greater than in Greece. Wallace, in his dissertation on the numbers of mankind, after alluding to the multitudes which fell by the sword in these times,
observes, "On an accurate review of the history of the Italians during this
" period, we shall wonder how such vast multitudes could be raised as
" were engaged in those continual wars till Italy was entirely subdued."[1]
And Livy expresses his utter astonishment that the Volsei and Æqui, so
often as they were conquered, should have been able to bring fresh armies
into the field.[2] But these wonders will perhaps be sufficiently accounted
for, if we suppose, what seems to be highly probable, that the constant
drains from wars had introduced the habit of giving nearly full scope to the
power of population, and that a much greater number of youths, in proportion to the whole people, were yearly rising into manhood, and becoming
fit to bear arms, than is usual in other states not similarly circumstanced. It
was, without doubt, the rapid influx of these supplies, which enabled them,
like the ancient Germans, to astonish future historians, by renovating in so
extraordinary a manner their defeated and half-destroyed armies.

Yet there is reason to believe, that the practice of infanticide prevailed in
Italy as well as in Greece, from the earliest times. A law of Romulus forbad
the exposing of children before they were three years old,[3] which implies,
that the custom of exposing them as soon as they were born had before prevailed. But this practice was of course never resorted to but when the drains
from wars were insufficient to make room for the rising generation; and
consequently, though it may be considered as one of the positive checks
to the full power of increase, yet, in the actual state of things, it certainly
contributed rather to promote than impede population.

Among the Romans themselves, engaged as they were in incessant
wars, from the beginning of their republick to the end of it, many of which
were dreadfully destructive, the positive check to population from this
cause alone, must have been enormously great. But this cause alone, great

---

1. Dissertation, p. 62. 8vo. 1763, Edinburgh.   2. Lib. vi. c. xii.
3. Dionysius Halicarn. lib. ii. 15.

as it was, would never have occasioned that want of Roman citizens, under the emperors, which prompted Augustus and Trajan to issue laws for the encouragement of marriage and of children, if other causes still more powerful in depopulation had not concurred.

When the equality of property, which had formerly prevailed in the Roman territory, had been destroyed by degrees, and the land had fallen into the hands of a few great proprietors, the citizens who were by this change successively deprived of the means of supporting themselves, would naturally have no resource to prevent them from starving, but that of selling their labour to the rich, as in modern states; but from this resource they were completely cut off by the prodigious number of slaves, which, increasing by constant influx with the increasing luxury of Rome, filled up every employment both in agriculture and manufactures. Under such circumstances, so far from being astonished that the number of free citizens should decrease, the wonder seems to be, that any should exist besides the proprietors. And, in fact, many could not have existed, but for a strange and preposterous custom, which however, perhaps, the strange and unnatural state of the city required, that of distributing vast quantities of corn to the poorer citizens gratis. Two hundred thousand received this distribution in Augustus's time; and it is highly probable that a great part of them had little else to depend upon. It is supposed to have been given to every man of full years; but the quantity was not enough for a family, and too much for an individual.[4] It could not therefore enable them to increase; and, from the manner in which Plutarch speaks of the custom of exposing children among the poor,[5] there is great reason to believe that many were destroyed in spite of the jus trium liberorum. The passage in Tacitus in which, speaking of the Germans, he alludes to this custom in Rome, seems to point to the same conclusion.[6] What effect, indeed, could such a law have among a set of people who appear to have been so completely barred out from all the means of acquiring a subsistence, except that of charity, that they would be scarcely able to support themselves, much less a wife and two or three chil-

---

4. Hume, Essay xi. p. 488.   5. De amore prolis.

6. De moribus Germanorum, 19. How completely the laws relating to the encouragement of marriage and of children were despised, appears from a speech of Minucius Felix in Octavio, cap. 30. "Vos enim video procreatos filios nunc feris et
" avibus exponere, nunc adstrangulatos misero mortis genere elidere; sunt quæ in
" ipsis visceribus medicaminibus epotis originem futuri hominis extinguant, et par-
" ricidium faciant antequam pariant." This crime had grown so much into a custom in Rome that even Pliny attempts to excuse it; "Quoniam aliquarum fecundi-
" tas plena liberis tali veniâ indiget." Lib. xxix. c. iv.

dren. If half of the slaves had been sent out of the country, and the people had been employed in agriculture and manufactures, the effect would have been to increase the number of Roman citizens with more certainty and rapidity than ten thousand laws for the encouragement of children.

It is possible that the jus trium liberorum, and the other laws of the same tendency, might have been of some little use among the higher classes of the Roman citizens; and, indeed, from the nature of these laws, consisting as they did principally of privileges, it would appear that they were directed chiefly to this part of society. But vicious habits of every possible kind, preventive of population,[7] seem to have been so generally prevalent at this period, that no corrective laws could have any considerable influence. Montesquieu justly observes, that "the corruption of manners had destroyed
"   the office of censor, which had been established itself to destroy the cor-
"   ruption of manners; but when the corruption of manners becomes gen-
"   eral, censure has no longer any force."[8] Thirty-four years after the passing of the law of Augustus respecting marriage, the Roman knights demanded its repeal. On separating the married and the unmarried, it appeared that the latter considerably exceeded in number the former; a strong proof of the inefficacy of the law.[9]

In most countries, vicious habits preventive of population appear to be rather a consequence than a cause of the infrequency of marriage; but in Rome the depravity of morals seems to have been the direct cause which checked the marriage union, at least among the higher classes. It is impossible to read the speech of Metellus Numidicus in his censorship without indignation and disgust. "If it were possible," he says, "entirely to go with-
"   out wives, we would deliver ourselves at once from this evil; but as the
"   laws of nature have so ordered it, that we can neither live happy with
"   them, nor continue the species without them, we ought to have more
"   regard for our lasting security than for our transient pleasures."[10]

Positive laws to encourage marriage and population, enacted on the urgency of the occasion, and not mixed with religion, as in China and some other countries, are seldom calculated to answer the end which they aim at, and therefore generally indicate ignorance in the legislator who proposes them; but the apparent necessity of them almost invariably indicates a very

7. Sed jacet aurato vix ulla puerpera lecto
   Tantum artes hujus, tantum medicamina possunt.
   Quæ steriles facit, atque homines in ventre necandos
   Conducit. Juvenal, fat. vi. 593.
8. Esprit des Loix, liv. xxiii. c. 21.   9. Ibid.   10. Aulus Gellius, lib. i. c. 6.

great degree of moral and political depravity in the state; and, in the countries in which they are most strongly insisted on, not only vicious manners will generally be found to prevail, but political institutions extremely unfavourable to industry, and consequently to population.

On this account, I cannot but agree with Wallace[11] in thinking that Hume was wrong in his supposition that the Roman world was probably the most populous during the long peace under Trajan and the Antonines.[12] We well know that wars do not depopulate much, while industry continues in vigour; and that peace will not increase the number of people when they cannot find the means of subsistence. The renewal of the laws relating to marriage under Trajan indicates the continued prevalence of vicious habits, and of a languishing industry, and seems to be inconsistent with the supposition of a great increase of population.

It might be said, perhaps, that the vast profusion of slaves would more than make up for the want of Roman citizens; but it appears that the labour of these slaves was not sufficiently directed to agriculture to support a very great population. Whatever might be the case with some of the provinces, the decay of agriculture in Italy seems to be generally acknowledged. The pernicious custom of importing great quantities of corn to distribute gratis to the people had given it a blow which it never afterwards recovered. Hume observes, that "when the Roman authors complain that Italy, which
" formerly exported corn, became dependent on all the provinces for its
" daily bread, they never ascribe this alteration to the increase of its in-
" habitants, but to the neglect of tillage and agriculture."[13] And in another place he says, "All ancient authors tell us, that there was a perpetual flux of
" slaves to Italy from the remoter provinces, particularly Syria, Cilicia,
" Cappadocia, and the Lesser Asia, Thrace, and Egypt; yet the number of
" people did not increase in Italy; and writers complain of the continual
" decay of industry and agriculture."[14] It seems but little probable that the peace under Trajan and the Antonines should have given so sudden a turn to the habits of the people as essentially to alter this state of things.

On the condition of slavery it may be observed, that there cannot be a stronger proof of its unfavourableness, to the propagation of the species in the countries where it prevails, than the necessity of this continual influx. This necessity forms at once a complete refutation of the observation of Wallace, that the antient slaves were more serviceable in raising up people

11. Dissertation, Appendix, p. 247.   12. Essay xi. p. 505.
13. Id. p. 504.   14. Hume, Essay xi. p. 433.

than the inferior ranks of men in modern times.[15] Though it is undoubtedly true, as he observes, that all our labourers do not marry, and that many of their children die, and become sickly and useless through the poverty and negligence of their parents;[16] yet notwithstanding these obstacles to increase, there is, perhaps, scarcely an instance to be produced, where the lower classes of society, in any country, if free, do not raise up people, fully equal to the demand for their labour.

To account for the checks to population which are peculiar to a state of slavery, and which render a constant recruit of numbers necessary, we must adopt the comparison of slaves to cattle, which Wallace and Hume have made; Wallace, to shew that it would be the interest of masters to take care of their slaves and rear up their offspring;[17] and Hume, to prove that it would more frequently be the interest of the master to prevent than to encourage their breeding.[18] If Wallace's observation had been just, it is not to be doubted that the slaves would have kept up their own numbers with ease by procreation; and as it is acknowledged that they did not do this, the truth of Hume's observation is clearly evinced. "To rear a child in London till he
" could be serviceable, would cost much dearer, than to buy one of the
" same age from Scotland or Ireland, where he had been raised in a cot-
" tage, covered with rags, and fed on oatmeal and potatoes. Those who
" had slaves, therefore, in all the richer and more populous countries,
" would discourage the pregnancy of the females, and either prevent or
" destroy the birth."[19] It is acknowledged by Wallace, that the male slaves greatly exceeded in number the females,[20] which must necessarily be an additional obstacle to their increase. It would appear, therefore, that the preventive check to population, must have operated with very great force among the Greek and Roman slaves; and as they were often ill treated, fed perhaps scantily, and sometimes great numbers of them confined together in close and unwholesome ergastula, or dungeons,[21] it is probable that the positive checks to population from disease, were also severe, and that when epidemicks prevailed they would be most destructive in this part of the society.

The unfavourableness of slavery to the propagation of the species in the country where it prevails, is not, however, decisive of the question respecting

15. Dissert. on the numbers of mankind, p. 91.
16. Id. p. 88.   17. Id. p. 89.   18. Hume, Essay xi. p. 433.   19. Hume, Essay xi. p. 433.   20. Appendix to Dissertation, p. 182.
21. Hume, Essay, xi. p. 430.

the absolute population of such a country, or, the greater question, respecting the populousness of antient and modern nations. We know that some countries could afford a great and constant supply of slaves, without being in the smallest degree depopulated themselves; and if these supplies were poured in, as they probably would be, exactly in proportion to the demand for labour in the nation which received them, the question respecting the populousness of this nation, would rest precisely on the same grounds as in modern states, and depend upon the number of people which it could employ and support. Whether the practice of domestick slavery, therefore, prevail or not, it may be laid down as a position not to be controverted, that, taking a sufficient extent of territory to include within it exportation and importation, and allowing some variation for the prevalence of luxury, or of frugal habits, that the population of these countries will always be in proportion to the food which the earth is made to produce. And no cause, physical or moral, unless it operate in an excessive and unusual manner,[22] can have any considerable and permanent effect on the population, except in as far as it influences the production and distribution of the means of subsistence.

In the controversy concerning the populousness of antient and modern nations, this point has not been sufficiently attended to, and physical and moral causes have been brought forward on both sides, from which no just inference in favour of either party could be drawn. It seems to have escaped the attention of both writers, that the more productive and populous a country is, in its actual state, the less probably will be its power of obtaining a further increase of produce, and consequently the more checks must necessarily be called into action to keep the population down to the level of this stationary, or slowly-increasing produce. From finding such checks, therefore, in antient or modern nations, no inference can be drawn against the absolute populousness of either. On this account, the prevalence of the small-pox, and of other disorders unknown to the antients, can by no means be considered as an argument against the populousness of modern nations, though to these physical causes, both Hume.[23] and Wallace[24] allow considerable weight.

---

22. The extreme insalubrity of Batavia, and perhaps the plague in some countries, may be considered as physical causes operating in an excessive degree. The extreme and unusual attachment of the Romans to a vicious celibacy, and the promiscuous intercourse in Otaheite, may be considered as moral causes of the same nature. Such instances may perhaps form exceptions to the general observation.

23. Essay xi. p. 425.   24. Dissertation, p. 80.

In the moral causes which they have brought forward, they have fallen into a similar error. Wallace introduces the positive encouragements to marriage among the antients, as one of the principal causes of the superior populousness of the antient world;[25] but the necessity of positive laws to encourage marriage, certainly rather indicates a want than an abundance of people; and in the instance of Sparta, to which he particularly refers, it appears from the passage in Aristotle, mentioned in the last chapter, that the laws to encourage marriage were instituted for the express purpose of remedying a marked deficiency of people. In a country with a crowded and overflowing population, a legislator would never think of making express laws to encourage marriage and the procreation of children. Other arguments of Wallace will be found upon examination to be almost equally ineffectual to his purpose.

Some of the causes which Hume produces, are in the same manner unsatisfactory, and rather make against the inference which he has in view than for it. The number of footmen, housemaids, and other persons remaining unmarried in modern states, he allows to be an argument against their populousness.[26] But the contrary inference of the two, appears to be the more probable. When the difficulties attending the rearing of a family are very great, and consequently, many persons of both sexes remain single, we may naturally enough infer that population is stationary, but by no means that it is not absolutely great; because the difficulty of rearing a family may arise from the very circumstance of a great absolute population, and the consequent fullness of all the channels to a livelihood; though the same difficulty may undoubtedly exist in a thinly-peopled country, which is yet stationary in its population. The number of unmarried persons in proportion to the whole number, may form some criterion by which we can judge whether population be increasing, stationary, or decreasing; but will not enable us to determine any thing respecting absolute populousness. Yet even in this criterion, we are liable to be deceived. In some of the southern countries early marriages are general, and very few women remain in a state of celibacy, yet the people not only do not increase, but the actual number is perhaps small. In this case the removal of the preventive check is made up by the excessive force of the positive check. The sum of all the positive and preventive checks taken together, forms undoubtedly the immediate cause which represses population; but we never can expect to obtain and estimate accurately this sum in any country; and we can certainly draw no safe conclusion from the contemplation of two or three of these checks taken by

25. Dissertation, p. 93.   26. Essay xi.

themselves, because it so frequently happens, that the excess of one check is balanced by the defect of some other. Causes which affect the number of births or deaths, may, or may not, affect the average population, according to circumstances; but causes which affect the production and distribution of the means of subsistence must necessarily affect population; and it is therefore only on these causes, besides actual enumerations, on which we can with any certainty rely.

All the checks to population which have been hitherto considered in the course of this review of human society, are clearly resolvable into moral restraint, vice, and misery.

Of moral restraint, though it might be rash to affirm that it has not had some share in repressing the natural power of population, yet it must be allowed to have operated very feebly indeed, compared to the others. Of the preventive check, considered generally, and without reference to its producing vice, though its effect appears to have been very considerable in the later periods of Roman History, and in some few other countries; yet, upon the whole, its operation seems to have been inferior to the positive checks. A large portion of the procreative power appears to have been called into action, the redundancy from which was checked by violent causes. Among these, war is the most prominent and striking feature; and after this, may be ranked famines and violent diseases. In most of the countries considered, the population seems to have been seldom measured accurately according to the average and permanent means of subsistence, but generally to have vibrated between the two extremes, and consequently the oscillations between want and plenty, are strongly marked, as we should naturally expect among less civilized nations.

ESSAY, &c.

BOOK II.

OF THE CHECKS TO POPULATION IN THE DIFFERENT STATES OF MODERN EUROPE.

CHAP. I.

Of the Checks to Population in Norway.

In reviewing the states of modern Europe, we shall be assisted in our inquiries by registers of births, deaths, and marriages, which, when they are complete and correct, point out to us with some degree of precision, whether the prevailing checks to population are of the positive, or of the preventive kind. The habits of most European nations, are of course much alike, owing to the similarity of the circumstances in which they are placed; and it is to be expected, therefore, that their tables of mortality should sometimes give the same results. Relying, however, too much upon this occasional coincidence, political calculators have been led into the error of supposing, that there is, generally speaking, an invariable order of mortality in all countries; but it appears, on the contrary, that this order is extremely variable; that it is very different in different places of the same country, and, within certain limits, depends upon circumstances, which it is in the power of man to alter.

Norway, during nearly the whole of the last century, was in a peculiar degree exempt from the drains of people by war. The climate is remarkably free from epidemick sicknesses, and, in common years, the mortality is less than in any other country in Europe, the registers of which are known to be correct.[1] The proportion of the annual deaths to the whole population, on an average throughout the whole country, is only as 1 to 48.[2] Yet the population of Norway never seems to have increased with great rapidity. It has made a start within the last ten or fifteen years, but, till that period, its progress must have been very slow, as we know that the country was peopled in very early ages, and in 1769 its population was only 723,141.[3]

Before we enter upon an examination of its internal economy, we must feel assured, that, as the positive checks to its population have been so small, the preventive checks must have been proportionably great; and we accordingly find from the registers, that the proportion of yearly marriages to the whole population, is as 1 to 130,[4] which is a smaller proportion of marriages than appears in the registers of any other country, except Switzerland.

One cause of this small number of marriages is the mode in which the enrolments for the army have been conducted, till within a very few years. Every man in Denmark and Norway born of a farmer or labourer is a soldier.[5] Formerly, the commanding officer of the district might take these peasants at any age he pleased, and he in general preferred those that were from twenty-five to thirty, to such as were younger. After being taken into the service, a man could not marry without producing a certificate signed by the minister of the parish, that he had substance enough to support a wife and family; and even then, it was further necessary for him to obtain the permission of the officer. The difficulty, and sometimes the expence, attendant on the obtaining of this certificate and permission, generally deterred those who were not in very good circumstances, from thinking of marriage till their service of ten years was expired; and as they might be enrolled at any age under thirty-six, and the officers were apt to take the oldest first, it would often be late in life before they could feel themselves at liberty to settle.

1. The registers for Russia give a smaller mortality; but it is supposed that they are defective.
2. Thaarup's Statistik der Danischen Monarchie, vol. ii. p. 4.
3. Id. Table ii. p. 5.   4. Id. vol. ii. p. 4.
5. The few particulars which I shall mention relating to Norway, were collected during a summer excursion in that country in the year 1799.

Though the minister of the parish had no legal power to prevent a man from marrying who was not enrolled for service; yet it appears, that custom had in some degree sanctioned a discretionary power of this kind, and the priest often refused to join a couple together, when the parties had no probable means of supporting a family.

Every obstacle, however, of this nature, whether arising from law or custom, has now been entirely removed. A full liberty is given to marry at any age, without leave either of the officer or priest; and in the enrolments for the army, all those of the age of twenty, are taken first, then all those at twenty-two, and so on till the necessary number is completed.

The officers in general disapprove of this change. They say that a young Norwegian has not arrived at his full strength, and does not make a good soldier at twenty. And many are of opinion, that the peasants will now marry too young, and that more children will be born than the country can support.

But, independently of any regulations respecting the military enrolments, the peculiar state of Norway throws very strong obstacles in the way of early marriages. There are no large manufacturing towns to take off the overflowing population of the country; and as each village naturally furnishes from itself a supply of hands more than equal to the demand, a change of place in search of work seldom promises any success. Unless, therefore, an opportunity of foreign emigration offer, the Norwegian peasant generally remains in the village in which he was born; and as the vacancies in houses and employments must occur very slowly, owing to the small mortality that takes place, he will often see himself compelled to wait a considerable time, before he can attain a situation which will enable him to rear a family.

The Norway farms have in general a certain number of married labourers employed upon them, in proportion to their size, who are called housemen. They receive from the farmer a house and a quantity of land nearly sufficient to maintain a family; in return for which, they are under the obligation of working for him at a low and fixed price whenever they are called upon. Except in the immediate neighbourhood of the towns, and on the seacoast, the vacancy of a place of this kind, is the only prospect which presents itself of providing for a family. From the small number of people, and the little variety of employment, the subject is brought distinctly within the view of each individual; and he must feel the absolute necessity of repressing his inclinations to marriage, till some such vacancy offer. If, from the plenty of materials, he should be led to build a house himself, it could not be expected that the farmer, if he had a sufficient number of labourers before, should give him an adequate portion of land with it; and though he would, in general, find employment for three or four months in the summer, yet there would be little chance of his earning enough to support a family during the whole year. It is probable, that it was in cases of this kind, where the impatience of the parties prompted them to build, or propose to build, a house themselves, and trust to what they could earn, that the parish priests exercised the discretionary power of refusing to marry.

The young men and women therefore, are obliged to remain with the farmers as unmarried servants, till a houseman's place becomes vacant: and of these unmarried servants, there is in every farm, and every gentleman's family, a much greater proportion than the work would seem to require. There is but little division of labour in Norway. Almost all the wants of domestick economy are supplied in each separate household. Not only the common operations of brewing, baking, and washing, are carried on at home, but many families make, or import, their own cheese and butter, kill their own beef and mutton, import their own grocery stores; and the farmers, and country people, in general, spin their own flax and wool, and weave their own linen and woollen clothes. In the largest towns, such as Christiania and Drontheim, there is nothing that can be called a market. It is extremely difficult to get a joint of fresh meat; and a pound of fresh butter is an article not to be purchased, even in the midst of summer. Fairs are held at certain seasons of the year, and stores of all kinds of provisions that will keep, are laid in at these times; and if this care be neglected, great inconveniences are suffered, as scarcely any thing is to be bought retail. Persons who make a temporary residence, in the country, or small merchants not possessed of farms, complain heavily of this inconvenience; and the wives of merchants who have large estates say, that the domestick economy of a Norway family is so extensive and complicated, that the necessary superintendence of it requires their whole attention, and that they can find no time for any thing else.

It is evident that a system of this kind must require a great number of servants. It is said besides, that they are not remarkable for diligence, and that to do the same quantity of work, more are necessary than in other countries. The consequence is, that in every establishment two or three times the number of servants will be found, as in a family, living at the same rate in England; and it is not uncommon for a farmer in the country, who, in his appearance, is not to be distinguished from any of his labourers, to have a household of twenty persons, including his own family.

The means of maintenance to a single man are, therefore, much less confined than to a married man; and under such circumstances, the lower classes of people cannot increase much, till the increase of mercantile stock, or the division and improvement of farms, furnishes a greater quantity of employment for married labourers. In countries more fully peopled this subject is always involved in great obscurity. Each man naturally thinks that he has as good a chance of finding employment as his neighbour, and that if he cannot get it in one place, he shall, in some other. He marries, therefore, and trusts to fortune; and the effect too frequently is, that the redundant population occasioned in this manner is repressed by the positive checks of poverty and disease. In Norway the subject is not involved in the same obscurity. The number of additional families which the increasing demand for labour will support, is more distinctly marked. The population is so small, that, even in the towns, it is difficult to fall into any considerable error on this subject; and in the country, the division and improvement of an estate, and the creation of a greater number of housemen's places, must be a matter of complete notoriety. If a man can obtain one of these places, he marries, and is able to support a family; if he cannot obtain one, he remains single. A redundant population is thus prevented from taking place, instead of being destroyed after it has taken place.

It is not to be doubted, that the general prevalence of the preventive check to population, owing to the state of society which has been described, together with the obstacles thrown in the way of early marriages from the enrolments for the army, have powerfully contributed to place the lower classes of people in Norway in a better situation, than could be expected from the nature of the soil and climate. On the seacoast, where, on account of the hopes of an adequate supply of food, from fishing, the preventive check does not prevail in the same degree, the people are very poor and wretched; and, beyond comparison, in a worse state, than the peasants in the interior of the country.

The greatest part of the soil in Norway is absolutely incapable of bearing corn, and the climate is subject to the most sudden and fatal changes. There are three nights about the end of August which are particularly distinguished by the name of iron nights, on account of their sometimes blasting the promise of the fairest crops. On these occasions, the lower classes of people necessarily suffer; but, as there are scarcely any independent labourers, except the housemen that have been mentioned, who all keep cattle, the hardship of being obliged to mix the inner bark of the pine with their bread, is mitigated, by the stores of cheese, of salt butter, of salt meat, salt fish, and bacon, which they were enabled to lay up for winter provision. The period in which the want of corn presses the most severely, is, generally, about two months before harvest; and at this time the cows, of which the poorest housemen have generally two or three, and many five or six, begin to give milk, which must be a great assistance to the family, particularly to the younger part of it. In the summer of the year 1799, the Norwegians appeared to wear a face of plenty and content, while their neighbours, the Swedes, were absolutely starving: and I particularly remarked, that the sons of housemen, and the farmers boys, were fatter, larger, and had better calves to their legs, than boys of the same age and in similar situations in England.

It is also, without doubt, owing to the prevalence of the preventive check to population, rather than to any peculiar healthiness of the air, that the mortality in Norway is so small. There is nothing in the climate, or the soil, that would lead to the supposition of its being in any extraordinary manner favourable to the general health of the inhabitants; but as in every country the principal mortality takes place among very young children, the smaller number of these in Norway, in proportion to the whole population, will naturally occasion a smaller mortality, than in other countries, supposing the climate to be equally healthy.

It may be said, perhaps, and with truth, that one of the principal reasons of the small mortality in Norway, is, that the towns are inconsiderable and few, and that few people are employed in unwholesome manufactories. In some of the agricultural villages in England, where the preventive check to population does not prevail in the same degree, the mortality is as small as in Norway. But it should be recollected, that the calculation, in this case, is for those particular villages alone; whereas in Norway the calculation of 1 in 48 is for the whole country. The redundant population of the villages in England is disposed of by constant emigrations to the towns, and the deaths of a great part of those that are born in the parish do not appear in the registers. But in Norway all the deaths are within the calculation, and it is clear that if more were born than the country could support, a great mortality must take place in some form or other. If the people were not destroyed by disease, they would be destroyed by famine. It is indeed well known that bad and insufficient food will produce disease and death in the purest air and the finest climate. Supposing, therefore, no great foreign emigration, and no extraordinary increase in the resources of the country, nothing but the more extensive prevalence of the preventive check to population in Norway could secure to her a smaller mortality than in other countries, however pure her air may be, or however healthy the employments of her people.

Norway seems to have been antiently divided into large estates or farms, called Gores; and as, according to the law of succession, all the brothers divide the property equally, it is a matter of surprise, and a proof how slowly the population has hitherto increased, that these estates have not been more subdivided. Many of them are indeed now divided into half gores, and quarter gores, and some still lower; but it has in general been the custom, on the death of the father, for a commission to value the estate at a low rate, and if the eldest son can pay his brothers' and sisters'[6] shares, according to this valuation, by mortgaging his estate, or otherwise, the whole is awarded to him; and the force of habit, and natural indolence, too frequently prompt him to conduct the farm after the manner of his forefathers, with few or no efforts at improvement.

Another great obstacle to the improvement of farms in Norway, is a law which is called Odel's right, by which, any lineal descendant can repurchase an estate which had been sold out of the family, by paying the original purchase-money. Formerly, collateral as well as lineal descendants had this power, and the time was absolutely unlimited, so that the purchaser could never consider himself as secure from claims. Afterwards, the time was limited to twenty years, and, in 1771, it was still further limited to ten years, and all the collateral branches were excluded. It must, however, be an uninterrupted possession of ten years; for if before the expiration of this term, a person who has a right to claim under the law, give notice to the possessor that he does not forego his claim, though he is not then in a condition to make the purchase, the possessor is obliged to wait six years more before he is perfectly secure. And as, in addition to this, the eldest in the lineal descent may reclaim an estate that has been repurchased by a younger brother, the law, even in its present amended state, must be considered as a very great bar to improvement; and in its former state when the time was unlimited, and the sale of estates in this way was more frequent, it seems as if it must have been a most complete obstacle to the amelioration of farms, and obviously accounts for the very slow increase of the population in Norway for many centuries.

A further difficulty in the way of clearing and cultivating the land, arises from the fears of the great timber merchants respecting the woods. When a farm has been divided among children and grandchildren, as each

6. A daughter's portion is the half of the son's portion.

proprietor has a certain right in the woods, each, in general, endeavours to cut as much as he can; and the timber is thus felled before it is fit, and the woods spoiled. To prevent this, the merchants buy large tracts of woods of the farmers, who enter into a contract, that the farm shall not be any further subdivided or more housemen placed upon it; at least, that if the number of families be increased, they should have no right in the woods. It is said, that the merchants who make these purchases are not very strict, provided the smaller farmers and housemen do not take timber for their houses. The farmers who fell these tracts of wood are obliged by law to reserve to themselves the right of pasturing their cattle, and of cutting timber sufficient for their houses, repairs, and firing.

A piece of ground round a houseman's dwelling cannot be inclosed for cultivation, without an application, first, to the proprietor of the woods, declaring that the spot is not fit for timber, and afterwards to a magistrate of the district, whose leave on this occasion is also necessary, probably for the purpose of ascertaining whether the leave of the proprietor had been duly obtained.

In addition to these obstacles to improved cultivation, which may be considered as artificial, the nature of the country presents an insuperable obstacle to a cultivation and population in any respect proportioned to the surface of the soil. The Norwegians, though not in a nomadic state, are still in a considerable degree in the pastoral state, and depend very much upon their cattle. The high grounds that border on the mountains, are absolutely unfit to bear corn, and the only use to which they can be put, is to pasture cattle upon them for three or four months during the summer. The farmers, accordingly, send all their cattle to these grounds at this time of the year, under the care of a part of their families; and it is here that they make all their butter and cheese for sale, or for their own consumption. The great difficulty is to support their cattle during the long winter, and for this purpose, it is necessary that a considerable proportion of the most fertile land in the vallies should be mowed for grass. If too much of it were taken into tillage, the number of cattle must be proportionably diminished, and the greatest part of the higher grounds would become absolutely useless; and it might be a question, in that case, whether the country, upon the whole, would support a greater population.

Notwithstanding, however, all these obstacles, there is a very considerable capacity of improvement in Norway, and of late years it has been called into action. I heard it remarked by a professor at Copenhagen, that the reason why the agriculture of Norway had advanced so slowly, was, that there were no gentlemen farmers who might set examples of improved cultivation, and break the routine of ignorance and prejudice in the conduct of farms, that had been handed down from father to son for successive ages. From what I saw of Norway, I should say that this want is now, in some degree, supplied. Many intelligent merchants and well-informed general officers are at present engaged in farming. In the country round Christiania, very great improvements have taken place in the system of agriculture; and even in the neighbourhood of Drontheim the culture of artificial grasses has been introduced, which, in a country where so much winter feed is necessary for cattle, is a point of the highest importance. Almost every where the cultivation of potatoes has succeeded, and they are growing more and more into general use, though in the distant parts of the country they are not yet relished by the common people.

It has been more the custom of late years, than formerly, to divide farms; and, as the vent for commodities in Norway is not perhaps sufficient to encourage the complete cultivation of large farms, this division of them has probably contributed to the improvement of the land. It seems, indeed, to be universally agreed, among those who are in a situation to be competent judges, that the agriculture of Norway in general has advanced considerably of late years; and the registers shew that the population has followed with more than equal pace. On an average of ten years, from 1775 to 1784, the proportion of births to deaths was 141 to 100.[7] But this seems to have been rather too rapid an increase; as the following year, 1785, was a year of scarcity and sickness, in which the deaths considerably exceeded the births; and for four years afterwards, particularly in 1789, the excess of births was not great. But in the five years from 1789 to 1794, the proportion of births to deaths was nearly 150 to 100.[8]

Many of the most thinking and best informed persons express their apprehensions on this subject, and on the probable result of the new regulations respecting the enrolments for the army, and the apparent intention of the court of Denmark to encourage, at all events, the population. No very unfavourable season has occurred in Norway since 1785; but it is feared that, in the event of such a season, the most severe distress might be felt from the increased population.

Norway is, I believe, almost the only country in Europe where a traveller will hear any apprehensions expressed of a redundant population, and where the danger to the happiness of the lower classes of people, from this cause, is, in some degree, seen and understood. This obviously arises from

7. Thaarup's Statistik der Danischen Monarchie, vol. ii. p. 4.
8. Id. table i. p. 4.

the smallness of the population altogether, and the consequent narrowness of the subject. If our attention were confined to one parish, and there were no power of emigrating from it, the most careless observer could not fail to remark that if all married at twenty, it would be perfectly impossible for the farmers, however carefully they might improve their land, to find employment and food for those that would grow up; but, when a great number of these parishes are added together in a populous kingdom, the largeness of the subject, and the power of moving from place to place, obscure and confuse our view. We lose sight of a truth which before appeared completely obvious; and, in a most unaccountable manner, attribute to the aggregate quantity of land a power of supporting people beyond comparison greater than the sum of all its parts.

CHAP. II.

Of the Checks to Population in Sweden.

SWEDEN is, in many respects, in a state similar to that of Norway. A very large proportion of its population is, in the same manner, employed in agriculture; and in most parts of the country the married labourers who work for the farmers, like the housemen of Norway, have a certain portion of land for their principal maintenance, while the young men and women that are unmarried, live as servants in the farmers' families. This state of things, however, is not so complete and general, as in Norway; and from this cause, added to the greater extent and population of the country, the superior size of the towns, and the greater variety of employment, it has not occasioned, in the same degree, the prevalence of the preventive check to population, and consequently the positive check has operated with more force, or the mortality has been greater.

According to a paper published by M. Wargentin in the *Memoires abrégés de l'Academie Royale des Sciences de Stockholm*,[1] the yearly average mortality in all Sweden, for nine years, ending in 1663, was to the population as 1 to $34\frac{3}{4}$.[2] M. Wargentin furnished Dr. Price with a continuance of these tables, and an average of 21 years gives a result of 1 to $34\frac{3}{8}$, nearly the same.[3] This is undoubtedly a very great mortality, considering the large proportion of the population in Sweden which is employed in agriculture. It appears from some calculations in Cantzlaer's account of Sweden, that the inhabitants of the towns are to the inhabitants of the country only as 1 to 13;[4] whereas, in well-peopled countries, the proportion is often as 1 to 3, or above.[5] The superior mortality of towns, therefore, could not much affect the general proportion in Sweden.

The average mortality of villages, according to Susmilch, is 1 in 40.[6] In Prussia and Pomerania, which include a number of great and unhealthy towns, and where the inhabitants of the towns are to the inhabitants of the

---

1. 1 vol. 4to. printed at Paris, 1772.   2. P. 27.
3. Price's Observ. on Revers. Paym. vol. ii. p. 126.
4. Memoires pour servir a la connoissance des affaires politiques et économiques du Royaume de Swede, 4to. 1776, ch. vi. p. 187. This work is considered as very correct in its information, and is in great credit at Stockholm.
5. Susmilch's Gottliche Ordnung, vol. i. ch. ii. sect. xxxiv. edit. 1798.
6. Susmilch's Gottliche Ordnung, vol. i. ch.ii. sect.xxxv. p. 91.

country as 1 to 4, the mortality is less than 1 in 37.[7] The mortality in Norway, as has been mentioned before, is 1 in 48, which is in a very extraordinary degree less than in Sweden, though the inhabitants of the towns in Norway bear a greater proportion to the inhabitants of the country than in Sweden.[8] The towns in Sweden are indeed larger, and more unhealthy, than in Norway; but there is no reason to think that the country is naturally more unfavourable to the duration of human life. The mountains of Norway are in general not habitable. The only peopled parts of the country are the vallies. Many of these vallies are deep and narrow clefts in the mountains; and the cultivated spots in the bottom, surrounded as they are by almost perpendicular cliffs of a prodigious height,[9] which intercept the rays of the fun for many hours, do not seem as if they could be so healthy, as the more exposed and drier soil of Sweden.

It is difficult, therefore, entirely to account for the mortality of Sweden, without supposing that, the habits of the people, and the continual cry of the government for an increase of subjects, tend to press the population too hard against the limits of subsistence, and, consequently, to produce diseases which are the necessary effect of poverty and bad nourishment; and this, from observation, appears to be really the case.

Sweden does not produce food sufficient for its population. Its annual want in the article of grain, according to a calculation made from the years 1768 and 1772, is 440,000 tuns.[10] This quantity, or near it, has in general been imported from foreign countries, besides pork, butter, and cheese, to a considerable amount.[11]

The distillation of spirits in Sweden is supposed to consume above 400,000 tuns of grain; and when this distillation has been prohibited by government, a variation in defect appears in the tables of importations;[12]

---

7. Id. vol. iii. p. 60.

8. Thaarup's Statistik der Danischen Monarchie, vol. ii. tab. ii. p. 5. 1765.

9. Some of these vallies are strikingly picturesque. The principal road from Christiania to Drontheim leads, for nearly 180 English miles, through a continued valley of this kind, by the side of a very fine river, which in one part stretches out into the extensive lake Miosen. I am inclined to believe that there is not any river in all Europe, the course of which, affords such a constant succession of beautiful and romantic scenery. It goes under different names in different parts. The verdure in the Norway vallies is peculiarly soft, the foliage of the trees luxuriant, and in summer, no traces appear of a northern climate.

10. Memoires du Royaume de Suede, table xvii. p. 174.

11. Id. c. vi. p. 198.

12. Id. table xlii. p. 418. c. vi. p. 201. I did not find out exactly the measure of the Swedish tun. It is rather less than our sack or half quarter.

but no great variations in excess are observable, to supply the deficiencies in years of scanty harvests, which, it is well known, occur frequently. In years the most abundant, when the distillation has been free, it is asserted, that 388,000 tuns have in general been imported.[13] It follows, therefore, that the Swedes consume all the produce of their best years, and nearly 400,000 more; and that, in their worst years, their consumption must be diminished by nearly the whole deficiency in their crops. The mass of the people appears to be too poor to purchase nearly the same quantity of corn at a very advanced price. There is no adequate encouragement, therefore, to corn merchants to import in great abundance; and the effect of a deficiency of one fourth, or one third, in the crops, is, to oblige the labourer to content himself with nearly three-fourths or two thirds of the corn which he used before, and to supply the rest by the use of any substitutes which necessity, the mother of invention, may suggest. I have said, nearly, because it is difficult to suppose that the importations should not be something greater in years of scarcity than in common years, though no marked differences of this kind appear in the tables published by Cantzlaer. The greatest importation, according to these tables, was in the year 1768, when it amounted to 590,265 tuns of grain;[14] but even this greatest importation is only 150,000 tuns above the average wants of the country; and what is this, to supply a deficiency of one fourth or one third of a crop? The whole importation is indeed in this respect trifling.

The population of Sweden, at the time that Cantzlaer wrote, was about two millions and an half.[15] He allows four tuns of grain to a man.[16] Upon this supposition the annual wants of Sweden would be ten millions of tuns, and four or five hundred thousand would go but a little way in supplying a deficiency of two millions and a half, or three millions; and, if we take only the difference from the average importation, it will appear, that the assistance which the Swedes receive from importation in a year of scarcity is perfectly futile.

The consequence of this state of things is, that the population of Sweden is in a peculiar manner affected by every variation of the seasons; and we cannot be surprised at a very curious and instructive remark of M. Wargentin, that the registers of Sweden shew, that the population and the mortality increase or decrease, according as the harvests are abundant or deficient. From the nine years of which he had given tables, he instances the following.

13. Memoires du Royaume de Suede, c. vi. p. 201.
14. Memoires du Royaume de Suede, table xlii. p. 418.
15. Id. ch. vi. p. 184.   16. Id. p. 196.

		Marriages.	Births.	Deaths.
Barren	1757	18799	81878	68054
years.	1758	19584	83299	74370
Abundant	1759	23210	85579	62662
years.	1760	23383	90635	60083.[17]

Here it appears, that in the year 1760 the births were to the deaths as 15 to 10; but in the year 1758 only as 11 to 10. By referring to the enumerations of the population in 1757 and 1760,[18] which M. Wargentin has given, it appears, that the number of marriages in the year 1760, in proportion to the whole population, was as 1 to 101; in the year 1757, only as 1 to about 124. The deaths in 1760, were to the whole population as 1 to 39; in 1757 as 1 to 32, and in 1758 as 1 to 31.

In making some observations on the tables which had been produced, M. Wargentin says, that in the unhealthy years about 1 in 29 have died annually, and in the healthy years 1 in 39; and that, taking a middle term, the average mortality might be considered at 1 in 36.[19] But this inference does not appear to be just, as a mean between 29 and 39 would give 34; and indeed the tables which he has himself brought forward, contradict an average mortality of 1 in 36, and prove that it is about 1 in $34\frac{3}{4}$.

The proportion of yearly marriages to the whole population, appears to be, on an average, nearly as 1 to 112, and to vary between the extremes of 1 to 101, and 1 to 124, according to the temporary prospect of a support for a family. Probably, indeed, it varies between much greater extremes, as the period from which these calculations are made is merely for nine years.

In another paper which M. Wargentin published in the same collection, he again remarks, that in Sweden, the years which are the most fruitful in produce, are the most fruitful in children.[20]

If accurate observations were made in other countries, it is highly probable that differences of the same kind would appear, though not to the same extent.[21] With regard to Sweden, they clearly prove that its population has a very strong tendency to increase; and that it is not only always ready to follow with the greatest alertness any average increase in the means of subsistence, but that it makes a start forwards at every temporary and oc-

17. Memoires Abrégés de l'Académie de Stockholm, p. 29.
18. Id. p. 21, 22.   19. Id. p. 29.
20. Memoires abrégés de l'Acad. de Stockholm, p. 31.
21. This has been confirmed, with regard to England, by the abstracts of parish registers which have lately been published. The years 1795 and 1800, are marked by a diminution of marriages and births, and an increase of deaths.

casional increase of food, by which means, it is continually going beyond the average increase, and is repressed by the periodical returns of severe want, and the diseases arising from it.

Yet notwithstanding this constant and striking tendency to overflowing numbers, strange to say! the government and the political economists of Sweden, are continually calling out for population, population. Cantzlaer observes, that the government, not having the power of inducing strangers to settle in the country, or of augmenting at pleasure the number of births, has occupied itself since 1748 in every measure which appeared proper to increase the population of the country.[22] But suppose, that the government really possessed the power of inducing strangers to settle, or of increasing the number of births at pleasure, what would be the consequence? If the strangers were not such as to introduce a better system of agriculture, they would either be starved themselves, or cause more of the Swedes to be starved; and if the yearly number of births were considerably increased, it appears to me perfectly clear, from the tables of M. Wargentin, that the principal effect would be merely an increase of mortality. The actual population might, perhaps, even be diminished by it, as when epidemicks have once been generated by bad nourishment and crowded houses, they do not always stop when they have taken off the redundant population, but take off with it a part, and sometimes a very considerable part, of that which the country might be able properly to support.

In all very northern climates, in which the principal business of agriculture must necessarily be compressed into the small space of a few summer months, it will almost inevitably happen, that during this period a want of hands is felt; but this temporary want should be carefully distinguished from a real and effectual demand for labour, which includes the power of giving employment and support through the whole year, and not merely for two or three months. The population of Sweden in the natural course of its increase, will always be ready fully to answer this effectual demand; and a supply beyond it, whether from strangers or an additional number of births, could only be productive of misery.

It is asserted by Swedish authors, that a given number of men and of days, produces, in Sweden, only a third part of what is produced by the same number of each, in some other countries;[23] and heavy accusations are in consequence brought against the national industry. Of the general grounds for such accusations, a stranger cannot be a competent judge; but

22. Memoires du Royaume de Suede, c. vi. p. 188.
23. Memoires du Royaume de Suede, (Cantzlaer) ch. vi. p. 191.

in the present instance, it appears to me, that more ought to be attributed to the climate and soil, than to an actual want of industry in the natives. For a large portion of the year their exertions are necessarily cramped by the severity of the climate; and during the time when they are able to engage in agricultural operations, the natural indifference of the soil, and the extent of surface required for a given produce, inevitably employ a great proportional quantity of labour. It is well known in England, that a farm of large extent consisting of a poor soil, is worked at a much greater expence for the same produce, than a small one of rich land. The natural poverty of the soil in Sweden, generally speaking, cannot be denied.

In a journey up the western side of the country, and afterwards in crossing it from Norway to Stockholm, and thence up the eastern coast to the passage over to Finland, I confess that I saw fewer marks of a want of national industry than I should have expected. As far as I could judge, I very seldom saw any land uncultivated which would have been cultivated in England, and I certainly saw many spots of land in tillage, which never would have been touched with a plough here. These were lands in which, every five or ten yards, there were large stones or rocks, round which the plough must necessarily be turned, or be lifted over them; and the one or the other is generally done according to their size. The plough is very light, and drawn by one horse, and in ploughing among the stumps of the trees when they are low, the general practice is to lift it over them. The man who holds the plough does this very nimbly, with little or no stop to the horse.

Of the value of those lands for tillage, which are at present covered with immense forests, I could be no judge; but both the Swedes and the Norwegians are accused of clearing these woods away too precipitately, and without previously considering what is likely to be the real value of the land when cleared. The consequence is, that, for the sake of one good crop of rye, which may always be obtained from the manure afforded by the ashes of the burnt trees, much growing timber is sometimes spoiled, and the land, perhaps, afterwards, becomes almost entirely useless. After the crop of rye has been obtained, the common practice is to turn cattle in upon the grass, which may accidentally grow up. If the land be naturally good, the feeding of the cattle prevents fresh firs from rising; but if it be bad, the cattle of course cannot remain long in it, and the seeds with which every wind is surcharged, sow the ground again thickly with firs.

On observing many spots of this kind both in Norway and Sweden, I could not help being struck with the idea, that, though for other reasons, it was very little probable, such appearances certainly made it seem possible, that these countries might have been better peopled formerly, than at present; and that lands, which are now covered with forests, might have produced corn a thousand years ago. Wars, plagues, or that greater depopulator than either, a tyrannical government, might have suddenly destroyed, or expelled, the greatest part of the inhabitants, and a neglect of the land for twenty or thirty years in Norway or Sweden, would produce a very strange difference in the face of the country. But this is merely an idea which I could not help mentioning, but which the reader already knows has not had weight enough with me, to make me suppose the fact in any degree probable.

To return to the agriculture of Sweden. Independently of any deficiency in the national industry, there are certainly some circumstances in the political regulations of the country, which tend to impede the natural progress of its cultivation. There are still some burdensome corvées remaining, which the possessors of certain lands are obliged to perform for the domains of the crown.[24] The posting of the country is undoubtedly very cheap and convenient to the traveller; but is conducted in a manner to occasion a great waste of labour to the farmer, both in men and horses. It is calculated by the Swedish economists, that the labour which would be saved by the abolition of this system alone, would produce annually 300,000 tuns of grain.[25] The very great distance of the markets in Sweden, and the very incomplete division of labour which is almost a necessary consequence of it, occasion also a great waste of time and exertion. And, if there be no marked want of diligence and activity among the Swedish peasants, there is certainly a want of knowledge in the best modes of regulating the rotation of their crops, and of manuring and improving their lands.[26]

If the government were employed in removing these impediments, and in endeavours to encourage and direct the industry of the farmers, and circulate the best information on agricultural subjects, it would do much more for the population of the country, than by the establishment of five hundred foundling hospitals.

According to Cantzlaer, the principal measures in which the government had been engaged for the encouragement of the population, were, the establishment of colleges of medicine, and of lying-in and foundling hospitals.[27] The establishment of colleges of medicine, for the cure of the poor, gratis, may in many cases be extremely beneficial, and was so, probably, in the particular circumstances of Sweden; but the example of the hospitals of France, which have the same object, may create a doubt, whether even such

---

24. Memoires du Royaume de Suede, ch. vi. p. 202.   25. Id. p. 204.
26. Memoires du Royaume de Suede, ch. vi.   27. Id. p. 188.

establishments are universally to be recommended. Lying-in hospitals, as far as they have an effect, are probably rather prejudicial than otherwise, as, according to the principle on which they are generally conducted, their tendency is certainly to encourage vice. Foundling hospitals, whether they attain their professed and immediate object, or not, are in every view hurtful to the state; but the mode in which they operate, I shall have occasion to discuss more particularly in another chapter.

The Swedish government, however, has not been exclusively employed in measures of this nature. By an edict in 1776, the commerce of grain was rendered completely free throughout the whole interior of the country, and, with regard to the province of Scania, which grows more than its consumption, exportation free of every duty was allowed.[28] Till this period, the agriculture of the southern provinces had been checked by the want of vent for their grain, on account of the difficulty of transport, and the absolute prohibition of selling it to foreigners at any price. The northern provinces are still under some little difficulties in this respect, though, as they never grow a quantity sufficient for their consumption, these difficulties are not so much felt.[29] It may be observed, however, in general, that there is no check more fatal to improving cultivation, than any difficulty in the vent of its produce, which prevents the farmer from being able to obtain, in good years, a price for his corn, not much below the general average.

But what perhaps has contributed more than any other cause to the increasing population of Sweden, is the abolition of a law in 1748, which limited the number of persons to each henman, or farm.[30] The object of this law appears to have been, to force the children of the proprietors to undertake the clearing and cultivation of fresh lands, by which, it was thought, that the whole country would be sooner improved. But it appeared from experience, that these children being without sufficient funds for such undertakings, were obliged to seek their fortune in some other way, and great numbers, in consequence, are said to have emigrated. A father may now, however, not only divide his landed property into as many shares as he thinks proper; but these divisions are particularly recommended by the government, and, considering the immense size of the Swedish henmans, and the impossibility of their being cultivated completely by one family, such divisions must in every point of view be highly useful.

The population of Sweden in 1751, was 2,229,661.[31] In 1799, according to an account which I received in Stockholm from professor Nicander, the

28. Id. p. 204.   29. Memoires du Royaume de Suede, ch. vi. p. 204.
30. Id. p. 177.   31. Id. p. 184.

successor to M. Wargentin, it was 3,043,731. This is a very considerable addition to the permanent population of the country, which has followed a proportional increase in the produce of the soil, as the imports of corn are not greater than they were formerly, and there is no reason to think that the condition of the people is, on an average, worse.

This increase, however, has not gone forwards, without periodical checks, which, if they have not, for the time, entirely stopped its progress, have always retarded the rate of it. How often these checks have recurred during the last 50 years, I am not furnished with sufficient data to be able to say, but I can mention some of them. From the paper of M. Wargentin,[32] already quoted in this chapter, it appears, that the years 1757 and 1758, were barren, and comparatively mortal years. If we were to judge from the increased importation of 1768,[33] this would also appear to be an unproductive year. According to the additional tables with which M. Wargentin furnished Dr. Price, the years 1771, 1772, and 1773, were particularly mortal.[34] The year 1789 must have been very highly so, as, in the accounts which I received from professor Nicander, this year alone materially affected the average proportion of births to deaths for the twenty years ending in 1795. This proportion, including the year 1789, was 100 to 77; but abstracting it, was 100 to 75; which is a great difference for one year to make in an average of twenty. To conclude the catalogue, the year 1799, when I was in Sweden, must have been a very fatal one. In the provinces bordering on Norway, the peasants called it the worst that they had ever remembered. The cattle had all suffered extremely during the winter, from the drought of the preceding year; and, in July, about a month before the harvest, a considerable portion of the people was living upon bread made of the inner bark of the fir, and of dried sorrel, absolutely without any mixture of meal, to make it more palatable and nourishing. The sallow looks, and melancholy countenances of the people, betrayed the unwholesomeness of their nourishment. Many had died, but the full effects of such a diet had not then been felt. They would probably appear afterwards in the form of some epidemick sickness.

The patience with which the lower classes of people in Sweden bear these severe pressures, is perfectly astonishing, and can only arise from their being left entirely to their own resources, and from the belief that they are submitting to the great law of necessity, and not to the caprices of

32. Memoires de l'Academic de Stockholm, p. 29.
33. Memoires du Royaume de Suede, table xlii.
34. Price's Observ. on Revers. Pay. vol. ii. p. 125.

their rulers. Most of the married labourers, as has been before observed, cultivate a small portion of land; and when, from an unfavourable season, their crops fail or their cattle die, they see the cause of their want, and bear it as the visitation of providence. Every man will submit, with becoming patience, to evils which he believes to arise from the general laws of nature; but when the vanity and mistaken benevolence of the government and the higher classes of society, have, by a perpetual interference with the concerns of the lower classes, endeavoured to persuade them, that all the good which they enjoy is conferred upon them by their rulers and rich benefactors, it is very natural that they should attribute all the evil which they suffer to the same sources, and patience, under such circumstances, cannot reasonably be expected. Though to avoid still greater evils, we may be allowed to repress this impatience by force, if it shew itself in overt acts, yet the impatience itself appears to be clearly justified in this case; and those are in a great degree answerable for its consequences, whose conduct has tended evidently to encourage it.

Though the Swedes had supported the severe dearth of 1799 with extraordinary resignation; yet afterwards, on an edict of the government to prohibit the distillation of spirits, it is said that there were considerable commotions in the country. The measure itself was certainly calculated to benefit the people; and the manner in which it was received, affords a curious proof of the different temper with which people bear an evil, arising from the laws of nature, or a privation caused by the edicts of a government.

The sickly periods in Sweden which have retarded the rate of its increase in population, appear in general to have arisen from the unwholesome nourishment occasioned by severe want. And this want has been caused by unfavourable seasons falling upon a country which was without any reserved store, either in its general exports, or in the liberal division of food to the labourer in common years, and which was therefore peopled fully up to its produce, before the occurrence of the scanty harvest. Such a state of things is a clear proof, that if, as some of the Swedish economists assert, their country ought to have a population of nine or ten millions,[35] they have nothing further to do, than to make it produce food sufficient for such a number, and they may rest perfectly assured that they will not want mouths to eat it, without the assistance of lying-in, and foundling hospitals.

35. Memoires du Royaume de Suede, ch. vi. p. 196.

Notwithstanding the mortal year of 1789, it appeared from the accounts which I received from professor Nicander, that the general healthiness of the country had increased. The average mortality for the twenty years ending 1795, was 1 in 37, instead of 1 in less than 35, which had been the average of the preceding twenty years. As the rate of increase had not been accelerated in the twenty years ending in 1795, the diminished mortality must have been occasioned by the increased operation of the preventive check. Another calculation which I received from the professor, seemed to confirm this supposition. According to M.Wargentin, as quoted by Susmilch,[36] standing marriages produced yearly 1 child; but in the latter period, the proportion of standing marriages to annual births, was as $5\frac{1}{10}$ and subtracting illegitimate children, as $5\frac{3}{10}$ to 1; a proof, that in the latter period the marriages had not been quite so early and so prolifick.

36. Gottliche Ordnung, vol. i. c. vi. s. 120. p. 231.

CHAP. III.

Of the Checks to Population in Russia.

THE lists of births, deaths, and marriages, in Russia, present such extraordinary results, that it is impossible not to receive them with a considerable degree of suspicion; at the same time, the regular manner in which they have been collected, and their agreement with each other in different years, entitle them to attention.

In a paper presented in 1786, by B. F. Herman, to the academy of Petersburgh, and published in the *Nova Acta Academiæ, tom. iv.* a comparison is made of the births, deaths, and marriages, in the different provinces and towns of the empire, and the following proportions are given:

In Petersburgh the births are to the burials, as	13 to	10
In the government of Moscow, - -	21 —	10
District of Moscow, excepting the town,	21 —	10
Tver, - - - - - -	26 —	10
Novogorod, - - - - -	20 —	10
Pskovsk, - - - - -	22 —	10
Resan, - - - - - -	20 —	10
Veronesch, - - - - -	29 —	10
Archbishopric of Vologda, - -	23 —	10
Kostroma, - - - - -	20 —	10
Archangel, - - - - -	13 —	10
Tobolsk, - - - - -	21 —	10
Town of Tobolsk, - - - -	13 —	10
Reval, - - - - - -	11 —	10
Vologda, - - - - -	12 —	10

Some of these proportions, it will be observed, are extraordinarily high. In Veronesch, for instance, the births are to the deaths, nearly as 3 to 1, which is as great a proportion, I believe, as ever was known in America. The average result, however, of these proportions, has been confirmed by subsequent observations. Mr. Tooke, in his View of the Russian Empire, makes the general proportion of births to burials throughout the whole country, as 225 to 100,[1] which is 2 and $\frac{1}{4}$ to 1; and this proportion is taken from the lists of 1793.[2]

---

1. Vol. ii. b. iii. p. 162.   2. Id. p. 145.

From the number of yearly marriages, and yearly births, M. Herman draws the following conclusions:

In Petersburgh one marriage yields -	4 children,
In the government of Moscow, about -	3
Tver, - - - - - -	3
Novogorod, - - - - -	3
Pskovsk, - - - - - -	3
Resan, - - - - - -	3
Veronesch, - - - - - -	4
Vologda, - - - - - -	4
Kostroma, - - - - - -	3
Archangel, - - - - - -	4
Reval, - - - - - -	4
Government of Tobolsk, - - -	4
Town of Tobolsk, from 1768 to 1778, -	3
.... from 1779 to 1783, -	5
.... in 1783, - - -	6

M. Herman observes, that the fruitfulness of marriages in Russia, does not exceed that of other countries, though the mortality is much less; as appears from the following proportions, drawn from a rough calculation of the number of inhabitants in each government:

In Petersburgh, - - -	1 in 28 dies annually.
In the government of Moscow, -	1 — 32
District of Moscow, - -	1 in 74 dies annually.
Tver, - - - - -	1 — 75
Novogorod, - - - -	1 — $68\frac{6}{7}$
Pskovsk, - - - -	1 — $70\frac{4}{5}$
Resan, - - - - -	1 — 50
Vcronesch, - - - -	1 — 79
Vologda, - - - -	1 — 65
Kostroma, - - - -	1 — 59
Archangel, - - - -	1 — $28\frac{3}{5}$
Reval, - - - - -	1 — 29
Government of Tobolsk, - -	1 — 44
Town of Tobolsk, - - -	1 — 32
.... in 1783,	1 — $22\frac{1}{4}$

It may be concluded, M. Herman says, that in the greatest number of the Russian provinces, the yearly mortality is 1 in 60.[3]

3. Nova Acta Academiæ, tom. iv.

This average number is so high, and some of the proportions in the particular provinces are so extraordinary, that it is almost impossible to believe them accurate. They have been nearly confirmed, however, by subsequent lists, which, according to Mr. Tooke, make the general mortality in all Russia, 1 in 58.[4] But Mr. Tooke himself seems to doubt the accuracy of this particular department of the registers; and I have since heard from good authority, that there is reason to believe, that the omissions in the burials are in all the provinces much greater than the omissions in the births, and consequently, that the very great excess of births, and very small mortality, are more apparent than real. It is supposed that many children, particularly in the Ukraine, are privately interred by their fathers without information to the priest. The numerous and repeated levies of recruits take off great numbers whose deaths are not recorded. From the frequent emigrations of whole families to different parts of the empire, and the transportation of malefactors to Siberia, great numbers necessarily die on journies, or in parts where no regular lists are kept; and some omissions are attributed to the neglect of the parish priests who have an interest in recording the births, but not the deaths.

To these reasons I should add, that the population of each province, is probably estimated by the number of boors belonging to each estate in it; but it is well known that a great part of them has leave to reside in the towns. Their births, therefore, appear in the province, but their deaths do not. The apparent mortality of the towns is not proportionably increased by this emigration, because it is estimated according to actual enumeration. The bills of mortality in the towns express correctly the numbers dying out of a certain number known to be actually present in these towns; but the bills of mortality in the provinces, purporting to express the numbers dying out of the estimated population of the province, do really only express the numbers dying out of a much smaller population, because a considerable part of the estimated population is absent.

In Petersburgh, it appeared by an enumeration in 1784, that the number of males was 126,827, and of females only 65,619.[5] The proportion of males was therefore very nearly double, arising from the numbers who came to the town, to earn their capitation tax, leaving their families in the country, and from the custom among the lords, of retaining a prodigious number of their boors as household servants, in Petersburgh and Moscow.

4. View of the Russian Empire, vol. ii. b. iii, p. 148.
5. Memoire par W. L. Krafft, Nova Acta Academiæ tom. iv.

The number of births in proportion to the whole population in Russia, is not different from a common average in other countries, being about 1 in 26.[6]

According to the paper of M. Herman, already quoted, the proportion of boys dying within the first year, is, at Petersburgh, $\frac{1}{5}$. In the government of Tobolsk $\frac{1}{10}$. In the town of Tobolsk $\frac{1}{5}$. In Vologda $\frac{1}{14}$. In Novogorod $\frac{1}{31}$. In Veronesch $\frac{1}{24}$. In Archangel $\frac{1}{5}$. The very small mortality of infants in some of these provinces, particularly, as the calculation does not seem to be liable to much error, makes the smallness of the general mortality more credible. In Sweden, throughout the whole country, the proportion of infants which dies within the first year, is $\frac{1}{5}$ or more.[7]

The proportion of yearly marriages in Russia to the whole population, is, according to M. Herman, in the towns, about 1 in 100, and in the provinces about 1 in 70 or 80. According to Mr. Tooke, in the fifteen governments of which he had lists, the proportion was 1 in 92.[8] This is not very different from other countries. In Petersburgh, indeed, the proportion was 1 in 140;[9] but this is clearly accounted for, by what has already been said of the extraordinary number of the males in comparison of the females.

The registers for the city of Petersburgh are supposed to be such as can be entirely depended upon; and these tend to prove the general salubrity of the climate. But there is one fact recorded in them, which is directly contrary to what has been observed in all other countries. This is a much greater mortality of female children than of male. In the period from 1781 to 1785, of 1000 boys born, 147 only, died within the first year, but of the same number of girls 310.[10] The proportion is as 10 to 21, which is inconceivable, and must indeed have been, in some measure, accidental, as, in the preceding periods, the proportion was only as 10 to 14; but even this is very extraordinary, as it has been generally remarked, that, in every stage of life, except during the period of childbearing, the mortality among females is less than among males. The climate of Sweden does not appear to be very different from that of Russia; and M. Wargentin observes, with respect to the Swedish tables, that it appears from them, that the smaller mortality of females, is not merely owing to a more regular and less laborious life, but is a natural law which operates constantly from infancy to old age.[11]

6. Tooke's View of Russian Empire, vol. ii. b. iii. p. 147.

7. Memoires Abrégés de l'Academie de Stockholm, p. 28.

8. View of Russ. Emp. vol. ii. b. iii. p. 146.

9. Memoire par W. L. Krafft, Nova Acta Academiæ, tom. iv.

10. Id. tom. iv.   11. Memoires Abrégés de l'Academie de Stockholm, p. 28.

According to M. Krafft,[12] the half of all that are born in Petersburgh, live to 25; which shews a degree of healthiness in early life very unusual for so large a town; but after twenty, a mortality, much greater than in any other town in Europe, takes place, which is justly attributed to the immoderate use of brandy.[13] The mortality between 10 and 15 is so small, that only 1 in 47 males, and 1 in 29 females, die. From 20 to 25, the mortality is so great, that 1 in 9 males, and 1 in 13 females, die. The tables shew, that this extraordinary mortality is occasioned principally by pleuresies, high fevers, and consumptions. Pleuresies destroy $\frac{1}{4}$, high fevers $\frac{1}{3}$, and consumptions $\frac{1}{6}$, of the whole population. The three together take off $\frac{5}{7}$ of all that die.

The general mortality during the period from 1781 to 1785, was, according to M. Krafft, 1 in 37. In a former period, it has been 1 in 35, and in a subsequent period, when epidemick diseases prevailed, 1 in 29.[14] This average mortality is small for a large town; but there is reason to think, from a passage in M. Krafft's memoir,[15] that the deaths in the hospitals, the prisons, and in the *maison des Enfans trouvés,* are either entirely omitted, or not given with correctness; and undoubtedly, the insertion of these deaths might make a great difference in the apparent healthiness of the town.

In the *maison des Enfans trouvés* alone, the mortality is prodigious. No regular lists are published, and verbal communications are always liable to some uncertainty. I cannot, therefore, rely upon the information which I collected on the subject; but, from the most careful inquiries which I could make of the attendants at the house in Petersburgh, I understood that 100 a month was the common average. In the preceding winter, which was the winter of 1788, it had not been uncommon to bury 18 a day. The average number received in the day, is about 10; and though they are all sent into the country to be nursed three days after they have been in the house, yet, as many of them are brought in a dying state, the mortality must necessarily be great. The number said to be received, appears, indeed, almost incredible; but, from what I saw myself, I should be inclined to believe, that both this and the mortality before mentioned, might not be far from the truth. I was at the house about noon, and four children had been just received, one of which was evidently dying, and another did not seem as if it would long survive.

12. Nova Acta Academiæ, tom. iv.
13. Tooke's View of the Russian Empire, vol. ii. b. iii. p. 155.
14. Id. p. 151.
15. See a Note in Tooke's View of Russ. Emp. vol. ii. b. iii. p. 150.

A part of the house is destined to the purpose of a lying-in hospital, where every woman that comes is received, and no questions are asked. The children which are thus born, are brought up by nurses in the house, and are not sent into the country like the others. A mother, if she chuse it, may perform the office of nurse to her own child, in the house, but is not permitted to take it away with her. A child brought to the house, may at any time be reclaimed by its parents, if they can prove themselves able to support it; and all the children are marked and numbered on being received, that they may be known and produced to the parents, when required, who, if they cannot reclaim them, are permitted to visit them.

The country nurses receive only two roubles a month, which, as the current paper rouble is seldom worth more than half a crown, is only about fifteen pence a week; yet, the general expences are said to be 100,000 roubles a month. The regular revenues belonging to the institution are not nearly equal to this sum; but the government takes on itself the management of the whole affair, and consequently bears all the additional expences. As the children are received without any limit, it is absolutely necessary, that the expences should also be unlimited. It is evident that the most dreadful evils must result from an unlimited reception of children, and only a limited fund to support them. Such institutions, therefore, if managed properly, that is, if the extraordinary mortality do not prevent the rapid accumulation of expence, cannot exist long except under the protection of a very rich government; and even under such protection there must ultimately be a limit.

At six or seven years old the children who have been sent into the country, return to the house, where they are taught all sorts of trades, and manual operations. The common hours of working are, from 6 to 12, and from 2 till 4. The girls leave the house at 18, and the boys at 20 or 21. When the house is too full, some of those which have been sent into the country are not brought back.

The principal mortality, of course, takes place among the infants who are just received, and the children which are brought up in the house; but there is a considerable mortality among those which are returned from the country, and are in the firmest stages of life. I was, in some degree, surprised at hearing this, after having been particularly struck with the extraordinary degree of neatness, cleanliness, and sweetness, which appeared to prevail in every department. The house itself had been a palace, and all the rooms were large, airy, and even elegant. I was present while 180 boys were dining. They were all dressed very neatly; the table-cloth was clean, and each had a separate napkin to himself. The provisions appeared to be extremely good, and there was not the smallest disagreeable smell in the room. In the dormitories there was a separate bed for each child; the bedsteads were of iron without tester or curtains, and the coverlids and sheets particularly clean.

This degree of neatness, almost inconceivable in a large institution, was to be attributed principally to the present empress dowager, who interested herself in all the details of the management; and, when at Petersburgh, seldom passed a week without inspecting them in person. The mortality which takes place in spite of all these attentions, is a clear proof, that the constitution, in early youth, cannot support confinement and work for 8 hours in the day. The children had all rather a pale and sickly countenance, and if a judgment had been formed of the national beauty from the girls and boys in this establishment, it would have been most unfavourable.

It is evident, that if the deaths belonging to this institution be omitted, the bills of mortality for Petersburgh cannot give a representation, in any degree near the truth, of the real state of the city, with respect to healthiness. At the same time, it should be recollected, that some of the observations which attest its healthiness, such as the number dying in a thousand, &c. are not influenced by this circumstance; unless indeed we say, what is perhaps true, that nearly all those who would find any difficulty in rearing their children, send them to the foundling hospital, and the mortality among the children of those who are in easy circumstances, and live in comfortable houses, and airy situations, will of course be much less than a general average taken from all that are born.

The *maison des Enfans trouvés,* at Moscow, is conducted exactly upon the same principles as that at Petersburgh; and Mr. Tooke gives an account of the surprising loss of children which it had sustained in twenty years, from the time of its first establishment to the year 1786. On this occasion, he observes, that if we knew precisely the number of those who died immediately after reception, or who brought in with them the germ of dissolution, a small part only of the mortality would probably appear to be fairly attributable to the foundling-hospital; as none would be so unreasonable, as to lay the loss of these certain victims to death to the account of a philanthropical institution, which enriches the country from year to year with an ever-increasing number of healthy, active, and industrious burghers.[16]

It appears to me, however, that the greatest part of this premature mortality is clearly to be attributed to these institutions, miscalled philanthropical. If any reliance can be placed on the accounts which are given of the

16. View of the Russian Empire, vol. ii. b. iii. p. 201.

infant mortality in the Russian towns and provinces, it would appear to be unusually small. The greatness of it, therefore, at the foundling hospitals, may justly be laid to the account of institutions which encourage a mother to desert her child, at the very time, when of all others, it stands most in need of her fostering care. The frail tenure by which an infant holds its life, will not allow of a remitted attention, even for a few hours.

The surprising mortality which takes place at these two foundling hospitals of Petersburgh and Moscow, which are managed in the best possible manner, as all who have seen them, with one consent, assert, appears to me incontrovertibly to prove, that the nature of these institutions is not calculated to answer the immediate end that they have in view, which I conceive to be, the preservation of a certain number of citizens to the state, which might otherwise, perhaps, perish from poverty or false shame. It is not to be doubted, that if the children received into these hospitals, had been left to the management of their parents, taking the chance of all the difficulties in which they might be involved, a much greater proportion of them would have reached the age of manhood, and have become useful members of the state.

When we look a little deeper into this subject, it will appear, that these institutions not only fail in their immediate object, but by encouraging, in the most marked manner, habits of licentiousness, discourage marriage, and thus weaken the main spring of population. All the well-informed men with whom I conversed on this subject, at Petersburgh, agreed invariably, that the institution had produced this effect in a surprising degree. To have a child, was considered as one of the most trifling faults which a girl could commit. An English merchant at Petersburgh told me, that a Russian girl, living in his family, under a mistress, who was considered as very strict, had sent six children to the foundling hospital without the loss of her place.

It should be observed, however, that generally speaking, six children are not common in this kind of intercourse. Where habits of licentiousness prevail, the births are never in the same proportion to the number of people, as in the married state; and therefore the discouragement to marriage, arising from this licentiousness, and the diminished number of births which is the consequence of it, will much more than counterbalance any encouragement to marriage, from the prospect held out to parents of disposing of the children which they cannot support.

Considering the extraordinary mortality which occurs in these institutions, and the habits of licentiousness which they have an evident tendency to create, it may be said, perhaps, with truth, that if a person wished to check population, and were not solicitous about the means, he could not propose a more effectual measure, than the establishment of a sufficient number of foundling hospitals, unlimited in their reception of children. And with regard to the moral feelings of a nation, it is difficult to conceive that they must not be very sensibly impaired by encouraging mothers to desert their offspring, and endeavouring to teach them, that their love for their new-born infants is a prejudice, which it is the interest of their country to eradicate. An occasional child-murder, from false shame, is saved at a very high price, if it can only be done by the sacrifice of some of the best and most useful feelings of the human heart in a great part of the nation.

On the supposition that foundling hospitals attained their proposed end, the state of slavery in Russia would, perhaps, render them more justifiable in that country than in any other; because, every child brought up at the foundling hospitals becomes a free citizen, and in this capacity is likely to be more useful to the state, than if it had merely increased the number of slaves belonging to an individual proprietor. But in countries not similarly circumstanced, the most complete success in institutions of this kind would be a glaring injustice to other parts of the society. The true encouragement to marriage is, the high price of labour, and an increase of employments, which require to be supplied with proper hands; but if the principal part of these employments, apprenticeships, &c. be filled up by foundlings, the demand for labour among the legitimate part of the society must be proportionally diminished, the difficulty of supporting a family be increased, and the best encouragement to marriage removed.

Russia has great natural resources. Its produce is, in its present state, above its consumptiòn, and it wants nothing but greater freedom of industrious exertion, and an adequate vent for its commodities in the interior parts of the country, to occasion an increase of population astonishingly rapid. The principal obstacle to this, is, the vassalage, or rather slavery, of the peasants, and the ignorance and indolence, which almost necessarily accompany such a state. The fortune of a Russian nobleman is measured by the number of boors that he possesses, which in general are saleable, like cattle, and not *adscripti glebœ*. His revenue arises from a capitation tax on all the males. When the boors upon an estate are increasing, new divisions of land are made at certain intervals, and either more is taken into cultivation, or the old shares are subdivided. Each family is awarded such a portion of land as it can properly cultivate, and will enable it to pay the tax. It is evidently the interest of the boor not to improve his lands much, and appear to get considerably more than is necessary to support his family and pay the poll-tax; because the natural consequence will be, that in the next division that takes place, the farm, which he before possessed, will be considered as capable of supporting two families, and he will be deprived of the half of it. The indolent cultivation that such a state of things must produce, is easily conceivable. When a boor is deprived of much of the land which he had before used, he makes complaints of inability to pay his tax, and demands permission for himself, or his sons, to go and earn it in the towns. This permission is in general eagerly sought after, and is granted without much difficulty by the seigneurs, in consideration of a small increase of the poll-tax. The consequence is, that the lands in the country are left half cultivated, and the genuine spring of population impaired in its source.

A Russian nobleman at Petersburgh, of whom I asked some questious, respecting the management of his estate, told me, that he never troubled himself to inquire whether it was properly cultivated or not, which he seemed to consider as a matter in which he was not in the smallest degree concerned. *Cela m'est egal,* says he, *cela me fait ni bien ni mal.* He gave his boors permission to earn their tax how and where they liked, and as long as he received it, he was satisfied. But it is evident, that, by this kind of conduct, he sacrificed the future population of his estate, and the con-sequent future increase of his revenues, to considerations of indolence and present convenience.

It is certain, however, that of late years many noblemen have attended more to the improvement and population of their estates, instigated, prin-cipally, by the precepts and examples of the empress Catherine, who made the greatest exertions to advance the cultivation of the country. Her im-mense importations of German settlers, not only contributed to people her state with free citizens, instead of slaves, but what was perhaps of still more importance, to set an example of industry, and of modes of directing that industry, totally unknown before to the Russian peasants.

These exertions have been crowned, upon the whole, with great success; and it is not to be doubted, that, during the reign of the late empress, and since, a very considerable increase of cultivation and of population has been going forward, in almost every part of the Russian empire.

In the year 1763, an enumeration of the people, estimated by the poll-tax, gave a population of 14,726,696; and the same kind of enumeration in 1783, gave a population of 25,677,000, which, if correct, shews a very ex-traordinary increase; but it is supposed, that the enumeration in 1783, was more correct and complete than the one in 1763. Including the provinces not subject to the poll-tax, the general calculation for 1763, was 20,000,000, and for 1796, 36,000,000.[17]

17. Tooke's View of the Russian Empire, vol. ii. book iii. sect. i. p. 126, et seq.

CHAP. IV.

On the fruitfulness of Marriages.

NOTWITHSTANDING the extraordinary proportions of births to deaths in Russia, which have been noticed in the last chapter, and the confirmation of these proportions, in a considerable degree, by actual enumerations, which establish a very rapid increase, it appears, that, in most of the provinces, each marriage yields only three children.

But if we reflect a moment, it will be clear, that to prevent the population of a country from regularly decreasing, it is absolutely necessary that each marriage, on an average, should yield a marriage, that is, yield two children who live to be married. If the result fall short of this, the number of marriages must be gradually diminishing, and the number of children to each marriage remaining the same, the population, of course, will continue decreasing. If each marriage yield accurately two marrying children, the number of marriages, and the number of children, being the same in every generation, the population can be neither retrograde nor progressive, but must remain exactly stationary.

Supposing each marriage to produce three children, as appears to be the case, according to the lists in some of the provinces of Russia, it will be granted, that one, out of three, is but a small proportion to allow for all who die in infancy and celibacy. But admitting this proportion, which may perhaps be true in the present instance, though it is very rarely so in other situations, it will follow that exactly two children, and no more, from every marriage, live to form a fresh union; in which case, from what has been before observed, no increase is possible. And yet in these same provinces, the proportion of the births to the deaths is given as 26 to 10; 22 to 10; 21 to 10; 20 to 10, &c: which implies a very rapid increase. The lists therefore involve a most complete contradiction. Yet there is no reason to suspect the accuracy of the statements respecting the births and marriages; and, allowing for some omissions in the burials, the excess of births will still be great, and indeed, the increasing state of the population has been ascertained by the enumerations, mentioned in the last chapter.

Contradictory as these lists appear, they do not involve a greater contradiction than the lists of other countries, which purport to express the number of births which each marriage yields. And it may perhaps contribute to the better understanding of the tables, which I shall have occasion to notice in the next chapter, if I endeavour to explain a very important error into which all the writers in political arithmetic, that I have ever met with, have fallen, relative to this subject.

These lists are, in reality, enumerations of the annual marriages and the annual births; and the proportion between them, of course, accurately expresses the proportion of births to marriages which takes place in the year; but this proportion has been assumed to express the number of births which each individual marriage in the course of its duration yields. On what grounds this assumption has been made, will appear from the following considerations.

If, in a country where there were no exports or imports of people, we could obtain the number of births and of marriages that had taken place in the course of a very long period, it is evident, that double the number of marriages, or, which is the same thing, the number of married people, would express accurately the proportion of the born which had lived to be married; and the difference between this number and the number of births, would also express accurately, the proportion of the born which had died in infancy and celibacy. But the whole numbers of births and marriages, during this period, are evidently nothing more than the sum of the annual births, and the sum of the annual marriages. If, therefore, in any country, an average proportion can be obtained between the annual births and annual marriages, this proportion will manifestly express the same thing as the whole numbers; that is, the number of persons annually married, compared with the number of annual births, will accurately express the proportion of the born which lives to be married; and the difference between them, the proportion of the born which dies in infancy and celibacy. For instance, if the average proportion of annual marriages to annual births, in any country, be as 1 to 4, this will imply, that, out of four children born, two of them live to marry, and the other two die in infancy and celibacy. This is a most important and interesting piece of information, from which the most useful inferences are to be drawn; but it is totally different from the number of births which each individual marriage yields in the course of its duration; so much so, that on the supposition which has been just made, that half of the born live to be married, which is a very usual proportion, the annual marriages would be to the annual births as 1 to 4, whether each individual marriage yielded 4 births, 2 births, or 100 births. If the latter number be taken, then, according to the present supposition, 50 would live to be married; and out of every 100 births there would be 25 marriages, and the marriages would still be to the births as 1 to 4. The same proportion would evidently hold good in the case of two births yielded by each marriage, as this proportion is not in the smallest degree affected by the number of children which a marriage in the course of its duration may yield, but merely relates to the number of these children who live to be married, or the number of births from which one marriage results.

The only case in which the proportion of annual births to annual marriages, is the same, as the proportion of births which each individual marriage yields, is, when the births and deaths are exactly equal; and the reason of their being the same in this case is, that, in order to make the births and deaths exactly equal, we must assume, that each marriage yields exactly another marriage, and that, whatever be the number of children born from each union, they all die in infancy and celibacy, except one pair. Thus, if each marriage yield five children, two of which only live to form a fresh union, the proportion of annual marriages, to annual births, will be as 1 to 5, which is the same as the number of births yielded by each individual marriage, by hypothesis. But whenever each marriage yields either more or less than one marrying pair, that is, whenever the population is either increasing or decreasing, then the proportion of annual births to annual marriages, can never be the same, as the proportion of births yielded by each individual marriage in the course of its duration.

Hence it follows, that whenever we assume them to be the same, any increase of population is impossible. Thus, if the foregoing reasoning be admitted, and it be granted that the proportion of persons yearly married, to the number of children yearly born, truly expresses the proportion of the born which lives to be married; then, assuming at the same time, what is assumed by those who produce these lists, that they express the number of births yielded by each individual marriage, it is evident, that all such lists prove that the population is stationary; whereas, perhaps, from other accounts, it is known with certainty, that a rapid increase is going forwards. Thus, in Sweden, if we allow that the proportion of yearly marriages to yearly births, which is as 1 to 4 and $\frac{1}{10}$, expresses, what it really does, that out of 4 and $\frac{1}{10}$ births, one pair lives to marry; and suppose, at the same time, according to Wargentin, Susmilch, Crome, Price, and others, that each marriage, in the course of its duration, yields only $4\frac{1}{10}$ births, it would follow, that, out of $4\frac{1}{10}$ births, 2 and $\frac{1}{10}$ die in infancy and celibacy, and only two children from each marriage live to form a fresh union, in which case no increase would be possible, though, from the excess of births above the deaths, and even from actual enumerations, it might be completely ascertained, that the progress of the population was considerable.

Dr. Price had considered this subject sufficiently to see, that, in countries where an increase or decrease of population was taking place, these lists did not accurately express the number of births yielded by each marriage; but that he was very far from coming at what I conceive to be the just conclusion on this point, appears, from his observing that, on the supposition that half of the born live to marry, if the prolifickness of marriages were to increase, the births would rise above quadruple the weddings;[1] whereas, in fact, as long as exactly half of the born live to be married, the annual births will always be exactly quadruple the annual weddings, let the prolifickness of marriages vary in any conceivable degree.[2]

As a further proof that Dr. Price did not understand this subject, though he has a long and elaborate note on it, he often mentions the lists of the yearly births and marriages, as expressing the number of children born to each marriage, and particularly notices the proportion in Sweden, as shewing the degree of prolifickness in the marriages of that country.[3] He merely thought that the lists of annual births and marriages, did not, in all cases, express accurately the prolifickness of marriages; but he does not seem to have been in the smallest degree aware, that they had absolutely nothing to do with it; and that, so far from being merely inaccurate, it would be impossible, from such lists, unaccompanied by other information, to tell with certainty, whether the prolifickness in the marriages of any country were such as to yield 2 births, or 100 births in the course of their duration.

Such lists, therefore, considered as expressing the prolifickness of marriages, must be rejected as perfectly useless; but considered as expressing the proportion of the born which lives to be married, should be preserved as highly valuable, and as giving a most interesting and desirable piece of information.

The late empress Catherine, in her instructions for a new code of laws in Russia, says, "our peasants have for the most part twelve, fifteen, and " even as far as twenty children from one marriage."[4] This is certainly an exaggeration; but the probability is, that the assertion was founded on a knowledge that the Russian women were generally prolifick; and yet, according to the lists which have been produced, it would appear that in most

1. Observations on Revers. Paym. vol. i. p. 270, note.
2. That is, when a sufficient time has elapsed, to let the births affect the marriages. Before this period, indeed, Dr. Price's observation would be just; but, practically, it seldom happens that the women of a country become all at once more prolifick than usual; and in the general tables of mortality from which the deductions are made, if they be not such, as for the births to affect the marriages, they cannot express a just average of any kind, and are in every point of view almost entirely useless.
3. Observations on Revers. Paym. vol. i. p. 275.
4. Chap. xii. p. 188. 4to. 1770. Petersburgh.

of the provinces, one marriage yields only three children, which is perfectly irreconcileable with the assertions of the empress. But, according to the foregoing reasonings, these lists merely express that, out of three children born, two live to be married, which agrees with the extraordinary healthiness in early life noticed in some of the provinces. The probability is, that each marriage in these provinces, yields about 6 births, 4 of which live to marry; and this supposition, which retains the proper proportion of the births to the marriages, according to the lists, will account for the excess of the births above the deaths, and the rapid increase of the population.

In those provinces where the annual births are to the annual marriages as 4 to 1, there, according to the principles laid down, only 2 out of 4, instead of 2 out of 3, live to be married; and to produce the excess of births, observed in some of these provinces, even after making great allowances for omissions in the burials,[5] it will be necessary to suppose, that there were full as many as 8 births to each marriage in the course of its duration.

Taking the general proportion of annual births to marriages for the whole country, as given by Mr. Tooke, then it would appear, that, out of 362 births, 200 lived to marry,[6] and to produce a proportion of births to deaths, as 2 to 1, instead of $2\frac{1}{4}$ to 1, as given by Mr. Tooke, that is, allowing the $\frac{1}{4}$ for the omissions in the burials, it will be necessary to suppose 7 or $7\frac{1}{2}$ births to each marriage, which may in some degree justify the assertions of the empress.[7]

These are rough calculations, formed by constructing tables on the plan of one produced by Wallace, in his Dissertation on the Numbers of Mankind, and observing the proportions of births to deaths, which result from different suppositions respecting the number of children born, and the number which live to be married. As this dissertation is not in every person's hands, I insert the table, in order that the reader may see the grounds on which I have gone in these calculations.

5. I am inclined to believe, that where only half of the born live to be married, the proportion of the births to the deaths can never rise quite so high as 2 to 1, whatever may be the number of children to a marriage. The lists, therefore, such as those of Veronesch, which imply that only half of the born live to be married, at the same time that the births are to the deaths in the proportion of above 2 to 1, can only be accounted for by great omissions in the deaths, and by emigrations.

6. Tooke's View of Russian Empire, vol. ii. b. iii. p. 147.

7. On the supposition that I have not assumed the proper proportions of births to deaths, which, from not knowing how to estimate the acknowledged omissions in the burials, is very probable, the results of course will be changed, and therefore too much stress should not be laid on them.

TABLE I.

Periods of the scheme.	Years of the scheme.	Born since the last period.	Of whom died since last period.	And remain in life to propagate.	Died since the last period at an advanced age.	The sum of all who are alive at the respective periods.	The sum of the last column collected.
Col. 1	Col. 2.	Col. 3.	Col. 4.	Col. 5.	Col. 6	Col. 7.	Col. 8.
0	1	0	0	0	0	2	2
1	$33\frac{1}{3}$	6	2	4	0	2+4	6
2	$66\frac{2}{3}$	12	4	8	2	6+8−2	12
3	100	24	8	16	4	12+16−4	24
4	$133\frac{1}{3}$	48	16	32	8	24+32−8	48
5	$166\frac{2}{3}$	96	32	64	16	48+64−16	96
6	200	192	64	128	32	96+128−32	192

It sets out with a single pair, but of course it is the same thing, whether we begin with 2 people or 2 millions of people. There are 8 columns, the contents of which are explained at the top of each.

The object of Mr. Wallace, in this table, was merely to shew the progress of population from a single pair, and the period of doubling; but, if no essential fault be found with the construction of it, it may be applied more extensively and usefully.

The periods are taken at $33\frac{1}{3}$ years; but the real period of a generation will, of course, vary in different countries, according to the average age of marriage. Each marriage is supposed to yield 6 children, 2 of whom, or one third, die in infancy or celibacy; and 4, or two thirds, forming two marriages, are left alive to breed.

If we examine the numbers in the second period, we shall find 12, in the 3d column, which expresses the births; 4, in the 4th column, which expresses the deaths in infancy and celibacy; and 2, in the 6th column, which expresses the deaths of the parents. Consequently the births are to the deaths, in the same period, as 12 to 4+2, as 12 to 6, or 2 to 1, and the proportions continue the same in all the other periods. From which, I think, we may safely infer, that, if in any country the births be to the deaths as 2 to 1, and two thirds of the born live to marry, that each marriage must yield exactly 6 children.

If we examine the births and marriages in any of the contemporaneous periods, we shall find, in the second period, 12 births, and 8 marrying persons, or the proportion of 12 births to 4 marriages; in the third period, 24 births and 16 marrying persons, or the proportion of 24 births to 8 marriages; and so on always in the proportion of 3 to 1. But the proportion of the sum of births to the sum of marriages, during these periods, must be the same, as any correct annual average; and consequently, the annual births are to the annual marriages as 3 to 1; from which, according to the usual mode of calculation, it would be inferred, that each marriage yielded 3 children, though we set out with the supposition of 6 children to each marriage; a contradiction, which strongly confirms the reasonings of the foregoing part of this chapter, and shews, that the proportion of annual births to annual marriages does not express the number of children to each marriage, but a very different thing, namely, the number of the born which live to marry.

If, instead of two thirds, as in the present instance, we suppose that only half of the born live to marry, which is a more common proportion; then, for the second period, we shall have in the third column, expressing the births, the number 9, and in the fifth column, expressing the marrying persons $4\frac{1}{2}$: consequently, the marriages will be to the births as 1 to 4, which is the most usual average of Europe; though, in the present instance, we still suppose, that each marriage yields six children in the course of its duration. On the same supposition, the births will be to the deaths, as 9 to $4\frac{1}{2} + 2$, as 18 to 13, or about $13\frac{4}{5}$ to 10; and consequently it may be inferred, that, when the births are to the deaths as $13\frac{4}{5}$ to 10, or 138 to 100, and half of the born live to marry, each marriage must yield six births.

If we suppose five births to a marriage, and that half of the born live to marry, then, according to the table, the births will be to the deaths, as, about $12\frac{1}{5}$ to 10; and consequently we may infer, in the same manner, that when the births are to the deaths as $12\frac{1}{5}$ to 10, and half of the born live to marry, that each marriage must yield 5 children.

Upon these principles, if we can obtain, in any country, the proportion of births to deaths, and of births to marriages, we may calculate pretty nearly the number of children born to each marriage.[8] This number will indeed turn out to be very different from the results of the old mode of calculation; but this circumstance is rather in favour of its correctness; because the known facts respecting population, cannot possibly be accounted for, according to the usual mode of estimating the number

8. That is, upon the supposition, that there is no incorrectness in the construction of the table, or in the inferences which I think may be drawn from it. At present I do not see any.

of births to a marriage, which gives less than four, for the general average of Europe.

Buffon has inserted in his work some tables of mortality, which he means should be considered as applicable to the whole human race. By these, it appears, that half of the born die under eight years and one month old.[9] If we apply the average of four children to a marriage, to Buffon's estimate of mortality, it would appear, that the population of Europe, instead of having a strong tendency to increase, is in danger of being extinct in the course of some years. Instead of increasing in a geometrical ratio, it would be decreasing in a geometrical ratio. If two, out of the four children allowed to each marriage, were to die under 8 years and a month old, the utmost that we could possibly expect, is, that $1\frac{1}{2}$ should survive, to form a fresh union, or that four present marriages should yield three in the next generation; a ratio of decrease, which would, in no very long period, unpeople Europe.

But the truth is, that both the calculations are incorrect. Buffon's tables were taken from the registers of Paris, and its neighbouring villages, and can by no means be considered as generally applicable. The source of the other error has been attempted to be pointed out in this chapter.

It is only in unhealthy towns, or villages very peculiarly circumstanced, that half of the born die under 8 or 9 years of age. Taking an average throughout Europe, I have little doubt, that not only above half of the born live beyond the age of puberty, but that each marriage yields considerably above four births, I should think, more than five. The poverty which checks population, tends much more powerfully to increase the number of deaths, than to diminish the number of births.

In forming conclusions respecting the proportion of the born which lives to be married from the lists of annual births and annual marriages, which, according to the principles laid down, is the only point of view in which they are useful; there is one circumstance, which, if not particularly attended to, may lead to considerable error.

In country parishes, from which there are emigrations, the proportion which lives to be married will be given too small, and in towns which receive continually an accession of strangers, this proportion will be given much too great. The proportion of annual births to annual marriages, is in general higher, in the country, than in towns; but if there were no changing of inhabitants, the proportion in the towns would be much the highest. If, in a country parish, the births be to the weddings, as 4, or $4\frac{1}{2}$, to 1, this implies, that, out of 4 or $4\frac{1}{2}$ births, in that place, 2 lived to be married in

9. Histoire Naturelle de l'Homme, tom. iv. p. 420. 12mo. 1752.

that place; but many probably emigrated and married in other places, and therefore we cannot positively infer, from this proportion, that only 2 out of the 4, or $4\frac{1}{2}$, lived to be married.

In towns, the proportion of births to marriages is very often only 3, and $3\frac{1}{2}$, to 1, which would seem to imply that, out of 3, or $3\frac{1}{2}$ children, 2 lived to be married; but in these towns, it is known perhaps from the bills of mortality, that much above half of the born die under the age of puberty. The proportion which has been mentioned, therefore, cannot possibly express the real proportion of the children born in the town, which lives to be married, but is caused by the accession of strangers, whose marriages appear in the registers, though not their births. In towns, where there is a great mortality in early life, if no marriages were registered but of those who were born in the place, the proportion of annual births to annual marriages, would be greater than the proportion of children born to each marriage, in the course of its duration, and would amount, perhaps, to 6 or 7 to 1, instead of 3, or $3\frac{1}{2}$, to 1.

In Leipsic, the proportion of births to weddings, is only 2 and $\frac{8}{10}$ to 1;[10] and Susmilch, supposing this to imply that there were only 2 and $\frac{8}{10}$ children born to each marriage, puzzles himself to account for this extraordinary unfruitfulness; but this appearance in the registers, without doubt, arises, either from a great accession of strangers, or from a custom among the inhabitants of the neighbouring country, of celebrating their marriages in the town.

At Geneva, where the registers are supposed to be kept with considerable care, the number of marriages, from the year 1701 to 1760, was 21,493, and the number of births in the same period, 42,076; from which it is inferred, that each marriage had yielded, on an average, less than two children. The author of a valuable paper in the Bibliotheque Britannique, who mentions these numbers,[11] naturally expresses some surprise at the result, but still adopts it as the measure of the fruitfulness of the Geneva women. The circumstance, however, arises undoubtedly from the constant influx of new settlers, whose marriages appear in the registers but not their births. If the number of children from each individual mother were traced with care in the bills of mortality at Geneva, I am confident that the result would be very different.

In Paris the proportion of annual births to annual marriages, is about $4\frac{1}{2}$ to 1,[12] and the women have, in consequence, been considered as more

10. Susmilch's Gottliche Ordnung, vol.i. c. v. s. lxxxiii. p. 171.
11. Tom. iv. p. 38. note.
12. Susmilch's Gottliche Ordnung, vol. i. c. v. s. lxxxv. p. 174.

prolifick than usual for a large town; but no such inference can properly be
drawn from this proportion, which is probably caused, merely by the infrequency of marriages among persons not born in the town, and the custom
of celebrating marriages in the neighbouring villages. The small number
of weddings which takes place in Paris, in proportion to the whole population,[13] and the more than usual number in the villages round Paris, seem to
confirm this supposition.

The rapidity of the increase in population depends upon the number of
children born to each marriage, and the proportion of that number which
lives to form a fresh union. The measure of this rapidity is the proportion, which the excess of the births above the deaths, bears to the whole
population.

That the reader may see at once the tendency to increase, and the period
of doubling, which would result from any observed proportion of births
to deaths, and of these to the whole population, I subjoin two tables from
Susmilch, calculated by Euler, which I believe are very correct. The first is
confined to the supposition of a mortality of 1 in 36, and therefore can only
be applied to countries where such a mortality is known to take place. The
other is general, depending solely upon the proportion, which the excess
of the births above the burials, bears to the whole population, and therefore
may be applied universally to all countries, whatever may be the degree of
their mortality.

It will be observed, that when the proportion between the births and
burials is given, the period of doubling will be shorter, the greater the mortality; because the births, as well as deaths, are increased by this supposition, and they both bear a greater proportion to the whole population, than
if the mortality were smaller, and there were a greater number of people in
advanced life.

The general mortality of Russia, according to Mr. Tooke, as has before
been stated, is 1 in 58, and the proportion of births 1 in 26. Allowing something for the omissions in the burials, if we assume the mortality to be 1 in
52, then the births will be to the deaths as 2 to 1, and the proportion, which
the excess of births bears to the whole population, will be $\frac{1}{52}$. According to

13. In Paris the proportion of annual marriages to the whole population, is, according to Susmilch, 1 to 137; according to Crome, 1 to 160. In Geneva, it is as 1 to
64; and this extraordinary proportion of marriages, is certainly owing principally to
the great influx of foreign settlers. In places, where the proportion of annual births
to annual marriages is much influenced by new settlers, or emigrations, few accurate
inferences can be drawn from them, in any way. They neither express the fruitfulness of marriages, nor the proportion of the born which lives to be married.

Table III. the period of doubling will, in this case, be about 36 years. But if we were to keep the proportion of births to deaths as 2 to 1, and suppose a mortality of 1 in 36, as in Table II. the excess of births above the burials would be $\frac{1}{36}$ of the whole population, and the period of doubling would be only 25 years.

It is evident, that in countries which are very healthy, and where, in consequence, the number of grown up people is great, the births can never bear the same proportion to the whole population, as where the number of grown people is smaller; and therefore the excess of births above the deaths, cannot, in so short a time, produce a number equal to the former population.

TABLE II.

When in any country there are 100,000 persons
living and the mortality is 1 in 36.

If the propor-tion of deaths to births be as		Then the excess of the births will be	The proportion of the excess of the births, to the whole population, will be	And therefore the period of doubling will be
10:	11	277	$\frac{1}{361}$	250 years.
	12	555	$\frac{1}{180}$	125
	13	833	$\frac{1}{120}$	$83\frac{1}{2}$
	14	1110	$\frac{1}{90}$	$62\frac{3}{4}$
	15	1388	$\frac{1}{72}$	$50\frac{1}{4}$
	16	1666	$\frac{1}{60}$	42
	17	1943	$\frac{1}{51}$	$35\frac{3}{4}$
	18	2221	$\frac{1}{45}$	$31\frac{2}{3}$
	19	2499	$\frac{1}{40}$	28
	20	2777	$\frac{1}{36}$	$25\frac{3}{10}$
	22	3332	$\frac{1}{30}$	$21\frac{1}{8}$
	25	4165	$\frac{1}{24}$	17
	30	5554	$\frac{1}{18}$	$12\frac{4}{5}$

TABLE III.

The proportion of the excess of births above the deaths, to the whole of the living.		Periods of doubling in years, and ten thousandth parts.	The proportion of the excess of births above the deaths, to the whole of the living.		Periods of doubling in years, and ten thousandth parts.
I:	10	7.2722	I:	21	14.9000
	11	7.9659		22	15.5932
	12	8.6595		23	16.2864
	13	9.3530		24	16.9797
	14	10.0465		25	17.6729
	15	10.7400		26	18. 3662
	16	11.4333		27	19.0594
	17	12.1266		28	19.7527
	18	12.8200		29	20.4458
	19	13.5133		30	21.1391
	20	14.2066			
I:	32	22.5255	I:	210	145.9072
	34	23.9119		220	152.8387
	36	25.2983		230	159.7702
	38	26.6847		240	166.7017
	40	28.0711		250	173.6332
	42	29.4574		260	180.5647
	44	30.8438		270	187.4961
	46	32.2302		280	194.4275
	48	33.6165		290	201.3590
	50	35.0029		300	208.2905
I:	55	38.4687	I:	310	215.2220
	60	41.9345		320	222.1535
	65	45.4003		330	229.0850
	70	48.8661		340	236.0164
	75	52.3318		350	242.9479
	80	55.7977		360	249.8794
	85	59.2634		370	256.8109
	90	62.7292		380	263.7425
	95	66.1950		390	270.6740
	100	69.6607		400	277.6055

(*continued*)

TABLE III. (*continued*)

The proportion of the excess of births above the deaths, to the whole of the living.	Periods of doubling in years, and ten thousandth parts.	The proportion of the excess of births above the deaths, to the whole of the living.	Periods of doubling in years, and ten thousandth parts.
I: { 110	76.5923	I: { 410	284. 5370
120	83.5238	420	291.4685
130	90.4554	430	298.4000
140	97.3868	440	305.3314
150	104.3183	450	312.2629
160	111.2598	460	319.1943
170	118.1813	470	326.1258
180	125.1128	480	333.0573
190	132.0443	490	339.9888
200	138.9757	500	346.9202
		I : 1000	693.49

CHAP. V.

Of the Checks to Population in the middle parts of Europe.

I HAVE dwelt longer on the northern states of Europe, than their relative importance might, to some, appear to demand, because their internal economy is, in many respects, essentially different from our own, and a personal, though slight, acquaintance with these countries, has enabled me to mention a few particulars which have not yet been before the publick. In the middle parts of Europe, the division of labour, the distribution of employments, and the proportion of the inhabitants of towns to the inhabitants of the country, differ so little from what is observable in England, that it would be in vain to seek for the checks to their population in any peculiarity of habits and manners sufficiently marked to admit of description. I shall, therefore, endeavour to direct the reader's attention, principally, to some inferences drawn from the lists of births, marriages, and deaths in different countries; and these data will, in many important points, give us more information respecting their internal economy than we could receive from the most observing traveller.

One of the most curious and instructive points of view in which we can consider lists of this kind, appears to me to be, in the dependence of the marriages on the deaths. It has been justly observed by Montesquieu, that wherever there is a place for two persons to live comfortably, a marriage will certainly ensue:[1] but in most of the countries in Europe, in the present state of their population, experience will not allow us to expect any sudden and great increase in the means of supporting a family. The place, therefore, for the new marriage must, in general, be made by the dissolution of an old one; and we find, in consequence, that, except after some great mortality, from whatever cause it may have proceeded, or some sudden change of policy peculiarly favourable to cultivation and trade, the number of annual marriages is regulated principally by the number of annual deaths. They reciprocally influence each other. There are few countries in which the common people have so much foresight, as to defer marriage, till they have a fair prospect of being able to support properly all their children. Some of the mortality, therefore, in almost every country, is forced by the too great frequency of marriage; and in every country, a great mortality,

---

1. Esprit des Loix, liv. xxiii. c. x.

whether arising principally from this cause, or occasioned by the number of great towns and manufactories, and the natural unhealthiness of the situation, will necessarily produce a great frequency of marriage.

A most striking exemplification of this observation occurs in the case of some villages in Holland. Susmilch has calculated the mean proportion of annual marriages, compared with the number of inhabitants, as between 1 in 107, and 1 in 113, in countries which have not been thinned by plagues or wars, or in which there is no sudden increase in the means of subsistence.[2] And Crome, a later statistical writer, taking a mean between 1 in 92 and 1 in 122, estimates the average proportion of marriages to inhabitants as 1 to 108.[3] But in the registers of 22 Dutch villages the accuracy of which, according to Susmilch, there is no reason to doubt, it appears that out of 64 persons there is 1 annual marriage.[4] This is a most extraordinary deviation from the mean proportion. When I first saw this number mentioned, not having then adverted to the mortality in these villages, I was much astonished, and very little satisfied with Susmilch's attempt to account for it, by talking of the great number of trades, and the various means of getting a livelihood, in Holland,[5] as it is evident, that, the country having been long in the same state, there would be no reason to expect any great yearly accession of new trades and new means of subsistence, and the old ones would of course all be full. But the difficulty was immediately solved, when it appeared that the mortality was between 1 in 22, and 1 in 23,[6] instead of being 1 in 36, as is usual when the marriages are in the proportion of 1 to 108. The births and deaths were nearly equal. The extraordinary number of marriages was not caused by the opening of any new sources of subsistence, and therefore produced no increase of population. It was merely occasioned by the rapid dissolution of the old marriages by death, and the consequent vacancy of some employment by which a family might be supported.

It might be a question, in this case, whether the too great frequency of marriage, that is, the pressure of the population too hard against the limits of subsistence, contributed most to produce the mortality, or the mortality, occasioned naturally by the employments of the people and unhealthiness of the country, the frequency of marriage. In the present instance, I should, without doubt, incline to the latter supposition, particularly, as it seems

---

2. Susmilch, Gottliche Ordnung, vol. i. c. iv. sect. lvi. p. 126.
3. Crome, uber die Gröffe und Bevölkerung der Europ. Staaten, p. 88. Leips. 1785.   4. Susmilch, Gottliche Ordnung, vol. i. c. iv. sect. lviii, p. 127.
5. Susmilch, Gottliche Ordnung, vol. i. c. iv. sect. lviii. p. 128.
6. Id. c. ii. sect. xxxvi. p. 92.

to be generally agreed, that the common people in Holland are, upon the whole, well off. The great mortality probably arises, partly from the natural marshiness of the soil, and the number of canals, and partly from the very great proportion of the people, which is engaged in sedentary occupations, and the very small number in the healthy employments of agriculture.

A very curious and striking contrast to these Dutch villages, tending to illustrate the present subject, will be recollected in what was said respecting the state of Norway. In Norway, the mortality is 1 in 48, and the marriages 1 in 130. In the Dutch villages, the mortality 1 in 23, and the marriages 1 in 64. The difference both in the marriages and deaths is above double. They maintain their relative proportions in a very exact manner, and shew how much the deaths and marriages mutually depend upon each other, and that, except where some sudden start in the agriculture of a country enlarges the means of subsistence, an increase of marriages will only produce an increase of mortality, and *vice versá.*

In Russia, this sudden start in agriculture has, in great measure, taken place; and consequently, though the mortality is very small, yet, the proportion of marriages is not so. But in the progress of the population of Russia, if the proportion of marriages remain the same as at present, the mortality will inevitably increase, or if the mortality remain nearly the same, the proportion of marriages will diminish.

Susmilch has produced some striking instances of this gradual decrease in the proportional number of marriages, in the progress of a country to a fuller population, and a more complete occupation of all the means of gaining a livelihood.

In the town of Halle, in the year 1700, the number of annual marriages was to the whole population as 1 to 77. During the course of the 55 following years, this proportion changed gradually, according to Susmilch's calculation, to 1 in 167.[7] This is a most extraordinary difference, and, if the calculation were quite accurate, would prove to what a degree the preventive check to population had operated, and how completely it had measured itself to the means of subsistence. As, however, the number of people is estimated by calculation, and not taken from enumerations, this very great difference in the proportions may not be perfectly correct, or may be occasioned in part by other causes.

In the town of Leipsic, in the year 1620, the annual marriages were to the population as 1 to 82 : from the year 1741 to 1756, they were as 1 to 120.[8]

7. Susmilch, Gottliche Ordnung, vol. i. c. iv. sect. lxii. p. 132.
8. Susmilch, Gottliche Ordnung, vol. i. c. iv. sect. lxiii. p. 134.

In Augsburgh, in 1510, the proportion of marriages to the population was as 1 to 86; in 1750, as 1 to 123.[9]

In Dantzic, in the year 1705, the proportion was as 1 to 89; in 1745 as 1 to 118.[10]

In the dukedom of Magdeburgh in 1700, the proportion was as 1 to 87; from 1752 to 1755, as 1 to 125.

In the principality of Halberstadt, in 1690, the proportion was as 1 to 88; in 1756, as 1 to 112.

In the dukedom of Cleves, in 1705, the proportion was 1 to 83; in 1755, 1 to 100.

In the Churmark of Brandenburgh, in 1700, the proportion was 1 to 76; in 1755, 1 to 108.[11]

More instances of this kind might be produced; but these are sufficient to shew that, in countries where, from a sudden increase in the means of subsistence, arising either from a great previous mortality, or from improving cultivation and trade, room has been made for a number of marriages much beyond those dissolved by death; this additional number will annually decrease, in proportion as all the new employments are filled up, and there is no further room for an increasing population.

But in countries which have long been fully peopled, and in which no new sources of subsistence are opening, the marriages being regulated principally by the deaths, will generally bear nearly the same proportion to the whole population, at one period as at another. And the same constancy will take place, even in countries where there is an annual increase in the means of subsistence, provided this increase be uniform and permanent. Supposing it to be such, as for half a century, to allow every year of a fixed number of marriages beyond those dissolved by death, the population would then be increasing, and perhaps rapidly; but it is evident, that the proportion of marriages to the whole population, would remain the same during the whole period.

This proportion Susmilch has endeavoured to ascertain in different countries and different situations. In the villages of the Churmark of Brandenburgh, 1 marriage out of 109 persons takes place annually;[12] and the general proportion for agricultural villages, he thinks, may be taken at between 1 in 108, and 1 in 115.[13] In the small towns of the Churmark where the mortality is greater, the proportion is 1 to 98:[14] in the Dutch villages

9. Id. sect. lxiv. p. 134.   10. Id. sect. lxv, p. 135.   11. Id. sect. lxxi. p. 140.
12. Susmilch, Gottliche Ordnung, vol. i. c. iv. sect. lvi. p. 125.
13. Id. sect. lxxv. p. 147.   14. Id. sect. lx. p. 129.

mentioned before, 1 to 64: in Berlin 1 to 110:[15] in Paris 1 to 137:[16] according to Crome in the *unmarrying* cities of Paris and Rome, the proportion is only 1 to 160.[17]

All general proportions, however, of every kind, should be applied with considerable caution, as it seldom happens that the increase of food and of population is uniform; and when the circumstances of a country are varying, either from this cause, or from any change in the habits of the people with respect to prudence and cleanliness, it is evident, that a proportion which is true at one period, will not be so at another.

Nothing is more difficult than to lay down rules on these subjects that do not admit of exceptions. Generally speaking, it might be taken for granted, that an increased facility in the means of gaining a livelihood, either from a great previous mortality, or from improving cultivation and trade, would produce a greater proportion of annual marriages; but this effect might not perhaps follow. Supposing the people to have been before in a very depressed state, and much of the mortality to have arisen from the want of foresight which usually accompanies such a state, it is possible, that the sudden improvement of their condition, might give them more of a decent and proper pride; and the consequence would be, that the proportional number of marriages might remain nearly the same, but they would all rear more of their children, and the additional population that was wanted, would be supplied by a diminished mortality, instead of an increased number of births.

In the same manner, if the population of any country had been long stationary, and would not easily admit of an increase, it is possible that a change in the habits of the people, from improved education, or any other cause, might diminish the proportional number of marriages; but as fewer children would be lost in infancy, from the diseases consequent on poverty, the diminution in the number of marriages would be balanced by the diminished mortality, and the population would be kept up to its proper level by a smaller number of births.

Such changes, therefore, in the habits of a people should evidently be taken into consideration.

The most general rule that can be laid down on this subject is, perhaps, that any *direct* encouragements to marriage must be accompanied by an increased mortality. The natural tendency to marriage is, in every country, so great, that, without any encouragements whatever, a proper place for a

15. Ibid.   16. Id. sect. lxix. p. 137.
17. Crome, uber die Gróffe und Bevölkerung der Europaischen Staaten, p. 89.

marriage will always be filled up. Such encouragements, therefore, must be either perfectly futile, or produce a marriage where there is not a proper place for one, and the consequence must necessarily be, increased poverty and mortality. Montesquieu, in his Lettres Persanes, says, that in the past wars of France, the fear of being inrolled in the militia, tempted a great number of young men to marry, without the proper means of supporting a family, and the effect was, the birth of a crowd of children, "que l'on cher-
" che encore en France, et que la misère la famine et les maladies en ont
" fait disparoître."[18]

After so striking an illustration of the necessary effects, of direct encouragements to marriage, it is perfectly astonishing, that in his Esprit des Loix, he should say that Europe is still in a state to require laws which favour the propagation of the human species.[19]

Susmilch adopts the same ideas, and though he contemplates the case of the number of marriages coming necessarily to a stand, when the food is not capable of further increase, and examines some countries, in which, the number of contracted marriages is exactly measured by the number dissolved by death, yet he still thinks that it is one of the principal duties of government to attend to the number of marriages. He cites the examples of Augustus and Trajan, and thinks that a prince or a statesman would really merit the name of father of his people, if, from the proportion of 1 to 120 or 125, he could increase the marriages to the proportion of 1 to 80 or 90.[20] But as it clearly appears, from the instances which he himself produces, that in countries which have been long tolerably well peopled, death is the most powerful of all the encouragements to marriage, the prince or statesman who should succeed in thus greatly increasing the number of marriages, might, perhaps, deserve much more justly the title of destroyer, than father, of his people.

The proportion of yearly births to the whole population, must evidently depend principally upon the proportion of the people marrying annually; and, therefore, in countries which will not admit of a great increase of population, must, like the marriages, depend principally on the deaths. Where an actual decrease of population is not taking place, the births will always supply the vacancies made by death, and exactly so much more, as the increasing agriculture and trade of the country will admit. In almost every part of Europe during the intervals of the great plagues, epidemicks, or unusually destructive wars, with which it is occasionally visited, the

18. Lettre cxxii.   19. Esprit des Loix, liv. xxiii. c. xxvi.
20. Susmilch, Gottliche Ordnung, vol. i. c. iv. sect. lxxviii. p. 151.

births exceed the deaths; but as the mortality varies very much in different countries and situations, the births will be found to vary in the same manner, though from the excess of births above deaths, which most countries can admit, not in the same degree.

In 39 villages of Holland, where the deaths are about 1 in 23, the births are also about 1 in 23.[21] In 15 villages round Paris, the births bear the same, or even a greater proportion to the whole population, on account of a still greater mortality. The births are 1 in $22\frac{7}{10}$, and the deaths the same.[22] In the small towns of Brandenburgh, which are in an increasing state, the mortality is 1 in 29, and the births 1 in $24\frac{7}{10}$.[23] In Sweden, where the mortality is about 1 in 35, the births are 1 in 28.[24] In 1056 villages of Brandenburgh, in which the mortality is about 1 in 39 or 40, the births are about 1 in 30.[25] In Norway, where the mortality is 1 in 48, the births are 1 in 34.[26] In all these instances, the births are evidently measured by the deaths, after making a proper allowance for the excess of births which the state of each country will admit. In Russia this allowance must be great, as, although the mortality may perhaps be taken as only 1 in 48 or 50, the births are as high as 1 in 26, owing to the present rapid increase of the population.

Statistical writers have endeavoured to obtain a general measure of mortality for all countries taken together; but, if such a measure could be obtained, I do not see what good purpose it could answer. It would be but of little use in ascertaining the population of Europe, or of the world; and it is evident, that, in applying it to particular countries or particular places, we might be led into the grossest errors. When the mortality of the human race, in different countries, and different situations, varies so much as from 1 in 20, to 1 in 60, no general average could be used with safety in a particular case, without such a knowledge of the circumstances of the country, with respect to the number of towns, the habits of the people, and the healthiness of the situation, as would probably supersede the necessity of resorting to any general proportion, by the knowledge of the particular proportion suited to the country.

There is one leading circumstance, however, affecting the mortality of countries, which may be considered as very general, and which is, at the same time, completely open to observation. This is the number of towns in any state, which has been before alluded to, and the proportion of town

21. Susmilch, Gottliche Ordnung, vol. i. c. vi. s. cxvi. p. 225.

22. Ibid. and c. ii. s. xxxvii. p. 93.

23. Id. c. ii. s. xxviii. p. 80. and c. vi. s. cxvi. p. 225.

24. Id. c. vi. s. cxvi. p. 225.   25. Ibid.   26. Thaarup's Statistik, vol. ii. p. 4.

to country inhabitants. The unfavourable effects of close habitations and sedentary employments on the health are universal; and therefore, on the number of people living in this manner, compared with the number employed in agriculture, will much depend the general mortality of the state. Upon this principle it has been calculated, that when the proportion of the people in the towns, to those in the country, is as 1 to 3. then the mortality is about 1 in 36, which rises to 1 in 35, or 1 in 33, when the proportion of townsmen to villagers is 2 to 5, or 3 to 7; and falls below 1 in 36, when this proportion is 2 to 7, or, 1 to 4. On these grounds the mortality in Prussia is 1 in 38; in Pomerania, 1 in $37\frac{1}{2}$; in the Neumark, 1 in 37; in the Churmark, 1 in 35; according to the lists for 1756.[27]

The nearest average measure of mortality for all countries, taking towns and villages together, is, according to Susmilch, 1 in 36.[28] But Crome thinks that this measure, though it might possibly have suited the time at which Susmilch wrote, is not correct at present, when in most of the states of Europe both the number and the size of towns have increased.[29] He seems to be of opinion, indeed that this mortality was rather below the truth in Susmilch's time, and that now 1 in 30 would be found to be nearer the average measure. It is not improbable that Susmilch's proportion is too small, as he had a little tendency, with many other statistical writers, to throw out of his calculations epidemick years; but Crome has not advanced proofs sufficient to establish a general measure of mortality in opposition to that proposed by Susmilch. He quotes Busching, who states the mortality of the whole Prussian monarchy to be 1 in 30.[30] But it appears that this inference was drawn from lists for only three years, a period much too short to determine any general average. This proportion for the Prussian monarchy is, indeed, completely contradicted by subsequent observations mentioned by Crome. According to lists for five years, ending in 1784, the mortality was only 1 in 37.[31] During the same period the births were to the deaths as 131 to 100. In Silesia the mortality from 1781 to 1784, was 1 in 30; and the births to deaths as 128 to 100. In Gelderland, the mortality from 1776 to 1781 was 1 in 27, and the births 1 in 26. These are the two provinces of the monarchy in which the mortality is the greatest. In some others it is very small. From 1781 to 1784, the average mortality in Neuffchatel and Ballengin, was only 1 in 44, and the births 1 in 31. In the principality of

27. Susmilch, Gottliche Ordnung, vol. iii. p. 60.
28. Vol. i. c. ii. s. xxx. p. 91.
29. Crome, uber die Gróffe und Bevölkerung der Europaischen Staaten, p. 116.
30. Crome, uber die Bevölkerung der Europaisch. Staat. p. 118.
31. Id. p. 120.

Halberstadtz, from 1778 to 1784, the mortality was still less, being only 1 in 45 or 46, and the proportion of births to deaths 137 to 100.[32]

The general conclusion that Crome draws, is, that the states of Europe may be divided into three classes, to which a different measure of mortality ought to be applied. In the richest and most populous states, where the inhabitants of towns are to the inhabitants of the country, in so high a proportion as 1 to 3, the mortality may be taken as 1 in 30. In those countries, which are in a middle state, with regard to population and cultivation, the mortality may be considered as 1 in 32. And in the thinly-peopled northern states, Susmilch's proportion of 1 in 36 may be applied.[33]

These proportions seem to make the general mortality rather too great, even after allowing epidemick years to have their full effect in the calculations.

32. Id. p. 122.   33. Crome's Europaischen Staaten, p. 127.

CHAP. VI.

Effects of Epidemicks on Tables of Mortality.

IT appears clearly, from the very valuable tables of mortality which Susmilch has collected, and which include periods of 50 or 60 years, that all the countries of Europe are subject to periodical sickly seasons, which check their increase; and very few are exempt from those great and wasting plagues, which, once or twice, perhaps, in a century, sweep off the third or fourth part of their inhabitants. The way in which these periods of mortality affect all the general proportions of births, deaths, and marriages, is strikingly illustrated in the tables for Prussia and Lithuania, from the year 1692 to the year 1757.[1]

The table, from which this is copied, contains the marriages, births, and deaths, for every particular year during the whole period; but to bring it into a smaller compass, I have retained only the general average drawn from the shorter periods of five and four years, except where the numbers for the individual years presented any fact worthy of particular observation. The year 1711, immediately succeeding the great plague, is not included by Susmilch in any general average; but he has given the particular numbers, and if they be accurate, they shew the very sudden and prodigious effect of a great mortality on the number of marriages.

Susmilch calculates that above one third of the people was destroyed by the plague; and yet, notwithstanding this great diminution of the population, it will appear, by a reference to the table, that the number of marriages in the year 1711, was very nearly double the average of the six years preceding the plague.[2] To produce this effect, we must suppose, that almost all who were at the age of puberty were induced, from the demand for labour, and the number of vacant employments, immediately to marry. This

---

1. Susmilch, Gottliche Ordnung, vol. i. table xxi. p. 83, of the tables.
2. The number of people before the plague, according to Susmilch's calculation, (vol. i. ch. ix. sect. 173.) was 570,000; from which, if we subtract 247,733, the number dying in the plague, the remainder 322,267 will be the population after the plague; which, divided by the number of marriages and the number of births for the year 1711, makes the marriages about one twenty-sixth part of the population, and the births about one tenth part. Such extraordinary proportions could only occur, in any country, in an individual year. If they were to continue, they would double the population in less than ten years.

TABLE IV.

Annual average.	Marriages.	Births.	Deaths.	Proportion of births to marriages.	Proportion of deaths to births.
5 yrs to 1697	5747	19715	14862	10 : 34	100 : 132
5 yrs — 1702	6070	24112	14474	10 : 39	100 : 165
6 yrs — 1708	6082	26896	16430	10 : 44	100 : 163
In 1709 and 1710	a plague	number destroyed in 2 years.	247733		
In 1711	12028	32522	10131	10 : 27	100 : 320
In 1712	6267	22970	10445	10 : 36	100 : 220
5 yrs to 1716	4968	21603	11984	10 : 43	100 : 180
5 yrs — 1721	4324	21396	12039	10 : 49	100 : 177
5 yrs — 1726	4719	21452	12863	10 : 45	100 : 166
5 yrs — 1731	4808	29554	12825	10 : 42	100 : 160
4 yrs — 1735	5424	22692	15475	10 : 41	100 : 146
In 1736	5280	21859	26371	Epidemic	
In 1737	5765	18930	24480	years.	
5 yrs to 1742	5582	22099	15255	10 : 39	100 : 144
4 yrs — 1746	5469	25275	15117	10 : 46	100 : 167
5 yrs — 1751	6423	28235	17272	10 : 43	100 : 163
5 yrs — 1756	5599	28392	19154	10 : 50	100 : 148
In the 16 yrs before the plague	95585	380516	245763	10 : 39	100 : 154
In 46 yrs after the plague	248777	1083872	690324	10 : 43	100 : 157
In 62 good years	344361	1464388 936087	936087	10 : 43	100 : 156
More born than died		528301			
In the 2 plague yrs	5477	23977	247733		
In all the 64 yrs including the plague	340838	1488365 1183820	1183820	10 : 42	100 : 125
More born than died		304745			

immense number of marriages in the year, could not possibly be accompanied by a great proportional number of births, because we cannot suppose that the new marriages could each yield more than one birth in the year, and the rest must come from the marriages which had continued unbroken through the plague. We cannot, therefore, be surprised, that the proportion of births to marriages in this year should be only 2 and $\frac{7}{10}$ to 1, or 27 to 10. But though the proportion of births to marriages could not be great; yet, on account of the extraordinary number of marriages, the absolute number of births must be great; and as the number of deaths would naturally be small, the proportion of births to deaths is prodigious, being 320 to 100; an excess of births, as great, perhaps, as has ever been known in America.

In the next year, 1712, the number of marriages must of course diminish exceedingly, because, nearly all who were at the age of puberty having married the year before, the marriages of this year would be supplied principally by those who had arrived at this age, subsequent to the plague. Still, however, as *all* who were marriageable had not probably married the year before, the number of marriages, in the year 1712, is great in proportion to the population; and, though not much more than half of the number which took place during the preceding year, is greater than the average number in the last period before the plague. The proportion of births to marriages in 1712, though greater than in the preceding year, on account of the smaller comparative number of marriages, is, with reference to other countries, not great, being, as $3\frac{6}{10}$ to 1, or 36 to 10. But the proportion of births to deaths, though less than in the preceding year, when so very large a proportion of the people married, is, with reference to other countries, still unusually great, being as 220 to 100; an excess of births which, calculated on a mortality of 1 in 36, would double the population of a country (according to Table II. page 190) in 21 $\frac{1}{8}$ years.

From this period the number of annual marriages begins to be regulated by the diminished population, and of course to sink considerably below the average number of marriages before the plague, depending principally on the number of persons rising annually to a marriageable state. In the year 1720, about nine or ten years after the plague, the number of annual marriages, either from accident, or the beginning operation of the preventive check, is the smallest; and it is at this time, as might be expected, that the proportion of births to marriages rises very high. In the period from 1717 to 1721 the proportion, as appears by the Table, is 49 to 10; and, in the particular years 1719 and 1720, it is 50 to 10, and 55 to 10.

Susmilch draws the attention of his readers to the fruitfulness of marriages in Prussia after the plague, and mentions the proportion of 50 annual births to 10 annual marriages as a proof of it. There are the best reasons for supposing that the marriages in Prussia at this time, were very fruitful; but certainly this proportion by itself is no proof of it, being evidently caused by the smaller number of marriages taking place in the year, and not by the greater number of births.[3] In the two years immediately succeeding the plague, when the excess of births above the deaths was so astonishing, the births bore a small proportion to the marriages, and, according to the usual mode of calculating, it would have followed, that each marriage yielded only $2\frac{7}{10}$, or $3\frac{6}{10}$ children. In the last period of the table, from 1752 to 1756, the births are to the marriages as 5 to 1, and in the individual year 1756, as $6\frac{1}{10}$ to 1; and yet, during this period, the births are to the deaths only as 148 to 100; which could not have been the case, if the high proportion of births to marriages, had indicated a greater number of births than usual, instead of a smaller number of marriages.

The variations in the proportion of births to deaths in the different periods of the 64 years included in the table, deserve particular attention. If we were to take an average of the four years immediately succeeding the plague, the births would be to the deaths, in the proportion of above 22 to 10, which, supposing the mortality to be 1 in 36, would double the population in less than 21 years. If we take the 20 years from 1711 to 1731, the average proportion of the births to deaths will appear to be about 17 to 10; a proportion which (according to Table II. page 190) would double the population in about 35 years. But if, instead of 20 years, we were to take the whole period of 64 years, the average proportion of births to deaths turns out to be but a little more than 12 to 10; a proportion which would not double the population in less than 125 years. If we were to include the mortality of the plague, or even of the epidemick years 1736 and 1737, in too short a period, the deaths might exceed the births, and the population would appear to be decreasing.

Susmilch thinks that instead of 1 in 36, the mortality in Prussia after the plague might be 1 in 38; and it may appear perhaps to some of my readers, that the plenty, occasioned by such an event, ought to make a still greater difference. Dr. Short has particularly remarked, that an extraordinary healthiness generally succeeds any very great mortality,[4] and I have no doubt that the observation is just, comparing similar ages together. But under the most favourable circumstances, infants under three years, are more subject to death than at other ages; and the extraordinary proportion

3. Susmilch, Gottliche Ordnung, vol. i. c. v. s. lxxxvi. p. 175.
4. History of air, seasons, &c. vol. ii. p. 344.

of children which usually follows a very great mortality, counterbalances the natural healthiness of the period, and prevents it from making much difference in the general mortality.

If we divide the population of Prussia, after the plague, by the number of deaths in the year 1711, it will appear that the mortality was nearly 1 in 31, and was therefore increased, rather than diminished, owing to the prodigious number of children born in that year. And, in general, we shall observe, that, from this cause, a great previous mortality produces a much more sensible effect on the births than on the deaths. By referring to the table, it will appear that the number of annual deaths regularly increases with the increasing population, and nearly keeps up the same relative proportion all the way through. But the number of annual births is not very different during the whole period, though, in this time, the population had more than doubled itself; and therefore the *proportion* of births to the whole population, at first, and at last, must have changed in an extraordinary degree.

On an average of the 46 years after the plague, the proportion of annual births to annual marriages is as 43 to 10, that is, according to the principles laid down in the fourth chapter of this book, out of 43 children born, 20 of them live to be married. The average proportion of births to deaths during this period is 157 to 100. But to produce such an increase, on the supposition that only 20 children out of 43, or 2 out of $4\frac{3}{10}$ live to be married, each marriage, I am persuaded, for the reasons given in that chapter, must have yielded 8 births.

Crome observes, that when the marriages of a country yield less than 4 births, the population is in a very precarious state,[5] and, like the other writers on this subject, he estimates the number of children from each marriage by the proportion of yearly births to yearly marriages. But I should say, on the contrary, that the population was in a more precarious state, when the yearly marriages in these lists appeared to give more than four children. If less than half of the born live to be married, which would then be the case, an extraordinary number of children to each marriage is necessary to produce any considerable increase. In Prussia, the marriages were so fruitful, as to allow of a considerable mortality among the children, without stopping the increase; but this mortality in itself cannot be considered as a favourable sign; and, in other countries in which a rapid increase is going on, the proportion of yearly births to yearly marriages is generally not so high as 4 to 1, or, according to the common mode of calculating, each marriage yields less than 4 children.

5. Uber die Bevölkerung der Europais. Staat. p. 91.

In the Churmark of Brandenburgh, for 15 years after 1694, the proportion of births to deaths was nearly 17 to 10, which, if it had continued, would have doubled the population in 35 years; yet the proportion of yearly births to yearly marriages was only 37 to 10. In the whole period from 1692 to 1756, in which the population had actually more than doubled itself, notwithstanding many epidemick years, this proportion was nearly the same, or about $37\frac{1}{2}$ to 10.[6]

In the dutchy of Pomerania from 1694 to 1756, the population had doubled itself, and the average proportion of yearly births to yearly marriages was 38 to 10.[7]

In the Newmark of Brandenburgh from 1694 to 1756, there were some periods of rapid increase, though it was checked more frequently and effectually by epidemicks. In 30 years, to 1726, the average proportion of births to deaths was 148 to 100, and the proportion of annual births to annual marriages 38 to 10. In the whole period, the births were to the deaths as 136 to 100, and the proportion of births to marriages the same as in the period of thirty years.[8]

In Russia, we know that a very rapid increase is going forwards, though the proportion of annual births to annual marriages is only about 36 to 10. And, if we had lists for America, where the progress of population is still more rapid, I should expect to find that the proportion of annual births to annual marriages was less than 4 to 1.[9]

6. Susmilch, Gottliche Ordnung, vol. i. table xxii. p. 88. of the tables.

7. Id. table xxiii. p. 91.   8. Id. table xxv. p. 99.

9. From a paper in the Transactions of the Society at Philadelphia (vol. iii. N° vii. p. 25.) by Mr. Barton, entitled, *Observations on the probability of life in the United States,* which I have seen since this was written, I am not sure that I might not be disappointed in the expectation here expressed. If, indeed, Mr. Barton's calculations were to be considered as true for the United States in general, it would appear that half of the born die under 13 or 14; and therefore half of the born could not live to marry. But the fact is, that Mr. Barton's calculations, which he applies generally, are merely taken from the town of Philadelphia, and one or two small towns or villages which are certainly not healthy. Our largest European towns are, of course, not so healthy as Philadelphia, where it appears that half of the born die under $12\frac{1}{2}$, but many of our moderate towns are much more healthy. Mr. Barton's calculations of a mortality of 1 in 45, at Philadelphia, and 1 in 47 at Salem, certainly contradict his other estimates, and can therefore only have been taken for short periods, and rejecting epidemick years; indeed, he acknowledges the having made this kind of rejection in one or two instances, and of course his calculations are not to be relied on. He mentions $6\frac{1}{2}$ births to a marriage, but his numbers give only $4\frac{1}{2}$: and, supposing this to be the true proportion of children to a marriage, if, at the same time we were to suppose that half of the born die under 14, all increase in the population

On the contrary, in Silesia, where the proportion of births to deaths is only 13 to 10, and where consequently the progress of the population is not rapid, the proportion of yearly births to yearly marriages is $4\frac{1}{10}$ to 1, or 41 to 10.[10] And in France, this proportion before the revolution, was $4\frac{1}{2}$ to 1, though the progress of population was slower than in Silesia. In Corsica, the births are said to be to the marriages as 5 to 1, though the population of Corsica cannot possibly be in a continued state of rapid increase. The proportion of births to deaths in Norway, is greater than in Sweden, though in Norway the annual births are to the annual marriages as 38 to 10, and in Sweden, as 41 to 10.

It cannot therefore be said, that the population of a country is in a precarious state when the proportion of yearly births to yearly marriages is less than 4 to 1. Such a proportion is, on the contrary, favourable to population, and is found to exist in many countries, where the increase of people is very rapid. A proportion greater than 4 to 1 is in itself unfavourable to the progress of population, and though it may occasionally exist in countries which are increasing rapidly, owing to an extraordinary fruitfulness of the marriages, yet it will be found more frequently in countries where the progress of population is slow.

I take every opportunity that occurs of illustrating this subject, because so many respectable writers have fallen into the error of estimating the number of children produced by each marriage in the course of its duration, by the proportion of yearly births to yearly marriages, and I am willing to give ample reasons to the reader for differing from such united authority. All these writers themselves express their surprise at the results that the lists, which they thus make use of, give. Susmilch and Crome particularly remark, that the average of 4 or $4\frac{1}{2}$ children to a marriage, contradicts the experience we have of the fruitfulness of particular women, many of whom bear above 12 children,[11] though a considerable part of them may die in

of America would be impossible. On the whole, though we cannot imagine that the calculations in this paper are applicable to the United States in general, and that half of the born die under 14, instead of living to 25 or 30 and above, as in Europe; yet, if we suppose, that they imply a considerable mortality under puberty, we must believe that each marriage yields full as many as 7 or 8 births, to account for the rapid progress of population which we know for a certainty is going forwards in America. Dr. Franklin supposes 8 births to a marriage in America, and that half of the born live to marry, which probably is not far from the truth. (Miscell. p. 3.)

10. Susmilch, Gottliche Ordnung, vol. i. table xx. p. 81.

11. Gottliche Ordnung, vol. i. c. v. s. lxxxiii. p. 169. Crome, p. 91.

the rearing. And Wargentin takes notice of the smallness of this number, in reference to the reputed fecundity of the Northern women.[12]

I feel strongly persuaded, that it has been principally owing to this error in the mode of estimating the fruitfulness of marriages, that Dr. Price, and almost all the writers in political arithmetick, have so totally misapprehended the principle of population. If indeed this mode of calculation were just, the fears of depopulation would really be well founded.

When it appears, from the lists of any country, that the annual births are to the annual marriages in a higher proportion than 4 to 1, that is, according to the principles laid down, when less than half of the born live to be married, it cannot be determined from such a proportion alone, whether this effect arises from a number of persons above the age of puberty dying unmarried, the operation of the preventive check; or from a considerable mortality among children, the operation of the positive check. But the proportion of deaths and births will generally ascertain, to which class it ought to be referred. In Prussia, it is undoubtedly occasioned principally by the mortality among children; and it does not seem improbable, that where so many children are born to each marriage, many should perish for want of sufficient attention, though there might be no want of food. I think it is generally to be observed, that when the women in the lower classes of life marry very young, they not only have more children, but lose a greater proportion of them, than when they marry later, and from having a smaller number, are able to take better care of them. It appears, from a table given by Susmilch, that in Prussia, during this period, half of the born died under 24.[13] And as not much less than half of the born lived to be married, the marriages must have been early, and the preventive check could not have operated much.

In Sweden, half of the born live to 33,[14] and as about half, or rather less, live to be married, the preventive check would operate much more than in Prussia, though still not to a great degree. In France, where a smaller proportion of the born lives to be married, the operation of the preventive check is probably not very different from what it is in Sweden, though I should think that it was certainly rather less. According to Necker,[15] the proportion of marriages to the population in France is as 1 to $113\frac{1}{3}$.

12. Susmilch, vol. i. c. v. s. lxxxv. p. 173.
13. Gottliche, Ordnung, vol. iii. tab. xxi. p. 29.
14. Price's Observ. on Revers. Paym. tab. xliii. p.132.
15. De l'Administration des Finances, tom. i. c. ix. p.255. 12mo. 1785.

The operation of the preventive check is best measured by the proportion which the whole population bears to the yearly marriages,[16] but though this proportion be obtained by multiplying the number of annual births in proportion to each annual marriage, by the number of inhabitants in proportion to each annual birth; yet it does not follow that it will be small, because less than half of the born live to be married, or be great, because more than half of the born live to be married. In that part of the Prussian dominions included in the table that has been given, and during the period there mentioned, less than half of the born lived to be married, yet the proportion of annual marriages to the whole population was as high as 1 to 92.[17] In Norway, where more than half of the born live to be married, the proportion of annual marriages to the whole population is as low as 1 to 130. The reason is, that the proportion of the population to annual births, which is the multiplier, is, in the two cases, extremely different.

In Norway, it is probable, that half of the born live to forty-three, forty-four, or above; and therefore, though rather more than half of the born live to be married, there will necessarily be many persons between the ages of 20 and 44 living unmarried, that is, the preventive check will prevail to a considerable degree. In a part of the Pays de Vaud in Switzerland, half of the born live to 45; and therefore if none married before 40, and all married

16. Even from this measure, the inferences are not entirely to be depended upon, as it is liable to be influenced by the fruitfulness of marriages, and the proportion of the population which is under the age of puberty. If all the marriages which take place in a country, be they few or many, take place young, and be consequently prolifick, it is evident that to produce the same proportion of births, a smaller proportion of marriages will be necessary; or with the same proportion of marriages a greater proportion of births will be produced. This latter case seems to be applicable to France, where both the births and deaths are greater than in Sweden, though the proportion of marriages is nearly the same, or rather less. And when in two countries compared, one of them has a much greater proportion of its population under the age of puberty, than the other, it is evident, that any general proportion of annual marriages to the whole population, will not imply the same operation of the preventive check among those of a marriageable age. It is, in part, the small proportion of the population in towns under the age of puberty, as well as the influx of strangers, which makes it appear in the registers, that the preventive check operates less in towns than in the country; whereas there can be little doubt, that the number of unmarried persons of a marriageable age is the greatest in towns. The converse of this will of course be true, and consequently, in such a country as America, where above half of the population is under sixteen, the proportion of yearly marriages to the whole population will not accurately express, how little the preventive check really operates. The subject is intricate, and requires some attention.

17. Susmilch, Gottliche Ordnung, vol. i. c. iv. s. lxxi. p. 141.

when they reached that age, more than half of the born would live to be married; yet all being unmarried under 40, the preventive check might be said to prevail to a very great degree.

It is evident, therefore, that we cannot infer the absence of the preventive check, because a considerable proportion of the born lives to be married. And it is equally evident, that we cannot infer the contrary.

In Holland, it would appear from the registers, that more than half of the born live to be married;[18] yet, from the proportion of annual marriages, to the whole population in the Dutch villages, mentioned before, it is clear, that the preventive check cannot operate much. In the Churmark of Brandenburgh, from 1694 to 1756, more than half of the born lived to be married. But it appears from a table given by Susmilch, that, in the Churmark, half of the born die under 22.[19] The marriages, therefore, must have been very early indeed. And, from the proportion of the marriages, for the Churmark, which he has given in one place, it appears that it was greater in comparison of the whole population, than in any other country, which he has mentioned, except Holland.[20] Still, however, if it be true, that half of the born die under 22, it is rather difficult to conceive that more than half should live to be married.

There is one circumstance not yet noticed, which may contribute to smooth this difficulty, and which should be attended to in all cases. This is the number of second and third marriages. In the dukedom of Pomerania, it was observed, during a period of seven years, from 1748 to 1754, that out of 23,324 marriages, that were contracted, 6170 of them were between persons, one of which had been married before, and 1214, between persons, both of which had been married before.[21] The whole of the latter number, therefore, and half of the former, ought to be subtracted, in order to find the number of the born which lived to be married. And, from this cause,

18. Susmilch, Gottliche Ordnung, vol. i. table xvii. p. 51.

19. Id. vol. iii. table xxii. p. 35.

20. Susmilch's proportions and calculations for the same countries, appear now and then a little to contradict each other. This arises from their being formed at different periods. The proportion of marriages to the population for the Churmark of Brandenburgh, from 1700 to 1755, (vol. i. ch. iv. sec. lxxi. p. 141.) appears to be 1 in 90, and up to the year 1722, 1 in 87. But in another calculation, which includes only the period from 1738 to 1748, the proportion for the villages of the Churmark is 1 in 109, and for the small towns, 1 in 98, (sec. lx, p. 129).

The table, which makes half of the born in the Churmark die under 22, was not formed from the period when the increase was so rapid, and when the lists appeared to shew that above half of the born lived to be married.

21. Susmilch, Gottliche Ordnung, vol. i. c. v. s. xc. p. 183.

all the lists will give the proportion of the born which lives to be married, greater than the truth. In the present instance, probably, full as many as half of the born died unmarried; and this correction, I am persuaded, ought to be applied to the Dutch villages, in particular, where the proportion of marriages is so great, as it is difficult to conceive, that a mortality of 1 in 23, should not destroy more than half of the born before they reach the age of twenty. In addition to this, I have little doubt that many of the marriages in the Dutch villages, are, as in towns, between persons not born in the place. There is a constant influx of strangers into all parts of Holland. It has been called the church-yard of Germany.

For the periodical, though irregular, returns of sickly seasons, I refer the reader to the valuable tables of mortality which Susmilch has collected. The common epidemical years that are interspersed throughout these tables, will not, of course, have the same effects on the marriages and births, as the great plague in the table for Prussia; but in proportion to their magnitude, their operation will in general be found to be similar. From the registers of many other countries, and particularly of towns, it appears, that the visitations of the plague were frequent at the latter end of the 17th, and the beginning of the 18th centuries.

In contemplating the plagues, and sickly seasons which occur in these tables, after a period of rapid increase, it is impossible not to be impressed with the idea that the number of inhabitants had, in these instances, exceeded the food and the accomodations necessary to preserve them in health. The mass of the people would, upon this supposition, be obliged to live more hardly, and a greater number of them would be crowded together in one house; and these natural causes would evidently contribute to produce sickness, even though the country, absolutely considered, might not be crowded and populous. In a country, even thinly inhabited, if an increase of population take place, before more food is raised, and more houses are built, the inhabitants must be distressed for room and subsistence. If, in the Highlands of Scotland, for the next ten or twelve years, the marriages were to be either more frequent, or more prolifick, and no emigration were to take place, instead of five to a cottage, there might be seven, and this, added to the necessity of worse living, would evidently have a most unfavourable effect on the health of the common people.

CHAP. VII.

Of the Checks to Population in Switzerland.

THE situation of Switzerland, is, in many respects, so different from the other states of Europe; and some of the facts that have been collected respecting it, are so curious, and tend so strongly to illustrate the general principles of this work, that it seems to merit a separate consideration.

About 35 or 40 years ago, a great and sudden alarm appears to have prevailed in Switzerland, respecting the depopulation of the country; and the transactions of the Economical Society of Berne, which had been established some years before, were crowded with papers deploring the decay of industry, arts, agriculture, and manufactures, and the imminent danger of a total want of people. The greater part of these writers considered the depopulation of the country as a fact so obvious as not to require proof. They employed themselves therefore chiefly in proposing remedies, and among others, the importation of midwives, the establishment of foundling hospitals, the portioning of young virgins, the prevention of emigration, and the encouragement of foreign settlers.[1]

A paper, containing very valuable materials, was, however, about this time published, by a Mons. Muret, minister of Vevey, who, before he proceeded to point out remedies, thought it necessary to substantiate the existence of the evil. He made a very laborious and careful research into the registers of different parishes up to the time of their first establishment, and compared the number of births which had taken place during three different periods of 70 years each, the first ending in 1620, the second in 1690, and the third in 1760.[2] Finding, upon this comparison, that the number of births was rather less in the second than in the first period, (and by the help of supposing some omissions in the second period, and some redundances in the third,) that the number of births in the third was also less than in the second, he considered the evidence for a continued depopulation of the country from the year 1550, as incontrovertible.

Admitting all the premises, the conclusion is not perhaps so certain as he imagined it to be, and, from other facts which appear in his memoir, I am strongly disposed to believe, that Switzerland, during this period, came

1. See the different Memoirs for the year 1766.
2. Memoires, &c. par la Societé Economique de Berne. Année 1766, premiere partie, p. 15. et seq. octavo. Berne.

under the case supposed in page 197, and that the improving habits of the people, with respect to prudence, cleanliness, &c. had added gradually to the general healthiness of the country, and by enabling them to rear up to manhood a greater proportion of their children, had furnished the requisite increase of population with a smaller number of births. Of course, the proportion of annual births to the whole population, in the latter period, would be less than in the former.

From accurate calculations of M. Muret, it appears, that, during the last period, the mortality was extraordinarily small, and the proportion of children reared from infancy to puberty, extraordinarily great.[3] In the former periods, this could not have been the case in the same degree. M. Muret himself, observes, that, "The ancient depopulation of the country was to be " attributed to the frequent plagues which in former times desolated it;" and adds, "if it could support itself, notwithstanding the frequency of so " dreadful an evil, it is a proof of the goodness of the climate, and of the " certain resources which the country could furnish, for a prompt recov- " ery of its population."[4] He neglects to apply this observation as he ought, and forgets that such a prompt repeopling could not take place without an unusual increase of births, and that, to enable a country to support itself against such a source of destruction, a greater proportion of births to the whole population would be necessary than at other times.

In one of his tables, he gives a list of all the plagues that had prevailed in Switzerland, from which it appears, that this dreadful scourge desolated the country, at short intervals, during the whole of the first period, and extended its occasional ravages to within 22 years of the termination of the second.[5]

It would be contrary to every rule of probability, to suppose, that, during the frequent prevalence of this disorder, the country could be particularly healthy, and the general mortality extremely small. Let us suppose it to have been such, as at present takes place in many other countries which are exempt from this calamity, about 1 in 32, instead of 1 in 45, as in the last period. The births would, of course, keep their relative proportion, and instead of 1 in 36,[6] be about 1 in 26. In estimating the population of the country by the births, we should thus have two very different multipliers for the different periods; and though the absolute number of births might be

---

3. Id. table xiii. p. 120. Année 1766.
4. Memoires, &c. par la Societé Econ. de Berne. Année 1765. premiere partie, p. 22.   5. Id. table iv. p. 22.   6. Id. table i. p. 21.

greater in the first period, yet the fact would by no means imply a greater population.

In the present instance, the sum of the births in 17 parishes during the first 70 years, is given as 49,860, which annually would be about 712. This, multiplied by 26, would indicate a population of 18,512. In the last period, the sum of the births is given 43,910,[7] which will be about 626 annually. This, multiplied by 36, will indicate a population of 22,536: and if the multipliers be just, it will thus appear, that, instead of the decrease which was intended to be proved, there had been a considerable increase.

That I have not estimated the mortality too high, during the first period, I have many reasons for supposing, particularly, a calculation respecting the neighbouring town of Geneva, in which it appears, that in the 16th century, the probability of life, or the age to which half of the born live, was only 4.883, rather less than four years and $\frac{9}{10}$ths; and the mean life 18.511, about 18 years and a half. In the 17th century, the probability of life was 11.607, above 11 years and a half; the mean life 23.358. In the 18th century, the probability of life had increased to 27.183, 27 years and nearly a fifth, and the mean life to 32 years and a fifth.[8]

It is highly probable, that a diminution of mortality, of the same kind, though, perhaps, not in the same degree, should have taken place in Switzerland; and we know from the registers of other countries, which have been already noticed, and most particularly from that of Prussia, that the period of the greater mortality naturally produces a greater proportion of births.

Of this dependence of the births on the deaths, M. Muret himself produces many instances; but not being aware of the true principle of population, they only serve to astonish him, and he does not apply them.

Speaking of the want of fruitfulness in the Swiss women, he says, that Prussia, Brandenburgh, Sweden, France, and indeed every country, the registers of which he had seen, give a greater proportion of baptisms to the number of inhabitants, than the Pays de Vaud, where this proportion is only as 1 to 36.[9] He adds, that, from calculations lately made in the Lyonois, it appeared, that in Lyons itself, the proportion of baptisms was 1 in 28; in the small towns, 1 in 25; and in the parishes, 1 in 23 or 24. What a prodigious difference, he exclaims, between the Lyonois and the Pays de Vaud,

7. Id. p. 16.
8. See a paper in the Bibliotheque Britannique, published at Geneva. tom. iv. p. 328.
9. Memoires, &c. par la Societé Econ. de Berne. Année, 1766, premiere partie, p. 47, 48.

where the most favourable proportion, and that only in two small parishes of extraordinary fecundity, is not above 1 in 26, and in many parishes it is considerably less than 1 in 40.[10] *The same difference,* he remarks, takes place in the *mean life.* In the Lyonois, it is a little above 25 years, while in the Pays de Vaud, the lowest mean life, and that only in a single marshy and unhealthy parish, is $29\frac{1}{2}$ years, and in many places it is above 45 years.[11]

"But whence comes it," he says, "that the country where children escape
" the best from the dangers of infancy, and where the mean life, in what-
" ever way the calculation is made, is higher than in any other, should be
" precisely that, in which the fecundity is the smallest? How comes it
" again, that, of all our parishes, the one which gives the mean life the
" highest, should also be the one, where the tendency to increase is the
" smallest?

"To resolve this question, I will hazard a conjecture, which, however, I
" give only as such. Is it not, that, in order to maintain in all places the
" proper equilibrium of population, God has wisely ordered things in such
" a manner, as that the force of life, in each country, should be in the in-
" verse ratio of its fecundity.[12]

"In effect, experience verifies my conjecture. Leyzin (a village in the
" Alps) with a population of 400 persons, produces but a little above eight
" children a year. The Pays de Vaud, in general, in proportion to the same
" number of inhabitants, produces 11, and the Lyonois 16. But if it hap-
" pen, that at the age of 20 years, the 8, the 11, and the 16, are reduced to
" the same number, it will appear, that the force of life gives in one place,
" what fecundity does in another. And thus the most healthy countries,
" having less fecundity, will not overpeople themselves, and the unhealthy
" countries, by their extraordinary fecundity, will be able to sustain their
" population."

We may judge of the surprise of M. Muret, at finding from the registers, that the most healthy people were the least prolifick, by his betaking himself to a miracle in order to account for it. But the *nodus* does not seem in the present instance to be worthy of such an interference.[13] The fact may be accounted for, without resorting to so strange a supposition, as that the fruitfulness of women should vary inversely as their health.

---

10. Memoires, &c. par la Societé Econ. de Berne. Année 1766, premiere partie, p. 48.   11. Ibid.   12. Id. p. 48. et seq.
13. Nec deus intersit nisi dignus vindice nodus.

There is certainly a considerable difference in the healthiness of different countries, arising partly from the soil and situation, and partly from the habits and employments of the people. When, from these, or any other causes whatever, a great mortality takes place, a proportional number of births immediately ensues, owing both to the greater number of yearly marriages, from the increased demand for labour, and the greater fecundity of each marriage, from being contracted at an earlier, and naturally a more prolifick, age.

On the contrary, when, from opposite causes, the healthiness of any country or parish is extraordinarily great; if, from the habits of the people, no vent for an overflowing population be found in emigration, the absolute necessity of the preventive check will be forced so strongly on their attention, that they must adopt it, or starve; and consequently, the marriages being very late, the number annually contracted will not only be small, in proportion to the population, but each individual marriage will naturally be less prolifick.

In the parish of Leyzin, noticed by M. Muret, all these circumstances appear to have been combined in a very high degree. Its situation in the Alps, but yet not too high, gave it probably the most pure and salubrious air; and the employments of the people being all pastoral, were consequently of the most healthy nature. From the calculations of M. Muret, the accuracy of which there is no reason to doubt, the probability of life in this parish, appeared to be so extraordinarily high as 61 years.[14] And the average number of the births, being, for a period of 30 years, almost accurately equal to the number of deaths,[15] clearly proved, that the habits of the people had not led them to emigrate, and that the resources of the parish for the support of population had remained nearly stationary. We are warranted, therefore, in concluding, that the pastures were limited, and could not easily be increased, either in quantity or quality. The number of cattle which could be kept upon them, would of course be limited; and, in the same manner, the number of persons required for the care of these cattle.

Under such circumstances, how would it be possible for the young men who had reached the age of puberty, to leave their father's houses, and marry, till an employment of herdsman, dairy-man, or something of the kind, became vacant by death. And as, from the extreme healthiness of the people, this must happen very slowly, it is evident, that the majority of

14. Memoires par la Societé Econ. de Berne. Année 1766, table v. p. 64.
15. Id. table i. p. 15.

them must wait during a great part of their youth, in their bachelor state, or run the most obvious risk of starving themselves and their families. The case is still stronger than in Norway, and receives a particular precision from the circumstance of the births and deaths being so nearly equal.

If a father had, unfortunately, a larger family than usual, the tendency of it would be rather to decrease, than increase, the number of marriages. He might, perhaps, with economy, be just able to support them all at home, though he could not probably find adequate employment for them on his small property; but it would evidently be long before they could quit him; and the first marriage among the sons would probably be after the death of the father; whereas, if he had had only two children, one of them might perhaps have married without leaving the parental roof, and the other, on the death of the father. And, in a general view, it may be said, that the absence or presence of four grown up unmarried people, will make the difference of there being room, or not, for the establishment of another marriage and a fresh family.

As the marriages in this parish would, with few exceptions, be very late, and yet, from the extreme healthiness of the situation, be very slowly dissolved by the death of either of the parties, it is evident, that a very large proportion of the subsisting marriages would be among persons so far advanced in life, that most of the women would have ceased to bear children; and in consequence, the whole number of subsisting marriages, was found to be, to the number of annual births, in the very unusual proportion of 12 to 1. The births were only about a 49th part of the population; and the number of persons above sixteen, was to the number below that age, nearly as 3 to 1.[16]

As a contrast to this parish, and a proof how little the number of births can be depended upon, for an estimate of population, M. Muret produces the parish of St. Cergue in the Jura, in which the subsisting marriages were, to the annual births, only in the proportion of 4 to 1, the births were a 26th part of the population, and the number of persons above and below sixteen just equal.[17]

Judging of the population of these parishes, from the proportion of their annual births, it would appear, he says, that Leyzin did not exceed St. Cergue by above one fifth at most; whereas, from actual enumeration, the population of the former turned out to be 405, and of the latter, only 171.[18]

16. Memoires, &c. par la Societé Econ. de Berne. Année 1766, p. 11 and 12.
17. Ibid.   18. Id. p. 11.

I have chosen, he observes, the parishes where the contrast is the most striking; but though the difference be not so remarkable in the rest, yet it will always be found true, that, from one place to another, even at very small distances, and in situations apparently similar, the proportions will vary considerably.[19]

It is strange, that, after making these observations, and others of the same tendency, which I have not produced, he should rest the whole proof of the depopulation of the Pays de Vaud on the proportion of births. There is no good reason for supposing that this proportion should not be different, at different periods, as well as in different situations. The extraordinary contrast in the fecundity of the two parishes of Leyzin and St. Cergue, depends upon causes within the power of time and circumstances to alter. From the great proportion of infants which was found to grow up to maturity in St. Cergue, it appeared that its natural healthiness was not much inferior to that of Leyzin.[20] The proportion of its births to deaths, was 7 to 4,[21] but as the whole number of its inhabitants did not exceed 171, it is evident, that this great excess of births could not have been regularly added to the population during the last two centuries. It must have arisen, therefore, either from a sudden increase of late years in the agriculture, or trade, of the parish, or from a habit of emigration. The latter supposition I conceive to be the true one, and it seems to be confirmed by the small proportion of adults which has already been noticed. The parish is situated in the Jura, by the side of the high road from Paris to Geneva, a situation which would evidently tend to facilitate emigration; and in effect, it seems to have acted the part of a breeding parish for the towns and flat countries, and the annual drain of a certain portion of the adults, made room for all the rest to marry, and to rear a numerous offspring.

A habit of emigration in a particular parish, will not only depend on situation, but probably often on accident. I have little doubt that three or four very successful emigrations have frequently given a spirit of enterprize to a whole village; and three or four unsuccessful ones, a contrary spirit. If a habit of emigration were introduced into the village of Leyzin, it is not to be doubted that the proportion of births would be immediately changed; and at the end of twenty years, an examination of its registers might give results as different from those at the time of M. Muret's calculations, as they were then, from the contrasted parish of St. Cergue. It will hence appear, that other causes besides a greater mortality, will concur to make an

19. Memoires, &c. par la Societé Econ. de Berne. Année 1766, p. 13.
20. Id. table xiii. p. 120.   21. Id. table i. p. 11.

estimate of population, at different periods, from the proportion of births, liable to great uncertainty.

The facts which M. Muret has collected are all valuable, though his inferences cannot always be considered in the same light. He made some calculations at Vevey, of a nature really to ascertain the question, respecting the fecundity of marriages, and to shew the fallacy of the usual mode of estimating it, though without this particular object in view at the time. He found that 375 mothers, had yielded 2093 children, all born alive, from which it followed, that each mother had produced $5\frac{10}{12}$, or nearly six children.[22] These, however, were all actually mothers, which every wife is not; but allowing for the usual proportion of barren wives at Vevey, which he had found to be 20 out of 478, it will still appear that the married women, one with another, produced above $5\frac{1}{3}$ children. And yet this was in a town, the inhabitants of which, he seems to accuse of not entering into the marriage state at the period when nature called them, and when married, of not having all the children which they might have.[23] The general proportion of the annual marriages to the annual births in the Pays de Vaud is as 1 to 3.9,[24] and, of course, according to the common mode of calculation, the marriages would appear to yield 3.9 children each.

In a division of the Pays de Vaud into eight different districts, M. Muret found, that, in seven towns, the mean life was 36 years; and the probability of life, or the age to which half of the born live, 37. In 36 villages, the mean life was 37, and the probability of life 42. In nine parishes of the Alps the mean life was 40, and the probability of life 47. In seven parishes of the Jura, these two proportions were 38 and 42: in 12 corn parishes, 37 and 40: in 18 parishes among the great vineyards, 34 and 37: in 6 parishes of mixed vines and hills, $33\frac{9}{10}$ and 36: and in one marshy, 29 and 24.[25]

From another table, it appears, that the number of persons dying under the age of puberty, was less than $\frac{1}{5}$ in the extraordinary parish of Leyzin; and less than $\frac{1}{4}$ in many other parishes of the Alps and the Jura. For the whole of the Pays de Vaud it was about $\frac{1}{3}$.[26]

In some of the largest towns, such as Lausanne and Vevey, on account of the number of strangers above the age of puberty settling in them, the proportion of adults to those under 15, was nearly as great as in the parish of Leyzin, and not far from 3 to 1. In the parishes from which there were

22. Memoires, &c. par la Societé Econ. de Berne. Année 1766, p. 29. et seq.
23. Id. p. 32.   24. Id. table i. p. 21.
25. Memoires, &c. par la Societé de Berne. Année 1766, table viii. p. 92. et seq.   26. Id. table xiii. p. 120.

not many emigrations, this proportion was about 2 to 1. And in those which furnished inhabitants for other countries, it approached more towards an equality.[27]

The whole population of the Pays de Vaud, M. Muret estimated at 113 thousand, of which 76 thousand were adults. The proportion of adults, therefore, to those under the age of puberty, for the whole country, was 2 to 1. Among these 76 thousand adults, there were 19 thousand subsisting marriages, and consequently 38 thousand married persons; and the same number of persons unmarried, though of the latter number nine thousand, according to M. Muret, would probably be widows or widowers.[28] With such an average store of persons not in the actual state of marriage, amounting to the half of all the adults, there was little ground for apprehension, that any probable emigrations, or military levies, would affect the number of annual marriages, and check the progress of population.

The proportion of annual marriages to inhabitants in the Pays de Vaud, according to M. Muret's tables, was only 1 to 140,[29] which is even less than in Norway.

All these calculations of M. Muret, imply the operation of the preventive check to population in a very considerable degree, throughout the whole of the district which he considered; and there is reason to believe, that the same habits prevail in other parts of Switzerland, though varying considerably from place to place, according as the situation or the employments of the people render them more or less healthy, or the resources of the country make room, or not, for an increase.

In the town of Berne, from the year 1583 to 1654, the sovereign council had admitted into the Bourgeoisie 487 families, of which 379 became extinct in the space of two centuries, and in 1783 only 108 of them remained. During the hundred years, from 1684 to 1784, 207 Bernoise families became extinct. From 1624 to 1712, the Bourgeoisie was given to 80 families. In 1623, the sovereign council united the members of 112 different families, of which 58 only remain.[30]

The proportion of unmarried persons in Berne, including widows and widowers, is considerably above the half of the adults, and the proportion of those below sixteen, to those above, is nearly as 1 to 3.[31] These are strong proofs of the powerful operation of the preventive check.

27. Id. table xii.   28. Id. p. 27.
29. Mem. Soc. de Berne, Année 1766, tab. i.
30. Statistique de la Suisse, Durand, tom. iv. p. 405. 8vo. 4 vols. Lausanne, 1796.   31. Beschreibung von Bern, vol. ii. tab. i. p. 35. 2 vols. 8vo. Bern, 1796.

The peasants in the canton of Berne have always had the reputation of being rich, and, without doubt, it is greatly to be attributed to this cause. A law has for some time prevailed, which makes it necessary for every peasant to prove himself in possession of the arms and accoutrements necessary for the militia, before he can obtain permission to marry. This at once excludes the very poorest from marriage; and a very favourable turn may be given to the habits of many others, from a knowledge that they cannot accomplish the object of their wishes, without a certain portion of industry and economy. A young man, who, with this end in view, had engaged in service, either at home, or in a foreign country, when he had gained the necessary sum, might feel his pride rather raised, and not be contented merely with what would obtain him permission to marry, but go on till he could obtain something like a provision for a family.

I was much disappointed, when in Switzerland, at not being able to procure any details respecting the smaller cantons, but the disturbed state of the country made it impossible. It is to be presumed, however, that as they are almost entirely in pasture, they must resemble in a great measure, the alpine parishes of the Pays de Vaud, in the extraordinary health of the people, and the absolute necessity of the preventive check; except where these circumstances may have been altered by a more than usual habit of emigration, or by the introduction of manufactures which has taken place in some parts.

The limits to the population of a country strictly pastoral, are strikingly obvious. There are no grounds less susceptible of improvement than mountainous pastures. They must necessarily be left chiefly to nature; and when they have been adequately stocked with cattle little more can be done. The great difficulty in these parts of Switzerland, as in Norway, is to procure a sufficient quantity of fodder for the winter support of the cattle which have been fed on the mountains in the summer. For this purpose, every bit of grass is collected with the greatest care. In places inaccessible to cattle, the peasant sometimes makes hay with crampons on his feet; grass is cut not three inches high, in some places, three times a year; and in the vallies, the fields are seen shaven as close as a bowling-green, and all the inequalities clipped as with a pair of scissars. In Switzerland, as in Norway, for the same reasons, the art of mowing seems to be carried to its highest pitch of perfection. As, however, the improvement of the lands in the vallies must depend principally upon the manure arising from the stock; it is evident, that the quantity of hay and the number of cattle, will be mutually limited by each other; and as the population will of course be limited by the produce of the stock, it does not seem possible to increase it beyond a certain point, and that, at no great distance. Though the population, therefore, in the flat parts of Switzerland, has increased during the last century, there is reason to believe that it has been stationary, in the mountainous parts. According to M. Muret, it has decreased very considerably in the Alps of the Pays de Vaud; but his proofs of this fact have been noticed as extremely uncertain. It is not probable that the Alps are less stocked with cattle than they were formerly: and if the inhabitants be really rather fewer in number, it is probably owing to the smaller proportion of children, and to the improvement which has taken place in the mode of living.

In some of the smaller cantons, manufactures have been introduced, which, by furnishing a greater quantity of employment, and, at the same time, a greater quantity of exports for the purchase of corn, have, of course, considerably increased their population. But the Swiss writers seem generally to agree, that the districts where they have been established, have, upon the whole, suffered in point of health, morals, and happiness.

It is the nature of pasturage to produce food for a much greater number of people than it can employ. In countries, strictly pastoral, therefore, many persons will be idle, or at most be very inadequately occupied. This state of things naturally disposes to emigration, and has been a chief cause that the Swiss have been so much engaged in foreign service. When a father had more than one son, it would rarely happen, that some of the rest did not enrol themselves as soldiers, or emigrate in some other way.

It is possible, though not probable, that a more than usual spirit of emigration, operating upon a country, in which, as it has appeared, the preventive check prevailed to a very considerable degree, might have produced a temporary check to increase at the period when there was such a universal cry about depopulation. If this were so, it without doubt contributed to improve the condition of the lower classes of people. All the foreign travellers in Switzerland, soon after this time, invariably take notice of the state of the Swiss peasantry as superior to that of other countries. In a late excursion to Switzerland, I was rather disappointed not to find it so superior as I had been taught to expect. The greatest part of the unfavourable change might justly be attributed to the losses and sufferings of the people during the late troubles; but a part, perhaps, to the ill-directed efforts of the different governments to increase the population, and to the ultimate consequences even of efforts well directed, and for a time, calculated to advance the comforts and happiness of the people.

I was very much struck with an effect of this last kind, in an expedition to the *Lac de Joux* in the Jura. The party had scarcely arrived at a little inn at the end of the lake, when the mistress of the house began to complain of the poverty and misery of all the parishes in the neighbourhood. She said that the country produced little, and yet was full of inhabitants; that boys and girls were marrying who ought still to be at school; and that, while this habit of early marriages continued, they should always be wretched, and distressed for subsistence.

The peasant, who afterwards conducted us to the source of the Orbe, entered more fully into the subject, and appeared to understand the principle of population almost as well as any man I ever met with. He said, that the women were prolifick, and the air of the mountains so pure and healthy, that very few children died, except from the consequences of absolute want; that the soil, being barren, was inadequate to yield employment and food for the numbers that were yearly growing up to manhood; that the wages of labour were consequently very low, and totally insufficient for the decent support of a family; but that the misery and starving condition of the greater part of the society did not operate properly as a warning to others, who still continued to marry and to produce a numerous offspring which they could not support. This habit of early marriages might really, he said, be called *le vice du pays;* and he was so strongly impressed with the necessary and unavoidable wretchedness that must result from it, that he thought a law ought to be made restricting men from entering into the marriage state before they were forty years of age, and then allowing it only with *"des vielles filles,"* who might bear them two or three children instead of six or eight.

I could not help being diverted with the carnestness of his oratory on this subject, and particularly, with his concluding proposition, which went far beyond even my ideas respecting the necessity of the preventive check. He must have seen and felt the misery arising from redundant population, most forcibly, to have proposed so violent a remedy. I found, upon inquiry, that he had himself married very young.

The only point in which he failed, as to his philosophical knowledge of the subject, was, in confining his reasonings too much to barren and mountainous countries, and not extending them into the plains; in fertile situations, he thought, perhaps, that the plenty of corn and employment might remove the difficulty, and allow of early marriages. Not having lived much in the plains, it was natural for him to fall into this error; particularly, as in such situations, the difficulty is not only more concealed from the extensiveness of the subject; but is in reality less, from the greater mortality, naturally occasioned by low grounds, towns, and manufactories.

On inquiring into the principal cause of what he had named the *predominant vice* of his country, he explained it with great philosophical precision. He said, that a manufacture for the polishing of stones, had been established some years ago, which for a time had been in a very thriving state, and had furnished high wages and employment to all the neighbourhood; that the facility of providing for a family, and of finding early employment for children, had encouraged, to a great degree, early marriages; and that the same habit had continued, when, from a change of fashion, accident, and other causes, the manufacture was almost at an end. Very great emigrations, he said, had of late years taken place, but the breeding system went on so fast, that they were not sufficient to relieve the country of its superabundant mouths, and the effect was such as he had described to me, and as I had in part seen.

In other conversations which I had with the lower classes of people in different parts of Switzerland and Savoy, I found many, who, though not sufficiently skilled in the principle of population, to see its effects on society, like my friend of the *Lac de Joux,* yet saw them clearly enough, as affecting their own individual interests, and were perfectly aware of the evils which they should probably bring upon themselves by marrying before they could have a tolerable prospect of being able to maintain a family. From the general ideas which I found to prevail on these subjects, I should by no means say that it would be a difficult task to make the common people comprehend the principle of population, and its effect in producing low wages and poverty.

Though there is no absolute provision for the poor in Switzerland, yet each parish generally possesses some seigneural rights, and property in land, for the public use, and is expected to maintain its own poor. These funds, however, being limited, will of course often be totally insufficient, and, occasionally, voluntary collections are made for this purpose. But the whole of the supply being comparatively scanty and uncertain, has not the same bad effects as the parish rates of England. Of late years much of the common lands belonging to parishes, has been parcelled out to individuals, which has, of course, tended to improve the soil and increase the number of people; but, from the manner in which it has been conducted, it has operated perhaps too much as a systematic encouragement of marriage; and has contributed to increase the number of poor. In the neighbourhood of the richest *communes,* I often observed the greatest quantity of beggars.

There is reason to believe, however, that the efforts of the Economical Society of Berne to promote agriculture were crowned with some success, and that the increasing resources of the country have made room for an additional population, and furnished an adequate support for the greatest part, if not the whole, of that increase which has of late taken place.

In 1764, the population of the whole canton of Berne, including the Pays de Vaud, was estimated at 336,689. In 1791, it had increased to 414,420. From 1764 to 1777, its increase proceeded at the rate of 2000 each year; and, from 1778 to 1791, at the rate of 3109 each year.[32]

32. Beschreibung von Bern, vol. ii. p. 40.

CHAP. VIII.

Of the Checks to Population in France.

As the tables of mortality in France, before the revolution, were not kept with peculiar care, nor for any great length of time, and as the few, which have been produced, exhibit no very extraordinary results, I should not have made this country the subject of a distinct chapter, but for a circumstance attending the revolution which has excited considerable surprise. This is, the undiminished state of the population, in spite of the losses sustained during so long and destructive a contest.

A great national work, founded on the reports of the Prefects in the different departments, is at present in some state of forwardness at Paris, and, when completed, it may reasonably be expected to form a very valuable accession to the materials of statistical science in general. The returns of all the Prefects are not, however, yet complete; but I was positively assured by the person who has the principal superintendence of them, that enough is already known, to be certain, that the population of the old territory of France has rather increased than diminished during the revolution.

Such an event, if true, very strongly confirms the general principles of this work; and assuming it, for the present, as a fact, it may tend to throw some light on the subject, to trace, a little in detail, the manner in which such an event might happen.

In every country, there is always a considerable body of unmarried persons, formed by the gradual accumulation of the excess of the number rising annually to the age of puberty, above the number of persons annually married. The stop to the further accumulation of this body, is when its number is such, that the yearly mortality equals the yearly accessions that are made to it. In the Pays de Vaud, as appeared in the last chapter, this body, including widows and widowers, persons who are not actually in the state of marriage, equals the whole number of married persons. But in a country like France, where both the mortality, and the tendency to marriage, are much greater than in Switzerland, this body does not bear so large a proportion to the population.

According to a calculation in an *Essai d' une Statitisque Generale,* published at Paris in 1800, by M. Peuchet, the number of unmarried males in France between 18 and 50 is estimated at 1,451,063, and the number of males, whether married or not, between the same ages, at 5,000,000.[1] It does not appear at what period exactly this calculation was made. The number of unmarried persons seems to be too great for any period after some years of the revolution had elapsed; and rather too small for the period before the revolution. Let us suppose, however, that this number of 1,451,063, expresses the collective body of unmarried males of a military age at the commencement of the revolution.

The population of France, before the beginning of the war, was estimated by the National Assembly, at 26,363,074;[2] and there is no reason to believe that this calculation was too high. Necker, though he mentions the number 24,800,000, expresses his firm belief that the yearly births, at that time, amounted to above a million, and consequently, according to his multiplier of $25\frac{3}{4}$, that the whole population was nearly 26 millions,[3] and this calculation was made ten years previous to the estimate of the National Assembly.

Taking then the annual births at rather above a million, and estimating that rather above $\frac{2}{5}$ would die under 18, which appears to be the case from some calculations of M. Peuchet,[4] it will follow, that 600,000 persons will annually arrive at the age of 18.

The annual marriages, according to Necker, are 213,774;[5] but as this number is an average of ten years, taken while the population was increasing, it is probably too low. If we take 220,000, then 440,000 persons will be supposed to marry out of the 600,000 rising to a marriageable age; and consequently, the excess of those rising to the age of 18, above the number wanted to complete the usual proportion of annual marriages, will be 160,000, or 80,000 males. It is evident, therefore, that the accumulated body of 1,451,063, unmarried males, of a military age, and the annual supply of 80,000 youths of 18, might be taken for the service of the state, without affecting, in any degree, the number of annual marriages. But we cannot suppose that the 1,451,063 should be taken all at once, and many soldiers are married, and in a situation not to be entirely useless to the population. Let us suppose 600,000 of the corps of unmarried males to be embodied at once; and this number to be kept up by the annual supply of 150,000 persons, taken partly from the 80,000, rising annually to the age of

---

1. P. 32. 8vo. 78 pages.
2. A. Young's Travels in France, vol. i. c. xvii. p. 466. 4to. 1792.
3. De l'Administration des Finances, tom. i. c. ix. p. 256. 12mo. 1785.
4. Essai, p. 31.   5. De l'Administration des Finances, tom. i. c. ix. p. 255.

18, and not wanted to complete the number of annual marriages, and partly, from the 851,063 remaining of the body of unmarried males which existed at the beginning of the war.

It is evident, that, from these two sources, 150,000 might be supplied each year, for ten years, and yet allow of an increase in the usual number of annual marriages of above 10,000. It is true, that, in the course of the 10 years, many of the original body of unmarried males will have passed the military age; but this will be balanced, and, indeed, much more than balanced, by their utility in the married life. From the beginning, it should be taken into consideration, that though a man of fifty be generally considered as past the military age, yet if he marry a fruitful subject, he may by no means be useless to the population; and in fact, the supply of 150,000 recruits each year, would be taken principally from the 300,000 males rising annually to 18, and the annual marriages would be supplied, in great measure, from the remaining part of the original body of unmarried persons. Widowers and bachelors of forty and fifty, who, in the common state of things, might have found it difficult to obtain an agreeable partner, would probably see these difficulties removed in such a scarcity of husbands; and the absence of 600,000 persons, would of course make room for a very considerable addition to the number of annual marriages. This addition in all probability took place. Many, among the remaining part of the original body of bachelors, who might otherwise have continued single, would marry under this change of circumstances; and it is known, that a very considerable portion of youths under 18, in order to avoid the military conscriptions, entered prematurely into the married state. This was so much the case, and contributed so much to diminish the number of unmarried persons, that, in the beginning of the year 1798, it was found necessary to repeal the law which had exempted married persons from the conscriptions; and those who married subsequently to this new regulation, were taken indiscriminately with the unmarried. And though after this, the levies fell, in part, upon those who were actually engaged in the peopling of the country; yet the number of marriages untouched by these levies might still remain greater than the usual number of marriages before the revolution; and the marriages which were broken by the removal of the husband to the armies, would not probably have been entirely barren.

Sir Francis D'Ivernois, who had certainly a tendency to exggerate, and probably has exaggerated considerably, the losses of the French nation, estimates the total loss of the troops of France both by land and sea, up to the year 1799, at a million and a half.[6] The round numbers which I have allowed, for the sake of illustrating the subject, exceed Sir Francis D'Ivernois's estimate by six hundred thousand. He calculates, however, a loss of a million of persons more, from the other causes of destruction attendant on the revolution; but as this loss fell indiscriminately on all ages and both sexes, it would not affect the population in the same degree, and will be much more than covered by the 600,000 men in the full vigour of life, which remain above Sir Francis's calculation. It should be observed also, that in the latter part of the revolutionary war, the military conscriptions were probably enforced with still more severity in the newly acquired territories, than in the old state; and, as the population of these new acquisitions is estimated at 5 or 6 millions, it would bear a considerable proportion of the million and a half supposed to be destroyed in the armies. And, although the law, which facilitated divorces to so great a degree, be radically bad, both in a moral and political view, yet, under the circumstance of a great scarcity of men, it would operate a little like the custom of polygamy, and increase the number of children in proportion to the number of husbands. In addition to this, the women without husbands do not appear all to have been barren, as the proportion of illegitimate births is now raised to $\frac{1}{12}$ of the whole number of births, from $\frac{1}{47}$,[7] which it was before the revolution; and though this be a melancholy proof of the depravation of morals, yet it would certainly contribute to increase the number of births; and as the female peasants in France were enabled to earn more than usual during the revolution, on account of the scarcity of hands, it is probable, that a considerable portion of these children would survive.

Under all these circumstances, it cannot appear impossible, and scarcely even improbable, that the population of France should remain undiminished, in spite of all the causes of destruction which have operated upon it during the course of the revolution, provided, that the agriculture of the country has been such, as to continue the means of subsistence unimpaired.

6. Tableau des Pertes, &c. c. ii. p. 7. Mons. Garnier, in the notes to his edition of Adam Smith, calculates, that only about a sixtieth part of the French population was destroyed in the armies. He supposes only 500,000 embodied at once, and that this number was supplied by 400,000 more in the course of the war; and allowing for the number which would die naturally, that the additional mortality occasioned by the war, was only about 45,000 each year. Tom. v. note xxx. p. 284. If the actual loss were no more than these statements make it, a small increase of births would have easily repaired it; but I should think that these estimates are probably as much below the truth as Sir F. D'Ivernois's are above.

7. Essai de Peuchet, p. 28.

And it seems now to be generally acknowledged, that, however severely the manufactures of France may have suffered, her agriculture has increased rather than diminished. At no period of the war, can we suppose, that the number of embodied troops exceeded the number of men employed before the revolution in manufactures. Those who were thrown out of work by the destruction of these manufactures, and who did not go to the armies, would of course betake themselves to the labours of agriculture; and it was always the custom in France for the women to work much in the fields, which custom was probably increased during the revolution. At the same time, the absence of a large portion of the best and most vigorous hands, would raise the price of labour; and as, from the new land brought into cultivation, and the absence of a considerable part of the greatest consumers,[8] in foreign countries, the price of provisions did not rise in proportion; this advance in the price of labour would not only operate as a powerful encouragement to marriage, but would enable the peasants to live better, and to rear a greater number of their children.

At all times, the number of small farmers and proprietors in France was great; and though such a state of things be by no means favourable to the clear surplus produce, or disposeable wealth, of a nation; yet, sometimes, it is not unfavourable to the absolute produce, and it has always a most powerful tendency to encourage population. From the sale and division of many of the large domains of the nobles and clergy, the number of landed proprietors has considerably increased during the revolution; and as a part of these domains consisted of parks and chaces, new territory has been given to the plough. It is true, that the land tax has been not only too heavy, but injudiciously imposed. It is probable, however, that this disadvantage has been nearly counter-balanced by the removal of the former oppressions under which the cultivator laboured, and that the sale and division of the great domains, may be considered as a clear advantage on the side of agriculture, or, at any rate; of the gross produce, which is the principal point with regard to mere population.

These considerations make it appear probable, that the means of subsistence have at least remained unimpaired, if they have not increased, during the revolution; and a view of the cultivation of France in its present state, certainly rather tends to confirm this supposition.

8. Supposing the increased number of children, at any period, to equal the number of men absent in the armies, yet these children being all very young, could not be supposed to consume a quantity equal to that which would be consumed by the same number of grown up persons.

We shall not, therefore, be inclined to agree with Sir Francis D'Ivernois, in his conjecture, that the annual births in France have diminished by one seventh during the revolution.[9] On the contrary, it is much more probable, that they have increased by this number. The average proportion of births, to the population in all France, before the revolution, was, according to Necker, as 1 to $25\frac{3}{4}$.[10] It has appeared in the reports of some of the Prefects which have been returned, that the proportion in many country places, was raised to 1 to 21, 22, $22\frac{1}{2}$, and 23;[11] and though these proportions might, in some degree, be caused by the absence of a part of the population in the armies, yet I have little doubt that they are principally to be attributed to the birth of a greater number of children than usual. If, when the reports of all the Prefects are put together, it should appear, that the number of births has not increased in proportion to the population, and yet, that the population is undiminished; it will follow, either that Necker's multiplier for the births was too small, which is extremely probable, as from this cause he appears to have calculated the population too low; or that the mortality among those not exposed to violent deaths, has been less than usual, which, from the high price of labour, and the desertion of the towns for the country, is not unlikely.

According to Necker and Moheau, the mortality in France, before the revolution, was 1 in 30 or $30\frac{1}{8}$.[12] Considering that the proportion of the population which lives in the country, is, to that in the towns, as $3\frac{1}{2}$ to 1,[13] this mortality is extraordinarily great, caused, probably, by the misery arising from an excess of population; and from the remarks of Arthur Young on the state of the peasantry in France,[14] which are completely sanctioned by Necker,[15] this appears to have been really the case. If we suppose, that from the removal of a part of this redundant population, the mortality should have decreased from 1 in 30, to 1 in 35,[16] this favourable change would go a considerable way in repairing the breaches made by war on the frontiers.

9. Tableau des Pertes, &c. c. ii. p. 14.   10. De l'Administration des Finances, tom. i. c.ix. p. 254.   11. Essai de Peuchet, p. 28.

12. De l'Administration des Finances, tom. i. c. ix. p. 255. Essai de Peuchet, p. 29.

13. Young's Travels in France, vol. i. c. xvii. p. 466.

14. See generally, c. xvii. vol. i. and the just observations on these subjects, interspersed in many other parts of his very valuable tour.

15. De l'Administration des Finances, tom. i. c. ix. p. 262. et seq.

16. If it should appear that the mortality among those remaining in the country has not diminished, it will be attributable to the greater proportion of infants, a circumstance noticed in reference to the Prussian table, in c. vi. of this book.

The probability is, that both the causes mentioned have operated in part. The births have increased, and the deaths of those remaining in the country have diminished; so that, putting the two circumstances together, it will probably appear, when the results of all the reports of the Prefects are known, that, including those who have fallen in the armies, and by violent means, the deaths have not exceeded the births in the course of the revolution.

The returns of the Prefects are to be given for the year 9 of the republick, and to be compared with the year 1789; but if the proportion of births to the population be given merely for the individual year 9, it will not shew with precision the average proportion of births to the population during the course of the revolution. In the confusion occasioned by this event, it is not probable that any very exact registers should have been kept; but, from theory, I should be inclined to expect, that, soon after the beginning of the war, and at other periods during the course of it, the proportion of births to the whole population would be greater, than in 1800 and 1801. If it should appear by the returns, that the number of annual marriages has not increased during the revolution, the circumstance will be obviously accounted for by the extraordinary increase in the illegitimate births, mentioned before in this chapter, which amount, at present, to one eleventh of all the births, instead of one forty-seventh, according to the calculation of Necker before the revolution.[17]

Sir Francis D'Ivernois observes, that "those have yet to learn the first
" principles of political arithmetick, who imagine that it is in the field of
" battle and the hospitals, that an account can be taken of the lives which
" a revolution or a war has cost. The number of men it has killed, is of
" much less importance than the number of children which it has pre-
" vented, and will still prevent, from coming into the world. This is the
" deepest wound which the population of France has received." – "Sup-
" posing," he says, "that, of the whole number of men destroyed, only two
" millions had been united to as many females; according to the calcula-
" tion of Buffon, these two millions of couples ought to bring into the
" world twelve millions of children, in order to supply, at the age of thirty-
" nine, a number equal to that of their parents. This is a point of view, in
" which the consequences of such a destruction of men becomes almost

17. Essai de Peuchet, p. 28. It is highly probable that this increase of illegitimate births occasioned a more than usual number of children to be exposed in those dreadful receptacles, *Les Hopiteaux des Enfans trouvés,* as noticed by Sir Francis D'Ivernois; but probably this cruel custom was confined to particular districts, and the number exposed, upon the whole, might bear no great proportion to the sum of all the births.

" incalculable; because they have much more effect with regard to the
" twelve millions of children, which they prevent from coming into exis-
" tence, than with regard to the actual loss of the two millions and a half
" of men, for whom France mourns. It is not till a future period, that she
" will be able to estimate this dreadful breach."[18]

And yet, if the circumstances on which the foregoing reasonings are founded, should turn out to be true, it will appear, that France has not lost a single birth by the revolution. She has the most just reason to mourn the two millions and a half of individuals which she may have lost, but not their posterity: because, if these individuals had remained in the country, a proportionate number of children, born of other parents, which are now living in France, would not have come into existence. If, in the best governed country in Europe, we were to mourn the posterity which is prevented from coming into being, we should always wear the habit of grief.

It is evident, that the constant tendency of the births, in every country, to supply the vacancies made by death, cannot, in a moral point of view, afford the slightest shadow of excuse for the wanton sacrifice of men. The positive evil that is committed, in this case, the pain, misery, and wide-spreading desolation and sorrow, that are occasioned to the existing inhabitants, can by no means be counterbalanced by the consideration, that the numerical breach in the population will be rapidly repaired. We can have no other right, moral or political, except that of the most urgent necessity, to exchange the lives of beings in the full vigour of their enjoyments, for an equal number of helpless infants.

It should also be remarked, that though the numerical population of France may not have suffered by the revolution; yet, that if her losses have been in any degree equal to the conjectures on the subject, her military strength cannot be unimpaired. Her population at present must consist of a much greater proportion than usual of women and children; and the body of unmarried persons of a military age, must be diminished in a very striking manner. This, indeed, is known to be the case, from the returns of the Prefects which have already been received.

It has appeared, that the point at which the drains of men will begin essentially to affect the population of a country, is, when the original body of unmarried persons is exhausted, and the annual demands are greater than the excess of the number of males rising annually to the age of puberty, above the number wanted to complete the usual proportion of annual marriages. France was probably at some distance from this point, at the conclu-

18. Tableau des Pertes, &c. ii. p. 13, 14.

sion of the war; but, in the present state of her population, with an increased proportion of women and children, and a great diminution of males of a military age, she could not make the same gigantic exertions which were made at one period, without trenching on the sources of her population.

At all times, the number of males of a military age in France, was small in proportion to the population, on account of the tendency to marriage,[19] and the great number of children. Necker takes particular notice of this circumstance. He observes, that the effect of the very great misery of the peasantry, is, to produce a dreadful mortality of infants under three or four years of age; and the consequence is, that the number of young children will always be in too great a proportion to the number of grown up people. A million of individuals, he justly observes, will, in this case, neither present the same military force, nor the same capacity of labour, as an equal number of individuals in a country where the people are less miserable.[20]

Switzerland, before the revolution, could have brought into the field, or have employed in labour appropriate to grown up persons, one third more in proportion to her population, than France, at the same period.

It will be but of little consequence, if any of the facts or calculations which have been assumed in the course of this chapter, should turn out to be false. The reader will see, that the reasonings are of a general nature, and may be true, though the facts taken to illustrate them may prove to be inapplicable.[21]

19. The proportion of marriages to the population in France, according to Necker, is 1 to 113, tom. i. c. ix. p. 255.

20. De l'Administration des Finances, tom. i. c. ix. p. 263.

21. Since I wrote this chapter I have had an opportunity of seeing the *Analyse des Procès Verbaux des Conseils Generaux de Departement,* which gives a very particular, and highly curious account of the internal state of France for the year 8. With respect to the population, out of 69 departments, the reports from which are given, in 16, the population is supposed to be increased; in 42, diminished; in 9, stationary; and in 2, the active population is said to be diminished, but the numerical to remain the same. It appears, however, that most of these reports are not founded on actual enumerations; and without such positive data, the prevailing opinions on the subject of population, together with the necessary and universally acknowledged fact, of a very considerable diminution in the males of a military age, would naturally dispose people to think that the numbers, upon the whole, must be diminished. Judging merely from appearances, the substitution of a hundred children, for a hundred grown up persons, would certainly not produce the same impression, with regard to population. I should not be surprised, therefore, if, when the enumerations for the year 9 are completed, it should appear, that the population, upon the whole, has not diminished. In some of the reports, *l'aisance generale repandue sur le peuple,* and *la division des grands proprietaires,* are mentioned as the causes of increase; and

almost universally, *les mariages prematurès,* and *les mariages multipliées par la crainte des loix militaires,* are particularly noticed.

With respect to the state of agriculture, out of 78 reports, 6 are of opinion that it is improved; 10, that it is deteriorated; 70 demand that it should be encouraged in general; 32 complain *de la multiplicitè des defrichements;* and 12 demand *des encouragements pour les defrichements.* One of the reports mentions, *la quantitè prodigieuse de terres vagues mise en culture depuis quelque tems, et les travaux multipliées, au de la de ce peuvent executer les bras employes en agriculture;* and others speak of *les defrichements multipliées qui ont eu lieu depuis plusieurs annèes,* which appeared to be successful at first; but it was soon perceived, that it would be more profitable to cultivate less, and cultivate well. Many of the reports notice the cheapness of corn, and the want of sufficient vent for this commodity; and in the discussion of the question respecting the division of the *biens communaux,* it is observed, that "le partage en operant le defrichement de ces biens, a sans doute " produit une augmentation rèelle de denrèes, mais d'un autre cotè, les vaines pa- " tures n'existent plus, et les bestiaux sont peutètre diminuès." On the whole, therefore, I should be inclined to infer, that though the agriculture of the country does not appear to have been conducted judiciously, so as to obtain a large *surplus* produce, yet that the *absolute* produce had by no means been diminished during the revolution, and that the attempt to bring so much new land under cultivation, had contributed to make the scarcity of labourers still more sensible. And if it be allowed, that the food of the country did not decrease during the revolution, the high price of labour, which is very generally noticed, must have operated as a most powerful encouragement to population among the labouring part of the society.

The land tax, or *contribution fonciere,* is universally complained of; indeed, it appears to be extremely heavy, and to fall very unequally. It was intended to be only a fifth of the net produce; but, from the unimproved state of agriculture in general, the number of small proprietors, and, particularly, the attempt to cultivate too much surface in proportion to the capital employed, it often amounts to a fourth, a third, or even a half. The state of agriculture in France has never been such, as to yield a surplus produce in proportion to the gross produce, in any respect equal to what it yields in England; and, therefore, a land tax bearing the same relation to the gross produce, would cause a very different degree of pressure in the two countries. And, when property is so much divided, that the rent and profit of a farm must be combined, in order to support a family upon it, a land tax must necessarily greatly impede cultivation; though it has little or no effect of this kind, when farms are large, and let out to tenants, as is most fequently the case in England. Among the impediments to agriculture mentioned in the reports, the two great division of lands from the new laws of succession is noticed. The partition of some of the great domains would probably contribute to the improvement of agriculture; but subdivisions of the nature here alluded to, would certainly have a contrary effect, and would tend most particularly to diminish surplus produce, and make a land tax both oppressive and unproductive. If all the land in England were divided into farms of 20l. a year, we should probably be more populous than we are at present; but, as a nation, we should be extremely poor. We should be almost without disposeable revenue, and should be under a total inability of maintaining the same number of manufactures, or collecting the same taxes, as at present. All the departments demand a diminution of the *contribution fonciere* as absolutely necessary to the prosperity of agriculture.

Of the state of the hospitals, and charitable establishments, of the prevalance of beggary, and the mortality among the exposed children, a most deplorable picture is drawn in almost all the reports. From which, we should at first be disposed to infer, a greater degree of poverty and misery among all the lower classes of people in general. It appears, however, that the hospitals and charitable establishments lost almost the whole of their revenues during the revolution; and this sudden subtraction of support from a great number of people who had no other reliance, together with the known failure of manufactures in the towns, and the very great increase of illegitimate children, might produce all the distressing appearances described in the reports, without impeaching the great fact of the ameliorated condition of agricultural labourers in general, necessarily arising from the acknowledged high price of labour, and comparative cheapness of corn; and it is from this part of the society that the effective population of a country is principally supplied. If the poor's rates of England were suddenly abolished, there would undoubtedly be the most complicated distress among those who were before supported by them; but I should not expect, that either the condition of the labouring part of the society in general, or the population of the country, would suffer from it. As the proportion of illegitimate children in France has risen so extraordinarily, as from $\frac{1}{47}$ of all the births to $\frac{1}{11}$, it is evident that more might be abandoned in hospitals, and more out of these die than usual, and yet a more than usual number be reared at home, and escape the mortality of these dreadful receptacles. It appears that, from the low state of the funds in the hospitals, the proper nurses could not be paid, and numbers of children died from absolute famine. Some of the hospitals, at last, very properly refused to receive any more.

The reports, upon the whole, do not present a favourable picture of the internal state of France; but something is undoubtedly to be attributed to the nature of these reports, which, consisting as they do of observations explaining the state of the different departments, and of particular demands with a view to obtain assistance or relief from government, it is to be expected that they should lean rather to the unfavourable side. When the question is respecting the imposition of new taxes, or the relief from old ones, people will generally complain of their poverty. On the subject of taxes indeed, it would appear as if the French government must be a little puzzled. For though it very properly recommended to the *conseils generaux* not to indulge in vague complaints, but to mention specifick grievances, and propose specifick remedies, and particularly not to advise the abolition of one tax, without suggesting another; yet all the taxes, appear to me, to be reprobated and most frequently in general terms, without the proposal of any substitute. *La contribution fonciere, la taxe mobiliare, les barrieres, les droits de douâne,* all excite bitter complaints, and the only new substitute that struck me, was a tax upon game, which, being at present almost extinct in France, cannot be expected to yield a revenue sufficient to balance all the rest. The work, upon the whole, is extremely curious, and as shewing the wish of the government to know the state of each department; and to listen to every observation, and proposal, for its improvement, is highly creditable to the ruling power. It was published for a short time, but the circulation of it was soon stopped, and confined to the ministers, *les conseils generaux,* &c. Indeed the documents are evidently more of a private than of a publick nature, and certainly have not the air of being intended for general circulation.

For the state of population in Spain, I refer the reader to the valuable, and entertaining travels of Mr. Townsend, in that country, in which he will often find the principle of population very happily illustrated. I should have made it the subject of a distinct chapter, but was fearful of extending this part of the work too much, and of falling, almost unavoidably, into too many repetitions, from the necessity of drawing the same kind of inference from so many different countries. I could expect, besides, to add very little to what has been so well done by Mr. Townsend.

C H A P .   IX.

Of the Checks to Population in England.

THE most cursory view of society in this country, must convince us, that throughout all ranks, the preventive check to population prevails in a considerable degree. Those among the higher classes, who live principally in towns, often want the inclination to marry, from the facility with which they can indulge themselves in an illicit intercourse with the sex. And others are deterred from marrying, by the idea of the expences that they must retrench, and the pleasures of which they must deprive themselves, on the supposition of having a family. When the fortune is large, these considerations are certainly trivial; but a preventive foresight of this kind, has objects of much greater weight for its contemplation as we go lower.

A man of liberal education, with an income only just sufficient to enable him to associate in the rank of gentlemen, must feel absolutely certain, that if he marry, and have a family, he shall be obliged, if he mix in society, to rank himself with farmers and tradesmen. The woman, that a man of education would naturally make the object of his choice, is one brought up in the same habits and sentiments with himself, and used to the familiar intercourse of a society totally different from that to which she must be reduced by marriage. Can a man easily consent to place the object of his affection in a situation so discordant, probably, to her habits and inclinations. Two or three steps of descent in society, particularly at this round of the ladder, where education ends and ignorance begins, will not be considered by the generality of people as a chimerical, but a real evil. If society be desirable, it surely must be free, equal, and reciprocal society, where benefits are conferred as well as received, and not such as the dependent finds with his patron, or the poor with the rich.

These considerations certainly prevent a great number in this rank of life, from following the bent of their inclinations in an early attachment. Others, influenced either by a stronger passion, or a weaker judgment, disregard these considerations; and it would be hard indeed, if the gratification of so delightful a passion as virtuous love, did not sometimes more than counterbalance all its attendant evils. But I fear that it must be acknowledged, that the more general consequences of such marriages are rather calculated to justify, than to disappoint, the forebodings of the prudent.

The sons of tradesmen and farmers, are exhorted not to marry, and generally find it necessary to comply with this advice, till they are settled in some business or farm, which may enable them to support a family. These events may not, perhaps, occur till they are far advanced in life. The scarcity of farms is a very general complaint; and the competition in every kind of business is so great, that it is not possible that all should be successful. Among the clerks in counting houses, and the competitors for all kinds of mercantile and professional employment, it is probable, that the preventive check to population prevails more than in any other department of society.

The labourer who earns eighteen-pence or two shillings a day, and lives at his ease as a singleman, will hesitate a little, before he divides that pittance among four or five, which seems to be not more than sufficient for one. Harder fare, and harder labour, he would perhaps be willing to submit to, for the sake of living with the woman that he loves; but he must feel conscious, that, should he have a large family, and any ill fortune whatever, no degree of frugality, no possible exertion of his manual strength, would preserve him from the heart-rending sensation of seeing his children starve, or of being obliged to the parish for their support. The love of independence is a sentiment that surely none would wish to see eradicated; though the parish law of England, it must be confessed, is a system of all others the most calculated gradually to weaken this sentiment, and in the end will probably destroy it completely.

The servants who live in the families of the rich, have restraints yet stronger to break through in venturing upon marriage. They possess the necessaries, and even the comforts, of life, almost in as great plenty as their masters. Their work is easy, and their food luxurious, compared with the work and food of the class of labourers; and their sense of dependence is weakened by the conscious power of changing their masters, if they feel themselves offended. Thus comfortably situated at present, what are their prospects if they marry. Without knowledge, or capital, either for business, or farming, and unused, and therefore unable, to earn a subsistence by daily labour, their only refuge seems to be a miserable alehouse, which certainly offers no very enchanting prospect of a happy evening to their lives. The greater number of them, therefore, deterred by this uninviting view of their future situation, content themselves with remaining single where they are.

If this sketch of the state of society in England be near the truth, it will be allowed, that the preventive check to population operates with considerable force throughout all the classes of the community. And this observation is further confirmed by the abstracts from the registers returned in consequence of the late Population Act. The results of these abstracts shew, that the annual marriages in England and Wales, are to the whole population as 1 to $123\frac{1}{5}$,[1] a smaller proportion of marriages than obtains in any of the countries which have been examined, except Norway and Switzerland.

In the earlier part of the last century, Dr. Short estimated this proportion at about 1 to 115.[2] It is probable that this calculation was then correct, and the present diminution in the proportion of marriages notwithstanding an increase of population more rapid than formerly, owing to the more rapid progress of commerce and agriculture, is partly a cause, and partly a consequence, of the diminished mortality that has been observed of late years.

The returns of the marriages, pursuant to the late act, are supposed to be less liable to the suspicion of inaccuracy, than any other parts of the registers.

Dr. Short in his *New Observations on Town and Country Bills of Mortality,* says, he will "conclude with the observation of an eminent Judge of " this nation, that the growth and increase of mankind is more stinted " from the cautious difficulty people make to enter on marriage, from the " prospect of the trouble and expences in providing for a family, than " from any thing in the nature of the species." And, in conformity to this idea, Dr. Short proposes to lay heavy taxes and fines, on those who live single, for the support of the married poor.[3]

The observation of the eminent Judge is, with regard to the numbers which are prevented from being born, perfectly just; but the inference that the unmarried ought to be punished, does not appear to be equally so. It will not, I believe, be very far from the truth, to say, that, in this country, not more than half of the prolifick power of nature is called into action, and yet, that there are more children born than the country can properly support.

1. Observ. on the Results of the Population Act, p. 11. The answers to the Population Act, have at length happily rescued the question of the population of this country from the obscurity in which it has been so long involved, and have afforded some very valuable data to the political calculator. At the same time, it must be confessed, that they are not so complete, as entirely to exclude reasonings and conjectures, respecting the inferences which are to be drawn from them. It is earnestly to be hoped, that the subject may not be suffered to drop after the present effort. Now that the first difficulty is removed, an enumeration, every ten years, might be rendered easy and familiar; and the registers of births, deaths, and marriages, might be received every year, or at least, every five years. I am persuaded that more inferences are to be drawn, respecting the internal state of a country, from such registers, than we have yet been in the habit of supposing.

2. New Observ. on Bills of Mortality, p. 265. 8vo. 1750.   3. Id. p. 247.

If we suppose that the yearly births were $\frac{1}{20}$ part of the population, a proportion, which, for short periods, obtains frequently on the continent,[4] and constantly, perhaps, in many parts of America; and allowing one third for the mortality under 20, which is a moderate supposition, as, according to Dr. Short, this mortality, in some places, is only one fifth or one fourth;[5] then if all were to marry at 20, which is by no means so early an age as is possible, $\frac{1}{30}$th part of the population would, in that case, marry annually; that is, there would be one annual marriage out of 60 persons, instead of one marriage out of 123 persons, as is the case at present. It may fairly be said, therefore, that not more than one half of the prolifick power of nature is called into action in this country. And yet, when we contemplate the insufficiency of the price of labour to maintain a large family, and the quantum of mortality which arises directly and indirectly from poverty; and add to this, the crowds of children, which are cut off prematurely in our great towns, our manufactories, and our workhouses, we shall be compelled to acknowledge, that if the number born annually, were not greatly thinned by this premature mortality, the funds for the maintenance of labour must increase with much greater rapidity than they have ever done hitherto in this country, in order to find work and food for the additional numbers that would then grow up to manhood.

Those, therefore, who live single, or marry late, do not, by such conduct, contribute, in any degree, to diminish the actual population; but merely to diminish the proportion of premature mortality which would otherwise be excessive; and consequently in this point of view do not seem to deserve any very severe reprobation or punishment.

The returns of the births and deaths are supposed, on good grounds, to be deficient, and it will therefore be difficult to estimate, with any degree of accuracy, the proportion which they bear to the whole population.

If we divide the existing population of England and Wales, by the average of burials for the five years ending in 1800, it would appear, that the mortality was only 1 in 49;[6] but this is a proportion so extraordinarily small, considering the number of our great towns and manufactories, that it cannot be considered as approaching to the truth.

4. On an average of five years, after the plague in Prussia, rejecting the first extraordinary year, the proportion of births to the whole population was above 1 to 18, (table iv. page 253). In New Jersey, according to Dr. Price (Observ. on Revers. Paym. vol i. p. 283.) it was 1 to 18, and in the back settlements probably 1 to 15.

5. New Observ. on Bills of Mortality, p. 59.

6. The population is taken at 9,168,000, and the annual deaths at 186,000. (Obs. on the Results of Pop. Act. p. 6 & 9.)

Whatever may be the exact proportion of the inhabitants of the towns to the inhabitants of the country, the southern part of this island certainly ranks in that class of states, where this proportion is greater than 1 to 3; indeed, there is ample reason to believe, that it is greater than 1 to 2. According to the rule laid down by Crome, the mortality ought, consequently, to be above 1 in 30;[7] according to Susmilch, above 1 in 33.[8] In the *Observations on the Results of the Population Act,*[9] many probable causes of deficiency in the registry of the burials, are pointed out; but no calculation is offered respecting the sum of these deficiencies, and I have no data whatever to supply such a calculation. I will only observe, therefore, that if we suppose them altogether to amount to such a number, as will make the present annual mortality about 1 in 40, this must appear to be the lowest proportion of deaths that can well be supposed, considering the circumstances of the country; and if true, would indicate a most astonishing superiority over the generality of other states, either in the habits of the people with respect to prudence and cleanliness, or in natural healthiness of situation.[10] Indeed, it seems to be nearly ascertained, that both these causes, which tend to diminish mortality, operate in this country to a considerable degree. The small proportion of annual marriages mentioned before, indicates, that habits of prudence, extremely favourable to happiness, prevail through a large part of the community, in spite of the poor-laws; and it appears from the clearest evidence, that the generality of our country parishes are very healthy. Dr. Price quotes an account of Dr. Percival, collected from the ministers of different parishes, and taken from positive enumerations, according to which, in some villages, only a 45th, a 50th, a 60th, a 66th, and even a 75th part, dies annually. In many of these parishes the births are to the deaths above 2 to 1, and in a single parish above 3 to 1.[11] These, however, are

7. Uber die Bevölkerung der Europaischen Staaten, p. 127.
8. Susmilch, Gottliche Ordnung, vol. iii. p. 60.   9. P. 6.
10. It is by no means surprising that our population should have been underrated formerly, at least by any person who attempted to estimate it from the proportion of births or deaths. Till the late Population Act, no one would have imagined, that the actual returns of annual deaths, which might naturally have been expected to be as accurate in this country as in others, would turn out to be less than a 49th part of the population. If the actual returns for France, even so long ago as the ten years ending with 1780, had been multiplied by 49, she would have appeared at that time to have a population of above 40 millions. The average of annual deaths, was 818,491. Necker, de l'Administration des Finances, tom. i. c. ix. p. 255. 12mo. 1785.
11. Price's Observ. on Revers. Paym. vol. ii. note, p. 10. First additional Essay. In particular parishes, private communications are perhaps more to be depended

particular instances, and cannot be applied to the agricultural part of the country in general. In some of the flat situations, and particularly those near marshes, the proportions are found very different, and in a few, the deaths exceed the births. In the 54 country parishes, the registers of which, Dr. Short collected, chusing them purposely in a great variety of situations, the average mortality was as high as 1 in 37.[12] This is certainly much above the present mortality of our agricultural parishes, in general. The period which Dr. Short took, included some considerable epidemicks, which may possibly have been above the usual proportion. But sickly seasons should always be included, or we shall fall into great errors. In 1056 villages of Brandenburgh, which Susmilch examined, the mortality for 6 good years, was 1 in 43; for 10 mixed years, about 1 in $38\frac{1}{2}$.[13] In the villages of England, which Sir F. M. Eden mentions, the mortality seems to be about 1 in 47 or 48;[14] and in the late returns pursuant to the Population Act, a still greater degree of healthiness appears. Combining these observations together, if we take 1 in 46, or 1 in 48, as the average mortality of the agricultural part of the country including sickly seasons, this will be the lowest that can be supposed with any degree of probability. But this proportion will certainly be raised to 1 in 40, when we blend it with the mortality of the towns, and the manufacturing part of the community, in order to obtain the average for the whole kingdom.

The mortality in London, which includes so considerable a part of the inhabitants of this country, was, according to Dr. Price, at the time he made his calculations, 1 in $20\frac{1}{4}$; in Norwich 1 in $24\frac{1}{2}$; in Northampton 1 in $26\frac{1}{2}$; in Newbury 1 in $27\frac{1}{2}$;[15] in Manchester 1 in 28; in Liverpool 1 in $27\frac{1}{2}$,[16] &c. He observes, that the number dying annually in towns is seldom so low as 1 in 28, except in consequence of a rapid increase produced by an influx of people at those periods of life when the fewest die, which is the case with Manchester and Liverpool,[17] and other very flourishing manufacturing towns. In general he thinks, that the mortality in great towns may be stated

upon than public returns; because in general those clergymen only are applied to, who are in some degree interested in the subject, and of course take more pains to be accurate.

12. New Observations on bills of Mortality, table ix. p. 133.

13. Gottliche Ordnung, vol. i. c. ii. s. xxi. p. 74.

14. Estimate of the number of Inhabitants in G. Britain.

15. Price's Observ. on Revers. Paym. vol. i. note p. 272.

16. Id. vol. ii. First additional Essay, note, p. 4.　　17. Ibid.

at from 1 in 19[18] to 1 in 22 and 23; in moderate towns, from 1 in 24 to 1 in 28; and, in country villages, from 1 in 40, to 1 in 50.[19]

The tendency of Dr. Price to exaggerate the unhealthiness of towns may justly be objected to these statements; but the objection seems to be only of weight with regard to London. The accounts from the other towns which are given, are from documents which his particular opinions could not influence. It should be remarked, however, that there is good reason to believe, that not only London, but the other towns in England, and probably also country villages, were, at the time of these calculations, less healthy than at present. Dr. William Heberden remarks, that the registers of the ten years from 1759 to 1768,[20] from which Dr. Price calculated the probabilities of life in London, indicate a much greater degree of unhealthiness than the registers of late years. And the returns pursuant to the population act, even after allowing for great omissions in the burials, exhibit in all our provincial towns, and in the country, a degree of healthiness much greater than had before been calculated. At the same time I cannot but think, that 1 in 31, the proportion of mortality for London, mentioned in the *Observations on the Results of the Population Act*,[21] is smaller than the truth. Five thousand may not, perhaps, be enough to allow for the omissions in the burials; or, perhaps, the absentees in the employments of war and commerce, may not be included in these omissions. In estimating the proportional mortality the resident population alone should be considered.

There certainly seems to be something in great towns, and even in moderate towns, peculiarly unfavourable to the very early stages of life; and the part of the community on which the mortality principally falls, seems to indicate, that it arises more from the closeness and foulness of the air, which may be supposed to be unfavourable to the tender lungs of children, and the greater confinement, which they almost necessarily experience, than from the superior degree of luxury and debauchery, usually, and justly, attributed to towns. A married pair, with the best constitutions, who lead the most regular and quiet life, seldom find that their children enjoy the same health in towns as in the country.

In London, according to former calculations, one half of the born died under three years of age; in Vienna and Stockholm under two; in Manchester, under five; in Norwich, under five; in Northampton, under

18. The Mortality at Stockholm was, according to Wargentin, 1 in 19.
19. Observ. on Revers. Paym. vol. ii. First additional Essay, p. 4.
20. Increase and Decrease of Diseases, p. 32. 4to. 1801.   21. P. 13.

ten.[22] In country villages, on the contrary, half of the born live till thirty, thirty-five, forty, forty-six, and above. In the parish of Ackworth, in Yorkshire, it appears, from a very exact account kept by Dr. Lee of the ages at which all died there for 20 years, that half of the inhabitants live to the age of 46,[23] and there is little doubt, that, if the same kind of account had been kept in some of those parishes before mentioned, in which the mortality is so small as 1 in 60, 1 in 66, and even 1 in 75, half of the born would be found to have lived till 50 or 55.

As the calculations respecting the ages to which half of the born live in towns, depend more upon the births and deaths which appear in the registers, than upon any estimates of the number of people, they are on this account less liable to uncertainty, than the calculations respecting the proportion of the inhabitants of any place which dies annually.

To fill up the void occasioned by this mortality in towns, and to answer all further demands for population, it is evident, that a constant supply of recruits from the country is necessary, and this supply appears, in fact, to be always flowing in from the redundant births of the country. Even in those towns, where the births exceed the deaths, this effect is produced by the marriages of persons not born in the place. At a time when our provincial towns were increasing much less rapidly than at present, Dr. Short calculated that $\frac{9}{19}$ of the married were strangers.[24] Of 1618 married men, and 1618 married women, examined at the Westminster Infirmary, only 329 of the men, and 495 of the women, had been born in London.[25]

Dr. Price supposes, that London, with its neighbouring parishes, where the deaths exceed the births, requires a supply of 10,000 persons annually. Graunt, in his time, estimated this supply for London alone at 6000;[26] and he further observes, that let the mortality of the city be what it will, arising from plague, or any other great cause of destruction, that it always fully repairs its loss in two years.[27]

As all these demands, therefore, are supplied from the country, it is evident, that we should fall into a very great error, if we were to estimate the proportion of births to deaths for the whole kingdom, by the proportion observed in country parishes, from which there must be such numerous emigrations.

22. Price's Observ. on Revers. Paym. vol. i. p. 264–266.
23. Id. vol. i. p. 268.   24. New Observations on bills of Mortality, p. 76.
25. Price's Observ. on Revers. Paym. vol. ii. p. 17.
26. Short's New Observ. Abstract from Graunt, p 277.   27. Id. p. 276.

We need not, however, accompany Dr. Price in his apprehensions, that the country will be depopulated by these emigrations, at least, as long as the funds for the maintenance of agricultural labour remain unimpaired. The proportion of births, as well as the proportion of marriages, clearly proves, that in spite of our increasing towns and manufactories, the demand on the country for people is by no means very pressing.

If we divide the present population of England and Wales, by the average number of baptisms for the last five years, it will appear, that the baptisms are to the population, as 1 to very nearly 36;[28] but it is supposed, with reason, that there are great omissions in the baptisms; and it is conjectured, that these omissions are greater than in the burials. On this point, however, I should be inclined to think differently, at least, with respect to the last twenty years, though probably it was the case formerly. It would appear, by the present proportion of marriages, that the more rapid increase of population, supposed to have taken place since the year 1780, has arisen more from the diminution of deaths, than the increase of the births.

Dr. Short estimated the proportion of births to the population of England as 1 to 28.[29] In the agricultural report of Suffolk, the proportion of births to the population was calculated at 1 to 30. For the whole of Suffolk, according to the late returns, this proportion is not much less than 1 to 33.[30] According to a correct account of thirteen villages from actual enumerations, produced by Sir F. M. Eden, the proportion of births to the population was as 1 to 33; and from another account, on the same authority, taken from towns and manufacturing parishes, as 1 to $27\frac{3}{4}$.[31] If, combining all these circumstances, and adverting, at the same time, to the acknowledged deficiency in the registry of births, and the known increase of our population of late years, we suppose the true proportion of the births to the population to be as 1 to 30; then, assuming the present mortality to be 1 in 40, as before suggested, we shall nearly keep the proportion of baptisms to burials, which appears in the late returns. The births will be to the deaths

28. Average medium of baptisms for the last five years 255, 426. Pop. 9,168,000. (Observ. on Results, p. 9.)

29. New Observ. p. 267.

30. In private inquiries, dissenters, and those who do not christen their children, will not of course be reckoned in the population, and consequently such inquiries, as far as they extend, will more accurately express the true proportion of births; and we are fairly justified in making use of them, in order to estimate the acknowledged deficiency of births in the public returns.

31. Estimate of the number of Inhabitants in G. Britain, &c. p. 27.

as 4 to 3 or $13\frac{1}{3}$ to 10, a proportion more than sufficient to account for the increase of population which has taken place since the American war, after allowing, for those who may be supposed to have died abroad, and for a greater general mortality, in the earlier part of this period.

In the *Observations on the Results of the Population Act,* it is remarked, that the average duration of life in England appears to have increased in the proportion of 117 to 100,[32] since the year 1780. So great a change, in so short a time, if true, would be a most striking phenomenon. But I am inclined to suspect, that the whole of this proportional diminution of burials does not arise from increased healthiness, but is occasioned, in part, by the greater number of deaths which must necessarily have taken place abroad, owing to the very rapid increase of our foreign commerce since this period; and to the great number of persons absent in naval and military employments, during the late war, and the constant supply of fresh recruits necessary to maintain undiminished so great a force. A perpetual drain of this kind, would certainly have a tendency to produce the effect observed in the returns, and might keep the burials stationary, while the births and marriages were increasing with some rapidity. At the same time, as the increase of population since 1780 is incontrovertible, and the present mortality extraordinarily small, I should still be disposed to believe, that the greater part of the effect is to be attributed to increased healthiness.

If we suppose, that the mortality about the year 1780 was 1 in 36, instead of 1 in 40, as at present, this will be making a great allowance for increased healthiness, though not so much as the proportion of 117 to 100; and assuming the proportion of births to have been nearly the same as at present, the births about the year 1780, will appear to have been to the deaths, as 36 to 30, or 12 to 10; a proportion, which, calculated on a mortality of 1 in 36, doubles the population of a country, in 125 years,[33] and is, therefore, as great a proportion, as can be true for the average of the whole century. The highest estimates of our population do not make it double of what it was at the revolution.

We must not suppose, however, that this proportion of births to deaths, or of births and deaths to the whole population, continued uniform before 1780. It appears from the registers of every country which have been kept for any length of time, that considerable variations occur at different periods. Dr. Short, about the middle of the century, estimated the proportion

32. P. 6.　　33. See table ii. p. 238.

of births to deaths at 11 to 10;[34] and if the births were at the same time a twenty-eighth part of the population, the mortality was then as high as 1 in 30$\frac{4}{5}$. We now suppose that the proportion of births to deaths is above 13 to 10; but if we were to assume this proportion as a criterion by which to estimate the increase of population for the next thirty or forty years, we should probably fall into a very gross error. The effects of the late scarcities are strongly marked, in the returns of the *Population Act,* by a decrease of births, and an increase of burials, and should such seasons frequently recur, they would soon destroy the great excess of births which has been observed during the last twenty years; and indeed we cannot reasonably suppose, that the resources of this country should increase, for any long continuance, with such rapidity, as to allow of a permanent proportion of births to deaths as 13 to 10, unless, indeed, this proportion were principally caused by great foreign drains.

From all the data that could be collected, the proportion of births, to the whole population of England and Wales, has been assumed to be as 1 to 30; but this is a smaller proportion of births than has appeared, in the course of this review, to take place in any other country, except Norway and Switzerland; and it has been hitherto usual with political calculators to consider a great proportion of births, as the surest sign of a vigorous and flourishing state. It is to be hoped, however, that this prejudice will not last long. In countries circumstanced like America or Russia, or in other countries after any great mortality, a large proportion of births may be a favourable symptom; but in the average state of a well-peopled territory, there cannot well be a worse sign than a large proportion of births, nor can there well be a better sign than a small proportion.

Sir Francis D'Ivernois very justly observes, that "if the various states of
" Europe kept and published annually an exact account of their popula-
" tion, noting carefully in a second column the exact age at which the
" children die, this second column would shew the relative merit of the
" governments, and the comparative happiness of their subjects. A simple
" arithmetical statement would then, perhaps, be more conclusive, than
" all the arguments that could be adduced."[35] In the importance of the inferences to be drawn from such tables, I fully agree with him: and to make these inferences, it is evident, that we should attend less to the column

34. New Observ. tables ii. & iii. p. 22 & 44. Price's Observ. on Revers. Paym. vol. ii. p. 311.
35. Tableau des Pertes, &c. c. ii. p. 16.

expressing the number of children born, than to the column expressing the number which survived the age of infancy and reached manhood; and this number will, almost invariably, be the greatest, where the proportion of the births to the whole population is the least. In this point, we rank next after Norway and Switzerland, which, considering the number of our great towns and manufactories, is certainly a very extraordinary fact. As nothing can be more clear, than that all our demands for population are fully supplied, if this be done with a small proportion of births, it is a decided proof of a very small mortality, a distinction on which we may justly pride ourselves. Should it appear from future investigations, that I have made too great an allowance for omissions, both in the births and in the burials, I shall be extremely happy to find, that this distinction which, other circumstances being the same, I consider as the surest test of happiness and good government, is even greater than I have supposed it to be. In despotic, miserable, or naturally unhealthy countries, the proportion of births to the whole population will generally be found very great.

According to one of Sir F. M. Eden's calculations, taken from towns and manufacturing parishes, the annual births are to the annual marriages as 3 to 1.[36] In 111 agricultural parishes for 12 years, ending in 1799, the annual births are to the annual marriages in the proportion of above 4 to 1.[37] From which it might appear, that, in our towns, more than half of the born live to be married, and in the country less. But for the reasons mentioned in page 187, the contrary is probably true. In our towns, from the mortality that takes place in the early stages of life, it is not to be doubted that less than half of the born live to be married, and the great proportion of marriages is occasioned merely by new settlers. In the country, on account of the emigrants that marry in other places, more than half of the born live to be married, though, allowing for second and third marriages, probably not much more. But from what was said in page 209, the degree in which the preventive check operates cannot be determined by the proportion of the born which lives to be married; but depends upon the proportion of annual marriages, and the proportion of annual births to the whole population; and till the first of these proportions rises from 1 in 123 to 1 in 80, or 1 in 70, and the second from 1 in 30 to 1 in 24, 22 or 20, it cannot be said, that the towns draw hard upon the country for population.

If taking the towns and country together, and rejecting at present second and third marriages and illegitimate children, we suppose, that accurately

36. Estimate of the Number of Inhabitants in Great Britain, p. 10.
37. Id. p. 79.

half of the born live to be married, then, according to table i. page 185, each marriage must yield five births, in order to produce a proportion of births to deaths, as $12\frac{1}{5}$ to 10. And if the proportion of our births to deaths be above this, or $13\frac{1}{3}$ to 10, then, including all circumstances, it does not appear that we can allow less than $5\frac{1}{2}$ births to each marriage.

In judging of the proportion of the born which lives to be married, by the proportion of annual births to annual marriages, the number of second and third marriages, and the number of illegitimate children, tend to correct each other. The second and third marriages tend to give the proportion which lives to be married too great, and the illegitimate children too small. It must depend on the particular circumstances of the country, which of these two causes of irregularity preponderates.

According to the late returns, it would appear, that, in this country, considerably more than half of the born live to be married; but when the deficiency in the births is assumed to be such as is suggested in this chapter, the result is rather on the contrary side.

On an average of the five years ending in 1780, the proportion of births to marriages is 350 to 100. In 1760, it was 362 to 100, from which, an inference is drawn, that the registers of births, however deficient, were certainly not more deficient formerly, than at present.[38] But a change of this nature, in the appearance of the registers, might arise from a cause totally unconnected with deficiencies. If from the acknowledged greater healthiness of the latter part of the century, compared with the middle of it, a greater number of children survived the age of infancy, a greater proportion of the born would of course live to marry; and this circumstance would produce exactly the effect observed in the registers. From what has already been said on this subject, the reader will be aware, that this change may take place without diminishing the operation of the preventive check. If half of the born live to 40 instead of 30, it is evident, that a greater proportion might live to marry, and yet the marriages be later.

It has been made a question, whether we have just grounds for supposing, that the registry of births and deaths was in general more deficient in the former part of the century, than in the latter part. It appears to me, that the late returns tend to confirm the suspicion of former inaccuracy, and to shew that the registers of the earlier part of the century, in every point of view, afford very uncertain data on which to ground any estimates of past population. In the years 1710, 1720, and 1730, it appears from the returns, that the deaths exceeded the births; and taking the six periods ending in

38. Observations on the Results of the Population Act, p. 8.

1750,[39] including the first half of the century, if we compare the sum of the births with the sum of the deaths, the excess of the births is so small, as to be perfectly inadequate to account for the increase of a million, which, upon a calculation from the births alone, is supposed to have taken place in that time.[40] Consequently, either the registers are very inaccurate, and the deficiencies in the births greater than in the deaths; or these periods, each at the distance of ten years, do not express the just average. These particular years may have been more unfavourable with respect to the proportion of births to deaths than the rest; indeed one of them, 1710, is known to have been a year of great scarcity and distress. But if this suspicion, which is very probable, be admitted, so as to affect the six first periods, we may justly suspect the contrary accident to have happened with regard to the three following periods ending with 1780, in which thirty years, it would seem by the same mode of calculation, that an increase of a million and an half had taken place.[41] At any rate it must be allowed that the three separate years, taken in this manner, can by no means be considered as sufficient to establish a just average; and what rather encourages the suspicion that these particular years might be more than usually favourable with regard to births, is, that the increase of births from 1780 to 1785, is unusually small,[42] which would naturally take place, without supposing a slower progress than before, if the births in 1780 had been accidentally above the average.

On the whole, therefore, considering the probable inaccuracy of the earlier registers, and the very great danger of fallacy, in drawing general inferences from a few detached years, I do not think that we can depend upon any estimates of past population, founded on a calculation from the births, till after the year 1780, when every following year is given, and a just average of the births may be obtained. As a further confirmation of this remark, I will just observe, that in the final summary of the abstracts from the registers of England and Wales, it appears, that in the year 1790, the total number of births was 248,774, in the year 1795, 247,218, and in 1800, 247,147.[43] Consequently, if we had been estimating the population from the births, taken at three separate periods of five years, it would have appeared that the population during the last ten years, had been regularly decreasing, though we have very good reason to believe, that it has increased considerably.

---

39. Population Abstract Parish Registers. Final Summary, p. 455.
40. Observations on the Results of the Population Act, p. 9.
41. Ibid.   42. Ibid.   43. Population Abstract Parish Registers, p. 455.

In the *Observations on the Results of the Population Act*,[44] a table is given of the population of England and Wales throughout the last century calculated from the births; but, for the reasons given above, little reliance can be placed on it, and for an estimate of the population at the revolution, I should be inclined to place more dependance on the old calculations from the number of houses.

It must, indeed, have appeared to the reader, in the course of this work, that registers of births or deaths, excluding any suspicion of deficiencies, must at all times afford very uncertain data for an estimate of population. On account of the varying circumstances of every country, they are both very precarious guides in this respect; but of the two, perhaps, the births still more so, than the deaths; though from the greater apparent regularity of the former, political calculators have generally adopted them as the ground of their estimates, in preference to the latter. Necker, in estimating the population of France, observes, that an epidemick disease, or an emigration, may occasion temporary differences in the deaths, and that therefore the number of births is the most certain criterion.[45] But the very circumstance of the apparent regularity of the births in the registers will now and then lead into the grossest errors. If in any country we can obtain registers of burials for two or three years together, a plague or mortal epidemick will always shew itself, from the very sudden increase of the deaths during its operation, and the still greater diminution of them afterwards. From these appearances we should of course be directed not to include the whole of a great mortality, in any very short term of years. But there would be nothing of this kind to guide us in the registers of births; and, after a country had lost an eighth part of its population by a plague, an average of the five or six subsequent years would probably shew an increase in the number of births, and our calculations would give the population the highest at the very time that it was the lowest. This appears very strikingly, in many of Susmilch's tables, and most particularly in the table for Prussia and Lithuania, which I have inserted in chap. vi. of this book, where, in the year subsequent to the loss of one third of the population, the births were considerably increased, and in an average of five years, but very little diminished; and this, at a time, when, of course, the country could have made but a very small progress towards recovering its former population.

44. P. 9.   45. De l'Administration des Finances, tom. i. c. ix. p. 252. 12mo. 1785.

We do not know indeed of any extraordinary mortality which has occurred in England since 1700; and there are reasons for supposing that the
proportions of the births and deaths to the population during the last century, have not experienced such great variations as in many countries on the
continent; at the same time it is certain, that the sickly seasons which are
known to have occurred, would, in proportion to the degree of their fatality, produce similar effects; and the change which has been observed in the
mortality of late years, should dispose us to believe that similar changes
might formerly have taken place respecting the births, and should instruct
us to be extremely cautious in applying any proportions which are observed
to be true at present, to past or future periods.

CHAP. X.

Of the Checks to Population in Scotland and Ireland.

An examination, in detail, of the statistical account of Scotland, would furnish numerous illustrations of the principle of population; but I have already extended this part of the work so much, that I am fearful of tiring the patience of my readers; and shall therefore confine my remarks in the present instance to a few circumstances which have happened to strike me.

On account of the acknowledged omissions in the registers of births, deaths, and marriages, in most of the parishes of Scotland, few just inferences can be drawn from them. Many give extraordinary results. In the parish of Crossmichael[1] in Kircudbright, the mortality appears to be only 1 in 98, and the yearly marriages 1 in 192. These proportions would imply the most unheard-of healthiness, and the most extraordinary operation of the preventive check; but there can be little doubt, that they are principally occasioned by omissions in the registry of burials, and the celebration of a part of the marriages in other parishes.

In general, however, it appears from registers that are supposed to be accurate, that in the country parishes the mortality is small; and that the proportions of 1 in 45, 1 in 50, and 1 in 55, are not uncommon. According to a table of the probabilities of life, calculated from the bills of mortality in the parish of Kettle, by Mr. Wilkie; the expectation of an infant's life is 46.6,[2] which is very high, and the proportion which dies in the first year is only $\frac{1}{10}$. Mr. Wilkie further adds, that, from 36 parish accounts, published in the first volume, the expectation of an infant's life appears to be 40.3. But in a table, which he has produced in the last volume, calculated for the whole of Scotland from Dr. Webster's survey, the expectation at birth appears to be only 31 years.[3] This, however, he thinks, must be too low, as it exceeds but little the calculations for the town of Edinburgh.

The Scotch registers appeared to be, in general, so incomplete, that the returns of 99 parishes only, are published in the Population Abstract; and, if any judgment can be formed from these, they shew a very extraordinary degree of healthiness, and a very small proportion of births. The sum

---

1. Statistical Account of Scotland, vol. i. p. 167.
2. Statistical Account of Scotland, vol. ii. p. 407.
3. Id. vol. xxi. p. 383.

of the population of these parishes in 1801, was 217,873;[4] the average of burials for 5 years ending in 1800, was about 3815; and of births, 4928:[5] from which it would appear that the mortality in these parishes was only 1 in 56, and the proportion of births 1 in 44. But these proportions are so extraordinary, that it is difficult to conceive, that they approach near the truth. Combining them with the calculations of Mr. Wilkie, it will not appear probable, that the proportion of deaths and births in Scotland, should be smaller than what has been allowed for England and Wales; namely, 1 in 40 for the deaths, and 1 in 30 for the births; and it seems to be generally agreed that the proportion of births to deaths is 4 to 3.[6]

With respect to the marriages, it will be still more difficult to form a conjecture. They are registered so irregularly, that no returns of them are given in the Population. Abstract. I should naturally have thought, from the Statistical Account, that the tendency to marriage in Scotland, was, upon the whole, greater than in England; but if it be true, that the births and deaths bear the same proportion to each other, and to the whole population, in both countries, the proportion of marriages cannot be very different. It should be remarked, however, that, supposing the operation of the preventive check to be exactly the same, in both countries, and the climates to be equally salubrious, a greater degree of want and poverty would take place in Scotland, before the same mortality was produced as in England, owing to the smaller proportion of towns and manufactories in the former country than in the latter.

From a general view of the statistical accounts, the result seeme clearly to be, that the condition of the lower classes of people in Scotland, has been considerably improved of late years. The price of provisions has risen; but, almost, invariably, the price of labour has risen in a greater proportion; and it is remarked in most parishes, that more butcher's meat is consumed among the common people than formerly; that they are both better lodged and better clothed; and that their habits, with respect to cleanliness, are decidedly improved.

A part of this improvement is probably to be attributed to the increase of the preventive check. In some parishes, a habit of later marriages is noticed, and in many places, where it is not mentioned, it may be fairly inferred, from the proportions of births and marriages, and other circumstances. The writer of the account of the parish of Elgin,[7] in enumerating

---

4. Population Abstract, Parish Registers, p. 459.
5. Id. p. 458.   6. Statistical Account of Scotland, vol. xxi. p. 383.
7. Vol. v. p. 1.

the general causes of depopulation in Scotland, speaks of the discouragement to marriage from the union of farms, and the consequent emigration
of the flower of their young men of every class and description, very few of
whom ever return. Another cause that he mentions, is, the discouragement
to marriage from luxury; at least, he observes, till people are advanced in
years, and then a puny race of children are produced. "Hence, how many
" men of every description remain single, and how many young women of
" every rank are never married, who, in the beginning of this century, or
" even so late as 1745, would have been the parents of a numerous and
" healthy progeny."

In those parts of the country where the population has been rather diminished, by the introduction of grazing, or an improved system of husbandry
which requires fewer hands, this effect has chiefly taken place; and I have
little doubt, that, in estimating the decrease of their population, since the
end of the last, or the beginning of the present century, by the proportion of
births at the different periods, they have fallen into the error which has been
particularly noticed, with regard to Switzerland, and have, in consequence,
made the difference greater than it really is.[8]

The general inference on this subject, which I should draw from the different accounts is, that the marriages are rather later than formerly. There
are, however, some decided exceptions. In those parishes where manufactures have been introduced, which afford employment to children as soon
as they have reached their 6th or 7th year, a habit of marrying early naturally follows; and while the manufacture continues to flourish and increase,
the evil arising from it is not very perceptible; though humanity must confess with a sigh, that one of the reasons why it is not so perceptible, is, that
room is made for fresh families, by the unnatural mortality which takes
place among the children so employed.

There are other parts of Scotland, however, particularly the Western
Isles, and some parts of the Highlands, where population has considerably increased from the subdivision of possessions, and where, perhaps,
the marriages may be earlier than they were formerly, though not caused
by the introduction of manufactures. Here, the poverty which follows is but
too conspicuous. In the account of Delting in Shetland,[9] it is remarked, that
the people marry very young, and are encouraged to this by their landlords,

8. One writer takes notice of this circumstance, and observes, that formerly the
births seem to have born a greater proportion to the whole population than at present. Probably, he says, more were born, and there was a greater mortality. Parish of
Montquitter, vol. vi. p. 121.

9. Vol. i. p. 385.

who wish to have as many men on their grounds as possible to prosecute the ling fishery; but that they generally involve themselves in debt and large families. The writer further observes, that formerly there were some old regulations called country acts, by one of which, it was enacted, that no pair should marry unless possessed of 40l. Scots, of free gear. This regulation is not now enforced. It is said that these regulations were approved and confirmed by the parliament of Scotland, in the reign of Queen Mary, or James VI.

In the account of Bressay Burra and Quarff in Shetland,[10] it is observed, that the farms are very small, and few have a plough. The object of the proprietors is to have as many fishermen on their lands as possible – a great obstacle to improvements in agriculture. They fish for their masters, who either give them a fee totally inadequate, or take their fish at a low rate. The writer remarks, that, "in most countries the increase of population is reck-
"   oned an advantage, and justly. It is, however, the reverse, in the present
"   state of Shetland. The farms are split. The young men are encouraged to
"   marry without having any stock. The consequence is poverty and dis-
"   tress. It is believed that there is at present in these islands, double the
"   number of people that they can properly maintain."

The writer of the account of Auchterderran,[11] in the county of Fife, says, that the meagre food of the labouring man is unequal to oppose the effects of incessant hard labour upon his constitution, and by this means his frame is worn down before the time of nature's appointment, and adds, "That
"   people continue voluntarily to enter upon such a hard situation by mar-
"   rying, shews how far the union of the sexes, and the love of indepen-
"   dence, are principles of human nature." In this observation, perhaps, the love of independence had better have been changed for the love of a progeny.

The island of Jura[12] appears to be absolutely overflowing with inhabitants in spite of constant and numerous emigrations. There are sometimes 50 or 60 on a farm. The writer observes, that such a swarm of inhabitants, where manufactures and many other branches of industry are unknown, are a very great load upon the proprietors, and useless to the state.

Another writer[13] is astonished at the rapid increase of population, in spite of a considerable emigration to America in 1770, and a large drain of young men during the late war. He thinks it difficult to assign adequate causes for it, and observes, that if the population continue to increase, in

10. Vol. x. p. 194.   11. Vol. i. p. 449.   12. Vol. xii. p. 317.
13. Parish of Lochalsh, county of Ross, vol. xi. p. 422.

this manner, unless some employment be found for the people, the country will soon be unable to support them. And in the account of the parish of Callander,[14] the writer says, that the villages of this place, and other villages in similar situations, are filled with naked and starving crowds of people, who are pouring down for shelter or for bread; and then observes that whenever the population of a town or village exceeds the industry of its inhabitants, from that moment the place must decline.

A very extraordinary instance of a tendency to rapid increase, occurs in the register of the parish of Duthil,[15] in the county of Elgin; and as errors of excess are not so probable, as errors of omission, it seems to be worthy of attention. The proportion of annual births to the whole population is as 1 to 12; of marriages, as 1 to 55; and of deaths the same. The births are to the deaths as 70 to 15, or $4\frac{2}{3}$ to 1. We may suppose some inaccuracy respecting the number of deaths, which seems to err on the side of defect; but the very extraordinary proportion of the annual births, amounting to $\frac{1}{12}$ of the whole population, does not seem to be easily liable to error; and the other circumstances respecting the parish, tend to confirm the statement. Out of a population of 830, there were only 3 bachelors, and each marriage yielded 7 children. Yet with all this, the population is supposed to have decreased considerably since 1745; and it appears, that this excessive tendency to increase, had been occasioned by an excessive tendency to emigrate. The writer mentions very great emigrations; and observes, that whole tribes who enjoyed the comforts of life in a reasonable degree, had of late years emigrated from different parts of Scotland, from mere humour, and a fantastical idea of becoming their own masters and freeholders.

Such an extraordinary proportion of births caused evidently by habits of emigration, shews the extreme difficulty of depopulating a country merely by taking away its people. Take but away its industry, and the sources of its subsistence, and it is done at once.

It may be observed, that in this parish, the average number of children to a marriage is said to be 7, though, from the proportion of annual births to annual marriages, it would appear to be only $4\frac{2}{3}$. This difference occurs in many other parishes, from which we may conclude, that the writers of these accounts very judiciously adopted some other mode of caculation, than the proportion of annual births and marriages; and probably founded the results they give, either on personal inquiries, or researches into their registers, to find the number of children which had been born to each mother in the course of her marriage.

14. Vol. xi. p. 574.   15. Vol. iv. p. 308.

The women of Scotland appear to be prolifick. The average of 6 children to a marriage is frequent; and of 7, and even $7\frac{1}{2}$, not very uncommon. One instance is very curious, as it appears as if this number was actually living to each marriage, which would of course imply, that a much greater number had been, and would be, born. In the parish of Nigg,[16] in the county of Kincardine, the account says, that there are 57 land families, and 405 children; which gives nearly $7\frac{1}{9}$ each; 42 fisher families, and 314 children; nearly $7\frac{1}{2}$ each. Of the land families, which have had no children, there were 7; of the fishers, none. If this statement be just, I should conceive that each marriage must have yielded, or would yield, in the course of its duration, as many as 9 or 10 births.

When, from any actual survey, it appears, that there is about 3 living children to each marriage, or 5 persons, or only $4\frac{1}{2}$ to a house, which are very common proportions, we must not infer that the average number of births to a marriage is not much above 3. We must recollect that all the marriages, or establishments, of the present year, are of course without children; all of the year before, have only one; all of the year before that, can hardly be expected to have as many as two, and all of the fourth year preceding will certainly, in the natural course of things, have less than three. One out of five children is a very unusually small proportion to lose in the course of ten years; and after ten years, it may be supposed that the eldest begin to leave their parents; so that if each marriage be supposed accurately to yield 5 births in the course of its duration, the families which had increased to their full complement would only have 4 children, and a very large proportion of those which were in the stages of increase would have less than three;[17] and consequently, taking into consideration the number of families where one of the parents may be supposed to be dead, I much doubt, whether in this case, a survey would give $4\frac{1}{2}$ to a family. In the parish of Duthil,[18] already noticed, the number of children to a marriage is mentioned as 7, and the number of persons to a house, as only 5.

I have taken notice of this circumstance, to obviate an objection which might perhaps appear to arise from the result of such surveys, to the proofs which have been adduced, that marriages are in general more prolifick than they have been usually supposed to be. The accounts of many of the parishes in Scotland, which mention 6, 7, and $7\frac{1}{2}$, as the average number of children to a marriage tend very strongly to confirm these proofs; and as in

16. Vol. vii. p. 194.
17. It has been calculated that, on an average, the difference of age in the children of the same family is about two years.   18. Vol. iv. p. 308.

these same parishes, the proportion of annual births to annual marriages, is seldom above $3\frac{1}{2}$, 4, or $4\frac{1}{2}$, to 1; they prove at the same time the fallacy of this mode of estimating the fruitfulness of marriages. In those parishes where the authors have adopted this mode, they generally mention, as might be expected, 3, $3\frac{1}{2}$, 4, and $4\frac{1}{2}$, as the average number of children to a marriage.

The poor of Scotland are in general supported by voluntary contributions, distributed under the inspection of the minister of the parish; and it appears, upon the whole, that they have been conducted with considerable judgment. Having no claim of right to relief, and the supplies, from the mode of their collection, being necessarily uncertain, and never abundant, the poor have considered them merely as a last resource in cases of extreme distress, and not as a fund on which they might safely rely, and an adequate portion of which belonged to them by the laws of their country, in all difficulties.

The consequence of this is, that the common people make very considerable exertions to avoid the necessity of applying for such a scanty and precarious relief. It is observed, in many of the accounts, that they seldom fail of making a provision for sickness and for age; and in general, the grown-up children and relations of persons, who are in danger of falling upon the parish, step forward, if they be in any way able, to prevent such a degradation, which is universally considered as a disgrace to the family.

The writers of the accounts of the different parishes, frequently reprobate, in very strong terms, the system of English assessments for the poor, and give a decided preference to the Scotch mode of relief. In the account of Paisley,[19] though a manufacturing town, and with a numerous poor, the author still reprobates the English system, and makes an observation on this subject, in which, perhaps, he goes too far. He says, that though there are in no country such large contributions for the poor as in England, yet there is no where so great a number of them; and their condition, in comparison of *the poor of other countries, is truly most miserable.*

In the account of Caerlaverock,[20] in answer to the question, How ought the poor to be supplied? it is most judiciously remarked, "that distress and " poverty multiply in proportion to the funds created to relieve them; that " the measures of charity ought to remain invisible, till the moment when " it is necessary that they should be distributed; that in the country parishes of Scotland, in general, small occasional voluntary collections are " sufficient; that the legislature has no occasion to interfere to augment the

19. Vol. vii. p. 74.   20. Vol. vi. p. 21.

" stream which is already copious enough; in fine, that the establishment
" of a poors rate would not only be unnecessary, but hurtful, as it would
" tend to oppress the landholder, without bringing relief on the poor."

These, upon the whole, appear to be the prevailing opinions of the clergy of Scotland. There are, however, some exceptions; and the system of assessments is sometimes approved, and the establishment of it proposed. But this is not to be wondered at. In many of these parishes, the experiment had never been made; and without being thoroughly aware of the principle of population, from theory, or having fully seen the evils of poor laws, in practice, nothing seems, on a first view of the subject, more natural, than the proposal of an assessment, to which the uncharitable, as well as the charitable, should be made to contribute, according to their abilities, and which might be increased or diminished, according to the wants of the moment.

The endemick and epidemick diseases in Scotland, fall chiefly, as is usual, on the poor. The scurvy is in some places extremely troublesome and inveterate; and in others it arises to a contagious leprosy, the effects of which are always dreadful, and not unfrequently mortal. One writer calls it the scourge and bane of human nature.[21] It is generally attributed to cold and wet situations, meagre and unwholesome food, impure air from damp and crowded houses, indolent habits, and the want of attention to cleanliness.

To the same causes, in great measure, are attributed the rheumatisms which are general, and the consumptions which are frequent among the common people. Whenever, in any place, from particular circumstances, the condition of the poor has been rendered worse, these disorders, particularly the latter, have been observed to prevail with greater force.

Low nervous fevers, and others of a more violent and fatal nature, are frequently epidemick, and sometimes take off considerable numbers; but the most fatal epidemick, since the extinction of the plague, which formerly visited Scotland, is the small-pox, the returns of which, are, in many places, at regular intervals; in others, irregular, but seldom at a greater distance than 7 or 8 years. Its ravages are dreadful, though in some parishes not so fatal as they were some time ago. The prejudices against inoculation are still great; and as the mode of treatment must almost necessarily be bad, in small and crowded houses, and the custom of visiting each other during the disorder still subsists in many places, it may be imagined that the mortality must be considerable, and the children of the poor the principal

---

21. Parishes of Forbes and Kearn, County of Aberdeen, vol. xi. p. 189.

sufferers. In some parishes of the Western Isles, and the Highlands, the number of persons to a house has increased from $4\frac{1}{2}$, and 5, to $6\frac{1}{2}$, and 7. It is evident, that if such a considerable increase, without the proper accommodations for it, do not absolutely generate the disease, it must give to its devastations tenfold force when it arrives.

Scotland has at all times been subject to years of scarcity, and occasionally even to dreadful famines. The years 1635, 1680, 1688, the concluding years of the seventeenth century, the years 1740, 1756, 1766, 1778, 1782, and 1783, are all mentioned in different places, as years of very great sufferings from want. In the year 1680, so many families perished from this cause, that, for six miles, in a well-inhabited extent, there was not a smoke remaining.[22] The seven years at the end of the seventeenth century were called the ill years. The writer of the account of the parish of Montquhitter,[23] says, that of 16 families on a farm in that neighbourhood, 13 were extinguished; and on another, out of 169 individuals, only 3 families, the proprietors included, survived. Extensive farms, now containing a hundred souls, being entirely desolated, were converted into a sheep walk. The inhabitants of the parish in general were diminished by death to one half, or as some affirm to one fourth, of the preceding number. Until 1709 many farms were waste. In 1740, another season of scarcity occurred, and the utmost misery was felt by the poor, though it fell short of death. Many offered in vain to serve for their bread. Stout men accepted thankfully twopence a day in full for their work. Great distress was also suffered in 1782 and 1783, but none died. "If, at this critical period," the author says, "the " American war had not ceased; if the copious magazines, particularly of " pease, provided for the navy, had not been brought to sale, what a scene " of desolation and horror would have been exhibited in this country!"

Many similar descriptions occur in different parts of the Statistical Account; but these will be sufficient to shew the nature and intensity of the distress which has been occasionally felt from want.

The year 1783 depopulated some parts of the Highlands, and is mentioned as the reason why in these places the number of people was found to have diminished since Dr. Webster's survey. Most of the small farmers in general, as might be expected, were absolutely ruined by the scarcity; and those of this description, in the Highlands, were obliged to emigrate to the Lowlands as common labourers,[24] in search of a precarious support. In some parishes at the time of the last survey, the effect of the ruin of the

22. Parish of Duthil, vol. iv. p. 308.   23. Vol. vi. p. 121.
24. Parish of Kincardine, County of Ross, vol. iii. p. 505.

farmers during this bad year, was still visible in their depressed condition, and the increased poverty and misery of the common people which is a necessary consequence of it.

In the account of the parish of Grange,[25] in the county of Banff, it is observed, that the year 1783 put a stop to all improvements by green crops, and made the farmers think of nothing but raising grain. Tenants were most of them ruined. Before this period, consumptions were not near so frequent as they have been since. This may be justly attributed to the effects of the scarcity and bad victual in the year 1783, to the long inclement harvests in 1782 and 1787, in both which seasons, the labourers were exposed to much cold and wet during the three months that the harvests continued; but principally to the change that has of late taken place in the manner of living among the lower ranks. Formerly every householder could command a draught of small beer, and killed a sheep now and then, out of his own little flock; but now the case is different. The frequent want of the necessaries of life among the poor, their damp and stinking houses, and dejection of mind among the middling classes, appear to be the principal causes of the prevailing distempers, and mortality of this parish. Young people are cut off by consumptions, and the more advanced by dropsies and nervous fevers.

The state of this parish, which, though there are others like it, may be considered as an exception to the average state of Scotland, was, without doubt, occasioned by the ruin of the tenants; and the effect is not to be wondered at, as no greater evil can easily happen to a country, than the loss of agricultural stock and capital.

We may observe, that the diseases of this parish are said to have increased, in consequence of the scarcity and bad victual of 1783. The same circumstance is noticed in many other parishes, and it is remarked, that though few people died of absolute famine, yet that mortal diseases almost universally followed.

It is remarked, also, in some parishes, that the number of births and marriages are affected by years of scarcity and plenty.

Of the parish of Dingwall,[26] in the county of Ross, it is observed, that, after the scarcity of 1783, the births were 16 below the average, and 14 below the lowest number of late years. The year 1787 was a year of plenty, and the following year the births increased in a similar proportion, and were 17 above the average, and 11 above the highest of the other years.

25. Vol. ix. p. 550.   26. Vol. iii. p. 1.

In the account of Dunrossness,[27] in Orkney, the writer says, that the annual number of marriages depends much on the seasons. In good years they may amount to thirty or upwards; but when crops fail, will hardly come up to the half of that number.

The whole increase of Scotland since the time of Dr. Webster's survey in 1755, is about 260,000,[28] for which a proportionate provision has been made in the improved state of agriculture and manufactures, and in the increased cultivation of potatoes, which in some places form two-thirds of the diet of the common people. It has been calculated that the half of the surplus of births in Scotland is drawn off in emigrations; and it cannot be doubted that this drain tends greatly to relieve the country, and to improve the condition of those which remain. Scotland is certainly still overpeopled, but not so much as it was a century or half a century ago, when it contained fewer inhabitants.

The details of the population of Ireland are but little known. I shall only observe, therefore, that the extended use of potatoes, has allowed of a very rapid increase of it during the last century. But the cheapness of this nourishing root, and the small piece of ground, which, under this kind of cultivation, will, in average years, produce the food for a family, joined to the ignorance and barbarism of the people, which have prompted them to follow their inclinations with no other prospect than an immediate bare subsistence, have encouraged marriage to such a degree, that the population is pushed much beyond the industry and present resources of the country; and the consequence naturally is, that the lower classes of people are in the most depressed and miserable state. The checks to the population are of course chiefly of the positive kind, and arise from the diseases occasioned by squalid poverty, by damp and wretched cabins, by bad and insufficient clothing, by the filth of their persons, and occasional want. To these positive checks, have, of late years, been added the vice and misery of intestine commotion, of civil war, and of martial law.

All the checks to population which have been observed to prevail in society, in the course of this review of it, are clearly resolvable into moral restraint, vice, and misery.

27. Vol. vii. p. 391.
28. According to the returns in the late estimate, the whole population of Scotland is above 1,590,000, and therefore the increase up to the present time is above 320,000.

CHAP. XI.

General deductions from the preceding view of Society.

THAT the checks, which have been mentioned, are the true causes of the slow increase of population, and that these checks result principally from an insufficiency of subsistence, will be evident from the comparatively rapid increase, which has invariably taken place, whenever, by some sudden enlargement in the means of subsistence, these checks have been in any considerable degree removed.

It has been universally remarked, that all new colonies, settled in healthy countries, where room and food were abundant, have constantly made a rapid progress in population. Many of the colonies from antient Greece, in the course of one or two centuries, appear to have rivalled, and even surpassed, their mother cities. Syracuse and Agrigentum in Sicily; Tarentum and Locri in Italy; Ephesus and Miletus in Lesser Asia; were, by all accounts, at least equal to any of the cities of antient Greece.[1] All these colonies had established themselves in countries inhabited by savage and barbarous nations, which easily gave place to the new settlers, who had of course plenty of good land. It is calculated that the Israelites, though they increased very slowly, while they were wandering in the land of Canaan, on settling in a fertile district of Egypt, doubled their numbers every fifteen years during the whole period of their stay.[2] But not to dwell on remote instances, the European settlements in America, bear ample testimony to the truth of a remark, that has never, I believe, been doubted. Plenty of rich land, to be had for little or nothing, is so powerful a cause of population, as generally to overcome all obstacles.

No settlements could easily have been worse managed than those of Spain, in Mexico, Peru, and Quito. The tyranny, superstition, and vices, of the mother country, were introduced in ample quantities among her children. Exorbitant taxes were exacted by the crown; the most arbitrary restrictions were imposed on their trade; and the governors were not behind hand, in rapacity and extortion for themselves as well as their master. Yet under all these difficulties, the colonies made a quick progress in population. The city of Quito, which was but a hamlet of Indians, is represented

1. Smith's Wealth of Nations, vol. ii. p. 360.
2. Short's New Observ. on Bills of Mortality, p. 259, 8vo. 1750.

by Ulloa as containing fifty or sixty thousand inhabitants above fifty years ago.[3] Lima, which was founded since the conquest, is mentioned by the same author, as equally or more populous, before the fatal earthquake in 1746. Mexico is said to contain a hundred thousand inhabitants, which, notwithstanding the exaggerations of the Spanish writers, is supposed to be five times greater than what it contained in the time of Montezuma.[4]

In the Portuguese colony of Brazil, governed with almost equal tyranny, there were supposed to be, above thirty years ago, six hundred thousand inhabitants of European extraction.[5]

The Dutch and French colonies, though under the government of exclusive companies of merchants, which, as Dr. Smith justly observes, is the worst of all possible governments, still persisted in thriving under every disadvantage.[6]

But the English North American colonies, now the powerful people of the United States of America, far outstripped all the others, in the progress of their population. To the quantity of rich land, which they possessed in common with the Spanish and Portuguese colonies, they added a greater degree of liberty and equality. Though not without some restrictions on their foreign commerce, they were allowed the liberty of managing their own internal affairs. The political institutions which prevailed, were favourable to the alienation and division of property. Lands, which were not cultivated by the proprietor within a limited time, were declared grantable to any other person. In Pensylvania, there was no right of primogeniture; and, in the provinces of New England, the eldest son had only a double share. There were no tythes in any of the States, and scarcely any taxes. And an account of the extreme cheapness of good land, a capital could not be more advantageously employed than in agriculture, which, at the same time that it affords the greatest quantity of healthy work, supplies the most valuable produce to the society.

The consequence of these favourable circumstances united, was, a rapidity of increase almost without parallel in history. Throughout all the northern provinces the population was found to double itself in 25 years. The original number of persons which had settled in the four provinces of New England in 1643 was 21,200. Afterwards, it was calculated, that more left them than went to them. In the year 1760, they were increased to half a million. They had, therefore, all along, doubled their number in

3. Voy. d'Ulloa, tom. i. liv. v. ch. v. p. 229. 4to. 1752.
4. Smith's Wealth of Nations, vol. ii. b. iv. ch. vii. p. 363.
5. Id. p. 365.   6. Id. p. 368, 369.

25 years. In New Jersey, the period of doubling appeared to be 22 years; and in Rhode Island still less. In the back settlements, where the inhabitants applied themselves solely to agriculture, and luxury was not known, they were supposed to double their number in fifteen years. Along the sea-coast, which would naturally be first inhabited, the period of doubling was about 35 years, and in some of the maritime towns the population was absolutely at a stand.[7] From the late census made in America, it appears, that, taking all the States together, they have still continued to double their numbers every 25 years; and, as the whole population is now so great, as not to be materially affected by the emigrations from Europe; and as it is known, that in some of the towns, and districts near the sea-coast, the progress of population has been comparatively slow; it is evident, that in the interior of the country, in general, the period of doubling from procreation only, must have been considerably less than 25 years.

The population of the United States of America, according to the late census, is 5,172,312.[8] We have no reason to believe that Great Britain is

7. Price's Observ. on Revers. Paym. vol. i. p. 282, 283, and vol. ii. p. 260. I have lately had an opportunity of seeing some extracts from the sermon of Dr. Styles, from which Dr. Price has taken these facts. Speaking of Rhode Island, Dr. Styles says, that though the period of doubling for the whole colony is 25 years, yet that it is different in different parts, and within land is 20 and 15 years. The five towns of Gloucester, Situate, Coventry, Westgreenwich, and Exeter, were 5033, A. D. 1748, and 6986 A. D. 1755; which implies a period of doubling of 15 years only. He mentions afterwards that the county of Kent doubles in 20 years; and the county of Providence in 18 years.

I have also lately seen a paper of *Facts and calculations respecting the population of the United States,* which makes the period of doubling for the whole of the States, since their first settlement, only 20 years. I know not of what authority this paper is; but, far as it goes upon publick facts and enumerations, I should think, that it must be to be depended on. One period is very striking. From a return to Congress in 1782, the population appeared to be 2,389,300, and in the census of 1790, 4,000,000: increase in 9 years, 1,610,700: from which deduct ten thousand per annum for European settlers, which will be 90,000; and allow for their increase at 5 per cent. for $4\frac{1}{2}$ years, which will be 20,250: the remaining increase during these 9 years, from procreation only, will be 1,500,450, which is very nearly 7 per cent.; and consequently the period of doubling at this rate would be less than 16 years.

If this calculation for the whole population of the States be in any degree near the truth, it cannot be doubted, that, in particular districts, the period of doubling from procreation only, has often been less than 15 years. The period immediately succeeding the war was likely to be a period of very rapid increase.

8. One small State is mentioned as being omitted in the census; and I understand that the population is generally considered at above this number. It is said to

less populous, at present, for the emigration of the small parent stock which produced these numbers. On the contrary, a certain degree of emigration is known to be favourable to the population of the mother country. It has been particularly remarked that the two Spanish provinces from which the greatest number of people emigrated to America, became in consequence more populous.

Whatever was the original number of British emigrants which increased so fast in North America; let us ask, Why does not an equal number produce an equal increase in the same time in Great Britain? The obvious reason to be assigned is, the want of food; and that this want is the most efficient cause of the three great checks to population, which have been observed to prevail in all societies, is evident, from the rapidity with which even old states recover the desolations of war, pestilence, famine, and the convulsions of nature. They are then, for a short time, placed a little in the situation of new colonies, and the effect is always answerable to what might be expected. If the industry of the inhabitants be not destroyed, subsistence will soon increase beyond the wants of the reduced numbers; and the invariable consequence will be, that population, which before, perhaps, was nearly stationary, will begin immediately to increase, and will continue its progress till the former population is recovered.

The fertile province of Flanders, which has been so often the seat of the most destructive wars, after a respite of a few years, has always appeared as rich and as populous as ever. The undiminished population of France, which has before been noticed, is an instance very strongly in point. The tables of Susmilch afford continual proofs of a very rapid increase, after great mortalities; and the table for Prussia and Lithuania, which I have inserted,[9] is particularly striking in this respect. The effects of the dreadful plague in London, in 1666, were not perceptible 15 or 20 years afterwards. It may even be doubted, whether Turkey and Egypt are, upon an average, much less populous for the plagues which periodically lay them waste. If the number of people which they contain be considerably less now, than formerly, it is rather to be attributed to the tyranny and oppression of the governments under which they groan, and the consequent discouragements to agriculture, than to the losses which they sustain by the plague. The traces of the most destructive famines in China, Indostan, Egypt, and other

approach towards 6,000,000. But such vague opinions cannot of course be much relied on.

9. See p. 203.

countries, are by all accounts very soon obliterated; and the most tremendous convulsions of nature, such as volcanic eruptions and earthquakes, if they do not happen so frequently as to drive away the inhabitants, or destroy their spirit of industry, have been found to produce but a trifling effect on the average population of any state.

It has appeared from the registers of different countries which have already been produced, that the progress of their population is checked by the periodical, though irregular, returns of plagues and sickly seasons. Dr. Short, in his curious researches into bills of mortality, often uses the expression of "terrible correctives of the redundance of mankind;"[10] and in a table of all the plagues, pestilences, and famines, of which he could collect accounts, shews the constancy and universality of their operation.

The epidemical years in his table, or the years in which the plague or some great and wasting epidemick prevailed, for smaller sickly seasons, seem not to be included, are 431,[11] of which 32 were before the Christian æra.[12] If we divide, therefore, the years of the present æra by 399, it will appear, that the periodical returns of such epidemicks, to some country that we are acquainted with, have been on an average only at the interval of about $4\frac{1}{2}$ years.

Of the 254 great famines and dearths, enumerated in the table, 15 were before the Christian æra,[13] beginning with that which occurred in Palestine, in the time of Abraham. If, subtracting these 15, we divide the years of the present æra by the remainder, it will appear that the average interval between the visits of this dreadful scourge has been only about $7\frac{1}{2}$ years.

How far these "terrible correctives to the redundance of mankind," have been occasioned by the too rapid increase of population, is a point which it would be very difficult to determine with any degree of precision. The causes of most of our diseases appear to us to be so mysterious, und probably are really so various, that it would be rashness to lay too much stress on any single one: but it will not, perhaps, be too much to say, that, *among* these causes, we ought certainly to rank crowded houses, and insufficient or unwholesome food, which are the natural consequences of an increase of population, faster, than the accommodations of a country, with respect to habitations and food, will allow.

Almost all the histories of epidemicks which we have, tend to confirm this supposition, by describing them in general as making their principal

10. New Observ. on Bills of Mortality, p. 96.
11. Hist. of Air, Seasons, &c. vol. ii. p. 366.   12. Id. vol. ii. p. 202.
13. Id. vol. ii. p. 206.

ravages among the lower classes of people. In Dr. Short's tables, this circumstance is frequently mentioned;[14] and it further appears, that a very considerable proportion of the epidemick years, either followed, or were accompanied by seasons of dearth and bad food.[15] In other places he also mentions great plagues as diminishing particularly the numbers of the lower or servile sort of people;[16] and, in speaking of different diseases, he observes, that those which are occasioned by bad and unwholesome food, generally last the longest.[17]

We know, from constant experience, that fevers are generated in our jails, our manufactories, our crowded workhouses, and in the narrow and close streets of our large towns; all which situations appear to be similar in their effects to squalid poverty: and we cannot doubt that causes of this kind, aggravated in degree, contributed to the production and prevalence of those great and wasting plagues formerly so common in Europe, but which now, from the mitigation of these causes, are every where considerably abated, and in many places appear to be completely extirpated.

Of the other great scourge of mankind, famine, it may be observed, that it is not in the nature of things, that the increase of population should absolutely produce one. This increase, though rapid, is necessarily gradual; and as the human frame cannot be supported, even for a very short time, without food, it is evident, that no more human beings can grow up, than there is provision to maintain. But though the principle of population cannot absolutely produce a famine, it prepares the way for one in the most complete manner; and, by obliging all the lower classes of people to subsist nearly on the smallest quantity of food that will support life, turns even a slight deficiency from the failure of the seasons into a severe dearth; and may be fairly said, therefore, to be one of the principal causes of famine. Among the signs of an approaching dearth, Dr. Short mentions one or more years of luxuriant crops together;[18] and this observation is probably just, as we know that the general effect of years of cheapness and abundance is to dispose a greater number of persons to marry, and under such circumstances, the return to a year, merely of an average crop, might produce a scarcity.

The small-pox, which at present may be considered as the most prevalent and fatal epidemick in Europe, is of all others, perhaps, the most difficult to account for, though the periods of its return are in many places regular.[19] Dr. Short observes, that from the histories of this disorder, it seems to have

14. Hist. of Air, Seasons, &c. vol. ii. p. 206. et seq.
15. Ibid, and p. 366.　16. New Observ. p. 125.　17. Id. p. 108.
18. Hist. of Air, Seasons, &c, vol. ii. p. 367.　19. Id. vol. ii. p. 411.

very little dependence upon the past or present constitution of the weather or seasons, and that it appears epidemically at all times, and in all states of the air, though not so frequently in a hard frost. We know of no instances, I believe, of its being clearly generated under any circumstances of situation. I do not mean, therefore, to insinuate, that poverty and crowded houses ever absolutely produced it; but I may be allowed to remark, that in those places where its returns are regular, and its ravages among children, particularly among those of the lower class, are considerable, it necessarily follows, that these circumstances, in a greater degree than usual, must always precede and accompany its appearance; that is, from the time of its last visit, the average number of children will be increasing, the people will, in consequence, be growing poorer, and the houses will be more crowded, till another visit removes this superabundant population.

In all these cases, how little soever force we may be disposed to attribute to the effects of the principle of population in the actual production of disorders, we cannot avoid allowing their force as predisposing causes to the reception of contagion, and as giving very great additional force to the extensiveness and fatality of its ravages.

It is observed by Dr. Short, that a severe mortal epidemick is generally succeeded by an uncommon healthiness, from the late distemper having carried off most of the declining worn-out constitutions.[20] It is probable, also, that another cause of it, may be, the greater plenty of room and food, and the consequently ameliorated condition of the lower classes of the people. Sometimes, according to Dr. Short, a very fruitful year is followed by a very mortal and sickly one, and mortal ones often succeeded by very fruitful, as though Nature sought either to prevent or quickly repair the loss by death. In general the next year after sickly and mortal ones is prolifick in proportion to the breeders left.[21]

This last effect we have seen most strikingly exemplified in the table for Prussia and Lithuania.[22] And from this and other tables of Susmilch, it also appears, that when the increasing produce of a country and the increasing demand for labour, so far ameliorate the condition of the labourer, as greatly to encourage marriage, the custom of early marriages is generally continued, till the population has gone beyond the increased produce, and sickly seasons appear to be the natural and necessary consequence. The continental registers exhibit many instances of rapid increase, interrupted in this manner by mortal diseases, and the inference seems to be, that those

20. Hist. of Air, Weather [Seasons], &c. vol. ii. p. 344.
21. New Observ. p. 191.   22. p. 203.

countries where subsistence is increasing sufficiently to encourage population, but not to answer all its demands, will be more subject to periodical
epidemicks, than those where the increase of population is more nearly
accommodated to the average produce.

The converse of this will of course be true. In those countries which are
subject to periodical sicknesses, the increase of population, or the excess
of births above the deaths, will be greater, in the intervals of these periods,
than is usual in countries not so much subject to these diseases. If Turkey
and Egypt have been nearly stationary in their average population for the
last century, in the intervals of their periodical plagues, the births must have
exceeded the deaths in a much greater proportion than in such countries as
France and England.

It is for these reasons, that no estimates of future population or depopulation, formed from any existing rate of increase or decrease, can be depended upon. Sir William Petty calculated that, in the year 1800, the city of
London would contain 5,359,000[23] inhabitants, instead of which, it does not
now contain a fifth part of that number. And Mr. Eton has lately prophesied
the extinction of the population of the Turkish empire in another century;[24]
an event which will, as certainly, fail of taking place. If America were to
continue increasing at the same rate as at present, for the next 150 years,
her population would exceed the population of China; but though prophe-
cies are dangerous, I will venture to say, that such an increase will not take
place in that time, though it may perhaps in five or six hundred years.

Europe was, without doubt, formerly more subject to plagues and wasting epidemicks than at present, and this will account, in great measure, for
the greater proportion of births to deaths in former times, mentioned by
many authors, as it has always been a common practice, to estimate these
proportions from too short periods, and generally to reject the years of
plague as accidental.

The highest average proportion of births to deaths in England may be
considered as about 12 to 10, or 120 to 100. The proportion in France for
ten years, ending in 1780, was about 115 to 100.[25] Though these proportions have undoubtedly varied, at different periods, during the last century,
yet we have reason to think that they have not varied in any very considerable degree; and it will appear, therefore, that the population of France
and England has accommodated itself more nearly to the average produce

23. Political Arithmetick, p. 17.
24. Survey of the Turkish Empire, c. vii. p. 281.
25. Necker de l'Administration des Finances, tom. i. c. ix. p. 255.

of each country than many other states. The operation of the preventive check, vicious manners, wars, the silent, though certain, destruction of life in large towns and manufactures, and the close habitations and insufficient food of many of the poor, prevent population from outrunning the means of subsistence; and if I may use an expression, which certainly at first appears strange, supersede the necessity of great and ravaging epidemicks to destroy what is redundant. If a wasting plague were to sweep off two millions in England, and six millions in France, it cannot be doubted, that after the inhabitants had recovered from the dreadful shock, the proportion of births to deaths would rise much above the usual average in either country during the last century.[26]

In New Jersey the proportion of births to deaths, on an average of 7 years, ending 1743, was 300 to 100. In France and England, the highest average proportion cannot be reckoned at more than 120 to 100. Great and astonishing as this difference is, we ought not to be so wonder-struck at it, as to attribute it to the miraculous interposition of heaven. The causes of it are not remote, latent, and mysterious, but near us, round about us, and open to the investigation of every inquiring mind. It accords with the most liberal spirit of philosophy to believe, that not a stone can fall, or plant rise, without the immediate agency of divine power. But we know, from experience, that these operations of what we call nature, have been conducted almost invariably according to fixed laws. And since the world began, the causes of population and depopulation have been probably as constant as any of the laws of nature with which we are acquainted.

The passion between the sexes has appeared in every age to be so nearly the same, that it may always be considered, in algebraic language, as a given quantity. The great law of necessity, which prevents population from increasing in any country beyond the food which it can either produce or acquire, is a law, so open to our view, so obvious and evident to our understandings, that we cannot for a moment doubt it. The different modes which nature takes to repress a redundant population, do not appear indeed to us so certain and regular; but though we cannot always predict the mode, we may with certainty predict the fact. If the proportion of the births to the deaths for a few years, indicate an increase of numbers much beyond the proportional increased or acquired food of the country, we may be perfectly certain, that unless an emigration take place, the deaths will shortly exceed the births, and that the increase that had been observed for a few

26. This remark has been, to a certain degree, verified of late in France, by the increase of births which has taken place since the revolution.

years, cannot be the real average increase of the population of the country. If there were no other depopulating causes, and if the preventive check did not operate very strongly, every country would, without doubt, be subject to periodical plagues or famines.

The only true criterion of a real and permanent increase in the population of any country, is the increase of the means of subsistence. But even this criterion is subject to some slight variations, which however are completely open to our observation. In some countries population seems to have been forced; that is, the people have been habituated, by degrees, to live almost upon the smallest possible quantity of food. There must have been periods in such countries when population increased permanently without an increase in the means of subsistence. China, India, and the countries possessed by the Bedoween Arabs, as we have seen in the former part of this work, appear to answer to this description. The average produce of these countries seems to be but barely sufficient to support the lives of the inhabitants, and of course any deficiency from the badness of the seasons must be fatal. Nations in this state must necessarily be subject to famines.

In America, where the reward of labour is at present so liberal, the lower classes might retrench very considerably in a year of scarcity, without materially distressing themselves. A famine, therefore, seems to be almost impossible. It may be expected, that in the progress of the population of America, the labourers will in time be much less liberally rewarded. The numbers will in this case permanently increase without a proportional increase in the means of subsistence.

In the different countries of Europe, there must be some variations in the proportion of the number of inhabitants, and the quantity of food consumed, arising from the different habits of living which prevail in each state. The labourers of the South of England are so accustomed to eat fine wheaten bread, that they will suffer themselves to be half-starved, before they will submit to live like the Scotch peasants. They might, perhaps, in time, by the constant operation of the hard law of necessity, be reduced to live, even like the lower classes of the Chinese, and the country would then, with the same quantity of food, support a greater population. But to effect this, must always be a difficult, and every friend to humanity will hope, an abortive attempt.

I have mentioned some cases where population may permanently increase, without a proportional increase in the means of subsistence. But it is evident, that the variation in different states, between the food, and the numbers supported by it, is restricted to a limit beyond which it cannot pass.

In every country, the population of which is not absolutely decreasing, the food must be necessarily sufficient to support and to continue the race of labourers.

Other circumstances being the same, it may be affirmed, that countries are populous according to the quantity of human food which they produce, or can acquire; and happy, according to the liberality with which this food is divided, or the quantity which a day's labour will purchase. Corn countries are more populous than pasture countries; and rice countries more populous than corn countries. But their happiness does not depend either upon their being thinly or fully inhabited, upon their poverty or their riches, their youth or their age; but on the proportion which the population and the food bear to each other. This proportion is generally the most favourable in new colonies, where the knowledge and industry of an old state, operate on the fertile unappropriated land of a new one. In other cases the youth, or the age, of a state is not, in this respect, of great importance. It is probable that the food of Great Britain is divided in more liberal shares to her inhabitants at the present period, than it was, two thousand, three thousand, or four thousand years ago. And it has appeared that the poor and thinly-inhabited tracts of the Scotch Highlands are more distressed by a redundant population, than the most populous parts of Europe.

If a country were never to be over-run by a people more advanced in arts, but left to its own natural progress in civilization; from the time that its produce might be considered as an unit, to the time that it might be considered as a million, during the lapse of many thousand years, there would not be a single period, when the mass of the people could be said to be free from distress, either directly or indirectly, for want of food. In every state in Europe, since we have first had accounts of it, millions and millions of human existences have been repressed from this simple cause, though perhaps, in some of these states, an absolute famine may never have been known.

Famine seems to be the last, the most dreadful resource of nature. The power of population is so superior to the power in the earth to produce subsistence for man, that, unless arrested by the preventive check, premature death must in some shape or other visit the human race. The vices of mankind are active and able ministers of depopulation. They are the precursors in the great army of destruction, and often finish the dreadful work themselves. But should they fail in this war of extermination, sickly seasons, epidemicks, pestilence, and plague, advance in terrifick array, and sweep off their thousands and ten thousands. Should success be still incomplete, gigantick inevitable famine stalks in the rear, and, with one mighty blow, levels the population with the food of the world.

Must it not then be acknowledged, by an attentive examiner of the histories of mankind, that, in every age, and in every state, in which man has existed, or does now exist,

The increase of population is necessarily limited by the means of subsistence.

Population invariably increases when the means of subsistence increase, unless prevented by powerful and obvious checks.

These checks, and the checks which keep the population down to the level of the means of subsistence, are, moral restraint, vice, and misery.

In comparing the state of society which has been considered in this second book with that which formed the subject of the first, I think it appears, that in modern Europe the positive checks to population prevail less, and the preventive checks more, than in past times, and in the more uncivilized parts of the world.

War, the predominant check to the population of savage nations, has certainly abated, even including the late unhappy revolutionary contests: and since the prevalence of a greater degree of personal cleanliness, of better modes of clearing and building towns, and of a more equable distribution of the products of the soil from improving knowledge in political economy, plagues, violent diseases, and famines, have been certainly mitigated, and have become less frequent.

With regard to the preventive checks to population, though it must be acknowledged, that moral restraint does not at present prevail much among the male part of society; yet I am strongly disposed to believe that it prevails more than in those states which were first considered; and it can scarcely be doubted, that in modern Europe, a much larger proportion of women pass a considerable part of their lives in the exercise of this virtue, than in past times and among uncivilized nations. But however this may be, taking the preventive check in its general acceptation, as implying an infrequency of the marriage union from the fear of a family, without reference to its producing vice, it may be considered, in this light, as the most powerful of the checks, which in modern Europe keep down the population to the level of the means of subsistence.

ESSAY, &c.

BOOK III.

OF THE DIFFERENT SYSTEMS OR EXPEDIENTS WHICH HAVE BEEN PROPOSED OR HAVE PREVAILED IN SOCIETY, AS THEY AFFECT THE EVILS ARISING FROM THE PRINCIPLE OF POPULATION.

CHAP. I.

Of Systems of Equality. Wallace. Condorcet.

To a person who views the past and present states of mankind in the light in which they have appeared in the two preceding books, it cannot but be a matter of astonishment, that all the writers on the perfectibility of man and of society, who have noticed the argument of the principle of population, treat it always very slightly, and invariably represent the difficulties arising from it, as at a great, and almost immeasurable distance. Even Mr. Wallace, who thought the argument itself of so much weight, as to destroy his whole system of equality, did not seem to be aware that any difficulty would arise from this cause, till the whole earth had been cultivated like a garden, and was incapable of any further increase of produce. Were this really the case, and were a beautiful system of equality in other respects practicable, I cannot think that our ardour in the pursuit of such a scheme ought to be damped by the contemplation of so remote a difficulty. An event at such a distance might fairly be left to providence. But the truth is, that if the view of the argument given in this essay be just, the difficulty, so far from being remote, would be imminent and immediate. At every period during the progress of cultivation, from the present moment to the time when the whole earth was become like a garden, the distress for want of food would be constantly pressing on all mankind, if they were equal. Though the produce of the earth would be increasing every year, population would be increasing much faster, and the redundancy must necessarily be checked by the periodical, or constant action, of moral restraint, vice, or misery.

M. Condorcet's *Esquisse d'un tableau historique des progrès de l'esprit humain,* was written, it is said, under the pressure of that cruel proscription which terminated in his death. If he had no hopes of its being seen during his life, and of its interesting France in his favour, it is a singular instance of the attachment of a man to principles, which every day's experience was, so fatally for himself, contradicting. To see the human mind, in one of the most enlightened nations of the world, debased by such a fermentation of disgusting passions, of fear, cruelty, malice, revenge, ambition, madness, and folly, as would have disgraced the most savage nations in the most barbarous age, must have been such a tremendous shock to his ideas of the necessary and inevitable progress of the human mind, that nothing but the firmest conviction of the truth of his principles, in spite of all appearances, could have withstood.

This posthumous publication is only a sketch of a much larger work which he proposed should be executed. It necessarily wants, therefore, that detail and application, which can alone prove the truth of any theory. A few observations will be sufficient to shew how completely this theory is contradicted, when it is applied to the real and not to an imaginary state of things.

In the last division of the work, which treats of the future progress of man towards perfection, M. Condorcet says, that, comparing in the different civilized nations of Europe, the actual population with the extent of territory; and observing their cultivation, their industry, their divisions of labour, and their means of subsistence, we shall see, that it would be impossible to preserve the same means of subsistence, and consequently the same population, without a number of individuals who have no other means of supplying their wants than their industry.

Having allowed the necessity of such a class of men, and adverting afterwards to the precarious revenue of those families that would depend so entirely on the life and health of their chief,[1] he says very justly, "There " exists then a necessary cause of inequality, of dependence, and even of " misery, which menaces, without ceasing, the most numerous and active " class of our societies." The difficulty is just, and well stated; but his mode of removing it, will, I fear, be found totally inefficacious.

By the application of calculations to the probabilities of life, and the interest of money, he proposes that a fund should be established, which should assure to the old an assistance, produced in part by their own former savings, and in part by the savings of individuals, who, in making the same sacrifice, die before they reap the benefit of it. The same, or a similar fund, should give assistance to women and children, who lose their husbands or fathers; and afford a capital to those who were of an age to found a new family, sufficient for the development of their industry. These establishments, he observes, might be made in the name, and under the protection, of the society. Going still further, he says, that by the just application of calculations, means might be found of more completely preserving a state of equality, by preventing credit from being the exclusive privilege of great fortunes, and yet giving it a basis equally solid, and by rendering the progress of industry and the activity of commerce, less dependent on great capitalists.

Such establishments and calculations may appear very promising upon paper; but when applied to real life, they will be found to be absolutely nugatory. M. Condorcet allows, that a class of people which maintains itself entirely by industry is necessary to every state. Why does he allow this? No other reason can well be assigned, than because he conceives, that the labour necessary to procure subsistence for an extended population, will not be performed without the goad of necessity. If by establishments, upon the plans that have been mentioned, this spur to industry be removed; if the idle and negligent be placed upon the same footing with regard to their credit, and the future support of their wives and families, as the active and industrious, can we expect to see men exert that animated activity in bettering their condition, which now forms the master-spring of publick prosperity. If an inquisition were to be established to examine the claims of each

---

1. To save time and long quotations, I shall here give the substance of some of M. Condorcet's sentiments, and I hope that I shall not misrepresent them; but I refer the reader to the work itself, which will amuse if it do not convince him.

individual, and to determine whether he had, or had not, exerted himself to the utmost, and to grant or refuse assistance accordingly, this would be little else than a repetition upon a larger scale, of the English poor laws, and would be completely destructive of the true principles of liberty and equality.

But independently of this great objection to these establishments, and supposing, for a moment, that they would give no check to production, the greatest difficulty remains yet behind.

Were every man sure of a comfortable provision for a family, almost every man would have one; and were the rising generation free from the "killing frost" of misery, population must increase with unusual rapidity. Of this, M. Condorcet seems to be fully aware himself; and, after having described further improvements, he says,

"But in this progress of industry and happiness, each generation will be
" called to more extended enjoyments, and, in consequence, by the physi-
" cal constitution of the human frame, to an increase in the number of
" individuals. Must not there arrive a period then, when these laws,
" equally necessary, shall counteract each other? when the increase of the
" number of men surpassing their means of subsistence, the necessary
" result must be, either a continual diminution of happiness, and popula-
" tion – a movement truly retrograde; or, at least, a kind of oscillation be-
" tween good and evil? In societies arrived at this term, will not this oscil-
" lation be a constantly subsisting cause of periodical misery? Will it not
" mark the limit when all further amelioration will become impossible,
" and point out that term to the perfectibility of the human race, which it
" may reach in the course of ages, but can never pass?" He then adds,

"There is no person who does not see how very distant such a period
" is from us. But shall we ever arrive at it? It is equally impossible
" to pronounce for, or against, the future realization of an event, which
" cannot take place but at an æra, when the human race will have
" attained improvements of which we can, at present, scarcely form a
" conception."

M. Condorcet's picture of what may be expected to happen, when the number of men shall surpass their means of subsistence, is justly drawn. The oscillation which he describes will certainly take place, and will, without doubt, be a constantly subsisting cause of periodical misery. The only point in which I differ from M. Condorcet in this description, is, with regard to the period when it may be applied to the human race. M. Condorcet thinks that it cannot possibly be applicable, but at an æra extremely distant. If the proportion between the natural increase of population and food, which was stated in the beginning of this essay, and which has received considerable confirmation from the poverty that has been found to prevail in every stage and department of human society, be in any degree near the truth, it will appear, on the contrary, that the period when the number of men surpass their means of subsistence, has long since arrived; and that this necessary oscillation, this constantly subsisting cause of periodical misery, has existed ever since we have had any histories of mankind, does exist at present, and will for ever continue to exist, unless some decided change take place in the physical constitution of our nature.

M. Condorcet, however, goes on to say, that should the period which he conceives to be so distant ever arrive, the human race, and the advocates of the perfectibility of man, need not be alarmed at it. He then proceeds to remove the difficulty in a manner which I profess not to understand. Having observed, that the ridiculous prejudices of superstition would by that time have ceased to throw over morals a corrupt and degrading austerity, he alludes either to a promiscuous concubinage, which would prevent breeding, or to something else as unnatural. To remove the difficulty in this way, will surely, in the opinion of most men, be, to destroy that virtue and purity of manners, which the advocates of equality, and of the perfectibility of man, profess to be the end and object of their views.

The last question which M. Condorcet proposes for examination, is, the organic perfectibility of man. He observes, that if the proofs which have been already given, and which, in their development, will receive greater force in the work itself, are sufficient to establish the indefinite perfectibility of man, upon the supposition, of the same natural faculties, and the same organization which he has at present; what will be the certainty, what the extent of our hopes, if this organization, these natural faculties themselves, be susceptible of amelioration?

From the improvement of medicine; from the use of more wholesome food, and habitations; from a manner of living, which will improve the strength of the body by exercise, without impairing it by excess; from the destruction of the two great causes of the degration of man, misery, and too great riches; from the gradual removal of transmissible and contagious disorders, by the improvement of physical knowledge, rendered more efficacious, by the progress of reason and of social order; he infers, that though man will not absolutely become immortal, yet that the duration between his birth, and natural death, will increase without ceasing, will have no assignable term, and may properly be expressed by the word indefinite. He then defines this word to mean, either a constant approach to an unlimited extent, without ever reaching it; or, an increase in the immensity of ages to an extent greater than any assignable quantity.

But surely the application of this term in either of these senses, to the duration of human life, is in the highest degree unphilosophical, and totally unwarranted by any appearances in the laws of nature. Variations from different causes are essentially distinct from a regular and unretrograde increase. The average duration of human life will, to a certain degree, vary, from healthy or unhealthy climates, from wholesome or unwholesome food, from virtuous or vicious manners, and other causes; but it may be fairly doubted, whether there has been really the smallest perceptible advance in the natural duration of human life, since first we had any authentic history of man. The prejudices of all ages have, indeed, been directly contrary to this supposition; and though I would not lay much stress upon these prejudices, they will in some measure tend to prove, that there has been no marked advance in an opposite direction.

It may perhaps be said, that the world is yet so young, so completely in its infancy, that it ought not to be expected that any difference should appear so soon.

If this be the case, there is at once an end of all human science. The whole train of reasonings from effects to causes will be destroyed. We may shut our eyes to the book of nature, as it will no longer be of any use to read it. The wildest and most improbable conjectures may be advanced with as much certainty as the most just and sublime theories, founded on careful and reiterated experiments. We may return again to the old mode of philosophising, and make facts bend to systems, instead of establishing systems upon facts. The grand and consistent theory of Newton, will be placed upon the same footing as the wild and eccentric hypotheses of Descartes. In short, if the laws of nature be thus fickle and inconstant; if it can be affirmed, and be believed, that they will change, when for ages and ages they have appeared immutable, the human mind will no longer have any incitements to inquiry, but must remain fixed in inactive torpor, or amuse itself only in bewildering dreams, and extravagant fancies.

The constancy of the laws of nature, and of effects and causes, is the foundation of all human knowledge; and, if without any previous observable symptoms or indications of a change, we can infer that a change will take place, we may as well make any assertion whatever, and think it as unreasonable to be contradicted, in affirming that the moon will come in contact with the earth to-morrow, as in saying, that the sun will rise at its appointed time.

With regard to the duration of human life, there does not appear to have existed, from the earliest ages of the world, to the present moment, the smallest permanent symptom, or indication, of increasing prolongation. The observable effects of climate, habit, diet, and other causes, on length of life, have furnished the pretext for asserting its indefinite extension; and the sandy foundation on which the argument rests, is, that because the limit of human life is undefined; because you cannot mark its precise term, and say so far exactly shall it go, and no further; that therefore its extent may increase for ever, and be properly termed, indefinite or unlimited. But the fallacy and absurdity of this argument will sufficiently appear from a slight examination of what M. Condorcet calls the organic perfectibility, or degeneration, of the race of plants and animals, which, he says, may be regarded as one of the general laws of nature.

I am told, that it is a maxim among the improvers of cattle, that you may breed to any degree of nicety you please; and they found this maxim upon another, which is, that some of the offspring will possess the desirable qualities of the parents in a greater degree. In the famous Leicestershire breed of sheep, the object is to procure them with small heads and small legs. Proceeding upon these breeding maxims, it is evident, that we might go on till the heads and legs were evanescent quantities; but this is so palpable an absurdity, that we may be quite sure that the premises are not just, and that there really is a limit, though we cannot see it, or say exactly where it is. In this case, the point of the greatest degree of improvement, or the smallest size of the head and legs, may be said to be undefined; but this is very different from unlimited, or from indefinite, in M. Condorcet's acceptation of the term. Though I may not be able, in the present instance, to mark the limit, at which further improvement will stop, I can very easily mention a point at which it will not arrive. I should not scruple to assert, that were the breeding to continue for ever, the heads and legs of these sheep would never be so small as the head and legs of a rat.

It cannot be true, therefore, that among animals, some of the offspring will possess the desirable qualities of the parents in a greater degree; or that animals are indefinitely perfectible.

The progress of a wild plant, to a beautiful garden flower, is perhaps more marked and striking, than any thing that takes place among animals; yet even here, it would be the height of absurdity to assert, that the progress was unlimited or indefinite. One of the most obvious features of the improvement is the increase of size. The flower has grown gradually larger by cultivation. If the progress were really unlimited, it might be increased ad infinitum; but this is so gross an absurdity, that we may be quite sure, that among plants, as well as among animals, there is a limit to improvement, though we do not exactly know where it is. It is probable that the gardeners who contend for flower prizes have often applied stronger dressing without success. At the same time, it would be highly presumptuous in any man to say, that he had seen the finest carnation or anemone that could ever be made to grow. He might however assert without the smallest chance of being contradicted by a future fact, that no carnation or anemone could ever by cultivation be increased to the size of a large cabbage; and yet there are assignable quantities greater than a cabbage. No man can say that he has seen the largest ear of wheat, or the largest oak that could ever grow; but he might easily, and with perfect certainty, name a point of magnitude, at which they would not arrive. In all these cases, therefore, a careful distinction should be made, between an unlimited progress, and a progress where the limit is merely undefined.

It will be said, perhaps, that the reason why plants and animals cannot increase indefinitely in size, is, that they would fall by their own weight. I answer, how do we know this but from experience? from experience of the degree of strength with which these bodies are formed. I know that a carnation, long before it reached the size of a cabbage, would not be supported by its stalk; but I only know this from my experience of the weakness, and want of tenacity in the materials of a carnation stalk. There are many substances in nature, of the same size, that would support as large a head as a cabbage.

The reasons of the mortality of plants are at present perfectly unknown to us. No man can say why such a plant is annual, another biennial, and another endures for ages. The whole affair in all these cases, in plants, animals, and in the human race, is an affair of experience; and I only conclude that man is mortal, because the invariable experience of all ages has proved the mortality of those materials of which his visible body is made.

"What can we reason but from what we know."

Sound philosophy will not authorize me to alter this opinion of the mortality of man on earth, till it can be clearly proved, that the human race has made, and is making, a decided progress towards an illimitable extent of life. And the chief reason why I adduced the two particular instances from animals and plants, was, to expose, and illustrate, if I could, the fallacy of that argument, which infers an unlimited progress, merely because some partial improvement has taken place, and that the limit of this improvement cannot be precisely ascertained.

The capacity of improvement in plants and animals, to a certain degree, no person can possibly doubt. A clear and decided progress has already been made; and yet, I think it appears, that it would be highly absurd to say, that this progress has no limits. In human life, though there are great variations from different causes, it may be doubted, whether, since the world began, any organic improvement whatever of the human frame can be clearly ascertained. The foundations, therefore, on which the arguments for the organic perfectibility of man rest, are unusually weak, and can only be considered as mere conjectures. It does not, however, by any means, seem impossible, that by an attention to breed, a certain degree of improvement, similar to that among animals, might take place among men. Whether intellect could be communicated may be a matter of doubt: but size, strength, beauty, complexion, and perhaps even longevity, are in a degree transmissible. The error does not seem to lie, in supposing a small degree of improvement possible, but in not discriminating between a small improvement, the limit of which is undefined, and an improvement really unlimited. As the human race, however, could not be improved in this way, without condemning all the bad specimens to celibacy, it is not probable, that an attention to breed should ever become general; indeed, I know of no well-directed attempts of the kind, except in the ancient family of the Bickerstaffs, who are said to have been very successful in whitening the skins, and increasing the height of their race by prudent marriages, particularly by that very judicious cross with Maud the milk-maid, by which some capital defects in the constitutions of the family were corrected.

It will not be necessary, I think, in order more completely to shew the improbability of any approach in man towards immortality on earth, to urge the very great additional weight that an increase in the duration of life would give to the argument of population.

M. Condorcet's book may be considered, not only as a sketch of the opinions of a celebrated individual, but of many of the literary men in France, at the beginning of the revolution. As such, though merely a sketch, it seems worthy of attention.

Many, I doubt not, will think that the attempting gravely to controvert so absurd a paradox, as the immortality of man on earth, or indeed, even the perfectibility of man and society, is a waste of time and words; and that such unfounded conjectures are best answered by neglect. I profess, however, to be of a different opinion. When paradoxes of this kind are advanced by ingenious and able men, neglect has no tendency to convince them of their mistakes. Priding themselves on what they conceive to be a mark of the reach and size of their own understandings, of the extent and comprehensiveness of their views; they will look upon this neglect merely as an indication of poverty, and narrowness, in the mental exertions of their contemporaries; and only think, that the world is not yet prepared to receive their sublime truths.

On the contrary, a candid investigation of these subjects, accompanied with a perfect readiness to adopt any theory, warranted by sound philosophy, may have a tendency to convince them, that, in forming improbable and unfounded hypotheses, so far from enlarging the bounds of human science, they are contracting it; so far from promoting the improvement of the human mind, they are obstructing it: they are throwing us back again almost into the infancy of knowledge; and weakening the foundations of that mode of philosophising, under the auspices of which, science has of late made such rapid advances. The late rage for wide and unrestrained speculation, seems to have been a kind of mental intoxication, arising, perhaps, from the great and unexpected discoveries which had been made in various branches of science. To men, elate and giddy with such successes, every thing appeared to be within the grasp of human powers; and, under this illusion, they confounded subjects where no real progress could be proved, with those, where the progress had been marked, certain, and acknowledged. Could they be persuaded to sober themselves with a little severe and chastized thinking, they would see, that the cause of truth, and of sound philosophy, cannot but suffer, by substituting wild flights and unsupported assertions, for patient investigation, and well authenticated proofs.

C H A P . II.

Of Systems of Equality. Godwin.

In reading Mr. Godwin's ingenious work on political justice, it is impossible not to be struck with the spirit and energy of his style, the force and precision of some of his reasonings, the ardent tone of his thoughts, and particularly with that impressive earnestness of manner, which gives an air of truth to the whole. At the same time it must be confessed, that he has not proceeded in his inquiries with the caution that sound philosophy requires. His conclusions are often unwarranted by his premises. He fails sometimes in removing objections which he himself brings forward. He relies too much on general and abstract propositions which will not admit of application. And his conjectures certainly far outstrip the modesty of nature.

The system of equality which Mr. Godwin proposes, is, on a first view, the most beautiful and engaging of any that has yet appeared. An amelioration of society to be produced merely by reason and conviction, gives more promise of permanence, than any change effected, and maintained by force. The unlimited exercise of private judgement, is a doctrine grand and captivating, and has a vast superiority over those systems, where every individual is in a manner the slave of the publick. The substitution of benevolence, as the masterspring and moving principle of society, instead of self-love, appears, at first sight, to be a consummation devoutly to be wished. In short, it is impossible to contemplate the whole of this fair picture without emotions of delight and admiration, accompanied with an ardent longing for the period of its accomplishment. But alas! that moment can never arrive. The whole is little better than a dream – a phantom of the imagination. These "gorgeous palaces" of happiness and immortality, these "solemn temples" of truth and virtue, will dissolve, "like the baseless fabric of a vision," when we awaken to real life, and contemplate the genuine situation of man on earth.

Mr. Godwin, at the conclusion of the third chapter of his eighth book, speaking of population, says, "There is a principle in human society, by
" which population is perpetually kept down to the level of the means of
" subsistence. Thus, among the wandering tribes of America and Asia, we
" never find, through the lapse of ages, that population has so increased as

" to render necessary the cultivation of the earth."[1] This principle, which Mr. Godwin thus mentions as some mysterious and occult cause, and which he does not attempt to investigate, has appeared to be the grinding law of necessity – misery, and the fear of misery.

The great error under which Mr. Godwin labours, throughout his whole work, is, the attributing of almost all the vices and misery that prevail in civil society to human institutions. Political regulations, and the established administration of property, are, with him, the fruitful sources of all evil, the hotbeds of all the crimes that degrade mankind. Were this really a true state of the case, it would not seem an absolutely hopeless task, to remove evil completely from the world; and reason seems to be the proper and adequate instrument, for effecting so great a purpose. But the truth is, that, though human institutions appear to be the obvious and obtrusive causes of much mischief to mankind, they are, in reality, light and superficial, in comparison with those deeper-seated causes of evil which result from the laws of nature.

In a chapter on the benefits attendant upon a system of equality, Mr. Godwin says, "The spirit of oppression, the spirit of servility, and the spirit of
" fraud, these are the immediate growth of the established administration
" of property. They are alike hostile to intellectual improvement. The
" other vices of envy, malice, and revenge, are their inseparable compan-
" ions. In a state of society where men lived in the midst of plenty, and
" where all shared alike the bounties of nature, these sentiments would
" inevitably expire. The narrow principle of selfishness would vanish. No
" man being obliged to guard his little store, or provide with anxiety and
" pain for his restless wants, each would lose his individual existence in
" the thought of the general good. No man would be an enemy to his
" neighbours, for they would have no subject of contention; and of conse-
" quence philanthropy would resume the empire which reason assigns
" her. Mind would be delivered from her perpetual anxiety about corporal
" support, and free to expatiate in the field of thought which is congenial
" to her. Each would assist the inquiries of all."[2]

This would indeed be a happy state. But that it is merely an imaginary picture, with scarcely a feature near the truth, the reader, I am afraid, is already too well convinced.

Man cannot live in the midst of plenty. All cannot share alike the bounties of nature. Were there no established administration of property, every man would be obliged to guard with force his little store. Selfishness would

1. p. 460. 8vo. 2d edit.   2. Political Justice, b. viii. c. iii. p. 458.

be triumphant. The subjects of contention would be perpetual. Every individual would be under a constant anxiety about corporal support, and not a single intellect would be left free to expatiate in the field of thought.

How little Mr. Godwin has turned his attention to the real state of human society, will sufficiently appear from the manner in which he endeavours to remove the difficulty of an overcharged population. He says, "The
" obvious answer to this objection is, that to reason thus, is to foresee dif-
" ficulties at a great distance. Three-fourths of the habitable globe is now
" uncultivated. The parts already cultivated are capable of immeasurable
" improvement. Myriads of centuries of still increasing population may
" pass away, and the earth be still found sufficient for the subsistence of
" its inhabitants."[3]

I have already pointed out the error of supposing that no distress or difficulty would arise from a redundant population, before the earth absolutely refused to produce any more. But let us imagine, for a moment, Mr. Godwin's system of equality realized in its utmost extent, and see how soon this difficulty might be expected to press, under so perfect a form of society. A theory that will not admit of application cannot possibly be just.

Let us suppose all the causes of vice and misery in this island removed. War and contention cease. Unwholesome trades and manufactories do not exist. Crowds no longer collect together in great and pestilent cities, for purposes of court intrigue, of commerce, and vicious gratification. Simple, healthy, and rational amusements, take place of drinking, gaming, and debauchery. There are no towns sufficiently large, to have any prejudicial effects on the human constitution. The greater part of the happy inhabitants of this terrestrial paradise live in hamlets and farm houses, scattered over the face of the country. All men are equal. The labours of luxury are at an end; and the necessary labours of agriculture are shared amicably among all. The number of persons and the produce of the island we suppose to be the same as at present. The spirit of benevolence guided by impartial justice, will divide this produce among all the members of society according to their wants. Though it would be impossible that they should all have animal food every day, yet vegetable food, with meat occasionally, would satisfy the desires of a frugal people, and would be sufficient to preserve them in health, strength, and spirits.

Mr. Godwin considers marriage as a fraud, and a monopoly.[4] Let us suppose the commerce of the sexes established upon principles of the most perfect freedom. Mr. Godwin does not think himself, that this freedom

3. Polit. Justice, b. viii. c. ix. p. 510.   4. Id. b. viii. c. viii. p. 498. et seq.

would lead to a promiscuous intercourse; and in this, I perfectly agree with him. The love of variety is a vicious, corrupt, and unnatural taste, and could not prevail, in any great degree, in a simple and virtuous state of society. Each man would probably select for himself a partner, to whom he would adhere, as long as that adherence continued to be the choice of both parties. It would be of little consequence, according to Mr. Godwin, how many children a woman had, or to whom they belonged. Provisions and assistance would spontaneously flow from the quarter in which they abounded, to the quarter in which they were deficient.[5] And every man, according to his capacity, would be ready to furnish instruction to the rising generation.

I cannot conceive a form of society so favourable, upon the whole, to population. The irremediableness of marriage, as it is at present constituted, undoubtedly deters many from entering into this state. An unshackled intercourse, on the contrary, would be a most powerful incitement to early attachments: and as we are supposing no anxiety about the future support of children to exist, I do not conceive that there would be one woman in a hundred, of twenty-three years of age, without a family.

With these extraordinary encouragements to population, and every cause of depopulation, as we have supposed, removed, the numbers would necessarily increase faster than in any society that has ever yet been known. I have before mentioned, that the inhabitants of the back settlements of America appear to double their numbers in fifteen years. England is certainly a more healthy country than the back settlements of America; and as we have supposed every house in the island to be airy and wholesome, and the encouragements to have a family, greater even than in America, no probable reason can be assigned, why the population should not double itself, in less, if possible, than fifteen years. But to be quite sure that we do not go beyond the truth, we will only suppose the period of doubling to be twenty-five years; a ratio of increase which is well known to have taken place throughout all the northern states of America.

There can be little doubt, that the equalization of property which we have supposed, added to the circumstance of the labour of the whole community being directed chiefly to agriculture, would tend greatly to augment the produce of the country. But to answer the demands of a population increasing so rapidly, Mr. Godwin's calculation of half an hour a day would certainly not be sufficient. It is probable, that the half of every man's time must be employed for this purpose. Yet with such, or much greater

5. Political Justice, b. viii. c. viii. p. 504.

exertions, a person who is acquainted with the nature of the soil in this country, and who reflects on the fertility of the lands already in cultivation, and the barrenness of those that are not cultivated, will be very much disposed to doubt, whether the whole average produce could possibly be doubled in twenty-five years from the present period. The only chance of success would be from the ploughing up most of the grazing countries, and putting an end almost entirely to animal food. Yet this scheme would probably defeat itself. The soil of England will not produce much without dressing; and cattle seem to be necessary to make that species of manure which best suits the land.

Difficult, however, as it might be, to double the average produce of the island in twenty-five years, let us suppose it effected. At the expiration of the first period, therefore, the food, though almost entirely vegetable, would be sufficient to support in health the doubled population of 22 millions.

During the next period, where will the food be found to satisfy the importunate demands of the increasing numbers? Where is the fresh land to turn up? Where is the dressing necessary to improve that which is already in cultivation? There is no person with the smallest knowledge of land, but would say, that it was impossible that the average produce of the country could be increased during the second twenty-five years, by a quantity equal to what it at present yields. Yet we will suppose this increase, however improbable, to take place. The exuberant strength of the argument allows of almost any concession. Even with this concession, however, there would be eleven millions at the expiration of the second term unprovided for. A quantity equal to the frugal support of 33 millions would be to be divided among 44 millions.

Alas! what becomes of the picture, where men lived in the midst of plenty, where no man was obliged to provide with anxiety and pain for his restless wants; where the narrow principle of selfishness did not exist; where the mind was delivered from her perpetual anxiety about corporeal support, and free to expatiate in the field of thought which is congenial to her. This beautiful fabrick of the imagination vanishes at the severe touch of truth. The spirit of benevolence, cherished and invigorated by plenty, is repressed by the chilling breath of want. The hateful passions that had vanished reappear. The mighty law of self-preservation expels all the softer, and more exalted emotions of the soul. The temptations to evil are too strong for human nature to resist. The corn is plucked before it is ripe, or secreted in unfair proportions; and the whole black train of vices that belong to falsehood are immediately generated. Provisions no longer flow in for the support of a mother with a large family. The children are sickly from insufficient food. The rosy flush of health gives place to the pallid cheek, and hollow eye of misery. Benevolence, yet lingering in a few bosoms, makes some faint expiring struggles, till at length self-love resumes his wonted empire, and lords it triumphant over the world.

No human institutions here existed, to the perverseness of which Mr. Godwin ascribes the original sin of the worst men.[6] No opposition had been produced by them between publick and private good. No monopoly had been created of those advantages which reason directs to be left in common. No man had been goaded to the breach of order by unjust laws. Benevolence had established her reign in all hearts. And yet in so short a period as fifty years, violence, oppression, falsehood, misery, every hateful vice, and every form of distress, which degrade and sadden the present state of society, seem to have been generated by the most imperious circumstances, by laws inherent in the nature of man, and absolutely independent of all human regulations.

If we be not yet too well convinced of the reality of this melancholy picture, let us but look for a moment into the next period of twenty-five years, and we shall see 44 millions of human beings without the means of support: and at the conclusion of the first century, the population would be 176 millions, and the food only sufficient for 55 millions, leaving 121 millions unprovided for. In these ages, want, indeed, would be triumphant, and rapine and murder must reign at large: and yet all this time we are supposing the produce of the earth absolutely unlimited, and the yearly increase greater than the boldest speculator can imagine.

This is undoubtedly a very different view of the difficulty arising from the principle of population, from that which Mr. Godwin gives, when he says, "Myriads of centuries of still increasing population may pass " away, and the earth be still found sufficient for the subsistence of its " inhabitants."

I am sufficiently aware, that the redundant millions, which I have mentioned, could never have existed. It is a perfectly just observation of Mr. Godwin, that, "there is a principle in human society by which popula- " tion is perpetually kept down to the level of the means of subsistence." The sole question is, what is this principle? Is it some obscure and occult cause? Is it some mysterious interference of heaven, which at a certain period strikes the men with impotence, and the women with barrenness? Or is it a cause, open to our researches, within our view; a cause, which has constantly been observed to operate, though with varied force, in every

6. Polit. Justice, b. viii. c. iii. p. 340.

state in which man has been placed. Is it not misery, and the fear of misery, the necessary and inevitable results of the laws of nature, which human institutions, so far from aggravating, have tended considerably to mitigate, though they can never remove.

It may be curious to observe, in the case that we have been supposing, how some of the principal laws which at present govern civilized society, would be successively dictated by the most imperious necessity. As man, according to Mr. Godwin, is the creature of the impressions to which he is subject, the goadings of want could not continue long, before some violations of publick or private stock would necessarily take place. As these violations increased in number and extent, the more active and comprehensive intellects of the society would soon perceive, that, while population was fast increasing, the yearly produce of the country would shortly begin to diminish. The urgency of the case would suggest the necessity of some immediate measures being taken for the general safety. Some kind of convention would then be called, and the dangerous situation of the country stated in the strongest terms. It would be observed, that while they lived in the midst of plenty, it was of little consequence who laboured the least, or who possessed the least, as every man was perfectly willing and ready to supply the wants of his neighbour. But, that the question was no longer, whether one man should give to another, that which he did not use himself; but whether he should give to his neighbour the food which was absolutely necessary to his own existence. It would be represented, that the number of those which were in want, very greatly exceeded the number and means of those who should supply them; that these pressing wants, which, from the state of the produce of the country, could not all be gratified, had occasioned some flagrant violations of justice; that these violations had already checked the increase of food, and would, if they were not by some means or other prevented, throw the whole community into confusion; that imperious necessity seemed to dictate, that a yearly increase of produce should, if possible, be obtained at all events; that, in order to effect this first great and indispensable purpose, it would be adviseable to make a more complete division of land, and to secure every man's property against violation, by the most powerful sanctions.

It might be urged, perhaps, by some objectors, that, as the fertility of the land increased, and various accidents occurred, the shares of some men might be much more than sufficient for their support; and that, when the reign of self-love was once established, they would not distribute their surplus produce without some compensation in return. It would be observed, in answer, that this was an inconvenience greatly to be lamented; but that it was an evil, which would bear no comparison to the black train of distresses which would inevitably be occasioned by the insecurity of property; that the quantity of food which one man could consume, was necessarily limited by the narrow capacity of the human stomach; that it was not certainly probable that he should throw away the rest; and if he exchanged his surplus produce for the labour of others, this would be better than that these others should absolutely starve.

It seems highly probable, therefore, that an administration of property, not very different from that which prevails in civilized states at present, would be established, as the best, though inadequate, remedy, for the evils which were pressing on the society.

The next subject which would come under discussion, intimately connected with the preceding, is, the commerce of the sexes. It would be urged by those who had turned their attention to the true cause of the difficulties under which the community laboured, that while every man felt secure that all his children would be well provided for by general benevolence, the powers of the earth would be absolutely inadequate to produce food for the population, which would inevitably ensue; that, even if the whole attention and labour of the society were directed to this sole point, and if, by the most perfect security of property, and every other encouragement that could be thought of, the greatest possible increase of produce were yearly obtained; yet still, the increase of food would by no means keep pace with the much more rapid increase of population; that some check to population, therefore, was imperiously called for; that the most natural and obvious check seemed to be, to make every man provide for his own children; that this would operate in some respect as a measure and a guide in the increase of population, as it might be expected that no man would bring beings into the world, for whom he could not find the means of support; that, where this, notwithstanding, was the case, it seemed necessary, for the example of others, that the disgrace and inconvenience attending such a conduct, should fall upon that individual, who had thus inconsiderately plunged himself and his innocent children into want and misery.

The institution of marriage, or at least of some express or implied obligation on every man to support his own children, seems to be the natural result of these reasonings, in a community under the difficulties that we have supposed.

The view of these difficulties, presents us with a very natural reason why the disgrace which attends a breach of chastity, should be greater in a woman than in a man. It could not be expected that women should have resources sufficient to support their own children. When, therefore, a woman had lived with a man, who had entered into no compact to maintain her children; and aware of the inconveniences that he might bring upon himself, had deserted her, these children must necessarily fall upon the society for support, or starve. And to prevent the frequent recurrence of such an inconvenience, as it would be highly unjust to punish so natural a fault by personal restraint or infliction, the men might agree to punish it with disgrace. The offence is, besides, more obvious and conspicuous in the woman, and less liable to any mistake. The father of a child may not always be known; but the same uncertainty cannot easily exist with regard to the mother. Where the evidence of the offence was most complete, and the inconvenience to the society, at the same time, the greatest; there, it was agreed, that the largest share of blame should fall. The obligation on every man to support his children, the society would enforce by positive laws; and the greater degree of inconvenience or labour to which a family would necessarily subject him, added to some portion of disgrace, which every human being must incur, who leads another into unhappiness, might be considered as a sufficient punishment for the man.

That a woman should, at present, be almost driven from society, for an offence which men commit nearly with impunity, seems to be, undoubtedly, a breach of natural justice. But the origin of the custom, as the most obvious and effectual method of preventing the frequent recurrence of a serious inconvenience to a community, appears to be natural, though not perhaps, perfectly justifiable. This origin, however, is now lost in the new train of ideas, that the custom has since generated. What at first might be dictated by state necessity, is now supported by female delicacy; and operates with the greatest force on that part of the society, where, if the original intention of the custom were preserved, there is the least real occasion for it.

When these two fundamental laws of society, the security of property, and the institution of marriage, were once established, inequality of conditions must necessarily follow. Those who were born, after the division of property, would come into a world already possessed. If their parents, from having too large a family, were unable to give them sufficient for their support, what could they do in a world where every thing was appropriated. We have seen the fatal effects that would result to society, if every man had a valid claim to an equal share of the produce of the earth. The members of a family which was grown too large for the original division of land appropriated to it, could not then demand a part of the surplus produce of others as a debt of justice. It has appeared, that, from the inevitable laws of human nature, some human beings will be exposed to want. These are the unhappy persons who in the great lottery of life have drawn a blank. The number of these persons would soon exceed the ability of the surplus produce to supply. Moral merit is a very difficult criterion, except in extreme cases. The owners of surplus produce would, in general, seek some more obvious mark of distinction; and it seems to be both natural and just, that, except upon particular occasions, their choice should fall upon those, who were able, and professed themselves willing, to exert their strength in procuring a further surplus produce, which would at once benefit the community, and enable the proprietors to afford assistance to greater numbers. All who were in want of food, would be urged by imperious necessity to offer their labour in exchange for this article, so absolutely necessary to existence. The fund appropriated to the maintenance of labour, would be the aggregate quantity of food possessed by the owners of land beyond their own consumption. When the demands upon this fund were great and numerous, it would naturally be divided into very small shares. Labour would be ill paid. Men would offer to work for a bare subsistence; and the rearing of families would be checked by sickness and misery. On the contrary, when this fund was increasing fast; when it was great in proportion to the number of claimants, it would be divided in much larger shares. No man would exchange his labour without receiving an ample quantity of food in return. Labourers would live in ease and comfort, and would consequently be able to rear a numerous and vigorous offspring.

On the state of this fund, the happiness, or the degree of misery, prevailing among the lower classes of people, in every known state, at present chiefly depends; and on this happiness, or degree of misery, depends principally the increase, stationariness, or decrease, of population.

And thus, it appears, that a society constituted according to the most beautiful form that imagination can conceive, with benevolence for its moving principle, instead of self-love, and with every evil disposition in all its members corrected by reason, not force, would, from the inevitable laws of nature, and not from any original depravity of man, or of human institutions, degenerate, in a very short period, into a society, constructed upon a plan, not essentially different from that which prevails in every known state at present; a society, divided into a class of proprietors and a class of labourers, and with self-love for the mainspring of the great machine.

In the supposition which I have made, I have undoubtedly taken the increase of population smaller, and the increase of produce greater, than they really would be. No reason can be assigned why, under the circumstances supposed, population should not increase faster than in any known instance. If, then, we were to take the period of doubling at fifteen years, instead of twenty-five years, and reflect upon the labour necessary to double the produce in so short a time, even if we allow it possible; we may venture to pronounce with certainty, that, if Mr. Godwin's system of society were established in its utmost perfection, instead of myriads of centuries, not thirty years could elapse, before its utter destruction from the simple principle of population.

I have taken no notice of emigration in this place, for obvious reasons. If such societies were instituted in other parts of Europe, these countries would be under the same difficulties, with regard to population, and could admit no fresh members into their bosoms. If this beautiful society were confined to this island, it must have degenerated strangely from its original purity, and administer but a very small portion of the happiness it proposed, before any of its members would voluntarily consent to leave it, and live under such governments as at present exist in Europe, or submit to the extreme hardships of first settlers in new regions.

C H A P . III.

Observations on the Reply of Mr. Godwin.

MR. Godwin, in a late publication, has replied to those parts of the Essay on the Principle of Population, which he thinks bear the hardest on his system. A few remarks on this reply will be sufficient.

In a note to an early part of his pamphlet, he observes, that the main attack of the essay, is not directed against the principles of his work, but its conclusion.[1] It may be true, indeed, that, as Mr. Godwin had dedicated one particular chapter towards the conclusion of his work, to the consideration of the objections to his system, from the principle of population, this particular chapter is most frequently alluded to: but certainly, if the great principle of the essay be admitted, it affects his whole work, and essentially alters the foundations of political justice. A great part of Mr. Godwin's book consists of an abuse of human institutions, as productive of all, or most of, the evils which afflict society. The acknowledgment of a new and totally unconsidered cause of misery, would evidently alter the state of these arguments, and make it absolutely necessary that they should be either newly modified, or entirely rejected.

In the first book of Political Justice, chap. iii. entitled, "The Spirit of " Political Institutions," Mr. Godwin observes, that "Two of the greatest " abuses relative to the interior policy of nations which at this time prevail " in the world, consist in the irregular transfer of property, either first, by " violence, or secondly, by fraud." And he goes on to say, that if there existed no desire in individuals to possess themselves of the substance of others, and if every man could, with perfect facility, obtain the necessaries of life, civil society might become what poetry has feigned of the golden age. Let us inquire, he says, into the principles to which these evils are indebted for existence. After acknowledging the truth of the principal argument in the essay on population, I do not think that he could stop in this inquiry at mere human institutions. Many other parts of his work would be affected by this consideration in a similar manner.

As Mr. Godwin seems disposed to understand, and candidly to admit the truth of, the principal argument in the essay, I feel the more mortified,

---

1. Reply to the attacks of Dr. Parr, Mr. Mackintosh, the author of an Essay on Population, and others, p. 10.

that he should think it a fair inference from my positions, that the political superintendents of a community are bound to exercise a paternal vigilance and care over the two great means of advantage and safety to mankind, misery and vice; and that no evil is more to be dreaded than that we should have too little of them in the world, to confine the principle of population within its proper sphere.[2] I am at a loss to conceive what class of evils Mr. Godwin imagines is yet behind, which these salutary checks are to prevent. For my own part, I know of no stronger or more general terms than vice and misery; and the sole question is, respecting a greater or less degree of them. The only reason why I object to Mr. Godwin's system, is, my full conviction that an attempt to execute it, would very greatly increase the quantity of vice and misery in society. If Mr. Godwin will undo this conviction, and prove to me, though it be only in theory, provided that theory be consistent, and founded on a knowledge of human nature, that his system will really tend to drive vice and misery from the earth, he may depend upon having me one of its steadiest and warmest advocates.

Mr. Godwin observes, that he should naturally be disposed to pronounce that man strangely indifferent to schemes of extraordinary improvement in society, who made it a conclusive argument against them, that, when they were realized, they might peradventure be of no permanence and duration. And yet, what is morality, individual or political, according to Mr. Godwin's own definition of it, but a calculation of consequences? Is the physician the patron of pain, who advises his patient to bear a present evil, rather than betake himself to a remedy, which, though it might give momentary relief, would afterwards greatly aggravate all the symptoms? Is the moralist to be called an enemy to pleasure, because he recommends to a young man just entering into life, not to ruin his health and patrimony in a few years, by an excess of present gratifications, but to economize his enjoyments, that he may spread them over a longer period? Of Mr. Godwin's system, according to the present arguments by which it is supported, it is not enough to say, *peradventure* it will be of no permanence; but we can pronounce with *certainty* that it will be of no permanence: and under such circumstances an attempt to execute it would unquestionably be a great political immorality.

Mr. Godwin observes, that after recovering from the first impression made by the Essay on Population, the first thing that is apt to strike every reflecting mind, is, that the excess of power in the principle of population over the principle of subsistence, has never, in any past instance, in any

2. Reply, &c. p. 60.

quarter, or age, of the world, produced those great and astonishing effects, that total breaking-up of all the structures and maxims of society, which the essay lead us to expect from it in certain cases in future.[3] This is undoubtedly true; and the reason is, that, in no past instance, nor in any quarter, or age, of the world, has an attempt been made to establish such a system as Mr. Godwin's, and without an attempt of this nature, none of these great effects will follow. The convulsions of the social system, described in the last chapter, appeared by a kind of irresistible necessity, to terminate in the establishment of the laws of property and marriage; but in countries, where these laws are already established, as they are in all the common constitutions of society, with which we are acquainted, the operation of the principle of population will always be silent and gradual, and not different to what we daily see in our own country. Other persons, besides Mr. Godwin, have imagined, that I looked to certain periods in future, when population would exceed the means of subsistence in a much greater degree than at present, and that the evils arising from the principle of population were rather in contemplation, than in existence; but this is a total misconception of the argument.[4] Poverty, and not absolute famine, is the specifick effect of the principle of population, as I have before endeavoured to shew. Many countries are now suffering all the evils that can ever be expected to flow from this principle, and even, if we were arrived at the absolute limit to all further increase of produce, a point, which we shall certainly never reach, I should by no means expect that these evils would be in any marked manner aggravated. The increase of produce in most European countries is so very slow, compared with what would be required to support an unrestricted increase of people, that the checks which are constantly in action to repress the population to the level of a produce increasing so slowly, would have very little more to do in wearing it down to a produce absolutely stationary.

But Mr. Godwin says, that if he looks into the past history of the world, he does not see that increasing population has been controlled and confined by vice and misery alone. In this observation I cannot agree with him. I will thank Mr. Godwin to name to me any check, which in past ages has contributed to keep down the population to the level of the means of subsistence, that does not fairly come under some form of vice or misery; except indeed the check of moral restraint, which I have mentioned in the course of this work; and which, to say the truth, whatever hopes we may entertain

3. Reply, p. 70.
4. In other parts of his Reply, Mr. Godwin does not fall into this error.

of its prevalence in future, has undoubtedly in past ages operated with very inconsiderable force.

I do not think that I should find it difficult to justify myself in the eyes of my readers from the imputation of being the patron of vice and misery; but I am not clear, that Mr. Godwin would find such a justification so easy. For though he has positively declared that he does not "regard them with " complacency;" and "hopes that it may not be considered as a taste abso- " lutely singular in him that he should entertain no vehement partialities " for vice and misery;"[5] yet he has certainly exposed himself to the suspicion of having this singular taste, by suggesting the organization of a very large portion of them for the benefit of society in general. On this subject I need only observe, that I have always ranked the two checks[6] which he first mentions, among the worst forms of vice and misery.

In one part of his Reply, Mr. Godwin makes a supposition respecting the number of children that might be allowed to each prolifick marriage; but as he has not entered into the detail of the mode by which a greater number might be prevented, I shall not notice it further, than merely to observe, that although he professes to acknowledge the geometrical and arithmetical ratios of population and food, yet in this place he appears to think that, practically applied, these different ratios of increase, are not of a nature to make the evil resulting from them urgent, or alarmingly to confine the natural progress of population.[7] This observation seems to contradict his former acknowledgment.

5. Reply, p. 76.

6. Mr. Godwin does not acknowledge the justice of Hume's observation respecting infanticide; and yet the extreme population and poverty in China, where this custom prevails, tends strongly to confirm the observation. It is still, however, true, as Mr. Godwin observes, that the expedient is, in its own nature, adequate to the end for which it was cited, (p. 66.); but, to make it so in fact, it must be done by the magistrate, and not left to the parents. The almost invariable tendency of this custom to increase population, when it depends entirely on the parents, shews the extreme pain which they must feel, in making such a sacrifice, even when the distress arising from excessive poverty may be supposed to have deadened in great measure their sensibility. What must this pain be then, upon the supposition of the interference of a magistrate or of a positive law, to make parents destroy a child, which they feel the desire, and think they possess the power, of supporting? The permission of infanticide is bad enough, and cannot but have a bad effect on the moral sensibility of a nation; but, I cannot conceive any thing much more detestable, or shocking to the feelings, than any direct regulation of this kind, although sanctioned by the names of Plato and Aristotle.

7. Reply, p. 70.

The last check which Mr. Godwin mentions, and which, I am persuaded, is the only one which he would seriously recommend, is, "that sentiment, " whether virtue, prudence, or pride, which continually restrains the uni- " versality and frequent repetition of the marriage contract."[8] On this sentiment, which I have already noticed under the name of moral restraint, and of the more comprehensive title, the preventive check, it will appear, that in the sequel of this work I shall lay considerable stress. Of this check therefore itself, I entirely approve; but I do not think that Mr. Godwin's system of political justice is by any means favourable to its prevalence. The tendency to early marriages is so strong that we want every possible help that we can get to counteract it; and a system which in any way whatever tends to weaken the foundation of private property, and to lessen in any degree the full advantage and superiority which each individual may derive from his prudence, must remove the only counteracting weight to the passion of love, that can be depended upon for any essential effect. Mr. Godwin acknowledges that in his system, "the ill consequences of a numerous family " will not come so coarsely home to each man's individual interest as they " do at present."[9] But I am sorry to say that, from what we know hitherto of the human character, we can have no rational hopes of success, without this coarse application to individual interest, which Mr. Godwin rejects. If the whole effect were to depend merely on a sense of duty, considering the powerful antagonist that is to be contended with, in the present case, I confess that I should absolutely despair. At the same time, I am strongly of opinion that a sense of duty, superadded to a sense of interest, would by no means be without its effect. There are many noble and disinterested spirits, who, though aware of the inconveniences which they may bring upon themselves by the indulgence of an early and virtuous passion, feel a kind of repugnance to listen to the dictates of mere worldly prudence, and a pride in rejecting these low considerations. There is a kind of romantick gallantry in sacrificing all for love, naturally fascinating to a young mind; and, to say the truth, if all is to be sacrificed, I do not know, in what better cause it can be done. But if a strong sense of duty could, in these instances, be added to prudential suggestions, the whole question might wear a different colour. In delaying the gratification of passion, from a sense of duty, the most disinterested spirit, the most delicate honour, might be satisfied. The romantick pride might take a different direction, and the dictates of worldly prudence might be followed with the cheerful consciousness of making a virtuous sacrifice.

8. Id. p. 72.   9. Id. p. 74.

If we were to remove or weaken the motive of interest, which would be the case in Mr. Godwin's system, I fear we should have but a weak substitute in a sense of duty. But if to the present beneficial effects, known to result from a sense of interest, we could superadd a sense of duty, which is the object of the latter part of this work, it does not seem absolutely hopeless that some partial improvement in society should result from it.

CHAP. IV.

Of Emigration.

ALTHOUGH the resource of emigration seems to be excluded from such a society as Mr. Godwin has imagined; yet in that partial degree of improvement which alone can rationally be expected, it may fairly enter into our consideration. And as it is not probable, that human industry should begin to receive its best direction, throughout all the nations of the earth at the same time, it may be said, that in the case of a redundant population in the more cultivated parts of the world, the natural and obvious remedy that presents itself, is, emigration to those parts that are uncultivated. As these parts are of great extent, and very thinly peopled, this resource might appear, on a first view of the subject, an adequate remedy, or at least of a nature to remove the evil to a distant period: but, when we advert to experience, and to the actual state of the uncivilized parts of the globe, instead of any thing like an adequate remedy, it will appear but a very weak palliative.

In the accounts which we have of the peopling of new countries, the dangers, difficulties, and hardships, that the first settlers have had to struggle with, appear to be even greater, than we can well imagine that they could be exposed to, in their parent state. The endeavour to avoid that degree of unhappiness arising from the difficulty of supporting a family, might long have left the new world of America unpeopled by Europeans, if those more powerful passions, the thirst of gain, the spirit of adventure, and religious enthusiasm, had not directed and animated the enterprize. These passions enabled the first adventurers to triumph over every obstacle; but in many instances in a way to make humanity shudder, and to defeat the true end of emigration. Whatever may be the character of the Spanish inhabitants of Mexico and Peru at the present moment, we cannot read the accounts of the first conquests of these countries, without feeling strongly, that the race destroyed, was, in moral worth, as well as numbers, highly superior to the race of their destroyers.

The parts of America settled by the English, from being thinly peopled, were better adapted to the establishment of new colonies; yet even here, the most formidable difficulties presented themselves. In the settlement of Virginia, begun by Sir Walter Raleigh, and established by Lord Delaware, three attempts completely failed. Nearly half of the first colony was destroyed by the savages, and the rest consumed and worn down by fatigue and famine, deserted the country, and returned home in despair. The second colony was cut off to a man, in a manner unknown; but they were supposed to be destroyed by the Indians. The third experienced the same dismal fate; and the remains of the fourth, after it had been reduced by famine and disease, in the course of six months from 500 to 60 persons, were returning in a famishing and desperate condition to England, when they were met in the mouth of the Chesapeak bay, by Lord Delaware, with a squadron loaded with provisions, and every thing for their relief and defence.[1]

The first puritan settlers in New England were few in number. They landed in a bad season, and they were only supported by their private funds. The winter was premature, and terribly cold; the country was covered with wood, and afforded very little for the refreshment of persons, sickly with such a voyage, or for the sustenance of an infant people. Nearly half of them perished by the scurvy, by want, and the severity of the climate; but they who survived were not dispirited by their hardships; but, supported by their energy of character, and the satisfaction of finding themselves out of the reach of the spiritual arm, reduced this savage country, by degrees, to yield them a comfortable subsistence.[2]

Even the plantation of Barbadoes, which increased afterwards with such extraordinary rapidity, had at first to contend with a country utterly desolate, an extreme want of provisions, a difficulty in clearing the ground unusually great, from the uncommon size and hardness of the trees, a most disheartening scantiness and poverty in their first crops, and a slow and precarious supply of provisions from England.[3]

The attempt of the French, in 1663, to form at once a powerful colony in Guiana, was attended with the most disastrous consequences. Twelve thousand men were landed in the rainy season, and placed under tents and miserable sheds. In this situation, inactive, weary of existence, and in want of all necessaries, exposed to contagious distempers, which are always occasioned by bad provisions, and to all the irregularities which idleness produces among the lower classes of society, almost the whole of them ended their lives in all the horrors of despair. The attempt was completely abortive. Two thousand men, whose robust constitutions had enabled them to resist the inclemency of the climate, and the miseries to which they had

1. Burke's America, vol. ii. p. 219. Robertson, b. ix. p. 83, 86.
2. Burke's America, vol. ii. p. 144.   3. Id. p. 85.

been exposed, were brought back to France; and the 25,000,000 of livres which had been expended in the expedition were totally lost.[4]

In the last settlement at Port Jackson, in New Holland, a melancholy and affecting picture is drawn by Collins, of the extreme hardships which, for some years, the infant colony had to struggle with, before the produce was equal to its support. These distresses were undoubtedly aggravated by the character of the settlers; but those which were caused by the unhealthiness of a newly-cleared country, the failure of first crops, and the uncertainty of supplies from so distant a mother country, were of themselves sufficiently disheartening, to place in a strong point of view, the necessity of great resources, as well as unconquerable perseverance, in the colonization of savage countries.

The establishment of colonies, in the more thinly peopled regions of Europe and Asia would evidently require still greater resources. From the power, and warlike character, of the inhabitants of these countries, a considerable military force would be necessary to prevent their utter and immediate destruction. Even the frontier provinces of the most powerful states, are defended with considerable difficulty from such restless neighbours; and the peaceful labours of the cultivator, are continually interrupted by their predatory incursions. The late Empress Catharine of Russia found it necessary to protect, by regular fortresses, the colonies which she had established in the districts near the Wolga; and the calamities which her subjects suffered by the incursions of the Crim Tartars furnished a pretext, and perhaps a just one, for taking possession of the whole of the Crimea, and expelling the greatest part of these turbulent neighbours, and reducing the rest to a more tranquil mode of life.

The difficulties attending a first establishment, from soil, climate, and the want of proper conveniences, are of course nearly the same in these regions as in America. Mr. Eton, in his account of the Turkish Empire, says, that 75,000 Christians were obliged by Russia to emigrate from the Crimea, and sent to inhabit the country abandoned by the Nogai Tartars; but the winter coming on before the houses built for them were ready, a great part of them had no other shelter from the cold, than what was afforded them by holes dug in the ground, covered with what they could procure, and the greatest part of them perished. Only seven thousand remained a few years afterwards. Another colony from Italy to the banks of the Borysthenes, had, he says, no better fate, owing to the bad management of those who were commissioned to provide for them.

---

4. Raynal, Hist. des Indes, tom. vii. liv. xiii. p. 43. 10 vols 8vo. 1795.

It is needless to add to these instances, as the accounts given of the difficulties experienced in new settlements are all nearly similar. It has been justly observed, by a correspondent of Dr. Franklin, that one of the reasons why we have seen so many fruitless attempts to settle colonies at an immense publick and private expence, by several of the powers of Europe, is, that the moral and mechanical habits adapted to the mother country are frequently not so, to the new-settled one, and to external events, many of which are unforeseen; and that it is to be remarked, that none of the English colonies became any way considerable, till the necessary manners were born and grew up in the country. Pallas particularly notices the want of proper habits in the colonies, established by Russia, as one of the causes why they did not increase so fast as might have been expected.

In addition to this, it may be observed, that the first establishment of a new colony, generally presents an instance of a country, peopled considerably beyond its actual produce; and the natural consequence seems to be, that this population, if not amply supplied by the mother country, should, at the beginning, be diminished to the level of the first scanty productions, and not begin permanently to increase till the remaining numbers had so far cultivated the soil, as to make it yield a quantity of food, more than sufficient for their own support; and which consequently they could divide with a family. The frequent failures in the establishment of new colonies tend strongly to show the order of precedence between food and population.

It must be acknowledged then, that the class of people on whom the distress arising from a too rapidly increasing population would principally fall, could not possibly begin a new colony in a distant country. From the nature of their situation, they must necessarily be deficient in those resources, which alone could ensure success: and unless they could find leaders among the higher classes, urged by the spirit of avarice or enterprize; or of religious or political discontent; or were furnished with means and support by government; whatever degree of misery they might suffer in their own country, from the scarcity of subsistence, they would be absolutely unable to take possession of any of those uncultivated regions, of which there is yet such an extent on the earth.

When new colonies have been once securely established, the difficulty of emigration is, indeed, very considerably diminished; yet, even then, some resources are necessary to provide vessels for the voyage, and support and assistance till the emigrants can settle themselves, and find employment in their adopted country. How far it is incumbent upon a government to furnish these resources, may be a question; but whatever be its duty in this particular, perhaps it is too much to expect, that except where any particular colonial advantages are proposed, emigration should be actively assisted.

The necessary resources for transport and maintenance, are, however, frequently furnished by individuals, or private companies. For many years before the American war, and for some few since, the facilities of emigration to this new world, and the probable advantages in view, were unusually great; and it must be considered undoubtedly as a very happy circumstance for any country, to have so comfortable an asylum for its redundant population. But I would ask, whether, even during these periods, the distress among the common people in this country was little or nothing, and whether every man felt secure before he ventured on marriage, that however large his family might be, he should find no difficulty in supporting it without parish assistance? The answer, I fear, could not be in the affirmative.

It will be said, that when an opportunity of advantageous emigration is offered, it is the fault of the people themselves, if, instead of accepting it, they prefer a life of celibacy, or extreme poverty in their own country. Is it then a fault for a man to feel an attachment to his native soil, to love the parents that nurtured him, his kindred, his friends, and the companions of his early years? or is it no evil that he suffers, because he consents to bear it, rather than snap these cords which nature has wound in close and intricate folds round the human heart? The great plan of providence seems to require, indeed, that these ties should sometimes be broken; but the separation does not, on that account, give less pain; and, though the general good may be promoted by it, it does not cease to be an individual evil. Besides, doubts and uncertainty must ever attend all distant emigrations, particularly in the apprehensions of the lower classes of people. They cannot feel quite secure, that the representations made to them of the high price of labour, or the cheapness of land, are accurately true. They are placing themselves in the power of the persons who are to furnish them with the means of transport and maintenance, who may perhaps have an interest in deceiving them; and the sea which they are to pass, appears to them like the separation of death from all their former connexions, and in a manner to preclude the possibility of return in case of failure, as they cannot expect the offer of the same means to bring them back. We cannot be surprised then, that, except where a spirit of enterprise is added to the uneasiness of poverty, the consideration of these circumstances, should frequently,

"   Make them rather bear the ills they suffer,
"   Than fly to others which they know not of."

If a tract of rich land as large as this island were suddenly annexed to it, and sold in small lots, or let out in small farms, the case would be very different, and the amelioration of the state of the common people would be sudden and striking; though the rich would be continually complaining of the high price of labour, the pride of the lower classes, and the difficulty of getting work done. These, I understand, are not unfrequent complaints among the men of property in America.

Every resource, however, from emigration, if used effectually, as this would be, must be of short duration. There is scarcely a state in Europe, except perhaps Russia, the inhabitants of which do not often endeavour to better their condition by removing to other countries. As these states therefore have nearly all rather a redundant, than deficient population, in proportion to their produce, they cannot be supposed to afford any effectual resources of emigration to each other. Let us suppose, for a moment, that in this more enlightened part of the globe, the internal economy of each state were so admirably regulated, that no checks existed to population, and the different governments provided every facility for emigration. Taking the population of Europe, excluding Russia, at a hundred millions, and allowing a greater increase of produce than is probable, or even possible, in the mother countries, the redundancy of parent stock in a single century, would be eleven hundred millions, which, added to the natural increase of the colonies, during the same time, would be more than double what has been supposed to be the present population of the whole earth.

Can we imagine, that in the uncultivated parts of Asia, Africa, or America, the greatest exertions, and the best directed endeavours, could in so short a period, prepare a quantity of land, sufficient for the support of such a population. If any sanguine person should feel a doubt upon the subject, let him only add 25 or 50 years more, and every doubt must be crushed in overwhelming conviction.

It is evident, therefore, that the reason why the resource of emigration has so long continued to be held out as a remedy to redundant population, is, because, from the natural unwillingness of people to desert their native country, and the difficulty of clearing and cultivating fresh soil, it never is, nor can be, adequately adopted. If this remedy were indeed really effectual, and had power so far to relieve the disorders of vice and misery in old states, as to place them in the condition of the most prosperous new colonies, we should soon see the phial exhausted, and when the disorders returned with increased virulence, every hope from that quarter would be for ever closed.

It is clear, therefore, that with any view of making room for an unrestricted increase of population, emigration is perfectly inadequate; but as a partial and temporary expedient, and with a view to the more general cultivation of the earth, and the wider spread of civilization, it seems to be both useful and proper; and if it cannot be proved that governments are bound actively to encourage it, it is not only strikingly unjust, but in the highest degree impolitick, in them to prevent it. There are no fears so totally ill-grounded, as the fears of depopulation from emigration. The *vis inertiæ* of people in general, and their attachment to their homes, are qualities so strong, and general, that we may rest assured that they will not emigrate, unless, from political discontents, or extreme poverty, they are in such a state, as will make it as much for the advantage of their country as of themselves that they should go out of it. The complaints of high wages in consequence of emigrations are, of all others, the most unreasonable, and ought the least to be attended to. If the wages of labour in any country be such, as to enable the lower classes of people to live with tolerable comfort, we may be quite certain, that they will not emigrate; and if they be not such, it is cruelty and injustice to detain them.

CHAP. V.

Of the English Poor Laws.

To remedy the frequent distresses of the poor, laws to enforce their relief have been instituted; and in the establishment of a general system of this kind, England has particularly distinguished herself. But it is to be feared, that though it may have alleviated a little the intensity of individual misfortune, it has spread the evil over a much larger surface.

It is a subject often started in conversation, and mentioned always as a matter of great surprise, that, notwithstanding the immense sum which is annually collected for the poor in this country, there is still so much distress among them. Some think that the money must be embezzled for private use; others, that the churchwardens and overseers consume the greatest part of it in feasting. All agree, that somehow or other, it must be very ill managed. In short, the fact, that, even before the late scarcities, three millions were collected annually for the poor, and yet that their distresses were not removed, is the subject of continual astonishment. But a man who looks a little below the surface of things, would be much more astonished, if the fact were otherwise than it is observed to be; or even if a collection universally of eighteen shillings in the pound, instead of four, were materially to alter it.

Suppose, that by a subscription of the rich, the eighteen-pence, or two shillings, which men earn now, were made up five shillings, it might be imagined, perhaps, that they would then be able to live comfortably, and have a piece of meat every day for their dinner. But this would be a very false conclusion. The transfer of three additional shillings a day to each labourer would not increase the quantity of meat in the country. There is not at present enough for all to have a moderate share. What would then be the consequence? The competition among the buyers in the market of meat, would rapidly raise the price from eight pence or nine pence, to two or three shillings in the pound, and the commodity would not be divided among many more than it is at present. When an article is scarce, and cannot be distributed to all, he that can shew the most valid patent, that is, he that offers the most money, becomes the possessor. If we can suppose the competition among the buyers of meat, to continue long enough for a greater number of cattle to be reared annually, this could only be done at the expence of the corn, which would be a very disadvantageous exchange;

for it is well known, that the country could not then support the same population; and when subsistence is scarce in proportion to the number of people, it is of little consequence, whether the lowest members of the society possess two shillings or five. They must, at all events, be reduced to live upon the hardest fare, and in the smallest quantity.

It might be said, perhaps, that the increased number of purchasers in every article would give a spur to productive industry, and that the whole produce of the island would be increased. But the spur that these fancied riches would give to population, would more than counterbalance it; and the increased produce would be to be divided among a more than proportionably increased number of people.

A collection from the rich, of eighteen shillings in the pound, even if distributed in the most judicious manner, would have an effect similar to that resulting from the supposition which I have just made; and no possible sacrifices of the rich, particularly in money, could, for any time, prevent the recurrence of distress among the lower members of society, who ever they were. Great changes might indeed be made. The rich might become poor, and some of the poor rich; but, while the present proportion between population and food continues, a part of society must necessarily find it difficult to support a family, and this difficulty will naturally fall on the least fortunate members.

It may at first appear strange, but I believe it is true, that I cannot by means of money, raise the condition of a poor man, and enable him to live much better than he did before, without proportionably depressing others in the same class. If I retrench the quantity of food consumed in my house, and give him what I have cut off, I then benefit him without depressing any but myself and family, who perhaps may be well able to bear it. If I turn up a piece of uncultivated land, and give him the produce, I then benefit both him and all the members of society, because what he before consumed is thrown into the common stock, and, probably, some of the new produce with it. But if I only give him money, supposing the produce of the country to remain the same, I give him a title to a larger share of that produce than formerly, which share he cannot receive without diminishing the shares of others. It is evident, that this effect in individual instances must be so small as to be totally imperceptible; but still it must exist, as many other effects do, which, like some of the insects that people the air, elude our grosser perceptions.

Supposing the quantity of food in any country, to remain the same for many years together, it is evident, that this food must be divided according to the value of each man's patent, or the sum of money which he can afford to spend in this commodity so universally in request. It is a demonstrative truth, therefore, that the patents of one set of men could not be increased in value, without diminishing the value of the patents of some other set of men. If the rich were to subscribe, and give five shillings a day to five hundred thousand men, without retrenching their own tables, no doubt can exist that as these men would live more at their ease, and consume a greater quantity of provisions, there would be less food remaining to divide among the rest; and consequently, each man's patent would be diminished in value, or the same number of pieces of silver would purchase a smaller quantity of subsistence, and the price of provisions would universally rise.

These general reasonings have been strikingly confirmed during the late scarcities. The supposition which I have made of a collection from the rich of eighteen shillings in the pound, has been nearly realized; and the effect has been such as might have been expected. If the same distribution had been made, when no scarcity existed, a considerable advance in the price of provisions would have been a necessary consequence; but following as it did a scarcity, its effect must have been doubly powerful. No person, I believe, will venture to doubt, that, if we were to give three additional shillings a day to every labouring man in the kingdom, as I before supposed, in order that he might have meat for his dinner, the price of meat would rise in the most rapid and unexampled manner. But surely, in a deficiency of corn, which renders it impossible for every man to have his usual share, if we still continue to furnish each person with the means of purchasing the same quantity as before, the effect must be in every respect similar.

It seems in great measure to have escaped observation, that the price of corn in a scarcity, will depend much more upon the obstinacy with which the same degree of consumption is persevered in, than on the degree of the actual deficiency. A deficiency of one half of a crop, if the people could immediately consent to consume only one half of what they did before, would produce little or no effect on the price of corn. A deficiency of one twelfth, if exactly the same consumption were to continue for ten or eleven months, might raise the price of corn to almost any height. The more is given in parish assistance, the more power is furnished of persevering in the same consumption, and of course the higher will the price rise before the necessary diminution of consumption is effected.

It has been asserted by some people that high prices do not diminish consumption. If this were really true, we should see the price of a bushel of corn at a hundred pounds or more, in every deficiency, which could not be fully and completely remedied by importation. But the fact is, that high prices do ultimately diminish consumption; but, on account of the riches of the country, the unwillingness of the people to resort to substitutes, and the immense sums, which are distributed by parishes, this object cannot be attained till the prices become excessive, and force even the middle classes of society, or at least those immediately above the poor, to save in the article of bread from the actual inability of purchasing it in the usual quantity. The poor who were assisted by their parishes had no reason whatever to complain of the high price of grain; because it was the excessiveness of this price, and this alone, which, by enforcing such a saving, left a greater quantity of corn, for the consumption of the lowest classes, which corn, the parish allowances enabled them to command. The greatest sufferers in the scarcity were undoubtedly the classes immediately above the poor; and these were in the most marked manner depressed by the excessive bounties given to those below them. Almost all poverty is relative; and I much doubt, whether these people would have been rendered so poor, if a sum equal to half of those bounties had been taken directly out of their pockets, as they were, by that new distribution of the money of the society which actually took place.[1] This distribution by giving to the poorer classes a command of food, so much greater than their degree of skill and industry entitled them to, in the actual circumstances of the country, diminished, exactly in the same proportion, that command over the necessaries of life, which the classes above them, by their superior skill and industry, would naturally possess; and it may be a question, whether the degree of assistance which the poor received, and which prevented them from resorting to the use of those substitutes, which, in every other country, on such occasions, the great law of necessity teaches, was not more than overbalanced by the severity of the pressure on so large a body of people from the extreme high prices, and the permanent evil which must result from forcing so many persons on the parish, who before thought themselves almost out of the reach of want.

1. Supposing the lower classes to earn on an average ten shillings a week, and the classes just above them, twenty, it is not to be doubted, that, in a scarcity, these latter would be more straightened in their power of commanding the necessaries of life, by a donation of ten shillings a week to those below them, than by the subtraction of five shillings a week from their own earnings. In the one case, they would be all reduced to a level; the price of provisions would rise in an extraordinary manner from the greatness of the competition; and all would be straightened for subsistence. In the other case, the classes above the poor would still maintain a considerable part of their relative superiority; the price of provisions would by no means rise in the same degree; and their remaining fifteen shillings would purchase much more than their twenty shillings in the former case.

If we were to double the fortunes of all those who possess above a hundred a year, the effect on the price of grain would be slow and inconsiderable; but if we were to double the price of labour throughout the kingdom, the effect, in raising the price of grain, would be rapid and great. The general principles on this subject will not admit of dispute; and that in the particular case which we have been considering, the bounties to the poor were of a magnitude to operate very powerfully in this manner, will sufficiently appear, if we recollect, that, before the late scarcities, the sum collected for the poor was estimated at three millions, and that during the year 1801 it was said to be ten millions. An additional seven millions acting at the bottom of the scale,[2] and employed exclusively in the purchase of provisions, joined to a considerable advance in the price of wages in many parts of the kingdom, and increased by a prodigious sum expended in voluntary charity, must have had a most powerful effect in raising the price of the necessaries of life, if any reliance can be placed on the clearest general principles, confirmed as much as possible by appearances. A man with a family, has received, to my knowledge, fourteen shillings a week from the parish. His common earnings were ten shillings a week, and his weekly revenue, therefore, twenty-four. Before the scarcity, he had been in the habit of purchasing a bushel of flour a week with eight shillings perhaps, and consequently had two shillings out of his ten, to spare for other necessaries. During the scarcity, he was enabled to purchase the same quantity at nearly three times the price. He paid twenty-two shillings for his bushel of flour, and had, as before, two shillings remaining for other wants. Such instances could not possibly have been universal, without raising the price of wheat very much higher than it really was during any part of the dearth. But similar instances were by no means infrequent, and the system itself, of measuring the relief given by the price of grain, was general.

If the circulation of the country had consisted entirely of specie, which could not have been immediately increased; it would have been impossible to give such an additional sum as seven millions to the poor, without embarrassing, to a great degree, the operations of commerce. On the

2. See a small pamphlet published in November 1800, entitled, *An investigation of the cause of the present high price of provisions.* This pamphlet was mistaken by some for an inquiry into the cause of the scarcity, and as such, it would naturally appear to be incomplete, adverting, as it does, principally to a single cause. But the sole object of the pamphlet was, to give the principal reason for the extreme high price of provisions, in proportion to the degree of the scarcity, admitting the deficiency of one fourth, as stated in the Duke of Portland's letter, which, I am much inclined to think, was very near the truth.

commencement, therefore, of this extensive relief, which would necessarily occasion a proportionate expenditure in provisions throughout all the ranks of society, a great demand would be felt for an increased circulating medium. The nature of the medium then principally in use, was such, that it could be created immediately on demand. From the accounts of the bank of England, as laid before Parliament, it appeared that no very great additional issues of paper took place from this quarter. The three millions and a half added to its former average issues, were not probably much above what was sufficient to supply the quantity of specie that had been withdrawn from the circulation. If this supposition be true, and the small quantity of gold which made its appearance at that time, furnishes the strongest reason for believing that as much as this must have been been withdrawn, it would follow, that the part of the circulation originating in the bank of England, though changed in its nature, had not been increased in its quantity; and with regard to the effect of the circulating medium on the price of all commodities, it cannot be doubted that it would be precisely the same, whether it were made up principally of guineas, or of pound notes and shillings, which would pass current for guineas.

The demand, therefore, for an increased circulating medium was left to be supplied by the country banks, and it could not be expected that they should hesitate in taking advantage of so profitable an opportunity. The paper issues of a country bank are, as I conceive, measured by the quantity of its notes which will remain in circulation; and this quantity is again measured, supposing a confidence to be established, by the sum of what is wanted to carry on all the money transactions of the neighbourhood. From the high price of provisions, all these transactions became more expensive. In the single article of the weekly payment of labourers' wages, including the parish allowances, it is evident, that a very great addition to the circulating medium of the neighbourhood would be wanted.[3] Had the country banks attempted to issue the same quantity of paper. without such a particular demand for it, they would quickly have been admonished of their error by its rapid and pressing return upon them; but at this time, it was

3. A rise of wages, or of parish allowances, amounting to any particular sum, would occasion a much greater demand for the current circulating medium, than an increase of commercial transactions to the same amount; because, in the first case, it is the common currency alone which can be used; in the latter, much is done by the bills of exchange, &c.; in the first also, much money is actually wanted, in proportion to the amount of the increased payments; in the latter, a little will go a great way.

wanted for immediate and daily use, and was therefore eagerly absorbed into the circulation.

It may even admit of a question, whether, under similar circumstances, the country banks would not have issued nearly the same quantity of paper, if the bank of England had not been restricted from payment in specie. Before this event, the issues of the country banks in paper were regulated by the quantity that the circulation would take up, and after, as well as before, they were obliged to pay the notes which returned upon them in bank of England circulation. The difference in the two cases, would arise principally from the pernicious custom, adopted since the restriction of the bank, of issuing one and two pound notes, and from the little preference that many people might feel, if they could not get gold, between country bank paper and bank of England paper.

The very great issue of country bank paper during the years 1800 and 1801 was evidently, therefore, in its origin rather a consequence than a cause of the high price of provisions; but being once absorbed into the circulation, it must necessarily affect the price of all commodities, and throw very great obstacles in the way of returning cheapness.[4] This is the great mischief of the system. During the scarcity itself, it is not to be doubted, that the increased circulation, by preventing the embarrassments which commerce and speculation must otherwise have felt, enabled the country to continue all the branches of its trade with less interruption, and to import a much greater quantity of grain, than it could have done otherwise; but to overbalance these temporary advantages, a lasting evil might be entailed upon the community, and the prices of a time of scarcity might become permanent, from the difficulty of re-absorbing this increased circulation.

In this respect, however, it is much better that the great issue of paper should have come from the country banks, than from the bank of England. During the restriction of payment in specie, there is no possibility of forcing the bank to retake its notes, when too abundant; but with regard to the country banks, as soon as their notes are not wanted in the circulation, they will be returned; and if the bank of England notes be not increased, which they probably will not be, the whole circulating medium will thus be diminished.

---

4. It does not appear to me that Mr. Thornton in his valuable publication on paper credit, has taken sufficient notice of the effects of the great paper issues of the country banks, in raising the price of commodities, and producing an unfavourable state of exchange with foreigners.

We may consider ourselves as peculiarly fortunate that the two years of scarcity were succeeded by two events the best calculated to restore plenty and cheapness – an abundant harvest, and a peace; which, together, produced a general conviction of plenty, in the minds both of buyers and sellers; and, by rendering the first slow to purchase, and the others eager to sell, occasioned a glut in the market, and a consequent rapid fall of price, which has enabled parishes to take off their allowances to the poor, and thus to prevent a return of high prices when the alarm among the sellers was over.

If the two years of scarcity had been succeeded merely by years of average crops, I am strongly disposed to believe, that as no glut would have taken place in the market, the price of grain would have fallen only in an inconsiderable degree, the parish allowances could not have been resumed, the increased quantity of paper would still have been wanted, and the prices of all commodities might by degrees have been regulated, permanently, according to the increased circulating medium.

If instead of giving the temporary assistance of parish allowances, which might be withdrawn on the first fall of price, we had raised universally the wages of labour, it is evident, that the obstacles to a diminution of the circulation, and to returning cheapness, would have been still further increased; and the high price of labour would have become permanent, without any advantage whatever to the labourer.

There is no one that more ardently desires to see a real advance in the price of labour than myself; but the attempt to effect this object by forcibly raising the nominal price, which was practised to a certain degree, and recommended almost universally during the late scarcities, every thinking man must reprobate as puerile and ineffectual.

The price of labour, when left to find its natural level, is a most important political barometer, expressing the relation between the supply of provisions, and the demand for them; between the quantity to be consumed, and the number of consumers; and taken on the average, independently of accidental circumstances, it further expresses, clearly, the wants of the society respecting population; that is, whatever may be the number of children to a marriage necessary to maintain exactly the present population, the price of labour will be just sufficient to support this number, or be above it, or below it, according to the state of the real funds for the maintenance of labour, whether stationary, progressive, or retrograde. Instead, however, of considering it in this light, we consider it as something which we may raise or depress at pleasure, something which depends principally upon his majesty's justices of the peace. When an advance in the price of provisions already expresses that the demand is too great for the supply, in order to put the labourer in the same condition as before, we raise the price of labour, that is, we increase the demand, and are then much surprised that the price of provisions continues rising. In this, we act much in the same manner, as if, when the quicksilver in the common weather-glass stood at *stormy,* we were to raise it by some forcible pressure to *settled fair,* and then be greatly astonished that it continued raining.

Dr. Smith has clearly shewn, that the natural tendency of a year of scarcity, is, either to throw a number of labourers out of employment, or to oblige them to work for less than they did before, from the inability of masters to employ the same number at the same price. The raising of the price of wages tends necessarily to throw more out of employment, and completely to prevent the good effects which, he says, sometimes arise from a year of moderate scarcity, that of making the lower classes of people do more work, and become more careful and industrious. The number of servants out of place, and of manufacturers wanting employment during the late scarcities, were melancholy proofs of the truth of these reasonings. If a general rise in the wages of labour had taken place proportioned to the price of provisions, none but farmers and a few gentlemen could have afforded to employ the same number of workmen as before. Additional crowds of servants and manufacturers would have been turned off; and those who were thus thrown out of employment, would, of course, have no other refuge than the parish. In the natural order of things, a scarcity must tend to lower, instead of to raise, the price of labour.

After the publication, and general circulation of such a work as Dr. Smith's, I confess, that it appears to me strange, that so many men who would yet aspire to be thought political economists, should still think, that it is in the power of the justices of the peace, or even of the omnipotence of parliament, to alter by a *fiat* the whole circumstances of the country; and when the demand for provisions is greater than the supply, by publishing a particular edict, to make the supply at once equal to, or greater, than the demand. Many men who would shrink at the proposal of a maximum, would propose themselves, that the price of labour should be proportioned to the price of provisions, and do not seem to be aware, that the two proposals are very nearly of the same nature, and that both tend directly to famine. It matters not, whether we enable the labourer to purchase the same quantity of provisions which he did before, by fixing their price, or by raising in proportion the price of labour. The only advantage on the side of raising the price of labour, is, that the rise in the price of provisions which necessarily follows it, encourages importation: but putting importation out of the question, which might possibly be prevented by war, or other circumstances, a universal rise of wages in proportion to the price of provisions, aided by adequate parish allowances to those who were thrown out of work, would, by preventing any kind of saving, in the same manner as a maximum, cause the whole crop to be consumed in nine months, which ought to have lasted twelve, and thus produce a famine.

As the inefficacy of poor laws, and of attempts forcibly to raise the price of labour, are most conspicuous in a scarcity, I have thought myself justified in considering them under this view; and as these causes of increased price received great additional force during the late scarcity from the increase of the circulating medium, I trust that the few observations which I have made on this subject, will be considered as an allowable digression.

C H A P . VI.

Subject of Poor Laws continued.

INDEPENDENTLY of any considerations respecting a year of deficient crops, it is evident, that an increase of population, without a proportional increase of food, must lower the value of each man's earnings. The food must necessarily be distributed in smaller quantities, and consequently, a day's labour will purchase a smaller quantity of provisions. An increase in the price of provisions will arise, either from an increase of population faster than the means of subsistence, or from a different distribution of the money of the society. The food of a country which has been long peopled, if it be increasing, increases slowly and regularly, and cannot be made to answer any sudden demands; but variations in the distribution of the money of the society, are not unfrequently occurring, and are undoubtedly among the causes which occasion the continual variations in the prices of provisions.

The poor laws of England tend to depress the general condition of the poor in these two ways. Their first obvious tendency is to increase population without increasing the food for its support. A poor man may marry with little or no prospect of being able to support a family without parish assistance. They may be said, therefore, to create the poor which they maintain; and as the provisions of the country must, in consequence of the increased population, be distributed to every man in smaller proportions, it is evident, that the labour of those who are not supported by parish assistance, will purchase a smaller quantity of provisions than before, and consequently more of them must be driven to apply for assistance.

Secondly, the quantity of provisions consumed in workhouses, upon a part of the society, that cannot in general be considered as the most valuable part, diminishes the shares that would otherwise belong to more industrious and more worthy members, and thus, in the same manner, forces more to become dependent. If the poor in the workhouses were to live better than they do now, this new distribution of the money of the society, would tend more conspicuously to depress the condition of those out of the workhouses by occasioning an advance in the price of provisions.

Fortunately for England, a spirit of independence still remains among the peasantry. The poor laws are strongly calculated to eradicate this spirit. They have succeeded in part; but had they succeeded as completely as might have been expected, their pernicious tendency would not have been so long concealed.

Hard as it may appear in individual instances, dependent poverty ought to be held disgraceful. Such a stimulus seems to be absolutely necessary to promote the happiness of the great mass of mankind; and every general attempt to weaken this stimulus, however benevolent its apparent intention, will always defeat its own purpose. If men be induced to marry from the mere prospect of parish provision, they are not only unjustly tempted to bring unhappiness and dependence upon themselves and children, but they are tempted, without knowing it, to injure all in the same class with themselves.

The parish laws of England appear to have contributed to raise the price of provisions, and to lower the real price of labour. They have therefore contributed to impoverish that class of people whose only possession is their labour. It is also difficult to suppose, that they have not powerfully contributed to generate that carelessness and want of frugality observable among the poor, so contrary to the disposition generally to be remarked among petty tradesmen and small farmers. The labouring poor, to use a vulgar expression, seem always to live from hand to mouth. Their present wants employ their whole attention; and they seldom think of the future. Even when they have an opportunity of saving, they seldom exercise it; but all that they earn beyond their present necessities, goes, generally speaking, to the alehouse. The poor laws may, therefore, be said to diminish both the power, and the will, to save, among the common people, and thus to weaken one of the strongest incentives to sobriety and industry, and consequently to happiness.

It is a general complaint among master manufacturers that high wages ruin all their workmen; but it is difficult to conceive that these men would not save a part of their high wages for the future support of their families, instead of spending it in drunkenness and dissipation, if they did not rely on parish assistance for support in case of accidents. And that the poor employed in manufactures consider this assistance as a reason why they may spend all the wages which they earn, and enjoy themselves while they can, appears to be evident, from the number of families that, upon the failure of any great manufactory, immediately fall upon the parish; when, perhaps, the wages earned in this manufactory while it flourished, were sufficiently above the price of common country labour, to have allowed them to save enough for their support, till they could find some other channel for their industry.

A man who might not be deterred from going to the alehouse, from the consideration that, on his death, or sickness, he should leave his wife and family upon the parish, might yet hesitate in thus dissipating his earnings, if he were assured that, in either of these cases, his family must starve, or be left to the support of casual bounty.

The mass of happiness among the common people cannot but be diminished, when one of the strongest checks to idleness and dissipation is thus removed; and positive institutions, which render dependent poverty so general, weaken that disgrace, which for the best and most humane reasons ought to be attached to it.

The poor laws of England were undoubtedly instituted for the most benevolent purpose; but it is evident, that they have failed in attaining it. They certainly mitigate some cases of severe distress, which might otherwise occur, though the state of the poor who are supported by parishes, considered in all its circumstances, is very miserable. But one of the principal objections to the system, is, that for the assistance which some of the poor receive, in itself almost a doubtful blessing, the whole class of the common people of England is subjected to a set of grating, inconvenient, and tyrannical laws, totally inconsistent with the genuine spirit of the constitution. The whole business of settlements, even in its present amended state, is contradictory to all ideas of freedom. The parish persecution of men whose families are likely to become chargeable, and of poor women who are near lying-in, is a most disgraceful and disgusting tyranny. And the obstructions continually occasioned in the market of labour by these laws, have a constant tendency to add to the difficulties of those who are struggling to support themselves without assistance.

These evils attendant on the poor laws seem to be irremediable. If assistance be to be distributed to a certain class of people, a power must be lodged somewhere of discriminating the proper objects, and of managing the concerns of the institutions that are necessary; but any great interference with the affairs of other people, is a species of tyranny; and, in the common course of things, the exercise of this power may be expected to become grating to those who are driven to ask for support. The tyranny of justices, churchwardens, and overseers, is a common complaint among the poor; but the fault does not lie so much in these persons, who, probably, before they were in power, were not worse than other people, but in the nature of all such institutions.

It will scarcely admit of a doubt, that if the poor laws had never existed in this country, though there might have been a few more instances of very severe distress, the aggregate mass of happiness among the common people would have been much greater than it is at present.

The radical defect of all systems of the kind, is, that of tending to increase population, without increasing the means for its support, and, by thus depressing the condition of those that are not relieved by parishes, to create more poor. If, indeed, we examine some of our statutes, strictly, with reference to the principle of population, we shall find that they attempt an absolute impossibility; and we cannot be surprised therefore, that they should constantly fail in the attainment of their object.

The famous 43d of Elizabeth, which has been so often referred to, and admired, enacts, that the overseers of the poor, "shall take order from time
" to time, by and with the consent of two or more justices, for setting to
" work the children of all such whose parents shall not, by the said per-
" sons, be thought able to keep and maintain their children; and also such
" persons married or unmarried, as, having no means to maintain them,
" use no ordinary and daily trade of life to get their living by. And also to
" raise, weekly or otherwise, by taxation of every inhabitant, and every
" occupier of lands in the said parish, (in such competent sums as they
" shall think fit,) a convenient stock of flax, hemp, wool, thread, iron, and
" other necessary ware and stuff, to set the poor to work."

What is this but saying, that the funds for the maintenance of labour in this country may be increased at will, and without limit, by a *fiat* of government, or an assessment of the overseers. Strictly speaking, this clause is as arrogant and as absurd, as if it had enacted that two ears of wheat should in future grow, where one only had grown before. Canute, when he commanded the waves not to wet his princely foot, did not, in reality, assume a greater power over the laws of nature. No directions are given to the overseers how to increase the funds for the maintenance of labour; the necessity of industry, economy, and enlightened exertion, in the management of agricultural and commercial capital is not insisted on, for this purpose; but it is expected, that a miraculous increase of these funds should immediately follow an edict of the government, used at the discretion of some ignorant parish officers.

If this clause were really, and *bona fide,* put in execution, and the shame attending the receiving of parish assistance worn off, every labouring man might marry as early as he pleased, under the certain prospect of having all his children properly provided for; and as, according to the supposition, there would be no check to population from the consequences of poverty after marriage, the increase of people would be rapid beyond example in old states. After what has been said in the former parts of this work, it is submitted to the reader, whether the utmost exertions of the most en-lightened government could, in this case, make the food keep pace with the population, much less a mere arbitrary edict, the tendency of which is certainly rather to diminish than to increase the funds for the maintenance of productive labour.

In the actual circumstances of every country, the principle of population seems to be always ready to exert nearly its full force; but, within the limit of possibility, there is nothing perhaps more improbable, or more out of the power of any government to effect, than the direction of the industry of its subjects in such a manner, as to produce the greatest quantity of human sustenance that the earth could bear. It evidently could not be done without the most complete violation of the law of property, from which every thing that is valuable to man has hitherto arisen. Such is the disposition to marry, particularly in very young people, that, if the difficulties of providing for a family were entirely removed, very few would remain single at twenty-two. But what statesman, or rational government, could propose, that, all animal food should be prohibited, that no horses should be used for busi-ness or pleasure, that all the people should live upon potatoes, and that the whole industry of the nation should be exerted in the production of them, except what was necessary for the mere necessaries of clothing and houses. Could such a revolution be effected, would it be desirable; particularly, as in a few years, notwithstanding all these exertions, want, with less resource than ever, would inevitably recur.

After a country has once ceased to be in the peculiar situation of a new colony, we shall always find, that, in the actual state of its cultivation, or in that state, which may rationally be expected from the most enlightened government, the increase of its food can never allow, for any length of time, an unrestricted increase of population; and therefore, the due execution of the clause in the 39th of Elizabeth, as a permanent law, is a physical impossibility.

It will be said, perhaps, that the fact contradicts the theory, and that the clause in question has remained in force, and has been executed during the last two hundred years. In answer to this, I should say without hesitation, that it has not really been executed; and that it is merely owing to its incom-plete execution, that it remains on our statute book at present.

The scanty relief granted to persons in distress, the capricious and in-sulting manner in which it is sometimes distributed by the overseers, and the natural and becoming pride not yet quite extinct among the peasantry of England, have deterred the more thinking and virtuous part of them, from venturing on marriage, without some better prospect of maintaining their families, than mere parish assistance. The desire of bettering our condition and the fear of making it worse, like the *vis medicatrix naturæ* in physick, is the *vis medicatrix reipublicæ* in politicks, and is continually counteracting the disorders arising from narrow human institutions. In spite of the prejudices in favour of population, and the direct encouragements to marriage from the poor laws, it operates as a preventive check to increase; and happy for this country is it that it does so.

Those who are not deterred for a time from marriage, by considerations of this nature, are either relieved very scantily at their own homes, where they suffer all the consequences arising from squalid poverty; or they are crowded together in close and unwholesome workhouses, where a great mortality almost universally takes place, particularly among the young children. The dreadful account given by Jonas Hanway of the treatment of parish children in London, is too well known to need a comment; and it appears from Mr. Howlett, and other writers, that in some parts of the country they are not very much better off. A great part of the redundant population occasioned by the poor laws, is thus taken off by the operation of the laws themselves, or at least by their ill execution. The remaining part which survives, by causing the funds for the maintenance of labour to be divided among a greater number than can be properly maintained by them, and by turning a considerable share from the support of the diligent and careful workman, to the support of the idle and the negligent, depresses the condition of all those who are out of the workhouses, forces more every year into them, and has ultimately produced the enormous evil which we all so justly deplore, that of the great and unnatural proportion of the people which is now become dependent upon charity.

If this be a just representation of the manner in which the clause in question has been executed, and of the effects which it has produced, it must be allowed that we have practised an unpardonable deceit upon the poor, and have promised what we have been very far from performing. It may be asserted, without danger of exaggeration, that the poor laws have destroyed many more lives than they have preserved.

The attempts to employ the poor on any great scale in manufactures have almost invariably failed, and the stock and materials have been wasted. In those few parishes which, by better management, or larger funds, have been enabled to persevere in this system, the effect of these new manufactures in the market, must have been, to throw out of employment many independent workmen who were before engaged in fabrications of a similar nature. This effect has been placed in a strong point of view by Daniel de Foe, in an address to parliament, entitled, *Giving alms no charity*. Speaking of the employment of parish children in manufactures, he says, For every skein of worsted these poor children spin, there must be a skein the less spun by some poor family that spin it before; and for every piece of bays so made in London, there must be a piece the less made at Colchester, or somewhere else.[1] Sir F. M. Eden, on the same subject, observes, that whether mops and brooms are made by parish children, or by private workmen, no more can be sold than the publick is in want of.[2]

It will be said, perhaps, that the same reasoning might be applied to any new capital brought into competition in a particular trade or manufacture, which can rarely be done without injuring, in some degree, those that were engaged in it before. But there is a material difference in the two cases. In this, the competition is perfectly fair, and what every man, on entering into business, must lay his account to. He may rest secure that he shall not be supplanted, unless his competitor possess superior skill and industry. In the other case, the competition is supported by a great bounty, by which means, notwithstanding very inferior skill and industry, on the part of his competitors, the independent workman may be undersold, and unjustly excluded from the market. He himself, perhaps, is made to contribute to this competition against his own earnings, and the funds for the maintenance of labour are thus turned, from the support of a trade which yields a proper profit, to one which cannot maintain itself without a bounty. It should be observed, in general, that when a fund for the maintenance of labour is raised by assessment, the greatest part of it is not a new capital brought into trade, but an old one, which before was much more profitably employed, turned into a new channel. The farmer pays to the poor's rates, for the encouragement of a bad and unprofitable manufacture, what he would have employed on his land with infinitely more advantage to his country. In the one case, the funds for the maintenance of labour, are daily diminished; in

1. See extracts from Daniel de Foe, in Sir F. M. Eden's valuable work on the poor, vol. i. p. 261.

2. Sir F. Eden speaking of the supposed right of the poor to be supplied with employment while able to work, and with a maintenance when incapacitated from labour, very justly remarks, "It may, however, be doubted, whether any right, the " gratification of which seems to be impracticable, can be said to exist," vol. i. p. 447. No man has collected so many materials for forming a judgment on the effects of the poor laws as Sir F. Eden, and the result he thus expresses. "Upon the " whole, therefore, there seems to be just grounds for concluding that the sum of " good to be expected from a compulsory maintenance of the poor, will be far " outbalanced by the sum of evil which it will inevitably create," vol. i. p. 467. I am happy to have the sanction of so practical an inquirer to my opinion of the poor laws.

the other, daily increased. And this obvious tendency of assessments for the employment of the poor, to decrease the real funds for the maintenance of labour in any country, aggravates the absurdity of supposing that it is in the power of a government to find employment for all its subjects, however fast they may increase.

It is not intended that these reasonings should be applied against every mode of employing the poor on a limited scale, and with such restrictions, as might not encourage, at the same time, their increase. I would never wish to push general principles too far, though I think that they ought always to be kept in view. In particular cases, the individual good to be obtained may be so great, and the general evil so slight, that the former may clearly overbalance the latter.

The intention is merely to shew, that the poor laws, as a general system, are founded on a gross error; and that the common declamation on the subject of the poor, which we see so often in print, and hear continually in conversation, namely, that the market price of labour ought always to be sufficient decently to support a family, and that employment ought to be found for all those who are willing to work, is in effect to say, that the funds for the maintenance of labour, in this country, are not only infinite, but might be made to increase with such rapidity, that, supposing us to have at present six millions of labourers, including their families, we might have 96 millions in another century; or if these funds had been properly managed since the beginning of the reign of Edward I. supposing that there were then only two millions of labourers, we might now have possessed above four million millions of labourers, or about four thousand times as many labourers as it has been calculated that there are people now on the face of the earth.

C H A P . VII.

Of increasing Wealth as it affects the Condition of the Poor.

THE professed object of Dr. Smith's inquiry, is, the nature and causes of the wealth of nations. There is another, however, perhaps still more interesting, which he occasionally mixes with it, the causes which affect the happiness and comfort of the lower orders of society, which is the most numerous class in every nation. I am sufficiently aware of the near connexion of these two subjects, and that, generally speaking, the causes which contribute to increase the wealth of a state, tend also to increase the happiness of the lower classes of the people. But perhaps Dr. Smith has considered these two inquiries, as still more nearly connected than they really are; at least, he has not stopped to take notice of those instances, where the wealth of a society may increase, according to his definition of wealth, without having any tendency to increase the comforts of the labouring part of it.

I do not mean to enter into any philosophical discussion of what constitutes the proper happiness of man, but shall merely consider two universally acknowledged ingredients, the command of the necessaries and comforts of life, and the possession of health.

The comforts of the labouring poor must necessarily depend upon the funds destined for the maintenance of labour; and will generally be in proportion to the rapidity of their increase. The demand for labour, which such increase occasions, will of course raise the value of labour; and till the additional number of hands required are reared, the increased funds will be distributed to the same number of persons as before, and therefore, every labourer will live comparatively at his ease. The error of Dr. Smith lies in representing every increase of the revenue or stock of a society, as an increase of these funds. Such surplus stock or revenue, will indeed always be considered by the individual possessing it, as an additional fund from which he may maintain more labour: but it will not be a real and effectual fund for the maintenance of an additional number of labourers, unless the whole, or at least a great part of it, be convertible into a proportional quantity of provisions; and it will not be so convertible where the increase has arisen merely from the produce of labour, and not from the produce of land. A distinction will in this case occur between the number of hands which the stock of the society could employ, and the number which its territory can maintain.

Dr. Smith defines the wealth of a state to be, the annual produce of its land and labour. This definition evidently includes manufactured produce, as well as the produce of the land. Now, supposing a nation, for a course of years, to add what it saved from its yearly revenue to its manufacturing capital solely, and not to its capital employed upon land, it is evident that it might grow richer according to the above definition, without a power of supporting a greater number of labourers, and therefore, without any increase in the real funds for the maintenance of labour. There would, notwithstanding, be a demand for labour, from the power that each manufacturer would possess, or at least think he possessed, of extending his old stock in trade, or of setting up fresh works. This demand, would of course raise the price of labour; but if the yearly stock of provisions in the country were not increasing, this rise would soon turn out to be merely nominal, as the price of provisions must necessarily rise with it. The demand for manufacturing labourers might, indeed, entice many from agriculture, and thus tend to diminish the annual produce of the land; but we will suppose any effects of this kind to be compensated by improvements in the instruments, or mode, of agriculture, and the quantity of provisions therefore to remain the same. Improvements in manufacturing machinery would of course take place; and this circumstance, added to the greater number of hands employed in manufactures, would augment considerably the annual produce of the labour of the country. The wealth, therefore, of the country would be increasing annually, according to the definition, and might not be increasing very slowly.

The question is, how far, wealth, increasing in this way, has a tendency to better the condition of the labouring poor. It is a self-evident proposition that any general advance in the price of labour, the stock of provisions remaining the same, can only be a nominal advance, as it must shortly be followed by a proportional rise in provisions. The increase in the price of labour which we have supposed, would have no permanent effect therefore in giving to the labouring poor a greater command over the necessaries of life. In this respect, they would be nearly in the same state as before. In some other respects, they would be in a worse state. A greater proportion of them would be employed in manufactures, and fewer consequently in agriculture. And this exchange of professions will be allowed, I think, by all to be very unfavourable, in respect of health, one essential ingredient of happiness, and also with regard to the greater uncertainty of manufacturing labour, arising from the capricious taste of man, the accidents of war, and other causes, which occasionally produce very severe distress among the lower classes of society. On the state of the poor employed in manufactories, with respect to health and other circumstances which affect their happiness, I will beg leave to quote a passage from Dr. Aikin's description of the country round Manchester.

"The invention and improvements of machines to shorten labour, have
" had a surprising influence to extend our trade, and also to call in hands
" from all parts, especially children for the cotton mills. It is the wise plan
" of Providence, that in this life there shall be no good without its atten-
" dant inconvenience. There are many which are too obvious in these cot-
" ton mills and similar factories, which counteract that increase of popu-
" lation usually consequent on the improved facility of labour. In these,
" children of very tender age are employed, many of them collected from
" the workhouses in London and Westminster, and transported in crowds,
" as apprentices to masters resident many hundred miles distant, where
" they serve unknown, unprotected, and forgotten by those to whose care,
" nature, or the laws, had consigned them. These children are usually too
" long confined to work in close rooms, often during the whole night. The
" air they breathe from the oil, &c. employed in the machinery, and other
" circumstances, is injurious; little attention is paid to their cleanliness;
" and frequent changes from a warm and dense, to a cold and thin atmo-
" sphere, are predisposing causes to sickness and disability, and particu-
" larly to the epidemick fever which is so generally to be met with in these
" factories. It is also much to be questioned, if society does not receive
" detriment, from the manner in which children are thus employed during
" their early years. They are not generally strong to labour, or capable of
" pursuing any other branch of business when the term of their appren-
" ticeship expires. The females are wholly uninstructed in sowing, knit-
" ting, and other domestick affairs, requisite to make them notable, and
" frugal wives and mothers. This is a very great misfortune to them and
" the publick, as is sadly proved by a comparison of the families of la-
" bourers in husbandry, and those of manufacturers in general. In the for-
" mer we meet with neatness, cleanliness and comfort; in the latter, with
" filth, rags, and poverty, although their wages may be nearly double to
" those of the husbandman. It must be added that the want of early reli-
" gious instruction and example, and the numerous and indiscriminate
" association in these buildings, are very unfavourable to their future con-
" duct in life.[1]"

---

1. P. 219. Endeavours have been made, Dr. Aikin says, to remedy these evils, and in some factories they have been attended with success. An act of parliament has of late also passed on this subject, from which it is hoped, that much good will result.

In addition to the evils mentioned in this passage, we all know how subject particular manufactures are to fail, from the caprice of taste, or the accident of war. The weavers of Spitalfields were plunged into the most severe distress by the fashion of muslins instead of silks; and numbers of the workmen in Sheffield and Birmingham were, for a time, thrown out of employment, from the adoption of shoe-strings and covered buttons, instead of buckles and metal buttons. Our manufactures, taken in the mass, have increased with great rapidity, but, in particular places, they have failed, and the parishes, where this has happened, are invariably loaded with a crowd of poor, in the most distressed and miserable condition. In the work of Dr. Aikin just alluded to, it appears that the register for the collegiate church at Manchester, from Christmas 1793 to Christmas 1794, stated a decrease of 168 marriages, 538 christenings, and 250 burials. And in the parish of Rochdale, in the neighbourhood, a still more melancholy reduction, in proportion to the number of people, took place. In 1792, the births were 746, the burials 646, and the marriages 339. In 1794, the births were 373, the burials 671, and the marriages 199. The cause of this sudden check to population, was the commencement of the war, and the failure of commercial credit, which occurred about this time; and such a check could not have taken place, in so sudden a manner, without being occasioned by the most severe distress.

Under such circumstances of situation, unless the increase of the riches of a country from manufactures, give the lower classes of the society, on an average, a decidedly greater command over the necessaries and conveniencies of life, it will not appear that their condition is improved.

It will be said, perhaps, that the advance in the price of provisions will immediately turn some additional capital into the channel of agriculture, and thus occasion a much greater produce. But from experience, it appears, that this is an effect which takes place very slowly, particularly when, as in the present instance, an advance in the price of labour had preceded the advance in the price of provisions, and would therefore tend to impede the good effects upon agriculture, which the increased value of the produce of land might otherwise have occasioned.

It may also be said, that the additional capital of the nation would enable it to import provisions, sufficient for the maintenance of those whom its stock could employ. A small country, with a large navy, and great accommodations for inland carriage, may indeed import and distribute an effectual quantity of provisions: but in large landed nations, if they may be so called, an importation adequate at all times to the demand, is scarcely possible. It seems in great measure to have escaped attention, that a nation, which, from its extent of territory and population, must necessarily support the greater part of its people on the produce of its own soil; but which yet, on average years, draws a small portion of its corn from abroad, is in a much more precarious situation with regard to the constancy of its supplies, than such states as draw almost the whole of their provisions from other countries. The demands of Holland and Hamburgh may be known with considerable accuracy by those who supply them. If they increase, they increase gradually, and are not subject, from year to year, to any great and sudden variations. But it is otherwise with such a country as England. Supposing it, in average years, to want about four hundred thousand quarters of wheat. Such a demand will of course be very easily supplied. But a year of deficient crops occurs, and the demand is suddenly two millions of quarters. If the demand had been, on an average, two millions, it might perhaps have been adequately supplied, from the extended agriculture of those countries which are in the habit of exporting corn: but we cannot expect that it can easily be answered thus suddenly; and indeed, we know from experience, that an unusual demand of this nature, in a nation capable of paying for it, cannot exist, without raising the price of wheat very considerably in all the ports of Europe. Hamburgh, Holland, and the ports of the Baltic, felt very sensibly the high prices of England during the late scarcity; and I have been informed from very good authority, that the price of bread in New York was little inferior to the highest price in London.

A nation, possessed of a large territory, is unavoidably subject to this uncertainty in its means of subsistence, when the commercial part of its population is either equal to, or has increased beyond, the surplus produce of its cultivators. No reserve being, in these cases, left in exportation, the full effect of every deficiency from unfavourable seasons must necessarily be felt; and though the riches of such a country may enable it, for a certain period, to continue raising the nominal price of wages, so as to give the lower classes of the society a power of purchasing imported corn at a high price; yet, as a sudden demand can very seldom be fully answered, the competition in the market will invariably raise the price of provisions, in full proportion to the advance in the price of labour; the lower classes will be but little relieved; and the dearth will operate severely throughout all the ranks of society.

According to the natural order of things, years of scarcity must occasionally recur, in all landed nations. They ought always therefore to enter into our consideration; and the prosperity of any country may justly be considered as precarious, in which the funds for the maintenance of labour are liable to great and sudden fluctuations, from every unfavourable variation in the seasons.

But putting, for the present, years of scarcity out of the question; when the commercial population of any country increases so much beyond the surplus produce of the cultivators, that the demand for imported corn is not easily supplied, and the price rises in proportion to the price of wages, no further increase of riches will have any tendency to give the labourer a greater command over the necessaries of life. In the progress of wealth, this will naturally take place; either from the largeness of the supply wanted; the increased distance from which it is brought, and consequently the increased expence of importation; the greater consumption of it in the countries in which it is usually purchased; or what must unavoidably happen, the necessity of a greater distance of inland carriage, in these countries. Such a nation, by increasing industry, and increasing ingenuity in the improvement of machinery, may still go on increasing the yearly quantity of its manufactured produce; but its funds for the maintenance of labour, and consequently its population, will be perfectly stationary. This point is the natural limit to the population of all commercial states.[2]

That every increase of the stock or revenue of a nation cannot be considered as an increase of the real funds for the maintenance of labour, and therefore, cannot have the same good effect upon the condition of the poor, will appear in a strong light, if the argument be applied to China.

Dr. Smith observes, that China has probably long been as rich as the nature of her laws and institutions will admit; but that, with other laws and institutions, and if foreign commerce were held in honour, she might still be much richer. The question is, would such an increase of wealth, be an increase of the real funds for the maintenance of labour, and consequently tend to place the lower classes of people in China in a state of greater plenty?

If trade and foreign commerce were held in great honour in China, it is evident, that, from the great number of labourers, and the cheapness of labour, she might work up manufactures for foreign sale to an immense amount. It is equally evident, that, from the great bulk of provisions, and the amazing extent of her inland territory, she could not in return import such a quantity, as would be any sensible addition to the annual stock of subsistence in the country. Her immense amount of manufactures, therefore, she would exchange chiefly for luxuries collected from all parts of the world. At present it appears, that no labour whatever is spared in the

2. Sir James Steuart's Political Œconomy, vol. i. b. i. c. xviii. p. 119.

production of food. The country is rather overpeopled in proportion to what its stock can employ, and labour is therefore so abundant, that no pains are taken to abridge it. The consequence of this is probably the greatest production of food that the soil can possibly afford; for it will be generally observed, that processes for abridging labour, though they may enable a farmer to bring a certain quantity of grain cheaper to market, tend rather to diminish than increase the whole produce. An immense capital could not be employed in China in preparing manufactures for foreign trade, without taking off so many labourers from agriculture, as to alter this state of things, and, in some degree, to diminish the produce of the country. The demand for manufacturing labourers would naturally raise the price of labour; but as the quantity of subsistence would not be increased, the price of provisions would keep pace with it, or even more than keep pace with it, if the quantity of provisions were really decreasing. The country would, however, be evidently advancing in wealth; the exchangeable value of the annual produce of its land and labour would be annually augmented; yet the real funds for the maintenance of labour would be stationary, or even declining; and consequently the increasing wealth of the nation would tend rather to depress than to raise the condition of the poor.[3] With regard to the command over the necessaries of life, they would be in the same, or rather worse state, than before; and a great part of them would have exchanged the healthy labours of agriculture for the unhealthy occupations of manufacturing industry.

The argument, perhaps, appears clearer when applied to China, because it is generally allowed, that its wealth has been long stationary, and its soil cultivated nearly to the utmost. With regard to any other country, it might always be a matter of dispute, at which of the two periods compared, wealth was increasing the fastest, as it is upon the rapidity of the increase of wealth, at any particular period, that, Dr. Smith says, the condition of the poor depends. It is evident, however, that two nations might increase exactly with the same rapidity in the exchangeable value of the annual produce of their land and labour; yet, if one had applied itself chiefly to agriculture, and the other chiefly to commerce, the funds for the maintenance of labour, and consequently the effect of the increase of wealth in each nation, would

3. The condition of the poor in China is, indeed, very miserable at present; but this is not owing to their want of foreign commerce, but to their extreme tendency to marriage and increase; and if this tendency were to continue the same, the only way in which the introduction of a greater number of manufacturers could possibly make the lower classes of people richer, would be, by increasing the mortality amongst them, which is certainly not a very desirable mode of growing rich.

be extremely different. In that, which had applied itself chiefly to agriculture, the poor would live in greater plenty, and population would rapidly increase. In that, which had applied itself chiefly to commerce, the poor would be comparatively but little benefited, and consequently, population would either be stationary, or increase very slowly.

CHAP. VIII.

Of the Definitions of Wealth. Agricultural and Commercial Systems.

A QUESTION seems naturally to arise here, whether the exchangeable value of the annual produce of the land and labour, is the proper definition of the wealth of a country, or whether merely the produce of land, according to the French Economists, may not be a more correct definition. Certain it is, that every increase of wealth, according to this definition, will be an increase of the funds for the maintenance of labour, and consequently will always tend to ameliorate the condition of the labouring poor, and increase population; though an increase of wealth, according to Dr. Smith's definition, will by no means invariably have the same tendency. And yet it may not follow, from this consideration, that Dr. Smith's definition is false.

The Economists consider all labour employed in manufactures as unproductive; and in endeavouring to disprove this position, Dr. Smith has been accused of arguing obscurely and inconclusively. He appears to me, however, only incorrect in applying his own definition to try the reasoning, by which the Economists support theirs; when, in fact, the question was, respecting the truth or falsehood of the definitions themselves; and, of course, one could not be applied as a test to the other. Nothing can be more clear than that manufactures increase the wealth of a state according to Dr. Smith's definition; and it is equally clear, that they do not increase it, according to the definition of the Economists. The question of the productiveness or unproductiveness of manufactures, is allowed by the Economists to be a question respecting net produce; and the determination of this question either way, would not affect Dr. Smith's definition, which includes produce of every kind, whether net, or otherwise. And in the same manner, the proof of a net produce arising to individuals from manufactures, would not really invalidate the definition of the Economists, though they have laid themselves open to objections from this quarter, by the manner in which they have defended their position.

They say, that labour employed upon land is productive, because the produce, over and above completely paying the labourer and the farmer, affords a clear rent to the landlord; and that the labour employed upon a piece of lace is unproductive, because it merely replaces the provisions that the workman had consumed while making it, and the stock of his employer, without affording any clear rent whatever. But supposing the value of the

wrought lace to be such, as that besides paying in the most complete manner, the workman and his employer, it could afford a clear rent to a third
person, the state of the case would not really be altered. Though, according
to this mode of reasoning, the man employed in the manufacture of lace,
would, upon the present supposition, appear to be a productive labourer;
yet, according to their definition of the wealth of a state, he ought not to
be considered in that light. He will have added nothing to the produce of
the land. He has consumed a portion of this produce, and has left a piece
of lace in return; and though he may sell this piece of lace for three times
the quantity of provisions which he consumed while he was making it, and
thus be a very productive labourer with regard to himself; yet he has added
nothing by his labour to the essential wealth of the state.

Suppose, that two hundred thousand men, who are now employed in
producing manufactures, that only tend to gratify the vanity of a few rich
people, were to be employed on some barren uncultivated land, and to produce only half of the quantity of food that they themselves consumed, they
might still be considered, in some respects, as more productive labourers
than they were before. In their former employment, they consumed a certain portion of the food of the country, and left in return some silks and
laces. In their latter employment, they consumed the same quantity of food,
and left in return, provision for a hundred thousand men. There can be little
doubt which of the two legacies would be the most really beneficial to the
country, and which, according to the definition of the Economists, would
add the most to the wealth of the state.

A capital employed upon land may be unproductive to the individual
that employs it, and yet be productive to the society. A capital employed in
trade, on the contrary, may be highly productive to the individual, and yet
be almost totally unproductive to the society. It is indeed impossible to see
the great fortunes that are made in commerce, and, at the same time, the
liberality with which so many merchants live, and yet agree in the statement of the Economists, that manufacturers can only grow rich by depriv-
ing themselves of the funds destined for their support. In many branches
of trade the profits are so great, as would allow of a clear rent to a third
person; but as there is no third person in the case, and all the profits centre
in the merchant or master manufacturer, he seems to have a fair chance
of growing rich without much privation, and we consequently see large
fortunes acquired in trade by persons who have not been remarked for their
parsimony.

These fortunes, however, by which individuals are greatly enriched, do
not enrich proportionally the whole society, and, in some respects, have

even a contrary tendency. The home trade of consumption is by far the most important trade of every nation. Putting then, for a moment, foreign trade out of the question, the man who, by an ingenious manufacture, obtains a double portion out of the old stock of provisions, will certainly not be so useful to the state, as the man, who, by his labour, adds a single share to the former stock. And this view of the subject, shews that manufactures are essentially different from the produce of the land, and that the question respecting their productiveness, or unproductiveness, by no means depends entirely upon the Iargeness of the profits upon them, or upon their yielding or not yielding a clear rent. If the Economists would allow, which, from the manner in which they express themselves, they might be sometimes supposed to do, that the value yielded by manufacturers was of the same nature as the produce of the land, though it were allowed to be only accurately equal to the value of their consumption, they certainly could not maintain the position that land is the only source of wealth. A marriage which produces two children, though it contain in itself no principle of increase, yet it adds to the sum of the actual population, which would have been less by two persons, if the marriage had been really barren. But the fact is, that though the language of the Economists has fairly warranted this illustration, which Dr. Smith gives; yet the illustration itself is incorrect. In the case of the marriage, the two children are really a new production, a completely new creation. But manufactures, strictly speaking, are no new production, no new creation, but merely a modification of an old one, and when sold must be paid for out of a revenue already in existence, and consequently the gain of the seller is the loss of the buyer. A revenue is transferred, but not created.

If, in asserting the productiveness, of the labour employed upon land, we look only to the clear monied rent yielded to a certain number of proprietors, we undoubtedly consider the subject in a very contracted point of view. The quantity of the surplus produce of the cultivators is, indeed, measured by this clear rent; but its real value consists in its capability of supporting a certain number of people, or millions of people, according to its extent, all exempted from the labour of procuring their own food, and who may, therefore, either live without manual exertions, or employ themselves in modifying the raw produce of nature into the forms best suited to the gratification of man.

A net monied revenue, arising from manufactures, of the same extent, and to the same number of individuals, would by no means be accompanied by the same circumstances. It would throw the country in which it existed into an absolute dependence upon the surplus produce of others; and if this foreign revenue could not be obtained, the clear monied rent, which we have supposed, would be absolutely of no value to the nation.

As manufactures are not a new production, but the modification of an old one, the most natural and obvious way of estimating them, is by the labour which this modification costs. At the same time, it may be doubted, whether we can say positively, that the price of this labour, added to the price of the raw material, is exactly their real value. The ultimate value of every thing, according to the general reasoning of the Economists, consists in being *propre a la jouissance*. In this view, some manufactures are of very high value; and in general, they may be said to be worth to the purchaser what that purchaser will consent to give. In the actual state of things, from monopolies, from superior machinery, or other causes, they are generally sold a price above what the Economists consider as their real worth; and with regard to a mere monied revenue to an individual, there is no apparent difference, between a manufacture which yields very large profits, and a piece of land which is farmed by the proprietor.[1]

Land, in an enlarged view of the subject, is incontrovertibly the sole source of all riches; but when we take individuals or particular nations into our view, the state of the question is altered, as both nations and individuals may be enriched by a transfer of revenue, without the creation of a new one.

There are none of the definitions of the wealth of a state that are not liable to some objections. If we take the gross produce of the land, it is evident that the funds for the maintenance of labour, the population, and the wealth, may increase very rapidly, while the nation is apparently poor, and has very little disposeable revenue. If we take Dr. Smith's definition, wealth may increase as has before been shewn, without tending to increase the funds for the maintenance of labour and the population. If we take the clear surplus produce of the land, according to most of the Economists; in this case, the funds for the maintenance of labour and the population may

---

1. I do not mean to say that the Economists do not fully comprehend the true distinction between the labour employed upon land, and the labour employed in manufactures, and really understand the value of the surplus produce of the cultivators, as totally distinct from the net monied revenue which it yields; but it appears to me that they have exposed themselves to be misunderstood, in their reasonings respecting the productiveness of land, and the unproductiveness of manufactures, by dwelling too much on the circumstance of a net rent to individuals. In an enlarged sense, it is certainly true, that land is the only source of net rent.

increase, without an increase of wealth, as in the instance of the cultivation of new lands, which will pay a profit but not a rent; and, *vice versa,* wealth may increase, without increasing the funds for the maintenance of labour, and the population, as in the instance of improvements in agricultural instruments, and in the mode of agriculture, which may make the land yield the same produce, with fewer persons employed upon it; and consequently the disposeable wealth, or revenue, would be increased, without a power of supporting a greater number of people.

The objections, however, to the two last definitions do not prove that they are incorrect; but merely that an increase of wealth, though generally, is not necessarily and invariably accompanied by an increase of the funds for the maintenance of labour; and consequently, by the power of supporting a greater number of people, or of enabling the former number to live in greater plenty and happiness.

Whichever of these two definitions is adopted, as the best criterion of the wealth, power, and prosperity of a state, the great position of the Economists will always remain true, that the surplus produce of the cultivators is the great fund which ultimately pays all those who are not employed upon the land. Throughout the whole world, the number of manufacturers, of proprietors, and of persons engaged in the various civil and military professions, must be exactly proportioned to this surplus produce, and cannot in the nature of things increase beyond it. If the earth had been so niggardly of her produce as to oblige all her inhabitants to labour for it, no manufacturers or idle persons could ever have existed. But her first intercourse with man was a voluntary present; not very large indeed, but sufficient as a fund for his subsistence, till by the proper exercise of his faculties he could procure a greater. In proportion as the labour and ingenuity of man, exercised upon the land, have increased this surplus produce, leisure has been given to a greater number of persons to employ themselves in all the inventions which embellish civilized life. And though, in its turn, the desire to profit by these inventions, has greatly contributed to stimulate the cultivators to increase their surplus produce; yet the order of precedence is clearly the surplus produce; because the funds for the subsistence of the manufacturer must be advanced to him, before he can complete his work: and if we were to imagine that we could command this surplus produce, whenever we willed it, by forcing manufactures, we should be quickly admonished of our gross error, by the inadequate support which the workman would receive, in spite of any rise that might take place in his nominal wages.

According to the system of the Economists, manufactures are an object on which revenue is spent, and not any part of the revenue itself.[2] But though from this description of manufactures, and the epithet sterile sometimes applied to them, they seem rather to be degraded by the terms of the Economists, it is a very great error to suppose that their system is really unfavourable to them. On the contrary, I am disposed to believe, that it is the only system by which commerce and manufactures can prevail to a very great extent, without bringing with them, at the same time, the seeds of their own ruin. Before the late revolution in Holland, the high price of the necessaries of life had destroyed many of its manufactures.[3] Monopolies are always subject to be broken; and even the advantage of capital and machinery, which may yield extraordinary profits for a time, is liable to be greatly lessened by the competition of other nations. In the history of the world, the nations, whose wealth has been derived principally from manufactures and commerce, have been perfectly ephemeral beings, compared with those, the basis of whose wealth has been agriculture. It is in the nature of things, that a state which subsists upon a revenue furnished by other countries, must be infinitely more exposed to all the accidents of time and chance, than one which produces its own.

No error is more frequent, than that of mistaking effects for causes. We are so blinded by the shewiness of commerce and manufactures, as to believe that they are almost the sole cause of the wealth, power, and prosperity of England. But perhaps, they may be more justly considered as the consequences, than the cause of this wealth. According to the definition of the Economists, which considers only the produce of land, England is the richest country in Europe in proportion to her size. Her system of agriculture is beyond comparison better, and consequently her surplus produce is more considerable. France is very greatly superior to England in extent of territory and population; but when the surplus produce, or disposeable

---

2. Even upon this system, there is one point of view, in which manufactures appear greatly to add to the riches of a state. The use of a revenue, according to the Economists, is to be spent; and a great part of it will of course be spent in manufactures. But if by the judicious employment of manufacturing capital, these commodities grow considerably cheaper, the surplus produce becomes proportionably of so much greater value, and the real revenue of the nation is virtually increased. There is no light, perhaps, in which we can view manufactures, where they appear to be so productive as in this; and if it do not completely justify Dr. Smith in calling manufacturing labour *productive* in the strict sense of that term; it fully warrants all the pains he has taken in explaining the nature and effects of commercial capital, and of the division of manufacturing labour.

3. Smith's Wealth of Nations, vol. iii, b. v. c. ii. p. 392.

revenue of the two nations are compared, the superiority of France almost vanishes. And it is this great surplus produce in England, arising from her agriculture, which enables her to support such a vast body of manufactures, such formidable fleets and armies, such a crowd of persons engaged in the liberal professions, and a proportion of the society living on money rents, very far beyond what has ever been known in any other country of the world. According to the returns lately made of the population of England and Wales, it appears that the number of persons employed in agriculture, is considerably less than a fifth part of the whole. There is reason to believe that the classifications in these returns are incorrect; but making very great allowances for errors of this nature, it can scarcely admit of a doubt, that the number of persons employed in agriculture is very unusually small in proportion to the actual produce. Of late years indeed, the part of the society, not connected with agriculture, has unfortunately increased beyond this produce; but the average importation of corn, as yet, bears but a small proportion to that which is grown in the country, and consequently the power which England possesses of supporting so vast a body of idle consumers must be attributed principally to the greatness of her surplus produce.

It will be said that it was her commerce and manufactures which encouraged her cultivators to obtain this great surplus produce, and therefore indirectly, if not directly, created it. That commerce and manufactures produce this effect in a certain degree, is true; but that they sometimes produce a contrary effect, and generally so, when carried to excess, is equally true. Undoubtedly agriculture cannot flourish without a vent for its commodities, either at home or abroad; but when this want has been adequately supplied, the interests of agriculture demand nothing more. When too great a part of a nation is engaged in commerce and manufactures, it is a clear proof, that, either from undue encouragement, or from other particular causes, a capital is employed in this way to much greater advantage than on land; and under such circumstances, it is impossible, that the land should not be robbed of much of the capital which would naturally have fallen to its share. Dr. Smith justly observes, that the navigation act, and the monopoly of the colony trade, necessarily forced into a particular and not very advantageous channel, a greater proportion of the capital of Great Britain than would otherwise have gone to it; and by thus taking capital from other employments, and at the same time universally raising the rate of British mercantile profit, discouraged the improvement of the land.[4] If the improvement of land, he goes on to say, affords a greater capital than what

4. Wealth of Nations, vol. ii. b. iv. c. vii. p. 435.

can be drawn from an equal capital in any mercantile employment, the land will draw capital from mercantile employments. If the profit be less, mercantile employments will draw capital from the improvement of land. The monopoly, therefore, by raising the rate of British mercantile profit, and thus discouraging agricultural improvement, has necessarily retarded the natural increase of a great original source of revenue, the rent of land.[5]

The East and West Indies, are indeed so great an object, and afford employment with high profits, to so great a capital, that it is impossible that they should not draw capital from other employments, and particularly from the cultivation of the soil, the profits upon which, in general, are unfortunately very small.

All corporations, patents, and exclusive privileges of every kind, which abound so much in the mercantile system, have in proportion to their extent the same effect. And the experience of the last twenty years seems to warrant us in concluding, that the high price of provisions arising from the abundance of commercial wealth, accompanied, as it has been, by very great variations, and by a great rise, in the price of labour, does not operate as an encouragement to agriculture, sufficient to make it keep pace with the rapid strides of commerce.

It will be said, perhaps, that land is always improved by the redundancy of commercial capital. But this effect is late and slow, and in the nature of things cannot take place till this capital is really redundant, which it never is, while the interest of money and the profits of mercantile stock are high. We cannot look forwards to any considerable effect of this kind till the interest of money sinks to 3 per cent. When men can get 5 or 6 per cent. for their money, without any trouble, they will hardly venture a capital upon land, where, including risks, and the profits upon their own labour and attendance, they may not get much more. Wars and loans, as far as internal circumstances are concerned, impede but little the progress of those branches of commerce where the profits of stock are high; but affect very considerably the increase of that more essential and permanent source of wealth, the improvement of the land. It is in this point, I am inclined to believe, that the national debt of England has been most injurious to her. By absorbing the redundancy of commercial capital, and keeping up the rate of interest, it has prevented this capital from overflowing upon the soil. And a large mortgage[6] has thus been established on the lands of England,

5. Id. p. 436.
6. One of the principal errors of the French Economists appears to be on the subject of taxation. Admitting, as I shall be disposed to do, that the surplus produce

the interest of which is drawn from the payment of productive labour, and dedicated to the support of idle consumers.

It must be allowed, therefore, upon the whole, that our commerce has not done much for our agriculture; but that our agriculture has done a great

---

of the land is the fund which pays every thing besides the food of the cultivators; yet it seems to be a mistake to suppose, that the owners of land are the sole proprietors of this surplus produce. It appears to me, that every man who has realized a capital in money, on which he can live without labour, has virtually a mortgage on the land for a certain portion of the surplus produce. This mortgage may not indeed be so well secured, as those which usually bear this title, or as the money rent of the land-owner; but while the power of obtaining this monied interest remains, its effect, or command over the surplus produce, is exactly the same. The landholders, therefore, are not the sole proprietors of surplus produce; and their joint proprietors, those who live upon the interest of money, certainly pay a general tax in the same manner as the landholders, and cannot throw it off from their shoulders, like those who live upon the profits of stock, or the wages of labour. Practically, indeed, it cannot be doubted that even the profits of stock and the wages of labour, particularly of professional labour, pay some taxes on necessaries, and many on luxuries, for a very considerable time. The real surplus produce of this country, or all the produce not actually consumed by the cultivators, is a very different thing, and should carefully be distinguished from the sum of the net rents of the landlords. This sum, it is supposed, does not much exceed a fifth part of the gross produce. The remaining four fifths, is certainly not consumed by the labourers and horses employed in agriculture; but a very considerable portion of it is paid by the farmer, in taxes, in the instruments of agriculture, and in the manufactures used in his own family, and in the families of his labourers. It is in this manner that a kind of mortgage is ultimately established on the land, by taxes, and the progress of commercial wealth; and in this sense, all taxes certainly fall upon the land. Before the existence of national debts, and the accumulation of monied capitals, the simple territorial impost would be the fairest and most eligible of all taxes; but when these mortgages alluded to have been actually established, and the interest of them cannot be changed with every new tax, which in many instances is the case, particularly with regard to government annuitants, the mortgagee will really and *bona fide* pay a part of the taxes on consumption; and though these taxes may still fall wholly on the land, they will not fall wholly on the landholders. It seems a little hard, therefore, in taxing surplus produce to make the landlords pay for what they do not receive. At the same time, it must be confessed, that, independently of these considerations, which makes a land tax partial, it is the best of all taxes, as it is the only one which does not tend to raise the price of commodities. Taxes on consumption, by which alone monied revenues can be reached, without an income tax, necessarily raise all prices to a degree greatly injurious to the country. A land tax, or tax upon net rent, has little or no effect in discouraging the improvement of land, as many have supposed. It is only a tithe, or a tax, in proportion to the gross produce, which does this. No man in his senses will be deterred from getting a clear profit of 20l. instead of 10l. because he is always to pay a fourth or fifth of his clear gains; but when he is to pay a tax in proportion to

deal for our commerce; and that the improved system of cultivation which has taken place, in spite of considerable discouragements, creates yearly a surplus produce, which enables the country, with but little assistance, to support so vast a body of people engaged in pursuits unconnected with the land.

---

his gross produce, which, in the case of capital laid out in improvements, is scarcely ever accompanied with a proportional increase of his clear gains, it is a very different thing, and must necessarily impede, in a great degree, the progress of cultivation. I am astonished that so obvious and easy a commutation for tithes, as a land tax on improved rents, has not been adopted. Such a tax would be paid by the same persons as before, only in a better form; and the change would not be felt, except in the advantage that would accrue to all the parties concerned, the landlord, the tenant, and the clergyman. Tithes undoubtedly operate as a high bounty on pasture, and a great discouragement to tillage, which in the present peculiar circumstances of the country is a very great disadvantage.

CHAP. IX

Different Effects of the Agricultural and Commercial Systems.

ABOUT the middle of the last century, we were genuinely, and in the strict sense of the Economists, an agricultural nation. Our commerce and manufactures were, however, then in a very respectable and thriving state; and if they had continued to bear the same relative proportion to our agriculture, they would evidently have gone on increasing considerably, with the improving cultivation of the country. There is no apparent limit to the quantity of manufactures which might in time be supported in this way. The increasing wealth of a country in such a state, seems to be out of the reach of all common accidents. There is no discoverable germ of decay in the system; and in theory, there is no reason to say, that it might not go on increasing in wealth and prosperity for thousands of years.

We have now, however, stepped out of the agricultural system, into a state, in which the commercial system clearly predominates; and there is but too much reason to fear, that even our commerce and manufactures will ultimately feel the disadvantage of the change. It has been already observed, that we are exactly in that situation, in which a country feels most fully the effect of those common years of deficient crops, which, in the natural course of things, are to be expected. The competition of increasing commercial wealth, operating upon a supply of corn not increasing in the same proportion, must at all times greatly tend to raise the price of labour; but when scarce years are taken into the consideration, its effect in this way must ultimately be prodigious. We know how extremely difficult it is in England to lower the wages of labour, after they have once been raised. During the late scarcities, the price of labour has been continually rising – not to fall again; the rents of land have been every where advancing – not to fall again; and of course, the price of produce must rise – not to fall again; as, independently of a particular competition from scarcity, or the want of competition from plenty, its price is necessarily regulated by the wages of labour, and the rent of land. We have no reason whatever for supposing that we shall be exempt in future from such scarcities as we have of late experienced. On the contrary, upon our present system, they seem to be unavoidable. And if we go on, as we have done lately, the price of labour and of provisions must soon increase in a manner out of all proportion to their price in the rest of Europe; and it is impossible that this should not ultimately check all our dealings with foreign powers, and give a fatal blow to our commerce and manufactures. The effect of capital, skill, machinery, and establishments, in their full vigour, is great; so great, indeed, that it is difficult to guess at its limit; but still it is not infinite, and without doubt has this limit. The principal states of Europe, except this fortunate island, have of late suffered so much by the actual presence of war; that their commerce and manufactures have been nearly destroyed, and we may be said in a manner to have the monopoly of the trade of Europe. All monopolies yield high profits, and at present, therefore, the trade can be carried on to advantage, in spite of the high price of labour. But when the other nations of Europe shall have had time to recover themselves, and gradually to become our competitors, it would be rash to affirm, that, with the prices of provisions and of labour still going on increasing, from what they are at present, we shall be able to stand the competition. Dr. Smith says, that, in his time, merchants frequently complained of the high price of British labour as the cause of their manufactures being undersold in foreign markets.[1] If such complaints were in any degree founded at that time, how will they be aggravated twenty years hence! And have we not some reason to fear that our present great commercial prosperity is temporary, and belongs a little to that worst feature of the commercial system, the rising by the depression of others.

When a country, in average years, grows more corn than it consumes, and is in the habit of exporting a part of it, its price, and the price of labour as depending on it, can never rise in any very extraordinary degree above the common price in other commercial countries; and under such circumstances, England would have nothing to fear from the fullest, and most open competition. The increasing prosperity of other countries, would only open to her a more extensive market for her commodities, and give additional spirit to all her commercial transactions.

The high price of corn and of rude produce in general, as far as it is occasioned by the freest competition among the nations of Europe, is a very great advantage, and is the best possible encouragement to agriculture; but when occasioned merely by the competition of monied wealth at home, its effect is totally different. In the one case, a great encouragement is given to production in general, and the more is produced, the better. In the other case, the produce is necessarily confined to the home consumption. The cultivators are justly afraid of growing too much corn, as a considerable loss will be sustained upon that part of it which is sold abroad; and a glut

---

1. Wealth of Nations, vol. ii. b. iv. c. vii. p. 413.

in the home market will universally make the price fall below the fair and proper recompence to the grower. It is impossible that a country, under such circumstances, should not be subject to great and frequent variations in the price of corn, and occasionally to severe scarcities.

If we were to endeavour to lower the price of labour by encouraging the importation of foreign corn, we should probably aggravate the evil tenfold. Experience warrants us in saying, that, from political fears, or other causes, the fall in the price of labour would be uncertain; but the ruin of our agriculture would be certain. The British grower of corn could not, in his own markets, stand the competition of the foreign grower, in average years. We should be daily thrown more and more into a dependence upon other countries for our support. Arable lands of a moderate quality would not pay the expence of cultivation. Rich soils alone would yield a rent. Round all our towns, the appearances would be the same as usual; but in the interior of the country, half of the lands would be neglected, and almost universally, where it was practicable, pasture would take place of tillage. How dreadfully precarious would our commerce and manufactures, and even our very existence be, under such circumstances! It could hardly be expected that a century should elapse without seeing our population repressed within the limits of our scanty cultivation; and suffering the same melancholy reverse, as the once flourishing population of Spain.

Nothing perhaps will shew more clearly the absurdity of that artificial system, which prompts a country, with a large territory of its own, to depend upon others for its food, than the supposition of the same system being pursued by many other states. If France, Germany, and Prussia, were to become manufacturing nations, and to consider agriculture as a secondary concern, how would their wants, in the indispensable article of food, be supplied. The increasing demand for corn, would tend certainly to encourage the growth of it in Russia and America; but we know that in these countries, at present, particularly in America, the natural progress of population is not very greatly checked; and that, as their towns and manufactories increase, the demand for their own corn will of course increase with them. The Russian nobleman, whose revenue depends upon the number of his boors, will hardly be persuaded to check their increase, in order to accommodate other nations; and the independent cultivator of America will surely feed his own family and servants, and probably supply the home market, before he begins to export. But allowing that at first, and for some time, the increasing demands of these manufacturing countries might be adequately supplied; yet this could not in the nature of things last long. The manufacturers, from the decay of agriculture in their own countries, would annually want more; and Russia and America, from their rapidly increasing population, and the gradual establishment of manufactures at home, would annually be able to spare less. From these causes and the necessity of drawing a part of such vast supplies of corn from a much greater distance inland, and loaded perhaps with the expence of land carriage, the price would ultimately rise so extravagantly high, that the poor manufacturers would be totally unable to pay it, and want and famine would convince them too late of the precarious and subordinate nature of their wealth. They would learn by painful experience, that, though agriculture may flourish considerably, and give plenty and happiness to great numbers, without many manufactures; yet, that manufactures cannot stir a single step, without their agricultural pay masters, either at home or abroad; and that therefore it is the height of folly and imprudence, to have these pay masters at a great distance, with different interests, and their payments precarious, instead of at home, with the same interests, and their payments always ready and certain. Nothing can be so hateful to a liberal mind, as the idea of being placed in a situation in which the growing prosperity of your neighbours will be the signal of your own approaching ruin. Yet this would be the situation of the principal countries of Europe, if they depended chiefly upon Russia and America, or any other nations for their corn. A system, which, like the present commercial system of England, throws a country into this state, without any physical necessity for it, cannot be founded on the genuine principles of the wealth of nations.

It seems almost impossible, that a country possessed of a considerable territory, should have its means of subsistence well assured, without growing at home more corn than it consumes. Nor can it be exempt from those great and sudden variations of price, which produce such severe distress throughout so large a part of the community, and are often attended with great and lasting disadvantages; unless this superfluity of produce bear some considerable proportion to the common deficiencies of unfavourable years. It has been almost universally acknowledged that there is no branch of trade, more profitable to a country, even in a commercial point of view, than the sale of rude produce. In general, its value bears a much greater proportion to the expence incurred in procuring it, than that of any other commodity whatever, and the national profit on its sale is in consequence greater. This is often noticed by Dr. Smith; but in combating the arguments of the Economists, he seems for a moment to forget it, and to speak of the superior advantage of exporting manufactures.

He observes, that a trading and manufacturing country exports what can subsist and accommodate but very few, and imports the subsistence and accommodation of a great number. The other, exports the subsistence and accommodation of a great number, and imports that of a very few only. The inhabitants of the one must always enjoy a much greater quantity of subsistence, than what their own lands in the actual state of their cultivation could afford. The inhabitants of the other must always enjoy a much smaller quantity.[2]

In this passage he does not seem to argue with his usual accuracy. Though the manufacturing nation may export a commodity which, in its actual shape, can only subsist and accommodate a very few; yet it must be recollected, that, in order to prepare this commodity for exportation, a considerable part of the revenue of the country had been employed in subsisting and accommodating a great number of workmen. And with regard to the subsistence and accommodation which the other nation exports, whether it be of a great or a small number, it is certainly no more than sufficient to replace the subsistence that had been consumed in the manufacturing nation, together with the profits of the master manufacturer and merchant, which, probably, are not so great as the profits of the farmer and the merchant in the agricultural nation. And though it may be true, that the inhabitants of the manufacturing nation enjoy a greater quantity of subsistence than what their own lands, in the actual state of their cultivation, could afford; yet an inference in favour of the manufacturing system by no means follows, because the adoption of the one, or the other system, will make the greatest difference in their actual state of cultivation. If, during the course of a century, two landed nations were to pursue these two different systems, that is, if one of them were regularly to export manufactures, and import subsistence; and the other to export subsistence, and import manufactures, there would be no comparison at the end of the period, between the state of cultivation in the two countries; and no doubt could rationally be entertained that the country which exported its raw produce, would be able to subsist and accommodate a much greater population than the other.

In the ordinary course of things, the exportation of raw produce is sufficiently profitable to the individuals concerned in it. But with regard to national profit, it possesses two peculiar and eminent advantages above any other kind of export. In the first place, raw produce, and more particularly corn, pays from its own funds the expences of procuring it, and the whole of what is sold is a clear national profit. If I set up a new manufacture, the persons employed in it must be supported out of the funds of subsistence already existing in the country, the value of which must be deducted from

2. Wealth of Nations, vol. iii. b. iv. c. ix. p. 27.

the price for which the commodity is sold, before we can estimate the clear national profit; and of course, this profit can only be the profit of the master manufacturer and the exporting merchant. But if I cultivate fresh land, or employ more men in the improvement of what was before cultivated, I increase the general funds of subsistence in the country. With a part of this increase I support all the additional persons employed, and the whole of the remainder which is exported and sold, is a clear national gain; besides the advantage to the country, of supporting an additional population equal to the additional number of persons so employed, without the slightest tendency to diminish the plenty of the rest.

Secondly, it is impossible always to be secure of having enough, if we have not, in general, too much; and the habitual exportation of corn, seems to be the only practicable mode of laying by a store of sufficient magnitude to answer the emergencies, that are to be expected. The evil of scarcity is so dreadful, that any branch of commerce, the tendency of which is to prevent it, cannot but be considered, in a national point of view, as pre-eminently beneficial.

These two advantages, added to that which must necessarily accrue to manufactures from the steady and comparatively low price of provisions and of labour, are so striking, that it must be a point of the first consequence to the permanent prosperity of any country, to be able to carry on the export trade of corn, as one considerable branch of its commercial transactions.

But how to give this ability, how to turn a nation from the habit of importing corn, to the habit of exporting it, is the great difficulty. It has been generally acknowledged, and is frequently noticed by Dr. Smith, that the policy of modern Europe has led it to encourage the industry of the towns more than the industry of the country, or, in other words, trade more than agriculture. In this policy, England has certainly not been behind the rest of Europe; perhaps, indeed, except in one instance,[3] it may be said that she has been the foremost. If things had been left to take their natural course, there is no reason to think that the commercial part of the society would have increased beyond the surplus produce of the cultivators; but the high profits of commerce from monopolies, and other peculiar encouragements, have altered this natural course of things; and the body politick is in an artificial, and in some degree, diseased state, with one of its principal members out of proportion to the rest. Almost all medicine is in itself bad; and one of the great evils of illness is, the necessity of taking it. No person can well be more averse to medicine in the animal economy, or a system of expedients

3. The bounty on the exportation of corn.

in political economy, than myself; but in the present state of the country, something of the kind may be necessary to prevent greater evils. It is a matter of very little comparative importance, whether we are fully supplied with broadcloth, linens, and muslins, or even with tea, sugar, and coffee; and no rational politician therefore, would think of proposing a bounty upon such commodities. But it is certainly a matter of the very highest importance, whether we are fully supplied with food; and if a bounty would produce such a supply, the most liberal political economist might be justified in proposing it; considering food as a commodity distinct from all others, and pre-eminently valuable.

CHAP. X.

Of Bounties on the Exportation of Corn.

IT is acknowledged by Dr. Smith, that the encouragement given to the industry of the towns has turned more capital into that channel than would otherwise have gone to it; and if this be true, it follows that the land must have had less than its natural share; and under such a discouragement, we cannot reasonably expect that agriculture should be able to keep pace with manufactures. The corn laws, as they were established in 1688 and 1700, did not do more than place them upon an equality.

The regulations respecting importation and exportation adopted in these corn laws, seemed to have the effect of giving that encouragement to agriculture, which it so much wanted, and the apparent result was gradually to produce a growth of corn in the country, considerably above the wants of the actual population, and consequently to lower greatly the prices of it, and give a steadiness to these prices that had never been experienced before.

During the seventeenth century, and indeed the whole period of our history previous to it, the prices of wheat were subject to great fluctuations, and the average price was very high. For fifty years before the year 1700, the average price of wheat per quarter was 3l. 11d. and before 1650 it was 6l. 8s. 10d.[1] From the time of the completion of the corn laws in 1700 and 1706, the prices became extraordinarily steady; and the average price for forty years previous to the year 1750, sunk so low as 1l. 16s. per quarter. This was the period of our greatest exportations. In the year 1757, the laws were suspended, and in the year 1773, they were totally altered. The exports of corn have since been regularly decreasing, and the imports increasing. The average price of wheat for the forty years ending in 1800, was 2l. 9s. 5d; and for the last five years of this period, 3l. 6s. 6d. During this last term, the balance of the imports of all sorts of grain is estimated at 2,938,357,[2] and the dreadful fluctuations of price which have occurred of late years, we are but too well acquainted with.

It is at all times dangerous to be hasty in drawing general inferences from partial experience; but, in the present instance, the period that has

1. Dirom's Inquiry into the Corn Laws, Appendix, No. I.
2. Anderson's Investigation of the Circumstances which led to Scarcity, table, p. 40.

been considered is of so considerable an extent, and the changes from fluc-
tuating and high prices, to steady and low prices, with a return to fluctuat-
ing and high prices again, correspond so accurately with the establishment
and full vigour of the corn laws, and with their subsequent alterations and
inefficacy, that it was certainly rather a bold assertion in Dr. Smith to say,
that the fall in the price of corn must have happened in spite of the bounty,
and could not possibly have happened in consequence of it.[3] We have a
right to expect that he should defend a position, so contrary to all apparent
experience, by the most powerful arguments. As in the present state of this
country, the subject seems to be of the highest importance, it will be worth
while to examine the validity of these arguments.

He observes, that both in years of plenty and in years of scarcity, the
bounty necessarily tends to raise the money price of corn somewhat higher
than it otherwise would be in the home market.[4]

That it does so, in years of plenty is undoubtedly true; but that it does
so in years of scarcity, appears to me as undoubtedly false. The only argument by which Dr. Smith supports this latter position, is, by saying, that
the exportation prevents the plenty of one year from relieving the scarcity
of another. But this is certainly a very insufficient reason. The scarce year
may not immediately follow the most plentiful year; and it is totally contrary to the habits and practice of farmers, to save the superfluity of six or
seven years for a contingency of this kind. Great practical inconveniences
generally attend the keeping of so large a reserved store. Difficulties often
occur from a want of proper accommodations for it. It is at all times liable
to damage from vermin, and other causes. When very large, it is apt to be
viewed with a jealous and grudging eye by the common people. And in
general the farmer may either not be able to remain so long without his returns; or may not be willing to employ so considerable a capital in a way, in
which the returns must necessarily be distant and precarious. On the whole,
therefore, we cannot reasonably expect, that, upon this plan, the reserved
store should in any degree be equal to that, which in a scarce year would be
kept at home, in a country which was in the habit of constant exportation to
a considerable amount; and we know that even a very little difference in the
degree of deficiency, will often make a very great difference in the price.

Dr. Smith then proceeds to state, very justly, that the defenders of the
corn laws do not insist so much upon the price of corn in the actual state
of tillage, as upon their tendency to improve this actual state, by opening
a more extensive foreign market to the corn of the farmer, and securing

3. Wealth of Nations, vol. ii. b. iv. c. v. p. 264.   4. Id. p. 265.

to him a better price than he could otherwise expect for his commodity: which double encouragement they imagine must, in a long period of years, occasion such an increase in the production of corn, as may lower its price in the home market much more than the bounty can raise it, in the state of tillage then actually existing.[5]

In answer to this, he observes, that whatever extension of the foreign market can be occasioned by the bounty, must, in every particular year, be altogether at the expence of the home market, as every bushel of corn, which is exported by means of the bounty, and which would not have been exported without the bounty, would have remained in the home market to increase the consumption, and to lower the price of that commodity.

In this observation he appears to me a little to misuse the term market. Because, by selling a commodity below its natural price, it is possible to get rid of a greater quantity of it, in any particular market, than would have gone off otherwise, it cannot justly be said that, by this process, such a market is proportionally extended. Though the removal of the two taxes mentioned by Dr. Smith, as paid on account of the bounty, would certainly rather increase the power of the lower classes to purchase; yet in each particular year the consumption must be ultimately limited by the population; and the increase of consumption from the removal of these taxes, might by no means be sufficient to take off the whole superfluity of the farmers, without lowering the general price of corn, so as to deprive them of their fair recompence.

Suppose, that the cultivators in England had a million quarters of wheat, beyond what would supply the country, at a price, for which they must sell their whole crop, or lose their fair profits. And suppose, at the same time, that, from the high price of land, the great taxes on consumption, and the consequent high price of labour, the British farmer cannot grow corn at the average price in Europe, which is always true when a bounty upon exportation is rendered necessary. Under these circumstances if the cultivators endeavoured to force the additional million of quarters on the home market, it is perfectly clear, that not only the price of this additional million, but the price of their whole crop, would fall very considerably; and, without a bounty, it could not answer to the farmer to export, till the prices in the home market had fallen below the average price in Europe, which we supposed to be lower, than what would properly pay to the British farmer the expences of cultivation. The purchasers in the home market would undoubtedly live for this year in great plenty. They might eat as

5. Wealth of Nations, vol. ii. b. iv. c. v. p. 265.

much bread as they pleased themselves, and perhaps even feed their hogs and their horses on wheat corn; but the farmers in the mean time would be ruined, and would dread, as the greatest of all evils, the growing of too much corn. Finding, therefore, that tillage would not answer to them, they would of course neglect the plough, and gradually lay more of their land into pasture, till the return of scarcity, or at least the total removal of the superfluity, had again raised the prices to such a height as would make it answer to them to grow corn, provided that they never overstocked the home market. An individual farmer cannot know the quantity of corn that is sown by his brother farmers in other counties. The state of the future supply, in proportion to the future demand, remains in a great measure concealed till the harvest; and the cheapness or dearness of the current year can alone regulate the conduct of the farmer in the management of his land for the following year. Under such circumstances, great variations in the supply of corn, and consequently in its price, must necessarily occur.

There cannot be a greater discouragement to the production of any commodity in a large quantity, than the fear of overstocking the market with it.[6] Nor can there be a greater encouragement to such a production, than the certainty of finding an effectual market for any quantity, however great, that can be obtained. It is obvious, that in the case which we have supposed, nothing but a bounty upon corn can extend the effectual market for it to the British farmer.

Dr. Smith goes on to say, that if the two taxes paid by the people on account of the bounty, namely, the one to the government to pay this bounty, and the other paid in the advanced price of the commodity, in the actual state of the crop, do not raise the price of labour, and thus return upon the farmer; they must reduce the ability of the labouring poor to bring up their children, and, by thus restraining the population and industry of the country, must tend to stunt and restrain the gradual extension of the home market, and thereby, in the long run, rather to diminish than to augment the whole market and consumption of corn.[7]

I think it has been shewn, and indeed it will scarcely admit of a doubt, that the system of exportation arising from the bounty, has an evident tendency in years of scarcity to increase the supplies of corn, or to prevent

6. I am sufficiently aware that, in common years, the farmer is apt to proceed in a regular routine of crops, without much attention to prices; but we cannot doubt for a moment, that this routine will yield to extreme cases. No man in his senses will long go on with any species of cultivation by which he loses.

7. Wealth of Nations, vol. ii. b. iv. c. v. p. 267.

their being so much diminished as they otherwise would be, which comes to the same thing. Consequently, the labouring poor will be able to live better, and the population will be less checked in these particular years, than they would have been without the system of exportation arising from the bounty. But if the effect of the bounty, in this view of the subject, be only to repress a little the population in years of plenty, while it encourages it comparatively in years of scarcity, its effect is evidently to regulate the population more equally according to that quantity of subsistence, which can permanently, and without occasional defalcations, be supplied. And this effect, I have no hesitation in saying, is one of the greatest advantages which can possibly occur to a society, and contributes more to the happiness of the labouring poor, than can easily be conceived by those who have not deeply considered the subject. In the whole compass of human events, I doubt if there be a more fruitful source of misery, or one more invariably productive of disastrous consequences, than a sudden start of population from two or three years of plenty, which must necessarily be repressed on the first return of scarcity, or even of average crops. With the present high price of labour, and the existing habits of the poor, in this country, I should consider it as a great misfortune, if from the late alarms respecting scarcity, and the unusual quantity of corn sown in consequence of them, the price of wheat, for the next two years, were to fall to ten or twelve pounds the load. It is not to be doubted, that in this case a more than usual number of marriages would take place among the common people. The mouths would be rapidly increasing; but as this price of corn, with the present advanced rents of land, accumulated taxes on consumption, and high price of labour, would certainly not repay the farmer, the supplies would be rapidly decreasing, and the consequences are but too obvious.

The most plausible argument that Dr. Smith adduces against the corn laws, is, that, as the money price of corn regulates that of all other home-made commodities, the advantage to the proprietor from the increased money price is merely apparent, and not real; since what he gains in his sales, he must lose in his purchases.[8]

This position, however, is not true, without many limitations.[9] The money price of corn, in a particular country, is undoubtedly by far the most

---

8. Wealth of Nations, vol. ii. b. iv. c. v. p. 269.

9. In the Physiocratie, by Dupont de Nemours, it is proposed as a problem in political economy, to determine, whether an advance in the money price of corn is a real or only nominal advantage: and the question is resolved, I think justly, on the side of the reality of the advantage. Tom. ii.

powerful ingredient in regulating the price of labour, and of all other commodities; but it is not the sole ingredient. Many parts of the raw produce
of land, though affected by the price of corn, do not, by any means, rise
and fall exactly in proportion to this price. When great improvements in
manufacturing machinery have taken place in any country, the part of
the expence arising from the wages of labour will bear a comparatively
small proportion to the whole value of the wrought commodity, and consequently, the price of it, though affected by the price of corn, will not
be affected proportionally. When great and numerous taxes on consumption exist in any country, those who live by the wages of labour must always receive wherewithal to pay them, at least all those upon necessaries, such as soap, candles, leather, salt, &c. A fall in the price of corn,
therefore, though it would decrease that part of the wages of labour which
resolves itself into food, evidently, would not decrease the whole in the
same proportion. And besides these, and other limitations that might be
named, the experienced difficulty of lowering wages when once they have
been raised, should be taken into consideration before the position can be
practically applied.

During the first half of the eighteenth century, the price of corn gradually fell, and that, in a very considerable degree; but it does not appear
that the price of labour fell in consequence of it. If this effect therefore
did not take place in the course of fifty years, we could hardly expect that
it would in seven or eight. And if with the view of lowering the price of
labour, the farmers were to push their superfluity on the home market,
the disappointment of this view would clearly disable them from growing the same quantity of corn in future: and under such circumstances,
it is obvious, that a bounty alone could encourage them to continue the
same growth of corn, and that this bounty is a great positive advantage
to them, and far from being merely apparent, as Dr. Smith endeavours
to prove.

Even supposing, that either by glutting the home market with British
corn, or by the importation of foreign corn, duty free, we could succeed
in lowering the wages of labour, the expences of the British farmer in
raising corn and bringing it to market, would not be lowered in proportion. One of the principal ingredients in the price of British corn, is the
high rent of land; another, the numerous taxes on consumption which the
farmer pays in his instruments of agriculture, his horses, his windows,
and the necessary expences of his establishment. While these ingredients of price remained the same, a fall in the wages of labour could not
proportionally affect the price at which British corn could be brought to

market:[10] and the British farmer would labour under a very considerable disadvantage in a competition with the farmers of America and the shores of the Baltic, where these two ingredients of price are comparatively trifling.

When Dr. Smith says, that the nature of things has stamped upon corn a real value, which cannot be altered by merely altering the money price; and that no bounty upon exportation, no monopoly of the home market, can raise that value; nor the freest competition lower it;[11] it is evident, that he changes the question from the profits of the growers of corn in any particular country, to the physical and absolute value of corn in itself. Nothing can be more obvious than that the competition of farmers who pay few or no taxes, and little comparative rent for their land, must lower the profits of those who labour under these disadvantages, and other things being equal, must ultimately justle them out of the market. And it is also obvious, that the bounty to those who labour under these disadvantages, must tend to raise their profits and give them a fairer chance of standing the competition with the others. But all this while, undoubtedly, the physical value of corn remains just the same, untouched either by competition, or bounty. I certainly do not mean to say, that the bounty alters the physical value of corn, and makes a bushel of it support a greater number of labourers for a day, than it did before; but I certainly do mean to say, that the bounty to the British cultivator does, in the actual state of things, really increase his profits on this commodity; and by thus making the growth of corn answer to him, encourages him to sow more than he otherwise would do, and enables him in consequence to employ more bushels of corn in the maintenance of a greater number of labourers. For, even supposing that the part of the price of labour which depends directly upon corn, were to rise and fall exactly with the variations in the price of this commodity, it is demonstrably evident, that the other two principal ingredients in the price remaining the same, every rise in the money price of corn would be a positive gain to the grower or proprietor, and every fall a positive loss. And were we to go still further, and suppose that the rent of land would vary in the same way, which might be the case in the long run; yet still the money taxes on consumption remaining unaltered, the effect of a rise or fall in the money price of corn, would be to benefit or injure the grower or proprietor

---

10. The immense tax paid in this country for the support of the poor, forms undoubtedly, another powerful ingredient in the price of British corn; but I have not mentioned it in the text, because it would always diminish immediately with the price of corn, which the other two ingredients would not.

11. Wealth of Nations, vol. ii. b. iv. c. v. p. 278.

though in a less degree than before. But in applying a theory to practice, all circumstances should certainly be taken into consideration; and in judging of the practical effects of the corn laws, or the opposite system, of importation duty free, not only, as was before observed, the difficulty of lowering the price of labour should be attended to, but also the length of time which it would require to lower the rents of land, and the probable ruin of agriculture before these two objects could be effected.

If Dr. Smith's theory be just, and if it be impossible in the nature of things to encourage the growth of corn by bounties, or any other human institutions, then it follows clearly, that every rich country must cease to grow corn, as soon as the price of labour, the rents of land, and the taxes on consumption, rise so high as to exceed the advantages of superior skill and a home market. As we cannot force people to raise a commodity which will not pay them, this point evidently forms an impassable limit to the agriculture of all modern countries which have a free intercourse with others; and, from this period, they must daily grow more and more dependent upon their less rich neighbours for their subsistence.

But if the reasons that have been adduced against this theory be judged valid, then it will appear, that though agriculture be not altogether so manageable as manufactures, yet that it is still capable of being encouraged and protected by human institutions. And that consequently a system of laws respecting bounties upon exportation, and duties upon importation, framed according to the circumstances of a particular country, with reference to the expence of bringing corn to market at home, and the average price of foreign corn, may make the production of this commodity answer to the farmers of such a country, however high may be, the taxes on consumption, the rent of land, and the price of labour.

And if it be admitted, that the cultivation of corn is susceptible of being encouraged by a bounty like other commodities, it will scarcely fail to follow, that the greater plenty, occasioned by this encouragement, will in the long run lower the price.

After all the circumstances which have been before mentioned as affecting price, have had their due weight, another cause must enter into our consideration capable of producing the greatest variations, and in its immediate effects more powerful than all the rest combined. This is, the proportion of the supply to the demand. A degree of plenty, indeed, which forces farmers to sell their corn below prime cost, evidently cannot last long; but the effects of scarcity are often permanent. The practical difficulty of lowering wages has before been noticed, but the same difficulty by no means exists with regard to raising them. Two or three years of high price from accidental causes are generally sufficient to do this; and when they are followed, as they generally are, by a rise in the rents of land, the extreme difficulty of a return to the former state of cheapness is obvious. Though it be allowed, therefore, that the growing of more corn, in average years, than is wanted for home consumption, in consequence of a bounty upon exportation, cannot permanently sink the price below what will fairly pay the British farmer; yet if it prevent that continual, and often permanent rise, occasioned by every slight deficiency of supply or increase of demand,[12] its effect will clearly be, to keep the average price of corn lower than it otherwise would be. When a habit of considerable exportation prevails in consequence of a bounty, a slight increase of demand, or deficiency of supply, will produce scarcely any perceptible effect in the price of corn in the home market. This price can never exceed the average price in the ports of the commercial world, with the addition of the bounty, whatever that may be; and this addition will be absolutely nothing, compared with the increase of price which arises from the slightest deficiency of supply; a deficiency which the system of importation in a large, rich, and populous country, such as Great Britain, will always render probable, not only in the home market, but in all the ports of the commercial world, as we have lately experienced to our cost.

And if the ultimate tendency of the bounty be clearly to lower the average price of corn in the home market, all Dr. Smith's just reasonings respecting the disadvantage of the cheapness of silver in any particular country, or the dearness of all other commodities, return upon himself, and are applicable in favour of the corn laws, not against them.

We are now indeed feeling the disadvantage of the cheapness of silver in this country, and in a few years, when our commercial competitors have recovered from their late depression, shall probably feel it much more than we do at present; but it certainly is not owing to a system of exporting corn in consequence of the corn laws; but, apparently, to our having altered these corn laws in such a manner as to make them fail in producing the effect of exportation.

That we can readily, and with perfect facility, turn ourselves from an importing, to an exporting nation, in the article of corn, I would by no means pretend to say; but both theory, and the experience of the first half of the last century, warrant us in concluding it practicable; and we cannot

12. An occasional increase of demand for the supply of government stores, produces, in the present state of things, a great effect upon the price of corn, but under a system of exportation, it would not be felt.

but allow that it is worth the experiment, as the continuance of our national greatness, and commercial prosperity, seem absolutely to depend upon it. If we proceed in our present course, let us but for a moment reflect on the probable consequences. There cannot be a doubt, that, in the course of a few years, we shall draw from America, and the nations bordering on the Baltic, as much as two millions quarters of wheat, besides other corn, the support of above two millions of people. If, under these circumstances, any commercial discussion, or other dispute, were to arise with these nations, with what a weight of power they would negotiate! Not the whole British navy could offer a more convincing argument than the simple threat of shutting all their ports. I am not unaware, that, in general, you may securely depend upon people's not acting directly contrary to their interest. But this consideration, all powerful as it is, will sometimes yield voluntarily to national indignation, and is sometimes forced to yield to the resentment of a sovereign. It is of sufficient weight in practice, when applied to manufactures; because a delay in their sale is not of such immediate consequence, and from their smaller bulk, they are easily smuggled. But in the case of corn, a delay of three or four months may produce the most complicated misery; and from the great bulk of corn, it will generally be in the power of a sovereign to execute almost completely his resentful purpose. Small commercial states which depend nearly for the whole of their supplies on foreign powers, will always have many friends. They are not of sufficient consequence to excite any general indignation against them, and if they cannot be supplied from one quarter, they will from another. But this is by no means the case with such a country as Great Britain, whose commercial ambition is peculiarly calculated to excite a general jealousy, and in fact has excited it, to a very great degree. If our commerce continue increasing for a few years, and our commercial population with it, we shall be laid so bare to the shafts of fortune, that nothing but a miracle can save us from being struck. The periodical return of such seasons of dearth, as those which we have of late experienced, I consider as absolutely certain, upon our present importing system: but, excluding from the question, at present, the dreadful distress that they occasion, which however no man of humanity can long banish from his mind, I would ask, is it politick, merely with a view to our national greatness, to render ourselves thus dependent upon others for our support, and put it in the power of a combination against us, to diminish our population two millions?

To restore our independence, and build our national greatness and commercial prosperity on the sure foundation of agriculture; it is evidently not sufficient, to propose premiums for tillage, to cultivate this or that waste, or even to pass a general inclosure bill, though these may be all good as far as they go. If the increase of the commercial population keep pace with these efforts, we shall only be where we were before, with regard to the necessity of importation. The object required, is to alter the relative proportion between the commercial and the agricultural population of the country, which can only be done by some system, which will permanently raise the profits of agriculture, encourage cultivators to employ more labour in the growing of corn, and completely secure them from all apprehensions of overstocking the market. I see no other way, at present, of effecting this object, but by a system of corn laws adapted to the peculiar circumstances of the country, and the state of foreign markets. All systems of peculiar restraints and encouragements are undoubtedly disagreeable, and the necessity of resorting to them may justly be lamented. But the objection which Dr. Smith brings against bounties in general, that, of forcing some part of the industry of the country into a channel less advantageous than that in which it would run of its own accord,[13] does not apply in the present instance, on account of the pre-eminent qualities of the products of agriculture, and the dreadful consequences that attend the slightest failure of them. The nature of things has, indeed, stamped upon corn a peculiar value,[14] and this remark, made by Dr. Smith for another purpose, may fairly be applied to justify the exception of this commodity from the objections against bounties in general. If, throughout the commercial world, every kind of trade were perfectly free, one should undoubtedly feel the greatest reluctance in proposing any interruption to such a system of general liberty; and indeed, under such circumstances, agriculture would not need peculiar encouragements. But under the present universal prevalence of the commercial system, with all its different expedients of encouragement and restraint, it is folly to except from our attention the great manufacture of corn which supports all the rest. The high duties paid on the importation of foreign manufactures, are so direct an encouragement to the manufacturing part of the society, that nothing but some encouragement of the same kind, operating with the same force, can place the manufacturers and cultivators of this country on a fair footing. Any system of encouragement, therefore, which might be found necessary for the commerce of grain, would evidently be owing to the prior encouragements which had been given to manufactures. We consider the woollen manufacture of England as of the first importance, and protect

13. Wealth of Nations, vol. ii. b. iv. c. v. p. 278.
14. Wealth of Nations, vol. ii. b. iv. c. v. p. 278.

and encourage it with peculiar care; but can any thinking man compare its influence on the strength and prosperity of the state, with the manufacture of corn, the scarcity or failure of which, will involve in it the failure of the favourite manufacture itself. If all be free, I have nothing to say; but if we protect and encourage, it seems to be folly not to encourage that production, which of all others is the most important and valuable.[15]

15. Though I have dwelt much on the importance of raising a quantity of corn in the country beyond the demands of the home consumption, yet I do not mean to recommend that general system of ploughing, which takes place in most parts of France, and defeats its own purpose. A large stock of cattle is not only necessary as a very valuable part of the food of the country, and as contributing very greatly to the comforts of a considerable portion of its population; but it is also necessary in the production of corn itself. A large surplus produce, in proportion to the number of persons employed, can never be obtained without a great stock of cattle. At the same time, it does not follow, that we should throw all the land that is fit for it into pasture. It is an observation of Arthur Young, and I should think a just one, that the first and most obvious improvement in agriculture, is to make the fallows of a country support the additional cattle and sheep wanted in it. (Travels in France, vol. i. p. 361.) I am by no means sanguine, however, as to the practicability of converting England again into an exporting country, while the demands for the products of pasture are daily increasing, from the increasing riches of the commercial part of the nation. But should this be really considered as impracticable, it seems to point out to us, one of the great causes of the decay of nations. We have always heard, that states and empires have their periods of declension; and we learn from history, that the different nations of the earth have flourished in a kind of succession; and that poor countries have been continually rising on the ruins of their richer neighbours. Upon the commercial system, this kind of succession seems to be in the natural and necessary course of things, independently of the effects of war. If from the increasing riches of the commercial part of any nation and the consequently increasing demands for the products of pasture, more lands were daily laid down to grass, and more corn imported from other countries, the unavoidable consequence seems to be, that the increasing prosperity of these countries, which their exportations of corn would contribute to accelerate, must ultimately destroy the population and power of the countries which had fostered them. The ancients always attributed this natural weakness and old age of states to luxury. But the moderns, who have generally considered luxury as a principal encouragement to commerce and manufactures, and consequently a powerful instrument of prosperity, have, with great appearance of reason, been unwilling to consider it as a cause of decline. But allowing with the moderns, all the advantages of luxury, and when it falls short of actual vice, they are certainly great; there seems to be a point, beyond which it must necessarily become prejudicial to a state, and bring with it the seeds of weakness and decay. This point is, when it is pushed so far, as to trench on the funds necessary for its support, and to become an impediment instead of an encouragement to agriculture. I should be much misunderstood, if, from anything that I have said in the four last chapters,

Let it not, however, be imagined, that the most enlightened system of agriculture, though it will undoubtedly be able to produce food beyond the demands of the actual population, can ever be made to keep pace with

---

I should be considered as not sufficiently aware of the advantages derived from commerce and manufactures. I look upon them as the most distinguishing characteristics of civilization, the most obvious and striking marks of the improvement of society, and calculated to enlarge our enjoyments, and add to the sum of human happiness. No great surplus produce of agriculture could exist without them, and if it did exist, it would be comparatively of very little value. But still they are rather the ornaments and embellishments of the political structure than its foundations. While these foundations are perfectly secure, we cannot be too solicitous to make all the apartments convenient and elegant; but if there be the slightest reason to fear that the foundations themselves may give way, it seems to be folly to continue directing our principal attention to the less essential parts. The most determined friend of commerce and manufactures must allow, that the persons employed in them cannot exist without the food to support them; and I cannot persuade myself to believe that they can be sufficiently secure of this food, if they depend for it principally on other countries. There has never yet been an instance in history, of a large nation continuing, with undiminished vigour, to support four or five millions of its people on imported corn; nor do I believe that there ever will be such an instance in future. England is, undoubtedly, from her insular situation, and commanding navy, the most likely to form an exception to this rule; but considering the subject as a general question in political economy, these advantages must evidently be looked upon as peculiar and incidental; and what might be applicable to England, would not be so to other countries. In spite, however, of the peculiar advantages of England, it appears to me clear that if she continue yearly to increase her importations of corn, she cannot ultimately escape that decline which seems to be the natural and necessary consequence of excessive commercial wealth; and the growing prosperity of those countries which supply her with corn, must, in the end, diminish her population, her riches, and her power. I am not now speaking of the next twenty or thirty years, but of the next two or three hundred. And though we are little in the habit of looking so far forwards, yet it may be questioned, whether we have a right knowingly to adopt a system which must necessarily terminate in the weakness and decline of our posterity. But whether we make any practical application of such a discussion or not, it is curious to contemplate the causes of those reverses in the fates of empires, which so frequently changed the face of the world in past times, and may be expected to produce similar, though perhaps not such violent, changes in future. War was, undoubtedly, in ancient times, the principal cause of these changes; but it frequently only finished a work which excess of luxury and the neglect of agriculture had begun. With regard to ourselves, we should recollect that it is only within the last twenty or thirty years, that we have become an importing nation. In so short a period, it could hardly be expected, that the evils of the system should be perceptible. We have, however, already felt some of its inconveniences; and if we persevere in it, its evil consequences may by no means be a matter of remote speculation. It has been before observed, that, if from the beginning every kind of trade had been left to

an unchecked population. The errors that have arisen from the constant appearance of a full supply, produced by the agricultural system, and the source of some other prejudices on the subject of population, will be noticed in the following chapter.

find its own level, agriculture would probably never have wanted any particular support; but when once this general and desirable liberty has been infringed, it seems to be clearly our interest to attend principally to those parts of the political structure, which in the actual circumstances of the country appear to be comparatively the weakest; and, upon this principle, we should be justified in giving particular encouragement to manufactures in such countries as Poland, and the southern parts of Siberia, and the same kind of encouragement to agriculture, in England.

CHAP. XI.

Of the principal Sources of the prevailing Errors on the Subject of Population.

IT has been observed, that many countries at the period of their greatest degree of populousness, have lived in the greatest plenty, and have been able to export corn; but at other periods, when their population was very low, have lived in continual poverty and want, and have been obliged to import corn. Egypt, Palestine, Rome, Sicily, and Spain, are cited as particular exemplifications of this fact: and it has been inferred, that an increase of population in any state, not cultivated to the utmost, will tend rather to augment than diminish the relative plenty of the whole society; and that, as Lord Kaimes observes, a country cannot easily become too populous for agriculture; because agriculture has the signal property of producing food in proportion to the number of consumers.[1]

The general facts from which these inferences are drawn, there is no reason to doubt; but the inferences by no means follow from the premises. It is the nature of agriculture, particularly when well conducted, to produce support for a considerable number above that which it employs; and consequently if these members of the society, or as Sir James Steuart calls them, the free hands, do not increase, so as to reach the limit of the number which can be supported by the surplus produce, the whole population of the country may continue for ages increasing with the improving state of agriculture, and yet always be able to export corn. But this increase, after a certain period, will be very different from the natural, and unrestricted, increase of population; it will merely follow the slow augmentation of produce from the gradual improvement of agriculture; and population will still be checked by the difficulty of procuring subsistence. It is very justly observed by Sir James Steuart, that the population of England in the middle of the last century when the exports of corn were considerable, was still checked for want of food.[2] The precise measure of the population in a country thus circumstanced, will not, indeed, be the quantity of food, because part of it is exported, but the quantity of employment. The state of this employment, however, will necessarily regulate the wages of labour,

---

1. Sketches of the History of Man, b. i. sketch i. p. 106, 107. 8vo. 1788.
2. Polit. Econ. vol. i. b. i. c. xv. p. 100.

on which depends the power of the lower classes of people to procure food; and according as the employment in the country is increasing, whether slowly, or rapidly, these wages will be such, as either to check, or to encourage, early marriages, such, as to enable a labourer to support, only two or three, or as many as five or six, children.

The quantity of employment in any country will not of course vary from year to year, in the same manner as the quantity of produce must necessarily do, from the variation of the seasons; and consequently the check from want of employment will be much more steady in its operation, and be much more favourable to the lower classes of people, than the check from the immediate want of food. The first will be the preventive check; the second the positive check. When the demand for labour is either stationary, or increasing very slowly, people, not seeing any employment open by which they can support a family, or the wages of common labour being inadequate to this purpose, will of course be deterred from marrying. But if a demand for labour continue increasing with some rapidity, although the supply of food be uncertain, on account of variable seasons, and a dependence on other countries, the population will evidently go on, till it is positively checked by famine, or the diseases arising from severe want.

Scarcity and extreme poverty, therefore, may, or may not, accompany an increasing population, according to circumstances. But they must necessarily accompany a permanently declining population; because there never has been, nor probably ever will be, any other cause than want of food, which makes the population of a country permanently decline. In the numerous instances of depopulation which occur in history, the causes of it may always be traced to the want of industry, or the ill direction of that industry, arising from violence, bad government, ignorance, &c. which first occasions a want of food, and of course depopulation follows. When Rome adopted the custom of importing all her corn, and laying all Italy into pasture, she soon declined in population. The causes of the depopulation of Egypt and Turkey have already been alluded to; and, in the case of Spain, it was certainly not the numerical loss of people, occasioned by the expulsion of the Moors; but the industry and capital thus expelled, which permanently injured her population. When a country has been depopulated by violent causes, if a bad government, with its usual concomitant, insecurity of property, ensue, which has generally been the case in all those countries which are now less peopled than formerly; neither the food nor the population can recover themselves, and the inhabitants will probably live in severe want. But when an accidental depopulation takes place, in a country which was before populous and industrious, and in the habit of exporting corn, if the remaining inhabitants be left at liberty to exert, and do exert, their industry in the same direction as before, it is a strange idea to entertain, that they would then be unable to supply themselves with corn in the same plenty; particularly, as the diminished numbers would, of course, cultivate principally the more fertile parts of their territory, and not be obliged, as in their more populous state, to apply to ungrateful soils. Countries in this situation would evidently have the same chance of recovering their former number, as they had originally of reaching this number; and indeed if absolute populousness were necessary to relative plenty, as some agriculturists have supposed,[3] it would be impossible for new colonies to increase with the same rapidity as old states.

The prejudices on the subject of population, bear a very striking resemblance to the old prejudices about specie, and we know how slowly, and with what difficulty, these last have yielded to juster conceptions. Politicians observing, that states which were powerful and prosperous, were almost invariably populous, have mistaken an effect for a cause, and concluded that their population was the cause of their prosperity, instead of their prosperity being the cause of their population, as the old political economists concluded, that the abundance of specie was the cause of

3. Among others, I allude more particularly to Mr. Anderson, who, in a *Calm Investigation of the Circumstances which have led to the present Scarcity of Grain in Britain,* (published in 1801,) has laboured, with extraordinary earnestness, and I believe with the best intentions possible, to impress this curious truth on the minds of his countrymen. The particular position which he attempts to prove is, *that an increase of population in any state whose fields have not been made to attain their highest possible degree of productiveness, (a thing that probably has never yet been seen on this globe,) will necessarily have its means of subsistence rather augmented, than diminished, by that augmentation of its population; and the reverse.* The proposition is, to be sure, expressed rather obscurely; but, from the context, his meaning evidently is, that every increase of population tends to increase relative plenty, and vice versà. He concludes his proofs by observing, that, if the facts which he has thus brought forward and connected, do not serve to remove the fears of those who doubt the possibility of this country producing abundance to sustain its increasing population, were it to augment in a ratio greatly more progressive than it has yet done, he should doubt, whether they could be convinced of it, were one even to rise from the dead to tell them so. Mr. A. is, perhaps, justified in this doubt, from the known incredulity of the age, which might cause people to remain unconvinced in both cases. I agree with Mr. A. however, entirely, respecting the importance of directing a greater part of the national industry to agriculture; but from the circumstance of its being possible for a country with a certain direction of its industry, always to export corn, although it may be very populous, he has been led into the strange error of supposing, that an agricultural country could support an unchecked population.

national wealth, instead of the effect of it. The annual produce of the land and labour, in both these instances, became, in consequence, a secondary consideration, and its increase, it was conceived, would naturally follow the increase of specie in the one case, or of population in the other. The folly of endeavouring, by forcible means, to increase the quantity of specie in any country, and the absolute impossibility of accumulating it beyond a certain level by any human laws that can be devised, are now fully established, and have been completely exemplified in the instances of Spain and Portugal; but the illusion still remains respecting population; and under this impression, almost every political treatise has abounded in proposals to encourage population, with little or no comparative reference to the means of its support. Yet, surely, the folly of endeavouring to increase the quantity of specie in any country without an increase of the commodities which it is to circulate, is not greater, than that of endeavouring to increase the number of people, without an increase of the food which is to maintain them; and it will be found, that the level above which no human laws can raise the population of a country, is a limit more fixed and impassable, than the limit to the accumulation of specie. However improbable, in fact, it is possible to conceive, that means might be invented of retaining a quantity of specie in a state, greatly beyond what was demanded by the produce of its land and labour; but when, by great encouragements, population has been raised to such a height, that this produce is meted out to each individual in the smallest portions that can support life, no stretch of ingenuity can even conceive the possibility of going further.

It has appeared, I think, clearly, in the review of different societies given in the former part of this work, that those countries, the inhabitants of which were sunk in the most barbarous ignorance, or oppressed by the most cruel tyranny, however low they might be in actual population, were very populous in proportion to their means of subsistence; and upon the slightest failure of the seasons generally suffered the severities of want. Ignorance and despotism seem to have no tendency to destroy the passion which prompts to increase; but they effectually destroy the checks to it from reason and foresight. The improvident barbarian who thinks only of his present wants, or the miserable peasant, who, from his political situation, feels little security of reaping what he has sown, will seldom be deterred from gratifying his passions by the prospect of inconveniences which cannot be expected to press on him under three or four years. But though this want of foresight, which is fostered by ignorance and despotism, tend thus rather to encourage the procreation of children, it is absolutely fatal to the industry which is to support them. Industry cannot exist without foresight and security. The indolence of the savage is well known; and the poor Egyptian or Abyssinian farmer, without capital, who rents land, which is let out yearly to the highest bidder, and who is constantly subject to the demands of his tyrannical masters, to the casual plunder of an enemy, and, not unfrequently, to the violation of his miserable contract, can have no heart to be industrious, and if he had, could not exercise that industry with success. Even poverty itself, which appears to be the great spur to industry, when it has once passed certain limits, almost ceases to operate. The indigence which is hopeless, destroys all vigorous exertion, and confines the efforts to what is sufficient for bare existence. It is the hope of bettering our condition, and the fear of want, rather than want itself, that is the best stimulus to industry, and its most constant and best directed efforts will almost invariably be found among a class of people above the class of the wretchedly poor.

The effect of ignorance and oppression will therefore always be to destroy the springs of industry, and consequently to diminish the annual produce of the land and labour in any country; and this diminution will inevitably be followed by a decrease of the population, in spite of the birth of any number of children whatever, annually. The desire of immediate gratification, and the removal of the restraints to it from prudence, may perhaps, in such countries, prompt universally to early marriages; but when these habits have once reduced the people to the lowest possible state of poverty, they can evidently have no further effect upon the population. Their only effect must be on the degree of mortality; and there is no doubt, that, if we could obtain accurate bills of mortality in those southern countries, where very few women remain unmarried, and all marry young, the proportion of the annual deaths would be 1 in 17, 18, or 20, instead of 1 in 34, 36, or 40, as in European states, where the preventive check operates.

That an increase of population, when it follows in its natural order, is both a positive good in itself, and absolutely necessary to a further increase in the annual produce of the land and labour of any country, I should be the last to deny. The only question is, what is the natural order of its progress? In this point, Sir James Steuart, who has in general explained this subject so well, appears to me to have fallen into an error. He determines that multiplication is the efficient cause of agriculture, and not agriculture of multiplication.[4] But though it may be allowed that the increase of people beyond what could easily subsist on the natural fruits of the earth, first prompted man to till the ground; and that the view of maintaining a family, or of obtaining some valuable consideration in exchange for the products of agri-

4. Polit. Econ. vol. i. b. i. c. xviii. p. 114.

culture, still operates as the principal stimulus to cultivation; yet it is clear, that these products in their actual state, must be beyond the lowest wants of the existing population, before any permanent increase can possibly be supported. And we know that multiplication has in numberless instances taken place, which has produced no effect upon agriculture, and has merely been followed by an increase of diseases; but perhaps there is no instance, where a permanent increase of agriculture, has not effected a permanent increase of population, somewhere or other. Consequently, agriculture may with more propriety be termed the efficient cause of population, than population of agriculture,[5] though they certainly re-act upon each other, and are mutually necessary to each other's support. This indeed seems to be the hinge on which the subject turns, and all the prejudices respecting population have, perhaps, arisen from a mistake about the order of precedence.

The author of *L'Ami des Hommes,* in a chapter on the effects of a decay of agriculture upon population, acknowledges that he had fallen into a fundamental error in considering population as the source of revenue; and that he was afterwards fully convinced that revenue was the source of population.[6] From a want of attention to this most important distinction, statesmen, in pursuit of the desireable object of population, have been led to encourage early marriages, to reward the fathers of families, and to disgrace celibacy; but this, as the same author justly observes, is to dress and water a piece of land without sowing it, and yet to expect a crop.

Among the other prejudices which have prevailed on the subject of population, it has been generally thought, that, while there is either waste among the rich, or land remaining uncultivated in any country, the complaints for want of food cannot be justly founded, or, at least, that the pressure of distress upon the poor is to be attributed to the ill-conduct of the higher classes of society, and the bad management of the land. The real effect, however, of these two circumstances, is merely to narrow the limit of the actual population; but they have little or no influence on what may be called the average pressure of distress on the poorer members of society. If our ancestors had been so frugal and industrious, and had transmitted such habits to their posterity, that nothing superfluous was now consumed by the higher classes, no horses were used for pleasure, and no land was left

<hr />

5. Sir James Steuart explains himself afterwards, by saying that he means principally the multiplication of those persons who have some valuable consideration to give for the products of agriculture; but this is evidently not mere increase of population, and such an explanation seems to admit the incorrectness of the general proposition.

6. Tom. viii. p. 84. 12mo. 9 vols. 1762.

uncultivated, a striking difference would appear in the state of the actual population; but probably none whatever, in the state of the lower classes of people, with respect to the price of labour, and the facility of supporting a family. The waste among the rich, and the horses kept for pleasure, have indeed a little the effect of the consumption of grain in distilleries, noticed before with regard to China. On the supposition that the food consumed in this manner may be withdrawn on the occasion of a scarcity, and be applied to the relief of the poor, they operate, certainly, as far as they go, like granaries which are only opened at the time that they are most wanted, and must therefore tend rather to benefit than to injure the lower classes of society.

With regard to uncultivated land, it is evident, that its effect upon the poor is neither to injure, nor to benefit them. The sudden cultivation of it, will indeed tend to improve their condition for a time, and the neglect of lands before cultivated, will certainly make their situation worse for a certain period; but when no changes of this kind are going forward, the effect of uncultivated land on the lower classes, operates merely like the possession of a smaller territory. It is, indeed, a point of very great importance to the poor, whether a country be in the habit of exporting or importing corn; but this point is not necessarily connected with the complete or incomplete cultivation of the whole territory, but depends upon the proportion of the surplus produce, to those who are supported by it; and, in fact, this proportion is generally the greatest, in countries which have not yet completed the cultivation of all their territory. If every inch of land in this country were well cultivated, there would be no reason to expect, merely from this circumstance, that we should be able to export corn. Our power in this respect would depend entirely on the proportion of the surplus produce to the commercial population; and this, of course, would in its turn depend on the direction of capital to agriculture, or commerce.

It is not probable that any country with a large territory should ever be completely cultivated; and I am inclined to think, that we often draw very inconsiderate conclusions against the industry and government of states from the appearance of uncultivated lands in them. It seems to be the clear and express duty of every government, to remove all obstacles, and give every facility, to the inclosure and cultivation of land; but when this has been done, the rest must be left to the operation of individual interest; and, upon this principle, it cannot be expected that any new land should be brought into cultivation, the manure and the labour necessary for which, might be employed to greater advantage on the improvement of land already in cultivation; and this is a case which will very frequently occur. In countries possessed of a large territory, there will always be a great quantity of land of a middling quality, which requires constant dressing to prevent it from growing worse; but which would admit of very great improvement, if a greater quantity of manure and labour could be employed upon it. The great obstacle to the amelioration of land is the difficulty, the expence, and, sometimes, the impossibility, of procuring a sufficient quantity of dressing. As this instrument of improvement, therefore, is in practice limited, whatever it may be in theory, the question will always be, how it may be most profitably employed; and in any instance where a certain quantity of dressing and labour employed to bring new land into cultivation, would have yielded a permanently greater produce if employed upon old land, both the individual and the nation are losers. Upon this principle it is not uncommon for farmers in some situations, never to dress their poorest land, but to get from it merely a scanty crop every three or four years, and to employ the whole of their manure, which they practically feel is limited, on those parts of their farms, where it will produce a greater proportional effect.

The case will be different, of course, in a small territory with a great population, supported on funds not derived from their own soil. In this case there will be little or no choice of land, and a comparative superabundance of manure; and under such circumstances the poorest soils may be brought under cultivation. But for this purpose, it is not mere population that is wanted, but a population which can obtain the produce of other countries, while it is gradually improving its own; otherwise, it would be immediately reduced in proportion to the limited produce of this small and barren territory; and the amelioration of the land might perhaps never take place; or if it did, it would take place very slowly indeed, and the population would always be exactly measured by this tardy state, and could not possibly increase beyond it.

This subject is illustrated in the cultivation of the Campine in Brabant, which, according to the Abbé Mann,[7] consisted originally of the most barren and arid sand. Many attempts were made by private individuals to bring it under cultivation, but without success; which prove that, as a farming project, and considered as a sole dependence, the cultivation of it would not answer. Some religious houses, however, at last settled there, and being supported by other funds, and improving the land merely as a secondary object, they, by degrees, in the course of some centuries, brought nearly the whole under cultivation, letting it out to farmers as soon as it was sufficiently improved.

7. Memoir on the Agriculture of the Netherlands, published in vol. i. of Communications to the Board of Agriculture, p. 225.

There is no spot, however barren, which might not be made rich this way, or by the concentrated population of a manufacturing town; but this is no proof whatever that with respect to population and food, population has the precedence, because this concentrated population could not possibly exist, without the preceding existence of an adequate quantity of food in the surplus produce of some other district.

In a country like Brabant or Holland, where territory is the principal want, and not manure, such a district as the Campine is described to be, may perhaps be cultivated with advantage. But in countries, possessed of a large territory, and with a considerable quantity of land of a middling quality, the attempt to cultivate such a spot, would be a palpable misdirection and waste, both of individual and national resources.

The French have already found their error in bringing under cultivation too great a quantity of poor land. They are now sensible that they have employed in this way a portion of labour and dressing, which would have produced a permanently better effect, if it had been applied to the further improvement of better land. Even in China, which is so fully cultivated and so fully peopled, barren heaths have been noticed in some districts; which prove, that, distressed as the people appear to be for subsistence, it does not answer to them to employ any of their manure on such spots. These remarks will be still further confirmed, if we recollect, that in the cultivation of a large surface of bad land, there must necessarily be a very great waste of seed corn.

We should not, therefore, be too ready to make inferences against the internal economy of a country, from the appearance of uncultivated heaths, without other evidence. But the fact is, that as no country has ever reached, or probably ever will reach, its highest possible acme of produce, it appears always, as if the want of industry, or the ill-direction of that industry, was the actual limit to a further increase of produce and population, and not the absolute refusal of nature to yield any more; but a man who is locked up in a room, may be fairly said to be confined by the walls of it, though he may never touch them; and with regard to the principle of population, it is never the question, whether a country will produce *any more,* but whether it may be made to produce a sufficiency to keep pace with an unchecked increase of people. In China, the question is not, whether a certain additional quantity of rice might be raised by improved culture, but whether such an addition could be expected during the next twenty-five years, as would be sufficient to support an additional three hundred millions of people. And in this country, it is not the question, whether by cultivating all our commons, we could raise considerably more corn than at present; but whether we could raise sufficient for a population of twenty millions in the next twenty-five years, and forty millions, in the next fifty years.

The allowing of the produce of the earth to be absolutely unlimited, scarcely removes the weight of a hair from the argument, which depends entirely upon the differently increasing ratios of population and food: and all that the most enlightened governments, and the most persevering and best guided efforts of industry can do, is to make the necessary checks to population operate more equably, and in a direction to produce the least evil; but to remove them, is a talk absolutely hopeless.

ESSAY, &c.

BOOK IV.

OF OUR FUTURE PROSPECTS RESPECTING THE REMOVAL OR MITIGATION OF THE EVILS ARISING FROM THE PRINCIPLE OF POPULATION.

CHAP. I.

Of moral restraint, and the foundations of our obligation to practise this virtue.

As it appears, that in the actual state of every society which has come within our review, the natural progress of population has been constantly and powerfully checked; and as it seems evident, that no improved form of government, no plans of emigration, no benevolent institutions, and no degree or direction of national industry, can prevent the continued action of a great check to increase in some form or other; it follows, that we must submit to it as an inevitable law of nature; and the only inquiry that remains, is, how it may take place with the least possible prejudice to the virtue and happiness of human society. The various checks to population which have been observed to prevail in the same and different countries, seem all to be resolvable into moral restraint, vice, and misery, and if our choice be confined to these three, we cannot long hesitate in our decision respecting which it would be most eligible to encourage.

In the former edition of this essay, I observed, that, as from the laws of nature it appeared, that some check to population must exist, it was better that this check should arise from a foresight of the difficulties attending a family, and the fear of dependent poverty, than from the actual presence of want and sickness. This idea will admit of being pursued further, and I am inclined to think, that, from the prevailing opinions respecting population, which undoubtedly originated in barbarous ages, and have been continued and circulated by that part of every community, which may be supposed to be interested in their support, we have been prevented from attending to the clear dictates of reason and nature on this subject.

Natural and moral evil seem to be the instruments employed by the Deity in admonishing us to avoid any mode of conduct, which is not suited to our being, and will consequently injure our happiness. If we be intemperate in eating and drinking, we are disordered; if we indulge the transports of anger, we seldom fail to commit acts of which we afterwards repent; if we multiply too fast, we die miserably of poverty and contagious diseases. The laws of nature in all these cases are similar and uniform. They indicate to us, that we have followed these impulses too far, so as to trench upon some other law which equally demands attention. The uneasiness we feel from repletion, the injuries that we inflict on ourselves or others in anger, and the inconveniencies we suffer on the approach of poverty, are all admonitions to us to regulate these impulses better; and if we heed not this admonition, we justly incur the penalty of our disobedience, and our sufferings operate as a warning to others.

From the inattention of mankind hitherto, to the consequences of increasing too fast, it must be presumed, that these consequences are not so immediately and powerfully connected with the conduct which leads to them, as in the other instances; but the delayed knowledge of any particular effects does not alter their nature, nor our obligation to regulate our conduct accordingly, as soon as we are satisfied of what this conduct ought to be. In many other instances it has not been till after long and painful experience, that the conduct most favourable to the happiness of man has been forced upon his attention. The kind of food, and the mode of preparing it, best suited to the purposes of nutrition and the gratification of the palate; the treatment and remedies of different disorders; the bad effects on the human frame, of low and marshy situations; the invention of the most convenient and comfortable clothing; the construction of good houses; and all the advantages and extended enjoyments which distinguish civilized life; were not pointed out to the attention of man at once; but were the slow and late result of experience, and of the admonitions received by repeated failures.

Diseases have been generally considered as the inevitable inflictions of Providence; but, perhaps, a great part of them may more justly be considered as indications that we have offended against some of the laws of nature. The plague at Constantinople, and in other towns of the East, is a constant admonition of this kind to the inhabitants. The human constitution cannot support such a state of filth and torpor; and as dirt, squalid poverty, and indolence, are in the highest degree unfavourable to happiness and virtue, it seems a benevolent dispensation, that such a state should by the laws of nature produce disease and death, as a beacon to others to avoid splitting on the same rock.

The prevalence of the plague in London till the year 1666, operated in a proper manner on the conduct of our ancestors; and the removal of nuisances, the construction of drains, the widening of the streets, and the giving more room and air to their houses, had the effect of eradicating completely this dreadful disorder, and of adding greatly to the health and happiness of the inhabitants.

In the history of every epidemick it has almost invariably been observed, that the lower classes of people, whose food was poor and insufficient, and who lived crowded together, in small and dirty houses, were the principal victims. In what other manner can nature point out to us, that if we increase too fast for the means of subsistence, so as to render it necessary for a considerable part of the society to live in this miserable manner, we have offended against one of her laws. This law she has declared exactly in the same manner, as she declares that intemperance in eating and drinking will be followed by ill health; and that, however grateful it may be to us at the moment to indulge these passions to excess, this indulgence will ultimately produce unhappiness. It is as much a law of nature that repletion is bad for the human frame, as that eating and drinking, unattended with this consequence, is good for it.

An implicit obedience to the impulses of our natural passions would lead us into the wildest and most fatal extravagancies; and yet we have the strongest reasons for believing that all these passions are so necessary to our being, that they could not be generally weakened or diminished, without injuring our happiness. The most powerful and universal of all our desires is the desire of food, and of those things, such as clothing, houses, &c. which are immediately necessary to relieve us from the pains of hunger and cold. It is acknowledged by all, that these desires put in motion the greatest part of that activity from which spring the multiplied improvements and advantages of civilized life; and that the pursuit of these objects and the gratification of these desires form the principal happiness of the larger half of mankind, civilized or uncivilized, and are indispensably necessary to the more refined enjoyments of the other half. We are all conscious, of the inestimable benefits that we derive from these desires when directed in a certain manner; but we are equally conscious, of the evils resulting from them when not directed in this manner; so much so, that society has taken upon itself to punish most severely, what it considers as an irregular gratification of them. And yet the desires in both cases are equally natural, and, abstractedly considered, equally virtuous. The act of the hungry man who satisfies his appetite by taking a loaf from the shelf of another, is in no respect to be distinguished from the act of him who does the same thing with a loaf of his own, but by its consequences. From the consideration of these consequences, we feel the most perfect conviction, that if people were not prevented from gratifying their natural desires with the loaves in the possession of others, that the number of loaves would universally diminish. This experience is the foundation of the laws relating to property, and of the distinctions of virtue and vice, in the gratification of desires, otherwise perfectly the same.

If the pleasure arising from the gratification of these propensities were universally diminished in vividness, violations of property would become less frequent; but this advantage would be greatly overbalanced by the narrowing of the sources of enjoyment. The diminution in the quantity of all those productions, which contribute to human gratification, would be much greater, in proportion, than the diminution of thefts; and the loss of general happiness on the one side, would be beyond comparison greater, than the gain to happiness on the other. When we contemplate the constant and severe toils of the greatest part of mankind, it is impossible not to be forcibly impressed with the reflection, that the sources of human happiness would be most cruelly diminished, if the prospect of a good meal, a warm house, and a comfortable fireside in the evening, were not incitements sufficiently vivid, to give interest and cheerfulness to the labours and privations of the day.

After the desire of food, the most powerful and general of our desires, is, the passion between the sexes, taken in an enlarged sense. Of the happiness spread over human life by this passion, very few are unconscious. Virtuous love, exalted by friendship, seems to be that sort of mixture of sensual and intellectual enjoyment, particularly suited to the nature of man, and most powerfully calculated to awaken the sympathies of the soul, and produce the most exquisite gratifications. Perhaps there is scarcely a man who has once experienced the genuine delight of virtuous love, however great his intellectual pleasures may have been, that does not look back to the period, as the sunny spot, in his whole life, where his imagination loves most to bask, which he recollects and contemplates with the fondest regret, and which he would most wish to live over again.

It has been said by Mr. Godwin, in order to shew the evident inferiority of the pleasures of sense, "Strip the commerce of the sexes of all its atten-
" dant circumstances, and it would be generally despised." He might as well say to a man who admired trees, strip them of their spreading branches, and lovely foliage, and what beauty can you see in a bare pole? But it was the tree with the branches and foliage, and not without them, that excited admiration. It is "the symmetry of person, the vivacity, the voluptuous soft-
" ness of temper, the affectionate kindness of feeling, the imagination and
" the wit"[1] of a woman, which excite the passion of love, and not the mere distinction of her being a female.

It is a very great mistake to suppose, that the passion between the sexes, only operates and influences human conduct, when the immediate gratification of it is in contemplation. The formation and steady pursuit of some particular plan of life, has been justly considered as one of the most permanent sources of happiness; but I am inclined to believe, that there are not many of these plans formed, that are not connected, in a considerable degree, with the prospect of the gratification of this passion, and with the support of children arising from it. The evening meal, the warm house, and the comfortable fireside, would lose half of their interest, if we were to exclude the idea of some object of affection with whom they were to be shared.

We have also great reason to believe, that the passion between the sexes has the most powerful tendency to soften and meliorate the human character, and keep it more alive to all the kindlier emotions of benevolence and pity. Observations on savage life have generally tended to prove, that nations in which this passion appeared to be less vivid, were distinguished by a ferocious and malignant spirit; and particularly by tyranny and cruelty to the sex. If, indeed, this bond of conjugal affection were considerably weakened, it seems probable, either that the man would make use of his superior physical strength, and turn his wife into a slave, as among the generality of savages; or at best, that every little inequality of temper which must necessarily occur between two persons, would produce a total alienation of affection; and this could hardly take place, without a diminution of parental fondness and care, which would have the most fatal effect on the happiness of society.

---

1. Political Justice, vol. i. b. i. c. v. p. 72. 8vo.

It may be further remarked, that observations on the human character in different countries, warrant us in the conclusion, that the passion is stronger, and its general effects in producing gentleness, kindness, and suavity of manners, much more powerful, where obstacles are thrown in the way of very early and universal gratification. In some of the southern countries where every impulse may be almost immediately indulged, the passion sinks into mere animal desire, is soon weakened and almost extinguished by excess; and its influence on the character is extremely confined. But in European countries, where, though the women are not secluded, yet manners have imposed considerable restraints on this gratification, the passion not only rises in force, but in the universality and beneficial tendency of its effects, and has often the most influence in the formation and improvement of the character, where it is the least gratified.

Considering then the passion between the sexes in all its bearings and relations, and including the endearing engagement of parent and child resulting from it, few will be disposed to deny that it is one of the principal ingredients of human happiness. Yet experience teaches us that much evil flows from the irregular gratification of it; and though the evil be of little weight in the scale, when compared with the good; yet its absolute quantity cannot be inconsiderable, on account of the strength and universality of the passion. It is evident, however, from the general conduct of all governments in their distribution of punishments, that the evil resulting from this cause is not so great, and so immediately dangerous to society, as the irregular gratification of the desire of property; but placing this evil in the most formidable point of view, we should evidently purchase a diminution of it at a very dear price, by the extinction or diminution of the passion which causes it; a change, which would probably convert human life, either into a cold and cheerless blank, or a scene of savage and merciless ferocity.

A careful attention to the remote as well as immediate effects of all the human passions, and all the general laws of nature, leads us strongly to the conclusion, that, under the present constitution of things, few or none of them would admit of being greatly diminished, without narrowing the sources of good, more powerfully than the sources of evil. And the reason seems to be obvious. They are, in fact, the materials of all our pleasures, as well as of all our pains; of all our happiness, as well as of all our misery; of all our virtues, as well as of all our vices. It must therefore be regulation and direction that are wanted, not diminution or extinction.

It is justly observed by Dr. Paley, that, "Human passions are either nec-
" essary to human welfare, or capable of being made, and in a great ma-
" jority of instances in fact made, conducive to its happiness. These

"   passions are strong and general; and perhaps would not answer their
"   purpose, unless they were so. But strength and generality, when it is
"   expedient that particular circumstances should be respected, become,
"   if left to themselves, excess and misdirection. From which excess and
"   misdirection, the vices of mankind (the causes no doubt of much mis-
"   ery) appear to spring. This account, while it shews us the principle
"   of vice, shews us at the same time, the province of reason and self-
"   government."[2]

Our virtue, therefore, as reasonable beings, evidently consists in educ-
ing, from the general materials which the Creator has placed under our guidance, the greatest sum of human happiness; and as all our natural impulses
are abstractedly considered good, and only to be distinguished by their consequences, a strict attention to these consequences, and the regulation of our
conduct conformably to them, must be considered as our principal duty.

The fecundity of the human species is, in some respects, a distinct consideration from the passion between the sexes, as it evidently depends more
upon the power of women in bearing children, than upon the strength or
weakness of this passion. It is, however, a law, exactly similar in its great
features to all the other laws of nature. It is strong and general, and apparently would not admit of any very considerable diminution, without
being inadequate to its object; the evils arising from it are incidental to
these necessary qualities of strength and generality; and these evils are
capable of being very greatly mitigated, and rendered comparatively light
by human energy and virtue. We cannot but conceive, that it is an object of
the Creator, that the earth should be replenished, at least to a considerable
degree; and it appears to me clear, that this could not be effected, without a
tendency in population to increase faster than food; and as with the present
law of increase, the peopling of the earth does not proceed very rapidly, we
have undoubtedly some reason to believe, that this law is not too powerful for its apparent object. The desire of the means of subsistence would
be comparatively confined in its effects, and would fail of producing that
general activity so necessary to the improvement of the human faculties,
were it not for the strong and universal effort of population, to increase
with greater rapidity than its supplies. If these two tendencies were exactly
balanced, I do not see what motive there would be, sufficiently strong, to
overcome the acknowledged indolence of man, and make him proceed in
the cultivation of the soil. The population of any large territory, however
fertile, would be as likely to stop at five hundred, or five thousand, as at five

2. Natural Theology, c. xxvi. p. 547.

millions, or fifty millions. Such a balance therefore, would clearly defeat one great purpose of creation; and if the question be merely a question of degree, a question of a little more, or a little less, strength, we may fairly distrust our competence to judge of the precise quantity necessary to answer the object, with the smallest sum of incidental evil. In the present state of things we appear to have under our guidance a great power, capable of peopling a desert region in a small number of years; and yet, under other circumstances, capable of being confined, by human energy and virtue, to any limits, however narrow, at the expence of a small comparative quantity of evil. The analogy of all the other laws of nature would be completely violated, if in this instance alone, there were no provision for accidental failures, no resources against the vices of mankind, or the partial mischiefs resulting from other general laws. To effect the apparent object without any attendant evil, it is evident, that a perpetual change in the law of increase would be necessary, varying with the varying circumstances of each country. But instead of this, it is not only more consonant to the analogy of the other parts of nature, but we have reason to think, that it is more conducive to the formation and improvement of the human mind, that the law should be uniform, and the evils, incidental to it under certain circumstances, be left to be mitigated or removed by man himself. His duties in this case vary with his situation; and he is thus kept more alive to the consequences of his actions, and his faculties have evidently greater play and opportunity of improvement, than if the evil were removed by a perpetual change of the law, according to circumstances.

Even if from passions too easily subdued, or the facility of illicit intercourse, a state of celibacy were a matter of indifference, and not a state of some privation, the end of nature in the peopling of the earth would be apparently liable to be defeated. It is of the very utmost importance to the happiness of mankind, that they should not increase too fast; but it does not appear that the object to be accomplished, would admit of any very considerable diminution in the desire of marriage. It is clearly the duty of each individual not to marry till he has a prospect of supporting his children; but it is at the same time to be wished, that he should retain undiminished his desire of marriage, in order that he may exert himself to realize this prospect, and be stimulated to make provision for the support of greater numbers.

It is evidently therefore, regulation and direction that is required with regard to the principle of population, not diminution or alteration. And if moral restraint be the only virtuous mode of avoiding the incidental evils arising from this principle, our obligation to practise it will evidently rest exactly upon the same foundation, as our obligation to practise any of the other virtues, the foundation of utility.

Whatever indulgence we may be disposed to allow to occasional failures in the discharge of a duty, of acknowledged difficulty; yet, of the strict line of duty, during the period of celibacy, whatever that may be, we cannot doubt. And, with regard to the necessity of this celibacy in countries that have been long peopled, or our obligation not to marry till we have a fair prospect of being able to support our children, it will appear to deserve the attention of the moralist, if it can be proved, that an attention to this obligation is of more effect in the prevention of misery, than all the other virtues combined; and that if, in violation of this duty, it were the general custom to follow the first impulse of nature, and marry at the age of puberty, the universal prevalence of every known virtue in the greatest conceivable degree, would fail of rescuing society from the most wretched and desperate state of want, and all the diseases and famines which usually accompany it.

C H A P . II.

*Of the Effects which would result to Society
from the general practice of this virtue.*

ONE of the principal reasons, which has prevented an assent to the doctrine of the constant tendency of population to increase beyond the means of subsistence, is, a great unwillingness to believe, that the Deity would, by the laws of nature, bring beings into existence, which, by the laws of nature, could not be supported in that existence. But if, in addition to that general activity and direction of our industry put in motion by these laws, we further consider, that the incidental evils arising from them, are constantly directing our attention to the proper check to population, moral restraint; and if it appear, that by a strict obedience to those duties which are pointed out to us by the light of nature and reason, and are confirmed and sanctioned by revelation, these evils may be avoided, the objection will, I trust, be removed, and all apparent imputation on the goodness of the Deity be done away.

The heathen moralists never represented happiness as attainable on earth, but through the medium of virtue; and among their virtues, prudence ranked in the first class, and by some was even considered as including every other. The christian religion places our present as well as future happiness in the exercise of those virtues which tend to fit us for a state of superior enjoyment; and the subjection of the passions to the guidance of reason, which, if not the whole, is a principal branch of prudence, is in consequence most particularly inculcated.

If, for the sake of illustration, we might be permitted to draw a picture of society, in which, each individual endeavoured to attain happiness by the strict fulfilment of those duties which the most enlightened of the ancient philosophers deduced from the laws of nature, and which have been directly taught, and received such powerful sanctions in the moral code of Christianity, it would present a very different scene from that which we now contemplate. Every act which was prompted by the desire of immediate gratification, but which threatened an ultimate overbalance of pain, would be considered as a breach of duty; and, consequently, no man whose earnings were only sufficient to maintain two children, would put himself in a situation in which he might have to maintain four or five, however he might be prompted to it by the passion of love. This prudential restraint, if it were generally adopted, by narrowing the supply of labour in the market, would, in the natural course of things, soon raise its price. The period of delayed gratification would be passed in saving the earnings which were above the wants of a single man, and in acquiring habits of sobriety, industry, and economy, which would enable him, in a few years, to enter into the matrimonial contract without fear of its consequences. The operation of the preventive check in this way, by constantly keeping the population within the limits of the food, though constantly following its increase, would give a real value to the rise of wages, and the sums saved by labourers before marriage, very different from those forced advances in the price of labour, or arbitrary parochial donations, which, in proportion to their magnitude and extensiveness, must of necessity be followed by a proportional advance in the price of provisions. As the wages of labour would thus be sufficient to maintain with decency a large family, and as every married couple would set out with a sum for contingencies, all squalid poverty would be removed from society, or, at least, be confined to a very few, who had fallen into misfortunes against which, no prudence or foresight could provide.

The interval between the age of puberty, and the period at which each individual might venture on marriage, must, according to the supposition, be passed in strict chastity; because the law of chastity cannot be violated without producing evil. The effect of any thing like a promiscuous intercourse, which prevents the birth of children, is evidently to weaken the best affections of the heart, and, in a very marked manner, to degrade the female character. And any other intercourse, would, without improper arts, bring as many children into the society as marriage, with a much greater probability of their becoming a burden to it.

These considerations shew, that the virtue of chastity is not, as some have supposed, a forced produce of artificial society; but that it has the most real and solid foundation in nature and reason; being apparently the only virtuous mean of avoiding the vice and misery which result from the principle of population.

In such a society as we have been supposing, it might be necessary for both sexes to pass many of the early years of life in the single state; and if this were general, there would certainly be room for a much greater number to marry afterwards, so that fewer, upon the whole, would be condemned to pass their lives in celibacy. If the custom of not marrying early prevailed generally, and if violations of chastity were equally dishonourable in both sexes, a more familiar and friendly intercourse between them might take place without danger. Two young people might converse together intimately, without its being immediately supposed, that they either intended marriage or intrigue; and a much better opportunity would thus be given to both sexes of finding out kindred dispositions, and of forming those strong and lasting attachments, without which, the married state is generally more productive of misery than of happiness. The earlier years of life would not be spent without love, though without the full gratification of it. The passion, instead of being extinguished, as it now too frequently is by early sensuality, would only be repressed for a time, that it might afterwards burn with a brighter, purer, and steadier flame; and the happiness of the married state, instead of an opportunity of immediate indulgence, would be looked forward to, as the prize of industry and virtue, and the reward of a genuine and constant attachment.[1]

The passion of love is a powerful stimulus in the formation of character, and often prompts to the most noble and generous exertions; but this is only when the affections are centered in one object; and generally, when full gratification is delayed by difficulties.[2] The heart is perhaps never so much disposed to virtuous conduct, and certainly at no time is the virtue of chastity so little difficult to men, as when under the influence of such a passion. Late marriages taking place in this way, would be very different from those of the same name at present, where the union is too frequently prompted solely by interested views, and the parties meet, not unfrequently, with exhausted constitutions, and generally with exhausted affections. The late marriages at present, are indeed principally confined to the men; and there are few, however advanced in life they may be, who, if they determine to

---

1. Dr. Currie, in his interesting observations on the character and condition of the Scotch Peasantry, which he has prefixed to his life of Burns, remarks, with a just knowledge of human nature, that "in appreciating the happiness and virtue of a
"   community, there is perhaps no single criterion on which so much dependence
"   may be placed, as the state of the intercourse between the sexes. Where this dis-
"   plays ardour of attachment, accompanied by purity of conduct, the character and
"   the influence of women rise, our imperfect nature mounts in the scale of moral
"   excellence; and, from the source of this single affection, a stream of felicity de-
"   scends, which branches into a thousand rivulets, that enrich and adorn the field
"   of life. Where the attachment between the sexes sinks into an appetite, the heri-
"   tage of our species is comparatively poor, and man approaches to the condition
"   of the brutes that perish." Vol. i. p. 18.

2. Dr. Currie observes, that the Scottish peasant, in the course of his passion, often exerts a spirit of adventure, of which a Spanish cavalier need not be ashamed. Burns' Works, vol. i. p. 16. It is not to be doubted, that this kind of romantic passion, which, Dr. C. says, characterizes the attachments of the humblest of the people of Scotland, and which has been greatly fostered by the elevation of mind given to them by a superior education, has had a most powerful and most beneficial influence on the national character.

marry, do not fix their choice on a very young wife. A young woman, without fortune, when she has passed her twenty-fifth year, begins to fear, and with reason, that she may lead a life of celibacy; and with a heart capable of forming a strong attachment, feels, as each year creeps on, her hopes of finding an object on which to rest her affections gradually diminishing, and the uneasiness of her situation aggravated by the silly and unjust prejudices of the world. If the general age of marriage among women were later, the period of youth and hope would be prolonged, and fewer would be ultimately disappointed.

That a change of this kind would be a most decided advantage to the more virtuous half of society, we cannot for a moment doubt. However impatiently the privation might be borne by the men, it would be supported by the women readily and cheerfully; and if they could look forwards with just confidence to marriage at twenty-eight or thirty, I fully believe, that if the matter were left to their free choice, they would clearly prefer waiting till this period, to the being involved in all the cares of a large family at twenty-five. The most eligible age of marriage, however, could not be fixed; but must depend on circumstances and situation, and must be determined entirely by experience. There is no period of human life at which nature more strongly prompts to an union of the sexes, than from seventeen or eighteen, to twenty. In every society above that state of depression which almost excludes reason and foresight, these early tendencies must necessarily be restrained; and if, in the actual state of things, such a restraint on the impulses of nature be found unavoidable, at what time can we be consistently released from it, but at that period, whatever it may be, when in the existing circumstances of the society a fair prospect presents itself of maintaining a family.

The difficulty of moral restraint, will perhaps be objected to this doctrine. To him who does not acknowledge the authority of the Christian religion, I have only to say, that, after the most careful investigation, this virtue appears to be absolutely necessary, in order to avoid certain evils which would otherwise result from the general laws of nature. According to his own principles, it is his duty to pursue the greatest good consistent with these laws; and not to fail in this important end, and produce an over-balance of misery, by a partial obedience to some of the dictates of nature while he neglects others. The path of virtue, though it be the only path which leads to permanent happiness, has always been represented by the heathen moralists, as of difficult ascent.

To the Christian I would say, that the scriptures most clearly and precisely point it out to us as our duty, to restrain our passions within the bounds of reason; and it is a palpable disobedience of this law, to indulge our desires in such a manner, as reason tells us, will unavoidably end in misery. The Christian cannot consider the difficulty of moral restraint as any argument against its being his duty; since in almost every page of the sacred writings, man is described as encompassed on all sides by temptations, which it is extremely difficult to resist; and though no duties are enjoined, which do not contribute to his happiness on earth as well as in a future state, yet an undeviating obedience is never represented as an easy task.

There is in general so strong a tendency to love in early youth, that it is extremely difficult, at this period, to distinguish a genuine, from a transient passion. If the earlier years of life were passed by both sexes in moral restraint, from the greater facility that this would give to the meeting of kindred dispositions, it might even admit of a doubt whether more happy marriages would not take place, and consequently more pleasure from the passion of love, than in a state such as that of America, the circumstances of which would allow of a very early union of the sexes. But if we compare the intercourse of the sexes in such a society as I have been supposing, with that which now exists in Europe, taken under all its circumstances, it may safely be asserted, that, independently of the load of misery which would be removed by the prevalence of moral restraint, the sum of pleasurable sensations from the passion of love would be increased in a very great degree.

If we could suppose such a system general, the accession of happiness to society in its internal economy, would scarcely be greater than in its external relations. It might fairly be expected that war, that great pest of the human race, would, under such circumstances, soon cease to extend its ravages so widely, and so frequently, as it does at present, and might ultimately perhaps cease entirely.

One of its first causes, and most powerful impulses, was undoubtedly an insufficiency of room and food; and, greatly as the circumstances of mankind have changed since it first began, the same cause still continues to operate, and to produce, though in a smaller degree, the same effects. The ambition of princes would want instruments of destruction, if the distresses of the lower classes of people did not drive them under their standards. A recruiting serjeant always prays for a bad harvest, and a want of employment, or, in other words, a redundant population.

In the earlier ages of the world, when war was the great business of mankind, and the drains of population from this cause were, beyond comparison, greater than in modern times, the legislators and statesmen of each country, adverting principally to the means of offence and defence, encouraged an increase of people in every possible way, fixed a stigma on barrenness and celibacy, and honoured marriage. The popular religions followed these prevailing opinions. In many countries, the prolifick power of nature was the object of solemn worship. In the religion of Mahomet, which was established by the sword, and the promulgation of which, in consequence, could not be unaccompanied by an extraordinary destruction of its followers, the procreation of children to glorify the Creator, was laid down as one of the principal duties of man; and he who had the most numerous offspring, was considered as having best answered the end of his creation. The prevalence of such moral sentiments had naturally a great effect in encouraging marriage; and the rapid procreation which followed, was partly the effect and partly the cause of incessant war. The vacancies occasioned by former desolations made room for the rearing of fresh supplies; and the overflowing rapidity, with which these supplies followed, constantly furnished fresh incitements and fresh instruments for renewed hostilities. Under the influence of such moral sentiments, it is difficult to conceive how the fury of incessant war should ever abate.

It is a pleasing confirmation of the truth and divinity of the Christian religion, and of its being adapted to a more improved state of human society, that it places our duties respecting marriage, and the procreation of children, in a different light from that in which they were before beheld.

Without entering minutely into the subject, which would evidently lead too far, I think it will be admitted, that if we apply the spirit of St. Paul's declarations respecting marriage, to the present state of society, and the known constitution of our nature, the natural inference seems to be, that when marriage does not interfere with higher duties, it is right; when it does, it is wrong. According to the genuine principles of moral science, "The method of coming at the will of God from the light of nature is to " inquire into the tendency of the action to promote or diminish the gen- " eral happiness."[3] There are perhaps few actions that tend so directly to diminish the general happiness, as to marry without the means of supporting children. He who commits this act, therefore, clearly offends against the will of God; and having become a burden on the society in which he lives, and plunged himself and family into a situation, in which virtuous habits are preserved with more difficulty than in any other, he appears to have violated his duty to his neighbours and to himself, and thus to have listened to the voice of passion in opposition to his higher obligations.

3. Paley's Moral Philosophy, vol. i. b. ii. c. iv. p. 65.

In a society, such as I have supposed, all the members of which endeavour to attain happiness by obedience to the moral code, derived from the light of nature, and enforced by strong sanctions in revealed religion, it is evident that no such marriages could take place; and the prevention of a redundant population, in this way, would remove one of the principal causes, and certainly the principal means of offensive war; and at the same time tend powerfully to eradicate those two fatal political disorders, internal tyranny and internal tumult, which mutually produce each other.

Weak in offensive war, in a war of defence, such a society would be strong as a rock of adamant. Where every family possessed the necessaries of life in plenty, and a decent portion of its comforts and conveniences, there could not exist that hope of change, or at best that melancholy and disheartening indifference to it, which sometimes prompts the lower classes of people to say, "let what will come, we cannot be worse off than we are " now." Every heart and hand would be united to repel an invader, when each individual felt the value of the solid advantages which he enjoyed, and a prospect of change presented only a prospect of being deprived of them.

As it appears, therefore, that it is in the power of each individual to avoid all the evil consequences to himself and society resulting from the principle of population, by the practice of a virtue clearly dictated to him by the light of nature, and expressly enjoined in revealed religion; and as we have reason to think that the exercise of this virtue to a certain degree, would rather tend to increase than diminish individual happiness; we can have no reason to impeach the justice of the Deity, because his general laws make this virtue necessary, and punish our offences against it by the evils attendant upon vice, and the pains that accompany the various forms of premature death. A really virtuous society, such as I have supposed, would avoid these evils. It is the apparent object of the Creator to deter us from vice by the pains which accompany it, and to lead us to virtue by the happiness that it produces. This object appears to our conceptions to be worthy of a benevolent Creator. The laws of nature respecting population, tend to promote this object. No imputation, therefore, on the benevolence of the Deity, can be founded on these laws, which is not equally applicable to any of the evils necessarily incidental to an imperfect state of existence.

C H A P .   III.

Of the only effectual mode of improving the condition of the Poor.

HE who publishes a moral code, or system of duties, however firmly he may be convinced of the strong obligation on each individual strictly to conform to it, has never the folly to imagine that it will be universally or even generally practised. But this is no valid objection against the publication of the code. If it were, the same objection would always have applied; we should be totally without general rules; and to the vices of mankind arising from temptation, would be added a much longer list, than we have at present, of vices from ignorance.

Judging merely from the light of nature, if we feel convinced of the misery arising from a redundant population, on the one hand, and of the evils and unhappiness, particularly to the female sex, arising from promiscuous intercourse, on the other, I do not see how it is possible for any person, who acknowledges the principle of utility as the great foundation of morals, to escape the conclusion that moral restraint, till we are in a condition to support a family, is the strict line of duty; and when revelation is taken into the question, this duty undoubtedly receives very powerful confirmation. At the same time, I believe that few of my readers can be less sanguine in their expectations of any great change in the general conduct of men on this subject than I am; and the chief reason, why, in the last chapter, I allowed myself to suppose the universal prevalence of this virtue, was, that I might endeavour to remove any imputation on the goodness of the Deity, by shewing that the evils arising from the principle of population were exactly of the same nature as the generality of other evils which excite fewer complaints, that they were increased by human ignorance and indolence, and diminished by human knowledge and virtue; and on the supposition, that each individual strictly fulfilled his duty, would be almost totally removed; and this, without any general diminution of those sources of pleasure, arising from the regulated indulgence of the passions, which have been justly considered as the principal ingredients of human happiness.

If it will answer any purpose of illustration, I see no harm in drawing the picture of a society in which each individual is supposed strictly to fulfil his duties; nor does a writer appear to be justly liable to the imputation of being visionary, unless he make such universal or general obedience necessary to the practical utility of his system, and to that degree of moderate and partial improvement, which is all that can rationally be expected from the most complete knowledge of our duties.

But in this respect, there is an essential difference between that improved state of society which I have supposed in the last chapter, and most of the other speculations on this subject. The improvement there supposed, if we ever should make approaches towards it, is to be effected in the way in which we have been in the habit of seeing all the greatest improvements effected, by a direct application to the interest and happiness of each individual. It is not required of us to act from motives, to which we are unaccustomed; to pursue a general good, which we may not distinctly comprehend, or the effect of which may be weakened by distance and diffusion. The happiness of the whole is to be the result of the happiness of individuals, and to begin first with them. No co-operation is required. Every step tells. He who persorms his duty faithfully will reap the full fruits of it, whatever may be the number of others who fail. This duty is express, and intelligible to the humblest capacity. It is merely that he is not to bring beings into the world for whom he cannot find the means of support. When once this subject is cleared from the obscurity thrown over it by parochial laws and private benevolence, every man must feel the strongest conviction of such an obligation. If he cannot support his children, they must starve; and if he marry in the face of a fair probability that he shall not be able to support his children, he is guilty of all the evils which he thus brings upon himself, his wife, and his offspring. It is clearly his interest, and will tend greatly to promote his happiness, to defer marrying, till, by industry and economy, he is in a capacity to support the children that he may reasonably expect from his marriage; and as he cannot in the mean time gratify his passions, without violating an express command of God, and running a great risk of injuring himself, or some of his fellow creatures, considerations of his own interest and happiness will dictate to him the strong obligation to moral restraint.

However powerful may be the impulses of passion, they are generally in some degree modified by reason. And it does not seem entirely visionary to suppose, that if the true and permanent cause of poverty were clearly explained, and forcibly brought home to each man's bosom, it would have some, and perhaps not an inconsiderable, influence on his conduct; at least, the experiment has never yet been fairly tried. Almost every thing that has been hitherto done for the poor, has tended, as if with solicitous care, to throw a veil of obscurity over this subject, and to hide from them the true cause of their poverty. When the wages of labour are hardly sufficient to maintain two children, a man marries and has five or six. He of course finds himself miserably distressed. He accuses the insufficiency of the price of labour to maintain a family. He accuses his parish for their tardy and sparing fulfilment of their obligation to assist him. He accuses the avarice of the rich, who suffer him to want what they can so well spare. He accuses the partial and unjust institutions of society, which have awarded him an inadequate share of the produce of the earth. He accuses perhaps the dispensations of Providence, which have assigned to him a place in society so beset with unavoidable distress and dependance. In searching for objects of accusation, he never adverts to the quarter from which all his misfortunes originate. The last person that he would think of accusing is himself, on whom, in fact, the whole of the blame lies, except in as far as he has been deceived by the higher classes of society. He may perhaps wish that he had not married, because he now feels the inconveniences of it; but it never enters into his head that he can have done any thing wrong. He has always been told that to raise up subjects for his king and country is a very meritorious act. He has done this act, and yet is suffering for it. He naturally thinks that he is suffering for righteousness sake; and it cannot but strike him as most extremely unjust and cruel in his king and country, to allow him thus to suffer, in return, for giving them what they are continually declaring that they particularly want.

Till these erroneous ideas have been corrected, and the language of nature and reason has been generally heard on the subject of population, instead of the language of error and prejudice, it cannot be said that any fair experiment has been made with the understandings of the common people; and we cannot justly accuse them of improvidence and want of industry, till they act as they do now, after it has been brought home to their comprehensions, that they are themselves the cause of their own poverty; that the means of redress are in their own hands, and in the hands of no other persons whatever; that the society in which they live, and the government which presides over it, are totally without power in this respect; and however ardently they may desire to relieve them, and whatever attempts they may make to do so, they are really and truly unable to execute what they benevolently wish, but unjustly promise; that when the wages of labour will not maintain a family, it is an incontrovertible sign that their king and country do not want more subjects, or at least that they cannot support them; that if they marry in this case, so far from fulfilling a duty to society, they are throwing a useless burden on it, at the same time that they are plunging themselves into distress; and that they are acting directly contrary to the will of God, and bringing down upon themselves various diseases, which might all, or in a great part, have been avoided, if they had attended to the repeated admonitions which he gives, by the general laws of nature, to every being capable of reason.

Dr. Paley, in his Moral Philosophy, observes, that "in countries in which " subsistence is become scarce, it behoves the state to watch over the " publick morals with increased solicitude; for nothing but the instinct of " nature, under the restraint of chastity, will induce men to undertake the " labour, or consent to the sacrifice of personal liberty and indulgence, " which the support of a family in such circumstances requires."[1] That it is always the duty of a state to use every exertion, likely to be effectual, in discouraging vice and promoting virtue, and that no temporary circumstances ought to cause any relaxation in these exertions, is certainly true. The means therefore proposed, are always good; but the particular end in view, in this case, appears to be absolutely criminal. We wish to force people into marriage, when, from the acknowledged scarcity of subsistence, they will have little chance of being able to support their children. We might as well force people into the water who are unable to swim. In both cases we rashly tempt Providence. Nor have we more reason to believe, that a miracle will be worked to save us from the misery and mortality resulting from our conduct, in the one case, than in the other.

The object of those who really wish to better the condition of the lower classes of society, must be, to raise the relative proportion between the price of labour and the price of provisions; so as to enable the labourer to command a larger share of the necessaries and comforts of life. We have hitherto principally attempted to attain this end, by encouraging the married poor, and consequently increasing the number of labourers, and overstocking the market with a commodity, which we still say that we wish to be dear. It would seem to have required no great spirit of divination to foretell the certain failure of such a plan of proceeding. There is nothing however, like experience. It has been tried in many different countries, and for many hundred years, and the success has always been answerable to the nature of the scheme. It is really time now to try something else.

When it was found, that oxygene, or pure vital air, would not cure consumptions, as was expected, but rather aggravated their symptoms; a trial was made of an air of the most opposite kind. I wish we had acted with the same philosophical spirit in our attempts to cure the disease of poverty; and having found that the pouring in of fresh supplies of labour, only tended to aggravate the symptoms, had tried what would be the effect of withholding a little these supplies.

1. Vol. ii. c, xi. p. 352.

In all old and fully-peopled states, it is from this method, and this alone, that we can rationally expect any essential and permanent amelioration in the condition of the lower classes of people.

In an endeavour to raise the proportion of the quantity of provisions to the number of consumers, in any country, our attention would naturally be first directed to the increasing of the absolute quantity of provisions; but finding that as fast as we did this, the number of consumers more than kept pace with it, and that, with all our exertions, we were still as far as ever behind, we should be convinced that our efforts, directed only in this way, would never succeed. It would appear to be setting the tortoise to catch the hare. Finding, therefore, that, from the laws of nature, we could not pro-portion the food to the population, our next attempt should naturally be to proportion the population to the food. If we can persuade the hare to go to sleep, the tortoise may have some chance of overtaking her.

We are not, however, to relax our efforts in increasing the quantity of provisions; but to combine another effort with it, that of keeping the popu-lation, when once it has been overtaken, at such a distance behind, as to effect the relative proportion which we desire; and thus unite the two grand desiderata, a great actual population, and a state of society in which squalid poverty and dependence are comparatively but little known; two objects which are far from being incompatible.

If we be really serious in what appears to be the object of such general research, the mode of essentially and permanently bettering the condition of the poor, we must explain to them the true nature of their situation, and show them, that the withholding of the supplies of labour is the only pos-sible way of really raising its price; and that they themselves being the pos-sessors of this commodity have alone the power to do this.

I cannot but consider this mode of diminishing poverty, as so perfectly clear in theory, and so invariably confirmed by the analogy of every other commodity that is brought to market, that nothing but its being shewn to be calculated to produce greater evils than it proposes to remedy, can justify us in not making the attempt to put it into execution.

CHAP. IV.

Objections to this mode considered.

ONE objection, which perhaps will be made to this plan, is that, from which alone it derives its value – a market rather understocked with labour. This must undoubtedly take place in a certain degree; but by no means in such a degree as to affect the wealth and prosperity of the country. The way in which we are going on at present, and the enormous increase in the price of provisions, which seems to threaten us, will tend much more effectually to enable foreigners to undersell us in the markets of Europe, than the plan now proposed. If the population of this country were better proportioned to its food, the nominal price of labour might be lower than it is now, and yet be sufficient to maintain a wife and six children. But putting this subject of a market understocked with labour, in the most unfavourable point of view, if the rich will not submit to a slight inconvenience necessarily attendant on the attainment of what they profess to desire, they cannot really be in earnest in their professions. Their benevolence to the poor, must be either childish play, or hypocrisy; it must be either to amuse themselves, or to pacify the minds of the common people with a mere shew of attention to their wants. To wish to better the condition of the poor, by enabling them to command a greater quantity of the necessaries and comforts of life, and then to complain of high wages, is the act of a silly boy who gives away his cake and then cries for it. A market overstocked with labour, and an ample remuneration to each labourer, are objects perfectly incompatible with each other. In the annals of the world they never existed together; and to couple them, even in imagination, betrays a gross ignorance of the simplest principles of political economy.

A second objection that may be made to this plan is, the diminution of population that it would cause. It is to be considered, however, that this diminution is merely relative; and when once this relative diminution had been effected, by keeping the population stationary, while the supply of food had increased, it might then start afresh, and continue increasing for ages, with the increase of food, maintaining always the same relative proportion to it. I can easily conceive, that this country with a proper direction of the national industry, might, in the course of some centuries, contain two or three times its present population, and yet, every man in the kingdom be much better fed and clothed than he is at present. While the springs of industry continue in vigour, and a sufficient part of that industry is directed to agriculture, we need be under no apprehensions of a deficient population; and nothing perhaps would tend so strongly to excite a spirit of industry and economy among the poor, as a thorough knowledge that their happiness must always depend principally upon themselves; and that if they obey their passions in opposition to their reason, or be not industrious and frugal while they are single men, to save a sum for the common contingencies of the married state, they must expect to suffer the natural evils which Providence has prepared for those who disobey its repeated admonitions.

A third objection which may be started to this plan, and the only one which appears to me to have any kind of plausibility, is, that, by endeavouring to urge the duty of moral restraint on the poor, we may increase the quantity of vice relating to the sex.

I should be most extremely sorry to say any thing which could, either directly or remotely be construed unfavourably to the cause of virtue: but I certainly cannot think that the vices which relate to the sex, are the only vices which are to be considered in a moral question; or that they are even the greatest and most degrading to the human character. They can rarely or never be committed without producing unhappiness somewhere or other, and therefore ought always to be strongly reprobated; but there are other vices, the effects of which are still more pernicious; and there are other situations, which lead more certainly to moral offences than the refraining from marriage. Powerful as may be the temptations to a breach of chastity, I am inclined to think that they are impotent, in comparison of the temptations arising from continued distress. A large class of women, and many men, I have no doubt, pass a considerable part of their lives in moral restraint; but I believe there will be found very few, who pass through the ordeal of squalid and hopeless poverty, or even of long continued embarrassed circumstances, without a considerable moral degradation of character.

In the higher and middle classes of society, it is a melancholy and distressing sight to observe, not unfrequently, a man of a noble and ingenuous disposition, once feelingly alive to a sense of honour and integrity, gradually sinking under the pressure of circumstances, making his excuses at first, with a blush of conscious shame, afraid of seeing the faces of his friends from whom he may have borrowed money, reduced to the meanest tricks and subterfuges, to delay or avoid the payment of his just debts; till ultimately grown familiar with falsehood, and at enmity with the world, he loses all the grace and dignity of man.

To the general prevalence of indigence, and the extraordinary encouragements which we afford in this country to a total want of foresight and prudence among the common people,[1] is to be attributed the principal part of those continual depredations on property, and other more atrocious crimes, which drive us to the painful resource of such a number of executions.[2] According to Mr. Colquhoun, above twenty thousand miserable individuals of various classes, rise up every morning, without knowing how, or by what means, they are to be supported during the passing day; or where, in many instances, they are to lodge on the succeeding night.[3] It is by these unhappy persons that the principal depredations on the public are committed; and, supposing but few of them to be married and driven to these acts, from the necessity of supporting their children; yet still it will not cease to be true, that the too great frequency of marriage among the poorest classes, is one of the principal causes of the temptations to these crimes. A considerable part of these unhappy wretches will probably be found to be the offspring of such marriages, educated in workhouses, where every vice is propagated, or bred up at home in filth and rags, and with an utter ignorance of every moral obligation.[4] A still greater part, perhaps, consists of persons, who, being unable for some time to get employment, owing to the full supply of labour, have been urged to these extremities by their temporary wants, and having thus lost their characters, are rejected, even when their labour may be wanted, by the well-founded caution of civil society.[5]

1. Mr. Colquhoun, speaking of the poor laws, observes, that, "in spite of all the
" ingenious arguments which have been used in favour of a system, admitted to be
" wisely conceived in its origin, the effects it has produced incontestably prove,
" that, with respect to the mass of the poor, there is something radically wrong in
" the execution. If it were not so, it is impossible that there could exist in the me-
" tropolis such an inconceivable portion of human misery amidst examples of mu-
" nificence and benevolence unparallelled in any age or country." Police of Metropolis, c. xiii. p. 359.

In the effects of the poor laws, I fully agree with Mr. Colquhoun; but I cannot agree with him in admitting that the system was well conceived in its origin. I attribute still more evil to the original ill conception, than to the subsequent ill execution.

2. Mr. Colquhoun observes, that, "Indigence, in the present state of society, may
" be considered as a principal cause of the increase of crimes." Police of Metropolis, c. xiii. p. 352.

3. Id. c. xi. p. 313.   4. Ibid. and c. xii. p. 355, 370.

5. Police of the Metropolis, c. xiii. p. 353. et seq. In so large a town as London, which must necessarily encourage a prodigious influx of strangers from the country, there must be always a great many persons out of work; and it is possible that some publick institution for the relief of the casual poor, upon a plan similar to that proposed by Mr. Colquhoun, (c. xiii. p. 371.) might, under very judicious management, produce more good than evil. But, for this purpose, it would be absolutely necessary, that if work were provided by the institution, the sum that a man could

When indigence does not produce overt acts of vice, it palsies every virtue. Under the continued temptations to a breach of chastity, occasional failures may take place, and the moral sensibility, in other respects, not be very strikingly impaired; but the continued temptations which beset hopeless poverty, and the strong sense of injustice that generally accompanies it from an ignorance of its true cause, tend so powerfully to sour the disposition, to harden the heart, and deaden the moral sense, that, generally speaking, virtue takes her flight clear away from the tainted spot, and does not often return.

Even with respect to the vices which relate to the sex, marriage has been found to be by no means a complete remedy. Among the higher classes, our Doctors Commons, and the lives that many married men are known to lead, sufficiently prove this; and the same kind of vice, though not so much heard of among the lower classes of people, owing to their indifference and want of delicacy on these subjects, is probably not very much less frequent.

Add to this, that squalid poverty, particularly when joined with idleness, is a state the most unfavourable to chastity that can well be conceived. The passion is as strong, or nearly so, as in other situations, and every restraint on it, from personal respect, or a sense of morality, is generally removed. There is a degree of squalid poverty, in which, if a girl was brought up, I should say that her being really modest at twenty was an absolute miracle. Those persons must have extraordinary minds indeed, and such as are not

---

earn by it, should be less than the worst paid common labour; otherwise the claimants would rapidly increase, and the funds would soon be inadequate to their object. In the institution at Hamburgh, which appears to have been the most successful of any yet established, the nature of the work was such, that, though paid above the usual price, a person could not easily earn by it, more than eighteen pence a week. It was the determined principle of the managers of the institution to reduce the support which they gave, lower than what any industrious man or woman in such circumstances could earn. (Account of the management of the poor in Hamburgh, by C. Voght, p. 18.) And it is to this principle that they attribute their success. It should be observed, however, that neither the institution at Hamburgh, nor that planned by Count Rumford in Bavaria, has subsisted long enough for us to be able to pronounce on their permanent good effects. It will not admit of a doubt that institutions for the relief of the poor, on their first establishment, remove a great quantity of distress. The only question is, whether, as succeeding generations arise, the increasing funds necessary for their support, and the increasing numbers that become dependent, are not greater evils, than that, which was to be remedied; and whether the country will not ultimately be left with as much mendicity as before, besides all the poverty and dependence accumulated in the publick institutions. This seems to be nearly the case in England at present. I do not believe that we should have more beggars, if we had no poor laws.

usually formed under similar circumstances, who can continue to respect themselves, when no other person whatever respects them. If the children thus brought up were even to marry at twenty, it is probable that they would have passed some years in vicious habits, before that period.

If after all, however, these arguments should appear insufficient; if we reprobate the idea of endeavouring to encourage the virtues of moral restraint and prudence among the poor, from a fear of producing vice; and if we think that to facilitate marriage by all possible means is a point of the first consequence to the morality and happiness of the people; let us act consistently, and, before we proceed, endeavour to make ourselves acquainted with the mode by which alone we can effect our object.

CHAP. V.

Of the consequences of pursuing the opposite mode.

It is an evident truth, that whatever is the state of increase in the means of subsistence, the increase of population must be limited by it, at least after the food has once been divided into the smallest shares that will support life. All the children born, beyond what would be required to keep up the population to this level, must necessarily perish, unless room be made for them by the deaths of grown persons. It has appeared, indeed, clearly in the course of this work, that in all old states, the marriages and births depend principally upon the deaths, and that there is no encouragement to early unions so powerful as a great mortality. To act consistently, therefore, we should facilitate, instead of foolishly and vainly endeavouring to impede, the operations of nature, in producing this mortality; and if we dread the too frequent visitation of the horrid form of famine, we should sedulously encourage the other forms of destruction which we compel nature to use. Instead of recommending cleanliness to the poor, we should encourage contrary habits. In our towns, we should make the streets narrower, crowd more people into the houses, and court the return of the plague. In the country, we should build our villages near stagnant pools, and particularly encourage settlements in all marshy and unwholesome situations.[1] But above all, we should reprobate specific remedies for ravaging diseases, and those benevolent, but much mistaken men, who have thought they were doing a service to mankind by projecting schemes for the total extirpation of particular disorders. If by these, and similar means, the annual mortality were increased from 1 in 36 or 40, to 1 in 18 or 20, we might, probably, every one of us marry at the age of puberty, and yet few be absolutely starved.

1. Necker, speaking of the proportion of the births in France, makes use of a new and instructive expression on this subject, though he hardly seems to be sufficiently aware of it himself. He says "Le nombre des naissances est a celui des habitans de " un a vingttrois et vingt-quatre dans les lieux *contrariés par la nature, ou par des* " *circonstances morales:* ce meme rapport dans la plus grande partie de la France, " est de un a 25, 25$\frac{1}{2}$, & 26." Administ. des Finances, tom. i. c. ix. p. 254. 12mo. It would appear, therefore, that we had nothing more to do, than to settle people in marshy situations, and oppress them by a bad government, in order to attain what politicians have hitherto considered as so desireable—a great proportion of marriages, and a great proportion of births.

If however, we all marry at this age, and yet still continue our exertions to impede the operations of nature, we may rest assured that all our efforts will be vain. Nature will not, nor cannot be defeated in her purposes. The necessary mortality must come, in some form or other; and the extirpation of one disease will only be the signal for the birth of another, perhaps more fatal. We cannot lower the waters of misery by pressing them down in different places which must necessarily make them rise somewhere else: the only way in which we can hope to effect our purpose is by drawing them off. To this course nature is constantly directing our attention by the chastisements which await a contrary conduct. These chastisements are more or less severe, in proportion to the degree in which her admonitions produce their intended effect. In this country, at present, these admonitions are by no means entirely neglected. The preventive check to population prevails to a considerable degree, and her chastisements are, in consequence, moderate: but if we were all to marry at the age of puberty, they would be severe indeed. Political evils would probably be added to physical. A people goaded by constant distress, and visited by frequent returns of famine, could not be kept down but by a cruel despotism. We should approach to the state of the people in Egypt or Abyssinia; and I would ask, whether, in that case, it is probable that we should be more virtuous?

Physicians have long remarked the great changes which take place in diseases; and that, while some appear to yield to the efforts of human care and skill, others seem to become, in proportion, more malignant and fatal. Dr. William Heberden published not long since, some valuable observations on this subject deduced from the London bills of mortality. In his preface, speaking of these bills, he says, "the gradual changes they exhibit in particu-
" lar diseases correspond to the alterations which in time are known to take
" place, in the channels through which the great stream of mortality is
" constantly flowing."[2] In the body of his work afterwards, speaking of some particular diseases, he observes with that candour which always distinguishes true science: "It is not easy to give a satisfactory reason for all the
" changes which may be observed to take place in the history of diseases.
" Nor is it any disgrace to physicians, if their causes are often so gradual
" in their operation, or so subtle, as to elude investigation."[3]

I hope I shall not be accused of presumption, in venturing to suggest, that, under certain circumstances, such changes must take place; and perhaps without any alteration in those proximate causes which are usually

2. Observations on the Increase and Decrease of different Diseases. Preface, p. v. 4to. 1801.   3. Id. p. 43.

looked to on these occasions. If this should appear to be true, it will not seem extraordinary that the most skilful and scientific physicians, whose business it is principally to investigate proximate causes, should sometimes search for these causes in vain.

In a country which keeps its population at a certain standard, if the average number of marriages and births be given, it is evident, that the average number of deaths will also be given; and, to use Dr. Heberden's metaphor, the channels through which the great stream of mortality is constantly flowing, will always convey off a given quantity. Now if we stop up any of these channels, it is most perfectly clear, that the stream of mortality must run with greater force through some of the other channels; that is, if we eradicate some diseases, others will become proportionally more fatal. In this case the only distinguishable cause is the damming up a necessary outlet of mortality.[4] Nature, in the attainment of her great purposes, seems always to seize upon the weakest part. If this part be made strong by human skill, she seizes upon the next weakest part, and so on in succession; not like a capricious deity, with an intention to sport with our sufferings, and constantly to defeat our labours; but like a kind though sometimes severe instructor, with the intention of teaching us to make all parts strong, and to chace vice and misery from the earth. In avoiding one fault we are too apt to run into some other; but we always find nature faithful to her great object, at every false step we commit, ready to admonish us of our errors, by the infliction of some physical or moral evil. If the prevalence of the preventive check to population, in a sufficient degree, were to remove many of those diseases which now afflict us, yet be accompanied by a considerable increase of the vice of promiscuous intercourse; it is probable that the disorders and unhappiness, the physical and moral evils arising from this vice, would increase in strength and degree, and, admonishing us severely of our error, would point to the only line of conduct approved by nature, reason, and religion, abstinence from marriage till we can support our children, and chastity till that period arrives.

In the case just stated, in which the population and the number of marriages are supposed to be fixed, the necessity of a change in the mortality of some diseases, from the diminution or extinction of others, is capable of mathematical demonstration. The only obscurity which can possibly involve this subject, arises from taking into consideration the effect that might be produced by a diminution of mortality, in increasing the population, or

4. The way in which it operates is probably by increasing poverty, in consequence of a supply of labour too rapid for the demand.

in decreasing the number of marriages. That the removal of any of the particular causes of mortality can have no further effect upon population, than the means of subsistence will allow; and that it has little or no influence on these means of subsistence, is a fact, of which, I hope, the reader is already convinced. Of its operation in tending to prevent marriage, by diminishing the demand for fresh supplies of children, I have no doubt; and there is reason to think that it had this effect, in no inconsiderable degree, on the extinction of the plague, which had so long and so dreadfully ravaged this country. Dr. Heberden draws a striking picture of the favourable change observed in the health of the people of England since this period; and justly attributes it to the improvements which have gradually taken place, not only in London, but in all great towns; and in the manner of living throughout the kingdom, particularly with respect to cleanliness and ventilation.[5] But these causes would not have been adequate to the effect observed, if they had not been accompanied by an increase of the preventive check; and, probably, the spirit of cleanliness, and better mode of living, which then began to prevail, by spreading more generally a decent and useful pride, principally contributed to this increase. The diminution in the number of marriages, however, was not sufficient to make up for the great decrease of mortality, from the extinction of the plague, and the striking reduction of the deaths in the dysentery.[6] While these, and some other disorders, became almost evanescent, consumption, palsy, apoplexy, gout, lunacy, and the small-pox, became more mortal.[7] The widening of these drains was necessary to carry off the population which still remained redundant, notwithstanding the increased operation of the preventive check, and the part which was annually disposed of, and enabled to exist, by the increase of agriculture.

Dr. Haygarth, in the sketch of his benevolent plan for the extermination of the casual small-pox, draws a frightful picture of the mortality which has been occasioned by this distemper; attributes to it the slow progress of population; and makes some curious calculations on the favourable effects which would be produced, in this respect, by its extermination.[8] His conclusions, however, I fear, would not follow from his premises. I am far from doubting that millions and millions of human beings have been destroyed by the small-pox. But were its devastations, as Dr. Haygarth supposes, many thousand degrees greater than the plague,[9] I should still doubt whether the average population of the earth had been diminished by them

5. Observ. on Inc. and Dec. of Diseases, p. 35.   6. Id. p. 34.

7. Id. p. 36. et seq.   8. Vol. i. part ii. sect. v. and vi.   9. Id. s. viii. p. 164.

a single unit. The small-pox is certainly one of the channels, and a very broad one, which nature has opened for the last thousand years, to keep down the population to the level of the means of subsistence; but had this been closed, others would have become wider, or new ones would have been formed. In antient times the mortality from war and the plague, was incomparably greater than in modern. On the gradual diminution of this stream of mortality, the generation, and almost universal prevalence, of the small-pox is a great and striking instance, of one of those changes in the channels of mortality, which ought to awaken our attention, and animate us to patient and persevering investigation. For my own part, I feel not the slightest doubt, that, if the introduction of the cow-pox should extirpate the small-pox, and yet the number of marriages continue the same, we shall find a very perceptible difference in the increased mortality of some other diseases. Nothing could prevent this effect, but a sudden start in our agriculture; and should this take place, which I fear we have not much reason to expect, it will not be owing to the number of children saved from death by the cow-pox inoculation, but to the alarms occasioned among the people of property by the late scarcities, and to the increased gains of farmers, which have been so absurdly reprobated. I am strongly, however, inclined to believe, that the number of marriages will not, in this case, remain the same; but that the gradual light which may be expected to be thrown, on this interesting topic of human inquiry, will teach us how to make the extinction of a mortal disorder, a real blessing to us, a real improvement in the general health and happiness of the society.

If, on contemplating the increase of vice which might contingently follow an attempt to inculcate the duty of moral restraint, and the increase of misery that must necessarily follow the attempts to encourage marriage and population, we come to the conclusion, not to interfere in any respect, but to leave every man to his own free choice, and responsible only to God for the evil which he does, in either way; this is all I contend for; I would on no account do more; but I contend that at present we are very far from doing this.

Among the lower classes, where the point is of the greatest importance, the poor laws afford a direct, constant, and systematical encouragement to marriage, by removing from each individual that heavy responsibility, which he would incur by the laws of nature, for bringing beings into the world which he could not support. Our private benevolence has the same direction as the poor laws, and almost invariably tends to facilitate the rearing of families, and to equalize, as much possible, the circumstances of married and single men.

Among the higher classes of people, the superior distinctions which married women receive, and the marked inattentions to which single women of advanced age are exposed, enable many men, who are neither agreeable in mind or person, and are besides in the wane of life, to choose a partner among the young and fair instead of being confined, as nature seems to dictate, to persons of nearly their own age and accomplishments. It is scarcely to be doubted, that the fear of being an old maid, and of that silly and unjust ridicule, which folly sometimes attaches to this name, drives many women into the marriage union, with men whom they dislike, or, at best, to whom they are perfectly indifferent. Such marriages must to every delicate mind appear little better than legal prostitutions; and they often burden the earth with unnecessary children, without compensating for it by any accession of happiness and virtue to the parties themselves.

Throughout all the ranks of society, the prevailing opinions respecting the duty and obligation of marriage, cannot but have a very powerful influence. The man who thinks that in going out of the world without leaving representatives behind him, he shall have failed in an important duty to society, will be disposed to force, rather than to repress, his inclinations on this subject; and when his reason represents to him the difficulties attending a family, he will endeavour not to attend to these suggestions, will still determine to venture, and will hope that, in the discharge of what he conceives to be his duty, he shall not be deserted by Providence.

In a civilized country, such as England, where a taste for the decencies and comforts of life prevail among a very large class of people, it is not possible that the encouragements to marriage from positive institutions and prevailing opinions, should entirely obscure the light of nature and reason on this subject; but still they contribute to make it comparatively weak and indistinct. And till this obscurity is entirely removed, and the poor are undeceived with respect to the principal cause of their past poverty, and taught to know that their future happiness or misery must depend chiefly upon themselves, it cannot be said, that, with regard to the great question of marriage, or celibacy, we leave every man to his own free and fair choice.

CHAP. VI.

Effect of the knowledge of the principal
cause of poverty on Civil Liberty.

IT may appear, perhaps, that a doctrine, which attributes the greatest part
of the sufferings of the lower classes of society exclusively to themselves,
is unfavourable to the cause of liberty; as affording a tempting opportunity to governments of oppressing their subjects at pleasure, and laying
the whole blame on the laws of nature and the imprudence of the poor.
We are not, however, to trust to first appearances; and I am strongly disposed to believe, that those who will be at the pains to consider this subject
deeply, will be convinced, that nothing would so powerfully contribute to
the advancement of rational freedom, as a thorough knowledge generally
circulated, of the principal cause of poverty; and that the ignorance of this
cause, and the natural consequences of this ignorance, form, at present, one
of the chief obstacles to its progress.

The pressure of distress on the lower classes of people, with the habit
of attributing this distress to their rulers, appears to me to be the rock of
defence, the castle, the guardian spirit, of despotism. It affords to the tyrant
the fatal and unanswerable plea of necessity. It is the reason that every
free government tends constantly to its destruction; and that its appointed
guardians become daily less jealous of the encroachments of power. It is
the reason that so many noble efforts in the cause of freedom have failed,
and that almost every revolution, after long and painful sacrifices, has terminated in a military despotism. While any dissatisfied man of talents has
power to persuade the lower classes of people, that all their poverty and
distress arise solely from the iniquity of the government, though perhaps
the greatest part of what they suffer is totally unconnected with this cause,
it is evident that the seeds of fresh discontents, and fresh revolutions, are
continually sowing. When an established government has been destroyed,
finding that their poverty is not removed, their resentment naturally falls
upon the successors to power; and when these have been immolated without producing the desired effect, other sacrifices are called for, and so on
without end. Are we to be surprised, that, under such circumstances, the
majority of well-disposed people, finding that a government, with proper
restrictions, was unable to support itself against the revolutionary spirit,
and weary and exhausted with perpetual change, to which they could see

no end, should give up the struggle in despair, and throw themselves into the arms of the first power which could afford them protection against the horrors of anarchy.

A mob, which is generally the growth of a redundant population, goaded by resentment for real sufferings, but totally ignorant of the quarter from which they originate, is, of all monsters, the most fatal to freedom. It fosters a prevailing tyranny, and engenders one where it was not; and though, in its dreadful fits of resentment, it appears occasionally to devour its unsightly offspring; yet no sooner is the horrid deed committed, than, however unwilling it may be to propagate such a breed, it immediately groans with the pangs of a new birth.

Of the tendency of mobs to produce tyranny, we may not be long without an example in this country. As a friend to freedom, and an enemy to large standing armies, it is with extreme reluctance that I am compelled to acknowledge, that, had it not been for the organized force in the country, the distresses of the people during the late scarcities, encouraged by the extreme ignorance and folly of many among the higher classes, might have driven them to commit the most dreadful outrages, and ultimately to involve the country in all the horrors of famine. Should such periods often recur, a recurrence which we have too much reason to apprehend from the present state of the country, the prospect which opens to our view is melancholy in the extreme. The English constitution will be seen hastening with rapid strides to the *Euthanasia* foretold by Hume; unless its progress be interrupted by some popular commotion; and this alternative presents a picture still more appalling to the imagination. If political discontents were blended with the cries of hunger, and a revolution were to take place by the instrumentality of a mob, clamouring for want of food, the consequences would be unceasing change, and unceasing carnage, the bloody career of which, nothing but the establishment of some complete despotism could arrest.

We can scarcely believe that the appointed guardians of British liberty should quietly have acquiesced in those gradual encroachments of power, which have taken place of late years, but from the apprehension of these still more dreadful evils. Great as has been the influence of corruption, I cannot yet think so meanly of the country gentlemen of England, as to believe that they would thus have given up a part of their birthright of liberty, if they had not been actuated by a real and genuine fear, that it was then in greater danger from the people, than from the crown. They appeared to surrender themselves to government on condition of being protected from the mob; but they never would have made this melancholy and disheartening surrender, if such a mob had not existed either in reality or in imagination. That the fears on this subject were artfully exaggerated, and increased beyond the limits of just apprehension, is undeniable; but I think it is also undeniable, that the frequent declamation which was heard against the unjust institutions of society, and the delusive arguments on equality which were circulated among the lower classes, gave us just reason to suppose, that if the *vox populi* had been allowed to speak, it would have appeared to be the voice of error and absurdity, instead of the *vox Dei.*

To say that our conduct is not to be regulated by circumstances, is to betray an ignorance of the most solid and incontrovertible principles of morality. Though the admission of this principle may sometimes afford a cloke to changes of opinion that do not result from the purest motives; yet the admission of a contrary principle would be productive of infinitely worse consequences. The phrase of existing circumstances has, I believe, not unfrequently created a smile in the English House of Commons; but the smile should have been reserved for the application of the phrase, and not have been excited by the phrase itself. A very frequent repetition of it, has indeed, of itself, rather a suspicious air; and its application should always be watched with the most jealous and anxious attention; but no man ought to be judged *in limine* for saying, that existing circumstances had obliged him to alter his opinions and conduct. The country gentlemen were perhaps too easily convinced that existing circumstances called upon them to give up some of the most valuable privileges of Englishmen; but, as far as they were really convinced of this obligation, they acted consistently with the clearest rule of morality.

The degree of power to be given to the civil government, and the measure of our submission to it, must be determined by general expediency; and in judging of this expediency, every circumstance is to be taken into consideration; particularly, the state of publick opinion, and the degree of ignorance and delusion prevailing among the common people. The patriot, who might be called upon by the love of his country, to join with heart and hand in a rising of the people for some specifick attainable object or reform, if he knew that they were enlightened respecting their own situation, and would stop short when they had attained their demand; would be called upon by the same motive, to submit to very great oppression, rather than give the slightest countenance to a popular tumult, the members of which, at least the greater number of them, were persuaded, that the destruction of the Parliament, the Lord Mayor, and the monopolizers, would make bread cheap, and that a revolution would enable them all to support their families. In this case, it is more the ignorance and delusion of the lower classes of people that occasions the oppression, than the actual disposition of the government to tyranny.

That there is, however, in all power a constant tendency to encroach is an incontrovertible truth, and cannot be too strongly inculcated. The checks which are necessary to secure the liberty of the subject, will always, in some degree, embarrass and delay the operations of the executive government. The members of this government feeling these inconveniences, while they are exerting themselves, as they conceive, in the service of their country, and conscious, perhaps, of no ill intention towards the people, will naturally be disposed, on every occasion, to demand the suspension or abolition of these checks; but if once the convenience of ministers be put into competition with the liberties of the people, and we get into a habit of relying on fair assurances, and personal character, instead of examining, with the most scrupulous and jealous care, the merits of each particular case, there is an end of British freedom. If we once admit the principle that the government must know better with regard to the quantity of power which it wants, than we can possibly do with our limited means of information, and that therefore, it is our duty to surrender up our private judgments, we may just as well, at the same time, surrender up the whole of our constitution. Government is a quarter in which liberty is not, nor cannot be, very faithfully preserved. If we are wanting to ourselves, and inattentive to our great interests in this respect, it is the height of folly and unreasonableness, to expect that government will attend to them for us. Should the British constitution ultimately lapse into a despotism, as has been prophesied, I shall think that the country gentlemen of England will have really much more to answer for than the ministers.

To do the country gentlemen justice, however, I should readily acknowledge, that, in the partial desertion of their posts as guardians of British freedom, which has already taken place, they have been actuated more by fear than treachery. And the principal reason of this fear was, I conceive, the ignorance and delusions of the common people, and the prospective horrors which were contemplated, if, in such a state of mind, they should, by any revolutionary movement, obtain an ascendant.

The circulation of Paine's Rights of Man, it is supposed, has done great mischief among the lower and middling classes of people in this country. This is probably true; but not because man is without rights, or that these rights ought not to be known; but because Mr. Paine has fallen into some fundamental errors respecting the principles of government, and in many important points has shewn himself totally unacquainted with the structure of society, and the different moral effects to be expected from the physical difference between this country and America. Mobs, of the same description as those collections of people known by this name in Europe, could not exist in America. The number of people without property, is, there, from the physical state of the country, comparatively small; and therefore the civil power which is to protect property, cannot require the same degree of strength. Mr. Paine very justly observes, that whatever the apparent cause of any riots may be, the real one is always want of happiness; but when he goes on to say, it shews that something is wrong in the system of government, that injures the felicity by which society is to be preserved, he falls into the common error of attributing all want of happiness to government. It is evident, that this want of happiness might have existed, and from ignorance might have been the principal cause of the riots, and yet be almost wholly unconnected with any of the proceedings of government. The redundant population of an old state furnishes materials of unhappiness, unknown to such a state as that of America; and if an attempt were to be made to remedy this unhappiness, by distributing the produce of the taxes to the poorer classes of society, according to the plan proposed by Mr. Paine, the evil would be aggravated a hundred fold, and in a very short time, no sum that the society could possibly raise, would be adequate to the proposed object.

Nothing would so effectually counteract the mischiefs occasioned by Mr. Paine's Rights of Man, as a general knowledge of the real rights of man. What these rights are, it is not my business at present to explain; but there is one right, which man has generally been thought to possess, which I am confident he neither does, nor can, possess, a right to subsistence when his labour will not fairly purchase it. Our laws indeed say, that he has this right and bind the society to furnish employment and food to those who cannot get them in the regular market; but in so doing, they attempt to reverse the laws of nature; and it is, in consequence, to be expected, not only that they should fail in their object, but that the poor who were intended to be benefited, should suffer most cruelly from this inhuman deceit which is practised upon them.

A man who is born into a world already possessed, if he cannot get subsistence from his parents on whom he has a just demand, and if the society do not want his labour, has no claim of *right* to the smallest portion of food, and, in fact, has no business to be where he is. At nature's mighty feast there is no vacant cover for him. She tells him to be gone, and will quickly execute her own orders, if he do not work upon the compassion of some of her guests. If these guests get up and make room for him, other intruders immediately appear demanding the same favour. The report of a provision for all that come, fills the hall with numerous claimants. The order and harmony of the feast is disturbed, the plenty that before reigned is changed into scarcity; and the happiness of the guests is destroyed by the spectacle of misery and dependence in every part of the hall, and by the clamorous importunity of those, who are justly enraged at not finding the provision which they had been taught to expect. The guests learn too late their error, in counteracting those strict orders to all intruders, issued by the great mistress of the feast, who, wishing that all her guests should have plenty, and knowing that she could not provide for unlimited numbers, humanely refused to admit fresh comers when her table was already full.

The Abbé Raynal has said, that "Avant toutes les loix sociales, l'homme " avoit le droit de subsister."[1] He might with just as much propriety have said, that, before the institution of social laws, every man had a right to live a hundred years. Undoubtedly he had then, and has still, a good right to live a hundred years, nay, a thousand, *if he can*, without interfering with the right of others to live; but the affair, in both cases, is principally an affair of power, not of right. Social laws very greatly increase this power, by enabling a much greater number to subsist, than could subsist without them, and so far very greatly enlarge *le droit de subsister;* but neither before nor after the institution of social laws, could an unlimited number subsist; and before, as well as since, he who ceased to have the power, ceased to have the right.

If the great truths on these subjects were more generally circulated, and the lower classes of people could be convinced, that, by the laws of nature, independently of any particular institutions, except the great one of property which is absolutely necessary in order to attain any considerable produce, no person has any claim of right on society for subsistence, if his labour will not purchase it, the greatest part of the mischievous declamation on the unjust institutions of society would fall powerless to the ground. The poor are by no means inclined to be visionary. Their distresses are always real, though they are not attributed to the real causes. If these real causes were properly explained to them, and they were taught to know how small a part of their present distress was attributable to government, and how great a part to causes totally unconnected with it, discontent and irritation among the lower classes of people would shew themselves much less frequently than at present; and when they did shew themselves, would be much less to be dreaded. The efforts of turbulent and discontented men in the middle classes of society, might safely be disregarded, if the poor

1. Raynal, Hist. des Indes, vol. x. s. x. p. 322. 8vo.

were so far enlightened respecting the real nature of their situation, as to be aware, that by aiding them in their schemes of renovation, they would probably be promoting the ambitious views of others, without, in any respect, benefiting themselves. And the country gentlemen, and men of property in England, might securely return to a wholesome jealousy of the encroachments of power; and, instead of daily sacrificing the liberties of the subject, on the altar of publick safety, might, without any just apprehension from the people, not only tread back all their late steps, but firmly insist upon those gradual reforms, which the lapse of time, and the storms of circumstances, have rendered necessary, to prevent the gradual destruction of the British constitution.

All improvements in government must necessarily originate with persons of some education, and these will of course be found among the people of property. Whatever may be said of a few, it is impossible to suppose that the great mass of the people of property should be really interested in the abuses of government. They merely submit to them, from the fear, that an endeavour to remove them, might be productive of greater evils. Could we but take away this fear, reform and improvement would proceed with as much facility, as the removal of nuisances, or the paving and lighting the streets. In human life we are continually called upon, to submit to a lesser evil, in order to avoid a greater; and it is the part of a wise man to do this readily and cheerfully; but no wise man will submit to any evil, if he can get rid of it, without danger. Remove all apprehension from the tyranny or folly of the people, and the tyranny of government could not stand a moment. It would then appear in its proper deformity, without palliation, without pretext, without protector. Naturally feeble in itself, when it was once stripped naked, and deprived of the support of publick opinion, and of the great plea of necessity, it would fall without a struggle. Its few interested defenders would hide their heads abashed; and would be ashamed any longer to advocate a cause for which no human ingenuity could invent a plausible argument.

The most successful supporters of tyranny are without doubt those general declaimers, who attribute the distresses of the poor, and almost all the evils to which society is subject, to human institutions and the iniquity of governments. The falsity of these accusations, and the dreadful consequences that would result from their being generally admitted and acted upon, make it absolutely necessary that they should at all events be resisted; not only on account of the immediate revolutionary horrors to be expected from a movement of the people acting under such impressions, a consideration which must at all times have very great weight; but on account of the extreme probability that such a revolution would terminate in a much worse despotism, than that which it had destroyed. On these grounds, a genuine friend of freedom, a zealous advocate for the real rights of man, might be found among the defenders of a considerable degree of tyranny. A cause bad in itself, might be supported by the good and the virtuous, merely because that which was opposed to it was much worse; and at the moment it was absolutely necessary to make a choice between the two. Whatever therefore may be the intention of those indiscriminate and wholesale accusations against governments, their real effect undoubtedly is, to add a weight of talents and principles to the prevailing power which it never would have received otherwise.

It is a truth, which I trust has been sufficiently proved in the course of this work, that, under a government constructed upon the best and purest principles, and executed by men of the highest talents and integrity, the most squalid poverty and wretchedness might universally prevail from the principle of population alone. And as this cause of unhappiness has hitherto been so little understood, that the efforts of society have always tended rather to aggravate than to lessen it, we have the strongest reasons for supposing, that, in all the governments with which we are acquainted, a very great part of the misery to be observed among the lower classes of the people, arises from this cause.

The inference, therefore, which Mr. Paine and others have drawn against governments from the unhappiness of the people, is palpably unfair; and before we give a sanction to such accusations, it is a debt we owe to truth and justice, to ascertain how much of this unhappiness arises from the principle of population, and how much is fairly to be attributed to government. When this distinction has been properly made, and all the vague, indefinite, and false accusations removed, government would remain, as it ought to be, clearly responsible for the rest. A tenfold weight would be immediately given to the cause of the people, and every man of principle would join in asserting and enforcing, if necessary, their rights.

I may be deceived; but I confess that if I were called to name the cause, which, in my conception, had more than any other contributed to the very slow progress of freedom, so disheartening to every liberal mind, I should say that it was the confusion that had existed, respecting the causes of the unhappiness and discontents which prevail in society; and the advantage which governments had been able to take, and indeed had been compelled to take, of this confusion, to confirm and strengthen their power. I cannot help thinking, therefore, that a knowledge generally circulated, that the principal cause of want and unhappiness is unconnected with government, and totally beyond its power to remove; and that it depends upon the conduct of the poor themselves; would, instead of giving any advantage to governments, give a great additional weight to the popular side of the question, by removing the dangers with which, from ignorance, it is at present accompanied; and thus tend, in a very powerful manner, to promote the cause of rational freedom.

CHAP. VII.

Plan of the gradual abolition of the Poor Laws proposed.

IF the principles in the preceding chapters should stand the test of examination, and we should ever feel the obligation of endeavouring to act
upon them, the next inquiry would be, in what way we ought practically to
proceed. The first grand obstacle which presents itself in this country, is the
system of the poor laws, which has been justly stated to be an evil, in comparison of which, the national debt, with all its magnitude of terror, is of
little moment.[1] The extraordinary rapidity with which the poors rates have
increased of late years, presents us, indeed, with the prospect of a mon-
strous deformity in society, which, if it did not really exist to a great degree
at present, and were not daily advancing in growth, would be considered
as perfectly incredible. It presents us with the prospect of a great nation,
flourishing in arts, and arms, and commerce, and with a government, which
has generally been allowed to be the best, which has hitherto stood the test
of experience, in any country, and yet the larger half of the people reduced
to the condition of paupers.[2]

Greatly as we may be shocked at such a prospect, and ardently as we
may wish to remove it, the evil is now so deeply seated, and the relief given
by the poor laws so widely extended, that no man of humanity could venture to propose their immediate abolition. To mitigate their effects, however, and stop their future increase, to which, if left to continue upon their
present plan, we can see no probable termination, it has been proposed to
fix the whole sum to be raised, at its present rate, or any other that might
be determined upon; and to make a law that on no account this sum should
be exceeded. The objection to this plan is, that a very large sum would be
still to be raised, and a great number of people to be supported; the consequence of which would be, that the poor would not be easily able to distinguish the alteration that had been made. Each individual would think that
he had as good a right to be supported when he was in want, as any other

1. Reports of the Society for bettering the condition of the poor, vol. iii. p. 21.
2. It has been said, that, during the late scarcities, half of the population of the
country received relief. If the poors rates continue increasing as rapidly as they have
done on the average of the last ten years, how melancholy are our future prospects?
The system of the poor laws has been justly stated by the French to be *la plaie politique de l'Angleterre la plus dévorante.* (Comitè de Mendicitè.)

person; and those who unfortunately chanced to be in distress when the fixed sum had been collected, would think themselves particularly ill used on being excluded from all assistance, while so many others were enjoying this advantage. If the sum collected, were divided among all that were in want, however their numbers might increase; though such a plan would be perfectly fair, with regard to those who became dependent, after the sum had been fixed, it would undoubtedly be rather hard upon those, who had been in the habit of receiving a more liberal supply, and had done nothing to justify its being taken from them.

I have reflected much on the subject of the poor laws, and hope, there-fore, that I shall be excused, in venturing to suggest a mode of their gradual abolition, to which, I confess, that at present I can see no material objec-tion. Of this, indeed, I feel nearly convinced, that, should we ever become sufficiently sensible of the wide-spreading tyranny, dependence, indolence, and unhappiness, which they create, as seriously to make an effort to abol-ish them, we shall be compelled to adopt the principle, if not the plan, which I shall mention. It seems impossible to get rid of so extensive a system of support, consistently with humanity, without applying ourselves directly to its vital principle, and endeavouring to counteract that deeply-seated cause, which occasions the rapid growth of all such establishments, and invariably renders them inadequate to their object.

To this end, I should propose a regulation to be made, declaring, that no child born from any marriage, taking place after the expiration of a year from the date of the law; and no illegitimate child born two years from the same date, should ever be entitled to parish assistance. And to give a more general knowledge of this law, and to enforce it more strongly on the minds of the lower classes of people, the clergyman of each parish should, previ-ously to the solemnization of a marriage, read a short address to the parties, stating the strong obligation on every man to support his own children; the impropriety, and even immorality, of marrying without a fair prospect of being able to do this; the evils which had resulted to the poor themselves, from the attempt which had been made to assist, by publick institutions, in a duty which ought to be exclusively appropriated to parents; and the absolute necessity which had at length appeared, of abandoning all such institutions, on account of their producing effects totally opposite to those which were intended.

This would operate as a fair, distinct, and precise notice, which no man could well mistake; and, without pressing hard on any particular individu-als, would at once throw off the rising generation from that miserable and helpless dependence upon the government and the rich, the moral as well as physical consequences of which are almost incalculable. When the poor are in the habit of constantly looking to these sources, for all the good or evil they enjoy or suffer, their minds must almost necessarily be under a continual state of irritation against the higher classes of society, whenever they feel distressed from the pressure of circumstances.

I have often heard great surprise expressed that the poor in this country should be with such difficulty persuaded to take to any substitutes during a period of scarcity; but I confess, that this fact never surprised me in the least. The poor are told that the parish is obliged to provide for them. This, they naturally conceive, is a rich source of supply; and when they are offered any kind of food to which they are not accustomed, they consider it as a breach of obligation in the parish, and as proceeding, not from the hard law of necessity from which there is no appeal; but from the injustice and hardheartedness of the higher classes of society, against which they would wish to appeal to the right of the strongest. The language which they generally make use of upon these occasions, is, "See what stuff *they* want to " make us eat, I wonder how *they* would like it *themselves*. I should like " to see some of *them* do a day's work upon it." The words *they* and *them* generally refer to the Parliament, the Lord Mayor, the Justices, the Parish, and in general to all the higher classes of society. Both the irritation of mind and the helplessness in expedients, during the pressure of want, arise in this instance from the wretched system of governing too much. When the poor were once taught, by the abolition of the poor laws, and a proper knowledge of their real situation, to depend more upon themselves, we might rest secure, that they would be fruitful enough in resources, and that the evils which were absolutely irremediable, they would bear with the fortitude of men, and the resignation of Christians.

After the publick notice which I have proposed had been given, and the system of poor laws had ceased with regard to the rising generation, if any man chose to marry, without a prospect of being able to support a family, he should have the most perfect liberty so to do. Though to marry, in this case, is in my opinion clearly an immoral act, yet it is not one, which society can justly take upon itself to prevent or punish; because the punishment provided for it by the laws of nature, falls directly and most severely upon the individual who commits the act, and, through him, only more remotely and feebly on the society. When nature will govern and punish for us, it is a very miserable ambition, to wish to snatch the rod from her hands, and draw upon ourselves the odium of executioner. To the punishment, therefore, of nature he should be left, the punishment of severe want. He has erred in the face of a most clear and precise warning, and can have no just reason to complain of any person but himself, when he feels the consequences of his error. All parish assistance should be most rigidly denied him: and if the hand of private charity be stretched forth in his relief, the interests of humanity imperiously require that it should be administered very sparingly. He should be taught to know that the laws of nature, which are the laws of God, had doomed him and his family to starve for disobeying their repeated admonitions; that he had no claim of right on society for the smallest portion of food, beyond that which his labour would fairly purchase; and that, if he and his family were saved from suffering the utmost extremities of hunger, he would owe it to the pity of some kind benefactor, to whom, therefore, he ought to be bound by the strongest ties of gratitude.

If this system were pursued, we need be under no apprehensions whatever, that the number of persons in extreme want would be beyond the power and the will of the benevolent to supply. The sphere for the exercise of private charity would, I am confident, be less than it is present; and the only difficulty would be, to restrain the hand of benevolence from assisting those in distress in so liberal a manner as to encourage indolence and want of foresight in others.

With regard to illegitimate children, after the proper notice had been given, they should on no account whatever be allowed to have any claim to parish assistance. If the parents desert their child, they ought to be made answerable for the crime. The infant is, comparatively speaking, of no value to the society, as others will immediately supply its place. Its principal value is on account of its being the object of one of the most delightful passions in human nature – parental affection. But if this value be disregarded, by those who are alone in a capacity to feel it, the society cannot be called upon to put itself in their place; and has no further business in its protection, than in the case of its murder or intentional ill-treatment to follow the general rules in punishing such crimes; which rules, for the interests of morality, it is bound to pursue, whether the object, in the particular instance, be of value to the state or not.

At present the child is taken under the protection of the parish,[3] and generally dies, at least in London, within the first year. The loss to the society, if it be one, is the same; but the crime is diluted by the number of people

---

3. I fully agree with Sir F. M. Eden, in thinking that the constant publick support which deserted children receive, is the cause of their very great numbers in the two most opulent countries of Europe, France and England. State of the Poor, vol. i. p. 339.

concerned, and the death passes as a visitation of Providence, instead of being considered as the necessary consequence of the conduct of its parents, for which they ought to be held responsible to God and to society.

The desertion of both parents, however, is not so common as the desertion of one. When a servant or labouring man has an illegitimate child, his running away is perfectly a matter of course; and it is by no means uncommon for a man with a wife and large family to withdraw into a distant county, and leave them to the parish; indeed, I once heard a hard-working good sort of man propose to do this, as the best mode of providing for a wife and six children.[4] If the simple fact of these frequent desertions were related in some countries, a strange inference would be drawn against the English character; but the wonder would cease when our publick institutions were explained.

By the laws of nature, a child is confided directly and exclusively to the protection of its parents. By the laws of nature, the mother of a child is confided almost as strongly and exclusively to the man who is the father of it. If these ties were suffered to remain in the state in which nature has left them, and the man were convinced, that the woman and the child depended solely upon him for support, I scarcely believe that there are ten men breathing so atrocious as to desert them. But our laws, in opposition to the laws of nature, say, that if the parents forsake their child, other persons will undertake to support it; or, if the man forsake the woman, she shall still meet with protection elsewhere; that is, we take all possible pains to weaken and render null the ties of nature, and then say, that men are unnatural. But the fact is, that the society itself, in its body politick, is the unnatural character, for framing laws that thus counteract the laws of nature, and give premiums to the violation of the best and most honourable feelings of the human heart.

It is a common thing, in most parishes, when the father of an illegitimate child can be seized, to endeavour to frighten him into marriage by the terrors of a jail; but such a proceeding cannot surely be too strongly reprobated. In the first place, it is a most shallow policy in the parish officers; for, if they succeed, the effect, upon the present system, will generally be, the having three or four children to provide for, instead of one. And, in the next place, it is difficult to conceive a more gross and scandalous profanation of a religious ceremony. Those who believe that the character of the woman

4. "That many of the poorer classes of the community avail themselves of the
" liberality of the law, and leave their wives and children on the parish, the reader
" will find abundant proof in the subsequent part of this work." Sir F. M. Eden on
the State of the Poor, vol. i. p. 339.

is salved by such a forced engagement, or that the moral worth of the man is enhanced by affirming a lie before God, have, I confess, very different ideas of delicacy and morality, from those which I have been taught to consider as just. If a man deceive a woman into a connexion with him under a promise of marriage, he has undoubtedly been guilty of a most atrocious act; and there are few crimes which merit a more severe punishment: but the last that I should choose is that which will oblige him to affirm another falsehood, which will probably render the woman that he is to be joined to miserable, and will burden the society with a family of paupers.

The obligation on every man to support his children, whether legitimate or illegitimate, is so clear and strong, that it would be just to arm society with any power to enforce it, which would be likely to answer the purpose. But I am inclined to believe, that no exercise of the civil power, however rigorous, would be half so effectual, as a knowledge generally circulated, that children were in future to depend solely for support upon their parents, and would perhaps starve if they were deserted.

It may appear to be hard, that a mother and her children, who had been guilty of no particular crime themselves, should suffer for the ill-conduct of the father; but this is one of the invariable laws of nature; and knowing this, we should think twice upon the subject, and be very sure of the ground on which we go, before we presume *systematically* to counteract it.

I have often heard the goodness of the Deity impeached on account of that part of the decalogue, in which he declares, that he will visit the sins of the father upon the children; but the objection has not perhaps been sufficiently considered. Without a most complete and fundamental change in the whole constitution of human nature; without making man an angel, or at least something totally different from what he is at present; it seems absolutely, necessary that such a law should prevail. Would it not require a perpetual miracle, which is, perhaps, a contradiction in terms, to prevent children from being affected in their moral and civil condition by the conduct of their parents? What man is there that has been brought up by his parents, who is not, at the present moment, enjoying something from their virtues, or suffering something from their vices; who, in his moral character, has not been elevated, in some degree, by their prudence, their justice, their benevolence, their temperance, or depressed by the contraries; who, in his civil condition, has not been raised by their reputation, their foresight, their industry, their good fortune; or lowered by their want of character, their imprudence, their indolence, and their adversity? And how much does a knowledge of this transmission of blessings contribute to excite and invigorate virtuous exertion? Proceeding upon this certainty, how ardent and incessant are the efforts of parents to give their children a good education, and to provide for their future situation in the world. If a man could neglect or desert his wife and children, without their suffering any injury, how many individuals there are, who, not being very fond of their wives, or being tired of the shackles of matrimony, would withdraw from household cares and difficulties, and resume their liberty and independence as single men. But the consideration that children may suffer for the faults of their parents has a strong hold even upon vice, and many who are in such a state of mind, as to disregard the consequences of their habitual course of life, as far as relates to themselves, are yet greatly anxious that their children should not suffer from their vices and follies. In the moral government of the world, it seems evidently necessary, that the sins of the fathers should be visited upon the children; and if in our overweening vanity we imagine that we can govern a private society better by endeavouring *systematically* to counteract this law, I am inclined to believe that we shall find ourselves very greatly mistaken.

If the plan, which I have proposed, were adopted, the poors rates in a few years would begin very rapidly to decrease, and in no great length of time would be completely extinguished; and yet, as far as it appears to me at present, no individual would be either deceived or injured, and consequently no person could have a just right to complain.

The abolition of the poor laws, however, is not of itself sufficient; and the obvious answer to those who lay too much stress upon this system, is, to desire them to look at the state of the poor in some other countries, where such laws do not prevail, and to compare it with their condition in England. But this comparison, it must be acknowledged, is in many respects unfair; and would by no means decide the question of the utility, or inutility, of such a system. England possesses very great natural and political advantages, in which, perhaps, the countries that we should, in this case, compare with her, would be found to be palpably deficient. The nature of her soil and climate is such, that those almost universal failures in the crops of grain, which are known in some countries, never occur in England. Her insular situation and extended commerce are peculiarly favourable for importation. Her numerous manufactures employ all the hands that are not engaged in agriculture, and afford the means of a regular distribution of the annual produce of the land and labour to the whole of her inhabitants. But above all, throughout a very large class of the people, a decided taste for the conveniencies and comforts of life, a strong desire of bettering their condition, that master-spring of publick prosperity, and,

in consequence, a most laudable spirit of industry and foresight, are observed to prevail. These dispositions, so contrary to the hopeless indolence
remarked in despotick countries, are probably generated, in great measure,
by the constitution of the English government, and the excellence of its
laws, which secure to every individual the produce of his industry. When,
therefore, on a comparison with other countries, England appears to have
the advantage in the state of her poor, the superiority is entirely to be attributed to these favourable circumstances, and not to the poor laws. A woman
with one bad feature may greatly excel in beauty some other who may have
this individual feature tolerably good; but it would be rather strange, to assert, in consequence, that the superior beauty of the former was occasioned
by this particular deformity. The poor laws have constantly tended, in the
most powerful manner, to counteract the natural and acquired advantages
of this country. Fortunately, these advantages have been so considerable,
that, though greatly weakened, they could not be entirely overcome; and to
these advantages, and these alone, it is owing, that England has been able
to bear up so long against this pernicious system. I am so strongly of this
opinion, that I do not think that any other country in the world, except perhaps Holland before the revolution, could have acted upon it so completely,
for the same period of time, without utter ruin.

It has been proposed by some, to establish poor laws in Ireland; but,
from the wretched and degraded state of the common people, and the total
want of that decent pride, which in England prevents so many from having recourse to parish assistance, there is little reason to doubt, that, on the
establishment of such laws, the whole of the landed property would very
soon be absorbed, or the system be given up in despair.

In Sweden, from the dearths which are not unfrequent, owing to the
general failure of crops in an unpropitious climate, and the impossibility
of great importations in a poor country, an attempt to establish a system of
parochial relief such as that in England, if it were not speedily abandoned
from the physical impossibility of executing it, would level the property of
the kingdom from one end to the other, and convulse the social system in
such a manner, as absolutely to prevent it from recovering its former state
on the return of plenty.

Even in France, with all her advantages of situation and climate, the tendency to population is so great, and the want of foresight among the lower
classes of the people so conspicuous, that if poor laws were established, the
landed property would soon sink under the burden, and the wretchedness
of the people at the same time be increased. On these considerations the

committee *de Mendicitè,* at the beginning of the revolution, very properly and judiciously rejected the establishment of such a system which had been proposed.

The exception of Holland, if it were an exception, would arise from very particular circumstances–her extensive foreign trade, and her numerous colonial emigrations, compared with the smallness of her territory; and the extreme unhealthiness of a great part of the country, which occasions a much greater average mortality than is common in other states. These, I conceive, were the unobserved causes which principally contributed to render Holland so famous for the management of her poor, and able to employ and support all who applied for relief.

No part of Germany is sufficiently rich to support an extensive system of parochial relief; but I am inclined to think, that, from the absence of it, the lower classes of the people in some parts of Germany, are in a better situation than those of the same class in England. In, Switzerland, for the same reason, their condition, before the late troubles, was perhaps universally superior. And in a journey through the dutchies of Holstein and Sleswick belonging to Denmark, the houses of the lower classes of people appeared to me to be neater and better, and, in general, there were fewer indications of poverty and wretchedness among them, than among the same ranks in this country.

Even in Norway, notwithstanding the disadvantage of a severe and uncertain climate, from the little that I saw in a few weeks residence in the country, and the information that I could collect from others, I am inclined to think, that the poor were, on the average, better off than in England. Their houses and clothing were superior, and, though they had no white bread, they had much more meat, fish, and milk, than our labourers; and I particularly remarked, that the farmers' boys were much stouter and healthier looking lads than those of the same description in England. This degree of happiness, superior to what could be expected from the soil and climate, arises almost exclusively from the degree in which the preventive check to population operates; and the establishment of a system of poor laws which would destroy this check, would at once sink the lower classes of the people into a state of the most miserable poverty and wretchedness; would diminish their industry, and consequently the produce of the land and labour of the country; would weaken the resources of ingenuity in times of scarcity; and ultimately involve the country in all the horrors of continual famines.

If, as in Ireland, and in Spain, and many of the southern countries, the people be in so degraded a state, as to propagate their species like brutes, totally regardless of consequences, it matters little, whether they have poor laws or not. Misery in all its various forms must be the predominant check to their increase. Poor laws, indeed, will always tend to aggravate the evil, by diminishing the general resources of the country, and, in such a state of things, could exist only for a very short time; but with, or without them, no stretch of human ingenuity and exertion could rescue the people from the most extreme poverty and wretchedness.

CHAP. VIII.

Of the modes of correcting the prevailing
opinions on the subject of Population.

IT is not enough to abolish all the positive institutions which encourage population; but we must endeavour, at the same time, to correct the prevailing opinions, which have the same, or perhaps even a more powerful, effect. This must necessarily be a work of time; and can only be done, by circulating juster notions on these subjects, in writings and conversation; and by endeavouring to impress as strongly as possible on the publick mind, that it is not the duty of man simply to propagate his species, but to propagate virtue and happiness; and that, if he has not a tolerably fair prospect of doing this, he is by no means called upon to leave descendants.

The merits of the childless, and of those who have brought up large families, should be compared without prejudice, and their different influence on the general happiness of society justly appreciated.

The matron who has reared a family of ten or twelve children, and whose sons, perhaps, may be fighting the battles of their country, is apt to think that society owes her much; and this imaginary debt, society is, in general, fully inclined to acknowledge. But if the subject be fairly considered, and the respected matron weighed in the scales of justice against the neglected old maid, it is possible that the matron might kick the beam. She will appear rather in the character of a monopolist, than of a great benefactor to the state. If she had not married and had so many children, other members of the society might have enjoyed this satisfaction; and there is no particular reason for supposing that her sons would fight better for their country than the sons of other women. She has therefore rather subtracted from, than added to, the happiness of the other parts of society. The old maid, on the contrary, has exalted others by depressing herself. Her self-denial has made room for another marriage, without any additional distress; and she has not, like the generality of men, in avoiding one error, fallen into its opposite. She has really and truly contributed more to the happiness of the rest of the society arising from the pleasures of marriage, than if she had entered in this union herself, and had besides portioned twenty maidens with a hundred pounds each; whose particular happiness would have been balanced, either by an increase in the general difficulties of rearing children and getting employment, or by the necessity of celibacy in twenty other maidens somewhere else. Like the truly benevolent man in an irremediable scarcity, she has diminished her own consumption, instead of raising up a few particular people, by pressing down the rest. On a fair comparison, therefore, she seems to have a better founded claim to the gratitude of society than the matron. Whether we could always completely sympathize with the motives of her conduct, has not much to do with the question. The particular motive which influenced the matron to marry, was certainly not the good of her country. To refuse a proper tribute of respect to the old maid, because she was not directly influenced in her conduct by the desire of conferring on society a certain benefit, which, though it must undoubtedly exist, must necessarily be so diffused as to be invisible to her, is in the highest degree impolitick and unjust. It is expecting a strain of virtue beyond humanity. If we never reward any persons with our approbation, but those who are exclusively influenced by motives of general benevolence, this powerful encouragement to good actions will not be very often called into exercise.

There are very few women who might not have married in some way or other. The old maid, who has either never formed an attachment, or has been disappointed in the object of it, has, under the circumstances in which she has been placed, conducted herself with the most perfect propriety; and has acted a much more virtuous and honourable part in society, than those women who marry without a proper degree of love, or at least of esteem, for their husbands; a species of immorality which is not reprobated as it deserves.

If, in comparisons of this kind, we should be compelled to acknowledge that, in considering the general tendency of population to increase beyond the means of subsistence, the conduct of the old maid had contributed more to the happiness of the society than that of the matron; it will surely appear, not only unjust, but strikingly impolitick, not to proportion our tribute of honour and estimation more fairly according to their respective merits. Though we should not go so far as to reward single women with particular distinctions; yet the plainest principles of equity and policy require, that the respect which they might claim from their personal character, should, in no way whatever, be impeded by their particular situation; and that, with regard to rank, precedence, and the ceremonial attentions of society, they should be completely on a level with married women.

It is still however true, that the life of a married person with a family, is of more consequence to society than that of a single person; because, when there is a family of children already born, it is of the utmost importance, that they should be well taken care of, and well educated; and of this there is very seldom so fair a probability when they have lost their parents. Our object should be merely to correct the prevailing opinions with regard to the duty of marriage; and, without positively discouraging it, to prevent any persons from being attracted, or driven into this state by the respect and honour which await the married dame, and the neglect and inconveniences attendant on the single woman.

It is perfectly absurd as well as unjust, that a giddy girl of sixteen should, because she is married, be considered by the forms of society as the protector of women of thirty, should come first into the room, should be assigned the highest place at table, and be the prominent figure to whom the attentions of the company are more particularly addressed. Those who believe that these distinctions, added to the very long confinement of single women to the parental roof, and their being compelled, on all occasions, to occupy the back ground of the picture, have not an influence in impelling many young women into the married state against their natural inclinations, and without a proper degree of regard for their intended husbands, do not, as I conceive, reason with much knowledge of human nature. And till these customs are changed, as far as circumstances will admit, and the respect and liberty which women enjoy, are made to depend more upon personal character and propriety of conduct, than upon their situation as married or single; it must be acknowledged, that among the higher ranks of life we encourage marriage by considerable premiums.

It is not, however, among the higher ranks of society, that we have most reason to apprehend the too great frequency of marriage. Though the circulation of juster notions on this subject might, even in this part of the community, do much good, and prevent many unhappy marriages; yet, whether we make particular exertions for this purpose, or not, we may rest assured, that the degree of proper pride, and spirit of independence, almost invariably connected with education and a certain rank in life, will secure the operation of the preventive check to a considerable extent. All that the society can reasonably require of its members is, that they should not have families without being able to support them. This may be fairly enjoined as a solemn duty. Every restraint beyond this, though in many points of view highly desirable, must be considered as a matter of choice and taste; but, from what we already know of the habits which prevail among the higher ranks of life, we have reason to think, that little more is wanted to attain the object required than to award a greater degree of respect and of personal liberty to single women, and to remove the distinctions in favour of married women, so as to place them exactly upon a level; a change which, independently of any particular purpose in view, the plainest principles of equity seem to demand.

If, among the higher classes of society, the object of securing the operation of the preventive check to population to a sufficient degree, appear to be attainable without much difficulty; the obvious mode of proceeding with the lower classes of society, where the point is of the principal importance, is, to endeavour to infuse into them a portion of that knowledge and foresight, which so much facilitates the attainment of this object in the educated part of the community.

The fairest chance of accomplishing this end, would probably be by the establishment of a system of parochial education upon a plan similar to that proposed by Dr. Smith.[1] In addition to the usual subjects of instruction, and those which he has mentioned, I should be disposed to lay considerable stress on the frequent explanation of the real state of the lower classes of society, as affected by the principle of population, and their consequent dependence on themselves, for the chief part of their happiness, or misery. If, in the course of time, a few of the simplest principles of political economy could be added to these instructions, the benefit to society would be almost incalculable.[2] In some conversations with labouring men, during the late scarcities, I confess that I was to the last degree disheartened, at observing their inveterate prejudices on the subject of grain; and I felt very strongly the almost absolute incompatibility of a government really free, with such

1. Wealth of Nations, vol. iii. b. v. c. i. p. 187.

2. Dr. Smith proposes that the elementary parts of geometry and mechanics should be taught in these parish schools; and I cannot help thinking that the common principles by which markets are regulated might be made sufficiently clear, to be of considerable use. It is certainly a subject, that, as it interests the lower classes of people nearly, would be likely to attract their attention. At the same time, it must be confessed, that it is impossible to be in any degree sanguine on this point, recollecting how very ignorant in general the educated part of the community is of these principles. If, however, political economy cannot be taught to the common people, I really think that it ought to form a branch of a university education. Scotland has set us an example in this respect, which we ought not to be so slow to imitate. It is of the very utmost importance, that the gentlemen of the country, and particularly the clergy, should not, from ignorance, aggravate the evils of scarcity every time that it unfortunately occurs. During the late dearths, half of the gentlemen and clergymen in the kingdom richly deserved to have been prosecuted for sedition. After inflaming the minds of the common people against the farmers and corn-dealers, by the manner in which they talked of them, or preached about them, it was but a feeble antidote to the poison which they had infused, coldly to observe, that however the poor might be oppressed or cheated, it was their duty to keep the peace. It was little better than Anthony's repeated declaration, that the conspirators were all honourable men; which did not save either their houses or their persons from the attacks of the mob. Political economy is perhaps the only science of which it may be said, that the ignorance of it is not merely a deprivation of good, but produces great positive evil.

a degree of ignorance. The delusions are of such a nature, that, if acted upon, they must, at all events, be repressed by force; and it is extremely difficult to give such a power to the government as will be sufficient at all times for this purpose, without the risk of its being employed improperly, and endangering the liberty of the subject. And this reflection cannot but be disheartening to every friend to freedom.

We have lavished immense sums on the poor, which we have every reason to think have constantly tended to aggravate their misery. But in their education, and in the circulation of those important political truths that most nearly concern them, which are perhaps the only means in our power of really raising their condition, and of making them happier men and more peaceable subjects, we have been miserably deficient. It is surely a great national disgrace, that the education of the lower classes of people in England should be left merely to a few sunday schools, supported by a subscription from individuals, who of course can give to the course of instruction in them, any kind of bias which they please. And even the improvement of sunday schools, for objectionable as they are in some points of view, and imperfect in all, I cannot but consider them as an improvement, is of very late date.

The arguments which have been urged against instructing the people, appear to me to be not only illiberal, but to the last degree feeble; and they ought, on the contrary, to be extremely forcible, and to be supported by the most obvious and striking necessity, to warrant us in withholding the means of raising the condition of the lower classes of people, when they are in our power. Those who will not listen to any answer to these arguments drawn from theory, cannot, I think, refuse the testimony of experience; and I would ask, whether the advantage of superior instruction which the lower classes of people in Scotland are known to possess, has appeared to have any tendency towards creating a spirit of tumult and discontent amongst them. And yet from the natural inferiority of its soil and climate, the pressure of want is more constant, and the dearths are not only more frequent, but more dreadful than in England. In the case of Scotland, the knowledge circulated among the common people, though not sufficient essentially to better their condition by increasing, in an adequate degree, their habits of prudence and foresight; has yet the effect of making them bear with patience the evils which they suffer, from being aware of the folly and inefficacy of turbulence. The quiet and peaceable habits of the instructed Scotch peasant, compared with the turbulent disposition of the ignorant Irishman, ought not to be without effect upon every impartial reasoner.

The principal argument that I have heard advanced against a system of national education in England, is, that the common people would be put in a capacity to read such works as those of Paine, and that the consequences would probably be fatal to government. But, on this subject, I agree most cordially with Dr. Smith[3] in thinking, that an instructed and well-informed people, would be much less likely to be led away by inflammatory writings, and would be much better able to detect the false declamation of interested and ambitious demagogues, than an ignorant people. One or two readers in a parish are sufficient to circulate any quantity of sedition; and if these be gained to the democratic side, they will probably have the power of doing much more mischief, by selecting the passages best suited to their hearers, and choosing the moments when their oratory is likely to have the most effect; than if each individual in the parish had been in a capacity to read and judge of the whole work himself; and, at the same time, to read and judge of the opposing arguments, which we may suppose would also reach him.

But in addition to this, a double weight would undoubtedly be added to the observation of Dr. Smith, if these schools were made the means of instructing the people in the real nature of their situation; if they were taught, what is really true, that, without an increase of their own industry and prudence, no change of government could essentially better their condition; that though they might get rid of some particular grievance, yet that, in the great point of supporting their families, they would be but little, or perhaps not at all benefited; that a revolution would not alter in their favour the proportion of the supply of labour to the demand, or the quantity of food to the number of the consumers; and that, if the supply of labour were greater than the demand, and the demand for food greater than the supply, they might suffer the utmost severity of want, under the freest, the most perfect, and best executed government that the human imagination could conceive.

A knowledge of these truths, so obviously tends to promote peace and quietness, to weaken the effect of inflammatory writings, and to prevent all unreasonable and ill-directed opposition to the constituted authorities, that those, who would still object to the instruction of the people, may fairly be suspected of a wish to encourage their ignorance, as a pretext for tyranny, and an opportunity of increasing the power and the influence of the executive government.

Besides correcting the prevailing opinions respecting marriage, and explaining the real situation of the lower classes of society, as depending

3. Wealth of Nations, vol. iii. b. v. c. i. p. 192.

almost entirely upon themselves for their happiness or misery; the parochial schools would, by early instruction and the judicious distribution of rewards, have the fairest chance of training up the rising generation in habits of sobriety, industry, independence, and prudence, and in a proper discharge of their religious duties; which would raise them from their present degraded state, and approximate them, in some degree, to the middle classes of society, whose habits, generally speaking, are certainly superior.

In most countries, among the lower classes of people, there appears to be something like a standard of wretchedness, a point below which, they will not continue to marry and propagate their species. This standard is different in different countries, and is formed by various concurring circumstances of soil, climate, government, degree of knowledge, and civilization, &c. The principal circumstances which contribute to raise it, are, liberty, security of property, the spread of knowledge, and a taste for the conveniences and the comforts of life. Those which contribute principally to lower it are despotism and ignorance.

In an attempt to better the condition of the lower classes of society, our object should be to raise this standard as high as possible, by cultivating a spirit of independence, a decent pride, and a taste for cleanliness and comfort among the poor. These habits would be best inculcated by a system of general education and, when strongly fixed, would be the most powerful means of preventing their marrying with the prospect of being obliged to forfeit such advantages; and would consequently raise them nearer to the middle classes of society.

C H A P .   IX.

Of the direction of our charity.

AN important and interesting inquiry yet remains, relating to the mode, by which we could direct our private charity, so as not to interfere with the great object in view, of ameliorating the condition of the lower classes of people, by preventing the population from pressing too hard against the limits of the means of subsistence.

The emotion which prompts us to relieve our fellow-creatures in distress, is like all our other natural passions, general, and in some degree indiscriminate and blind. Our feelings of compassion may be worked up to a higher pitch by a well-wrought scene in a play, or a fictitious tale in a novel, than by almost any events in real life; and if, among ten petitioners, we were to listen only to the first impulses of our feelings, without making further inquiries, we should undoubtedly give our assistance to the best actor of the party. It is evident, therefore, that the impulse of benevolence, like the impulses of love, of anger, of ambition, of eating and drinking, or any other of our natural propensities, must be regulated by experience, and frequently brought to the test of utility, or it will defeat its intended purpose.

The apparent object of the passion between the sexes is, the continuation of the species, and the formation of such an intimate union of views and interests between two persons, as will best promote their happiness, and at the same time secure the proper degree of attention to the helplessness of infancy and the education of the rising generation; but if every man were to obey at all times the impulses of nature in the gratification of this passion, without regard to consequences, the principal part of the important objects would not be attained, and even the continuation of the species might be defeated by a promiscuous intercourse.

The apparent end of the impulse of benevolence, is to draw the whole human race together, but more particularly that part of it which is of our own nation and kindred, in the bonds of brotherly love; and by giving men an interest in the happiness and misery of their fellow creatures, to prompt them, as they have power, to mitigate some of the partial evils arising from general laws, and thus to increase the sum of human happiness; but if our benevolence be indiscriminate, and the degree of apparent distress be made the sole measure of our liberality, it is evident, that it will be exercised almost exclusively upon common beggars, while modest unobtrusive merit, struggling with unavoidable difficulties, yet still maintaining some slight appearances of decency and cleanliness, will be totally neglected. We shall raise the worthless above the worthy; we shall encourage indolence and check industry; and, in the most marked manner, subtract from the sum of human happiness.

Our experience has, indeed, informed us, that the impulse of benevolence is not so strong as the passion between the sexes, and that, generally speaking, there is much less danger to be apprehended from the indulgence of the former than of the latter; but, independently of this experience, and of the moral codes founded upon it, a youth of eighteen would be as completely justified in indulging the sexual passion with every object capable of exciting it, as in following indiscriminately every impulse of his benevolence. They are both natural passions which are excited by their appropriate objects, and to the gratification of which, we are prompted by the pleasurable sensations which accompany them. As animals, or till we know their consequences, our only business is to follow these dictates of nature; but, as reasonable beings, we are under the strongest obligations to attend to their consequences; and if they be evil to ourselves or others, we may justly consider it as an indication that such a mode of indulging these passions is not suited to our state, or conformable to the will of God. As moral agents, therefore, it is clearly our duty to restrain their indulgence in these particular directions; and by thus carefully examining the consequences of our natural passions, and frequently bringing them to the test of utility, gradually to acquire a habit of gratifying them, only in that way, which, being unattended with evil, will clearly add to the sum of human happiness, and fulfil the apparent purpose of the Creator.

Though utility, therefore, can never be the immediate excitement to the gratification of any passion, it is the test by which alone we can know, whether it ought, or ought not, to be indulged; and is, therefore, the surest foundation of all morality which can be collected from the light of nature. All the moral codes which have inculcated the subjection of the passions to reason, have been, as I conceive, really built upon this foundation, whether the promulgators of them were aware of it or not.

I remind the reader of these truths, in order to apply them to the habitual direction of our charity; and, if we keep the criterion of utility constantly in view, we may find ample room for the exercise of our benevolence, without interfering with the great purpose which we have to accomplish.

One of the most valuable parts of charity, is its effect upon the giver. It is more blessed to give than to receive. Supposing it to be allowed, that the exercise of our benevolence in acts of charity is not, upon the whole, really beneficial to the poor, yet we could never sanction any endeavour to extinguish an impulse, the proper gratification of which has so evident a tendency to purify and exalt the human mind. But it is particularly satisfactory and pleasing to find, that the mode of exercising our charity, which, when brought to the test of utility, will appear to be most beneficial to the poor, is precisely that, which will have the best and most improving effect on the mind of the donor.

The quality of charity like that of mercy,

"   is not strained;
"   It droppeth as the gentle rain from heaven
"   Upon the earth beneath."

The immense sums distributed to the poor, in this country, by the parochial laws, are improperly called charity. They want its most distinguishing attribute; and, as it might be expected, from an attempt to force that which loses its essence the moment that it ceases to be voluntary, their effect upon those from whom they are collected are as prejudicial, as on those to whom they are distributed. On the side of the receivers of this miscalled charity, instead of real relief, we find accumulated distress and more extended poverty; on the side of the givers, instead of pleasurable sensations, unceasing discontent and irritation.

In the great charitable institutions supported by voluntary contributions, many of which are certainly of a prejudicial tendency, the subscriptions, I am inclined to fear, are sometimes given grudgingly, and rather because they are expected by the world from certain stations, and certain fortunes, than because they are prompted by motives of genuine benevolence; and as the greater part of the subscribers do not interest themselves in the management of the funds, or in the fate of the particular objects relieved, it is not to be expected that this kind of charity should have any strikingly beneficial influence on the minds of the majority who exercise it.

Even in the relief of common beggars, we shall find that we are more frequently influenced by the desire of getting rid of the importunities of a disgusting object, than by the pleasure of relieving it. We wish that it had not fallen in our way, rather than rejoice in the opportunity given us of assisting a fellow-creature. We feel a painful emotion at the sight of so much apparent misery; but the pittance we give does not relieve it. We know that it is totally inadequate to produce any essential effect. We know, besides, that we shall be addressed in the same manner at the corner of the next street; and we know that we are liable to the grossest impostures. We hurry, therefore, sometimes by them, and shut our ears to their importunate demands. We give no more than we can help giving without doing actual violence to our feelings. Our charity is in some degree forced, and, like forced charity, it leaves no satisfactory impression on the mind, and cannot, therefore, have any very beneficial and improving effect on the heart and affections.

But it is far otherwise with that voluntary and active charity, which makes itself acquainted with the objects which it relieves; which seems to feel, and to be proud of, the bond which unites the rich with the poor; which enters into their houses; informs itself not only of their wants, but of their habits and dispositions; checks the hopes of clamorous and obtrusive poverty, with no other recommendation but rags; and encourages with adequate relief the silent and retiring sufferer, labouring under unmerited difficulties. This mode of exercising our charity presents a very different picture from that of any other; and its contrast with the common mode of parish relief, cannot be better described than in the words of Mr. Townsend, in the conclusion of his admirable dissertation on the Poor Laws: "Nothing
" in nature can be more disgusting than a parish pay-table, attendant upon
" which, in the same objects of misery, are too often found combined,
" snuff, gin, rags, vermin, insolence, and abusive language; nor in nature,
" can any thing be more beautiful than the mild complacency of benevo-
" lence hastening to the humble cottage to relieve the wants of industry
" and virtue, to feed the hungry, to clothe the naked, and to soothe the
" sorrows of the widow with her tender orphans; nothing can be more
" pleasing, unless it be their sparkling eyes, their bursting tears, and their
" uplifted hands, the artless expressions of unfeigned gratitude for un-
" expected favours. Such scenes will frequently occur whenever men
" shall have power to dispose of their own property."

I conceive it to be almost impossible, that any person could be much engaged in such scenes without daily making advances in virtue. No exercise of our affections can have a more evident tendency to purify and exalt the human mind. It is almost exclusively this species of charity that blesseth him that gives; and, in a general view, it is almost exclusively this species of charity which blesseth him that takes; at least it may be asserted, that there is no other mode of exercising our charity, in which large sums can be distributed without a greater chance of producing evil than good.

The discretionary power of giving or withholding relief, which is, to a certain extent, vested in parish officers and justices, is of a very different nature, and will have a very different effect, from the discrimination which may be exercised by voluntary charity. Every man in this country, under certain circumstances, is entitled by law to parish assistance; and unless his disqualification be clearly proved, has a right to complain if it be withheld. The inquiries necessary to settle this point, and also the extent of the relief to be granted, too often produce evasion and lying on the part of the petitioner, and afford an opening to partiality and oppression in the overseer. If the proposed relief be given, it is of course received with unthankfulness; and if it be denied, the party generally thinks himself severely aggrieved, and feels resentment and indignation at his treatment.

In the distribution of voluntary charity, nothing of this kind can take place. The person who receives it, is made the proper subject of the pleasurable sensation of gratitude; and those who do not receive it, cannot possibly conceive themselves, in the slightest degree, injured. Every man has a right to do what he will with his own; and cannot, in justice, be called upon to render a reason why he gives in the one case, and abstains from it in the other. This kind of despotic power, essential to voluntary charity, gives the greatest facility to the selection of worthy objects of relief, without being accompanied by any ill consequences; and has further a most beneficial effect from the degree of uncertainty which must necessarily be attached to it. It is, in the highest degree, important to the general happiness of the poor, that no man should look to charity, as a fund on which he may confidently depend. He should be taught that his own exertions, his own industry and foresight, were his only just ground of dependence; that if these failed, assistance in his distresses could only be the subject of rational hope; and that even the foundation of this hope must be in his own good conduct, and the consciousness that he had not involved himself in these difficulties by his indolence or imprudence.

That, in the distribution of our charity, we are under a strong moral obligation to inculcate this lesson on the poor, by a proper discrimination, is a truth, of which I cannot feel a doubt. If all could be completely relieved, and poverty banished from the country, even at the expence of three-fourths of the fortunes of the rich, I would be the last to say a single syllable against relieving all, and making the degree of distress alone the measure of our bounty. But as experience has proved, I believe without a single exception, that poverty and misery have always increased in proportion to the quantity of indiscriminate charity; are we not bound to infer, reasoning as we usually do from the laws of nature, that it is an intimation, that such a mode of distribution is not the proper office of benevolence.

The laws of nature say, with St. Paul, "If a man will not work, neither " shall he eat." They also say, that he is not rashly to trust to Providence. They appear indeed to be constant and uniform for the express purpose of telling him what he is to trust to, and that if he marry, without being able to support a family, he must expect severe want. These intimations appear from the constitution of human nature to be absolutely necessary, and to have a strikingly beneficial tendency. If in the direction either of our publick or our private charity, we say, that though a man will not work, yet he shall eat; and though he marry, without being able to support a family, yet his family shall be supported; it is evident that we do not merely endeavour to mitigate some of the partial evils arising from general laws, but regularly and systematically to counteract the obviously beneficial effects of these general laws themselves. And we cannot easily conceive, that the Deity should implant any passion in the human breast for such a purpose.

In the great course of human events, the best-founded expectations will sometimes be disappointed; and industry, prudence, and virtue, not only fail of their just reward, but be involved in unmerited calamities. Those who are thus suffering in spite of the best directed endeavours to avoid it, and from causes which they could not be expected to foresee, are the genuine objects of charity. In relieving these, we exercise the appropriate office of benevolence, that of mitigating some of the partial evils arising from general laws; and in this direction of our charity, therefore, we need not apprehend any ill consequences. Such objects ought to be relieved according to our means liberally and adequately, even though the worthless were starving.

When indeed, this first claim on our benevolence was satisfied, we might then turn our attention to the idle and improvident: but the interests of human happiness most clearly require, that the relief which we afford them should be very scanty. We may perhaps take upon ourselves, with great caution, to mitigate, in some degree, the punishments which they are suffering from the laws of nature; but on no account to remove them entirely. They are deservedly at the bottom, in the scale of society; and, if we raise them from this situation, we not only palpably defeat the end of benevolence, but commit a most glaring injustice to those who are above them. They should on no account be enabled to command so much of the necessaries of life, as can be obtained by the worst-paid common labour. The brownest bread, with the coarsest and scantiest apparel, is the utmost which they should have the means of purchasing.

It is evident that these reasonings do not apply to those cases of urgent distress arising from disastrous accidents, unconnected with habits of indolence and improvidence. If a man break a leg or an arm, we are not to stop to inquire into his moral character before we lend him our assistance; but in this case we are perfectly consistent, and the touchstone of utility completely justifies our conduct. By affording the most indiscriminate assistance in this way, we are in little danger of encouraging people to break their arms and legs, According to the touchstone of utility, the high approbation which Christ gave to the conduct of the good Samaritan, who followed the immediate impulse of his benevolence in relieving a stranger, in the urgent distress of an accident, does not, in the smallest degree, contradict the expressions of St. Paul, "If a man will not work, neither shall " he eat."

We are not, however, in any case, to lose a present opportunity of doing good, from the mere supposition that we may possibly meet with a worthier object. In all doubtful cases, it may safely be laid down as our duty, to follow the natural impulse of our benevolence; but when, in fulfilling our obligation as reasonable beings, to attend to the consequences of our actions, we have, from our own experience and that of others, drawn the conclusion, that the exercise of our benevolence in one mode is prejudicial, and in another is beneficial, in its effects, we are certainly bound, as moral agents, to check our natural propensities in the one direction, and to encourage them, and acquire the habits of exercising them, in the other.

C H A P . X.

*Of the errors in different plans which have been
proposed, to improve the condition of the Poor.*

In the distribution of our charity, or in any efforts which we may make to
better the condition of the lower classes of society, there is another point
relating to the main argument of this work, to which we must be particularly attentive. We must on no account do any thing, which tends directly
to encourage marriage; or to remove, in any regular and systematic manner,
that inequality of circumstances, which ought always to exist between the
single man and the man with a family. The writers who have best understood the principle of population, appear to me all to have fallen into very
important errors on this point.

Sir James Steuart, who is fully aware of what he calls vicious procreation, and of the misery that attends a redundant population, recommends,
notwithstanding, the general establishment of foundling hospitals; the
taking of children, under certain circumstances, from their parents, and
supporting them at the expence of the state; and particularly laments
the inequality of condition between the married and single man, so ill-
proportioned to their respective wants.[1] He forgets, in these instances, that
if, without the encouragement to multiplication, of foundling hospitals, or
of publick support for the children of some married persons; and under the
discouragement of great pecuniary disadvantages on the side of the married man, population be still redundant; which is evinced by the inability
of the poor to maintain all their children; it is a clear proof, that the funds
destined for the maintenance of labour cannot properly support a greater
population; and that, if further, encouragements to multiplication be given,
and discouragements removed, the result must be, an increase, somewhere
or other, of that vicious procreation which he so justly reprobates.

Mr. Townsend, who, in his dissertation on the Poor Laws, has treated
this subject with great skill and perspicuity, appears to me to conclude
with a proposal, which violates the principles on which he had reasoned so
well. He wishes to make the benefit clubs, or friendly societies, which are
now voluntarily established in many parishes, compulsory and universal;
and proposes, as a regulation, that an unmarried man should pay a fourth

1. Political Œconomy, vol. i. b. i. c. xii.

part of his wages, and a married man with four children, not more than a thirtieth part.[2]

I must first remark, that the moment these subscriptions are made compulsory, they will necessarily operate exactly like a direct tax upon labour, which, as Dr. Smith justly states, will always be paid, and in a more expensive manner, by the consumer. The landed interest, therefore, would receive no relief from this plan, but would pay the same sum as at present, only in the advanced price of labour and of commodities, instead of in the parish rates. A compulsory subscription of this kind, would have almost all the ill effects of the present system of relief, and, though altered in name, would still possess the essential spirit of the poor laws.

Dean Tucker, in some remarks on a plan of the same kind, proposed by Mr. Pew, observed, that, after much talk and reflection on the subject, he had come to the conclusion, that they must be voluntary associations, and not compulsory assemblies. A voluntary subscription is like a tax upon a luxury, and does not necessarily raise the price of labour.

It should be recollected also, that in a voluntary association of a small extent, over which each individual member can exercise a superintendence, it is highly probable, that the original agreements will all be strictly fulfilled, or if they be not, every man may, at least, have the redress of withdrawing himself from the club. But in an universal compulsory subscription, which must necessarily become a national concern, there would be no security whatever for the fulfilment of the original agreements; and when the funds failed, which they certainly would do, when all the idle and dissolute were included, instead of some of the most industrious and provident, as at present, a larger subscription would probably be demanded, and no man would have the right to refuse it. The evil would thus go on increasing as the poor rates do now. If, indeed, the assistance given were always specific, and on no account to be increased, as in the present voluntary associations, this would certainly be a striking advantage; but the same advantage might be completely attained by a similar distribution of the sums collected by the parish rates. On the whole, therefore, it appears to me, that, if the friendly societies were made universal and compulsory, it would be merely a different mode of collecting parish rates; and any particular mode of distribution, might be as well adopted upon one system as upon the other.

With regard to the proposal of making single men pay a fourth part of their earnings weekly, and married men with families only a thirtieth part, it would evidently operate as a heavy fine upon bachelors, and a high

2. Dissertation on the Poor Laws, p. 89. 2d edit. 1787.

bounty upon children; and is therefore directly adverse to the general spirit in which Mr. Townsend's excellent dissertation is written. Before he introduces this proposal, he lays it down as a general principle, that no system for the relief of the poor can be good, which does not regulate population by the demand for labour,[3] but this proposal clearly tends to encourage population without any reference to the demand for labour, and punishes a young man for his prudence in refraining from marriage at a time, perhaps, when this demand is so small, that the wages of labour are totally inadequate to the support of a family. I should be averse to any compulsory system whatever for the poor; but, certainly, if single men were compelled to pay a contribution for the future contingencies of the married state, they ought, in justice, to receive a benefit, proportioned to the period of their privation; and the man who had contributed a fourth of his earnings for merely one year, ought not to be put upon a level with him who has contributed this proportion for ten years.

Arthur Young, in most of his works, appears clearly to understand the principle of population, and is fully aware of the evils which must necessarily result from an increase of people beyond the demand of labour, and the means of comfortable subsistence. In his tour through France, he has particularly laboured this point, and shewn most forcibly the misery, which results, in that country, from the excess of population occasioned by the too great division of property. Such an increase, he justly calls, merely a multiplication of wretchedness. "Couples marry and procreate on the idea, not " the reality, of a maintenance; they increase beyond the demand of towns " and manufactures; and the consequence is, distress, and numbers dying " of diseases arising from insufficient nourishment."[4]

In another place he quotes a very sensible passage from the report of the committee of mendicity, which, alluding to the evils of overpopulation, concludes thus, "Il faudroit enfin necessairement que le prix de travail bais- " sat par la plus grand concurrence de travailleurs, d'ou resulteroit un in- " digence complette pour ceux qui ne trouveroient pas de travail, et une " subsistence incomplette pour ceux mêmes aux quels il ne seroit pas re- " fusé." And in remarking upon this passage, he observes, "France itself " affords an irrefragable proof of the truth of these sentiments; for, I am " clearly of opinion, from the observations I made in every province of " the kingdom, that her population is so much beyond the proportion of " her industry and labour, that she would be much more powerful and " infinitely more flourishing, if she had five or six millions less of inhab-

3. P. 84.   4. Travels in France, vol. i. c. xii. p. 408.

" itants. From her too great population, she presents, in every quarter,
" such spectacles of wretchedness, as are absolutely inconsistent with that
" degree of national felicity, which she was capable of attaining, even
" under the old government. A traveller, much less attentive than I was to
" objects of this kind, must see at every turn most unequivocal signs of
" distress. That these should exist, no one can wonder, who considers the
" price of labour and of provisions, and the misery into which a small rise
" in the price of wheat throws the lower classes."[5]
"   "If you would see," he says, "a district with as little distress in it as is
" consistent with the political system of the old government of France,
" you must assuredly go where there are no little properties at all. You
" must visit the great farms in Beauce, Picardy, part of Normandy, and
" Artois, and there you will find no more population than what is regu-
" larly employed and regularly paid; and if in such districts, you should,
" contrary to this rule, meet with much distress, it is twenty to one, but
" that it is in a parish which has some commons, which tempt the poor to
" have cattle–to have property–and in consequence misery. When you
" are engaged in this political tour, finish it by seeing England, and I will
" shew you a set of peasants well clothed, well nourished, tolerably
" drunken from superfluity, well lodged, and at their ease; and yet,
" amongst them, not one in a thousand has either land or cattle."[6] A little
further on, alluding to encouragements to marriage, he says of France; "the
" predominant evil of the kingdom is the having so great a population,
" that she can neither employ nor feed it; why then encourage marriage?
" would you breed more people, because you have more already than you
" know what to do with? you have so great a competition for food, that
" your people are starving or in misery; and you would encourage the
" production of more to encrease that competition. It may almost be ques-
" tioned whether the contrary policy ought not to be embraced? whether
" difficulties should not be laid on the marriage of those who cannot make
" it appear that they have the prospect of maintaining the children that
" shall be the fruit of it? But why encourage marriages which are sure to
" take place in all situations in which they ought to take place? There is
" no instance to be found of plenty of regular employment being first es-
" tablished where marriages have not followed in a proportionate degree.
" The policy therefore, at best, is useless, and may be pernicious."
After having once so clearly understood the principle of population as
to express these and many other sentiments on the subject, equally just and

5. Travels in France, vol. i. c. xvii. p. 469.   6. Id. p. 471.

important, it is not a little surprising to find Mr. Young in a pamphlet, intitled, *The Question of Scarcity plainly stated, and Remedies considered,*
(*published in* 1800), observing, that "the means which would of all others
" perhaps tend most surely to prevent future scarcities so oppressive to the
" poor as the present, would be to secure to every country labourer in the
" kingdom, that has three children and upwards, half an acre of land for
" potatoes, and grass enough to feed one or two cows.[7] * * * * If each had
" his ample potatoe ground and a cow, the price of wheat would be of
" little more consequence to them, than it is to their brethren in Ireland."

"Every one admits the system to be good, but the question is, how to
" enforce it."

I was by no means aware, that the excellence of the system had been so
generally admitted. For myself I strongly protest against being included in
the general term of *every one,* as I should consider the adoption of this system, as the most cruel and fatal blow to the happiness of the lower classes
of people in this country, that they had ever received.

Mr. Young, however, goes on to say, that, "The magnitude of the object
" should make us disregard any difficulties, but such as are insuperable:
" none such would probably occur if something like the following means
" were resorted to:"

"I. Where there are common pastures, to give to a labouring man hav-
" ing   children, a right to demand an allotment proportioned to the
" family, to be set out by the parish officers, &c. * * * and a cow bought.
" Such labourer to have both for life, paying 40s. a year till the price of
" the cow, &c. was reimbursed: at his death to go to the labourer having
" the most numerous family, for life, paying   shillings a week to the
" widow of his predecessor."

"II. Labourers thus demanding allotments by reason of their families to
" have land assigned, and cows bought, till the proportion so allotted
" amounts to one of   the extent of the common."

"III. In parishes where there are no commons, and the quality of the
" land adequate, every cottager having   children, to whose cottage
" there is not within a given time land sufficient for a cow, and half an acre
" of potatoes, assigned at a fair average rent, subject to appeal to the ses-
" sions, to have a right to demand   shillings per week of the parish for
" every child, till such land be assigned; leaving to landlords and tenants
" the means of doing it. Cows to be found by the parish, under an annual
" reimbursement."[8]

7. P. 77.   8. P. 78.

"The great object is, by means of milk and potatoes, to take the mass
" of the country poor from the consumption of wheat, and to give them
" substitutes equally wholesome and nourishing, and as independent of
" scarcities, natural and artificial, as the providence of the Almighty will
" admit."[9]

Would not this plan operate, in the most direct manner, as an encouragement to marriage and bounty on children, which Mr. Young has with
so much justice reprobated in his travels in France? and does he seriously
think that it would be an eligible thing, to feed the mass of the people in this
country on milk and potatoes, and make them as independent of the price
of corn, and of the demand for labour, as their brethren in Ireland?

The specifick cause of the poverty and misery of the lower classes of
people in France and Ireland, is, that, from the extreme subdivision of
property in the one country, and the facility of obtaining a potatoe ground
in the other, a population is brought into existence, which is not demanded
by the quantity of capital and employment in the country; and the consequence of which must, therefore, necessarily be, as is very justly expressed
in the report of the committee of mendicity before mentioned, to lower
in general the price of labour by too great competition; from which must
result complete indigence to those who cannot find employment, and an
incomplete subsistence even to those who can.

The obvious tendency of Mr. Young's plan, is, by encouraging marriage and furnishing a cheap food, independent of the price of corn, and,
of course, of the demand for labour, to place the lower classes of people
exactly in this situation.

It may perhaps be said, that our poor laws, at present, regularly encourage marriage and children, by distributing relief in proportion to the size of
families; and that this plan, which is proposed as a substitute, would merely
do the same thing in a less objectionable manner. But surely, in endeavouring to get rid of the evil of the poor laws, we ought not to retain their most
pernicious quality: and Mr. Young must know, as well as I do, that the principal reason why poor laws have invariably been found ineffectual in the
relief of the poor, is, that they tend to encourage a population which is not
regulated by the demand for labour. Mr. Young himself, indeed, expressly
takes notice of this effect in England, and observes, that notwithstanding
the unrivalled prosperity of her manufactures, "population is sometimes
" too active, as we see clearly by the dangerous increase of poor's rates
" in country villages."[10]

9. P. 79.   10. Travels in France, vol. i. c. xvii. p. 470.

But the fact is, that Mr. Young's plan would be incomparably more powerful in encouraging a population beyond the demand for labour, than our present poor laws. A laudable repugnance to the receiving of parish relief, arising partly from a spirit of independence not yet extinct, and partly, from the disagreeable mode in which the relief is given, undoubtedly deters many from marrying with a certainty of falling on the parish; and the proportion of marriages to the whole population, which has before been noticed, clearly proves that the poor laws, though they have undoubtedly a considerable influence in this respect, do not encourage marriage so much as might be expected from theory. But the case would be very different, if, when a labourer had an early marriage in contemplation, the terrific forms of workhouses and parish officers, which might disturb his resolution, were to be exchanged for the fascinating visions of land and cows. If the love of property, as Mr. Young has repeatedly said, will make a man do much, it would be rather strange if it would not make him marry; an action to which, it appears from experience, that he is by no means disinclined.

The population which would be thus called into being, would be supported by the extended cultivation of potatoes, and would of course go on without any reference to the demand for labour. In the present state of things, notwithstanding the flourishing condition of our manufactures, and the numerous checks to our population, there is no practical problem so difficult as to find employment for the poor; but this difficulty would evidently be aggravated a hundred fold, under the circumstances here supposed.

In Ireland, or in any other country, where the common food is potatoes, and every man who wishes to marry may obtain a piece of ground, sufficient, when planted with this root, to support a family, prizes may be given till the treasury is exhausted, for essays on the best means of employing the poor; but till some stop to the progress of population, naturally arising from this state of things, take place, the object in view is really a physical impossibility.[11]

Mr. Young has intimated, that if the people were fed upon milk and potatoes, they would be more independent of scarcities than at present; but why this should be the case I really cannot comprehend. Undoubtedly,

11. Dr. Crumpe's prize essay on the best means of finding employment for the people, is an excellent treatise, and contains much valuable information; but, till the capital of the country is better proportioned to its population, it is perfectly chimerical to expect success in any project of the kind. I am also strongly disposed to believe that the indolent and turbulent habits of the lower Irish can never be corrected, while the potatoe system enables them to increase so much beyond the regular demand for labour.

people who live upon potatoes will not be much affected by a scarcity of wheat; but is there any contradiction in the supposition of a failure in the crops of potatoes? I believe it is generally understood, that they are more liable to suffer damage during the winter than grain. From the much greater quantity of food, yielded by a given piece of land, when planted with potatoes, than under any other kind of cultivation, it would naturally happen, that, for some time after the introduction of this root, as the general food of the lower classes of people, a greater quantity would be grown than was demanded, and they would live in plenty. Mr. Young, in his travels through France, observes, that, "In districts which contain immense quantities of
" waste land of a certain degree of fertility, as in the roots of the Pyrenees,
" belonging to communities ready to sell them, economy and industry,
" animated with the views of settling and marrying, flourish greatly; in
" such neighbourhoods something like an American increase takes place,
" and, if the land be cheap, little distress is found. But as procreation goes
" on rapidly under such circumstances, the least check to subsistence is
" attended with great misery; as wastes becoming dearer, or the best por-
" tions being sold, or difficulties arising in the acquisition; all which cir-
" cumstances I met with in those mountains. The moment that any im-
" pediment happens the distress of such people will be proportioned to the
" activity and vigour which had animated population."[12]

This description will apply exactly to what would take place in this country, on the distribution of small portions of land to the common people, and the introduction of potatoes as their general food. For a time, the change might appear beneficial, and, of course, the idea of property would make it, at first, highly acceptable to the poor; but as Mr. Young, in another place, says, "You presently arrive at the limit, beyond which, the earth,
" cultivate it as you please, will feed no more mouths; yet those simple
" manners which instigate to marriage still continue; what then is the con-
" sequence but the most dreadful misery imaginable?"[13]

When the commons were all divided and difficulties began to occur in procuring potatoe grounds, the habit of early marriages which had been introduced, would occasion the most complicated distress; and when, from the increasing population, and diminishing sources of subsistence, the average growth of potatoes was not more than the average consumption, a scarcity of potatoes would be, in every respect, as probable, as a scarcity of wheat at present, and when it did arrive, it would be, beyond all comparison, more dreadful.

12. Travels in France, vol. i. c. xvii. p. 409.   13. Ibid.

When the common people of a country live principally upon the dearest grain, as they do in England on wheat, they have great resources in a scarcity; and barley, oats, rice, cheap soups, and potatoes, all present themselves as less expensive, yet, at the same time, wholesome means of nourishment; but when their habitual food is the lowest in this scale, they appear to be absolutely without resource, except in the bark of trees, like the poor Swedes; and a great portion of them must necessarily be starved. Wheaten bread, roast beef, and turbot, which might not fail at the same time, are indeed, in themselves, unexceptionable substitutes for potatoes, and would probably be accepted as such, without murmuring by the common people; but the misfortune is, that a large population which had been habitually supported by milk and potatoes, would find it difficult to obtain these substitutes in sufficient quantities, even if the whole benevolence of the kingdom were called into action for the purpose.

The wages of labour will always be regulated by the proportion of the supply to the demand. And as, upon the potatoe system, a supply more than adequate to the demand would very soon take place, and this supply might be continued at a very cheap rate, on account of the cheapness of the food which would furnish it, the common price of labour would soon be regulated principally by the price of potatoes, instead of the price of wheat, as at present; and the rags and wretched cabins of Ireland would follow of course.

When the demand for labour occasionally exceeds the supply, and wages are regulated by the price of the dearest grain, they will generally be such as to yield something besides mere food, and the common people may be able to obtain decent houses and decent clothing. If the contrast between the state of the French and English labourers which Mr. Young has drawn, be in any degree near the truth, the advantage on the side of England has been occasioned, precisely and exclusively, by these two circumstances; and if, by the adoption of milk and potatoes as the general food of the common people, these circumstances were totally altered, so as to make the supply of labour constantly in a great excess above the demand for it, and regulate wages by the price of the cheapest food, the advantage would be immediately lost, and no efforts of benevolence could prevent the most general and abject poverty.

Upon the same principle, it would by no means be eligible that the cheap soups of Count Rumford should be adopted as the general food of the common people. They are excellent inventions for publick institutions, and as occasional resources; but if they were once universally adopted by the poor, it would be impossible to prevent the price of labour from being regulated by them; and the labourer, though at first he might have more to spare for other expences, besides food, would ultimately have much less to spare than before.

The desirable thing, with a view to the happiness of the common people, seems to be, that their habitual food should be dear, and their wages regulated by it; but that, in a scarcity, or other occasional distress, the cheaper food should be readily and cheerfully adopted.[14] With a view of rendering this transition easier, and at the same time of making a useful distinction between these who are dependent on parish relief, and those who are not, I should think that one plan which Mr. Young proposes, would be extremely eligible. This is "to pass an act prohibiting relief, so far as subsistence is " concerned, in any other manner than by potatoes, rice, and soup, not " merely as a measure of the moment, but permanently."[15] I do not think that this plan would necessarily introduce these articles as the common food of the lower classes; and if it merely made the transition to them in periods of distress easier, and, at the same time, drew a more marked line than at present, between dependence and independence, it would have a very beneficial effect.

As it is acknowledged that the introduction of milk and potatoes, or of cheap soups, as the general food of the lower classes of people, would lower the price of labour, perhaps some cold politician might propose to adopt the system, with a view of underselling foreigners in the markets of Europe. I should not envy the feelings which could suggest such a proposal. I really cannot conceive any thing much more detestable than the idea of knowingly condemning the labourers of this country to the rags and wretched cabins of Ireland, for the purpose of selling a few more broadcloths and calicoes.[16] The wealth and power of nations are, after all, only desirable as

14. It is certainly to be wished, that every cottage in England should have a garden to it, well stocked with vegetables. A little variety of food is in every point of view highly useful. Potatoes are undoubtedly a most valuable subsidiary, though I should be very sorry ever to see them the principal dependence of our labourers.

15. Question of Scarcity, &c. p. 80. This might be done, at least, with regard to workhouses. In assisting the poor at their own homes, it might be subject to some practical difficulties.

16. In this observation I have not the least idea of alluding to Mr. Young, who, I firmly believe, ardently wishes to ameliorate the condition of the lower classes of people, though I do not think that his plan would effect the object in view. He either did not see those consequences which I apprehend from it; or he has a better opinion of the happiness of the common people in Ireland, than I have. In his Irish tour he seemed much struck with the plenty of potatoes which they possessed, and the absence of all apprehension of want. Had he travelled in 1800 and 1801,

they contribute to happiness. In this point of view, I should be very far from undervaluing them, considering them, in general, as absolutely necessary means to attain the end; but if any particular case should occur, in which they appeared to be in direct opposition to each other, we cannot rationally doubt which ought to be postponed.

Fortunately, however, even on the narrowest political principles, the adoption of such a system would not answer. It has always been observed, that those who work chiefly on their own property, work very indolently and unwillingly when employed for others; and it must necessarily happen, when, from the general adoption of a very cheap food, the population of a country increases considerably beyond the demand for labour, that habits of idleness and turbulence will be generated, most peculiarly unfavourable to a flourishing state of manufactures. In spite of the cheapness of labour in Ireland, there are few manufactures which can be prepared in that country for foreign sale so cheap as in England: and this is evidently owing to the want of those industrious habits which can only be produced by regular employment.

---

his impressions would by all accounts have been very different. From the facility which has hitherto prevailed in Ireland of procuring potatoe grounds, scarcities have certainly been rare, and all the effects of the system have not yet been felt, though certainly enough to make it appear very far from desirable.

Mr. Young has since pursued his idea more in detail, in a pamphlet, entitled, *An Inquiry into the Propriety of applying Wastes to the better Maintenance and Support of the Poor.* But the impression on my mind is still the same; and it appears to me calculated to assimilate the condition of the labourers of this country to that of the lower classes of the Irish. Mr. Young seems, in a most unaccountable manner, to have forgotten all his general principles on this subject. He has treated the question of a provision for the poor, as if it was merely, How to provide in the cheapest and best manner for a *given number* of people? If this had been the sole question, it would never have taken so many hundred years to resolve. But the real question is, How to provide for those who are in want, in such a manner, as to prevent a continual accumulation of their numbers? and it will readily occur to the reader, that a plan of giving them land and cows cannot promise much success in this respect. If, after all the commons had been divided, the poor laws were still to continue in force, no good reason can be assigned, why the rates should not in a few years be as high as they are at present, independently of all that had been expended in the purchase of land and stock.

CHAP. XI.

Of the necessity of general principles on this subject.

IT has been observed by Hume, that of all sciences, there is none, where first appearances are more deceitful than in politicks.[1] The remark is undoubtedly very just, and is most peculiarly applicable to that department of the science, which relates to the modes of improving the condition of the lower classes of society.

We are continually hearing declamations against theory and theorists, by men who pride themselves upon the distinction of being practical. It must be acknowledged that bad theories are very bad things, and the authors of them useless, and sometimes pernicious members of society. But these advocates of practice do not seem to be aware, that they themselves very often come under this description, and that a great part of them may be classed among the most mischievous theorists of their time. When a man faithfully relates any facts which have come within the scope of his own observation, however confined it may have been, he undoubtedly adds to the sum of general knowledge, and confers a benefit on society. But when, from this confined experience, from the management of his own little farm, or the details of the workhouse in his neighbourhood, he draws a general inference, as is very frequently the case, he then at once erects himself into a theorist; and is the more dangerous; because experience being the only just foundation for theory, people are often caught merely by the sound of the word, and do not stop to make the distinction between that partial experience which, on such subjects, is no foundation whatever for a just theory, and that general experience, on which alone a just theory can be founded.

There are, perhaps, few subjects, on which human ingenuity has been more exerted, than in the endeavour to ameliorate the condition of the poor; and there is certainly no subject in which it has so completely failed. The question between the theorist who calls himself practical, and the genuine theorist, is, whether this should prompt us to look into all the holes and corners of workhouses, and content ourselves with mulcting the parish officers for their waste of cheese parings and candle ends, and with distributing more soups and potatoes; or to recur to general principles, which shew us at once the cause of the failure, and prove that the system has been from

1. Essay xi. vol. i. p. 431. 8vo.

the beginning radically erroneous. There is no subject to which general principles have been so seldom applied; and yet, in the whole compass of human knowledge, I doubt if there be one, in which it is so dangerous to lose sight of them; because the partial and immediate effects of a particular mode of giving assistance are so often directly opposite to the general and permanent effects.

It has been observed in particular districts, where cottagers are possessed of small pieces of land, and are in the habit of keeping cows, that, during the late scarcities, some of them were able to support themselves without parish assistance, and others with comparatively little.[2]

According to the partial view in which this subject has been always contemplated, a general inference has been drawn from such instances, that, if we could place all our labourers in a similar situation, they would all be equally comfortable, and equally independent of the parish. This is an inference, however, that by no means follows. The advantage which cottagers, who at present keep cows, enjoy, arises in a great measure from its being peculiar; and would be destroyed if it were made general.

A farmer or gentleman living in a grazing country has, we will suppose, a certain number of cottages on his farm. Being a liberal man, and liking to see all the people about him comfortable, he may join a piece of land to his cottages sufficient to keep one or two cows, and give, besides, high wages. His labourers will of course live in plenty, and be able to rear up large families; but a grazing farm requires few hands; and though the master may choose to pay those that he employs well, he will not probably wish to have more labourers on his farm than his work requires. He does not therefore build more houses; and the children of the labourers whom he employs must evidently emigrate and settle in other countries. While such a system continues peculiar to certain families, or certain districts, no great inconveniencies arise from it to the community in general; and it cannot be doubted, that the individual labourers employed on these farms are in an enviable situation, and such as we might naturally wish was the lot of all our labourers. But it is perfectly clear, that such a system could not, in the nature of things, possess the same advantages, if it were made general; because there would then be no countries to which the children could emigrate with any prospect of finding work. Population would evidently increase beyond the demand of towns and manufactories, and universal poverty must necessarily ensue.

2. See an Inquiry into the State of Cottagers in the Counties of Lincoln and Rutland by Robert Gourlay. Annals of Agriculture, vol, xxxvii. p. 514.

It should be observed also, that one of the reasons, why the labourers who at present keep cows, are so comfortable, is, that they are able to make a considerable profit of the milk which they do not use themselves; an advantage which would evidently be very much diminished if the system were universal. And though they were certainly able to struggle through the late scarcities with less assistance than their neighbours, as might naturally be expected, from their having other resources besides the article which in those individual years was scarce; yet if the system were universal, there can be no reason assigned, why they would not be subject to suffer as much from a scarcity of grass and a mortality among cows, as our common labourers do now from a scarcity of wheat. We should be extremely cautious therefore of trusting to such appearances, and of drawing a general inference from this kind of partial experience.

The main principle on which the society for increasing the comforts, and bettering the condition of the poor, professes to proceed, is excellent. To give effect to that masterspring of industry, the desire of bettering our condition,[3] is the true mode of improving the state of the lower classes; and we may safely agree with Mr. Bernard, in one of his able prefaces, that whatever encourages and promotes habits of industry, prudence, foresight, virtue, and cleanliness, among the poor, is beneficial to them and to the country; and whatever removes or diminishes the incitements to any of these qualities, is detrimental to the state, and pernicious to the individual.[4]

Mr. Bernard, indeed, himself, seems in general to be fully aware of the difficulties which the society has to contend with in the accomplishment of its object. But still it appears to be in some danger of falling into the error before alluded to, of drawing general inferences from insufficient experience. Without adverting to the plans, respecting cheaper foods and parish shops, recommended by individuals, the beneficial effects of which depend entirely upon their being peculiar to certain families or certain parishes, and would be lost if they were general, by lowering the wages of labour; I shall only notice one observation of a more comprehensive nature, which occurs in the preface to the second volume of the Reports. It is there remarked, that the experience of the society seemed to warrant the conclusion, that the best mode of relieving the poor, was, by assisting them at their own homes, and placing out their children as soon as possible in different employments, apprenticeships, &c. I really believe that this is the best, and it is certainly the most agreeable mode, in which occasional and

3. Preface to vol. ii. of the Reports.   4. Preface to vol. iii. of the Reports.

discriminate assistance can be given. But it is evident, that it must be done with caution, and cannot be adopted as a general principle, and made the foundation of universal practice. It is open exactly to the same objection as the cow system in pasture countries which has just been noticed, and that part of the act of the 43d of Elizabeth which directs the overseers to employ and provide for the children of the poor. A particular parish, where all the children, as soon as they were of a proper age, were taken from their parents, and placed out in proper situations, might be very comfortable; but if the system were general, and the poor saw that all their children would be thus provided for, every employment would presently be overstocked with hands, and the consequence need not be again repeated.

Nothing can be more clear, than that it is within the power of money, and of the exertions of the rich, adequately to relieve a particular family, a particular parish, and even a particular district. But it will be equally clear, if we reflect a moment on the subject, that it is totally out of their power to relieve the whole country in the same way; at least, without providing a regular vent for the overflowing numbers in emigration, or without the prevalence of a particular virtue among the poor, which the distribution of this assistance tends obviously to discourage.

Even industry itself, is, in this respect, not very different from money. A man who possesses a certain portion of it, above what is usually possessed by his neighbours, will, in the actual state of things, be almost sure of a competent livelihood; but if all his neighbours were to become at once as industrious as himself, the absolute portion of industry which he before possessed would no longer be a security against want. Hume fell into a very great error, when he asserted that "almost all the moral, as well as " natural evils of human life, arise from idleness;" and for the cure of these ills, required only that the whole species should possess naturally an equal diligence, with that which many individuals are able to attain by habit and reflection.[5] It is evident that this given degree of industry possessed by the whole species, if not combined with another virtue of which he takes no notice, would totally fail of rescuing society from want and misery, and would scarcely remove a single moral or physical evil, of all those to which he alludes.

I am aware of an objection, which will, with great appearance of justice, be urged against the general tenour of these reasonings. It will be said, that to argue thus, is at once to object to every mode of assisting the

5. Dialogues on Natural Religion, Part xi. p. 212.

poor, as it is impossible, in the nature of things, to assist people individually, without altering their relative situation in society, and proportionally depressing others; and that as those who have families, are the persons naturally most subject to distress, and as we are certainly not called upon to assist those who do not want our aid, we must necessarily, if we act at all, relieve those who have children, and thus encourage marriage and population.

I have already observed, however, and I here repeat it again, that the general principles on these subjects ought not to be pushed too far, though they should always be kept in view; and that many cases may occur, in which the good resulting from the relief of the present distress, may more than overbalance the evil to be apprehended from the remote consequence.

All relief in instances of distress, not arising from idle and improvident habits, clearly comes under this description; and in general it may be observed, that it is only that kind of systematic and certain relief, on which the poor can confidently depend, whatever may be their conduct, that violates general principles, in such a manner, as to make it clear that the general consequence is worse than the particular evil.

Independently of this discriminate and occasional assistance, the beneficial effects of which I have fully allowed in a preceding chapter, I have before endeavoured to shew, that much might be expected from a better and more general system of education. Every thing that can be done in this way, has indeed a very peculiar value; because education is one of those advantages, which not only all may share without interfering with each other, but the raising of one person may actually contribute to the raising of others. If, for instance, a man by education acquires that decent kind of pride, and those juster habits of thinking, which will prevent him from burdening society with a family of children, which he cannot support, his conduct, as far as an individual instance can go, tends evidently to improve the condition of his fellow labourers; and a contrary conduct from ignorance, would tend as evidently to depress it.

I cannot help thinking also, that something might be done towards bettering the situation of the poor, by a general improvement of their cottages; if care were taken, at the same time, not to make them so large, as to allow of two families settling in them; and not to increase their number faster than the demand for labour required. Perhaps one of the most salutary, and least pernicious checks, to the frequency of early marriages in this country, is the difficulty of procuring a cottage, and the laudable habits which prompt a labourer rather to defer his marriage some years, in the expectation of a vacancy, than to content himself with a wretched mud cabin, like those in Ireland.[6]

Even the cow system, upon a more confined plan, might not be open to objection. With any view of making it a substitute for the Poor Laws, and of giving labourers a right to demand land and cows in proportion to their families; or of taking the common people from the consumption of wheat, and feeding them on milk and potatoes; it appears to me, I confess, truly preposterous: but if it were so ordered as merely to provide a comfortable situation for the better and more industrious class of labourers, and to supply, at the same time, a very important want among the poor in general, that of milk for their children, I think that it would be extremely beneficial, and might be made a very powerful incitement to habits of industry, economy, and prudence. With this view, however, it is evident, that only a certain portion of the labourers in each parish could be embraced in the plan; that good conduct, and not mere distress, should have the most valid claim to preference; that too much attention should not be paid to the number of children; and that, universally, those who had saved money enough for the purchase of a cow, should be preferred, to those who required to be furnished with one by the parish.[7]

To facilitate the saving of small sums of money for this purpose, and encourage young labourers to economize their earnings with a view to a provision for marriage; it might be extremely useful to have country banks, where the smallest sums would be received, and a fair interest paid for them. At present, the few labourers who save a little money, are often greatly at a loss to know what to do with it; and under such circumstances we cannot be much surprised that it should sometimes be ill employed, and last but a short time. It would probably be essential to the success of any

---

6. Perhaps, however, this is not often left to his choice, on account of the fear which every parish has of increasing its poor. There are many ways by which our poor laws operate in counteracting their first obvious tendency to increase population, and this is one of them. I have little doubt that it is almost exclusively owing to these counteracting causes, that we have been able to persevere in this system so long, and that the condition of the poor has not been so much injured by it as might have been expected.

7. The act of Elizabeth which prohibited the building of cottages, unless four acres of land were annexed to them, is probably impracticable in a manufacturing country like England; but upon this principle, certainly the greatest part of the poor might possess land; because the difficulty of procuring such cottages would always operate as a powerful check to their increase. The effect of such a plan would be very different from that of Mr. Young's.

plan of this kind, that the labourer should be able to draw out his money whenever he wanted it, and have the most perfect liberty of disposing of it in every respect as he pleased. Though we may regret, that money so hardly earned should sometimes be spent to little purpose; yet it seems to be a case in which we have no right to interfere; nor if we had, would it, in a general view, be advantageous; because the knowledge of possessing this liberty would be of more use in encouraging the practice of saving, than any restriction of it, in preventing the misuse of money so saved.

One should undoubtedly be extremely unwilling, not to make as much use as possible of that known stimulus to industry and economy, the desire of, and the attachment to, property: but it should be recollected, that the good effects of this stimulus, show themselves principally, when this property is to be procured, or preserved, by personal exertions; and that they are by no means so general, under other circumstances. If any idle man with a family could demand, and obtain, a cow and some land, I should expect to see both very often neglected.

It has been observed, that those cottagers who keep cows, are more industrious and more regular in their conduct than those who do not. This is probably true, and what might naturally be expected; but the inference that the way to make all people industrious, is to give them cows, may by no means be quite so certain. Most of those who keep cows at present have purchased them with the fruits of their own industry. It is therefore more just to say, that their industry has given them a cow, than that a cow has given them their industry; though I would by no means be understood to imply, that the sudden possession of property never generates industrious habits.

The practical good effects which have been already experienced, from cottagers keeping cows,[8] arise in fact from the system being nearly such as the confined plan which I have mentioned. In the districts where cottagers of this description most abound, they do not bear a very large proportion to the population of the whole parish: they consist in general of the better sort of labourers, who have been able to purchase their own cows; and the peculiar comforts of their situation arise, more from the relative, than the positive advantages which they possess.

From observing, therefore, their industry and comforts, we should be very cautious of inferring that we could give the same industry and

8. Inquiry into the State of Cottagers in the Counties of Lincoln and Rutland, by Robert Gourlay. Annals of Agriculture, vol. xxxvii. p. 514.

comforts to all the lower classes of people, by giving them the same possessions. There is nothing that has given rise to such a cloud of errors, as a confusion between relative and positive, and between cause and effect.

It may be said, however, that any plan of generally improving the cottages of the poor, or of enabling more of them to keep cows, would evidently give them the power of rearing a greater number of children, and, by thus encouraging population, violate the principles which I have endeavoured to establish. But if I have been successful in making the reader comprehend the principal bent of this work, he will be aware, that the precise reason why I think that more children ought not to be born than the country can support, is, that the greatest possible number of those that are born may be supported. We cannot, in the nature of things, assist the poor, in any way, without enabling them to rear up to manhood a greater number of their children. But this is, of all other things, the most desirable, both with regard to individuals and the publick. Every loss of a child from the consequences of poverty, must evidently be preceded and accompanied by great misery to individuals; and, in a publick view; every child that dies under ten years of age, is a loss to the nation of all that had been expended in its subsistence till that period. Consequently, in every point of view, a decrease of mortality, at all ages, is what we ought to aim at. We cannot, however, effect this object, without first crowding the population in some degree by making more children grow up to manhood; but we shall do no harm in this respect, if, at the same time, we can impress these children with the idea that to possess the same advantages as their parents, they must defer marriage till they have a fair prospect of being able to maintain a family. And it must be candidly confessed that, if we cannot do this, all our former efforts will have been thrown away. It is not in the nature of things that any permanent and general improvement in the condition of the poor can be effected, without an increase in the preventive check: and unless this take place, either with, or without our efforts, every thing that is done for the poor must be temporary and partial: a diminution of mortality at present, will be balanced by an increased mortality in future; and the improvement of their condition in one place, will proportionally depress it in another. This is a truth so important, and so little understood, that it can scarcely be too often insisted on. The generality of charitable people and of the encouragers of marriage, are not in the smallest degree aware of the real effects of what they do.

Dr. Paley, in a chapter on population, provision, &c. in his Moral Philosophy, observes, that the condition most favourable to the population of a country, and, at the same time, to its general happiness, is, "that of a

" laborious frugal people ministering to the demands of an opulent, luxu-
" rious nation."[9] Such a form of society has not, it must be confessed, an
inviting aspect. Nothing but the conviction of its being absolutely necessary, could reconcile us to the idea of ten millions of people condemned to
incessant toil, and to the privation of every thing but absolute necessaries,
in order to minister to the excessive luxuries of the other million. But the
fact is, that such a form of society is by no means necessary. It is by no
means necessary, that the rich should be excessively luxurious, in order to
support the manufactures of a country, or that the poor should be deprived
of all luxuries, in order to make them sufficiently numerous. The best, and
in every point of view the most advantageous, manufactures in this country,
are those which are consumed by the great body of the people. The manufactures which are confined exclusively to the rich, are not only trivial on
account of the comparative smallness of their quantity; but are further liable to the great disadvantage of producing much occasional misery among
those employed in them, from changes of fashion. It is the spread of luxury,
therefore, among the mass of the people, and not an excess of it in a few,
that seems to be most advantageous, both with regard to national wealth
and national happiness; and what Dr. Paley considers as the true evil and
proper danger of luxury, I should be disposed to consider as its true good,
and peculiar advantage. If, indeed, it be allowed that in every society, not in
the state of a new colony, some powerful check to population must prevail;
and if it be observed, that a taste for the comforts and conveniences of life
will prevent people from marrying under the certainty of being deprived of
those advantages; it must be allowed that we can hardly expect to find any
check to marriage so little prejudicial to the happiness and virtue of society
as the general prevalence of such a taste; and consequently that the spread
of luxury[10] in this sense of the term, is particularly desirable; and one of

9. Vol. ii. c. xi. p. 359. From a passage in Dr. Paley's late work on Natural Theology, I am inclined to think, that subsequent reflection has induced him to modify
some of his former ideas on the subject of population. He has stated most justly,
(chap. xxv. p. 539.) that mankind will in every country breed up to a certain point
of distress. If this be allowed, that country will evidently be the happiest, where
the degree of distress at this point is the least, and consequently, if the spread of
luxury, by producing the check sooner, tend to diminish this degree of distress, it is
certainly desirable.

10. In a note to the tenth chapter of the last book, I have mentioned the point at
which, alone, it is probable that luxury becomes really prejudicial to a country. But
this point does not depend upon the spread of luxury, as diminishing the frequency
of marriage among the poor, but upon the proportion which those employed in preparing or procuring luxuries, bears to the funds which are to support them.

the best means of raising that standard of wretchedness, alluded to in the eighth chapter of this book.

It has been generally found that the middle parts of society are most favourable to virtuous and industrious habits, and to the growth of all kinds of talents. But it is evident, that all cannot be in the middle. Superior and inferior parts are, in the nature of things, absolutely necessary; and not only necessary, but strikingly beneficial. If no man could hope to rise, or fear to fall in society; if industry did not bring with it its reward, and indolence its punishment; we could not expect to see that animated activity in bettering our condition, which now forms the master-spring of publick prosperity. But in contemplating the different states of Europe, we observe a very considerable difference in the relative proportions of the superior, the middle, and the inferior parts; and from the effect of these differences, it seems probable, that our best grounded expectations of an increase in the happiness of the mass of human society, are founded in the prospect of an increase in the relative proportions of the middle parts. And if the lower classes of people had acquired the habit of proportioning the supplies of labour to a stationary, or even decreasing demand, without an increase of misery and mortality, as at present; we might even venture to indulge a hope, that at some future period the processes for abridging human labour, the progress of which has of late years been so rapid, might ultimately supply all the wants of the most wealthy society with less personal labour than at present; and if they did not diminish the severity of individual exertion, might, at least, diminish the number of those employed in severe toil. If the lowest classes of society were thus diminished, and the middle classes increased, each labourer might indulge a more rational hope of rising by diligence and exertion into a better station; the rewards of industry and virtue would be increased in number; human society would appear to consist of fewer blanks and more prizes; and the sum of social happiness would be evidently augmented.

To indulge, however, in any distant views of this kind, unaccompanied by the evils usually attendant on a stationary, or decreasing demand for labour, we must suppose the general prevalence of such prudential habits among the poor, as would prevent them from marrying, when the actual price of labour, joined to what they might have saved in their single state, would not give them the prospect of being able to support a wife and six children without assistance. And, in every point of view, such a degree of prudential restraint would be extremely beneficial; and would produce a very striking amelioration in the condition of the lower classes of people.

It may be said, perhaps, that even this degree of prudence might not always avail, as when a man marries he cannot tell what number of children he shall have, and many have more than six. This is certainly true; and in this case I do not think that any evil would result from making a certain allowance to every child above this number; not with a view of rewarding a man for his large family, but merely, of relieving him from a species of distress, which it would be unreasonable in us to expect that he should calculate upon. And with this view, the relief should be merely such, as to place him exactly in the same situation as if he had had six children. Montesquieu disapproves of an edict of Lewis the fourteenth, which gave certain pensions to those who had ten and twelve children, as being of no use in encouraging population.[11] For the very reason that he disapproves of it, I should think that some law of the kind might be adopted without danger, and might relieve particular individuals from a very pressing and unlooked-for distress, without operating in any respect as an encouragement to marriage.

If at some future period, any approach should be made towards the more general prevalence of prudential habits with respect to marriage among the poor, from which alone any permanent and general improvement of their condition can arise; I do not think that the narrowest politician need be alarmed at it, from the fear of its occasioning such an advance in the price of labour as will enable our commercial competitors to undersell us in foreign markets. There are four circumstances that might be expected to accompany it, which would probably either prevent, or fully counterbalance, any effect of this kind. These are, 1st, The more equable and lower price of provisions, from the demand being less frequently above the supply. 2dly, The removal of that heavy burden on agriculture, and that great addition to the present wages of labour, the poors rates. 3dly, The national saving of a great part of that sum, which is expended without return, in the support of those children who die prematurely, from the consequences of poverty. And, lastly, The more general prevalence of economical and industrious habits, particularly among unmarried men, which would prevent that indolence, drunkenness, and waste of labour, which at present are too frequently a consequence of high wages.

11. Esprit des Loix, liv. xxiii. c. xxvii.

CHAP. XII.

Of our rational expectations respecting the future improvement of Society.

IN taking a general and concluding view of our rational expectations respecting the mitigation of the evils arising from the principle of population, it may be observed, that though the increase of population in a geometrical ratio be incontrovertible, and the period of doubling, when unchecked, has been uniformly stated in this work, rather below than above the truth; yet there are some natural consequences of the progress of society and civilization, which necessarily repress its full effects. There are, more particularly, great towns and manufactures, in which we can scarcely hope, and certainly not expect, to see any very material change. It is undoubtedly our duty, and in every point of view highly desirable, to make towns and manufacturing employments as little injurious as possible to the duration of human life; but, after all our efforts, it is probable that they will always remain less healthy than country situations and country employments; and consequently, operating as positive checks, will diminish in some degree the necessity of the preventive check.

In every old state it is observed, that a considerable number of grown-up people, remain for a time unmarried. The duty of practising the common and acknowledged rules of morality during this period, has never been controverted in theory, however it may have been opposed in practice. This branch of the duty of moral restraint has scarcely been touched by the reasonings of this work. It rests on the same foundation as before, neither stronger nor weaker. And knowing how incompletely this duty has hitherto been fulfilled, it would certainly be visionary to expect any very material change for the better, in future.

The part which has been affected by the reasonings of this work is not, therefore, that which relates to our conduct during the period of celibacy, but to the duty of extending this period till we have a prospect of being able to maintain our children. And it is by no means visionary to indulge a hope of some favourable change in this respect; because it is found by experience, that the prevalence of this kind of prudential restraint is extremely different in different countries, and in the same countries at different periods.

It cannot be doubted, that throughout Europe in general, and most particularly in the northern states, a decided change has taken place in the operation of this prudential restraint, since the prevalence of those warlike and enterprising habits which destroyed so many people. In later times, the gradual diminution, and almost total extinction, of the plagues which so frequently visited Europe in the seventeenth and the beginning of the eighteenth centuries, produced a change of the same kind. And in this country it is not to be doubted that the proportion of marriages has become smaller, since the improvement of our towns, the less frequent returns of epidemicks, and the adoption of habits of greater cleanliness. During the late scarcities, it appears that the number of marriages diminished; and the same motives which prevented many people from marrying during such a period, would operate precisely in the same way, if, in future, the additional number of children reared to manhood from the introduction of the cow-pox, were to be such, as to crowd all employments, lower the price of labour, and make it more difficult to support a family.

Universally, the practice of mankind on the subject of marriage has been much superior to their theories; and however frequent may have been the declamations on the duty of entering into this state, and the advantage of early unions to prevent vice, each individual has practically found it necessary to consider of the means of supporting a family, before he ventured to take so important a step. That great *vis medicatrix reipublicæ,* the desire of bettering our condition, and the fear of making it worse, has been constantly in action, and has been constantly directing people into the right road in spite of all the declamations which tended to lead them aside. Owing to this powerful spring of health in every state, which is nothing more than an inference from the general course of the laws of nature, irresistibly forced on each man's attention, the prudential check to marriage has increased in Europe; and it cannot be unreasonable to conclude, that it will still make further advances. If this take place, without any marked and decided increase of a vicious intercourse with the sex, the happiness of society will evidently be promoted by it; and with regard to the danger of such increase, it is consolatory to remark, that those countries in Europe where marriages are the least frequent, are by no means particularly distinguished by vices of this kind. It has appeared that Norway, Switzerland, England, and Scotland, are above all the rest in the prevalence of the preventive check; and though I do not mean to insist particularly on the virtuous habits of these countries, yet I think that no person would select them as the countries most marked for profligacy of manners. Indeed, from the little that I know of the continent, I should have been inclined to select them as most distinguished for contrary habits, and as rather above than below their neighbours in the chastity of their women, and consequently in the virtuous habits of their men. Experience therefore seems to teach us, that it is possible for moral and physical causes to counteract the effects that might at first be expected from an increase of the preventive check; but allowing all the weight to these effects which is in any degree probable, it may be safely asserted, that the diminution of the vices arising from indigence, would fully counterbalance them; and that all the advantages of diminished mortality, and superior comforts, which would certainly result from an increase of the preventive check, may be placed entirely on the side of the gains to the cause of happiness and virtue.

It is less the object of the present work to propose new plans of improving society, than to inculcate the necessity of resting contented with that mode of improvement, which is dictated by the course of nature, and of not obstructing the advances which would otherwise be made in this way.

It would be undoubtedly highly advantageous, that all our positive institutions, and the whole tenour of our conduct to the poor, should be such as actively to co-operate with that lesson of prudence inculcated by the common course of human events; and if we take upon ourselves, sometimes, to mitigate the natural punishments of imprudence, that we should balance it by increasing the rewards of an opposite conduct. But much would be done, if merely the institutions which directly tend to encourage marriage were gradually changed, and we ceased to circulate opinions, and inculcate doctrines, which positively counteract the lessons of nature.

The limited good which it is sometimes in our power to effect, is often lost by attempting too much, and by making the adoption of some particular plan essentially necessary even to a partial degree of success. In the practical application of the reasonings of this work, I hope that I have avoided this error. I wish to press on the recollection of the reader, that, though I may have given some new views of old facts, and may have indulged in the contemplation of a considerable degree of *possible* improvement, that I might not absolutely shut out that prime cheerer hope; yet in my expectations of probable improvement, and in suggesting the means of accomplishing it, I have been very cautious. The gradual abolition of the poor laws has already often been proposed, in consequence of the practical evils which have been found to flow from them, and the danger of their becoming a weight absolutely intolerable on the landed property of the kingdom. The establishment of a more extensive system of national education, has neither the advantage of novelty with some, nor its disadvantage with others, to recommend it. The practical good effects of education have long been experienced in Scotland; and almost every person who has been placed in a situation to judge, has given his testimony, that education appears to have a considerable effect in the prevention of crimes,[1] and the promotion of industry, morality, and regular conduct. Yet these are the only plans which have been offered; and though the adoption of them in the modes suggested, would very powerfully contribute to forward the object of this work, and better the condition of the poor; yet if nothing be done in this way, I shall not absolutely despair of some partial good effects from the general tenour of the reasoning.

If the principles which I have endeavoured to establish be false, I most sincerely hope to see them completely refuted; but if they be true, the subject is so important, and interests the question of human happiness so nearly, that it is impossible that they should not in time be more fully known, and more generally circulated, whether any particular efforts be made for the purpose or not.

Among the higher and middle classes of society, the effect of this knowledge would, I hope, be to direct without relaxing their efforts in bettering the condition of the poor; to show them what they can, and what they cannot do; and that, although much may be done by advice and instruction, by encouraging habits of prudence and cleanliness, by occasional and discriminate charity, and by any mode of bettering the present condition of the poor, which is followed by an increase of the preventive check; yet that, without this last effect, all the former efforts would be futile; and that, in any old and well-peopled state, to assist the poor in such a manner as to enable them to marry as early as they please, and rear up large families, is a physical impossibility. This knowledge, by tending to prevent the rich from destroying the good effects of their own exertions, and wasting their efforts in a direction where success is unattainable, would confine their attention to the proper objects, and thus enable them to do more good.

Among the poor themselves, its effects would be still more important. That the principal and most permanent cause of poverty, has little or no relation to forms of government, or the unequal division of property; and that, as the rich do not in reality possess the power of finding employment and maintenance for the poor, the poor cannot, in the nature of things, possess the right to demand them, are important truths flowing from the principle of population, which, when properly explained, would by no means

---

1. Mr. Howard found fewer prisoners in Switzerland and Scotland, than in other countries, which he attributed to a more regular education among the lower classes of the Swiss and the Scotch. During the number of years which the late Mr. Fielding presided at Bow-street, only six Scotchmen were brought before him. He used to say that of the persons committed the greater part were Irish. Preface to vol. iii. of the Reports of the Society for bettering the condition of the poor, p. 32.

be above the most ordinary comprehensions. And it is evident, that every man in the lower classes of society, who became acquainted with these truths, would be disposed to bear the distresses in which he might be involved with more patience; would feel less discontent and irritation at the government and the higher classes of society on account of his poverty; would be on all occasions less disposed to insubordination and turbulence; and if he received assistance, either from any publick institution, or from the hand of private charity, he would receive it with more thankfulness, and more justly appreciate its value.

If these truths were by degrees more generally known, which in the course of time does not seem to be improbable, from the natural effects of the mutual interchange of opinions, the lower classes of people, as a body, would become more peaceable and orderly; would be less inclined to tumultuous proceedings in seasons of scarcity, and would at all times be less influenced by inflammatory and seditious publications, from knowing how little the price of labour, and the means of supporting a family, depend upon a revolution. The mere knowledge of these truths, even if they did not operate sufficiently to produce any marked change in the prudential habits of the poor, with regard to marriage, would still have a most beneficial effect on their conduct in a political light; and undoubtedly one of the most valuable of these effects would be, the power that would result to the higher and middle classes of society of gradually improving governments,[2] without the apprehension of those revolutionary excesses, the fear of which, at present, threatens to deprive Europe even of that degree of liberty, which she had before experienced to be practicable, and the salutary effects of which she had long enjoyed.

From a review of the state of society in former periods, compared with the present, I should certainly say, that the evils resulting from the principle of population have rather diminished, than increased, even under the disadvantage of an almost total ignorance of their real cause. And if we can indulge the hope that this ignorance will be gradually dissipated, it does not seem unreasonable to expect, that they will be still further diminished. The increase of absolute population which will of course take place, will

2. I cannot believe that the removal of all unjust grounds of discontent against constituted authorities would render the people torpid and indifferent to advantages which are really attainable. The blessings of civil liberty are so great, that they surely cannot need the aid of false colouring to make them desireable. I should be sorry to think that the lower classes of people could never be animated to assert their rights but by means of such illusory promises, as will generally make the remedy of resistance much worse than the disease that it was intended to cure.

evidently tend but little to weaken this expectation, as every thing depends upon the relative proportions between population and food, and not on the absolute number of people. In the former part of this work, it appeared, that the countries which possessed the fewest people, often suffered the most from the effects of the principle of population; and it can scarcely be doubted, that taking Europe throughout, fewer famines, and fewer diseases arising from want, have prevailed in the last century, than in those which preceded it.

On the whole, therefore, though our future prospects respecting the mitigation of the evils arising from the principle of population, may not be so bright as we could wish, yet they are far from being entirely disheartening, and by no means preclude that gradual and progressive improvement in human society, which, before the late wild speculations on the subject, was the object of rational expectation. To the laws of property and marriage, and to the apparently narrow principle of self-love, which prompts each individual to exert himself in bettering his condition, we are indebted for all the noblest exertions of human genius, for every thing that distinguishes the civilized from the savage state. A strict inquiry into the principle of population leads us strongly to the conclusion, that we shall never be able to throw down the ladder by which we have risen to this eminence; but it by no means proves that we may not rise higher by the same means. The structure of society, in its great features, will probably always remain unchanged. We have every reason to believe, that it will always consist of a class of proprietors, and a class of labourers; but the condition of each, and the proportion which they bear to each other, may be so altered as greatly to improve the harmony and beauty of the whole. It would, indeed, be a melancholy reflection, that, while the views of physical science are daily enlarging, so as scarcely to be bounded by the most distant horizon, the science of moral and political philosophy should be confined within such narrow limits, or at best be so feeble in its influence, as to be unable to counteract the increasing obstacles to human happiness arising from the progress of population. But however formidable these obstacles may have appeared in some parts of this work, it is hoped that the general result of the inquiry is such, as not to make us give up the cause of the improvement of human society in despair. The partial good which seems to be attainable, is worthy of all our exertions; is sufficient to direct our efforts and animate our prospects. And although we cannot expect that the virtue and happiness of mankind will keep pace with the brilliant career of physical discovery, yet if we are not wanting to ourselves, we may confidently indulge the hope, that, to no unimportant extent, they will be influenced by its progress, and will partake in its success.

Essays

Malthus and the History of Population

NIALL O'FLAHERTY

The truism that Robert Malthus's *Essay on the Principle of Population* (1803) was "more generally talked of than read" in the nineteenth century has long been offered as an explanation of why Malthus's critics (and some admirers) continued to misinterpret his views on population despite his repeated efforts throughout his career to clarify them.[1] A refinement of this diagnosis may be suggested, however, that chimes with the author's view of why he was so widely misunderstood. As early as 1806, an exasperated Malthus felt compelled to add an appendix to the third edition of the *Essay* "to correct some of the misrepresentations which have gone abroad" regarding the main points of the much-expanded second edition of the work published in 1803. Much of the declamation against the theory was so devoid of argument, in Malthus's view, that it was unworthy of a response. The appendix was aimed instead at those who not having "had leisure to read the whole work" might interpret it in the light of the "partial and incorrect statements which they have heard."[2] Malthus sensed that there was a large class of readers who were liable to misconstrue his opinions not because they had failed to read the book, but because they had read it too selectively. While he did not specify precisely which parts of the *Essay* he thought were being overlooked, a number of factors suggest that he may have had the first two books of the "Great Quarto" in mind. In the first place, and as is shown below, no one who had read this part of the work attentively would have made the main accusation that Malthus set out to deny in the appendix, that is, that he was an enemy of population. Furthermore, while these books were not entirely ignored in the myriad publications that engaged with the work in the nineteenth century, aside from the preface and the first two chapters, books 1 and 2 received scant attention relative to 3 and 4, suggesting that they made a more limited impression on the public imagination.[3] That the *first* half of a work should be neglected in this way seems less anomalous when we consider its contents and the role it was intended to fulfil.

The first *Essay on the Principle of Population* (1798) had been dashed off by Malthus following a debate with his father (a fanatical Rousseauian) about human perfectibility. Its main target was William Godwin, who in his *Enquiry Concerning Political Justice* (1793) had argued that most of society's evils stemmed from the inequality of riches occasioned by the institutions of property and marriage. Their gradual abolition, accompanied by an inevitable improvement in man's ability to control his destructive sexual and violent impulses, would lead to something akin to paradise on earth. In the *Essay,* Malthus argued that population growth tended to outstrip man's ability to increase the produce of the soil, condemning even the most advanced states to suffer perpetual oscillations between happiness and misery. The "strong law of necessity" would always act "as a check on the greater power." In old states, reason was brought to bear on the power of population in the form of preventive checks: the delaying of marriage from "a foresight of the difficulties attending the rearing of a family." In England, such checks operated at every level of society, but especially among the middle classes who, loath to accept the reduced circumstances that additional mouths entailed, deferred matrimony until they had built up a nest egg.[4] Positive checks, on the other hand, did their work almost exclusively among the poor. Arising principally from the inability of parents suffering from severe want to provide proper nutrition for their offspring, they produced high child-mortality and general ill health. Vice, in the form of "irregular gratifications," always accompanied the preventive check, while misery was the natural bedfellow of both positive and preventive checks. Since periods would always arise when population pressed hard upon the limits of subsistence, no great improvement could be expected in the long-term condition of the poor, nor would a more equal distribution of resources, along the lines advocated by Godwin, fix things. Assured that all would be provided for, and enjoying a more liberal commerce of the sexes, the citizens of Godwin's paradise would soon breed beyond their food supply; in the ensuing struggle for meager resources, the narrower affections would displace benevolence as the ruling passions, and, ultimately, "an administration of property, not very different from that which prevails in civilized States at present, would be established as the best, though inadequate, remedy for the evils which were pressing on the society."[5]

Reflecting on the first *Essay* in the preface to the second edition, Malthus recalled how "in the course of this discussion" about perfectibility, he had come to realize that population oscillations "account for much of that poverty and misery observable among the lower classes of people in every nation, and for those reiterated failures in the efforts of the higher classes

to relieve them," and he therefore resolved "to turn my leisure reading towards an historical examination of the principle of population on the past
and present state of society."[6] It is this historical examination, aimed at
lending "a more practical and permanent interest to the subject," that takes
up most of books 1 and 2.[7] Book 1 looks at checks to population in "less
civilised parts of the world, and in past times," while book 2 examines the
checks in the different states of modern Europe. Book 2 is largely centered
on the available statistical data for births, deaths, and marriages in modern
European states, though some chapters draw on information collected by
Malthus himself, on trips to Scandinavia and Russia in 1799, and France
and Switzerland in 1802. Book 1, on the other hand, is based almost entirely on travel writing and works of history.[8]

Despite Malthus's labors, however, it was the second half of the book
that received most attention. Patricia James noted how the attack on Godwin's theory of perfectibility (in book 3), which she saw as a relatively
unimportant part of the second edition of the *Essay,* continued to exercise
reviewers.[9] Equally, Malthus's prescribed remedy for overpopulation, detailed in book 4, provoked much debate. If the case against perfectibility
made in 1798 was "conclusive," by 1803 Malthus had come to entertain
more sanguine expectations about improving the lot of the poor, having
discovered evidence that the great amelioration which had taken place in
their condition in some European states was owing to their increasing tendency to practice prudential restraint. By lowering the number of souls in
proportion to the means of subsistence, preventive checks had increased
each individual's command of essentials. This upward trend was set to
continue in the future, according to Malthus, but at a pace determined by
prevailing opinions about population and the institutional factors influencing marriage customs in each country. If the governing classes were serious
about tackling poverty, they needed to inculcate opinions and develop institutions that encouraged the laborer to delay marriage until he had sufficient
funds to support a family. This would raise the price of labor by narrowing the supply. Furthermore, if the would-be couple could be persuaded to
refrain from "irregular gratifications" in the period between the onset of
sexual maturity and marriage – that is, to practice *moral* rather than merely
prudential restraint – they might avoid altogether the vice and misery that,
it was claimed in the 1798 edition, invariably accompanied population
checks. Whereas the social and religious implications of moral restraint
came in for intense scrutiny,[10] and much ink was also spilt on Malthus's
call for the gradual abolition of the Poor Laws, barring a few exceptions,[11]
the so-called factual part of the theory contained in books 1 and 2 was

dealt with perfunctorily by nineteenth commentators. And since most of the historical scholarship has been concerned with exploring the social, political, economic, and religious debates that Malthus was contributing to, it has understandably shared the bias in favor of the themes discussed in books 3 and 4.[12] Two glaring exceptions to the nineteenth-century pattern were Charles Darwin and Alfred Russel Wallace, for whom the description of "the struggle for existence" among men in book 1 of the *Essay* provided revelatory insights into the mechanisms underpinning natural selection in the plant and animal kingdoms.[13] Surprisingly, however, the profuse historical literature on this engagement has had little to say about the intentions underlying the early parts of the quarto, and those few scholarly treatments we do have of these sections are largely descriptive.[14]

It is argued here, however, that if we are to do justice to Malthus's authorial intentions, we need to reorient our view of the *Essay* so as to give the historical aspects of the theory their proper weight, most obviously because the principle of population purports to be an argument based on historical observation. It is this record of human experience that comprises the "scientific" underpinning of all of Malthus's practical recommendations and that forms the sole basis for his restored faith in "that gradual and progressive improvement in human society, which, before the late wild speculations on this subject, was the object of rational expectation."[15] But even if we accept that what really matters about the *Essay* are the social and political issues that concerned most of its nineteenth-century readers, it can also be shown that these arguments were never meant to be read in isolation from the historical demography of the earlier books. A second aim of this essay therefore is to restore this critical context to Malthus's social and political thought. It demonstrates that paying due attention to books 1 and 2 dramatically alters one's experience of the book, and that had readers engaged with them more seriously, the *Essay* would not have become "one of the most . . . misunderstood works published during the last two hundred years."[16]

Ironically, it was with a view to winning over the largest possible number of readers that Malthus decided to detail the effects of population pressure "at different times and on different occasions." Such an exposition might entail needless repetition and an overly detailed analysis of some facets of the problem, admitted Malthus, but without it he did not entertain "the slightest hope of producing conviction" regarding those conclusions that were "different from our usual habits of thinking."[17] In order to understand what Malthus was doing in the first half of the *Essay* of 1803, then, we need to identify the conclusions he was referring to and the habitual patterns of thought militating against their ready acceptance. Books 1 and 2 were principally aimed at establishing two strands of argument about the past and present effects of the principle of population. In the first place, the history of the poor revealed a progressive development in the ways in which human societies grappled with the principle of population, which brought to light the means by which they might escape its worst consequences. According to Malthus, the principal "scientific" objective of the opening books was to establish a typology of population checks with a view to assessing the likelihood of their "total or partial removal."[18] This analysis showed how the emergence of increasingly rational customs in relation to marriage had enabled certain European societies to escape the oscillations between feast and famine to which past and "savage" peoples were invariably condemned.[19] But the history of population checks also served the more basic purpose of establishing the existence of the principle of population in the first place.

Notwithstanding Malthus's remark in 1806 that the he considered the theory of population to have been "established in the first six pages" of the *Essay*, it was clearly one of the chief aims of the first half of the book to bring home to readers its material reality.[20] He needed to show, in the first place, that checks to population were in constant operation, and not something that would only occur in the distant future when the whole world had been fully cultivated. Godwin had appealed to the latter assumption in response to Robert Wallace's assertion that the sense of economic security occasioned by systems of perfect equality would inevitably encourage such unfettered reproduction that the world would soon be peopled up to the limits of its food supply.[21] Seeing that large portions of the globe remained uncultivated, and the cultivated parts were capable of "immeasurable improvement," replied Godwin, advocates of human perfectibility could take heart from the fact that "Myriads of centuries" must pass before the earth was overstocked.[22] By proving that such checks had existed always and everywhere, the first two books helped Malthus to reinforce the central argument of the first *Essay* that population pressure would present an "imminent and immediate" obstacle to schemes of human perfectibility.[23] But in the second *Essay,* Godwin's speculations were treated merely as *one* of the proposed answers to what was now the main question in hand – how to improve the condition of the poor. Previous efforts to ameliorate poverty had proven at best futile, at worst counterproductive, according to Malthus, because of a failure to identify its true causes. Another crucial aim of the demographic history, then, was to prove beyond doubt that population oscillations were to blame.

This diagnosis flew in the face of the universal consensus that population growth was the most important measure of economic improvement and the proper aim of government policy. In his Cambridge textbook, the *Principles of Moral and Political Philosophy* (1785), the Christian utilitarian William Paley had echoed Adam Smith and virtually every writer on the subject in deeming the increase of population to be "the object which ought, in all countries, to be aimed at in preference to every other political purpose whatsoever."[24] Exacerbating the difficulty of uprooting such views was the fact that they were widely believed to accord with Christian doctrine. As well as appearing to contradict the scriptural command to increase and multiply, Malthus's theory assailed the complacent optimism underlying some of the core strictures of the dominant strain of moral and religious thought in the period, the doctrine of utility, not least Paley's assumption that every increase in population advanced the providential plan by adding to the stock of human happiness.[25] Worse still, Malthus seemed to impugn the benevolence of the deity in the process – hence his concerted efforts in both editions of the *Essay* to justify the ways of God to man.[26] Not only did the theory rankle with deeply entrenched attitudes, however, but as Malthus explained in the first *Essay,* there was something about the demographic phenomenon itself that made it particularly hard for the reading public to swallow.

An oscillation was triggered when population increased before a growth in the food supply, diminishing each person's share of subsistence and reducing many to hardship. In modern states, the swell in numbers increased the supply of labor, lowering its price while the price of food remained the same, forcing the laborer to work harder for the same wages he had earned before. Birth rates would eventually return to their former levels as the difficulties of raising a family in such conditions discouraged laborers from marrying, while, at the same time, the cheapness and ready availability of labor would encourage cultivators to employ more hands to plow more soil and improve its general fertility. Equilibrium between the population and the food supply would thus be restored, and the conditions of the laborer would improve accordingly; but this would again loosen "the restraints to population" such that "the retrograde and progressive movements with respect to happiness are repeated." As Malthus frequently observed, however, there were a number of factors that concealed such vibrations "from common view" in modern societies, most importantly the difference of the real and nominal price of labor, which meant that the fall in the real price was often obscured by the nominal price remaining the same.[27] Unhappily, it was the positive checks among the rural poor, in particular, that tended to be hidden in this way. So whereas the high mortality of poor children in cities often provoked concerned comment,[28] a starry-eyed view of rural life endured, fostering complacency among the educated ranks about the condition of country children. Like a modern-day television charity appeal, Malthus presented readers with images designed to shock them into a sense of urgency about child poverty in the countryside, from the stunted sons of laborers to scrawny-calved plow-hands. "The sons and daughters of peasants" were clearly not "the rosy cherubs" described in the romances, and their sufferings could "only be attributed to a want either of proper or of sufficient nourishment."[29]

In this context an important clue as to the intentions behind the second *Essay* comes to light, as Malthus alleged that a principal reason for the widespread obliviousness to the sufferings of the rural poor was that the histories of man had focused exclusively on the higher classes, relating little about the lives of those among whom positive checks operated. Chapter 3 of the first *Essay* had presented a brief historical examination of such oscillations, but soon after its publication Malthus appears to have decided that this "cursory review" was inadequate to the broader purposes of the second edition.[30] The "faithful history" of the second *Essay* was aimed at writing the great mass of the people into history, and it needed to be comprehensive enough to leave readers in no doubt as to the unremitting effects of population pressure on their lives. The history begins then with Malthus's incredibly vivid descriptions of "the lowest stages of human existence" as represented by the indigenous peoples of America, New Zealand, and Australia–accounts based on the travel writings of Captain James Cook, David Collins, Mungo Park, and other explorers. "In savage life, where there is no regular price of labour," the "progressive and retrograde movements" are abundantly evident, as they everywhere produce scenes of unparalleled horror. Of the American Indians Malthus reports that, "like beasts of prey, they must either drive away or fly from every rival, and be engaged in perpetual contests with each other." New Zealanders, similarly, "live under perpetual apprehensions of being destroyed by each other."[31] In these opening chapters we read about "perpetual diseases," "perpetual wandering and hardship," "perpetual quarrels" between savages who live in "a perpetual state of war."[32] The reason for this endless struggle, according to Malthus, was that without prudential restraint to limit population or the technological means of increasing the food supply, any advantage in procuring subsistence, leading to an increase of numbers in one tribe, will inevitably result in the destruction of their competitors.

Lacking both the technology and foresight to increase subsistence, tribes of hunter-gatherers are rarely populous. Among pastoral nations, by contrast, unlimited access to fresh pastures unleashes mighty powers of increase, which have historically found vent in great barbarian conquests like those of the Huns, Moguls, and Tartars. Here the checks to population are "but too obvious," often involving "a whole people in indiscriminate massacre." Inquiries into the state of modern pastoral peoples revealed with equal clarity how population was distributed according to levels of subsistence. Tribes inhabiting barren desert regions lived further apart and were far more sparsely populated than those occupying land with a good covering of soil. This principle, "so obvious" in Grand Tartary, Syria, and Arabia, was "equally applicable to the whole earth," asserted Malthus, but "the commerce of civilized nations" tended to conceal it.[33] Nowhere were the oscillations more readily observable, however, than on islands inhabited by savage societies, for here economic simplicity combined with clearly defined barriers to population growth. It was customary for the upper echelons of Eareeoie societies, for example, to suffocate newborns with a wet cloth, both as a means of facilitating their licentious lifestyle and of limiting the numbers enjoying it. Frequent and devastating wars in which the vanquishers destroyed their enemy's means of subsistence, combined with libertinage and infanticide, served to decimate the Othaheite (Tahiti) population, such that when Captain Vancouver returned to the island in 1791, most of the friends he had made on the previous landing of 1777 were dead.[34] But the conspicuousness of vice and misery among islanders had led some commentators to erroneous and dangerous conclusions, which Malthus was anxious to refute. Notably, the French radical Abbé Raynal had argued that the population pressures endemic to islands had made them the cradles of numerous vicious customs that curbed population throughout every continent. Europe therefore had the British Isles to thank for "anthropophagy, the castration of males, the infibulation of females, late marriages, the consecration of virginity, the appropriation of celibacy, the punishments exercised against girls who become mothers at too early an age, &c."[35] What the Abbé had failed to realize was "that a savage tribe in America, surrounded by enemies, or a civilised and populous nation, hemmed in by others in the same state, is in many respects in a similar situation."[36] The whole world was like an island, according to Malthus, in the sense that the barriers to population growth in old states were scarcely less intractable than those afflicting the inhabitants of New Guinea, New Holland, and New Caledonia.

Readers of the *Essay* would have been sensitive to the deep political resonance of Malthus's accounts of "primitive life."[37] By depicting it as "a horrid mixture of famine and ferocity," he sought to counter "the frequent declamations in favour of savage life" found in radical literature, not least, that of Raynal, who in his *Histoire des deux Indes* (1770) had insisted in Rousseauian fashion that the savage life was happier than the civilized. The savage "seldom experiences . . . that weariness that arises from unsatisfied desires, or that emptiness and uneasiness of mind that is the offspring of prejudice and vanity." This comparison obviously had ideological connotations.[38] Even supposing, wrote Raynal, that civilized man was somehow less unhappy than the savage, "there would still remain a wide difference between the fate of the civilised man and the wild Indian, a difference entirely to the disadvantage of social life. This is the injustice that reigns in the partial distribution of fortunes and stations; an inequality which is at once the effect and the cause of oppression."[39] Responding to traveler accounts that described the natives of Formosa as living in a state of social equality and engaging in bloodless wars, Malthus asserted that an equal distribution of property must unleash the power of population by removing the fear of "*particular poverty* from a large family." The only means of preserving equality then would be to limit population by law, a measure more unconscionable, in Malthus's view, than any of the evils resulting from the institution of property.[40]

Fearing that assertions about the relative equanimity of savage life might have purchase among a reading public enchanted by traveler accounts of the South Sea Islands, Malthus insisted that visions of plenteous island paradises, like those of an idyllic English countryside, were mirages that would disappear on closer inspection. The journal of Captain Cook's third voyage and accounts from a British missionary voyage of 1796–1798 dispelled such myths by revealing the scarcity that stalked the islands at various times of the year.[41] This periodic dearth explained why visitors to the Sandwich Islands experienced none of the profuse hospitality offered to the first European guests of the Tahitians. And like the histories of European states, accounts of fleeting visits to savage kingdoms were liable to focus on the lives of the nobles, since it was they who formed the greeting parties and attended the welcoming feasts, but while these "principal proprietors" might have plenty of provisions to trade with, it was likely that "their vassals and slaves were suffering severely from want," surmised Malthus.[42] In savage societies where food was abundant, the distinctions of rank were so extreme and enforced so tyrannically that the lives of the lower orders were incomparably wretched. More egalitarian tribes, on the other hand, suffered incessant scarcity and war, and this overbalanced any advantage that might have accrued to "savage life" from their having more leisure time than the laboring poor in civilized countries. Nothing, however, placed the contrast between savage and civilized life in starker light than their respective modes of education. Whereas the civilized man was taught to nurture fellow feeling and expand the scope for agreeable affections, "Everything that can contribute to teach the most unmoved patience under the severest pains and misfortunes, everything that tends to harden the heart, and narrow all the sources of sympathy, is sedulously inculcated in the savage." Since virtues were like commodities in a market – those in greater demand being produced in greater abundance – "the obvious inference" from these different pedagogies was that while "the civilised man hopes to enjoy, the savage expects only to suffer."[43]

That the contrast between savage and civilized life was so central to Malthus's purposes in the *Essay* demonstrates that the first half of the quarto cannot be read as a discreet statement of *the facts* about population. The historical details were deeply intertwined with his political and social program.[44] Readers who bypassed the first half of the book neglected the most powerful evidence that the well-intentioned expedients for tackling the evils resulting from population pressure described in books 3 and 4 were doomed to fail, and that only his recommendations for their mitigation (i.e., prudential restraint and the gradual abolition of the Poor Laws) could work. The second aim of the historical volumes then was to establish the demographic principles on which these arguments turned, and this involved, first of all, discrediting the almost universal assumption that raw birthrates were a measure of national prosperity. Malthus insisted that high fertility was not even a reliable indicator of increasing population, as by diminishing each person's portion of subsistence it frequently led to soaring mortality. In a nation fearful of French invasion and in which a patriotic chorus exhorted Britons to boost the nation's power by adding to its numbers, it was an assertion as untimely as it was counterintuitive.[45] But here, again, Malthus trusted that a total immersion in the checks to population in "every age" and "every state" would counteract these prejudices, and that having observed the rapid succession of human beings (i.e., high birth- and death-rates) among the shepherds of northern Europe in the times of their constant emigrations and among present-day Abyssinians, readers would approach the second half of the book with a deep sense of "how little population depends on the birth of children, in comparison of the production of food, and of those circumstances of natural and political situation which influence this produce."[46] Again and again we are presented with instances of governments or families who encourage breeding, only to give rise to surplus population and its attendant vice and misery.[47] In answer to the suggestion that the dire poverty of large parts of Africa could be ascribed to their sparse population, Malthus observed that a bounty on children would increase war, slavery, and general misery but not the numbers of inhabitants, for population in such regions already pressed hard on the limits of subsistence. Driving the point home in characteristically gruesome fashion, he related how during the famines that plagued Cairo in 1784–1785, Constantin-François Volney had reported seeing "under the walls of ancient Alexandria, two miserable wretches seated on the carcase of a camel, and disputing with the dogs its putrid flesh."[48]

As part of a complex analysis of the natural and political factors affecting levels of food production – the true cause of population increase – Malthus ascribed the sufferings of Egyptians to the despotic government of the Mamelukes. Their failure to maintain the ancient irrigation system had crippled agricultural production, and their constant plundering removed all stimulus to industry and forethought among the people, for no one would accumulate capital where its possession invited destruction.[49] As detrimental as despotism was to the ratios between population and subsistence, Malthus wanted to show that well-meaning social policy could be just as pernicious. Mooted as a means of increasing population and thereby promoting the well-being of the nation, the foundling hospitals established in Russia in the reign of Catherine the Great were a case in point. "All the well-informed men" with whom Malthus discussed the matter during his visit to Saint Petersburg in 1799 agreed that these institutions greatly encouraged licentiousness by providing a relatively guilt-free means (in comparison to infanticide) of disposing of unwanted offspring.[50] In this way, not only were the institutions corrosive to maternal sympathy but they produced a large proportion of the country's child mortality. By filling the posts normally taken by "the legitimate part of the society," they reduced the price of labor, thereby spreading hardship throughout the working population. Not that the foundlings themselves prospered. Attendants at the Maison des Enfant Trouvé in Saint Petersburg told Malthus that in the winter of 1798, it had not been unusual to bury eighteen children a day, and all those he encountered on his visit were pale and sickly looking.[51] Such examples were intended to produce an intuitive sense in the reader that the Poor Laws on the one hand, and the egalitarian solutions examined in books 3 and 4 on the other, were doomed to fail.[52] Malthus forcefully brought home the human cost of such failure by granting intimate access to the lives of people who had to live with it.

But if by the time the reader gets to book 3 he has imbibed an almost instinctual sense of how *not* to promote the national welfare and population, he also has a keen sense of what works. Indeed, while much of book 4

was dedicated to establishing the expediency of prudential and moral restraint–defined in Paleyan terms as promoting the happiness of mankind
"in obedience to the will of God"–the foundations for these arguments
were laid in the historical account of population checks. Early in book 1,
for example, we are told that the Shangalla (Oromo) tribes in western Africa, whose efforts to increase the number of warriors through polygamy
yielded only hardship and misery, would be better off concentrating their
efforts on rearing just a few children, thus ensuring that more survived.[53]
And it was thanks to precisely this modus operandi that that the sons of
Norwegian "house-men" were "fatter, larger, and had better calves to their
legs, than boys of the same age and in similar situations in England."[54]
By showing that markedly low mortality rates occurred where early marriages were relatively rare, the Norwegian case was vital in helping Malthus to verify the efficacy of his partial remedy. For although he did not
say whether he considered the restraint practiced by Norwegian peasants
to be strictly "moral,"[55] the contrast between robust Norwegian children
and their emaciated English counterparts put the frustrations of temporary
chastity in moral perspective–poignantly establishing the obligation to
practice moral restraint.[56]

Aside from providing this comparative perspective, the chapter on Norway (strategically placed at the start of book 2) formed a vital part of the
historical framework within which Malthus believed the problem of poverty needed to be understood. The persuasive force of Malthus's utilitarian case for moral restraint made in book 4 is multiplied manifold when
preventive checks are viewed as preservatives of civilization itself. A central plank of this argument was that if widely adopted, such checks would
greatly diminish war (and even eliminate it entirely) by removing "one of
its first causes and most powerful impulses," "an insufficiency of room and
food."[57] The moral sentiments that made fecundity a primary virtue while
stigmatizing celibacy created the "redundant" population that supplied ambitious princes with their "instruments of destruction," there being no better recruiting sergeant than want. But the vital argument that such attitudes
were a relic of barbarous ages loses much of its power when divorced from
the grisly depictions of "the struggle for existence" among ancient pastoral
and present-day "savage" nations in book 1.[58] The concept of *struggle* may
not have been fundamental to the principle of population in the way that it
would become to the theory of natural selection, but the picture it conveyed
of the lives of barbarous peoples was integral to the historical argument
that frames all of Malthus's utilitarian prescriptions.[59]

Malthus's anticipation of the religious objections to moral restraint were also set against this natural historical backdrop, as he asserted that the simplistic interpretation which saw the divine command to increase and multiply as an incitement to unbridled breeding was also characteristic of less civilized peoples and epochs. "A Mahometan," says Malthus,

> is in some degree obliged to polygamy from a principle of obedience to his prophet, who makes one of the greatest duties of man to consist in procreating children to glorify the Creator. Fortunately, individual interest corrects in some degree, as in many other instances, the absurdity of the legislator; and the poor Arab is obliged to proportion his religious obedience to the scantiness of his resources. Yet still the direct encouragements to population are extraordinarily great; and nothing can place in a more striking point of view the futility and absurdity of such encouragements than the present state of those countries.[60]

Malthus goes on to describe the rigid poverty occasioned by such injunctions. These vignettes of human suffering built into a cumulative case for the utilitarian reassessment of some of the most hallowed edicts of scripture, a revision he later justified on the grounds that "every express command given to man by his Creator is given in subordination to those great and uniform laws of nature which he had previously established."[61] But the orthodoxies of natural law were also subject to reconsideration in the light of historical scrutiny, most notably the Paleyan conception of practical virtue as consisting primarily in nurturing charitable instincts. For the natural historical record confirmed the view, asserted by Malthus in the first *Essay,* that the partial affections were invariably a more reliable guide to right action. Whereas the indiscriminate charity provided by the Lama's bounty in Tibet had created a "mass of indigence and idleness," for example, reason pointing out private interest had compelled the "poor Arab" to defy wrongheaded religious customs for the sake of his family.[62]

The most convincing evidence, however, that the narrower affections were more likely to illuminate effective ways of diminishing want came again from Norway. The description of the conditions that induced Norwegians to marry later than their English counterparts is worth examining more closely, since it provided a blueprint for the widespread operation of preventive checks among the poor. Low mortality in the Norwegian villages meant that openings for laborers were scarce, and with no large manufacturers to provide an outlet for the excess population of the countryside, the Norwegian laborer often had to wait a long time before he could find a position that would enable him to raise a family. The system of "house-men," whereby the farmer provided a number of married laborers with small plots of land, and they in return were obliged to work for him at a low and fixed price when required, provided the only viable opportunity for the peasant to raise a family.[63] As there were no large manufacturing towns, nor even an extensive retail trade, to offer them work, young men and women had no option but to remain with the farmer as unmarried servants until such premises became available. "From the small number of people, and the little variety of employment, the subject is brought distinctly within the view of each individual; and he must feel the absolute necessity of repressing his inclination to marriage till some such vacancy offer." In more populous countries like England, by contrast, the complexity of the labor market occasioned by the greater division of labor meant the subject was shrouded in obscurity, such that "each man naturally thinks that he has as good a chance of finding employment as his neighbour, and that if he cannot get it in one place, he shall in some other." Trusting to fortune then, the laborer marries, too often producing a redundant population, replete with malnourished babies and scrawny plowboys.[64] What the Norwegian example demonstrated was that the laborer would only desist from such gambling where he was clear that losing spelled inescapable ruin for his family. Hence, prudential restraint was far less likely to become widespread where there was a safety net like the Poor Laws.[65] Because the rustic simplicity and demographic sparseness that brought population dynamics "so distinctly within the view" of the Norwegian could not be replicated in England, however, those interested in improving the conditions of the poor at home had to call for the establishment of "a system of general education" to inculcate the fundamentals of political arithmetic, and more generally to cultivate "a spirit of independence" and "decent pride."[66]

This focus on deeply practical objectives helps to explain why, despite its richly suggestive analysis of the various stages of civilization, Malthus's work has never been regarded as a major contribution to the "natural history of man." A history exclusively focused on revealing population cycles was never going to offer conclusions as far reaching as, say, Adam Smith's account of the retrograde order of economic development followed by European commercial societies in book 3 of the *Wealth of Nations* (1776).[67] Nor, for the same reason no doubt, was the prediction of the critic from the *Monthly Review* that Malthus was destined to cause "the history of every country, antient and modern, to be pursued with new interest" ever likely to come to fruition.[68] The *Essay* could not be categorized as a work of "philosophical history" in the tradition of Montesquieu or Edward Gibbon, for

while Malthus engaged critically with their respective accounts of the de-
mise of Rome, it was only to challenge their assumptions that the barbarian
hordes were fueled by "real" rather than redundant population in northern
Europe. Similarly, Malthus did not extrapolate into a broader anthropology
his profound suggestion that scarcity caused by population pressure was
the hidden underlying cause of countless customs, such as polygamy, cannibalism, the exposure of children, and the ferocity of martial codes among
savages, as well as "the double standard" that ostracized the adulteress
"for an offence, which men commit nearly with impunity" in old states.[69]
Rather, such customs featured as part of his typology of population checks,
as the immediate restraint on increase, indeed, where food shortages did
not express themselves as famine or epidemics.[70] In other words, Malthus
employed history in the service of practical demography but seldom vice
versa.[71] But if the *Essay* does not merit study as a work of history, it is
clear that the comparative historical perspective he labored so hard to provide was vital to his ultimate aim of dispelling the mist concealing the true
causes of want in commercial societies for the reading public, so that they
in turn could put the poor straight about where their true interests lay. One
important implication of this conclusion, given Malthus's sources for the
Essay, is that an important context for the book has been much understud-
ied, that of European overseas exploration and expansion.[72] The evidence
presented here also adds weight to Donald Winch's view that Malthus's
thought shared more with the eighteenth-century science of morals, with
its focus on the complex interrelations between the broad historical deter-
minants of economic and social progress, than with the narrower, more
technical political economy that emerged in the 1820s, which aimed at
solving the day-to-day problems of economic policy.[73] But it also places
Malthus in a long line of thinkers, including Locke, Montesquieu, and Vol-
taire, who appealed to traveler accounts of alien customs to undermine
deeply engrained cultural norms at home.

NOTES

1. Patricia James, *Population Malthus: His Life and Times* (London, 1979),
   115. See also the advertisement to T. R. Malthus, *A Summary View of the
   Principle of Population* (London, 1830).
2. T. R. Malthus, appendix to *An Essay on the Principle of Population* (London,
   1806), 1:506 (hereafter "1806 Appendix").
3. An overview of these preoccupations can be gleaned from the copious "List
   of Books, Pamphlets, and Articles on the Population Question, Published in

Britain in the Period 1793 to 1880," comp. J. A. Banks and D. V. Glass, in *Introduction to Malthus,* ed. D. V. Glass (London, 1953), 79–112.

4. T. R. Malthus, *An Essay on the Principle of Population as It Affects the Future Improvement of Society with Remarks on the Speculations of Mr. Godwin, M. Condorcet, and Other Writers* (1798) in *The Works of Thomas Robert Malthus,* ed. E. A. Wrigley and David Souden (London, 1986), 1:13, 26–27 (hereafter First *Essay*).

5. Ibid., 190, 198.

6. The most notable of these failures, in Malthus's view, was the Poor Laws of England, which by encouraging population growth without increasing the food supply, effectively "create the poor which they maintain." Ibid., 33.

7. T. R. Malthus, *An Essay on the Principle of Population; or, A View of Its Past and Present Effects on Human Happiness; with an Inquiry into Our Prospects Respecting the Future Removal or Mitigation of the Evils Which It Occasions. A New Edition, Very Much Enlarged,* 2nd ed. (London, 1803; reprint, New Haven, Conn., 2017), 3 (hereafter *Essay of 1803;* the page numbers cited for this work are to this book).

8. Malthus consulted 102 books in all when researching the first two volumes. James, *Population Malthus,* 93.

9. Ibid., 111.

10. While some lauded the duty of moral restraint as a divine decree promulgated through the sufferings of improvident breeders, others believed Malthus was risking damnation by *"resisting"* the biblical command to *"marry* or *burn."* See, respectively, Boyd Hilton, *The Age of Atonement: The Influence of Evangelicalism on Social and Economic Thought, 1785–1865* (Oxford, 1988), 79, 81, and "Simplex" [John Young], *An Inquiry into the Constitution, Government and Practices of the Church of Christ . . . with Strictures on . . . Mr. Malthus on Population* (Edinburgh, 1808), 211.

11. Important exceptions were the reviews in the *Monthly Review,* December 1803, 337–357, and January 1804, 56–70; and *British Critic,* January 1804, 59–69, and March 1804, 233–245.

12. The best accounts of these debates are Donald Winch, *Riches and Poverty: An Intellectual History of Political Economy in Britain, 1750–1834* (Cambridge, 1996), 221–422; A. M. C. Waterman, *Revolution, Economics, and Religion: Christian Political Economy, 1798–1833* (Cambridge, 1991), 1–170; Hilton, *Age of Atonement;* and Robert J. Mayhew, *Malthus: The Life and Legacies of an Untimely Prophet* (Cambridge, Mass., 2014). The same themes are generally emphasized in the numerous articles on the *Essay* collected in Jon Cunningham Wood, ed., *Thomas Robert Malthus: Critical Assessments* (Dover, N.H., 1986).

13. An equally notable exception was J. S. Mill, who paid close attention to Malthus's history of population checks. See, for example, Mill, *Principles of Political Economy* (1848), 8th ed. (London, 1878), 1:200, 429–430. The same can be said for commentators who were specifically interested in the demographic issues raised by the *Essay*. See *Malthus and the Population Controversy 1803–1830* (Bristol, 1994).

14. Since completing this essay, a work by Alison Bashford and Joyce E. Chaplin has appeared that does pay attention to the historical parts of the *Essay of 1803*. Where I differ from them is in viewing these books as largely intended to shed light on domestic social and political questions rather than "developments in other hemispheres" per se. See Alison Bashford and Joyce E. Chaplin, *The New Worlds of Thomas Robert Malthus: Rereading the Principle of Population* (Princeton, N.J., 2016), p. 6. On Darwin's Malthusian heritage, see, for example, Robert Young, "Malthus and the Evolutionists: The Common Context of Biological and Social Theory," *Past and Present* 43 (1969): 109–145; Peter Vorzimmer, "Darwin, Malthus, and the Theory of Natural Selection," *Journal of the History of Ideas* 30, no. 4 (1969): 527–542; P. J. Bowler, "Malthus, Darwin and the Concept of Struggle," *Journal of the History of Ideas* 37 (1976): 631–650; Donald Winch, "Darwin Fallen among Political Economists," *Proceedings of the American Philosophical Society* 145 (2001): 415–437; and Gregory Radick, "Is the Theory of Natural Selection Independent of History?" in *The Cambridge Companion to Darwin,* ed. Jonathan Hodge and Gregory Radick (Cambridge, 2003), 143–167. Patricia James's account of Malthus's research is rich in detail but offers little interpretation. James, *Population Malthus,* 92–98. A somewhat more analytical account of books 1 and 2 was given by James Bonar in *Malthus and His Work* (London, 1885), 85–207.

15. *Essay of 1803,* 473.

16. See the blurb on the back cover of T. R. Malthus, *An Essay on the Principle of Population; or, A View of Its Past and Present Effects on Human Society* (1803), ed. Donald Winch (Cambridge, 1992).

17. *Essay of 1803,* 4.

18. Ibid., 11.

19. For an account of these researches in relation to the practical aims of the book, see Niall O' Flaherty, "Malthus and the End of Poverty," in *New Perspectives on Malthus,* ed. Robert J. Mayhew (Cambridge, 2016), 74–104.

20. "1806 Appendix," 520n.

21. Wallace speculated that the earth might have already reached this point had perfect government been instituted since the creation of Adam. Robert Wallace, *Various Prospects of Mankind, Nature and Providence* (London, 1761), 115–116.

22. William Godwin, *An Enquiry Concerning Political Justice and Its Influence on General Virtue and Happiness* (London, 1793), 2:861.

23. First *Essay,* 53.

24. William Paley, *Principles of Moral and Political Philosophy* (London, 1785), 589.

25. Ibid., 587–589.

26. The theodicy that took up the last two chapters in the 1798 edition was dropped from later editions. However, the opening chapters of book 4 of the quarto were dedicated to reconciling the theory with Paleyan orthodoxy. See Waterman, *Revolution, Economics, and Religion,* chap. 4.

27. First *Essay,* 15, 16.

28. See, for example, Richard Price, *Observations on the Expectations of Lives, the Increase of Mankind, the Influence of Great Towns on Population, and Particularly the State of London with Respect to Healthfulness and Number of Inhabitants* (London, 1769).

29. First *Essay,* 78.

30. Ibid., 17.

31. *Essay of 1803,* 22–23, 29–30, 47.

32. Ibid., 34, 40, 44, 48.

33. Ibid., 76.

34. Ibid., 50–52.

35. Ibid., 46. The quotation is from G. T. Raynal, *Histoire philosophique et politique des établissemens et du commerce des Européens dans les deux Indes* (Paris, 1795), 2:liv; 3:3.

36. *Essay of 1803,* 46.

37. It would take another essay to explore how far Malthus's interpretation of his sources was shaped by his political aims, but also how far the views of the travelers themselves were framed by "anthropological" idioms drawn from political philosophy. Employing distinctly Hobbesian language, for example, David Collins characterized the natives of Botany Bay, Port Jackson, and Broken Bay as "living in that state of nature which must have been common to all men previous to their uniting in society, and acknowledging but one authority." Collins, appendix 1, in *An Account of the English Colony in New South Wales . . . to Which Are Added Some Particulars of New Zealand* (London, 1802), 1:544.

38. Most notably, it formed the basis of Thomas Paine's attack on "agrarian monopoly" in *Agrarian Justice* (London, 1797), 5–7.

39. G. T. Raynal, *A Philosophical and Political History of the British Settlements and Trade in North America* (Edinburgh, 1776), 38, 42.

40. *Essay of 1803,* 57n59.

41. Malthus's sources were William Wilson, *A Missionary Voyage to the Southern Pacific Ocean* (London, 1799), and a three-volume version of accounts of Cook's *Voyages* (n.p., 1784) compiled by John Hawkesworth, which is no longer extant.

42. *Essay of 1803*, 58.

43. Ibid.

44. This helps to explain why the *Essay* has so often been read as an ideological "move" rather than a "scientific" theory. Malthus claimed that had he merely set out his demographic principles and not ventured to speculate on their practical implications, he might have "entrenched" himself in "an impregnable fortress," but that an abstract treatise of this kind would have done little to promote the public good. Even if it tarnished the theory in some people's eyes, he hoped that the rancor which was sure to greet his practical proposals would ensure they were widely discussed. *Essay of 1803, 4.*

45. The worst invasion scares were in 1797–1798 and the summer of 1803.

46. *Essay of 1803*, 95.

47. See, for example, the chapter on China.

48. *Essay of 1803*, 98.

49. Ibid., 97.

50. "To have a child was considered as one of the most trifling faults," observed Malthus. Ibid., 177.

51. Ibid., 178, 174.

52. It was also a verdict on calls for the general establishment of foundling hospitals by the political economist James Steuart and others. Ibid., 446–447.

53. Ibid., 92.

54. Ibid., 154.

55. While much of his trip was spent quizzing locals on the details of their home economy and agricultural practices, he understandably shied away from enquiring about the prevalence of "irregular gratifications." For an account of the tour, see Patricia James, ed., *The Travel Diaries of T. R. Malthus* (Cambridge, 1966).

56. It is important to be clear about his priorities in this respect. While he strongly encouraged perfect chastity before marriage, Malthus believed that any increase in "the vices relating to sex" that might accompany an increase in prudential restraint was a price worth paying for the reduction in "squalid and hopeless poverty" it would occasion. *Essay of 1803*, 403.

57. Ibid., 394. In the sense that his main reason for imagining the universal practice of moral restraint in this chapter was to reconcile the principle of population with the idea of divine benevolence, it is one of the more speculative chapters in the book. But he was clearly in earnest in arguing that an increase

in prudential checks would reduce conflict. The overriding narrative of the *Essay,* after all, was that barbaric customs in relation to population, of which war was the most pervasive, were gradually being supplanted by more rational marital practices.

58. Just as Hobbes's insistence on the absolute nature of sovereignty in *Leviathan* would be weaker if abstracted from his depiction of the state of nature.

59. See Bowler, "The Concept of Struggle," 636.

60. *Essay of 1803,* 81.

61. "1806 Appendix," 506.

62. *Essay of 1803,* 120, 81.

63. Michael Drake argues that Malthus's conclusions were shaped by the fact that he only visited the richer parts of the country in the interior of the south. He also appears to have been selective in what published statistical data he chose to mention, omitting figures that did not accord with his claims. See Michael Drake, "Malthus on Norway," *Population Studies,* 20, no. 2 (November 1966): 175–196. According to Malthus, Norway also benefited from laws that only permitted Norwegian conscripts to marry on proof of being able to support a family. See *Essay of 1803,* 150.

64. *Essay of 1803,* 151, 153.

65. While Malthus believed that the "obvious tendency" of the English Poor Laws was to encourage marriage, the returns of the 1801 census forced him to concede that they did not appear to do so in practice. "1806 Appendix," 226.

66. *Essay of 1803,* 438.

67. Except, obviously, in relation to the problem of poverty, which, as Malthus saw it, was the principal subject of political economy.

68. *Monthly Review,* December 1803, 338. Malthus himself claimed that his demography "lead to the elucidation of some of the most obscure yet important points in the history of human society." *Essay of 1803,* 46–47.

69. *Essay of 1803,* 297; First *Essay,* 73.

70. *Essay of 1803,* 29–30.

71. Even his own lectures on British and European history at the East India Company were devoid of demographic insight. See J. M. Pullen and Trevor Hughes Parry, eds., *Malthus: The Unpublished Papers in the Collection of Kanto Gakuen University* (Cambridge, 2004), 2:159–212.

72. See note 14, above, on the recently published work by Alison Bashford and Joyce Chaplin, however. See also Alison Bashford, "Malthus and Colonial History," *Journal of Australian Studies* 36, no. 1 (March 2012): 99–110.

73. Donald Winch shows how the historical analysis of economic problems was also a feature of Malthus's writings on political economy. Winch, *Malthus* (Oxford, 1987), 56.

The Tortoise and the Hare

Thomas Robert Malthus as Natural Philosopher

DEBORAH VALENZE

One of the most curious aspects of Thomas Robert Malthus's *Essay on the Principle of Population* is its pessimistic view of even the most modern methods of food production. "The power of population is so superior to the power in the earth to produce subsistence for man that, unless arrested by the preventive check, premature death must in some shape or other visit the human race," he reasoned.[1] In his notoriously closed system, any attempt to adjust the food supply to fit the number of people led inexorably to the need for more food, which was followed only by further population growth. "The increasing of the absolute quantity of provisions," he wrote in 1803, "would appear to be setting the tortoise to catch the hare." Malthus softened this by adding an important qualification: "Finding therefore that, from the laws of nature, we could not proportion the food to the population, our next attempt should naturally be to proportion the population to the food. If we can persuade the hare to go to sleep, the tortoise may have some chance of overtaking her."[2]

A homely allusion to Aesop's tale did not disguise what was, at bottom, an unfriendly message, even though it served as an improvement over other metaphors offered up by the *Essay on Population*. (Malthus would remove his reference to "nature's mighty feast," a bountiful table from which the poor would be excluded, from the 1806 edition.[3]) Persuading the hare "to go to sleep"–that is, discouraging the poor from reproducing–should invite us to ask why Malthus had so little faith in the possibility of harnessing the productive potential of the natural world. Was this simply a case of jettisoning the optimism of an earlier age embodied in William Godwin's *An Enquiry Concerning Political Justice*? Or was there a particular way in which Malthus viewed the power of nature that explained this essential piece of the *Essay on the Principle of Population*?

Early critics challenged the geometrical and arithmetical ratios of the *Essay,* unconvinced by the ninth wrangler from Cambridge, who described himself as a Newtonian. The pseudonymous Piercy Ravenstone fulminated in 1821 that "if . . . the geometrical ratio was admitted on very slight proofs, the arithmetical ratio was asserted on no evidence at all. . . . It has no being but in the imagination of its author." Adjusting Malthus's metaphor, he identified the true "tortoise which supports the elephant" as the dual forces of "liberty" and the "diffusion of knowledge."[4] For some readers, an abiding belief in progress muted the mathematical register of Malthus. As a doctor of Manchester pointed out in 1806, why would food be any different from woolens? Rather than leaving an increasing population unclothed, manufacturing would respond by producing more commodities; likewise, agriculture (and perhaps the fishing industry) would develop to meet rising demand.[5]

Malthusian views of food production sat uncomfortably with contemporary works on agricultural improvement, which were enjoying popularity during the era of the French Revolution. The establishment of the Board of Agriculture in 1793 signaled the practical orientation of the times. Arthur Young, as its public-spirited spokesperson, employed a style of arithmetic decidedly different from that of the *Essay on Population* when he first embarked on his tours of England and Wales. The dynamic combination of enclosures and improvements promised to yield increases of produce by multiples that more than satisfied the demands of a growing population. "It is not difficult, even on such data as have been already obtained," reported Sir John Sinclair, the president of the board, in 1795, "to make calculations sufficiently accurate for every useful purpose, . . . in regard to income – capital – and population."[6] Laboring men and women might present an obstacle, not from their reproductive rate but rather from their claim to common rights to land use. "Let us not be satisfied with the liberation of Egypt, or the subjugation of Malta," Sinclair declared in 1803, "but let us subdue Finchley Common; let us conquer Hounslow Heath; let us compel Epping Forest to submit to the yoke of improvement."[7] The march of progress aimed to vanquish, in Arthur Young's words, the "Goths and Vandals" of the "open fields."[8]

Malthus, however, derived no reassurance from agricultural improvements. When it came to the possibility of converting pasture to arable land, he adhered to a relentlessly arithmetical (and hypothetical) approach not unlike his method of computing population. In refuting the low estimates of necessary agricultural labor proposed in Godwin's *Political Justice,* Malthus argued that the only way to meet the needs of double the population "would be from ploughing up most of the grazing countries, and putting an end almost entirely to animal food." Without cattle, he pointed out, Britain would be deprived of sufficient manure for crop enhancement. Deficiencies would follow. In one of the most famous passages preserved from the first edition, he calculated the impact of an extension of cultivated land: in their evolution as consumers, the British population, driven to a miserable adherence to vegetarianism, would eventually succumb to "the chilling breath of want" and "the whole black train of vices" belonging to a state of perpetual deprivation. "The rosy flush of health gives place to the pallid cheek and hollow eye of misery"–grim justice for the nation mistakenly dedicated to the task of feeding its fecund population.[9]

History was to leave behind this particular debate as economic theory, with continuing crucial contributions by Malthus, adopted new strategies of reasoning in the early nineteenth century. By 1815, the law of diminishing returns, derived in part from Malthus's writings on population, inserted an assumption of scarcity into formulas involving natural resources; agriculture and mining industries were thus redefined as belonging to a special category of production. Bringing poor, marginal land into cultivation would only act as a drag on capital accumulation within the wealthiest class of society. All consideration of the value of agricultural commodities was mediated by a theory of rent shaped by Malthus, David Ricardo, and a new generation of political economists. The effect of this was to leave undisturbed the existing terms of Malthus's discussion: the rights of private property, rent, prices, and wages governed subsequent economic debate. Scarcity in the marketplace thus operated as a check to ruinous claims of the poor on the resources of landowners.[10]

The power of nature over agriculture nevertheless remained as a wild-card within the mathematically plotted realm of political economy. Here was Malthus's means to a much larger, irrefutable argument about the future of humankind. According to Margaret Schabas, "inescapable laws of nature are essential to the telling of his population tale," and the topic repays closer investigation.[11] Like Adam Smith and the Physiocrats, Malthus saw agriculture as a primary source of wealth and prosperity, but he viewed its vulnerability to natural forces as a crucial determinant of its prospects. "We know from experience that these operations of what we call nature have been conducted almost according to fixed laws," he argued. "And since the world began, the causes of population and depopulation have been probably as constant as any of the laws of nature with which we are acquainted."[12] As with natural history, seasons of blight and adversity figured as inevitable features of human history, taking the form of scarcity and deprivation; this would continue even in the face of modern improvements, removing any guarantee of keeping pace with a multiplying population.

Historians have explained the absolutism of Malthus's argument through its connection to natural theology, which rendered "the laws of nature" and "the laws of God" as one.[13] If we want to come to grips with divine power, we are told, we must "turn our eyes to the book of nature, where alone we can read God as he is." Or, in a more famous turn of phrase eliminated from the second edition of the *Essay,* "we should reason from nature up to nature's God and not presume to reason from God to nature."[14] For Malthus and the Christian political economists who followed him, a reflexive exercise of contemplating a sublime divinity led to the conclusion that, in Boyd Hilton's words, God was "mad, bad, and dangerous" and "does not often meddle" with the capriciousness of earth's environmental events. The pummeling of nature was not necessarily out of character with the notion of a benevolent deity, for such hardships served as tests of morality and character placed before humankind as positive opportunities. As Malthus argued in the final two chapters of the first *Essay on Population,* the resulting activity, intellectual and physical, promised to exalt humanity in all its complexity.[15]

Even while theology enforced the foundation of the *Essay,* a particular methodological orientation enabled Malthus to assume authority and legitimacy in his argumentation. Here too the intertwining of natural and human history remained central to his project. Building on the excellent work of Schabas's *Natural Origins of Economics,* this essay looks beyond the specific intellectual arguments about nature built into the concerns of political economy to other aspects of Malthus's orientation toward natural history.[16] The following examination relates his active interest in seeing the world as a theater of natural forces to a broader social milieu in the final decades of the eighteenth century. Naturalists practiced a daily alertness to meteorology, flora, and fauna, and they held a conviction that progress entailed a series of identifiable stages of history from ancient to present times. A love of facts drawn from the natural world and relentless empiricism gird the arguments of the *Essay,* characteristics that represented reliable data to many of Malthus's contemporaries. As one admirer indicated in 1807, "It is quite delightful to find how closely he has taught himself to examine the circumstances of the lower classes of society, and what a scientific turn he gives the subject."[17] Malthus's search for "system" also reflected a naturalist's yearning for universal categories and laws. His reliance on premises drawn from the natural world enabled him to launch overarching generalizations about the fate of all humanity from very particular circumstances.

As a precocious child, Thomas Robert (always "Bob" among family members) was trained up as a student of nature from his earliest years. At the head of his "learned" and "accomplished" family was the fascinating figure of Daniel Malthus, a well-read man of enlightened and at times radical inclinations.[18] His ardent admiration for Jean-Jacques Rousseau fueled occasional decisions to shun convention (such as forbidding his wife to wear a wedding ring) and considerable efforts to court the philosopher, which overlap in interesting ways with the formative years of Robert's life. No biographer has ever solved the mystery of why the Malthus family sold their home soon after Rousseau's visit to England and "wandered about" for the next nineteen years; Daniel Malthus's intellectual proclivities surely had something to do with it. As he wrote to Rousseau after the philosopher's departure, he did not share the concerns of typical landlords, and, in the words of Patricia James, "he spent more time in cottages than in castles." Perhaps it was important to the older Malthus to deny himself (and his household) the complacency and security that would have been expected of persons in possession of their considerable wealth.[19]

This devotee of the late enlightenment was intent on guiding the education of his second son with a marked degree of precision. From birth, Robert's congenital cleft palate and hare-lip presented a painful commentary on the mysterious workings of nature, but early signs of intellectual gifts clearly provided an inspiring consolation to a parent who admired Rousseau. After several years at a school in Claverton in Somerset (which his brother, Sydenham, older by twelve years, had also attended), Robert was sent to a dissenting academy at Warrington, and later to the home of Gilbert Wakefield. Wakefield's fame in the history of radical dissent makes this choice an interesting one: he was an outspoken critic of the established church, who became a Unitarian and later a celebrated (and imprisoned) critic of the British government. Daniel Malthus, with his philosophical bent, probably applauded Wakefield's unusually liberal pedagogical principles, along with his stellar academic credentials. Distinguished as second wrangler at Cambridge and a scholar of classical literature and mathematics, Wakefield enjoyed success as a published author. The elder Malthus may have viewed Robert, however impeded in his speech, as his own private Émile, and Wakefield's tutelage offered an unmistakable opportunity.

The experiment backfired, at least in part. A remark made by Robert's good friend William (later Bishop) Otter suggests that Malthus "bore few marks and signs 'of the scenes and persons to which he had been entrusted for the specific purposes of education,'" a revealing, if psychologically naive, observation.[20] From these early years, Malthus carved out his own positions resolutely. His first schoolmaster, Richard Graves, captured the paradox of his young charge's character, which would someday generate scholarly debate: Malthus hated to offend or upset others (making him the consummate "gentleman," worthy of defense in the face of public opprobrium), yet he seemed also "to [love] fighting for fighting's sake" (rendering him closer to Robert Southey's characterization as a "mischievous booby").[21] One wonders if Malthus's pointed contrariness galled Wakefield. A strict pacifist, Wakefield harbored a reverence for nature and gave up fishing because of the pain it inflicted. What must he have thought of young Robert, who repeatedly demonstrated his relish for shooting while living with the Wakefields, once complaining in a letter to his father that the birds "are so wild, that you can seldom get a shot, & then at a very great distance."[22]

Malthus nevertheless complied in important ways, setting out for Wakefield's former college at Cambridge in the autumn of 1784, a move that would leave important imprints on his intellect. "The chief study is mathematics," Malthus reported to his father, "for all honour in taking a degree depends upon that science & the great aim of most of the men is to take an honorable degree."[23] Their correspondence shows how the issue of the breadth or narrowness of his education was a concern, as his father (who had never finished his studies at Oxford a generation earlier) strained to understand what his son was doing at university. His chief worry most likely arose from uncertainty about how Robert, who would inherit no part of the family estate on his father's death, would support himself in the future. Daniel extended a palm to his son, who felt unsupported in his choice of study, by elaborating his views on mathematics. "There is scarcely any part of learning which I esteem more, & all I have ever said to you which cou'd possibly be misunderstood . . . is that I cou'd always wish to see it applied, & that I desir'd to see you a surveyor, a mechanic, a navigator, a financier [this last inserted as an afterthought], a natural philosopher, an astronomer, & [not] a meer speculative *algebraist*."[24] Malthus answered by assuring his father that "I am rather remark'd in College for talking of what actually exists in nature, or may be put to real practical use." More than once, he pointed out that his course of mathematics was not confined to abstractions: "The greatest stress is laid on a thorough knowledge of the branches of natural philosophy," he explained, asking permission "to proceed in my own plan of reading for the next two years." "I promise you at the expiration of that time to be a decent natural philosopher, & not only to know a few principles, but to be able to apply those principles in a variety of useful problems."[25]

Malthus as natural philosopher was already practicing a daily form of scientific observation, evident in his correspondence with his father and throughout his travel journals: he recorded the weather, along with temperature, and regularly commented on his observations. This kind of enlightened exercise stretched back for a century, reflected in Robert Boyle's widely read *General History of the Air* (1692), which taught readers how to integrate temperature, pressure, and humidity into a broader search for the effects of the air. John Locke appended to that volume "a portion of his own weather diary, indicating that a Baconian natural history could take the form of a chronological record of weather phenomena."[26] According to historian Vladimir Janković, a growing number of lower-rung "clerical naturalists" who recorded meteorological data in the eighteenth century may have been trying to enhance their profiles in the eyes of potential patrons.[27] Malthus's elementary applications of what he knew about weather placed him among the dilettanti, particularly in the way he employed a deus ex machina in his narrative of natural occurrences. Among more serious students of nature, the second half of the century generated a keener sense of professional practices in science, in which "quantification displaced the narratives of meteoric tradition, averages were more relevant than extremes, and recurring phenomena more telling than singularities." But meteorologists had not yet hammered out general laws governing the atmosphere, rules similar to "Newton's accomplishments in celestial mechanics." Lacking a governing paradigm in earth science, weather diarists like Malthus were free to interpret natural disasters according to frameworks of causality of their own choosing.[28]

The fact that Malthus saw himself as a natural philosopher in a truth-seeking age, offering observations from a laboratory writ large, places him squarely among a late eighteenth-century generation of gentlemanly naturalists. An earlier generation engaged in enthusiastic combing of field and forest (along with far-flung colonial landscapes) in order to catalogue botanical specimens according to England's own guide, John Ray, as well as the rising star of Carl Linnaeus. "Natural History is now, by a kind of national establishment, become the favourite study of the time," proclaimed the *Critical Review* in 1763. The establishment of botanic gardens in Cambridge and Kew underscored the institutional support for such activity, vital and popular by the time of Malthus's years at university. This was an era of nature-clubbing and field excursions, along with a growing interest in geology and its power to reveal the "majestic unfolding of Creation's inexorable plan."[29] By the 1790s, natural history in all its forms inflated the sails of the Romantic movement, evident in a burgeoning passion for Rousseau's sojourns in the outdoors, Thomas Gray's poetry, and Edmund Burke's writings on the sublime. For the more empirically oriented, like Malthus, the trend toward sensibility spelled a diversion from accurate observation and less comfortable truths. In his reaction to Godwin, Malthus would marshal a distinctly rational approach to human nature combined with a renovated empiricism, what we might consider a nascent form of social science. Unlike the rationality associated with the late Enlightenment, however, his was a decidedly unsentimental and blunt instrument.[30]

An insistence on "what actually exists in nature" captures the spirit of Malthus's endeavor when, years later, he set upon Godwin's *Political Justice* as the fertile text from which he would generate his famous principle. In the first edition and more systematically in the second, Malthus mocked what he believed to be Godwin's chimerical construction of human nature, which, he objected, had no basis in observed behavior. His most trenchant statements about nature often appeared in conjunction with his descriptions of the twin forces of population, the "passion between the sexes" and the impact of natural and social forces on human offspring once they were born. "Since the world began, the causes of population and depopulation have been probably as constant as any of the laws of nature with which we are acquainted," he argued.[31] Nature "will not, cannot, be defeated in her purposes." Its workings were inseparable from theological imperatives: it acted "like a kind though sometimes severe instructor, with the intention of teaching us to make all parts strong, and to chase vice and misery from the earth." No matter what high-minded ideals informed the projects of philosophers like Godwin (and Rousseau, we might add), these were, in Adam Smith's words, the "impotent endeavors of man."[32]

Critics have had no trouble pointing out that the young man who wrote the first *Essay* had not seen much of the world in either its human or plant variety. Once his pamphlet had reached the public and created a stir, Malthus may have felt some belated humility. He most likely had little direct knowledge of the fixed laws of nature in the realm of sexuality. As Gail Bederman brilliantly argues, his agitated marginalia suggest that his anxiety in reading Godwin and Mary Wollstonecraft, particularly Godwin's account of sexual freedom, may well have fueled the bold and somewhat cavalier argumentation in the first edition. This same preoccupation may similarly account for his considerable recklessness in marshalling data. By his own account, Malthus had dashed off the first *Essay* with few books to hand. Now that his argument was, in a sense, history, he embarked on a mission to reinforce it with hard data from "what actually exists in nature."[33]

The remainder of this essay looks at two paths of research into the natural world used by Malthus in revising the *Essay*. As footnotes in the 1803 edition indicate, Malthus adopted a scholarly approach, enlisting evidence drawn from books on environmental conditions affecting food supplies. A brief examination of two works sheds light on Malthus's catastrophic mode of thought and its connection to the weather and the natural world. Secondly, consideration of Malthus's tour of Scandinavia shows how he was determined to go beyond mere book-learning to bolster his case. In 1799, he and two Cambridge friends, William Otter and Daniel Clarke, along with a pupil of Clarke, embarked on a tour of Scandinavia. The outbreak of the French Revolution, which limited travel on the Continent, suggested the alternative itinerary, which took them first through Germany and Denmark, then northward into Sweden and Norway.[34] To the budding theorist of population, the rugged landscape of Scandinavia, less well known to the educated public, held particular advantages. Untrammeled by agricultural improvers, inhabited by simple peasants versed in the ways of nature, the region offered Malthus the hope of gleaning information on reproduction and survival shaped by minimal interference of modernizing forces. This was worthwhile information indeed to the assiduous student of nature.

"As the frost detains you in Town, and me in the country; and as you were so kind as to make an offer of services . . . I will mention a few books which if you should hear of at any of the booksellers where you happen to call, I wish you would get for me," Malthus wrote to his father in London in February 1799. His list included items on population in German, French, Dutch, and English, and may also have yielded the copy of Benjamin Franklin's *Works* that resides now in the Jesus College Library.[35]

Malthus obviously had other means of obtaining books and pamphlets, many of which do not appear in the Cambridge library, yet nevertheless supplied him with the data he desired for his expanded second edition. In his search for periodical checks to population, he mined the pages of Thomas Short's two-volume *General Chronological History of the Air, Weather, Seasons, Meteors, &c.* (1749) and his *New Observations . . . on . . . Bills of Mortality* (1750). The Scottish-born doctor was an energetic advocate of the "empiric" method, which he defined as a necessary combination of reason and observation. Without the latter, he argued, reason is simply "wrangling." Short moved south to Sheffield and devoted his career to the study of fluids, particularly waters, but he also theorized about air, arguing that wind was the primary communicant of disease. For Short, the weather patterns of the globe were merely handmaidens of a larger, comprehensive system that science might discern through its enlightened methodologies. The "God of Nature most certainly has the Universe in his own Hands, and can dispose of his Creatures as he sees proper, either for the Destruction or Relief of Mankind," Short offered in the preface to his *History of Air*.[36] As the author of *A Comparative History of the Increase and Decrease of*

Mankind (1767), it is not surprising that his work came to Malthus's attention. Short's argument–that earlier marriages were beneficial to humankind–was no doubt less congenial to Malthus than Short's methodology. Malthus ultimately stood the doctor's argument on its head. But such arguments about the influence of extraordinary weather on humankind harmonized perfectly with Malthus's own views of the natural world.

In both works, Short's approach to natural history was encyclopedic, his picture of nature's workings endlessly punishing. The twenty-first-century reader may register something like surprise in perusing the good doctor's findings in his *History of the Air.* Beginning with Genesis, he collated information on catastrophic weather and peculiar celestial occurrences across the globe. His "Chronological Table" detailed "Unnatural Rains, Dews, or other Downfalls," including an occurrence in Rome in 3736 "A.M. [Anno Mundi]," in which "Milk rained from the Clouds and watered the Earth like Rain." Closer to home, in the year 688 A.D., it "Rained Blood 7 days together through all Britain" and "Milk, Cheese, Butter turned to Blood." In 1014, "A Heap of Clouds fell, and smothered Thousands."[37] Data on plagues and other less easily categorized events followed. More credibly, he demonstrated the absence of causality linking comets and meteors to outbreaks of disease in the more modern era. And in *New Observations,* he used recent, quotidian information to demonstrate a direct link between extreme weather occurrences and mortality from disease. Grasping at a bigger picture, Malthus fastened on Short's pungent characterization of these spectacular events–"terrible correctives of the redundance of mankind"–and employed the phrase in his second edition.[38]

Short's peculiar tables on famines and plagues appealed to Malthus and supplied supporting evidence for the revised *Essay.* Malthus simply tabulated the number of total years covered by Short's tables and divided the result by the number of plagues catalogued, arriving at a rate of epidemics "at the interval of about 4 ½ years."[39] As Malthus had explained in the first edition in a particularly vehement paragraph that was to vanish after 1807, "Famine seems to be the last, the most dreadful resource of nature." Much more powerful are "the vices of mankind" as "active and able ministers of depopulation." He added, "But should they fail in this war of extermination, sickly seasons, epidemics, pestilence, and plague, advance in terrific array, and sweep off their thousands and ten thousands. Should success be still incomplete, gigantick inevitable famine stalks in the rear, and, with one mighty blow, levels the population with the food of the world."[40]

Historians have been at pains to explain how such a catastrophic view of the conditions under which human society perpetuated itself could have been brewing in the mind of this seemingly placid young curate living at home with his parents. Besides its utter simplification (lacking any sense of medical or environmental improvements that might cushion the effects of physical misfortunes), such argumentation seemed to associate Malthus with the decriers of dark satanic mills in the industrial north. Social historians reexamining the *Essay* have linked his grim predictions to the deleterious effects of urbanization on the poor. Another explanatory strategy has pointed to the fact that within the span of Malthus's life, Britain had spent many years at war.[41] It is certainly true that the year 1795 provided direct evidence of wartime scarcity, but Malthus took this misery-inducing circumstance one step further: a key factor that year was bad weather that accentuated already existing shortages. Here was a direct example of his careful choreography of one bad thing leading to another. Too many people bearing down on food supplies, particularly among the poor, "turns even a slight deficiency from the failure of the seasons into a severe dearth; and may be fairly said, therefore, to be one of the principal causes of famine."[42]

Malthus was not imagining the intrusive power of European weather patterns during the eighteenth century. Works like Short's *New Observations,* written at midcentury, most likely reflected the experiences of markedly cold winters and recent episodes of extreme weather. As a Scot, Short's sensitivity to meteorological calamity could have sprung from events close to home. A sizeable diminution of upland cultivation took place in southern Scotland, apparent by the eighteenth century; cool summers caused consecutive harvest failures, particularly of oat crops, and thus changed the map of Scottish food production by forcing the abandonment of farms in upper elevations.[43] Malthus would have had no trouble finding evidence of catastrophic events in the earlier part of the century, such as the freeze of 1709, which reduced the area devoted to olive cultivation in France, or the subsistence crisis in Switzerland that qualified as a famine in 1770–1771. The year 1771 witnessed "an extremely snowy summer" across Europe, and weather historians have demonstrated that the 1780s was a notably weather-beaten decade.[44] "Placed at a critical phase during the closing stages of the Little Ice Age, the 1780s contain a number of outstanding temperature and rainfall extremes, . . . which must represent some very pronounced regional anomalies," John Kington argued in his collation of data from eighteenth-century observers. One factor promoting coolness was an increase in volcanic activity after 1780, which added dust to the upper atmosphere. Malthus himself had noted the unusually low temperatures of that decade in his correspondence with his father; both men watched their thermometers and remarked on the effects of the cold. "Then, as now,"

Kington points out, "an apparent increase in the variability of weather and climate from season to season and year to year was causing concern."[45]

Malthus's meteorological interests, as part of his general awareness of the power of nature, played a role in his tour of Scandinavia. In his search for data, Norway would provide him with a test case of how populations might best respond to the pummeling of nature. There, in a nation carved out of the upper latitudes, he found the correct balance between nature and prudential restraint. "Even in Norway, notwithstanding the disadvantage of a severe and uncertain climate," he wrote in the 1803 edition of the *Essay,*

> I am inclined to think that the poor were, on the average, better off than in England. Their houses and clothing were superior and, though they had no white bread, they had much more meat, fish, and milk than our labourers. . . . This degree of happiness, superior to what could be expected from the soil and climate, arises almost exclusively from the degree in which the preventive check to population operates.[46]

In fact, as Michael Drake has shown from the 1801 census, fertility measures at the time were high, indicating that preventive checks were not at all what Malthus thought them to be. Malthus's complete faith in his idiosyncratic interviews with contacts in Norway and Sweden led to several incorrect assumptions about deterrents to early marriage.[47] Once back in England, he also drew selectively from statistical works, concluding that in Norway, "mortality [was] less than in any other country in Europe." This assertion, too, was incorrect; so-called positive checks had kept the Norwegian population from growing, and only when the diminution of disease and infantile morbidity declined in the first half of the nineteenth century would the number of people rise.[48]

It seems counterintuitive that Malthus, with his bleak portrait of natural forces plaguing humankind, should make such inaccurate and even optimistic judgments about Norway. By his own account, the country endured "eight months of winter, [and] four months of bad weather."[49] What are we to make of this aberration of the "population story"? This was his first tour of a landscape and culture outside of England, and references to the "picturesque" and "sublime" suggest that he was determined to put a learned sensibility to the test. We know that he had read Mary Wollstonecraft's account of Sweden and Norway,[50] but crucial to the second edition of the *Essay* was his reading of Bishop Erich Pontoppidan's *Natural History of Norway,* translated from the Danish and published in England in 1755, along with William Coxe's *Travels into Poland, Russia, Sweden, and Den-*

mark (4th ed., 1792).[51] Malthus's findings on tour consistently confirm the arguments of these two works in their extravagant praise of Norwegian peasants; in many cases, his journal mirrors the very evidence used by Pontoppidan and Coxe. More important was the apparent proof they offered that in this vivid laboratory of nature, hard work and prudential restraint would save humankind from misfortune.

Pontoppidan's extraordinary two-volume work, a paean to the wonders of the natural world, included a bold and affirmative assessment of "the Norwegian nation." The common people received high marks for their "good appearance," their height and bravery, their light complexion (particularly among the women), "civility," "courteous behavior," and cheerfulness, even when doing "the work of horses." Their politeness reminded Pontoppidan of the French, while their love of "fine cloaths" and "elegant houses" proved that they "endeavour to imitate" the English, though he added that they were far more hospitable and friendly than that island nation. Their health was generally faultless, except for those affected by the dampness of coastal areas; their simple diet gave rise to many instances of astonishing longevity. Above all, the Norwegian peasant, in his enviable "state of liberty," showed a determination "to live independent of others, and without being in any body's debt." A critic of the English poor would find these traits indeed praiseworthy.[52]

Perhaps most remarkable was Pontoppidan's description of a forward-looking, self-help approach to times of scarcity, said to be common among peasants in the north:

> If grain be scarce, which generally happens after a severe winter, the peasants are obliged to have recourse to an old custom, as a disagreeable, but sure method of preserving life. Their bread, in time of scarcity, is made thus, they take the bark of the fir-tree, boil it and dry it before the fire, then they grind it to meal and mix a little oatmeal with it; of this mixture, they make a kind of bread, which has a bitterness and a resinous taste, and does not afford that nourishment, that their usual bread does. However, there are some people, that think it is not right to disuse this sort of bread entirely, and even in plentiful years they sometimes eat a little of it, that they may be prepared against a time of scarcity, which by the goodness of providence, does not happen in a century.[53]

In fact, the end of the eighteenth century proved to be one such time when peasants resorted to the notorious substitute. Bark bread, Malthus discovered on his tour, was sustaining peasants near Magnor at the border of Sweden, where a notably poor harvest had left "above thirty families" without oat bread for the first eight months of 1799. Malthus "collected some specimens," which boasted only a sprinkling of "a little oat flower." Ever the evidence-collector, he also noted that "the white bark of the best red firs is used for bread" and that "many of the finest trees are spoilt in this way."[54]

Clearly, the Norwegian peasant was one with nature. Malthus expressed wonderment at other practices that blended the inhabitants of this brisk climate with the landscape, such as dwellings with flat roofs topped with grass and sod, where he witnessed sheep grazing or villagers busily mowing hay. He registered a mixture of interest and dismay in the native attachment to oatcakes and milk. After weeks of refusing to eat the local bread, he dutifully consumed an oat biscuit and assiduously recorded its consistency as "more of chaff, than of oatmeal." Although he struggled to make sense of the scanty shifts commonly worn by women, also noted by Coxe and Pontoppidan (was it poverty or immodesty that had caused them to dress so minimally in chilly temperatures?), he regularly recorded glimpses of bare bodies beneath their folds. Malthus made his journal reflect as much of his empirical philosophy as possible, not knowing that the science he was approximating was late Enlightenment ethnography.[55]

In his role as natural philosopher, Malthus strained to collect as much hard data as possible. Each day, we hear of his familiar practice of recording the temperature twice and sometimes three and even four times. "Clouds low, misling [drizzling] rain at times," he wrote on 8 July; "at 9 in the evening a hard shower. Therm at half past 6 in the morning, 62; at 1, 65; at half past 7, 60."[56] At the prospect of beautiful Lake Wennerlind, the ever-zealous Malthus promptly plunged his thermometer into the water and recorded it at 61 degrees at eleven in the morning on 21 June. "Observed at Wennerburgh an apple tree in full blossom – rather late."[57] He was not immune to natural wonders: "Saw by far the most brilliant rainbow that I ever saw in my life," he enthused at one point, adding a painstaking description of its double character and "stripes." We can feel his "extreme mortification" when, on 1 August, he found his thermometer broken.[58]

Malthus's other textual guide, Coxe's *Travels*, informed him of a Norwegian practice of conscripting young men between the ages of sixteen and twenty-six. By the time Malthus toured the countryside, the strategy had been largely abandoned, but at least one of his hosts confirmed its existence, misleading the philosopher into believing that the institution of military service delayed marriage and thus reduced the number of children born to Norwegian peasants. Another customary arrangement impressed him by its stewardship: farmers provided lodging to unmarried servants and cottages and land to married male servants (*husmen*). At Drivthuen, he witnessed a particularly lavish breakfast taking place, which later bore the weight of his argument about prudential restraint. Seven men were feasting on

> fried bacon & veal, some fried fish, large bowls of milk, & oak cake and butter. Each had his knife & fork & spoon – the bowls of milk were in common. We enquired of the master of the house afterwards whether they were all his men – he said they were, and lived in his house, besides others. He had, he said, 20 altogether in family. . . . None of the men that lived with him were married. . . . The establishments of the farmers in this country appear to be much larger than with us, and it is probable that the sons of housemen & small farmers become the servants of farmers, and do not marry till they are able to obtain a houseman's place.[59]

Sample Norwegian census returns from 1801 show no farms hosting twenty servants.[60] Yet this powerful encounter convinced Malthus of a method of strict paternal oversight that kept reproductive rates at a minimum. The scene offered many powerful symbols to the wide-eyed Malthus: the meat and fish, the communal bowls of milk, the hearty all-male camaraderie amounted to the wish-list of a latter-day anthropologist, and also the perfect ammunition for the second edition of the *Essay*. Work hard, be obedient and chaste, and you will eat well, it promised, even in the face of belligerent weather and a fearsome climate.

With a whiff of Aesop, the tortoise and hare revealed more about the morality informing the second *Essay* than any likely prediction of how agriculture might perform in an increasingly commercial world. Malthus's understanding of rural life, supported by his empirical natural philosophy, belonged to a universe in which nature held the trump card capable of negating all efforts to match agricultural output with the level of population. Over time, the fury of Malthus's concept of nature diminished, as it hovered over a carefully planned notion of economic life only distantly related to the communal table in Norway. Later editions of the *Essay* implied that the blows of catastrophe might be avoided, as its author recognized the power of human nature to respond to incentives and rewards. Malthus was much less the natural philosopher and much more the political economist by then, though he never abandoned his advocacy of moral restraint.[61] His depiction of the inexorable laws of nature would support sweeping arguments about population and poverty for many years, despite the peculiar circumstances that gave birth to his views.

NOTES

1. T. R. Malthus, *An Essay on the Principle of Population; or, A View of Its Past and Present Effects on Human Happiness; with an Inquiry into Our Prospects Respecting the Future Removal or Mitigation of the Evils Which It Occasion. A New Edition, Very Much Enlarged,* 2nd ed. (London, 1803; reprint, New Haven, Conn., 2017), 276 (hereafter *Essay of 1803;* the page numbers cited for this work are to this book).

2. Ibid., 401.

3. Ibid., 417.

4. Piercy Ravenstone, "Of Subsistence," in *A Few Doubts as to the Correctness of Some Opinions Generally Entertained on the Subject of Population and Political Economy* (London, 1821), reprinted in *T. R. Malthus; Critical Responses,* ed. Geoffrey Gilbert (London, 1998), 2:11, 18, 22. Ravenstone was recognized by David Ricardo and, much later, Karl Marx, as a participant in serious debates over political economy. See Max Beer, *A History of British Socialism* (London, 1919, 1921; reprint, London, 2002), 1:251–258.

5. The argument is taken from Thomas Jerrold, *Dissertations on Man, Philosophical, Physiological and Political* (London, 1806), cited in Roy Porter, "The Malthusian Moment," in *Malthus, Medicine, and Morality: "Malthusianism" after 1798,* ed. Brian Dolan (Amsterdam, 2000), 65.

6. "Board of Agriculture. Letter to the Editor, from the President," *Annals of Agriculture* 23 (1795): 210.

7. Quoted in Michael Turner, "Corn Crises in the Age of Malthus," in *Malthus and His Time,* ed. Michael Turner (Houndmills, U.K., 1986), 120.

8. Arthur Young, *View of the Agriculture of Oxfordshire* (London, 1809), 36, quoted in Roy Porter, "The Environment and the Enlightenment: The English Experience," in *The Faces of Nature in Enlightenment Europe,* ed. Lorraine Daston and Gianna Pomata (Berlin, 2003), 27.

9. *Essay of 1803,* 294.

10. R. L. Meek, "Malthus—Yesterday and Today," in *Thomas Robert Malthus: Critical Assessments,* ed. John Cunningham Wood (London, 1986), 1:175–197; Donald Winch, *Riches and Poverty: An Intellectual History of Political Economy in Britain, 1750–1834* (Cambridge, 1996), chap. 13, *passim.*

11. Margaret Schabas, *The Natural Origins of Economics* (Chicago, 2005), 108.

12. *Essay of 1803,* 274.

13. D. L. LeMahieu, "Malthus and the Theology of Scarcity," *Journal of the History of Ideas* 40 (1979): 467–474.

14. T. R. Malthus, *Population: The First Essay* (Ann Arbor, Mich., 1959), 122–123. See also Mervyn Nicholson, "The Eleventh Commandment: Sex and

Spirit in Wollstonecraft and Malthus," *Journal of the History of Ideas* 51, no. 3 (1990): 406.

15. J. M. Pullen, "Malthus' Theological Ideas and Their Influence on His Principle of Population," *History of Political Economy* 13 (1981): 39–54; Boyd Hilton, *The Age of Atonement: The Influence of Evangelicalism on Social and Economic Thought* (Oxford, 1988), 17, 36–70.

16. Schabas, *Natural Origins,* 102–124. See also Paul B. Wood, "The Science of Man," in *Cultures of Natural History,* ed. N. Jardine, J. A. Secord, and E. C. Spary (Cambridge, 1996), 197–210.

17. Francis Horner to Lord Webb Seymour, 6 July 1807, quoted in Patricia James, *Population Malthus: His Life and Times* (London, 1979), 148–149.

18. Although a granddaughter perhaps unfairly typecast Daniel as "peculiar" and "eccentric," a grandson of George Berkeley, philosopher and bishop of Cloyne, thought it a "truly amiable family." James, *Population Malthus,* 13, 24.

19. Ibid., 11–13. Daniel went to some lengths to court Rousseau during his visit to England at the time of Robert's birth in February 1766. Just before leaving England during the summer of 1768, the philosopher finally found time to meet in Derbyshire, where Daniel promptly carried part of the family in order to pursue some recreational hours botanizing.

20. Ibid., 19, quoting from W. Otter, "Memoir of Robert Malthus," in T. R. Malthus, *Principles of Political Economy,* 2nd edn. (London, 1836), xxiv.

21. Richard Graves to Daniel Malthus, 10 August [1780?], in *T. R. Malthus: The Unpublished Papers in the Collection of Kanto Gakuen University,* ed. John Pullen and Trevor Hughes Parry (Cambridge, 1997), 1:5 (hereafter *Unpublished Papers*). On critics of Malthus, see James P. Huzel, *The Popularization of Malthus in Early Nineteenth-Century England: Martineau, Cobbett, and the Popular Press* (Aldershot, 2006), and Robert Southey, *New Letters of Robert Southey,* ed. Kenneth Curry (New York, 1965), 1:357.

22. T. R. Malthus to Daniel Malthus, 25 December 1783, in *Unpublished Papers,* 1:16. On Wakefield, see Bruce E. Graver, "Wakefield, Gilbert," in *Oxford Dictionary of National Biography* (Oxford, 2004), http://www.oxforddnb .com/view/article/28418; James, *Population Malthus,* 19–22; and Charles James Fox to Gilbert Wakefield, 14 September 1799, in *Correspondence of the Late Gilbert Wakefield, B.A. with Late Right Honourable Charles James Fox, in the Years 1796 . . . 1801 Chiefly, on Subjects of Classical Literature* (London, 1813), 80.

23. T. R. Malthus to Daniel Malthus, 14 November 1784, in *Unpublished Papers,* 1:29.

24. Daniel Malthus to T. R. Malthus, 19 December 1785, in ibid., 1:36.

25. T. R. Malthus to Daniel Malthus, 11 February 1786, in ibid., 1:41–42.

26. Jan Golinski, *British Weather and the Climate of Enlightenment* (Chicago, 2007), 204–205, 213.

27. Vladimir Janković, *Reading the Skies: A Cultural History of English Weather, 1650–1820* (Manchester, 2000), 113–116, 143. John Kington gives many clerical examples, high and low, ranging from an Augustinian monk in Munich to the bishop of Durham and Gilbert White of Selborne. Kington, *The Weather of the 1780s over Europe* (Cambridge, 1988), 2, 9–10, passim.

28. Golinski, *British Weather,* 205.

29. David Ellison Allen, *The Naturalist in Britain: A Social History,* 2nd ed. (Princeton, N.J., 1994), 35, 39, 48.

30. Ibid., 47. See also Joyce E. Chaplin, "Mark Catesby, a Skeptical Newtonian in America," in *Empire's Nature: Mark Catesby's New World Vision,* ed. Amy R. W. Meyers and Margaret Beck Pritchard (Chapel Hill, N.C., 1998), 38–47.

31. *Essay of 1803,* 274.

32. Ibid., 408–409; Adam Smith quoted in LeMahieu, "Malthus and the Theology of Scarcity," 468.

33. Gail Bederman, "Sex, Scandal, Satire, and Population in 1798: Revisiting Malthus's First *Essay,*" *Journal of British Studies* 47 (October 2008): 768–795. Without census data, Malthus had gotten the population of Great Britain wrong by 56 percent in the first *Essay.* New figures available to him, along with an altered perspective, influenced later revisions. E. A. Wrigley, "Malthus's Model of a Pre-Industrial Economy," in *Malthus Past and Present,* ed. J. Dupâquier, A. Fauve-Chamoux, and E. Grebenik (London, 1983), 114.

34. Patricia James, "Biographical Sketches," in *The Travel Diaries of T. R. Malthus,* ed. Patricia James (Cambridge, 1966), 16–17 (hereafter *Travel Diaries*). Clarke and his pupil eventually went their own way, leaving Otter and Malthus to complete their own itinerary. Michael Drake, "Malthus on Norway," *Population Studies* 20, no. 2 (November 1966): 175.

35. T. R. Malthus to Daniel Malthus, 4 February 1799, in *Unpublished Papers,* 1:63.

36. Thomas Short, "Praelegomena," in *A General Chronological History of the Air, Weather, Seasons, Meteors, &c.* (London, 1749), 1:x.

37. Ibid., 1:45; 2:180.

38. *Essay of 1803,* 270; Thomas Short, *New Observations, Natural, Moral, Civil, Political, and Medical, on City, Town, and Country Bills of Mortality* (London, 1750), 96. Quoted again in *Essay of 1803,* 270, as "terrible correctives to the redundance of mankind."

39. *Essay of 1803*, 270. Malthus cited the wrong page of *History of Air* for this point.

40. Ibid., 276–277.

41. M. W. Flinn, "Malthus and His Time," in Dupâquier, Fauve-Chamoux, and Grebenik, eds., *Malthus Past and Present*, 85–95.

42. *Essay of 1803*, 271.

43. Jean M. Grove, *Little Ice Ages, Ancient and Modern*, 2nd ed. (London, 2004), 2:622–627. Climate historians of the British Isles estimate that over 2 million hectares were abandoned for climatic reasons between 1300 and 1600 (2:627).

44. Ibid., 2:630.

45. Kington, *Weather*, 2.

46. *Essay of 1803*, 430.

47. Malthus incorrectly assumed that a particular system of military recruitment, which siphoned off young men in their twenties for service, deterred early marriages. In fact, the system had fallen into disuse by the time of his visit; moreover, certain aspects of its deployment had worked precisely in the opposite way Malthus thought, by encouraging early marriage. Drake, "Malthus on Norway," 176.

48. Ibid., 181–182, 187, 189.

49. *Travel Diaries*, 92.

50. Mary Wollstonecraft had traveled to Sweden and Norway in 1795 and enjoyed considerable success in publishing her letters in 1796. The work was in Malthus's personal collection and, as Gail Bederman has indicated (see note 33, above), contained unusually prolific marginalia in Malthus's handwriting.

51. *Travel Diaries*, 25.

52. Erich Pontoppidan, *Natural History of Norway* (London, 1755), 2:240–243, 248, 254–257.

53. Ibid., 2:268.

54. *Travel Diaries*, 217–218.

55. Ibid., 131, 134, 136, 187–196.

56. Ibid., 130.

57. Ibid., 81.

58. Ibid., 94, 211.

59. Ibid., 142.

60. Drake, "Malthus on Norway," 178–179.

61. Timothy L. Alborn, "Boys to Men: Moral Restraint at Haileybury College," in Dolan, ed., *Malthus, Medicine, and Morality*, 33–55.

The Preventive Check
and the Poor Law

The Malthusian Model and Its Implications

E. A. WRIGLEY

The three most eminent among the classical economists shared a common belief in the impossibility of bringing about an era in which there was exponential growth in the output of material goods. The reason was simple. All material production involved land, labor, and capital. Of these it was reasonable to suppose that the supply of labor and capital could, in suitable circumstances, be increased as required, but the supply of land was fixed. This implied an insuperable problem associated with increasing production. If output was to rise, more land must be taken into cultivation, but, since the best land would already be in use, this meant exploiting land of poorer quality. Alternatively, existing land could be used more intensively, or the two expedients might be combined. In any event, even allowing for the possibility of improvements in technology, returns both to labor and capital must decline and growth would be arrested. In short, the very process of growth ensured its eventual cessation.[1]

In considering this conclusion it is important to note that land was not just the source of food but also of virtually all the raw materials which entered material production. The productivity of the land set limits not just to the scale of food supply but also of industrial production. This is self-evidently true of raw materials such as cotton, wool, silk, leather, and wood but also, if indirectly, of all metals since the smelting of the ores from which the metals were derived required much heat, and the heat in question came from the burning of wood and charcoal. Adam Smith depicted the nature of the economies of his day as follows:

> The great commerce of every civilised society, is that carried on between the inhabitants of the town and those of the country. It consists in the exchange of rude for manufactured produce. . . . The country supplies the town with the means of subsistence, and the materials of manufacture. The town repays this supply by sending back a part of the manufactured produce to the inhabitants of the country. The town, in which there neither is nor can be any reproduction of substances, may

very properly be said to gain its whole wealth and subsistence from the country.[2]

Sir Thomas More encapsulated the nature of the fundamental problem facing all such organic economies in his famous comment in *Utopia* that the sheep were eating up the men: if the output of raw wool was to be increased, this must mean less land available to grow corn.[3] David Ricardo drove home the impossibility of escaping this problem at the end of his discussion of the inevitability of declining returns to capital and labor by noting, "This will necessarily be rendered permanent by the laws of nature, which have limited the productive powers of the land."[4] It was not defects in human institutions or an inadequate legal framework or human frailties that lay behind this gloomy conclusion: it was a feature of the natural world and beyond remedy.

Malthus shared with the other classical economists the same concern about the implications of the impossibility of overcoming the ceiling set to material production by the limited amount of cultivable land, but he added a further consideration that reinforced and extended this concern. As a young man in Cambridge he had studied mathematics and was familiar with the possibility of expressing a problem in mathematical terms. He depicted the nature and seriousness of the problem in a way that his critics found difficult to dismiss. He suggested that even on the most optimistic of assumptions it was impossible to suppose that any achievable rise in agricultural output could exceed an arithmetic progression, whereas it was rational to assume that populations would grow by geometric progression unless constrained by inadequate resources. Given the nature of the two progressions, tension between production and population was unavoidable. Except in areas where for a time the cultivable area could be expanded as fast as population grew, as in the young United States, living standards must be in danger of being reduced close to bare subsistence by a deteriorating balance between numbers and available nutrition. This insight of Malthus has not only proved of great value in studying all preindustrial, organic societies but has also proved to have a much wider relevance. It was reading Malthus's *Essay* that suggested to Charles Darwin a force which would drive the process of natural selection. Only a proportion of each rising generation of young plants, animals, fish, birds, or insects would survive to reproduce, and those that were successful in doing so would be the ones best adapted to meet the challenges presented by the environment in which they lived.

In the first *Essay* Malthus was concerned to drive home the implications of this insight in order to refute the views of men such as William Godwin and the Marquis de Condorcet, who believed that a radical improvement of the human condition could be achieved by institutional change and altered personal motivations. Malthus expressed his views trenchantly and with few qualifications. As time passed, however, he became increasingly alive to the importance of an issue to which he had referred in the first *Essay* and which was treated at length in the later versions of the work. Although population growth, in his analysis, must always be arrested by the difficulties of expanding output, it did not follow that the growth would always cease at the same size of population. He emphasized the importance of the distinction between the "positive" and "preventive" checks. The significance of this distinction is perhaps easiest to appreciate by presenting it in graphical form, as in figure 1.

In the upper half of figure 1, three combinations of fertility and mortality are shown, each of which results in population ceasing to grow. In the lower half the implications for living standards of each of the three possibilities are shown. F_1 shows a high level of fertility, which does not change as population growth continues. Eventually mortality, M, rises to the same level, but only when population has reached a total which implies (P_1) that living standards have been driven down to a low level. If fertility is at a lower level but is also invariant as population rises, as in the case of F_2, the intersection with M occurs at a somewhat smaller population total, which therefore results in a less severely depressed standard of living (P_2). If, however, fertility is responsive to reduced living standards (F_{2a}) and declines in sympathy, population growth will cease earlier and still higher living standards will result (P_{2a}). F_1 depicts the situation that might arise in a society in which marriage was early and universal, with women normally marrying soon after reaching sexual maturity. Here the positive check alone brings growth to a halt, and the population lives close to what is sometimes termed the Malthusian precipice. F_2 represents a variant that might describe the situation if marriage normally occurred later in life and where some men and women never married. In this case rising mortality brings population to a stop at a lower total than in the case of F_1 with benefit to living standards, even though fertility remains constant as population totals rise. However, if marriage age rises with deteriorating economic prospects, and a larger fraction of each rising generation remains single throughout life, the resultant reduction in fertility (F_{2a}), by arresting growth at a still earlier point, preserves living standards even more effectively. F_1 may be taken as exemplifying the perils that must arise if the positive check is the sole influence determining at what point population growth comes to

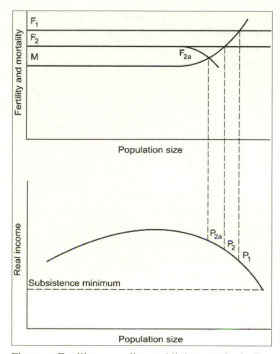

Figure 1. Fertility, mortality, and living standards. Reprinted with permission from E. A. Wrigley, *Continuity, Chance and Change: The Character of the Industrial Revolution in England,* (Cambridge: Cambridge
University Press, 1988), 21.

an end. F_{2a} shows the benefits that can be achieved if the preventive check
is effective.[5]

The world in which Malthus lived and the problems that were then
prominent were both very different from the situation in today's world.
In order to understand and at the same time to do justice to the views that
Malthus expressed, it is essential to take this point into account. As already
noted, for example, it was generally assumed that there was a ceiling set
by the limited supply of land to the scope for increased material production. Although the immediate problem in this analysis is the fixed supply
of land, the underlying problem is energy supply. Both heat energy and
mechanical energy in organic economies are derived almost exclusively

from plant photosynthesis. The annual quantum of plant growth resulting from such photosynthesis, therefore, is almost the sole source of the energy needed for all forms of material production.[6] This fact set a ceiling to the possible output of types of material production that were energy intensive. As an example, even if half the land surface of Britain were devoted to woodland, the annual yield of wood and charcoal would only suffice to produce about $1\frac{1}{4}$ million tons of bar iron on a sustained yield basis.[7]

Crucial to overcoming the barrier that made exponential growth in material production impossible was the increasing importance of a new source of energy in the form of coal. Coal itself is the product of photosynthesis, but in this case accumulated over hundreds of millions of years, whereas organic societies had access each year only to the product of photosynthesis in that year.[8] It is a striking example of the difficulty the classical economists had in realizing the significance of the changes which were in train in their midst that Adam Smith, in noting how industry was increasingly clustering on the coalfields, attributed this trend principally to the fact that wage costs were lowered on the coalfields because coal provided a cheap source of domestic heating![9]

The belief that sustained growth was out of the question is so foreign to the world of the twenty-first century that it may stand in the way of appreciating what was taken for granted in Malthus's day. Again, we take it as a matter of course that fertility both within marriage and more generally is readily controlled, and there is as much concern about the problems that societies face if fertility falls below the replacement level as about the dangers of excessive fertility. If, however, intercourse always carries the risk of pregnancy and yet it seems essential to control fertility levels, the available options are very limited. During her fecund years a married woman was always at risk to become pregnant. This implied that influencing nuptiality was the only practical method of controlling fertility.

When Malthus wrote the first *Essay* he was, so to speak, arguing from first principles, a fact that gave a particular cogency to the views he expressed. The later editions of the *Essay* were much longer and not without their *longueurs,* but the core argument remains the same in all of them. It may be helpful to describe the core argument further before commenting on its relation to other topics that attracted his attention, notably the Poor Laws.

Given the difference between the rates of growth in arithmetic and geometric progressions, there was a constant danger that excessive population growth would force down the living standards of the bulk of the population, since an excessive supply of labor would reduce wages for those fortunate enough to find employment and also increase the risk of unemployment.

In a peasant economy in which the play of the market was less important, subdivision of holding would produce a similar result. Mortality rates rose when the population size became excessive because nutritional levels declined and living conditions generally deteriorated. In a sense mortality could be regarded as a given; even if it were reduced for a time by human intervention, the resulting rise in the rate of population growth must generate the additional pressures associated with excessive numbers. Fertility was different. Reducing it could bring clear benefits, as illustrated in figure 1.[10] Moreover, if fertility remained low, improvements secured in this way were capable of being retained rather than being dissipated in the long run. Success in reducing and controlling fertility levels could only be achieved by limiting nuptiality. *Ceteris paribus,* where women married at, say, age twenty-five on average, fertility levels would be substantially lower than where the average age at marriage was eighteen. Similarly, if many men and women never married fertility would be lower than if marriage was universal. Limiting nuptiality was the only way to avoid excessive population pressure and a reduction in living standards. In expounding the advantages that might flow from the preventive check, Malthus showed himself, despite his reputation, to be less pessimistic than Adam Smith who wrote, "Every species of animals naturally multiplies in proportion to the means of their subsistence, and no species can ever multiply beyond it. But in every civilized society it is only among the inferior ranks of people that the scantiness of subsistence can set limits to the further multiplication of the human species; and it can do so in no other way than by destroying a great part of the children which their fruitful marriages produce."[11]

The key issue in Malthus's view was to encourage prudence when contemplating marriage. A man was not justified in contracting a marriage unless satisfied that he possessed the resources needed to support his wife and the children born to the marriage. Malthus was therefore stridently, at times bitterly, opposed to the English Poor Laws system, which, in affording support to a family in distress, adjusted the scale of support according to the number of children in the family, if the family were large. This practice, in his view, encouraged improvident marriages since it removed a consideration that would otherwise have induced greater caution on the part of men contemplating matrimony. As he put it in the first *Essay:*

> I entirely acquit Mr Pitt of any sinister intention in that clause of the Poor Bill which allows a shilling a week to every labourer for each child he has above three. I confess, that before the bill was brought into Parliament, and for some time after, I thought that such a regulation would

be highly beneficial; but further reflection on the subject has convinced me, that if its object be to better the condition of the poor, it is calculated to defeat the very purpose which it has in view.[12]

With the benefit of hindsight there is good reason to have doubts about several aspects of Malthus's attitude to the Poor Laws. One weakness in his argument was evident in his own day. To urge that a man should not contemplate marriage unless he was confident that he could support a wife and children only makes sense if it is possible in advance to calculate the approximate size of the prospective commitment. But a most important element in the prospective expense involved, perhaps the largest single element, turns on the number of children born to the marriage and whether or not they die in infancy and childhood. Given the scale of the intrinsic uncertainties in this regard, although the principle involved may be sound, it does not afford a practical basis for decision-making. In the penultimate chapter of the second edition of the *Essay,* Malthus somewhat belatedly recognized the problem and partially modified his stance. Having suggested that if it were the case that men based their calculation of making a prudential marriage on the assumption that they might have to support as many as six children, and in a given case the offspring proved more numerous, he suggested that "in this case I do not think that any evil would result from making a certain allowance to every child above this number; not with a view of rewarding a man for his large family, but merely of relieving him from a species of distress which it would be unreasonable in us to expect that he should calculate upon."[13]

Malthus was also ready to concede that there were other circumstances in which the existence of the Poor Laws had proved of great social benefit. This is apparent in his second publication, a pamphlet entitled "An Investigation of the Cause of the Present High Price of Provisions," which, like the first *Essay,* was published anonymously. "An Investigation" was also a remarkable piece of work in other ways. It displayed, for example, his ability both to detect an apparent paradox and to resolve it. In 1799, Malthus had made a lengthy tour through Norway and Sweden, and on his return to England discovered that there was widespread alarm about the level to which the price of bread had risen. During his journey through western Sweden in the province of Värmland he had seen very severe distress in the wake of harvest failure. The people were reduced to subsisting on dried sorrel and powdered tree bark. Suffering was greater than any experienced in England: "Yet as far as we could learn, the price of rye, which is the grain principally used for bread, had not risen above double its usual aver-

age; whereas in this country last year, in a scarcity that must be acknowledged to be greatly inferior in degree, wheat rose to above three times its
former price."[14]

Malthus's explanation of this paradox was essentially the same as that
of Amartya Sen when commenting on similar phenomena in recent years.[15]
Malthus wrote,

> To proceed to the point: I am most strongly inclined to suspect, that the
> attempt in most parts of the kingdom to increase the parish allowances
> in proportion to the price of corn, combined with the riches of the coun-
> try, which have enabled it to proceed as far as it has done in this attempt,
> is, comparatively speaking, the sole cause, which has occasioned the
> price of provisions in this country to rise so much higher than the degree
> of scarcity would seem to warrant, so much higher than it would do in
> any other country where this cause did not operate.[16]

He argued that the transfer of purchasing power into the hands of those
who would otherwise have suffered worst, effected through the Poor Laws,
was the reason that prices had risen so steeply: "The principal benefit
which they [the Poor Laws] have produced, is exactly that which is most
bitterly complained of – the high price of all the necessaries of life. The
poor cry out loudly at this price; but in so doing, they are very little aware
of what they are about; for it has undoubtedly been owing to this price that
a much greater number of them has not been starved."[17] Effective demand
was boosted by placing additional purchasing power in the hands of those
who would otherwise have been reduced to near starvation. The population
at large was obliged to pay a higher price for bread, but the poorest suffered
far less than would have been the case if they had not received increased
support. They continued to be able to buy bread and their presence in the
market for bread enhanced the rise in its price. Malthus emphasized that
he still heartily condemned the Poor Law system in general but explicitly
recognized that "their operation in the present scarcity has been advantageous to the country."[18]

Malthus's wish to dismantle the Poor Law system sprang, of course,
from his desire to strengthen the preventive check. Since he devoted so
much attention to the preventive check, it is of interest to note that there is
one respect in which his description of its operation largely lacks an element that figures prominently in recent discussions of the same topic. In recent decades work on family and household structure has given prominence
to the importance of the convention that no household should normally
contain more than one married couple. A man and woman contemplating

matrimony were therefore faced with the problem of ensuring that they had acquired sufficient resources to set up a new household. Elsewhere in the world it was usual for a couple on marriage to join an existing household.[19] The existence of this convention is taken to be central to the explanation both of the later average age at marriage in northwest Europe and the frequency with which men and women remained single rather than marrying. It was also closely linked to a feature of household structure and family life that would have been regarded with surprise and no doubt severe disapproval in much of the rest of the world. In seventeenth-century England it was normal both for young men and young women living in rural areas to leave the households of their parents in their teens and spend several years living as servants in the households of others. In the archetypal case a young man or woman would be hired at a local hiring fair to work for a year in farm service, during which time the master of the household would provide him or her with food, lodging, and a money payment, often given as a lump sum at the end of the year. The young person would then decide either to attend the annual hiring fair once more and work in another household for a further year, or, if he or she had found a prospective partner and the pair had assembled sufficient resources, instead of embarking on another year of service, would marry. In many parishes there was a marked surge in marriages in the weeks immediately after the hiring fair.[20] Perhaps because comparative data about household composition and family structures in different countries were scanty in the early nineteenth century, Malthus did not draw attention to this aspect of the functioning of the preventive check though it was still common in rural areas in much of the country in his youth.

The extent to which Malthus was handicapped by the limitations of the information that was available to him is apparent in other contexts.[21] Conscious that when writing the first *Essay* he lacked familiarity with much relevant literature, he set about extending his knowledge with great vigor. In the five years between the publication of the first and second editions of the *Essay* he read widely in the existing literature about population and conducted an extensive correspondence. The first two books in the second edition were largely devoted to describing the balance between population and productive capacity in countries throughout the world. The first book dealt with countries in Asia, Africa, the Americas, the Pacific islands, and the classical world of Greece and Rome; the second with European countries. They are testimony to the breadth of his reading and contain much of interest, but they also bring home forcibly the difficulty of obtaining accurate data either about population or about income and output levels at the beginning of the nineteenth century. Few countries had begun to take censuses, and vital registration data were even more difficult to secure. The same was true of data relating to many aspects of economic performance. This made it difficult for Malthus to test effectively the validity of some of the propositions he advanced. Furthermore it made it difficult for him to appreciate the slow but profound changes in the relationship between economic change and population growth taking place in England during his lifetime, which were reducing the relevance of his "model" of this relationship.[22] With the benefit of the striking increase in information about these two variables during the early modern period that has occurred in recent decades, the nature of the difficulty he was experiencing can be clarified. Once again a figure summarizes the point at issue.

Figure 2 plots the annual rate of population growth against changes in the real wage. During the first two centuries covered, from the mid-sixteenth to the mid-eighteenth century, their relationship was classically Malthusian. Productive capacity was rising, if slowly, and the trend line of the plotted points, stretching northwest to southeast, suggests that real wages could be maintained as long as the population was not growing faster than around 0.3–0.4 percent per annum. In other words, the economy in this period was expanding rapidly enough to make it possible for population to rise at a modest rate without harm to living standards. If growth rates were below this level, real wages rose. If, however, they exceeded this level, and especially if they rose to 0.5 percent per annum and above, real wages plummeted. In the seventy years from 1561 to 1631, the population of England increased from 3.04 million to 4.93 million, an increase of 62 percent, representing an annual rate of increase of 0.7 percent. The result was a sharp fall in real wages. The relationship between population growth rates and real incomes conformed closely to Malthus's expectations during the first two centuries covered in figure 2. From the mid-eighteenth century onward, however, a new world was slowly coming into existence in which the behavior of the two variables ceased to conform to his expectations. Population growth rates skyrocketed, approaching at their peak about 1.4 percent annually. The population rose from 6.31 million in 1761 to 14.94 million in 1841, an increase of 137 percent, or an annual growth rate of 1.1 percent.[23] Such a rate of growth in earlier centuries would have led to a disastrous fall in living standards, but in the new circumstances that had come to prevail, the real wage held steady and toward the end of the period even began to edge upward. The consistent negative relationship between the population growth rate and the real-wage trend, which had prevailed for two centuries and probably much longer, faded.[24]

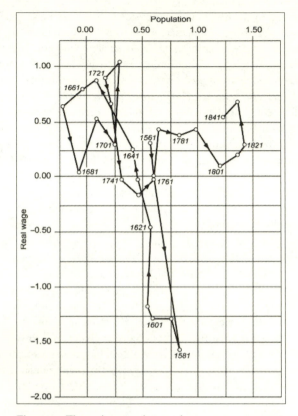

Figure 2. The points on the graph are ten years apart, and each point represents the annual rate of change over a third-year period centering on the date shown. Reprinted with permission from E. A. Wrigley, "Coping with Rapid Population Growth: How England Fared in the Century Preceding the Great Exhibition of 1851," in *Structures and Transformations in Modern British History,* ed. D. Feldman and J. Lawrence (Cambridge: Cambridge University Press, 2011), 27.

Malthus lived in a new age that was coming into being, but its character was initially very difficult to discern, and it is not surprising that, in trying to comprehend what was taking place, contemporaries carried over assumptions from an earlier era. Perhaps the most important single difference between what happened during the earlier population surge in the Tudor period and events in Malthus's lifetime is that in Tudor times the growth was relatively uniform throughout the land. Tudor England was still an essentially rural country and the bulk of the labor force was engaged in agriculture. As population pressure increased in rural areas, wages fell and employment became progressively harder to find. Parliament wrestled with the problem of the "sturdy beggars," men who were well able to labor but could find no one willing to employ them. In conformity with the assumptions of the preventive check model, nuptiality fell, causing fertility to decline in sympathy; population growth slowed and eventually halted. By the mid-eighteenth century England had greatly changed. Agriculture employed less than half the male labor force. Indeed, during the period of very rapid population growth that ensued, the number employed in agriculture was broadly stationary. Any increase was minor. Malthus's strictures on improvident marriage decisions would have had clear resonance when Elizabeth was on the throne but were less readily applicable in his own day. Young couples living in rural areas who could not find a viable "niche" in the local community solved their problem by migration. The growth of industrial and commercial centers was very rapid. The percentage of the population living in towns increased sharply. England moved from being one of the least urbanized countries in Europe in the sixteenth century to occupying pole position by the nineteenth century.[25] The nature of the contrast in growth rates made possible by large-scale internal migration is epitomized, to take an illustrative example, by the contrast between the two counties of Lancashire and Shropshire during the period 1761–1841. Lancashire's population increased from 324,000 to 1,695,000, or by 423 percent: Shropshire's population rose from 153,000 to 243,000, or by 59 percent.[26] That it was not necessarily imprudent to continue to marry at an early age despite the speed of population growth is demonstrated by the trend in the real wage during the period of dramatic population growth.

Malthus made the assumption that any significant rise in population must increase pressure on the land. In common with the other classical economists he supposed that this must involve declining returns both to capital and labor as poorer land was brought into cultivation and existing acreages were worked more intensively. But the land was the material base for a declining fraction of raw material supply and, crucially, no longer the dominant source of the energy needs of the population. Even as early as 1700 coal supplied half of the total energy consumed in England and Wales. By 1800 coal supplied four-fifths of the total.[27] A model of the relationship between population and production that was effective in capturing the constraints of all organic economies became progressively less relevant since the land was losing its monopoly in supplying raw materials and energy to production processes. A rapidly rising population, rather than being a reason for serious alarm, might mark a gradual escape from the constraints that had previously proved insuperable.

The nature of the relationship between productive capacity and population was changing during Malthus's lifetime in ways that made his model of their linkages increasingly inapplicable to the country in which he lived. Nevertheless his insistence on the potential benefits associated with the preventive check may well play a part in explaining the background to the changes that were gathering momentum as the eighteenth century progressed. In a famous passage he compared the relative speed of the growth of productive capacity and of population to a contest between a tortoise and a hare. But he added that the effect of the preventive check might be such that the hare was slowed to the point where the tortoise would have no difficulty in matching his speed. Where this was so, an improved standard of living might not only be attained but also preserved.[28] Both the evidence of inventories and the changing occupational structure of England in the early modern period strongly suggest that the aggregate structure of demand was changing substantially. It is not difficult to show that, because the income elasticity of demand for goods which the classical economists described as "comforts" and "luxuries" is higher than for basic necessities, a relatively minor increase in income levels could provide a disproportionate boost to the demand for goods such as pottery, window glass, clocks, curtains, cooking utensils, furniture, and bedclothes.[29] Occupational structure changed in response to the altered structure of aggregate demand. The operation of the preventive check, by bringing about a somewhat improved level of real incomes and helping to preserve any gains made, may account in part for the changes that occurred.

It is a striking and impressive feature of Malthus's research and writing that he was both eager to secure new knowledge and willing to modify his views as a result. This aspect of his work endeared him to John Maynard Keynes. He admired Malthus for his discussion of the possibility of a general glut and his reasoning in doubting Say's law, but still more for his openness of mind and his willingness to give greater prominence to what Malthus termed "experience," that is empirical evidence, than to theorizing. Keynes expressed forcibly his regret that as a discipline economics had followed the path trodden by Ricardo rather than that which Malthus took.[30] In deploring the "precipitate attempt to simplify and generalize" in much writing about economic affairs, Malthus himself had written, "The same tendency to simplify and generalize, produces a still greater disinclination to allow of modifications, limitations and exceptions to any rule or proposition, than to admit the operation of more causes than one . . . yet there is no truth of which I feel a stronger conviction than that there are many important propositions in political economy which absolutely require limitations and exceptions."[31]

It is worth stressing in conclusion that despite the apparent harshness of his views about support for the least fortunate members of society implied by the wish to abolish the Poor Law system, Malthus was strongly sympathetic to their sufferings and advocated a variety of reforms that would help them, notably the establishment of a universal system of school education. Ignorance and poverty were, in his view, closely intertwined (although he did not use the term, he had a good understanding of what would nowadays be called feedback mechanisms). He was an ardent advocate of the value of promoting savings banks. Their presence would help to inculcate the habit of prudent calculation, a habit of mind that must strengthen the preventive check.[32]

His concern for the sufferings of the poor was prominent even when he wrote about aspects of the economic and political life of the country that might appear far removed from this issue. For example, he was a firm advocate of the importance of what he termed the "principle of private property," and in that connection put forward an argument about one aspect of its functioning which suggested that, rather like the preventive check, its presence must tend to benefit the living standards of the laboring poor: "With a view to the individual interest, either of a landlord or farmer, no labourer can ever be employed on the soil, who does not produce more than the value of his wages; and if these wages be not on an average sufficient to maintain a wife, and rear two children to the age of marriage, it is evident that both population and produce must come to a stand."[33] In other words, a capitalist organization of economic life would promote a relatively favorable balance between population and resources by creating an institutional framework in which the minimum real wage would be adequate to support a family. This line of reasoning is reminiscent of the distinction drawn by development economists between a peasant economy in which family members may be retained on the farm until the *average* output of each family member is reduced to mere subsistence, and a market economy in which members will begin to leave the farmstead when the *marginal* member produces only what he or she consumes.[34] Private property in Malthus's view was one aspect of a more general *desideratum*, civil liberty:

Of all the causes which tend to generate prudential habits among the lower classes of society, the most essential is unquestionably civil liberty. No people can be much accustomed to form plans for the future, who do not feel assured that their industrious exertions, while fair and honourable, will be allowed to have free scope; and that the property which they either possess, or may acquire, will be secured to them by a known code of just laws impartially administered.[35]

Elsewhere, as if anxious to dispel any doubt about his motives in calling for an end to the Poor Law system, Malthus wrote as follows:

With regard to the large sum which is collected from the higher classes of society for the support of the poor, I can safely say, that in the discussion of the question it has always been with me a most subordinate consideration[.]

I should indeed think that the whole, or a much greater sum, was well applied, if it merely relieved the comparatively few that would be in want, if there were no public provision for them, with the fatal and unavoidable consequence of increasing their number, and depressing the condition of those who were struggling to maintain themselves in independence. Were it possible to fix the number of the poor and to avoid the further depression of the independent labourer, I should be the first to propose that those who were actually in want should be most liberally relieved, and that they should receive it as a right, and not as a bounty.[36]

NOTES

1. E. A. Wrigley, "The Classical Economists and the Industrial Revolution," in *People, Cities and Wealth*, ed. E. A. Wrigley (Oxford, 1987), 21–45.
2. Adam Smith, *An Inquiry into the Nature and Causes of the Wealth of Nations*, ed. E. C. Cannan (1776; Indianapolis, 1976), 1:401.
3. Sir Thomas More, *Utopia and a Dialogue of Comfort*, rev. edn. (London, 1951), 26.
4. David Ricardo, "On the Principles of Political Economy and Taxation," in *The Works and Correspondence of David Ricardo*, ed. P. Sraffa and M. H Dobb (Cambridge, 1951), 1:126.
5. Malthus was mistaken in supposing that early and universal marriage must result in high fertility and hence also high mortality. Recent research has discovered many instances of preindustrial Asian communities in which the levels of both variables was relatively modest. T. Bengtsson et al., *Life under*

Pressure: Mortality and Living Standards in Europe and Asia, 1700–1900 (Cambridge, Mass., 2004); N. Tsuya et al., *Prudence and Pressure: Reproduction and Human Agency in Europe and Asia, 1700–1900* (Cambridge, Mass., 2010).

6. Wind and water power were relatively unimportant sources of mechanical energy. P. Warde, *Energy Consumption in England and Wales, 1560–2000* (Rome, 2007), table 4, 69.

7. E. A. Wrigley, *Energy and the English Industrial Revolution* (Cambridge, 2010), 16.

8. This is a very brief summary of a large subject. It is treated at length in ibid., chaps. 1 and 2.

9. 'The price of fuel has so important an influence upon that of labour, that all over Great Britain manufactures have confined themselves principally to the coal countries; other part of the country, on account of the high price of this necessary article, not being able to work so cheap." Smith, *Wealth of Nations,* 2:404.

10. In some environments, however, because of the wide prevalence of fatal diseases, mortality might be immovably high, and in these circumstances, if a community was to survive, it had no option but to achieve an equally high level of fertility.

11. Ibid., 1:89.

12. T. R. Malthus, *An Essay on the Principle of Population as It Affects the Future Improvement of Society with Remarks on the Speculations of Mr. Godwin, M. Condorcet, and Other Writers* (1798), in *The Works of Thomas Robert Malthus,* ed. E. A Wrigley and David Souden (London, 1986), 1:50 (hereafter First *Essay*). Other volumes from this series are cited as *Works of Malthus.* Other editions of the *Essay* referenced here also cite the eight-volume Wrigley and Souden edition of the *Works of Malthus.*

13. T. R. Malthus, *An Essay on the Principle of Population; or, A View of Its Past and Present Effects on Human Happiness; with an Inquiry into Our Prospects Respecting the Future Removal or Mitigation of the Evils Which It Occasions. A New Edition, Very Much Enlarged,* 2nd ed. (London, 1803; reprint, New Haven, Conn., 2017), 467 (hereafter *Essay of 1803;* the page numbers cited for this work are to this book). See also *Works of Malthus,* vol. 3, *Essay on the Principle of Population,* 568.

14. Malthus, "An Investigation of the Cause of the High Price of Provisions," in *Works of Malthus,* vol. 7, *Essays on Political Economy,* 6.

15. A. Sen, *Poverty and Famines, an Essay on Entitlement and Deprivation* (Oxford, 1982).

16. "An Investigation of the Cause of the High Price of Provisions," 6–7.

17. Ibid., 13–14.

18. Ibid., 13. See E. A. Wrigley, "Corn and Crisis: Malthus on the High Price of Provisions," *Population and Development Review* 25 (1999): 121–128, for a fuller discussion of his pamphlet.

19. J. Hajnal, "Two Kinds of Pre-Industrial Household Formation System," in *Family Forms in Historic Europe,* ed. R. Wall with P. Laslett and J. Robin (Cambridge, 1983), 65–104.

20. The functioning and significance of these practices are described with authority in A. Kussmaul, *Servants in Husbandry in Early Modern England* (Cambridge, 1981).

21. It is amusing to note in this connection, for example, that Malthus accepted Bishop James Ussher's chronology of creation: "No move towards the extinction of the passion between the sexes has taken place in the five or six thousand years that the world has existed." First *Essay,* 76.

22. He was himself well aware of this problem. In describing the long, slow oscillations in the balance between population and production, and in trying to explain why they had not been more widely noticed, he wrote, "One principal reason is that the histories of mankind that we possess, are histories only of the higher classes. We have but few accounts that can be depended upon of the manners and customs of that part of mankind, where these retrograde and progressive movements chiefly take place." First *Essay,* 15.

23. The population data are taken from E. A. Wrigley et al., *English Population History from Family Reconstitution, 1580–1837* (Cambridge, 1997), table A9.1, 614–615.

24. The real-wage data are based primarily on male wages in a restricted range of industries. They do not therefore reflect the earnings of families, which, if available, would be a more relevant measure. They also assume constant levels and duration of employment. These points should be borne in mind in considering figure 2, but it is probable that the relationship they depict is valid.

25. England and Wales in 1550 had a smaller urban percentage (taken as the percentage of the total population living in towns with ten thousand or more inhabitants) than any other country in western Europe with the exception of Scandinavia, Switzerland, and Scotland and Ireland but by 1850 was a clear leader. J. De Vries, *European Urbanization, 1500–1800* (Cambridge, Mass., 1984), table 3.7, 39; table 3.8, 45. Some of these issues are examined in greater detail in E. A. Wrigley, "Coping with Rapid Population Growth: How England Fared in the Century Preceding the Great Exhibition," in *Structures and Transformations in Modern British History,* ed. D. Feldman and J. Lawrence (Cambridge, 2011), 24–53.

26. E. A. Wrigley, *The Early English Censuses* (Oxford, 2011), table 2.6, 224–225.

27. Wrigley, *Energy and the English Industrial Revolution*, table 2.1, 37.

28. *Essay of 1803*, 401. See also *Works of Malthus*, vol. 3, *Essay on the Principle of Population*, 486.

29. See, for example, M. Overton et al., *Production and Consumption in English Households, 1600–1750* (London, 2004).

30. Concerning Malthus's correspondence with Ricardo, Keynes remarked, "One cannot rise from a perusal of this correspondence without a feeling that the almost total obliteration of Malthus's line of approach and the complete domination of Ricardo's for a period of a hundred years has been a disaster to the progress of economics. Time after time in these letters Malthus is talking plain sense, the force of which Ricardo with his head in the clouds wholly fails to comprehend. Time after time a crushing refutation by Malthus is met by a mind so completely closed that Ricardo does not even see what Malthus is saying." Keynes, *Essays in Biography* (London, 1933), 140–141. Keynes himself is alleged, on an occasion when he had been accused of inconsistency, to have replied, "When the facts change, I change my mind. What do you do?" Malthus had the same mindset.

31. *Works of Malthus*, vol. 5, *Principles of Political Economy*, 7–8.

32. *Essay of 1803*, 462–463. See also *Works of Malthus*, vol. 3, *Essay on the Principle of Population*, 555.

33. Ibid., 405.

34. There is an illuminating discussion of this range of issues in R. Schofield, "Family Structure, Demographic Behaviour, and Economic Growth," in *Famine, Disease and the Social Order in Early Modern Society*, ed. J. Walter and R. Schofield (Cambridge, 1989), 279–304.

35. *Works of Malthus*, vol. 5, *Principles of Political Economy*, 184.

36. "The Amendment of the Poor Laws," in *Works of Malthus*, vol. 4, *Essays on Population*, 9.

Malthusian Economics

Right or Wrong?

KENNETH BINMORE

Robert Malthus famously argued that a human population will necessarily outgrow its capacity to feed itself.[1] Since the publication of his *Essay on the Principle of Population* in 1798, a sometimes furious debate has raged over whether he was right or wrong.

Charles Darwin thought Malthus was right, crediting him with being one of his sources of inspiration. As he wrote in the *Origin of Species:* "Even slow-breeding man has doubled in twenty-five years, and at this rate, in less than a thousand years, there would literally not be standing room for his progeny."[2] Friedrich Engels is more typical in denouncing the Malthusian doctrine as a vile and repulsive blasphemy against man and nature[3] (although Bertrand Russell argued that Karl Marx's labor theory of value was nevertheless derived by surreptitiously accepting Malthus's doctrine of population).[4] William Hazlitt similarly attributed Malthus's gloomy predictions to some personal defect: "Unless Mr Malthus can contrive to starve someone, he thinks that he does nothing."[5]

Modern writers tend to dismiss Malthus in less emotional terms, observing that he was unaware of the technical advances of the Industrial Revolution that were just around the corner in his time and continue to be made today.[6] Sometimes it is not only argued that the rate of food production can and will be stepped up enormously, but that increasing wealth is bound to lead to a natural decrease in the birthrate.[7]

My impression is that both the critics who criticize Malthus for being evil and those who criticize him for being ignorant or out of date are more interested in making rhetorical points than in responding to what he actually wrote. For example, it is commonplace to ignore the fact that the second edition of his *Essay* admits the possibility (discounted in the first edition) that birth control may eventually solve the problem.[8] This chapter therefore looks again at the Malthusian doctrine with a view to demonstrating that a suitably cleaned-up version is essentially tautological.

So much has been written on this subject that it is hard to say anything that has not been said many times before, but perhaps I can contribute by saying what is necessary without excluding readers who have no mathematical background. Is it really true that as Malthus suggests a population will necessarily increase exponentially (geometrically) if the birth- and death-rates are fixed so that the former exceeds the latter?[9] What does it mean to say that something increases exponentially? Journalists seem to think that "exponential" means very big, but mathematicians mean something much more precise by the term.

What of Malthus on food production? Is it really true that this can only increase linearly (arithmetically)? What does it mean that something increases linearly? Must something that increases exponentially necessarily outgrow something that increases linearly? What if Malthus's claim that food production can only increase linearly is mistaken? Does his claim that a human population will then necessarily outgrow its food supply consequently fail? If not, how long will it take?

Only the last of these questions is difficult if one can succeed in putting aside the religious and emotional issues that arise when scenarios of doom or birth control are on the table.

Exponential Growth

At the root of Malthus's argument is the incontestable proposition that something cannot grow without bound if there is a bound that it cannot exceed. When he argues that the birth- and death-rate of a human population cannot stay fixed if the former exceeds the latter, he therefore does not need to appeal to the fact that the population would then increase exponentially. If there were always just one more person alive on the earth every year than the year before, then there would eventually be nowhere left to stand.[10]

Malthus insisted that the population will increase exponentially (or geometrically) under his assumptions because he wanted to emphasize that the catastrophe he anticipated was not located in some far-distant future but was awaiting just around the corner. Events have shown that he was wrong to think that the catastrophe was as close as he thought at the time he wrote, but it does not follow that modern prophets of doom are wrong when they repeat his warnings after doing their best to take account of all the factors that he was in no position to evaluate

PUT NOT THY TRUST IN PRINCES

Something grows exponentially if there is a time period in which it doubles in size. For example, Benjamin Franklin (who was propounding the Malthusian doctrine long before Malthus) estimated that the population of the American colonies would double every 25 years – which turned out to be more or less correct for the next 150 years.[11] On the assumption that future resource constraints in the whole world could similarly be neglected today, Franklin would be led to a doubling-up period of about 54 years.[12]

Everybody has their favorite way of illustrating how fast exponential growth can be once it takes off. The story of a water lily that doubles its size every day is a popular conundrum for children. If it takes thirty-one days to cover half a pond, how many more days before it covers the whole pond? Charles Darwin preferred elephants to water lilies. He calculated that a single pair of elephants would have at least 19 million live progeny after 750 years if unhindered by resource constraints.

My own favorite is the story of an Indian potentate who offered the inventor of chess whatever reward he chose. The inventor proposed that he should be given one grain of rice on the first square of his chessboard and an amount on each subsequent square equal to double the amount on the previous square. The number of grains of rice on the final square would then mass more than one of the larger asteroids![13] The lesson that Malthus would draw is that, somewhere along the line, the impossibility of granting the inventor his chosen reward would necessarily become apparent. In the event, so the story goes, the inventor lost his head when the potentate broke his promise after finally realizing how he had been taken for a fool.

Sometimes critics seeking to discredit Malthus deny that there is a fixed bound to the resources available for feeding the world's population. It is airily said that technology will come to the rescue as it has is in the past. However, the mass of the earth is an ultimate bound that no new technology seems likely to overcome. I have heard it argued to the contrary that there are other planets out in space for us to colonize. But even if we could pack the world population into a squirming mass of humanity contained in a cube whose surface receded from the earth at the speed of light, there would still eventually not be room for a population that expands exponentially. The reason is that exponential growth is not only faster than linear growth as Malthus argued; it will eventually overtake anything that grows like the volume of a cube.[14]

Unless modern physics is hopelessly wrong about what is or is not physically impossible, it follows that Malthus's basic claim is unimpeachable. A population cannot increase forever with a fixed birthrate that exceeds its death-rate – no matter what technological advances may be made in the future. Something will therefore happen to change either the birth- or death-rate. We can do this ourselves – as the Chinese have done in their own country – or we can await the arrival of the four Horsemen of the Apocalypse.

CHANGING BIRTH- AND DEATH-RATES?

It is sometimes not appreciated that Malthus was making a *hypothetical* argument when discussing exponential growth. Critics point to various populations that have not in fact increased exponentially and seem to feel that this is enough to dispose of the Malthusian doctrine. But such critics miss the point that Malthus argues that the birth- and death-rates must necessarily adjust to lower the rate at which a population grows because people who cannot feed themselves cannot reproduce themselves. For example, at the time that Malthus wrote, the population of Great Britain was clearly not expanding exponentially like that of the United States. To see why not, it is enough to note that John Stuart Mill was converted to the need for birth control when he came across dead children abandoned in a London street.[15]

How can the birthrate be decreased without resorting to infanticide or equally repugnant measures? One method is for us all to follow the Chinese example by restricting the number of children a woman can have by government decree. Methods of enforcement less brutal than those sometimes reported from China could doubtless be found, but any kind of enforcement is bound to be unpleasant at best. However, this would need to be a global enterprise. Exponential growth is so relentless that the Chinese experiment in self-control, even if continued forever, would only reduce the long-run doubling-up period of the total world population by a negligible factor. China might perhaps be able to secure its boundaries against the war, famine, and disease that would inevitably afflict the rest of the world in this scenario, but it seems much more likely that it would only succeed in briefly delaying a similar fate.

Another unpleasant expedient would be to reduce the ratio of the death-rate to the birthrate by asking or requiring old folks to surrender their lives as new babies are born. It is said that elderly people on the island of Cos in classical times chose to drink hemlock because it was considered impolite to live too long, so perhaps something similar might eventually come to seem acceptable in our own culture. I certainly hope that I will have the courage to take my own life before I become a burden to myself and others, but who is likely to volunteer departing this life before they have become a burden?

A more popular expedient than birth control by government decree consists of doing nothing, on the grounds that increasing prosperity will spread throughout the world, with the result that people will choose to have fewer children. It is true that there is empirical support for the proposition that more prosperous societies nowadays have lower birthrates. It is also true that prosperity is a lot more widespread nowadays than in the past. But where is the evidence that these effects are strong enough to make any significant difference in the long run? Only the most naive Pollyanna would be willing to predict an inevitable continuation of the spread of prosperity at a time when our global resources are coming under increasing strain and the consequences of global warming are waiting in the wings.

It is evident that I am pessimistic about the future. The probability that events will sort themselves out without our active intervention seems negligible to me. Perhaps the human race will get its act together in time to take the repugnant steps necessary to get our birth- and death-rates under control, but this also seems unlikely. The mere fact that the essence of the Malthusian doctrine should be denied so vociferously by so many is just one of many problems standing in the way. I weep for the woes my great-grandchildren are likely to suffer, but nothing that people like me write in articles like this is going to make any difference. The question is not whether disaster is on the horizon but how long we have to wait before it strikes us down.

To answer this question, we need to make predictions about how long the world's food supply can keep up with population growth. It is here that Malthus went wrong in arguing that we cannot achieve more than linear (arithmetic) growth in food production.

Production

How long we have to wait for the coming population catastrophe depends on how fast we can increase our productivity. I am not one of the doom-sayers who think that we are already close to our productivity frontier, but nor am I one of the numerous commentators who think that we can count on technological advances to kick the problem into the long grass for our remote ancestors to solve. Such Pollyannas were doubtless predicting a utopian future for Easter Island just before its final collapse. The truth is that nobody – neither optimists nor pessimists – can predict scientific break-throughs in advance. So all I can do in this section is provide some back-ground in how economists think about production functions to provide a framework within which different scenarios can be evaluated.

ARITHMETIC INCREASE?

Malthus proposed treating food production as though it grows linearly (ar-ithmetically).[16] This amounts to assuming that annual food production in-creases by a fixed amount in every period. The fixed increment he proposed as being larger than anything actually possible was the current annual food production over a period of twenty-five years. Applying this reasoning to Britain in 1798, Malthus argued that there would be 77 million people after only a century who could not be fed.[17]

I suspect that Malthus chose to assume that the food supply can only grow linearly largely for rhetorical reasons. He could simply have said that food production is bounded (by the mass of the earth or one of many much smaller inescapable bounds), but then his readers would have consigned his warnings to the infinite future. He therefore chose to compare exponential growth in a population with linear growth in food production so that his audience would treat his warnings as relevant to their great-grandchildren.

Why did Malthus choose to assume that growth in food production would be no more than linear? I suspect for no better reason than that he could then appeal to the mathematical commonplace that exponential growth is much faster than linear growth without boring his readers with any tiresome algebra.

I have heard Malthus's assumption that the growth in food production can be no more than linear defended on the grounds that he was merely taking the law of diminishing returns for granted, but this defense misses the point that Malthus assumed food production to be linear with respect to *time* rather than more directly relevant inputs such as capital, labor, or land. But there seems little point in pursuing his reasoning in this matter, since events have now conclusively refuted his linearity assumption.

DIMINISHING RETURNS

A particularly naive version of the labor theory of value – too naive even for Karl Marx – makes labor the only relevant input in production.[18] If so, we would never need to worry about feeding the multitudes engendered by exponential growth, because the production of food would then increase linearly with the size of the population, and therefore exponentially with respect to time (rather than linearly, as in the story that Malthus offers). Perhaps this is what happened in Benjamin Franklin's America during the 150 years for which his prediction about its population growth turned out to be valid (inputs other than labor, notably capital and land, being relatively unimportant in the circumstances of the time).

However, the law of diminishing returns applies to labor as to any other factor of production. If all other factors of production are held constant, the law says that the extra output obtained by employing an extra worker will eventually start decreasing. For example, adding more workers to a job like growing tomatoes in a greenhouse will eventually result in their getting in each other's way.

RETURNS TO SCALE

The naive labor theory of value considered above makes labor the only relevant input to a production function with constant returns to scale. Economists say that constant returns to scale applies when scaling up all the inputs to a production process results in the output being scaled up by the same factor. There is a sense in which all production processes using a fixed technology necessarily have constant returns to scale, provided that all the inputs to the process have been listed. One then simply needs to duplicate whatever one did to make the last unit of output when making the next unit. When talking about increasing or decreasing returns to scale, economists are therefore taking for granted either a change in technology or else recognizing that some inputs have not been taken into account. For example, it would be easy to overlook the fact that oxygen is needed to smelt iron ore, since nobody (yet) needs to pay for the air we breathe. But nobody would neglect the need for oxygen if smelting iron ore on the moon.

Increasing returns to scale traditionally arise when operating at a larger scale allows something to be made more efficiently. Adam Smith famously used the manufacture of pins to illustrate this point.[19] With many workers, the labor of making a pin can be divided, so that each worker can specialize in just one of the necessary operations – such as cutting the wire into suitable lengths or sharpening one end of such a length into a point. Ten workers who specialize in this way produce many more than ten times the number of pins that a single worker who has to do all the operations alone could produce. However, the law of diminishing returns tells us that such efficiency gains must eventually taper off, unless all the other inputs (like factory space) are increased in proportion to the increases in labor.

A standard production function is therefore shaped like a forward-sloping letter S. It begins by showing increasing returns to scale, but eventually switches to decreasing returns to scale as shortages of inputs originally deemed to be available in infinite abundance begin to bite. In both phases, new technologies – ways of doing things – need to be continually brought online. At first, new ways of doing things are necessary to exploit the efficiency gains that operating on a larger scale make possible in the increasing-returns phase. But even in the decreasing-returns phase, the technology in use will need to adapt as the increasing scarcity of some inputs forces up their prices and so provides an incentive to use them less intensively. Of course, eventually the price of any resource will rise through the roof as it begins to run out.[20] All production functions are therefore necessarily bounded. No matter what technology may be employed, there is an absolute maximum on the output of all physical processes.

MAGIC PORRIDGE POTS?

Some critics react to the preceding discussion of production functions with disdain. It is said that such pieces of neoclassical economics have been rendered hopelessly out of date by the accelerating rate of scientific and technological advance in modern times.[21] It cannot be denied technological advances definitively refute Malthus's claim that linear growth in food production is the best that we can hope for. But although Malthus antedated the Industrial Revolution, the same is not true of neoclassical economics. Its commonsense precepts on the nature of production remain valid whatever technology may be applied.

Critics respond by drawing attention to all the many ways that food production has been increased since Malthus's time. We are reminded of rail transport and tractors, electricity and computers, fertilizers and the green revolution. These and all the other advances that have been made since 1798 certainly have delayed the disaster that Malthus predicted would happen if birth- and death-rates are not somehow brought under control, but they have not altered the fact that production functions are necessarily S-shaped and bounded above. All that has changed is the shape of the S and the height of the bound.

Can science be relied on to rescue us when the demand for food gets close to the current upper bound on production? Or to put the same point more tendentiously, is science a magic porridge pot that can produce porridge from nowhere as in the fairy story that so delighted my children when they were small? We have already seen why the answer is no. Modern physics constrains what is possible. For example, nothing can exceed the speed of light. Mass and energy are interchangeable, but the total cannot be created or destroyed. It is therefore possible to imagine an ideal production function that already incorporates all future technological advances. This ideal production function will necessarily be S-shaped and bounded above like its less-perfect brethren. Applying Malthus's argument to this ideally scientific production function will yield the longest period that we can hope to feed a population whose birthrate is fixed higher than its deathrate. Nothing says that output produced according to such an ideal production function may not initially match an exponentially growing population, but the law of diminishing returns will inexorably step in as soon as some vital resource begins to be exhausted.

To deny this conclusion is essentially to put one's faith in some supernatural resolution of the population problem. But I for one think it as unlikely that our progeny will be fed by manna from heaven as that modern physics will be refuted by the discovery of a magic porridge pot.

Uncertainty

The question left unanswered by the previous section is how long it would be before a population growing exponentially would exceed a food supply generated by an ideally scientific production process. One can always find gurus who claim to know the answers to such questions, but why should we imagine that they know any better than Malthus? The case of scientific advances is particularly telling. The memory of the astronomer royal in my own country who denied the possibility of space travel a few days before the Russians put the first Sputnik into orbit is especially sweet.

Uncertainties about future technology are just one of numerous other sources of uncertainty. What impact is global warming going to have on agriculture? Has the supply of fossil fuels peaked? What of future social and political developments? Who would have guessed a few decades ago that the Soviet Union would be replaced as our leading enemy by Al-Qaeda? Is it possible that wars can be avoided as squabbling over dwindling resources become more intense? What of the mass movement of refugees fleeing across borders in the hope of finding food and water? How can epidemics be avoided when undernourished people live huddled together in unsanitary conditions?

All I can say on this subject is that there is no point in looking to economists for adequate ways of modeling such uncertainties. The recent credit crunch ought to be enough to discredit the current Bayesian orthodoxy in which economic agents are assumed to be able to assign determinate probabilities to all relevant future events.[22] However, it is generally acknowledged that the current methodology fails to give sufficient weight to the possibility of "low probability" events which would have a large impact if they were to occur. For example, the Stern Report on global warming was explicitly motivated by the need to better incorporate such possibilities into a utilitarian evaluation of what climate change may entail for the human race.[23] Even financial economists recognize the need to replace their normal (bell curve) probability distributions by new distributions with "fat tails." These are movements in the right direction but hopelessly inadequate in my opinion.[24]

One may hope that the scientific advances we need to improve food production will also include advances in how we model uncertainties. Such advances would allow us to incorporate in our models not just the aversion to risk that is a staple of orthodox Bayesian decision theory but also the aversion to ambiguity that behavioral economists report arises when laboratory subjects are faced with situations in which there is uncertainty about what probability (if any) to assign to future events–such as whether physicists will finally come up with a source of cheap energy or an antigravity machine. However, current attempts to model ambiguity aversion are not very reassuring, since they commonly assume that people will proceed as though the worst-case scenario is going to happen. Applying this principle to Malthus's argument generates a prospect so gloomy that it is not surprising that nobody is willing to examine it too closely.

Conclusion

This essay puts the case for treating the essence of Malthus's argument as essentially tautological: something cannot grow without bound if there is a bound that it cannot exceed. The fact that a population with a birthrate fixed higher than its death-rate necessarily grows exponentially is a flourish which implies that the bound can be reached very fast unless the birth- and death-rates adjust to the depletion of resources soon enough. Malthus was wrong to argue that the increase of the food supply can only grow linearly with time, but he does not need this assumption for his argument to work.

How long it would it take for disaster to strike on the Malthusian hypothesis that birth- and death-rates remain unchanged? All I have to say on this subject is that economics offers no comfort. Various gurus to the contrary, the answer depends on which of many uncertain events, each of which is individually very unlikely, are realized in the future. We do not even know how to model such uncertainties in an adequate way.

Even the implicit assumption in the previous sentence that the existence of an economic model that adequately captured the realities of our predicament would result in the human race responding in a collectively rational manner seems unreasonably optimistic in a world in which fanatics of various stripes are virulently opposed to any kind of abortion or the genetic modification of crops. I am sorry not to be able to end on a more positive note, but I think that – as with global warming – the efforts that governments eventually make to deal with population growth will be too little and too late. Our great-grandchildren look likely to pay a terrible price for the folly of their ancestors.

NOTES

I am grateful for financial support from the European Research Council under the European Community's Seventh Framework Programme (FP7/2007–2013)/ERC grant 295449.

1. K. Binmore, *Rational Decisions* (Princeton, N.J.: Princeton University Press, 2009).

2. C. Darwin, *The Origin of Species by Means of Natural Selection* (Harmondsworth, U.K.: Penguin, 1985), 117.

3. F. Engels, "Outlines of a Critique of Political Economy" (1844), in *Collected Works of Karl Marx and Frederick Engels* (New York: International Publishers, 1975), 3:418–443.

4. B. Russell, "Why I Am Not a Communist," in *Portraits from Memory and Other Essays* (London: George Allen and Unwin, 1958), 224.

5. W. Hazlitt, "A Reply to the Essay on Population," in *The Complete Works of William Hazlitt* (London: J. M. Dent and Sons, 1930), 1:177–364, 328 (quotation).

6. For example, Fred Pearce in the *New Scientist,* 16 June 2012, 38–43.

7. I was recently on a panel with the psychologist Nicholas Humphries, who confidently announced that the human population will naturally level out at (only!) 10 billion, and so there is nothing to worry about. William Godwin felt that we could rely on cultural advances lessening passion between the sexes to bring about a similarly benign outcome. Godwin, *Enquiry Concerning Political Justice and Its Influence on Morals and Happiness* (London: Watson, 1842).

8. As a clergyman, Malthus restricted his advocacy of birth control to delayed marriage. See also T. R. Malthus, *An Essay on the Principle of Population; or, A View of Its Past and Present Effects on Human Happiness; with an Inquiry into Our Prospects Respecting the Future Removal or Mitigation of the Evils Which It Occasions. A New Edition, Very Much Enlarged,* 2nd ed. (London: J. Johnson, 1803; reprint, New Haven, Conn.: Yale University Press, 2017), 381, where an argument for "moral restraint" is developed (hereafter *Essay of 1803;* the page numbers cited for this work are to this book).

9. Ibid., 14.

10. In Malthus's terms, the population would then increase arithmetically (by a fixed amount in each time period). For what he calls geometric growth, the population needs always to double in size over some fixed time period. See ibid., 14, 16.

11. B. Franklin, "Observations Concerning the Increase of Mankind," in *Autobiography and Other Writings,* ed. O. Seavey (1851; New York: Oxford University Press, 1999), 251–260.

12. There were supposedly 6 billion people alive on the planet on 12 October 1999 and 7 billion on 31 October 2011 (in spite of the continuing one-baby-per-family policy in China). If the population increases by a factor of $f > 1$ in one day, the doubling-up period is $\ln 2 / \ln f$ days. (If the daily birthrate is b and the daily death-rate is d, then $f = 1 + b - d$ because the number of people tomorrow will be $N + bN - dN$ if the number of people today is N.)

13. On the assumption that each grain of rice weighs 2.5 mg. With 102 squares rather than 64, the mass of rice on the final square would be larger than the mass of the whole earth.

14. The quantity 2^n eventually overtakes any power of n. For example, $2^n \geq n^4$ for $n \geq 16$ because $2^{16} = (16)^4$.

15. Mill was later imprisoned for several days for offending Victorian sensibilities by helping to distribute birth-control literature in slum neighborhoods – an event that did not get into his *Autobiography*!

16. T. R. Malthus, *An Essay on the Principle of Population as It Affects the Future Improvement of Society with Remarks on the Speculations of Mr. Godwin, M. Condorcet, and Other Writers* (1798), in *The Works of Thomas Robert Malthus,* ed. E. A. Wrigley and David Souden (London: W. Pickering, 1986), 1:12; *Essay of 1803,* 16.

17. Critics who delight in how badly wrong Malthus was in this calculation fail to notice that it is hypothetical in character – valid only if the population were to keep doubling up every twenty-five years. But the essence of his argument is that the economics of diminishing food resources would necessarily alter the

birth- and death-rates long before there were millions of people with nothing to eat. However, the fact that he is criticized for wrong reasons on this count does not make his assumptions about the food supply any better.

18. The economist David Ricardo – Malthus's old friend and intellectual sparring partner – offered a less threadbare version of the labor theory of value. He argued that more-fertile land is likely to be brought into cultivation before less-fertile land. At the margin will be land that generates only enough income to pay off the labor necessary to cultivate it. The value of the food produced on such marginal land is then equal to the value of the labor needed to produce it – provided all the issues that are abstracted away in such an analysis are indeed negligible.

19. A. Smith, *An Inquiry into the Nature and Causes of the Wealth of Nations* (1776; Indianapolis: Liberty Classics, 1976), 1:14–15.

20. Pollyannas who appeal to the notion of infinite resources available in infinite space can be told some version of the story shared earlier about a sphere packed solid with people whose radius increases at the speed of light.

21. The term "neoclassical economics" refers to the modern synthesis in economic theory that was put together some fifty or more years ago. It remains the mainstream position in economics, although there are critics within the discipline who use the word "neoclassical" as a general term of abuse.

22. In his *Foundations of Statistics,* which is the bible for Bayesian decision theory. Leonard J. Savage says that it would be "ridiculous" and "utterly preposterous" to use his theory in a "large world" – which notion includes the worlds of macroeconomics and finance. But these warnings are almost universally ignored (Binmore, *Rational Decisions*). Fischer Black and Myron Scholes were even awarded a Nobel Prize for a contribution to finance which not only assumes that Bayesian decision theory applies but that economic agents are risk-neutral except when faced by bankruptcy. Savage, *The Foundations of Statistics* (New York: Wiley, 1954), 16.

23. N. Stern, *The Economics of Climate Change: The Stern Review* (Cambridge: Cambridge University Press, 2007). Its message was unfortunately obscured by a continuing squabble among environmental economists about the "correct" social discount factor to be used in comparing the welfare of those alive today with those who will be alive in the future.

24. Binmore, *Rational Decisions*.

The Cultural and Literary Significance of the 1803 *Essay*

KAREN O'BRIEN

The cultural and literary impact of Malthus's 1803 edition of the *Essay* was both considerable in itself and deeply enmeshed with contemporary circumstances in the first few decades after its publication: circumstances that included the Napoleonic wars, political controversy about poverty and food scarcity, cultural debates about the rate and age of marriage, and, more specifically, the significance of the findings of first British censuses of 1801, 1811, and 1821. Malthus's work and his very name (the adjective "Malthusian" was first used in the 1820s) became so entangled with issues of population measurement and poor relief that questions of impact and influence require careful and sequential reconstruction. Donald Winch and Philip Connell, for example, have shown how "Malthusianism" was the quickly established and patiently elaborated artifact of Malthus's Romantic and Tory critics.[1] Since then, the Malthus whom most of us have come to know is, to a large extent, the counter-creation of his enemies: a figure who appears to be more secular, more narrow and retrograde in his social thinking than the intellectually flexible, politically Whiggish Christian minister who published the 1803 *Essay*.

The Malthus of the 1803 *Essay* was more broadly influential than his Romantic critics allowed, not only among his fellow political economists but on pressing debates in the early nineteenth century. These debates concerned the national importance of marriage, the status of women, the social impact of overseas emigration, the social efficacy of enlightened self-interest, the relationship between a Christian ethics of personal responsibility and the national economy, and the meaning of history itself. In all of these discussions during the first three decades of the nineteenth century, and in the many places in which these debates took place – reviews, pamphlets, dissertations, novels, poems, and didactic tales – Malthus's *Essay* was a constant, shaping presence. Broad though these debates were, the *Essay* intervened in them with two haunting questions: What if it is really true that we are now living at the limit of our natural sustainability? And what are the moral consequences of either accepting or acting upon such a supposition? For imaginative writers in particular, there was a third question: how might it feel to be, in the modern, demographic sense, a redundant human being?

Reviewers of the 1803 *Essay* – an imposing quarto that appeared under Malthus's own name – were in agreement that it was quite different in meaning and significance from the 1798 edition. They saw the earlier version as a bravura polemic against Utopian radical philosophers such as William Godwin and the Marquis de Condorcet but viewed this new book as a serious and historically grounded economic analysis of the population problem. Although the 1803 *Essay* was not initially covered by the *Edinburgh Review,* it received lengthy and broadly favorable treatment in a number of other major publications, including the *Monthly Review, Gentleman's Magazine,* and *British Critic.* These all interested themselves greatly in what Malthus had to say about the "preventive" check of delayed marriage and how, at different eras and places, climate, culture, and political institutions create differing male attitudes toward women, marriage age, and family size.[2] The irony of a Christian minister urging readers *not* to go forth and multiply in too great a hurry was not lost on any of the reviewers. However, two reviews by major figures appeared in 1804, one by the statistician and agricultural writer Arthur Young and one by the poet Robert Southey. These fired the opening salvos in the long campaign against Malthus's timeserving justification of apathy and harshness toward the poor, and particularly Malthus's advocacy of the gradual withdrawal of poor relief, on the basis of his needlessly pessimistic extrapolations from the fact of population growth. That the population was growing, and that this had been demonstrated incontrovertibly by the findings of the 1801 census, all were agreed. But not, Southey insisted, to the point where there was at that moment so great a pressure of population on basic resources as to necessitate drastic reductions in poor relief: "If a country be over-peopled, and crowded, and distressed, in regard to its system of society, before it be half peopled in proportion to its size and power of production; the fault lies in the system of society, not in the system of nature. If, while not a tenth, nay not an hundredth part of the habitable world be cultivated, mankind be every where in want, the fault is their own."[3]

Measuring the Future

Southey's self-confidence as a reviewer was underpinned by his friendship with the architect of the first British census, the statistician and civil servant

John Rickman (as well as, for this particular review, direct help from Samuel Coleridge).[4] Rickman would later provide Southey with extensive assistance in honing further attacks on Malthus in the periodicals, notably Southey's landmark essay "On the State of the Poor, the Principle of Mr. Malthus's Essay on Population, and the Manufacturing System" for the *Quarterly Review* of December 1812. Rickman secured Tory political backing for the census at a time of acute national concern about food security and the size of the male fighting force: "No country can confidently pretend to provide the requisite quantity of food, till they know the number of consumers," he wrote.[5] He then personally oversaw the first four censuses of 1801, 1811, 1821, and 1831 (and the British census continues at decennial intervals to this day).[6] Rickman was among those more traditional pro-populationist thinkers, who associated larger numbers of people with national strength, and who believed that the census would reveal a large and increasing population. The first census pro-formas, filled out by local overseers of the poor, ascertained the numbers of residents, subdivided by sex and occupation (or lack of occupation, if on poor relief).[7] Separating those employed in agriculture from those engaged in "trade, manufactures, or handicraft," they gave some indication of national productivity. Including those not at home at the time (military and naval personnel, and convicts), the census revealed a population of 9.4 million in England and Wales. This figure did not entirely surprise Rickman or Malthus, but what did strike Malthus in particular was that, although in the mid-eighteenth century, "as far as can be collected from the births and marriages, the population was increasing but slowly," there had been a dramatic and accelerating takeoff in population from this point.[8] Malthus was able to comment on this rate of increase because a second strand of the 1801 census exercise required local clergymen to trawl through their parish registers and record numbers of baptisms and burials at ten-year intervals from 1700, along with annual numbers of marriages from 1754 (the date from which all marriages had to take place by formal ceremony). There is every likelihood, for example, that Jane Austen, a clergyman's daughter living in Steventon in Hampshire, helped with this process; she must certainly have known about it. Austen was at home on 10 March 1801 on the day of the enumeration; since she regularly acted as her father's parish clerk by making entries in the parish registers of his two livings, she may well have helped him to perform this arduous task.[9]

The data furnished by the census provided an imperfect yet transformative account of the state of the nation. When compounded by the finding of the 1811 census that the population of England and Wales had increased by over 1 million in only ten years, Britain found itself coming to terms, for

good or ill, with an entirely new vision of its own history. Earlier models of
the recent past, in terms of incremental progress or cyclical development
and decline, were supplanted by the visual model of a fairly flat line followed by a sudden upward curve. Added to this was the discovery, after the
1821 census first measured the age of the population in five- and ten-year
age groups, that Britain was a spectacularly young country, with almost
half the population under twenty years old. Reinhart Koselleck in *Futures
Past,* his study of the conceptualization of time and history in Western culture, associates the period from the late eighteenth to the mid-nineteenth
centuries with a crisis in historical consciousness whereby "the temporal
dimension within which experience had previously been developed and
collected became displaced."[10] An emerging new sense of historical time,
Koselleck argues, was underpinned by a "law of acceleration . . . on the
basis of which standards were continually altered, since the acceleration of
the future constantly foreshortened resort to the past. Population increased
in ever-decreasing intervals; technically – created velocities rose exponentially; the increase of production showed similar tendencies."[11]

To what extent did the census in Britain contribute to a collective sense
of temporal acceleration? Kathrin Levitan in her study *A Cultural History
of the British Census* has endeavored to gauge the cultural impact of these
extraordinary discoveries as they filtered through and were filtered by the
work of Malthus.[12] She documents the ambivalence about such explosive
growth, and the way in which census data crystallized anxieties about urbanization and urban mortality rates, as well as about the balance between
the agricultural and manufacturing sectors of the economy. Malthus's 1803
Essay was not the first or only work to confront these issues, but its impact
was distinctive, Levitan argues, in terms of the way it positioned population
surplus and redundancy not as an adventitious but as a structural feature of
economic history: "The political and intellectual life of Malthus's concept
of surplus population can be traced through the first half of the nineteenth
century through the perspective of the census. The census . . . helped make
surplus a national concept that was understood in terms of proportions of
people and national productivity."[13] This Malthusian perspective shone a
spotlight on unproductive or surplus individuals, and transposed older discussions of poverty, spinsterhood, bachelorhood, and marriage, and also of
emigration overseas into a new, nationally consequential economic idiom.
It allowed others to assess the extent of poverty notably Patrick Colquhoun,
who in his *Treatise of Indigence* (1806) used both census returns and the
national survey of paupers (1802–1803) to reveal in England and Wales
over a million paupers, nearly a quarter of a million in an underclass of

vagrants, prostitutes, and "gypsies," and over 1.5 million agricultural male and female laborers.[14]

Alternative Pasts and Futures

Ultimately, the combined question posed by Malthus and the census was about the extent to which the British past offered any guidance as to the future. As well as seeking to model mathematically rates of population increase in ways that would enable states to anticipate disaster, Malthus, as Murray Milgate and Shannon C. Stimson have argued, thought that the "capacity to calculate distant consequences and form reliable plans for the future is a fundamental part of the formation of moral character, or prudence."[15] Political economy – understood as an integrated science of politics, economics, and morals – was for Malthus as for Adam Smith a means of guiding both individuals and legislators through the dilemmas of an expanding commercial and manufacturing society. Although Malthus was far less optimistic than Smith about the possibilities of continuing economic growth and increased productivity enabled by the division of labor, contemporary reviewers immediately recognized the close affinity between these two writers. For Malthus, as for Smith, the purpose of political economy was to inform individual and state actors about how to promote "the gradual and progressive improvement in human society" (as opposed to the Utopian schemes for transformation favored by Godwin and Condorcet).[16] Recent accounts of Malthus's thought have explained his allegiance to an Anglican version of the British Whig Enlightenment of Smith, David Hume, and Edward Gibbon.[17] As the final chapter of the 1803 *Essay* makes clear, the domain of human history is one we can shape by a combination of individual responsibility, legislative intervention (creating a national system of education, for example), and also nonintervention (as a way to solve the problem of welfare dependency). Yet at the same time that Malthus offered a heavily modified version of Smith's vision of the future of human history, with population setting an absolute limit to progress and prosperity, he also showed, in the first two books of the 1803 *Essay*, the narrow class specificity of such notions of progress: "The histories of mankind which we possess," Malthus brilliantly observed, "are, in general, histories only of the higher classes."[18] Enlightenment thinkers had posited a model of economic and social development through a series of four stages, in which pastoral and agricultural societies were positioned as historically prior to commercial modernity. The reality, Malthus insisted, is that most people have always inhabited a separate history of "oscillation" between the "retrograde and progressive movements" associated with living close to the margins of subsistence and being subject to vicissitudes of scarcity, disease, and conflict.[19] The hidden, disconnected subhistory of the poorer part of mankind that Malthus depicted in the early parts of the *Essay* underscores humanity's biological participation in the natural world; its participants have no historical consciousness, no insight into what he called the "internal structure of human society," which is visible only to those with access to statistical and economic forms of analysis.[20]

The Hidden History of Poverty

The significance of the cognitive deficit that Malthus ascribed to those members of society most likely to be affected by positive population checks was not lost on early critics of the *Essay*. William Wordsworth repeatedly challenged distinctions between public lives and poor lives, between those whose relative economic insulation from natural "oscillation" gives them a privileged position of observation and the poor who simply live within the subhistorical domain. In many of his early poems, Wordsworth describes encounters between well-meaning but baffled middle-class figures and poor, vulnerable, usually itinerant characters. In his *Lyrical Ballads* of 1798, for example, in the poem "We are Seven," a man encounters an eight-year-old "cottage girl" from a family of seven children who insists repeatedly that, although two of her siblings have died, "we are seven." Wordsworth juxtaposes the speaker's simplistic logic of counting against the girl's tenacious sense of who counts, to the point where his privileged statistical reasoning seems far less humanly valid than her imaginative response to child mortality.[21] Having first encountered Malthus's work in 1798, Wordsworth later sought to bridge the gulf between the subjective lives of the poor and the privileged by espousing projects for national education as a means of rescuing the underclass from material and moral disaster.[22] A vignette of incomprehension in the *Lyrical Ballads* thus became, in later works such as his epic *The Excursion* (1814), a passionate plea for moral and religious education for all in order to induct all children, rich and poor, into the mental culture of a single community. The poem's authoritative speaker The Wanderer yearns for a time when

> this Imperial Realm. . . . shall admit
> An obligation, on her part, to *teach*

Them who are born to serve her and obey;
Binding herself by Statute to secure
For all the Children whom her soil maintains
The rudiments of Letters, and to inform
The mind with moral and religious truth
Both understood, and practised, – so that none,
However destitute, be left to droop
By timely culture unsustained, or run
Into wild a disorder; or be forced
To drudge through weary life without the aid
Of intellectual implements and tools;
A savage Horde among the civilized,
A servile Band among the lordly free![23]

Wordsworth's concern here is with the Malthusian specter of division between the "civilized" and the "savage Horde" who may live in a state of
cognitive, economic, and moral deprivation. Education must heal this rift
in human consciousness, or else, from Wordsworth's conservative perspective, "wild disorder" and social unrest may ensue.

For some commentators, Malthus's assertion of the ecological basis
of human history, beneath the superstructure of "progress," civilization,
and human historical consciousness, amounts to a fundamental break with
the Enlightenment. For the theologian John Milbank, Malthus's work has
"something of the character of an 'epistemic switch'" from the Enlightened era of Smith because it reinserts political economy into a providential
framework and replaces the unplanned collaboration of Smith's economy
with a more hectic vision of human striving. This striving, though it may
yield social progress, is really an end in itself.[24] For Gertrude Himmelfarb,
Malthus, though indebted to Smith, inaugurated an entirely new way of
thinking about poverty. Where Smith had posited a continuum between the
entire body of the poor and the nation as a whole, Malthus consigned poverty to a different realm of recurrent misery and scarcity, and rather than
restating the traditional view that the poor will always be with us, he set
out to demonstrate that poverty, though it might be greatly mitigated, could
never entirely be brought to an end.[25]

Malthus's Romantic critics undoubtedly saw the 1803 *Essay* as an entirely new and pernicious development in what came to be known as the
"dismal science." Even where they agreed that population checks would
eventually occur, they insisted that these would only take place in a very
distant future when the whole world had been cultivated and that it was

doom-mongering to suggest otherwise. The *Essay* came out at a key moment of transition for the first generation of Romantic writers, after they had acknowledged the failure of the French Revolution and had become disenchanted with Godwin's ideas of human perfectibility. Its publication coincided with Coleridge's and Southey's newfound identification with the Anglican Church and with a mood of popular patriotism amid fears of a French invasion.[26] Both Winch and Connell document in detail the role played by Malthus in the counter-elaboration of the Romantics' post-radical "anti-economism." This grew into the fully fledged conservatism of the 1820s and 1830s, encompassing wider issues such as the Corn Laws, Catholic emancipation, the Reform Act of 1832, and, above all, the 1834 Poor Law Amendment Act, and shaping a moral critique of industrial society that stretched to Thomas Carlyle and John Ruskin.[27] Tory anti-economism had a venerable literary history, stretching back to Jonathan Swift's *A Modest Proposal for Preventing the Children of Poor People from Being a Burden to Their Parents or Country* (1729) in which he mockingly ventriloquized the coldly reasonable voice of contemporary demographers such as William Petty and John Graunt, suggesting that the solution to the problem of Irish overpopulation was for parents to eat their own children. Another enormously popular Tory Irish writer, Oliver Goldsmith, sounded a similar, humanitarian note of protest against what he saw as the depopulating consequences of commercial modernization. In *The Deserted Village* (1770), a once idyllic village community is devastated by the local landlord's estate-building activities, forcing many of its poor inhabitants to emigrate to the Americas. It fell to the first generation of Romantic writers, however, to fashion this tradition of humanitarian Toryism into a coherent Romantic conservatism, as David Eastwood first explained.[28]

Kevin Gilmartin sees the Romantic anti-Malthusians engaged in a still wider project as they sought to mobilize and bring cultural depth to the opposition to the radical reform movements of early nineteenth-century political thinking, by reimagining the established order of church and state.[29] Although their adumbration of a new conservative politics was actuated by their antagonism, first toward Malthus and then toward David Ricardo, there were many twists and turns in the tale. Southey, Coleridge, Rickman, and Wordsworth in fact agreed with Malthus that the problem of scarcity was symptomatic of the transition from a landed economy to an increasingly urban one based on manufacturing and commerce.[30] In the long run, there was a surprising degree of convergence between Malthus and his Romantic critics, particularly on the need to create a national education system and to protect domestic agriculture.[31] Ironically, Rickman ultimately had a better claim to be the architect of the Poor Law Amendment Act than Malthus.[32]

Malthusian Responsibilities

If Romantic conservatism had its origins in the powerful negative inspiration of Malthus's ideas, there were other kinds of literary and didactic writings that drew heavily on Malthus for new kinds of literary realism and new ways of advocating individual moral responsibility in the face of hostile economic conditions. First among these was the work of the poet George Crabbe, whom William Hazlitt dubbed "a Malthus turned Metrical Romancer."[33] Crabbe (1754–1832) was from an earlier generation than the Romantics but remained popular until the mid-nineteenth century.[34] He came from humble beginnings in Suffolk and knew firsthand the harshness of life in rural areas far from the metropolis. Early and generous patronage by Edmund Burke cemented his broadly Whig affiliations and may well have occasioned discussions of poverty and famine, topics that preoccupied Burke long before his proto-Malthusian memorandum "Thoughts and Details on Scarcity" (1795).[35] Crabbe achieved early fame with "The Village" (1783), a poem that directly countered Goldsmith's idyllic portrait of village life by showing poverty to be endemic and grinding, neither caused nor remediable by individual intervention. Crabbe's subsequent works were suffused with the economic hardships of the Napoleonic Wars and with debates about the Poor Laws, overpopulation, and food scarcity. In *The Parish Register* (1807), Crabbe adopted the stance of a clergyman reviewing the registers of births, marriages, and deaths in his parish, as though taking a census, and recalling their human stories of struggle, deprivation, loss, and violence. The poem casts an unsentimental eye on the overcrowded, harsh lives of the poor and their abandoned and illegitimate children. In the *Edinburgh Review,* Francis Jeffrey saluted the social realism of *The Parish Register:* "Instead of conducting us through blooming groves and pastoral meadows, [he] had led us along filthy lanes and crowded wharfs, to hospitals, alms-houses and gin-shops."[36] Here, Jeffrey argues, is an emotional truthfulness sorely lacking in the Romantic Lake poets. Here, implicitly at least, is a Whig poetics of poverty and scarcity (the poem was read to Charles James Fox on his deathbed). Just as Malthus had done, Crabbe insinuated that the recognition of elite helplessness in the face of poverty might, in the long run, be more compassionate, more attuned to God's purpose, and–by avoiding well-intentioned interventions that serve only to perpetuate the causes of poverty – more effective than Romantic paternalism. Moreover, there exists for the poor the Malthusian remedy of what Crabbe called "prudent delay," exemplified in the "Marriages" section by the story of Reuben and Rachel, who wait for many years until they can afford to marry and have children:

> Reuben and Rachel though as fond as Doves,
> Were yet discreet and cautious in their Loves;
> Nor would attend to *Cupid's* wild Commands,
> Till cool Reflection bade them join their Hands;
> When both were poor, they thought it argued ill
> Of hasty Love to make them poorer still;
> Year after year, with Savings long laid by,
> They bought the future Dwelling's full Supply.[37]

Crabbe's poems gave dramatic embodiment to Malthus's prescription for individual moral restraint in conditions of scarcity, their human agency limited but not without some effectiveness in God's testing world.

Crabbe was a great favorite with Jane Austen, and his themes of moral restraint, individual agency, and delayed marriage were indeed topics still more native to the novel than to poetry.[38] Unlike poetry, the more recent genre of the novel was slower in the later eighteenth and early nineteenth centuries to grapple with issues of poverty and deprivation, and rarely depicted the full spectrum of society. However, as Ruth Perry has argued, novelists were nevertheless intensely preoccupied with economic vulnerability of various kinds: the threat of eviction, the loss of shelter, the pressure of rising rents, and the need to downsize to smaller homes.[39] By the early nineteenth century, novelists were painting society on an ever more broad social canvas, and the lives of villagers, cottagers, tenants, and shopkeepers increasingly surfaced within plots still dominated by the perspectives of middle-class protagonists. Some of the most influential writers to adopt this wider social purview were both novelists and amateur economists and social scientists. A prominent example is Maria Edgeworth. The daughter of the improving Anglo-Irish landlord, Lunar Society member, and educational writer Richard Lovell Edgeworth, she was an established educational theorist before publishing a novel that undoubtedly set the stage for wider debates about fertility, population, and food management. Her *Castle Rackrent* (1800) tells, in the voice of its Irish steward, the story of the mismanagement of an Anglo-Irish estate over four generations of feckless owners, to the point where the landowners are dispossessed by the steward's son. Edgeworth vividly dramatized the owners' exploitation of their peasantry as the estate becomes less and less able to support their most basic needs: Lady Murtagh Rackrent, for example, actually extorts gifts of food from them, even while she requires their children to work for her free of charge. Edgeworth recapitulated many of these themes in her subsequent fiction including her novel about exploitative Irish landlordism, *The Absentee* (1812).[40] She became a friend of David Ricardo in the 1820s, and the two of them corresponded extensively about Irish food security and other economic matters. She also came to know Malthus himself.[41]

Edgeworth was also acquainted with the celebrated Edinburgh University professor Dugald Stewart. In his enormously influential lectures on political economy and population, delivered in 1800–1801 to an audience of future luminaries of the *Edinburgh Review,* Stewart took explicit issue with Malthus by asserting that population growth was consistent with economic growth, social progress, and liberal political institutions, and that it posed no real threat to the future sustainability of any of these.[42] Edgeworth's subsequent fiction, therefore, embraced this lively context of debate in which Malthusian pessimism was tested and challenged, even while she accepted, for example in her *Popular Tales* (1804) for children, one key premise of the 1803 *Essay,* that all families should educate their children to take prudent cognizance of the conditions of scarcity in which they live. Edgeworth and Stewart were themselves the friends of the Scottish novelist and educational writer Elizabeth Hamilton, whose popular 1808 novel *The Cottagers of Glenburnie* descended to the filthy, chaotic farmstead of a Scots cottager and his family in order to explore the themes of scarcity, large family life, and disease among the lower classes. The novel tells how Mrs. Mason, a respectable but poor unmarried cousin of the cottager Mac-Clarty family, comes to live with them and tries unsuccessfully to save them from their poor hygiene, lack of discipline toward their numerous children, and failure to maximize their economic opportunities. At one point, Mrs. Mason advises her cousin to ask her children to help to cultivate the garden in order to provide more food for the family, and on another she wonders at the "perverted ingenuity which could contrive to give to the sleeping rooms of a country house, all the disadvantages which attend the airless abodes of poverty in the crowded lanes of great and populous cities."[43] To Mrs. Mason's mind, the MacClarty family needlessly condemn themselves to a crowded, disease-ridden, and improvident Malthusian existence. When disaster overtakes them – the husband dies, and one of the daughters abandons her illegitimate offspring – Mrs. Mason leaves and sets up a school for the poorer children of Glenburnie, with the support of her friend "Mr Stewart." As the *Edinburgh Review* enthusiastically recognized, the novel provides an education about the degree to which poverty can be mitigated by educated, religiously informed, prudent conduct.[44]

The Great Marriage Debate

Of equal relevance to the issue of family regulation is the figure of Mrs. Mason herself as a socially useful and morally influential single woman whose dignity in the face of rejection and financial precariousness is rendered by Hamilton with sympathy and insight. As I have written elsewhere, Malthus was in his 1803 *Essay* acutely aware that the logic of his argument for moral restraint demanded a rethinking of social attitudes toward unmarried women, widows, and women who do not have children.[45] In his chapter "Of the Modes of Correcting the Prevailing Opinions on the Subject of Population," he argued vigorously that society should stop stigmatizing old maids and treating wives as though they are the social superiors of much older unmarried women: "It is perfectly absurd, as well as unjust, that a giddy girl of sixteen should, because she is married, be considered by the forms of society as the protector of women of thirty, should come first into the room, should be assigned the highest place at the table, and be the prominent figure to whom the attentions of the company are more particularly paid."[46] Moreover, he argued, the male propensity to regard women past their mid-twenties as unmarriageable blinded them to the advantages of having few childbearing years within a marriage and drove women themselves to desperate and unhappy marriages. Female novelists such as Hamilton and Austen were able to give more positive and sympathetic embodiments to the predicaments that Malthus described: in *Pride and Prejudice,* the sixteen-year-old, newly married Lydia Bennett triumphs over her unmarried older sister Jane, insisting that she must take "her place" at her mother's right hand, "and you must go lower because I am a married woman." Likewise, Charlotte Lucas, aged twenty seven, makes the apparently bewildering decision to marry the odious Mr. Collins.[47]

Malthus's bold and explicit engagements with questions of human fertility, sexual desire, marriage age, and the social stigmatizing of unmarried women helped to transform public discourse about marriage in the early nineteenth century, from a private, household, and dynastic matter to one that emphasized the need for freely choosing individuals to make sensible marriages in the national interest. For some writers such as Edgeworth and Hamilton this was a matter of explicit engagement with Malthus, while for other popular writers of fiction it took the form of a more diffuse yet pervasive preoccupation with the relationship between personal decisions about marriage, child-rearing, and the management of the household economy and the stability and prosperity of society as a whole. Obliquely at least, fiction writers bore witness to the rising popularity of marriage as a life-style choice (by 1801 only around 6.8% of people in their early forties had never married, down from around 24.9% a century earlier), by thematizing the topic (Susan Ferrier's successful novel *Marriage* [1818] being one case in point), and by paying more attention to those women and men whose economic circumstances denied them access to marriage.

The politicization of the domestic sphere and the growing sense that the well-regulated household was the prerequisite for the well-functioning state was further reinforced by Malthus's emphasis on the need for families to justify their own economic viability, as well as his belief in the spiritual benefits of the economic struggle to survive.[48] The traditional fictional topics of marriage, heirs and spares, old maids, and seduced young women acquired peculiar national resonance during the early nineteenth century. This was particularly reinforced by the ways in which evangelical writers combined moral and religious prescriptions with Malthusian warnings. Before Malthus, the evangelical campaigner Hannah More prepared the ground with her *Cheap Repository Tracts* (1795–1798), which sold hundreds of thousands of copies and were in the main short, didactic fables about the endeavors of the poor to improve their lot through piety, hard work, self-restraint, and social acquiescence. The most enduring, the "Shepherd of Salisbury Plain" (1795), is about a family of eight warding off hunger and cold, ultimately rewarded for their resilience.[49] After Malthus's *Essay,* More, in her bestselling novel *Coelebs in Search of a Wife* (1808), took the theme of restraint and delay into a more middle-class arena. The young man of the title (Coelebs means bachelor) narrates the considered, lengthy courtship of himself and his lady, Lucilla, while introducing a wide range of female characters whose financial self-reliance or purposeful philanthropy enables them to delay marriage until the time is right.

More wrote at the height of a vogue for evangelical fiction that temporarily flooded the novel market in the first two decades of the nineteenth century. With starkly moralistic titles such as *Temper* (1812), *Self-Control* (1811), *Discipline* (1814), *Correction* (1818), and *A Father as He Should Be* (1815), these novels emphasized self-regulation and domestic prudence as essential to the economic and political health of the nation.[50] Female characters often had to face the reality of providing financially for their families, as, for example, in Barbara Hofland's three "widow" novels for children in which widowed mothers experience firsthand an adverse ratio of children to resources but learn to survive economically without remar-rying.[51] Such novels are Malthusian to the extent that they are imbued with a sense of the natural vicissitudes of disease and scarcity, and of economic calculation as both morally formative for the individual and part of God's plan for an educative world. Evangelical fiction, in other words, partook of the wider assimilation of Malthusian ideas into the evangelical religious thinking that took place in the years following the publication of the 1803 *Essay,* and that shaped the new Tory "Evangelical economics" described by Boyd Hilton in his *The Age of Atonement.*[52] Influential evangelical cler-ics such as Archbishop of Canterbury John Bird Sumner and the Scottish Presbyterian Thomas Chalmers endeavored to reconcile the principle of population with God's love for humanity; this theodicy works, in Chal-mers's words, by calling on humanity to exercise its powers of will and sexual self-restraint against "the demonstrable inadequacy in all the mate-rial resources which the globe can furnish, for the increasing wants of a recklessly increasing species," and so giving them a path to salvation.[53]

Despite Jane Austen's often quoted remark, "I do not like the Evan-gelicals," her novels also bear witness to the pervasiveness of intersect-ing evangelical and Malthusian themes in the early nineteenth century.[54] Austen certainly encountered Malthus's ideas either directly or through her reading of Charles Pasley's *Essay on the Military Policy . . . of the British Empire* (1810), which discusses his ideas.[55] Written at the height of the evangelical vogue, and taking the name of its heroine, Fanny Price, from Crabbe's *Parish Register,* Austen's *Mansfield Park* (1814) records Fanny's dignified reckoning against her own status as the superfluous daughter of a large family ("nobody at home seemed to want her"), and her struggle to earn her place at her wealthy uncle's table.[56] Fanny's adoption by her uncle's family happens as a result of her mother writing to her relations of her difficulties with "such a superfluity of children, and such a want of almost everything else."[57] Her impoverished parents' home in Portsmouth is vividly depicted in the novel as "the abode of noise, disorder and im-propriety," teeming with unwanted children and memories of a child who did not survive. In *Mansfield Park* and in her other novels, Austen engaged profoundly with the experience of what it means to be a redundant fe-male, to be one of too many: Elizabeth Bennet endures a rebuke from Lady Catherine de Bourgh on her family size of five daughters: "Daughters are never of much consequence to a father."[58] In a world that simply calculates the ratio of daughters to resources, Austen's heroines gain moral stature by refusing to rush into marriage, and by insisting, as Malthus insisted, that spinsterhood is a better option than the unhappy, over-fertile marriages of the Bennets or Prices. Austen also depicted sympathetically the social and psychological predicament of those women who did not marry, most memorably when Mr. Knightley rebukes Emma for making fun of the unmarried Miss Bates.

Austen's probing of parish registers may have given her a more than intuitive sense of what was later understood as the "surplus woman problem." It was not until the 1851 census that the marital status of household members was listed, prompting a wave of public agonizing over the still large numbers of unmarried, "excess" females.[59] Although Austen portrayed the dilution of parental feelings by a too numerous offspring, she did not examine the darker side of human superfluousness in the way that some of her contemporary and successor writers did. In *Child Murder and British Culture,* Josephine McDonagh explains how there came about in the nineteenth century a new Malthusian understanding of infanticide as something that only poverty and desperation could bring about, famously in George Eliot's *Adam Bede* (1859), when Hetty Sorrel leaves her illegitimate baby to die having been abandoned by her lover.[60] Other writers highlighted the Malthusian tragedy of enforced displacement, as for example in Walter Scott's *Guy Mannering* (1815) in which a tragic plot is set in motion by a laird's cruel displacement of a gypsy settlement from his lands.

Viewed from another angle, it occurred to many commentators that the eviction and emigration of surplus peoples might offer a potential solution to population pressure. Malthus himself stated in the 1803 *Essay* that he thought emigration "a very weak palliative" for the problem of overpopulation, but nevertheless found himself drawn into a series of public debates about the issue in the 1820s when British and Irish emigration to the colonies and North America was rising rapidly.[61] Malthus appeared before a Parliamentary Select Committee on emigration convened by the undersecretary of state for the colonies, Robert Wilmot-Horton, who was considering options for state-sponsored emigration as a way of alleviating poverty and overcrowding. Wilmot-Horton's project for a national colonization scheme as a means of indefinitely postponing Britain and Ireland's Malthusian future (often caricatured as "shovelling out paupers") was ably supported by Rickman, Southey, Wordsworth, and other Tories, although it was not ultimately funded.[62] The broader issue of displacement and migration became a prevalent topos in nineteenth-century fiction.[63] Some novelists followed Goldsmith's *Deserted Village* in their bleak portrayal of emigrant exile, but for many, emigration offered a real alternative to overcrowded life at home.

At the end of Elizabeth Gaskell's *Mary Barton* (1848), for instance, the protagonist and her husband leave behind congested, industrial Manchester for a new life in Canada, and in Dickens's *David Copperfield* (1850), the perpetually indigent Mr. Micawber and his numerous family successfully emigrate to Australia and become sheep farmers.[64]

In the 1803 edition, Malthus revised his *Essay on the Principle of Population* in such a way as to give his readers a sense of the choices available to humanity in the face of dark inevitabilities. Commentators have tended to focus on the inevitabilities more than the choices, ascribing to the *Essay* a persistent strain of pessimistic "Malthusian" thinking that underpinned the 1834 Poor Law Amendment Act and haunted the nineteenth-century conception of poverty. William Cobbett's anti-amendment act comedy *Surplus Population* (1831) features a Malthusian squire, Peter Thimble, who spends the entire play trying to dissuade a young country girl from marrying and having babies: "Nothing can save the country but plague, pestilence, famine, and sudden death. Government ought to import a ship-load of arsenic. [To her] But young woman, cannot you impose on yourself '*moral restraint*' for ten or a dozen years?"[65]

Although this caricature of Malthus is undoubtedly part of the story, closer attention to the contemporary reception of the *Essay* suggests that it helped to reframe discourse about life expectancy, marriage, women, and fertility in ways that emphasized the importance of human decision-making within a certain, limited compass. The Malthusian feminist Harriet Martineau, for example, in her bestselling *Illustrations of Political Economy* (1832–1834), tells the story of a Scottish widow who decides not to remarry and have more children; the widow recognizes that the populous island community in which she lives can no longer be supported by dwindling local fishing stocks and that famine may ensue if the community does not take charge of its destiny.[66] Other Malthusians advocated birth control. Accepting the diagnosis, but not the remedial actions, of the 1803 *Essay,* the radical Francis Place made the case in his *Illustrations and Proofs of the Principle of Population* (1822) that "it is not disreputable for married persons to avail themselves of such precautionary means as would, without being injurious to health, or destructive to female delicacy, prevent conception."[67] John Stuart Mill warmly espoused Place's neo-Malthusian birth-control campaign, on the radical grounds that the working classes, if they could regulate their own numbers, might command higher wages.[68] Contraception was a practice that Malthus classed among the "improper arts to conceal the consequences of irregular connexions," less, perhaps, from motives of Anglican prudishness than out of concern that it would distract society from its true obligation to confront the providential purpose served by population pressure.[69] Nevertheless, in this great revolution in the human shaping of natural destiny, the 1803 *Essay* certainly played its part.

NOTES

1. Donald Winch, *Riches and Poverty: An Intellectual History of Political Economy in Britain, 1750–1832* (Cambridge: Cambridge University Press, 1996); Philip Connell, *Romanticism, Economics and the Question of "Culture"* (Cambridge: Cambridge University Press, 2001).

2. The reviews of Malthus are usefully collected in Andrew Pyle, ed., *Population: Contemporary Responses to Thomas Malthus* (Bristol: Thoemmes Press, 1994). Francis Horner failed to deliver his commissioned review for the *Edinburgh Review,* but the *Edinburgh*'s editor, Francis Jeffrey, made up for this by publishing a number of reviews and articles (some by Malthus himself) subsequently.

3. Robert Southey, review of "An Essay on the Principles of Population," *Annual Review,* January 1804, in Pyle, ed., *Population,* 128.

4. See Winch, *Riches and Poverty,* 288, and Connell, *Romanticism,* 38–41.

5. John Rickman, "Thoughts on the Utility and Facility of a General Enumeration of the People of the British Empire" (1796), reprinted in D. V. Glass, *Numbering the People: The Eighteenth-Century Population Controversy and the Development of Census and Vital Statistics in Britain* (Farnborough, U.K.: D. C. Heath, 1973), 108.

6. See the website of the Office for National Statistics, www.ONS.gov.uk.

7. The schedule is reproduced in Edward Higgs, *Making Sense of the Census: The Manuscript Returns for England and Wales, 1801–1901* (London: Her Majesty's Stationary Office, 1989), 5, 114.

8. See discussion in T. R. Malthus, *An Essay on the Principle of Population; or, A View of Its Past and Present Effects on Human Happiness; with an Inquiry into Our Prospects Respecting the Future Removal or Mitigation of the Evils Which It Occasions. A New Edition, Very Much Enlarged,* 2nd ed. (London: J. Johnson, 1803; reprint, New Haven, Conn.: Yale University Press, 2017), 248–254 (hereafter *Essay of 1803;* the page numbers cited for this work are to this book).

9. The census returns were destroyed in 1904, and the documents used to compile these for George Austen's parishes of Steventon and Deane in Hampshire do not survive.

10. Reinhart Koselleck, *Futures Past: On the Semantics of Historical Time,* trans. Keith Tribe (New York: Columbia University Press, 2004), 41.

11. Ibid., 42.

12. Kathrin Levitan, *A Cultural History of the British Census: Envisioning the Multitude in the Nineteenth Century* (New York: Palgrave Macmillan, 2011). On the census and the state, see Stephen John Thompson, "Census-Taking, Political Economy and State Formation in Britain c. 1790–1840," Ph.D. thesis, University of Cambridge, 2010.

13. Levitan, *A Cultural History of the British Census,* 48.

14. Colquhoun's calculation of the social structure of England and Wales is reproduced in Boyd Hilton, *A Mad, Bad and Dangerous People? England, 1783–1846* (Oxford: Clarendon Press, 2006), 127–128.

15. Murray Milgate and Shannon C. Stimson, *After Adam Smith: A Century of Transformation in Politics and Political Economy* (Princeton, N.J.: Princeton University Press, 2009), 135.

16. *Essay of 1803,* 473. For the 1798 *Essay,* see T. R. Malthus, *An Essay on the Principle of Population as It Affects the Future Improvement of Society with Remarks on the Speculations of Mr. Godwin, M. Condorcet, and Other Writers* (1798), in *The Works of Thomas Robert Malthus,* ed. E. A Wrigley and David Souden (London: W. Pickering, 1986), vol. 1 (hereafter First *Essay*).

17. Winch, *Riches and Poverty,* 237–241; A. M. C. Waterman, *Political Economy and Christian Theology since the Enlightenment: Essays in Intellectual History* (Basingstoke, U.K.: Palgrave Macmillan, 2004).

18. *Essay of 1803,* 21.

19. Ibid.; First *Essay,* 15.

20. *Essay of 1803,* 21–22. This does not appear in the First *Essay.*

21. See Hollis Robbins, "'We Are Seven' and the First British Census," *English Language Notes* 48 (2010): 201–213, and Aaron Fogel, "Wordsworth's 'We Are Seven' and Crabbe's *The Parish Register:* Poetry and Anti-Census," *Studies in Romanticism* 48 (2009): 23–65.

22. Duncan Wu, *Wordsworth's Reading, 1770–1799* (Cambridge: Cambridge University Press, 1993), 94.

23. William Wordsworth, *The Excursion,* ed. Sally Bushell, James A. Butler, and David Garcia (1814; Ithaca, N.Y.: Cornell University Press, 2007), ix, lines 295–310.

24. John Milbank, *Theology and Social Theory: Beyond Secular Reason* (Oxford: Blackwell, 1990), 42.

25. Gertrude Himmelfarb, *The Idea of Poverty: England in the Early Industrial Age* (New York: Knopf, 1984); Gareth Stedman Jones, *An End to Poverty? A Historical Debate* (New York: Columbia University Press, 2008), 99–103.

26. Connell, *Romanticism,* 34–37.

27. Winch, *Riches and Poverty,* 227.

28. David Eastwood, "Robert Southey and the Intellectual Origins of Romantic Conservatism," *English Historical Review* 104 (1989): 308–331; Eastwood, "Ruinous Prosperity: Robert Southey's Critique of the Commercial System," *Wordsworth Circle* 25 (1994): 72–76.

29. Kevin Gilmartin, *Writing against Revolution: Literary Conservatism in Britain, 1790–1832* (Cambridge: Cambridge University Press, 2007), 207–210.

30. Connell, *Romanticism,* 31–33.

31. Winch, *Riches and Poverty,* 311, 332.

32. Ibid., 314.

33. William Hazlitt, *The Spirit of the Age* (1825), in *The Selected Writings of William Hazlitt,* ed. Duncan Wu (London: Pickering and Chatto, 1998), 7:167.

34. On Crabbe, see Colin Winbron, *The Literary Economy of Jane Austen and George Crabbe* (Aldershot, U.K.: Ashgate, 2004).

35. On this work, see Winch, *Riches and Poverty,* 198–205.

36. This and other reviews of Crabbe are in *George Crabbe: The Critical Heritage,* ed. Arthur Pollard (London: Routledge, 1972), 83.

37. "Marriages," *The Parish Register,* lines 435–442, in *George Crabbe: The Complete Poetical Works,* ed. Norma Dalrymple-Champneys and Arthur Pollard (Oxford: Clarendon Press, 1988), 1:249

38. Deirdre Le Faye, ed., *Jane Austen's Letters* (Oxford: Oxford University Press, 1995), 218, 220, 243.

39. Ruth Perry, "Home Economics: Representations of Poverty in Eighteenth-Century Fiction," in *A Companion to the Eighteenth-Century English Novel,* ed. Paula R. Backscheider and Catherine Ingrassia (Oxford: Blackwell, 2005), 441.

40. On Edgeworth, see Cliona Ò'Gallchoir, *Maria Edgeworth: Women, Enlightenment and Nation* (Dublin: University College Dublin Press, 2005), and Claire Connolly, *A Cultural History of the Irish Novel, 1790–1829* (Cambridge: Cambridge University Press, 2012).

41. Patricia James, *Population Malthus: His Life and Times* (London: Routledge and Kegan Paul, 1979), 367. Letters between Edgeworth and Ricardo are reprinted in volume 9 of *The Works and Correspondence of David Ricardo,* ed. Piero Sraffa and M. H. Dobb (Indianapolis: Liberty Fund, 2005).

42. On Stewart's lectures and Edgeworth, see Karen O'Brien, *Women and Enlightenment in Eighteenth-Century Britain* (Cambridge: Cambridge University Press, 2009), 229–230.

43. Elizabeth Hamilton, *The Cottagers of Glenburnie and Other Educational Writings,* ed. Pam Perkins (Glasgow: Association for Scottish Literary Studies, 2009), chap. 9.

44. On Jeffrey's review and Hamilton more generally, see Pam Perkins, *Women Writers and the Edinburgh Enlightenment* (Amsterdam: Rodopi, 2010), 125, chap. 1.

45. "Malthus's Old Maids," in O'Brien, *Women and Enlightenment,* 226–230.

46. *Essay of 1803,* 434.

47. Jane Austen, *Pride and Prejudice,* ed. Pat Rogers (Cambridge: Cambridge University Press, 2006), vol. 3, chap. 51.

48. See Harriet Guest, *Small Change: Women, Learning, Patriotism, 1750–1810* (Chicago: Chicago University Press, 2000).

49. See Anne Stott, *Hannah More: The First Victorian* (Oxford: Oxford University Press, 2003), chap. 8.

50. See Anthony Mandal, "Evangelical Fiction," in *The Oxford History of the Novel, 1750–1820,* ed. Peter Garside and Karen O'Brien (Oxford: Oxford University Press, 2015), 255–272.

51. *The History of an Officer's Widow and Her Young Family* (1809), *The History of a Clergyman's Widow and Her Young Family* (1812), and *The Merchant's Widow and Her Young Family* (1814). All were published by the Minerva Press and went through many editions.

52. Boyd Hilton, *The Age of Atonement: The Influence of Evangelicalism on Social and Economic Thought, 1795–1865* (Oxford: Oxford University Press, 1988).

53. Thomas Chalmers, *On the Power, Wisdom and Goodness of God* (1833), quoted in Hilton, *A Mad, Bad and Dangerous People,* 337.

54. Jane Austen to Cassandra Austen, 24 January 1809, in Le Faye, ed., *Jane Austen's Letters,* 177. See Anthony Mandal, *Jane Austen and the Popular Novel: The Determined Author* (Basingstoke, U.K.: Palgrave Macmillan, 2007), chap. 4.

55. C. W. Pasley, *An Essay on the Military Policy and Institutions of the British Empire* (London: Edmund Lloyd, 1810), 506–507; Le Faye, ed., *Jane Austen's Letters,* 198.

56. Jane Austen, *Mansfield Park,* ed. John Wiltshire (Cambridge: Cambridge University Press, 2009), book 1, chap. 2.

57. Ibid., book 1, chap. 1.

58. Austen, *Pride and Prejudice,* book 2, chap. 14.

59. Levitan, *A Cultural History of the British Census,* 132–138.

60. Josephine McDonagh, *Child Murder and British Culture, 1720–1900* (Cambridge: Cambridge University Press, 2003).

61. *Essay of 1803*, 306. See Marjory Harper, "British Migration," in *The Oxford History of the British Empire,* ed. Andrew Porter (Oxford: Oxford University Press, 1999), 75–87.

62. See Karen O'Brien, "Colonial Emigration, Public Policy and Tory Romanticism, 1783–1830," *Proceedings of the British Academy* 155 (2009): 161–179.

63. Charlotte Sussman, "Memory and Mobility: Fictions of Population in Defoe, Goldsmith and Scott," in Backscheider and Ingrassia, eds., *A Companion to the Eighteenth-Century English Novel,* 191–213.

64. See Josephine McDonagh, "Place, Region and Migration," in *The Oxford History of the Novel in English: The Nineteenth-Century Novel,* ed. John Kucich and Jenny Bourne Taylor (Oxford: Oxford University Press, 2012), 361–376.

65. William Cobbett, *Surplus Population: And Poor-Law Bill. A Comedy,* in *Political Register,* 28 May 1831, 496.

66. "Weal or Woe," discussed in Ella Dzelzainis, "Reason v. Revelation: Feminism, Malthus, and the New Poor Law in Narratives by Harriet Martineau and Charlotte Elizabeth Tonna," *Interdisciplinary Studies in the Long Nineteenth Century* 2 (2006): 1–15.

67. Francis Place, *Illustrations and Proofs of the Principle of Population, Including an Examination of the Proposed Remedies of Mr. Malthus* (London: Longman, 1822), 165.

68. Winch, *Riches and Poverty,* 282–284.

69. *Essay of 1803*, 19. On "Malthusian" advocates of birth control, see Robert Mayhew, *Malthus: The Life and Legacies of an Untimely Prophet* (Cambridge, Mass.: Harvard University Press, 2014), 150–154.

Bibliography

Alborn, T. L. "Boys to Men: Moral Restraint at Haileybury College." In *Malthus, Medicine, and Morality: "Malthusianism" after 1798,* ed. B. Dolan, 33–55. Amsterdam: Rodopi, 2000.

Allen, D. E. *The Naturalist in Britain: A Social History.* 2nd ed. Princeton, N.J.: Princeton University Press, 1994.

Anon, *The Monthly Review,* vol. XLII, December 1803, 337–357; Vol. XLIII, January 1804, 56–69.

Anon, *The British Critic,* vol. XXIII, January 1804, 59–69; March 1804, 233–245.

Austen, J. *Mansfield Park.* Ed. J. Wiltshire. Cambridge: Cambridge University Press, 2009.

Austen, J. *Pride and Prejudice.* Ed. P. Rogers. Cambridge: Cambridge University Press, 2006.

Bashford, A. "Malthus and Colonial History." *Journal of Australian Studies* 36, no. 1 (March 2012): 99–110.

Bashford, A., and J. E. Chaplin. *The New Worlds of Thomas Robert Malthus: Rereading the Principle of Population.* Princeton, N.J.: Princeton University Press, 2016.

Bederman, G. "Sex, Scandal, Satire, and Population in 1798: Revisiting Malthus's First Essay." *Journal of British Studies* 47 (October 2008): 768–795.

Beer, M. *A History of British Socialism.* 2 vols. London: George Allen and Unwin, 1919, 1921; reprint, London: Routledge, 2002.

Bengtsson, T., et al. *Life under Pressure: Mortality and Living Standards in Europe and Asia, 1700–1900.* Cambridge, Mass.: MIT Press, 2004.

Bergh, A. E., ed. *Writings of Jefferson.* 20 vols. Washington, D.C.: Jefferson Memorial Association, 1903–1904.

Binmore, K. *Rational Decisions.* Princeton, N.J.: Princeton University Press, 2009.

Board of Agriculture. "Letter to the Editor, from the President." *Annals of Agriculture* 23 (1795): 210.

Bonar, J. *Malthus and His Work.* London: Macmillan, 1885.

Bonar, J. *Malthus and His Work.* 2nd ed. London: Allen and Unwin, 1924.

Bowler, P. J. "Malthus, Darwin and the Concept of Struggle." *Journal of the History of Ideas* 37 (1976): 631–650.

Burrow, J. *Whigs and Liberals.* Oxford: Clarendon, 1988.

Chaplin, J. E. "Mark Catesby, a Skeptical Newtonian in America." In *Empire's Nature: Mark Catesby's New World Vision,* ed. A. R. W. Meyers and M. B. Pritchard, 38–47. Chapel Hill: University of North Carolina Press, 1998.

Cobbett, W. "Surplus Population: And Poor-Law Bill. A Comedy." *Cobbett's Weekly Political Register,* 28 May 1831, 493–511.

Collins, D. *An Account of the English Colony in New South Wales . . . to Which Are Added Some Particulars of New Zealand.* 2 vols. London: T. Cadell Jr. and W. Davies, 1802.

Connell, P. *Romanticism, Economics and the Question of "Culture."* Cambridge: Cambridge University Press, 2001.

Connolly, C. *A Cultural History of the Irish Novel, 1790–1829.* Cambridge: Cambridge University Press, 2012.

Dalrymple-Champneys, N., and A. Pollard, eds. *George Crabbe: The Complete Poetical Works.* 3 vols. Oxford: Clarendon Press, 1988.

Daly, H. E. *Steady-State Economics: The Economics of Biophysical Equilibrium and Moral Growth.* 2nd ed. Washington, D.C.: Island Press, 1991.

Darwin, C. *The Origin of Species by Means of Natural Selection.* Harmondsworth, U.K.: Penguin, 1985.

De Vries, J. *European Urbanization, 1500–1800.* Cambridge, Mass.: Harvard University Press, 1984.

Dolan, B., ed. *Malthus, Medicine, and Morality: "Malthusianism" after 1798.* Amsterdam: Rodopi, 2000.

Drake, M. "Malthus on Norway." *Population Studies* 20, no. 2 (November 1966): 175–196.

Dzelzainis, E. "Reason v. Revelation: Feminism, Malthus, and the New Poor Law in Narratives by Harriet Martineau and Charlotte Elizabeth Tonna." *Interdisciplinary Studies in the Long Nineteenth Century* 2 (2006): 1–15.

Eastwood, D. "Robert Southey and the Intellectual Origins of Romantic Conservatism." *English Historical Review* 104 (1989): 308–331.

Eastwood, D. "Ruinous Prosperity: Robert Southey's Critique of the Commercial System." *Wordsworth Circle* 25 (1994): 72–76.

Edgeworth, M. *Maria Edgeworth: Letters from England, 1813–1844.* Ed. C. Colvin. Oxford: Oxford University Press, 1971.

Engels, F. "Outlines of a Critique of Political Economy." In *Collected Works of Karl Marx and Frederick Engels,* 3:418–443. 1844; New York: International Publishers, 1975.

Flinn, M. W. "Malthus and His Time." In *Malthus Past and Present,* ed. J. Dupâquier, A. Fauve-Chamoux, and E. Grebenik, 85–96. London: Academic Press, 1983.

Fogel, A. "Wordsworth's 'We Are Seven' and Crabbe's *The Parish Register:* Poetry and Anti-Census." *Studies in Romanticism* 48 (2009): 23–65.

Fogel, R. *Without Consent or Contract: The Rise and Fall of American Slavery.* New York: Norton, 1989.

Franklin, B. "Observations Concerning the Increase of Mankind." In *Autobiography and Other Writings,* ed. O. Seavey, 252–260. 1851; New York: Oxford University Press, 1999.

Genovese, E., and E. Genovese. "Slavery, Economic Development, and the Law: The Dilemma of Southern Political Economists, 1800–1860." *Washington and Lee Law Review* 41, no. 1 (Winter 1984): 1–29.

Gilbert, G., ed. *T. R. Malthus: Critical Responses.* 4 vols. New York: Routledge, 1998.

Gilmartin, K. *Writing against Revolution: Literary Conservatism in Britain, 1790–1832.* Cambridge: Cambridge University Press, 2007.

Glass, D. V., ed. *Introduction to Malthus.* London: C. A. Watts and Company, 1953.

Glass, D. V. *Numbering the People: The Eighteenth-Century Population Controversy and the Development of Census and Vital Statistics in Britain.* Farnborough, U.K.: D. C. Heath, 1973.

Godwin, W. *The Enquirer. Reflections on Education, Manners, and Literature. In A Series of Essays.* London: G. G. and J. Robinson, 1797.

Godwin, W. *Enquiry Concerning Political Justice, and Its Influence on General Virtue and Happiness.* 2 vols. London: G. G. and J. Robinson, 1793.

Godwin, W. *Enquiry Concerning Political Justice, and Its Influence on General Virtue and Happiness.* 3rd ed. 2 vols. London: G. G. and J. Robinson, 1798.

Godwin. W. *An Enquiry Concerning Political Justice and Its Influence on Morals and Happiness.* 4th ed. London: Watson, 1842.

Golinski, J. *British Weather and the Climate of Enlightenment.* Chicago: University of Chicago Press, 2007.

Graver, B. E. "Wakefield, Gilbert." In *Oxford Dictionary of National Biography.* Oxford: Oxford University Press, 2004. www.oxforddnb.com/view/article/28418.

Grove, J. M. *Little Ice Ages, Ancient and Modern.* 2nd ed. 2 vols. London: Routledge, 2004.

Guest, H. *Small Change: Women, Learning, Patriotism, 1750–1810.* Chicago: Chicago University Press, 2000.

Hajnal, J. "Two Kinds of Pre-Industrial Household Formation System." In *Family Forms in Historic Europe,* ed. R. Wall, P. Laslett, and J. Robin, 65–104. Cambridge: Cambridge University Press, 1983.

Hamilton, E. *The Cottagers of Glenburnie and Other Educational Writings.* Ed. P. Perkins. Glasgow: Association for Scottish Literary Studies, 2009.

Hardin, G. "The Tragedy of the Commons." *Science,* 13 December 1968, 1243–1248.

Harper, M. "British Migration." In *The Oxford History of the British Empire,* vol. 3, *The Nineteenth Century,* ed. A. Porter, 75–87. Oxford: Oxford University Press, 1999.

Hazlitt, W. "A Reply to the Essay on Population." In *The Complete Works of William Hazlitt,* ed. P. P. Howe, 1:177–364. London: J. M. Dent and Sons, 1930.

Hazlitt, W. "The Spirit of the Age." In *The Selected Writings of William Hazlitt,* ed. D. Wu, 7:75–236. London: Pickering and Chatto, 1998.

Higgs, E. *Making Sense of the Census: The Manuscript Returns for England and Wales, 1801–1901.* London: Her Majesty's Stationery Office, 1989.

Hilton, B. *The Age of Atonement: The Influence of Evangelicalism on Social and Economic Thought, 1795–1865.* Oxford: Oxford University Press, 1988.

Hilton, B. *A Mad, Bad and Dangerous People? England, 1783–1846.* Oxford: Clarendon Press, 2006.

Hilton, B. "Malthus and the Dismal Science." *Times Literary Supplement,* 16 August 1996, 9.

Himmelfarb, G. *The Idea of Poverty: England in the Early Industrial Age.* New York: Knopf, 1984.

Holland, H. *Recollections of Past Life.* London: Longmans, 1872.

Huzel, J. P. *The Popularization of Malthus in Early Nineteenth-Century England: Martineau, Cobbett, and the Popular Press.* Aldershot, U.K.: Ashgate, 2006.

James, P. *Population Malthus: His Life and Time.* London: Routledge and Kegan Paul, 1979.

Janković, V. *Reading the Skies: A Cultural History of English Weather, 1650–1820.* Manchester: Manchester University Press, 2000.

Jerrold, T. *Dissertations on Man, Philosophical, Physiological and Political.* London: Cadell and Davies, 1806.

Keynes, J. M. *The Collected Writings of John Maynard Keynes.* Ed. Elizabeth Johnson and Donald Moggridge. Vol. 10. London: Macmillan, 1972.

Keynes, J. M. *Essays in Biography.* London: Macmillan, 1933.

Kington, J. *The Weather of the 1780s over Europe.* Cambridge: Cambridge University Press, 1988.

Koselleck, R. *Futures Past: On the Semantics of Historical Time.* Trans. K. Tribe. New York: Columbia University Press, 2004.

Kussmaul, A. *Servants in Husbandry in Early Modern England.* Cambridge: Cambridge University Press, 1981.

Le Faye, D., ed. *Jane Austen's Letters.* Oxford: Oxford University Press, 1995.

LeMahieu, D. L. "Malthus and the Theology of Scarcity." *Journal of the History of Ideas* 40 (1979): 467–474.

Levitan, K. *A Cultural History of the British Census: Envisioning the Multitude in the Nineteenth Century.* New York: Palgrave Macmillan, 2011.

Malthus, T. R. "The Crisis, a View of the Present State of Britain, by a Friend of the Constitution," surviving fragments in W. Empson, "Life, Writings, and Character of Mr. Malthus," in Bernard Semmel, ed., *Occasional Papers of T. R. Malthus on Ireland, Population and Political Economy from Contemporary Journals Written Anonymously and Hitherto Uncollected.* New York: Burt Franklin, 1963: 231–268.

Malthus, T. R. *An Essay on the Principle of Population.* 3rd ed. 2 vols. 1803; London: J. Johnson, 1806.

Malthus, T. R. *An Essay on the Principle of Population.* 2 vols. Ed. P. James. 1803; Cambridge: Cambridge University Press, 1989.

Malthus, T. R. *An Essay on the Principle of Population; or, A View of Its Past and Present Effects on Human Happiness; with an Inquiry into Our Prospects Respecting the Future Removal or Mitigation of the Evils Which It Occasions. A New Edition, Very Much Enlarged.* 2nd ed. London: J. Johnson, 1803.

Malthus, T. R. *An Essay on the Principle of Population; or, A View of Its Past and Present Effects on Human Happiness.* Ed. D. Winch. 1803; Cambridge: Cambridge University Press, 1992.

Malthus, T. R. *Population: The First Essay.* Ann Arbor: University of Michigan Press, 1959.

Malthus, T. R. "Review of J. R. McCulloch's 'Essay on Political Economy,' *Supplement to the Encyclopaedia Britannica,* vol. VI, part I (Edinburgh, 1823)," *Quarterly Review* 30, no. 6 (1828): 297–334.

Malthus, T. R. *A Summary View of the Principle of Population.* London: John Murray, 1830.

Malthus, T. R. *The Travel Diaries of T. R. Malthus.* Ed. P. James. Cambridge: Cambridge University Press, 1966.

Malthus, T. R. *The Works of Thomas Robert Malthus.* Ed. E. A. Wrigley and D. Souden. London: W. Pickering, 1986.

————. Vol. 1. *An Essay on the Principle of Population* (1798), 1st ed.

————. Vol. 2. *An Essay on the Principle of Population* (1826), 6th ed. with variant readings from the 2nd ed., part 1.

————. Vol. 3. *An Essay on the Principle of Population* (1826), 6th ed. with variant readings from the 2nd ed., part 2.

————. Vol. 4. *Essays on Population.*

————. Vol. 5. *Principles of Political Economy* (1836), 2nd ed. with variant readings from the 1st ed., part 1.

————. Vol. 6. *Principles of Political Economy* (1836), 2nd ed. with variant readings from the 1st ed., part 2.

————. Vol. 7. *Essays on Political Economy.*

————. Vol. 8. *Definitions in Political Economy* (1827).

Mandal, A. "Evangelical Fiction." In *The Oxford History of the Novel, 1750–1820.* Ed. P. Garside and K. O'Brien. Oxford: Oxford University Press, 2015.

Mandal, A. *Jane Austen and the Popular Novel: The Determined Author.* Basingstoke, U.K.: Palgrave Macmillan, 2007.

Martineau, Harriet. *Harriet Martineau's Autobiography.* 2nd ed. 3 vols. London: Smith, Elder, 1877.

Marx, K. *Capital.* Ed. E. Mandel. Vol. 1. New York: Vintage, 1977.

Mayhew, R. *Malthus: The Life and Legacies of an Untimely Prophet.* Cambridge, Mass.: Harvard University Press, 2014.

Mayhew, R., ed. *New Perspectives on Malthus.* Cambridge: Cambridge University Press, 2016.

McDonagh, J. *Child Murder and British Culture, 1720–1900.* Cambridge: Cambridge University Press, 2003.

McDonagh, J. "Place, Region and Migration." In *The Oxford History of the Novel in English: The Nineteenth-Century Novel.* Ed. J. Kucich and J. Bourne Taylor. Oxford: Oxford University Press, 2012.

Meek, R. L. "Malthus--Yesterday and Today." In *Thomas Robert Malthus: Critical Assessments,* ed. J. C. Wood, 1:175–197. London: Croom Helm, 1986.

Milbank, J. *Theology and Social Theory: Beyond Secular Reason.* Oxford: Blackwell, 1990.

Milgate, M., and S. C. Stimson. *After Adam Smith: A Century of Transformation in Politics and Political Economy.* Princeton, N.J.: Princeton University Press, 2009.

Milgate, M., and S. C. Stimson. *Ricardian Politics.* Princeton, N.J.: Princeton University Press, 1991.

Mill, J. S. *Principles of Political Economy.* 8th ed. 2 vols. 1848; London: Longmans, Green, Reader, and Dyer, 1878.

Mill, J. S. "Art. IX. *The Quarterly Review,* No. LX., Art. 1. *On the Essay on Political Economy, in the Supplement to the Encyclopaedia Britannica.*" *Westminster Review* 3, no. 5 (January 1825): 213–223.

More, T. *Utopia and a Dialogue of Comfort,* rev. edn. London: J. M. Dent, 1951.

Nicholson, M. "The Eleventh Commandment: Sex and Spirit in Wollstonecraft and Malthus." *Journal of the History of Ideas* 51, no. 3 (1990): 401–421.

O'Brien, K. "Colonial Emigration, Public Policy and Tory Romanticism, 1783–1830." *Proceedings of the British Academy* 155 (2009): 161–179.

O'Brien, K. *Women and Enlightenment in Eighteenth-Century Britain.* Cambridge: Cambridge University Press, 2009.

O'Flaherty, N. "Malthus and the End of Poverty." In *New Perspectives on Malthus,* ed. R. Mayhew, 52–73. Cambridge: Cambridge University Press, 2016.

Ò'Gallchoir, C. *Maria Edgeworth: Women, Enlightenment and Nation.* Dublin: University College Dublin Press, 2005.

Overton, M., et al. *Production and Consumption in English Households, 1600–1750.* London: Routledge, 2004.

Paine, T. *Agrarian Justice.* London: J. Adlard and J. Parsons, 1797.

Paley, W. *Principles of Moral and Political Philosophy.* London: Faulder, 1785.

Pasley, C. W. *An Essay on the Military Policy and Institutions of the British Empire.* London: Edmund Lloyd, 1810.

Pearce, F. "Peak Planet: Are We Starting to Consume Less?" *New Scientist* 2869 (16 June 2012): 38–43.

Perkins, P. *Women Writers and the Edinburgh Enlightenment.* Amsterdam: Rodopi, 2010.

Perry, R. "Home Economics: Representations of Poverty in Eighteenth-Century Fiction." In *A Companion to the Eighteenth-Century English Novel,* ed. P. R. Backscheider and C. Ingrassia, 441–458. Oxford: Blackwell, 2005.

Place, F. *Illustrations and Proofs of the Principle of Population, Including an Examination of the Proposed Remedies of Mr. Malthus.* London: Longman, 1822.

Pollard, A., ed. *George Crabbe: The Critical Heritage.* London: Routledge, 1972.

Pontoppidan, E. *Natural History of Norway.* 2 vols. London: A. Linde, 1755.

Porter, R. "The Environment and the Enlightenment: The English Experience." In *The Faces of Nature in Enlightenment Europe,* ed. L. Daston and G. Pomata, 17–38. Berlin: Berliner Wissenshcafts-Verlag, 2003.

Porter, R. "The Malthusian Moment." In *Malthus, Medicine, and Morality: "Malthusianism" after 1798,* ed. B. Dolan, 57–72. Amsterdam: Rodopi, 2000.

Price, R. "Observations on the Expectations of Lives, the Increase of Mankind, the Influence of Great Towns on Population, and Particularly the State of London with Respect to Healthfulness and Number of Inhabitants." *Philosophical Transactions* 59 (1769): 89–125.

Pullen, J. M. "Malthus' Theological Ideas and Their Influence on His Principle of Population." *History of Political Economy* 13, no. 1 (1981): 39–54.

Pullen, J. M., and T. H. Parry, eds. *T. R. Malthus: The Unpublished Papers in the Collection of Kanto Gakuen University.* 2 vols. Cambridge: Cambridge University Press, 1997–2004.

Pyle, A., ed. *Population: Contemporary Responses to Thomas Malthus.* Bristol, U.K.: Thoemmes Press, 1994.

Radick, G. "Is the Theory of Natural Selection Independent of History?" In *The Cambridge Companion to Darwin,* ed. J. Hodge and G. Radick, 143–168. Cambridge: Cambridge University Press, 2003.

Ravenstone, P. [pseudonym] "Of Subsistence." In *A Few Doubts as to the Correctness of Some Opinions Generally Entertained on the Subject of Population and Political Economy,* 152–189. London: John Andrews, 1821.

Raynal, G. T. *Histoire philosophique et politique des établissements et du commerce des Européens dans les deux Indes.* 10 vols. Geneva: L'Imprimerie des Associés, 1795.

Raynal, G. T. *A Philosophical and Political History of the British Settlements and Trade in North America.* Edinburgh: C. MacFarquhar, 1776.

Rickman, J. "Thoughts on the Utility and Facility of a General Enumeration of the People of the British Empire." 1796. Reprinted in D. V. Glass, *Numbering the People: The Eighteenth-Century Population Controversy and the Development of Census and Vital Statistics in Britain.* Farnborough: D. C. Heath, 1973, 106–113.

Robbins, H. "'We Are Seven' and the First British Census." *English Language Notes* 48, no. 2 (Fall–Winter 2010): 201–213.

Russell, B. "Why I Am Not a Communist." In *Portraits from Memory and Other Essays*, 224–227. London: George Allen and Unwin, 1958.

Savage, L. *The Foundations of Statistics*. New York: Wiley, 1954.

Schabas, M. *The Natural Origins of Economics*. Chicago: University of Chicago Press, 2005.

Schofield, R. "Family Structure, Demographic Behaviour, and Economic Growth." In *Famine, Disease and the Social Order in Early Modern Society*, ed. J. Walter and R. Schofield, 279–304. Cambridge: Cambridge University Press, 1989.

Semmel, B., ed. *Occasional Papers of T. R. Malthus on Ireland, Population, and Political Economy from Contemporary Journals Written Anonymously and Hitherto Uncollected*. New York: Burt Franklin, 1963.

Sen, A. *Poverty and Famines, an Essay on Entitlement and Deprivation*. Oxford: Clarendon Press, 1982.

Short, T. *A General Chronological History of the Air, Weather, Seasons, Meteors, &c.* 2 vols. London: T. Longman and A. Millar, 1749.

Short, T. *New Observations, Natural, Moral, Civil, Political, and Medical, on City, Town, and Country Bills of Mortality*. London: T. Longman and A. Millar, 1750.

"Simplex" [John Young]. *An Inquiry into the Constitution, Government and Practices of the Church of Christ . . . with Strictures on . . . Mr. Malthus on Population*. Edinburgh: D. Schaw and Son, 1808.

Smith, A. *An Inquiry into the Nature and Causes of the Wealth of Nations*. Ed. E. C. Cannan. 2 vols. in 1. 1776; Indianapolis: Liberty Classics, 1976.

Southey, R. *New Letters of Robert Southey*. Ed. K. Curry. 2 vols. New York: Columbia University Press, 1965.

Sraffa, P. and M. H. Dobb, eds. *The Works and Correspondence of David Ricardo*. Cambridge: Cambridge University Press, 1951.

Stedman Jones, G. *An End to Poverty? A Historical Debate*. New York: Columbia University Press, 2008.

Stern, N. *The Economics of Climate Change: The Stern Review*. Cambridge: Cambridge University Press, 2007.

Stimson, S. C. "From Invisible Hand to Moral Restraint: The Transformation of the Market Mechanism from Smith to Malthus." *Journal of Scottish Philosophy* 2, no.1 (Spring 2004): 22–47.

Stott, A. *Hannah More: The First Victorian*. Oxford: Oxford University Press, 2003.

Sussman, C. "Memory and Mobility: Fictions of Population in Defoe, Goldsmith and Scott." In *A Companion to the Eighteenth-Century English*

Novel and Culture, ed. P. R. Backscheider and C. Ingrassia, 191–213. Oxford: Blackwell, 2005.

Thompson, S. J. "Census-Taking, Political Economy and State Formation in Britain c.1790–1840." Ph.D. thesis, University of Cambridge, 2010.

Tsuya, N., et al. *Prudence and Pressure: Reproduction and Human Agency in Europe and Asia, 1700–1900.* Cambridge, Mass.: MIT Press, 2010.

Turner, M. "Corn Crises in the Age of Malthus." In *Malthus and His Time,* ed. M. Turner, 112–128. Houndmills, U.K.: Macmillan, 1986.

Vorzimmer, P. "Darwin, Malthus, and the Theory of Natural Selection." *Journal of the History of Ideas* 30, no. 4, (1969): 527–542.

Wakefield, G., and C. J. Fox. *Correspondence of the Late Gilbert Wakefield, B.A. with Late Right Honourable Charles James Fox, in the Years 1796 . . . 1801, Chiefly, on Subjects of Classical Literature.* London: T. Cadell and W. Davies, 1813.

Wallace, R. *Various Prospects of Mankind, Nature and Providence.* London: A. Millar, 1761.

Warde, P. *Energy Consumption in England and Wales, 1560–2000.* Rome: Consiglio Nazionale delle Ricerche, 2007.

Waterman, A. M. C. *Revolution, Economics, and Religion: Christian Political Economy, 1798–1833.* Cambridge: Cambridge University Press, 1991.

Wilson, W. *A Missionary Voyage to the Southern Pacific Ocean.* London: T. Chapman, 1799.

Winbron, C. *The Literary Economy of Jane Austen and George Crabbe.* Aldershot, U.K.: Ashgate, 2004.

Winch, D. "Darwin Fallen among Political Economists." *Proceedings of the American Philosophical Society* 145 (2001): 415–437.

Winch, D. *Malthus.* Oxford: Oxford University Press, 1987.

Winch, D. *Malthus: A Very Short Introduction.* Oxford: Oxford University Press, 2013.

Winch, D. *Riches and Poverty: An Intellectual History of Political Economy in Britain, 1750–1834.* Cambridge: Cambridge University Press, 1996.

Winch, D. "Robert Malthus: Christian Moral Scientist, Arch-Demoralizer, or Implicit Secular Utilitarian?" *Utilitas* 5, no. 2 (November 1993): 239–253.

Wood, J. C., ed. *Thomas Robert Malthus: Critical Assessments.* 4 vols. Dover, N.H.: Croom Helm, 1986.

Wood, P. B. "The Science of Man." In *Cultures of Natural History,* ed. N. Jardine, J. A. Secord, and E. C. Spary, 197–210. Cambridge: Cambridge University Press, 1996.

Woodward, C. Vann. *American Counter-Point: Slavery and Racism in the Noth-South Dialogue.* Boston: Little, Brown, 1971.

Wordsworth, W. *The Excursion.* Ed. S. Bushell, J. A. Butler, and D. Garcia. Ithaca, N.Y.: Cornell University Press, 2007.

Wrigley, E. A. "British Population during the 'Long' Eighteenth Century, 1680–1840." In *The Cambridge Economic History of Modern Britain,* ed. R. Floud and P. Johnson, 1:57–95. Cambridge: Cambridge University Press, 2004.

Wrigley, E. A. "The Classical Economists and the Industrial Revolution." In *People, Cities and Wealth,* 21–45. Oxford: Blackwell, 1987.

Wrigley, E. A. *Continuity, Chance and Change: The Character of the Industrial Revolution in England.* Cambridge: Cambridge University Press, 1988.

Wrigley, E. A. "Coping with Rapid Population Growth: How England Fared in the Century Preceding the Great Exhibition." In *Structures and Transformations in Modern British History,* ed. D. Feldman and J. Lawrence, 24–53. Cambridge: Cambridge University Press, 2011.

Wrigley, E. A. "Corn and Crisis: Malthus on the High Price of Provisions." *Population and Development Review* 25 (1999): 121–128.

Wrigley, E. A. *The Early English Censuses.* Oxford: Oxford University Press, 2011.

Wrigley, E. A. *Energy and the English Industrial Revolution.* Cambridge: Cambridge University Press, 2010.

Wrigley, E. A. "The Limits to Growth: Malthus and the Classical Economists." In *Population and Resources in Western Intellectual Traditions,* ed. M. S. Teitelbaum and J. M. Winter, 30–48. Cambridge: Cambridge University Press, 1989.

Wrigley, E. A. "Malthus's Model of a Pre-Industrial Economy." In *Malthus Past and Present,* ed. J. Dupâquier, A. Fauve-Chamoux, and E. Grebenik, 111–124. London: Academic Press, 1983.

Wrigley, E. A., et al. *English Population History from Family Reconstitution, 1580–1837.* Cambridge: Cambridge University Press, 1997.

Wu, D. *Wordsworth's Reading, 1770–1799.* Cambridge: Cambridge University Press, 1993.

Young, A. *View of the Agriculture of Oxfordshire.* London: Board of Agriculture, 1809.

Young, R. "Malthus and the Evolutionists: The Common Context of Biological and Social Theory." *Past and Present* 43 (1969): 109–114.

Index

The original index to the Malthus 1803 edition of the *Essay* has been reproduced here with minor alterations. Page numbers have been revised to reflect the present volume. For historical purposes, substantive content of the index has not been altered.

Rethinking the Western Tradition

ALSO AVAILABLE IN THE SERIES:

On Liberty
By John Stuart Mill
EDITED BY DAVID BROMWICH AND GEORGE KATEB

Groundwork for the Metaphysics of Morals
By Immanuel Kant
EDITED BY ALLEN W. WOOD

Sesame and Lilies
By John Ruskin
EDITED BY DEBORAH EPSTEIN NORD

"The Social Contract" and "The First and Second Discourses"
By Jean-Jacques Rousseau
EDITED BY SUSAN DUNN

Discourse on Method and Meditations on First Philosophy
By René Descartes
EDITED BY DAVID WEISSMAN

Culture and Anarchy
By Matthew Arnold
EDITED BY SAMUEL LIPMAN

The Idea of a University
By John Henry Newman
EDITED BY FRANK M. TURNER

The Prince
By Niccolò Machiavelli
TRANSLATED BY ANGELO CODEVILLA